# Educational Psychology
## Windows on Teaching

# Educational Psychology
## Windows on Teaching

*Thomas K.
Crowl*

*Sally
Kaminsky*

*David M.
Podell*

*The College of Staten Island, City University of New York*

Brown & Benchmark
PUBLISHERS

Madison, WI  Dubuque  Guilford, CT  Chicago  Toronto  London
Mexico City  Caracas  Buenos Aires  Madrid  Bogotá  Sydney

**Book Team**

Executive Publisher  *Edgar J. Laube*
Managing Editor  *Sue Pulvermacher-Alt*
Developmental Editor  *Suzanne M. Guinn*
Production Editor  *Gloria G. Schiesl*
Proofreading Coordinator  *Carrie Barker*
Art Editor  *Rita Hingtgen*
Photo Editor  *Rose Deluhery*
Permissions Coordinator  *Mavis M. Oeth*
Production Manager  *Beth Kundert*
Production/Costing Manager  *Sherry Padden*
Design and New Media Development Manager  *Linda Meehan Avenarius*
Visuals/Design Freelance Specialist  *Mary L. Christianson*
Marketing Manager  *Amy Halloran*
Copywriter  *Jennifer Smith*
Proofreader  *Mary Svetlik Anderson*

Basal Text  *10/12 Sabon*
Display Type  *Frutiger*
Typesetting System  *Macintosh*® *FrameMaker*
Paper Stock  *45# Restorecote*

Executive Vice President and General Manager  *Bob McLaughlin*
Vice President, Business Manager  *Russ Domeyer*
Vice President of Production and New Media Development  *Victoria Putman*
National Sales Manager  *Phil Rudder*
National Telesales Director  *John Finn*

**A Times Mirror Company**

Cover design by Ben Neff

Interior design by K. Wayne Harms and Christopher E. Reese

Cover image: Paul Klee, "Polyphon gefasstes Weiss" (Polyphonically enclosed white), Kunstmuseum Bern, Paul-Klee-Stiftung, photo by Peter Lauri.

Copyedited by Cindy Peck; proofread by Sarah Greer Bush

Library of Congress Catalog Card Number: 96-83184

ISBN 0-697-26816-0

Printed in the United States of America by Times Mirror Higher Education Group, Inc.
2460 Kerper Boulevard, Dubuque, IA 52001

10  9  8  7  6  5  4  3  2  1

To our families,
for their constant
support and
encouragement.

# Brief Contents

# CONTENTS

## PART I

© Laura Dwight

# Introduction to Educational Psychology

## CHAPTER 1

## CHAPTER 2

## PART III

© Jeffry Myers/Corbis Media

# Learner Characteristics

## CHAPTER 11

### Learning Difficulties: The Special Student    253

© Jim Whitmer Photography

# Shaping the Learning Environment

## CHAPTER 12

### Planning for Instruction    283

# PREFACE

Welcome to the revolution. This text is your field guide to the revolution. It's your tool to get the information you want—the way you want it—from a perspective that fits your course.

## Revolutionary Perspective

Three decades ago, cognitive psychologists created a major revolution in psychology. They began to pursue the question, "How does the mind work?" The emphasis shifted from the study of behavior to the study of thinking. Psychologists now ask, "How do people *construct* knowledge?" The cognitive approach now dominates educational psychology, but it is not the only way to look at the field. Although this text emphasizes the cognitive approach, it also thoroughly covers all major approaches to educational psychology.

With its strong cognitive orientation, our book includes coverage of Vygotsky, information processing theory, and culture and language to emphasize the most compelling and current issues in educational psychology. We use examples of real situations to highlight practical application of these topics.

## The Book

This text emphasizes the role of teachers as decision makers. Our goal is to prepare future teachers to be competent professionals who are well grounded in the principles of educational psychology and are ready to use this knowledge in their careers. How does our text do this?

We believe that a textbook is worthless if students feel intimidated or overwhelmed by the material in the book. An **easily accessible and understandable presentation** is a high priority. We deliberately use a style of language that is easy to understand and that makes even abstract ideas comprehensible.

The text provides comprehensive and **up-to-date coverage of the relevant topics in educational psychology**, including some topics (such as language development, information processing theory, and creativity) that others don't thoroughly address.

The book primarily follows a **cognitive approach**, reflecting the cognitive revolution in the field of educational psychology. We feel it is important to represent the other paradigms in the field (e.g., behaviorism, humanism), too, so prospective teachers know the many ways of understanding students and their development. The cognitive approach, currently the dominant school of thought in the field, provides a conceptual framework for future teachers to (1) organize the material in this book in a meaningful way, (2) understand more easily their subsequent study of teaching methods, and (3) enhance their effectiveness as classroom teachers.

We believe that future teachers need to know about topics that are not directly within the scope of cognitive science, but that have direct bearing on their future careers as teachers. To meet this need, we include traditional topics within educational psychology, including **social and emotional development, classroom management, motivation, and measurement,** which we consider essential to teacher preparation.

We firmly believe that an educational psychology textbook should demonstrate the **classroom applications of theory and research.** We do this through examples and discussion of practical issues throughout the text. Applications are not limited to boxed inserts—you will find them within the text, flagged by icons.

**Teachers Roundtables** appear throughout the textbook to help students relate their learning to real world situations they will face. This feature presents excerpts of conversations among a small group of teachers, giving students an opportunity to hear these topics discussed in teachers' own voices. Participants in the Teachers Roundtable include early childhood, elementary, and secondary teachers, and at least one special educator.

U.S. teachers are serving an increasingly heterogeneous population of students, but many feel poorly prepared to do so. **Diversity Makes a Difference** boxes address specific topics in educational psychology as they relate to multiculturalism. For example, the assessment chapter has a boxed insert on the cultural bias inherent in standardized tests. In the language development chapter, the boxed insert is about how nonverbal communication differs among different cultural groups. We believe boxed inserts highlight not only the content but the importance of the topic of multiculturalism for future teachers.

A growing trend is the **inclusion** of all students with various disabilities in regular early childhood, elementary, and secondary settings where future teachers will work. Our book addresses issues that relate to inclusion throughout the text, and we emphasize similarities rather than differences between nondisabled students and those with disabilities.

*Educational Psychology: Windows on Teaching* has five sections. The first section, *Introduction to Educational Psychology*, includes the introductory chapter and one on learning as a major focus of educational psychology. These chapters provide the necessary background information for understanding educational psychology as it exists today.

The second section, *Cognitive Processes*, describes how recent theories of cognition have altered the way psychologists and educators conceptualize the mind and study how it works. It includes chapters on the cognitive-developmental model; information-processing theory; culture and language; knowledge and comprehension; and problem solving, decision making, and critical thinking.

The third section, *Learner Characteristics*, focuses on important student characteristics that affect learning, such as intelligence, creativity, social and emotional development, motivation, and learning difficulties.

The fourth section, *Shaping the Learning Environment*, examines the context in which learning and teaching take place: the classroom. This section explains how to plan for instruction, assess and evaluate students, manage the classroom, and teach effectively.

# Text Features

Each chapter opens with an **outline, learning objectives,** and **preview** to alert readers to important concepts. All **key terms** are highlighted in the text and defined in the comprehensive glossary. Each chapter ends with a list of the chapter's **key points, self-study exercises, suggested further readings,** and a list of **references.** Each chapter also contains features that appear in the text page margin, and boxed features.

## Features in the Margin

These features in the margin will help students maximize their learning:

**A+ icons** highlight teaching applications of educational psychology principles.

**Learning objectives with icons** show exactly where the text addresses each learning objective.

**Marginal notes** provide students additional information, and encourage students to reflect on educational psychology concepts and apply them to their own experiences.

**Annual Edition: Educational Psychology icons** highlight areas of the text that relate to articles in Annual Editions.

## Boxed Features

**Windows on Teaching** provide students with practical ways to use principles of educational psychology in classroom teaching.

**Diversity Makes a Difference** describes ways that student ethnic diversity impacts classroom teaching.

**Teachers Roundtables** contain teachers' thoughts on issues in their own voices.

# Additional Items

*Student Study Guide* by Mina Berkowitz, Ph.D. Mina worked closely with us by contributing to the text and creating a study guide that reinforces the cognitive perspective of the text. The guide includes case studies with special questions for students. Chapter features are outline, key terms, comprehension check, critical thinking and application questions, final self-test, and answer key.

*Guide to the Internet: Educational Psychology* is a truly revolutionary resource! This guide introduces the Internet, explains terminology, then helps users explore the most valuable educational psychology resources on the net. Links described in the guide are accessible through the Brown & Benchmark Educational Psychology home page for point-and-click access to the best education and educational psychology sites. The guide is valuable for all skill levels, from web neophytes to web whizzes.

*Brown & Benchmark Educational Psychology Home Page* links you and your students to the best education and educational psychology sites on the web. Special features include **What's New, Internet Resources for Educators,** and more! Explore our home page at http://www.bbp.com/edpsych.html, or visit the Brown & Benchmark site at http://www.bbp.com to see what we're doing on the web right now.

# Acknowledgments

We acknowledge the contributions of our editor, Sue Pulvermacher-Alt, and our developmental editor, Suzanne Guinn, who were knowledgeable, professional, supportive, and a delight to work with. At Brown & Benchmark, Gloria Schiesl, Amy Halloran, Rose Deluhery, Rita Hingtgen, and Mavis Oeth were extremely helpful. We thank Dr. Mina Berkowitz for her many useful suggestions for improving this text and for producing the comprehensive Student Study Guide that accompanies it. We thank Kathleen Glawon of the Department of Education at the College of Staten Island for her on-going assistance, and Professors Raja Jayatilleke and Allen Natowitz of the College of Staten Island Library for their help in obtaining journal articles. We also thank John Behan for his expert advice.

We gratefully acknowledge the contributions of Angela Beckham, Donna Berry, Anthony Gasparo, Irwin Goldstein, and Mary Kelly who shared in the Teachers Roundtables their insights and ideas about teaching.

Thanks also to Theresa Deady-Kabbez for allowing us to use her lesson plans, and to the following colleagues who reviewed the many drafts of our chapters:

Keith W. Allred
*Brigham Young University*

Austin C. Archer
*Walla Walla College*

Mina Berkowitz
*Long Island University–Brooklyn*

Curtis J. Bonk
*University of Indiana*

Allen Colebank
*Fairmont State*

Betty Davenport
*Campbell University*

James Davidson
*Bowling Green State University*

Mariane Kistler Dove
*Youngstown State Univeristy*

David Dungan
*Emporia State University*

Keith Eicher
*University of Richmond*

Darwin F. Gale
*Brigham Young University*

D. L. Kirk
*Point Loma Nazarene College*

Jewel Linville-Cress
*Northeastern Oklahoma State University*

Leslie Soodak
*Adelphi University*

Colleen Willard-Holt
*Penn State–Harrisburg*

Finally, we thank our many students who over the years as preservice and inservice teachers helped us focus our thoughts and articulate the ideas expressed in this text.

# THE AUTHORS

## Thomas K. Crowl

Thomas K. Crowl is professor emeritus of education at the College of Staten Island of the City University of New York, where he taught educational psychology and educational research from 1970 to 1995. Prior to that, he taught sixth-, seventh-, and eighth-grade students. A graduate of Brown University, he received his Ph.D. in educational psychology from Teachers College, Columbia University. He has written extensively in the areas of educational psychology and communication, and has served as a reviewer for the *Journal of Educational Psychology*. He has been a Senior Fulbright Research Professor at the Psychological Institute of the Technical University of Berlin, and a Fulbright scholar in the Department of Psychology at the University of Vienna. He is also the author of *Fundamentals of Educational Research* (Brown & Benchmark, 1996).

## Sally Kaminsky

Sally Kaminsky is professor of education at the College of Staten Island of the City University of New York, where she teaches reading and educational research, and serves as Coordinator of Undergraduate Programs in Elementary and Secondary Education and Director of Student Teaching. After graduating from Upsala College, she received her M.A. from New York University and her Ed.D. in curriculum research and theory from Teachers College, Columbia University. She taught elementary students in the New York City public school system for several years and brings a strong classroom emphasis to this text. She has carried out research on students' perceptions of the role of student teacher, locus of control and reading achievement, and bilingual children's oral language and beginning reading processes. She has also worked directly with special education supervisors and evaluators in reading and language assessment and evaluated the academic impact of programs in which intermediate and high school students use microcomputers in the classroom.

## David M. Podell

David Podell is associate professor of education and chair of the Department of Education at the College of Staten Island of the City University of New York, where he teaches educational psychology, educational research, assessment, and psychology of exceptionality. He studied at the University of London, graduated from the University of Pennsylvania, received his Ed.M. from Harvard University, and received his Ph.D. in educational psychology from New York University. He has published research articles dealing with teacher efficacy, special education prevention and referral, and educational applications of technology. A certified psychologist, he assesses infants and children with suspected cognitive and language disabilities. He also created an international program for American teachers in Copenhagen, Denmark. He frequently consults with a number of organizations, including the Educational Testing Service and the New York City Board of Education.

# SAMPLE CHAPTER FROM THE STUDENT STUDY GUIDE

The following pages contain a sample chapter from the *Student Study Guide* that accompanies *Educational Psychology: Windows on Teaching* by Thomas K. Crowl, Sally Kaminsky, and David M. Podell. For this presentation, the original pages have been reduced in size. By working through each chapter of the guide, you will better understand the concepts presented in the text. Cases with questions written specifically for you appear at the end of the guide. Look for the complete guide at your bookstore, or talk to your bookstore manager.

*CHAPTER* **6 KNOWLEDGE AND COMPREHENSION**

**CHAPTER OUTLINE**

I.      There are three types of knowledge: declarative, procedural and conceptual. (lrng. obj. 6.1, p. 139)
   A.      Declarative knowledge or "knowing specific things," involves memorizing factual information. (pp. 138, 139)
   B.      Procedural knowledge, or "knowing how to do something," involves knowing the steps required to complete a task. (pp. 138, 140)
   C.      Conceptual knowledge, or "knowing about something," involves understanding the relationships between ideas. (pp. 138, 142)
II.     Declarative knowledge involves memorizing information and is best learned through practice and overlearning. (lrng. obj. 6.2, p. 139)
   A.      Students will retain information longer if they review it often and integrate it with what they already know. (p. 139)
   B.      Distributed practice, with breaks between study periods, is more effective than massed practice, with no breaks. (p. 139)
   C.      Once declarative knowledge is learned, it is automatically accessible. (p. 139)
III.    Declarative knowledge provides the foundation on which to build more complex information and to engage in higher order thinking. (lrng. obj. 6.3, p. 140)
IV.     Procedural knowledge is knowing how to do something; it involves knowing rules and how to apply them in order to complete a task. (lrng. obj. 6.4, p. 140)
   A.      Procedural knowledge is harder to learn than declarative knowledge because it involves mastering a sequence of steps and knowing when to use them. (p. 140)
   B.      Teachers can help students acquire procedural knowledge by explaining the goal of using the procedure, defining the set of problems for which the procedure is appropriate, demonstrating the procedure, allowing students to practice the procedure and giving students feedback about their performance. (p. 141)
V.      Conceptual knowledge is knowing about something; it involves categorizing related information into an organized idea and understanding the relationships between ideas. (lrng. obj. 6.5, pp. 138, 142)
   A.      The level of abstraction of a concept can vary--ranging from concrete (a concept that can be seen and touched) to abstract (a concept that does not have a physical existence). (lrng. obj. 6.5, p. 143)
   B.      Concepts can vary in generality--ranging from general to specific. (lrng. obj. 6.5, p. 144)
   C.      Concepts may vary in complexity--ranging from simple to complex, depending on the type and number of relationships they have with other concepts. (lrng. obj. 6.5, p. 144)
VI.     Four methods of teaching concepts are teaching attributes, using examples and non-examples, using discovery learning and using prototypes. (lrng. obj. 6.6, pp. 145-146)
   A.      Attributes are characteristics of a concept. Teachers can present students with a list of attributes that are and are not associated with a concept and have students identify the correct attributes. (p. 145)
   B.      By presenting examples of the concept (things that "belong") and also presenting nonexamples of the concepts (things that do not "belong"), teachers can help students to better understand a concept. (p. 145)
   C.      To help students learn concepts, teachers can use discovery learning; that is, teachers can structure situations that foster exploration, questioning, hypothesis testing and conclusion-drawing. (p. 146)
   D.      A prototype is the first instance of a concept that comes to mind and possesses the concept's most characteristic attributes, i.e., a model. Students can compare an object to their prototype to see if the object 'belongs' to the concept. (p. 146)
VII.    Schemata--mental structures that represent existing bodies of knowledge--can affect how people process and understand new information. (lrng. obj. 6.7, p. 149)

      A.        If students lack appropriate schemata, they will probably not understand the new information. (p. 149)

      B.        Information that contradicts a student's existing schemata may be resisted or rejected. (p. 149)

VIII.    Methods of helping students understand material include paraphrasing and summarizing, questioning, PQ4R, notetaking and using graphic organizers. (lrng. obj. 6.8, pp. 150-151)

      A.        Paraphrasing material--saying it in your own words--and summarizing material--condensing and reconstructing it--are both effective ways to increase comprehension. (p. 150)

      B.        By asking themselves questions, students can test their own understanding, evaluate their own knowledge and examine their own ideas, (p. 150)

      C.        PQ4R--preview, question, read, reflect, recite, review--combines a number of techniques for increasing comprehension, including paraphrasing and questioning. (p. 151)

      D.        Taking notes, or writing down ideas presented by others in ones own words, also enhances comprehension. (p. 151)

      E.        Graphic organizers--various types of charts and graphs--enhance comprehension by helping students analyze the structure of information and organize information in a meaningful way. (p. 151)

## KEY TERMS

In the space provided, write a definition for each of the following terms. You may check the accuracy of your definitions by referring to the answer key at the end of this chapter.

1.      Declarative knowledge:

2.      Rote learning:

3.      Distributed practice:

4.      Massed practice:

5.      Procedural knowledge:

6.      General knowledge:

7.      Domain-specific knowledge:

8.      Conceptual knowledge:

9.      Concepts:

10.      Concrete concept:

11.   Abstract concept:

12.   Attributes:

13.   Examples:

14.   Nonexamples:

15.   Discovery learning:

16.   Prototypes:

17.   Principles:

18.   Comprehension:

19.   Schema:

20.   Reciprocal questioning:

21.   Linear array:

22.   Hierarchies:

23.   Networks:

24.   Matrix:

## Comprehension Check

Read the paragraphs below. Fill in each of the blanks by selecting a word or phrase from the list of words provided. Note that not all of the words will be used and each word that is used will be used only once. Words are listed in alphabetical order. You may check your answers by referring to the answer key at the end of this chapter.

According to psychologists, there are three kinds of knowledge: knowing factual information or _____1_____; knowing how to do some, or _____2_____; and knowing about something, or _____3_____. Extensive practice, overlearning, and frequent review will help in remembering _____4_____ knowledge. Explaining the purpose of a procedure, describing the kinds of problems a procedure is designed for, demonstrating a procedure, and giving feed back while a procedure is practiced will enhance the acquisition of _____5_____ knowledge.

A general category of ideas, objects or people whose members share specific characteristics is called a(n) _____6_____. Concepts may vary in degree of _____7_____, _____8_____, _____9_____. Three ways of teaching concepts are: 1) by pointing out their _____10_____; 2) by using _____11_____; and by making use of _____12_____. Conceptual knowledge can provide an understanding of why a set of rules (procedural knowledge) is used.

The process by which we construct meaning from incoming information is called _____13_____. Activities for strengthening comprehension include _____14_____, _____15_____, _____16_____, _____17_____, and _____18_____.

abstraction
attributes
complexity
comprehension
concept
conceptual
conceptual knowledge
conditional
declarative
declarative knowledge
examples and nonexamples
generality
inert knowledge
notetaking
overgeneralization
paraphrasing
PQ4R
procedural
procedural knowledge
prototypes
questioning
rote memory
summarizing

## CRITICAL THINKING/APPLICATION QUESTIONS

1.  Use the content area of mathematics. Describe something that students have to learn that would be an example of declarative knowledge. Describe something that students have to learn that would be an example of procedural knowledge. Give an example of conceptual knowledge in mathematics.

2.  Choose a content area such as social studies. Give examples of social studies concepts that students need to know; for each concept, indicate the degree of abstraction, generality and complexity. List the attributes of each concept. Give examples and nonexamples of each concept.

3.  Think of a concept that you had to learn. Explain how your current schemata (or lack of them) affected your learning.

## FINAL SELF-TEST

Write your answers to each of the questions in the space provided.  You may check the accuracy and completeness of your answers by referring to the answer key at the end of this chapter.

1.   Name and define the three kinds of knowledge identified by psychologists.

2.   Explain how declarative knowledge is best learned.

3.   Describe the relationship between declarative knowledge and higher level tasks.

4.   Describe the dimensions along which concepts may vary.

5.   Describe four methods of teaching concepts.

6.   Explain the role of schemata in the comprehension of new material.

7.   Describe five ways to help students comprehend material.

## ANSWER KEY

**Definition of Key Terms**

1.   Declarative knowledge:  knowing specific things; involves memorizing factual information (pp. 138, 139)

2.   Rote learning:  remembering through repetition (p. 139)

3.   Distributed practice:  practice that occurs over time with breaks between study periods (p. 139)

4.   Massed practice:  practice that occurs in one long period with no breaks (p. 139)

5.   Procedural knowledge:  knowing how to do things; involves knowing rules and how to apply them in order to complete a task (pp. 138, 140)

6.   General knowledge:  knowledge used in a wide range of situations (p. 142)

7.   Domain-specific knowledge:  knowledge used in a limited, defined content area (p. 142)

8.   Conceptual knowledge:  knowing about something; involves categorizing related information into an organized idea and understanding the relationships between ideas (pp. 138, 142)

9.   Concepts:  classifications of a set of related ideas or events (p. 142)

10.   Concrete concept:  a concept that can be seen, that exists, that is tangible (p. 143)

11.     Abstract concept:  a concept that has no physical existence, that is intangible (p. 143)

12.     Attributes:  characteristics of a concept (p. 145)

13.     Examples:  members of the set described by a concept (p. 145)

14.     Nonexamples:  something that is not part of the set described by a concept (p. 145)

15.     Discovery learning:  the process in which students 'figure out' principles or relationships as a result of active learning and direct, hands-on experiences (p. 146)

16.     Prototypes:  the first instances of a concept that come to mind and possess the concept's most characteristic attributes--a model (p. 146)

17.     Principles:  generalizations that describe relationships between or among concepts (p. 148)

18.     Comprehension:  the process by which learners construct meaning from incoming information (p. 149)

19.     Schema:  an individual's existing organization of knowledge about a topic--one's understanding about how the world works (p. 149)

20.     Reciprocal questioning:  pairs of students ask each other questions about material they have learned (p. 150)

21.     Linear array:  a line on which events are placed in chronological order (p. 151)

22.     Hierarchies:  structures describing the relationships between ideas in terms of subordinate and superordinate categories (p. 151)

23.     Networks:  ways of organizing complex information that show how various ideas are linked to each other (p. 152)

24.     Matrix:  a graphic organizer that compares several topics along multiple dimensions (p. 153)


**Answers to Comprehension Check**

| | | |
|---|---|---|
| 1. | declarative knowledge | (p. 138) |
| 2. | procedural knowledge | (p. 138) |
| 3. | conceptual knowledge | (p. 138) |
| 4. | declarative | (p. 139) |
| 5. | procedural | (p. 141) |
| 6. | concept | (p. 142) |
| 7. | abstraction | (p. 143) |
| 8. | generality | (p. 144) |
| 9. | complexity | (p. 144) |
| 10. | attributes | (p. 145) |
| 11. | examples and nonexamples | (p. 145) |
| 12. | prototypes | (p. 146) |
| 13. | comprehension | (p. 149) |
| 14. | paraphrasing | (p. 150) |
| 15. | summarizing | (p. 150) |
| 16. | questioning | (p. 150) |

17.    notetaking                              (p. 151)
18.    PQ4R                                    (p. 151)


**Answers to Final Self-Test Questions**

1.    The three kinds of knowledge identified by psychologists are: 1) declarative knowledge, or knowing specific things, which involves memorizing factual information; 2) procedural knowledge, or knowing how to do something, which involves knowing the steps required to complete a task; and 3) conceptual knowledge, or knowing about something, which involves understanding the relationships between ideas. (p. 138)

2.    Declarative knowledge is best learned through practice and overlearning. (p. 139)

3.    Declarative knowledge provides the foundation on which to build more complex information and to engage in higher order thinking. (p. 140)

4.    Concepts may vary in degree of abstraction; they may range from concrete--a concept that can be seen and touched--to abstract--a concept that does not exist physically. Concepts may vary in degree of generality; they may range from general to specific. Concepts may also vary in degree of complexity; they may range from simple--with few relationships with other concepts--to complex--with many different kinds of relationships with other concepts. (pp. 143-144)

5.    Four methods of teaching concepts are: 1) presenting students with a list of attributes or characteristics of a concept; 2) presenting examples of the concept (things that belong to the concept) and also presenting nonexamples of the concept (things that do not belong to the concept); 3) using discovery learning, structuring situations that foster exploration, questioning, hypothesis testing and conclusion drawing; and 4) comparing an object to a prototype--the first instance of a concept that comes to mind and that possesses the concept's most characteristic attributes. (pp. 145-146)

6.    Schemata affect the processing and comprehension of new information. If students have appropriate schemata, they will understand and remember new information. If students lack appropriate schemata, they will probably not understand new information. Information that contradicts existing schemata may be resisted or rejected. (p. 149)

7.    Five methods of helping students comprehend material are: 1) paraphrasing material--putting it into one's own words; 2) summarizing material--condensing and reconstructing it; 3) self-questioning; 4) taking notes in one's own words; 5) using graphic organizers--various types of charts and graphs, and 6) PQ4R--preview, question, read, reflect, recite, review. (pp. 150-151)

# Introduction to Educational Psychology

© Jeff Greenberg/Unicorn Stock Photos

# Educational Psychology for Teachers: An Introduction

# USING THIS TEXT

This text was designed as your learning tool. The next few pages show how the special features can help you get the most from this text.

## Chapter Outlines

Provide a map of the chapter content, and list pages for easy reference.

### Chapter Outline

### Learning Objectives

2.1 Define the term *learning*.

2.2 Describe the philosophical roots of behavioral and cognitive approaches to learning.

2.3 Summarize the behavioral approach and distinguish between classical and operant conditioning.

2.4 Apply behaviorism to educational settings.

2.5 Describe the cognitive approach to learning and differentiate the cognitive-developmental from the information-processing model.

2.6 Discuss the principles of social learning theory and explain how models can influence learning.

2.7 Explain the ideas inherent in a humanist approach to learning and give examples of educational applications of humanism.

### Preview

Although the field of educational psychology is concerned with all psychological aspects of the educational process, its primary goal is to discover how people learn. Over the years, educational psychologists have used a variety of approaches in trying to describe and explain learning. In this chapter, we describe two approaches that have had the greatest impact on our understanding of learning: the *behavioral* and the *cognitive* approaches; in addition, we describe the *humanist* and *social learning* approaches.

Both the behavioral and cognitive approaches have had more influence on educational practice than have the social learning or humanist approaches. The behavioral approach

has been around the longest, but more and more educational psychologists are shifting to the cognitive approach.

Followers of the behavioral approach attempt to explain learning by studying behavior that is observable; behaviorists believe that internal mental processes are unobservable and consequently unknowable. Behaviorists use two types of conditioning to explain learning: *classical conditioning*, in which a response originally linked to one stimulus becomes linked to a different stimulus; and *operant conditioning*, in which the use of reinforcers leads to increases or decreases in the occurrence of a response.

According to the social learning approach, people learn by imitating

The cognitive approach tries to explain learning by examining the thought processes that underlie it. Cognitivists differ from behaviorists in a very fundamental way: Behaviorists do not address how the mind works, which is precisely the focus of cognitivists. There are two major models within the cognitive approach: (a) the *cognitive-developmental model*, which focuses on how individuals construct their own understanding and the stages that people go through in their cognitive development, and (b) the *information-processing model*, which examines the workings of the human mind as if it were a computer.

---

#### Differences Between Animal and Human Learning

Many psychologists question whether laws of animal learning offer much help in understanding human learning. There are many reasons to doubt the assumption that universal laws of learning apply equally well to animals and human beings, particularly because human beings have the ability to use language and exhibit a far greater degree of judgment and reasoning than pigeons and rats.

#### Extrinsic Versus Intrinsic Motivation

Some critics argue that the use of rewards to motivate students (extrinsic motivation) may dampen students' intrinsic motivation (Deci et al., 1991; Kohn, 1993). If students act in certain ways to receive rewards, they will not engage in the behavior for its own sake or because they know it to be the right thing to do (intrinsic motivation). Most educators want students to be self-motivated individuals who seek knowledge to satisfy their curiosity or because they love learning. If using rewards reduces students' intrinsic motivation, it may be a bad idea in the long run. Chance (1992; 1993) argues that both types of rewards have a place in educational settings and teachers need to strike a balance regarding use of extrinsic and intrinsic forms of motivation.

#### Individual Differences

Teachers are well aware that what students learn may vary from student to student, even when students are exposed to the same environment. Behaviorists claim that students who are placed in the same learning situation may respond differently because each student has a different set of previous experiences. As a result of these different experiences, some students have learned to make different responses than other students to the same stimuli, so that in any given situation, not all students will necessarily respond in the same way.

Cognitivists, however, argue that previous experiences are stored in memory and that even the same event is remembered differently by different people. The way in which a person remembers an experience is determined by how the person perceives the experience and thinks about it. According to cognitivists, a person's prior experience is not simply an accumulation of prior learning, but rather a body of knowledge that the person has created. How a person responds in a given situation is at least partially determined by the body of knowledge the person brings to the situation.

### The Cognitive Approach to Learning

**2.5**
*Describe the cognitive approach to learning and differentiate the cognitive-developmental from the information-processing model.*

The fundamental difference between behavioral and cognitive approaches to learning is the role that thinking plays. Thinking plays no role whatsoever in behavioral theories. In cognitive theories, however, thinking plays the central role (Schwartz & Reisberg, 1991).

Cognition is a term used to describe all of our mental processes, such as perception, memory, and judgment. The most important mental process is thinking, and cognitivists focus most of their attention on studying how people think. There are two major approaches to the study of thinking: the cognitive-developmental model and the information-processing model. A brief overview of these two approaches should help you grasp more clearly the theoretical contrast between cognitive and behavioral approaches to the study of learning.

#### The Cognitive-Developmental Model

The cognitive-developmental model focuses on changes that occur in how people think as they progress from infancy though childhood and adolescence and ultimately into adulthood. The best-known cognitive-developmental psychologist is Jean Piaget, who revolutionized our understanding of how children think and construct knowledge.

## Learning Objectives (with icons)

Clearly state objectives of the chapter. The icons show exactly where text meets the learning goals stated at the beginning of the chapter.

## Previews

Prime you for the chapter by introducing ideas and putting content into perspective. Previews answer the question "Why am I reading this chapter?"

## TEACHERS ROUNDTABLE

### "Every Year You Get Better"

**DMP:** Could you share some thoughts at this point with college students who are planning to be teachers? What are your recommendations to them?

**Donna:** I'd like to emphasize the small successes. You give your students an opportunity, and you encourage them to succeed. Also, it's important to remember that fair doesn't necessarily mean equal. I may give more help to one student and less to another. Some may not be able to do what every other child is doing; or they may not have the ability to sit and do work for the period of time you're asking them to. You have to provide them with the opportunities for success so they will want to go on and tackle the next lesson. You also have to be knowledgeable and sensitive to the social aspects. You have to know their personalities.

**Mary:** To new teachers, I would say count your successes. New teachers are often very hard on themselves. It's difficult to be the teacher. Sometimes it's frustrating. So, to help yourself, you have to focus on the successes.

**Anthony:** And remember that you can't be a perfect teacher the first year of teaching; you make improvements every year. And every year you get a little bit better. You do it a step at a time. There is no substitute for experience.

**Angela:** And continue to learn. Take a course; read journals. Not only do you get wonderful information, but you're learning about other teachers and what they have tried, faced with the same types of problem you may have. And as you grow as a person, you automatically grow as a teacher because you have more to share.

**Irwin:** The first thing I would tell teachers is that it is a very difficult job. It requires a great deal of work and a great deal of planning. You have to be prepared. You also have to learn from the students who are in front of you. You have to learn about them, their egos, their needs. You have to deal with all different kinds of kids in the classroom. So not only do you have to plan the material in order to be prepared (because otherwise you'll stumble), but you also have to learn continuously from the kids who are in front of you.

**Donna:** My first few weeks, my head was spinning. "She's doing this, but he's doing that." I kept thinking about how the kids *should* be and how I *should* be. Now, I'm really finding my own way. It's very difficult, but suddenly the days and weeks go by, and you realize you've found your own style.

**Irwin:** The single most important factor in the classroom is that the teacher must make connections with a class. You can always teach better—you can ask better questions and you can know the curriculum better. But when you connect with that class, when your personality is present, and the kids believe that you and they are in this together. Then you're a successful teacher.

---

## Teachers Roundtables

Put you at the table as teachers speak, in their own voices, about issues in classrooms and schools. You'll find these throughout the text, placed to fit with the chapter content.

---

## Diversity Makes a Difference

Explore issues of diversity, including how learners differ and the impact of diversity on classroom teaching. This feature helps you to see learners from various perspectives and to think about how you will approach diversity in your own classroom.

---

### DIVERSITY MAKES A DIFFERENCE

#### Where Do Stereotypes Come From?

Piaget's concepts of equilibration, assimilation, and accommodation help us understand how people develop stereotypes. A *stereotype* is a generalization on which prejudices are based. Often stereotypes are beliefs individuals hold about a group of people. You are no doubt familiar with common stereotypes people hold about men, women, African Americans, Asians, Hispanics, Jews, WASPs, teenagers, elderly people, homosexuals, librarians, lawyers, athletes, short people, fat people, and so forth. Clearly, not all members of each group have the same traits, but we cling to our stereotypes.

According to Piagetian theory, stereotypes represent schemata we have developed, either from our own experience or more likely from hearing or observing others' attitudes. Children may see librarians portrayed on television as middle-aged women who are quiet and timid and who wear glasses hanging around their neck. When visiting the library, children may notice some librarians who fit this image, thereby reinforcing the schema for "librarian."

Not every librarian fits this image, of course, so children eventually encounter librarians who are young, outspoken, male, or not wearing glasses. According to Piaget's theory, children reconcile their image of librarians who don't fit the stereotype by assimilating, that is, by regarding the librarian who doesn't fit the stereotype as simply an exception. When faced with a challenge to schemata, people tend to assimilate, not accommodate, frequently maintaining rigid stereotypes in the presence of contradictory evidence (Hamilton, 1981; Hamilton & Rose, 1980).

Stereotypes may cause people to behave in certain ways toward an individual simply because the individual belongs to a stereotyped group. Although Piaget's theory explains how stereotypes develop, we should treat others fairly and without bias, especially in schools, where teachers, students, and parents may come from a variety of ethnic, cultural, and language groups.

Peanuts reprinted by permission of United Feature Syndicate, Inc.

Lev Semenovich Vygotsky (1896–1934).
© James Wertsch/Washington University in St. Louis

skills and knowledge more efficiently; in other words, helping students learn to *think* allows them to learn more facts and skills than teaching them those facts and skills directly. Research tends to support this view (e.g., DeVries & Kohlberg, 1987).

#### Vygotsky's Approach to Cognitive Development

Lev Semenovich Vygotsky was a pioneering Russian cognitive psychologist who made an enormous contribution to our understanding of language and thinking even though he was only 38 years old when he died. Because of his genius and creativity, he has been called the "Mozart of psychology" (Toulmin, 1978). Vygotsky's work did not attract much attention in the United States until the 1980s, even though his work had been known for some time. The cognitive revolution led to the rediscovery of Piaget long before the rediscovery of Vygotsky, perhaps because Vygotsky's work was done in the Communist Soviet Union. As better translations of Vygotsky's work appeared, however, Vygotsky's genius has become recognized in the United States.

---

## Windows on Teaching

Help you make the leap from theory to practice by describing step-by-step practices for classroom teaching. Several of these boxes are in each chapter so you can immediately begin to develop your repertoire of teaching ideas.

---

### WINDOWS ON TEACHING

#### Presenting a Moral Dilemma

Gilligan presented elementary school children with a moral dilemma: On a cold, rainy night and a porcupine pokes its head into the home of a mole and asks to take shelter there. The mole then invites the porcupine in but soon discovers that sharing a small home with a porcupine can be extremely uncomfortable. The mole tells the porcupine to leave, but the porcupine says, "You invited me in and I'm going to stay." What should the porcupine do?

Consistent with her theory, Gilligan found that girls' responses concerned the responsibilities of the mole and the porcupine, but boys' responses concerned the rights of each. (It is important to note that some boys gave responses with a "responsibilities" orientation, some girls gave responses reflecting a "rights" orientation, and some children produced solutions that showed elements of both orientations.)

Now it's your turn: Read the "Mole and Porcupine" dilemma to some elementary school-age children and listen to their responses. Ask probing questions and see what orientation (or orientations) their responses reflect, and what stage they represent within the framework of Kohlberg's and Gilligan's theories.

---

### Self-Concept

**Self-concept**, or one's perception of oneself, probably develops at the moment the child is aware of his or her separateness (Stern, 1985). Early experiences with caregivers, parents, and family provide the backdrop from which attitudes about the self grow. Psychologists regard the early years as critical to the eventual sense of confidence, personal regard, and competence that an individual experiences (Markus & Wurf, 1987; Suls & Greenwald, 1986). Self-concept, however, is not simply an emotional response to experience; it is a complex cognitive schema that the individual creates from experience (Markus & Nurius, 1986).

Just as we develop schemata for other concepts, we develop a schema of the self. Our **self-schema** is a cognitive structure we construct as we receive information about ourselves (Markus & Nurius, 1986). Markus and Nurius contend that most self-concepts are **working self-concepts** that are open to change as we encounter new experiences that provide us new feedback. How we imagine ourselves now and in the future determines our self-concept. As a teacher you will be most concerned with the impact of students' self-concepts on their motivation to learn.

#### Academic Self-Concept and Academic Achievement

Most students enter school expecting to learn (Entwistle & Hayduk, 1981; Stipek, 1988), but negative school experiences often reverse their views. In particular, students who have learning difficulties begin to perceive themselves as unable to learn (Chapman, 1988).

Most people see themselves in several different roles. For example, students have varying beliefs about their athletic ability, their ability to make lasting friendships, their musical ability, and their academic ability. They also have a generalized self-concept, such as a propensity toward optimism or pessimism. General self-concept has only a small positive correlation with academic achievement. Some specific perceptions of self, such as athletic or social abilities, have no relationship to academic achievement (Hansford & Hattie, 1982; Marsh & Shavelson, 1985).

**9.5**
Summarize the research concerning self-concept and its role in academic achievement.

Students' self-concepts can change as a result of new experiences.

What are some school experiences that might negatively affect students at the elementary, junior high, and senior high school levels?

---

## Notes to Students

Encourage and challenge you to think about what you are reading. How does this content apply to your own experiences and beliefs? When you read these notes, answer the questions—either on your own or with others. By putting yourself into the content, you will gain a richer understanding of the text concepts. Notes are comments, questions, and suggestions.

The executive may say, "We are expecting a big delivery—we'd better move some workers from the production line to the loading dock." In our minds, the workers are analogous to the mental resources we devote to attention and rehearsal; the executive processes oversee how we use our resources and may decide to reallocate resources when needed.

### Metacognition as a Function of Age

As people get older their metacognitive abilities improve (Flavell, 1985). Young children have little metacognitive awareness and do not apply metacognitive strategies spontaneously, even though they are able to do so when reminded (Garner, 1990). You can teach elementary school students to use metacognitive strategies to improve their learning (Cross & Paris, 1988; Ghatala et al., 1985). Ormrod (1990) notes that, in general, as students get older, they

- become more realistic about their memory abilities
- are better able to develop and use effective learning strategies and
- are more accurate in knowing that they know something

Not all students improve their metacognitive abilities as they get older. In fact, a surprising number of older students are unaware of techniques they can use to check their knowledge and performance. You may sometimes have to encourage your students to learn self-checking techniques; indeed, programs such as Meichenbaum's "cognitive behavior modification" method (1986) have been designed to help students learn how to monitor their thinking.

### Other Models of Information Processing

Have you ever been heavily engaged in a conversation and, although you are aware that a nearby group is having another conversation, you have no knowledge of what that group is talking about? The linear model of information processing easily explains this phenomenon: Your limited capacity of attention is focused on your own conversation and does not permit the neighboring conversation to enter STM. However, if your name is mentioned in the neighboring conversation, you would be instantly aware of it!

A student who approaches learning passively may not engage in the metacognitive activities necessary for successful performance.

A+

Have you ever been engaged in a conversation and, although you are aware that another conversation is occurring nearby, you have no knowledge of what the other group is talking about?
© Unephoto, Inc.

---

## A+ Icons

Flag passages in the text that apply educational psychology concepts to classroom teaching.

## Annual Edition Icons

Show where sections or articles from *Annual Editions: Educational Psychology* directly apply to text content. *Annual Editions* feature the latest articles and the classics, compiled as the "best of the best" resources.

## Key Terms

Boldfaced in text and explained fully in the comprehensive glossary.

---

**Figure 3.6**
Class inclusion task.

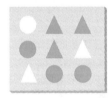

once could solve. Teaching preoperational students to perform logical operations associated with the stage of concrete operations has no lasting effect. Children can learn logical operations only when they are developmentally ready.

Casey (1990), for example, compared the performance of preschoolers attending an experimental preschool designed to "promote planning and problem-solving abilities" with the performance of similar children attending conventional preschools. After one year in their respective schools, children in the experimental program performed better on planning and problem-solving tasks than children in the conventional program, but the groups did not differ in their ability to conserve.

**Class inclusion**, the ability to classify objects according to more than one category simultaneously, is another operation that concrete operational children can perform but preoperational children can't. Preoperational children have difficulty determining if there are more shaded figures than triangles in figure 3.6 because they can't classify objects by color and shape simultaneously. Concrete operational children can easily give the correct answer.

### Formal Operations Stage

Concrete operational children can apply logic only to "here and now" situations. People in the **formal operations stage**, which begins around age 11 or 12 and continues through adulthood, can apply logic to abstract and hypothetical situations. At this stage, students can answer questions such as, "What would have happened if the Germans and Japanese had won World War II?" or "What might happen if we did not vote by secret ballot?" Concrete operational children cannot generate meaningful responses to these questions, but formal operational adolescents can.

Formal thinking requires the ability to think abstractly. Works of literature and art can take on abstract meaning only to someone in formal operations. Concrete operational children look at such works literally. Formal operational thinkers can also engage in hypothesis testing, or scientific thinking.

Suppose you ask students what controls the speed at which a pendulum moves back and forth. Some students may suggest that the weight at the end of the pendulum controls speed; others may believe that the length of the string is the important factor. To help the students experimentally determine the correct answer, you give them two weights, one weighing 1 gram and the other 2 grams, and two pieces of string, one 5 centimeters and the other 10 centimeters in length.

Concrete operational thinkers would try various combinations of weights and lengths of string haphazardly. They might stumble upon the correct answer, but they would not solve the problem efficiently and systematically. Formal operational thinkers, however, would test hypotheses: First, they might test the hypothesis that the weight controls speed. As shown in figure 3.7, testing this hypothesis involves two steps:

A+

---

Students bring diverse personalities to the classroom.
© Tom McCarthy/Unicorn Stock Photos

Just as individuals differ in terms of intelligence and creativity, they also differ in terms of personality. Some students are shy and withdrawn, whereas others are outgoing and enjoy the company of others. Some students are conscientious and cooperative; others are rebellious and uncooperative. It is not just students, however, who exhibit diverse personality characteristics. Teachers do, too.

You probably remember having some teachers who were warm and supportive and who made school a fun place to be. Perhaps such a teacher inspired you to become a teacher yourself. Unfortunately, you probably also remember some teachers who handled the classroom like drill sergeants.

In this chapter we discuss the nature of personality, including factors affecting its development and explain how you can help students acquire healthy emotions and appropriate social behaviors. This chapter will give you a framework for examining your own social and emotional behavior and also give you guidelines for helping students develop positive attitudes toward school and learning.

### Personality: Where Does It Come From?

Psychologists use the term **personality** to refer to "a broad collection of attributes—including temperament, attitudes, traits, values, and distinctive behavioral patterns (or habits)—that seem to characterize an individual" (Shaffer, 1988, p. 43). Various psychologists hold different views about how personality develops, depending on their philosophy about the nature of human beings and the relative importance of hereditary and environmental factors on personality development.

### Erikson's Theory of Psychosocial Development

Erik Erikson was one of the most distinguished students of Sigmund Freud, who believed that human beings are driven by *irrational* impulses. Erikson, however, believed human beings are inherently *rational* and that social aspects of culture, not instinctive biological drives, determine people's emotional and social behavior. Erikson also believed that despite cultural differences, all people progress through the same sequence of psychosocial development (Erikson, 1963).

Annual ✎ Edition
unit 2

9.1 ◉
*Define personality and identify where it comes from.*

*How does the psychological definition differ from other definitions of personality?*

9.2 ◉
*Describe Erikson's theory of psychosocial development and identify methods of promoting students' psychosocial development.*

**Figure 8.1**
Guilford's Structure of Intellect Model.

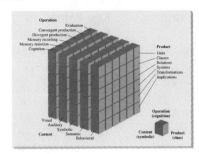

## Visuals

Highlight information through a different perspective than straight text, addressing various learning styles. A good visual can show an idea and help concepts click into place. Visuals include line art, photographs, and cartoons.

**Your Beliefs About Intelligence**

8.1

*Explain how your beliefs and your students' beliefs about intelligence influence classroom activity.*

Your views about intelligence may affect the way you deal with students. If you believe intelligence is a single entity, you may expect a student's academic performance in all subjects to be comparable. On the other hand, if you believe intelligence is multifaceted, you may expect students' performance levels to vary from one subject to another. Your beliefs about intelligence may also affect decisions you make about grouping students, designing lessons, and deciding the appropriate level of difficulty of assigned academic tasks.

### Guilford's Structure of Intellect Model

Of all the psychometric models, Guilford's Structure of Intellect (Guilford, 1988) has generated the most interest (see figure 8.1). Guilford's model contains 120 unique types of intelligence within a three-dimensional system. The first dimension is *operation*, or types of the mental processes; the second is *content*, or the types of information to which mental processes are applied; and the third is *product*, or the types of outcomes of mental processes. The model is difficult to apply in practical situations because it has so many different types of intelligence.

### Current Theories of Intelligence

8.2

*Describe six theories of human intelligence.*

Current theories, which regard intelligence as multidimensional, stem from cognitive psychology and neuropsychology, not from psychometrics. The leading theorists are Howard Gardner and Robert Sternberg.

### Gardner's Theory of Multiple Intelligences

Gardner (1983, 1993b) believes that people have seven kinds of intelligence, with high ability in some and low ability in others. These intelligences, shown in figure 8.2, are independent of one another.

## Self-Study Exercises

Ask you to interact with the chapter ideas. These exercises help you actively test your knowledge.

## Further Readings

List other references to help you achieve your reading and research assignments, or broaden your knowledge.

---

Teachers use individual, paired, or small group assignments to address the differing needs of students.
© 1996 Laura Dwight

### KEY POINTS

1. Although students with learning disabilities are a heterogeneous group, their major characteristics include hyperactivity, perceptual-motor difficulties, emotional instability, attention problems, and impulsivity.

2. To help students with learning disabilities learn more effectively, place them in a nondistracting environment, use direct instruction, and teach them general learning strategies.

3. Mental retardation is defined as subaverage intellectual functioning (IQ less than 70) that occurs concurrently with deficits in adaptive behavior and has a variety of causes, including lack of a stimulating environment in the early years and improper nutrition.

4. Behavior classified as emotionally disturbed must differ markedly from the norm. Students with emotional disturbance are frequently either extremely aggressive or withdrawn.

5. Teachers of students with emotional disturbance use behavior modification techniques, direct instruction of appropriate behaviors, and the Rogerian counseling technique.

6. Special education is designed for students whose needs cannot be met in regular educational settings.

7. *Mainstreaming* is the term used when a student in a special education classroom attends a regular classroom for part of the day.

8. IDEA mandates that all students, regardless of their disability, have a right to a free and appropriate education in the least restrictive environment.

9. Regular classroom teachers should exhaust all possible remedies before referring a student for possible special education placement.

10. Students from ethnic minorities are overrepresented in special education classes for a number of reasons unrelated to their learning difficulties.

11. Inclusion is the practice of placing students with disabilities in age-appropriate classes with appropriate supportive services.

---

### SELF-STUDY EXERCISES

1. Why is the term *learning disabled* so difficult to define? Give one definition of the term.

2. Contrast the developmental and difference theories of mental retardation.

3. Define the term *adaptive behavior* and explain why it is an important aspect of mental retardation.

4. How do emotional disabilities interfere with learning? Describe a behavior modification approach and the Rogerian approach to teaching students with emotional disturbance.

5. Explain how the age at which hearing loss occurs affects student learning. Describe the role of American Sign Language or total communication in teaching students with hearing loss.

6. Name two important instructional goals for students with visual impairments.

7. What are the legal rights of the student with special needs? What is meant by *least restrictive environment?*

8. What is an IEP? How does mainstreaming affect the regular teacher's role in determining students' educational needs?

9. How do mainstreaming and inclusion differ? What are the pros and cons of each?

10. List specific measures you can take to assure that students with disabilities have sufficient opportunities to learn in a regular classroom.

11. What should you do before deciding to refer a student to special education?

12. How does cultural bias affect student referral for possible special education placement? What accounts for the overrepresentation of minorities in special education?

13. Discuss possible causes for low academic achievement among students who are not disabled. Describe effective instructional techniques for low-achieving students. How can you help low achievers improve their self-esteem?

### FURTHER READINGS

Gartner, A., & Joe, T. (1986). *Images of the disabled/disabling images.* New York: Praeger.

Hallahan, D. P., & Kauffman, J. M. (1991). *Exceptional children: Introduction to special education* (5th ed.). Englewood Cliffs, NJ: Prentice Hall.

Larivee, B. (1985). *Effective teaching for successful mainstreaming.* New York: Longman.

Rogers, C. (1977). *Freedom to learn.* Columbus, OH: Merrill.

### REFERENCES

Algozzine, B., Christenson, S., & Ysseldyke, J. E. (1982). Probabilities associated with the referral to placement process. *Teacher Education and Special Education, 5,* 19–23.

Belmont, J. M., & Butterfield, E. C. (1971). What the development of short-term memory is. *Human Development, 14,* 236–248.

Biklen, D. (1992). *Schools without labels: Parents, educators, and inclusive education.* Philadelphia: Temple University Press.

Brooks, P. H., & McCauley, C. (1984). Cognitive research in mental retardation. *American Journal of Mental Deficiency, 88,* 479–486.

Campione, J. C., Brown, A. L., & Ferrara, R. A. (1982). Mental retardation and intelligence. In R. J. Sternberg (Ed.), *Handbook of human intelligence* (pp. 392–490). Cambridge: Cambridge University Press.

Cummins, J. (1984). *Bilingualism and special education: Issues in assessment and pedagogy.* Cleveland, Avon, England: Multilingual Matters, Ltd.

Duffy, F. H., & McAnulty, G. B. (1985). Brain electrical activity mapping (BEAM): The search for a physiological signature of dyslexia. In F. H. Duffy & N. Geschwind

(Eds.), *Dyslexia: A neuroscientific approach to clinical evaluation* (pp. 105–122). Boston: Little, Brown.

Dunn, L. M. (1968). Special education for the mildly retarded: Is much of it justifiable? *Exceptional Children, 35,* 5–22.

Ellis, E. S., Deshler, D. D., & Schumaker, J. B. (1989). Teaching adolescents with learning disabilities to generate and use task-specific strategies. *Journal of Learning Disabilities, 22,* 108–119, 130.

Ellis, N. R. (1970). Memory processes in retardates and normals. In N. R. Ellis (Ed.), *International review of research in mental retardation* (Vol. 4, pp. 1–32). New York: Academic Press.

Ellis, N. R., & Cavalier, A. R. (1982). Research perspectives in mental retardation. In E. Zigler & D. Balla (Eds.), *Mental retardation: The developmental-difference controversy* (pp. 121-152). Hillsdale, NJ: Erlbaum.

Engelmann, S., Carnine, L., Johnson, G., & Meyers, L. (1989). *Corrective reading: Comprehension.* Chicago: Science Research Associates.

Engelmann, S. E. (1977). Sequencing cognitive and academic tasks. In R. D. Kneedler & S. G. Tarver (Eds.), *Changing perspectives in special education* (pp. 46–61). Columbus, OH: Merrill.

## References

List resources we used in writing the chapter.

## Key Points

Summarize specific, important chapter concepts. Use them to review chapter ideas.

# Chapter Outline

# Learning Objectives ◉

1.1 Describe the improving status of teaching as a profession.

1.2 Summarize the reports of several national task forces that have recently studied education in the United States.

1.3 Identify factors that have contributed to criticism of education in the United States.

1.4 Summarize important social conditions that affect student achievement.

1.5 Describe the importance of higher-order thinking skills.

1.6 Explain how the current educational reform movement differs from previous ones.

1.7 List important requirements for professional development.

1.8 Describe how the cognitive revolution has affected education in U.S. schools.

1.9 Explain why educators in the United States are rethinking the curriculum.

# Preview

Chances are that if you are reading this book, you are enrolled as a student in an educational psychology course. And chances also are that you want to be a teacher. The purpose of this introductory chapter is to bring you up to date on what is happening in the field of teaching and to give you an overview of how educational psychology can help you become and remain a competent teacher.

The role of the teacher has changed markedly over the last 20 years or so, and even more dramatic changes will occur in the near future. By grasping the nature of these changes and the reasons underlying them, you can better prepare yourself for what lies ahead in your chosen profession.

The principles of educational psychology are among the most powerful tools you can use to increase your chances of succeeding as a beginning teacher. These principles will also help you continue to grow professionally and meet the challenges you will encounter as you pursue your career. We have included in this book the traditional core of knowledge that constitutes the field of educational psychology, as well as new information and ideas on the frontier of the field.

This chapter presents an overview of some fundamental and important concepts that will help you develop a frame of reference to guide your learning as you read the chapters that follow. There are numerous ways to approach educational psychology. We have chosen to approach the field from a cognitive perspective to help you organize what you learn into a coherent set of principles and enable you to know how and when to apply them when you become a teacher. ◉

# The Improving Status of Teaching

The United States Senate proclaimed 1985 as the Year of the Teacher, a symbolic tribute to the increased recognition that teachers in the United States have begun to receive for the vital role they play in society. A more tangible form of recognition is the substantial increase in salaries offered to teachers in a growing number of school districts. Although teaching still pays less than many other professions, the salary gains over the past few years are probably proportionately higher for teachers than for many other professionals.

## Thinking Skills in Modern Society

Largely as a result of our declining economy, we began in the 1980s to reassess our educational system at a national level to determine how well it was preparing students to contribute to society. Various national commissions and task forces, such as the National Commission on Excellence in Education (1983), the Commission on Reading (1985), and the Carnegie Forum on Education and the Economy (1986), issued a number of influential reports on the status of education in the United States.

Comparisons of the academic performance of U.S. students with that of students in other countries, particularly Japan, a country that has demonstrated sustained economic growth since World War II, revealed that in many academic areas our students lag behind students in other industrialized societies

Figure 1.1 shows the results of a U.S. Department of Education (1985) report that compared average math scores of eighth-graders from 14 countries in 1981–1982. Japanese students had the highest average score, 64 percent, while U.S. students scored an average of only 48 percent, placing *twelfth*. Comparisons of performance in various mathematical topics, such as measurement or geometry, showed that U.S. eighth-graders consistently scored below their Japanese counterparts.

The National Commission on Excellence in Education found in 1983 that, among students from various industrialized nations, U.S. students scored *lowest* on 7 of 19 academic tests and failed to score first or second on any test. A 1992 Educational Testing

**1.1** ◎

*Describe the improving status of teaching as a profession.*

**1.2** ◎

*Summarize the reports of several national task forces that have recently studied education in the United States.*

These reports were not intended to "bash" U.S. education, but to identify problems in our current system and recommend changes that would lead to improvement

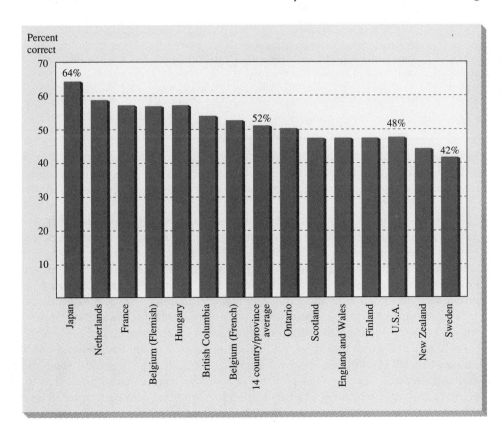

**Figure 1.1**

Average mathematics scores for students in the eighth grade: 1981–1982.

Source: U.S. Department of Education, National Center for Education Statistics (1985). Second International Mathematics Study.

# TEACHERS ROUNDTABLE

## "Children Are the Best Part of the Job"

The Teachers Roundtable feature is the result of a discussion between two of the authors and five practicing teachers. The teachers represent many different aspects of teaching: One is brand new; others are veterans; one teaches high school; another teaches special education. In the discussion, the teachers bring their different perspectives to bear on a variety of topics. This first portion describes these teachers' professional backgrounds and what motivated them to become teachers.

**DMP:** First, I think our readers would like to know something about your background in teaching, and then we'll talk more about what you think about students and about teaching.

**Irwin:** I started out many years ago as a junior high school teacher in Bedford Stuyvesant teaching social studies. From there, I moved on to the high school level. I came to my current school about 17 years ago as a social studies teacher, but I've taught the range of subjects; as a new teacher I taught math, Shakespeare, and even Business Arithmetic.

**Anthony:** I went in the other direction . . . I started in high school, but ended up in elementary school. I worked one year teaching high school biology and then stumbled into elementary school, intending to stay a short time, and spent 33 years there! I just enjoyed working with young children. I never thought I would—I wanted to work in high schools, but I just fell in love with the elementary school age group. I thought that they were just marvelous to work with. They are so honest and open.

**Angela:** I started with private schools in an open classroom environment for four or five years. And from there I came to the public schools and started working in special education. My first assignment was working with students with severe emotional disturbances, and I did that for four or five years. Then I went to the opposite end of the spectrum and currently work in a resource room with students with learning disabilities.

**Donna:** I'm at the beginning of the ladder, if that is what you want to call it. I'm just starting my first full-time teaching job and I am a language arts teacher. I teach what's called the language enrichment program . . . anything involving reading, writing, listening, or speaking. I teach classes in both special education and general education, and I teach all the grades. Last year, I spent half a year student teaching and half a year working as a substitute teacher, so this year is really the beginning for me.

**Mary:** I taught first in a parochial school, then in a public school, and I've taught first to fifth grade. Over the years, I've changed direction

---

The United States has a large and widely diverse school population. This diversity, which contributes to our strength as a nation, presents multifaceted problems to educators seeking complex solutions. In countries with more homogeneous populations, such as Japan, cultural values are shared by the majority and conflicts rarely arise about how and what students should be taught in schools.

Explore this important issue as you read on and identify the effects of language, culture, and curriculum on student learning.

Service study comparing students from the United States and those from other industrialized countries found similar results. Of even greater concern is the finding that nearly 40 percent of U.S. 17-year-olds can't perform higher-order thinking skills (Fantini, 1986).

Bracey (1996) argues that interpretations of the findings of studies that compare the academic performance of students in various industrialized societies (e.g., Merseth, 1993; Stevenson, Lee, & Stigler, 1986; Stevenson & Stigler, 1992) often inaccurately portray U.S. students as lagging far behind. International comparisons, however, often ignore the important finding that "most countries score together such that small differences in *scores* make large differences in *ranks*" (Bracey, 1996, p. 6). In other words, even though U.S. students rank lower than students from many other nations, their scores are not significantly lower.

Bracey also notes that the variability among scores of students from the same country exceeds that among scores of students from different countries, suggesting that students from all countries perform at a similar level. He also notes that it is often difficult to determine if students from other countries who participate in international studies represent biased samples consisting of high academic achievers.

from a basal reader to a whole language approach. I love, love, love what I'm doing.

**SK:** How did you get to the idea that you wanted to be a teacher in the first place? What was it that inspired you or made you think that teaching was a career for you?

**Anthony:** I think that you have to just love to be with children. If you have that initial love, teaching is something you just want to do.

**Mary:** I loved school. I was a good student, but I always felt sorry for the children who weren't. And I guess maybe, when I became a teacher, I wanted to recognize those children who didn't do well, such as my own sister who was left back. It was very difficult for her in school, but she had many other talents.

**Angela:** As a child, I was always playing teacher, and I was always put in the role where I was helping or counseling or dealing with others. And I guess that and the love for school motivated me to want to work with children. I worked as a camp counselor, and did tutoring and babysitting—all that encouraged me to become a teacher.

**Irwin:** In college, being a teacher was not foremost in my mind. I was a political science major and did not go into teaching when I graduated college. Shortly afterwards, I went into the army and when I came out of the army, I went into business. My evolution into teaching was quite interesting. My wife was student teaching when I first met her at Brooklyn College. I became very friendly with some teachers who were involved in a Ford Foundation project in a low-income area, an innovative project designed to give students equal opportunities. I felt this was more meaningful than working in business. I've been teaching ever since, and I never looked back.

**Donna:** I didn't come to teaching from the beginning. I was a case worker in child protective services investigating alleged child abuse. That work wasn't always fulfilling for me—sometimes it involved forcing people to get help they really didn't want. From time to time, I would hear from people I knew who were teachers about how exciting it was; I was really turned on and found out more about the teacher education programs at the local college. Teaching seems so much more meaningful to me and inspiring. And, in a somewhat selfish way, I have to say that I need to get a little something back.

**DMP:** Has teaching fulfilled your expectations?

**Donna:** About 99.8 percent probably; other than on those days that everybody has, I'm very happy. I like working with children and it's a very gratifying experience every day.

**Anthony:** Children are the best part of the job. As long as you can spend your time with the kids, it's great. The *adults* make it difficult! The children are the rewards.

**SK:** Is the same true when you're teaching older students?

**Irwin:** In my high school work, the kids are wonderful. Kids are the most honest people in the building. And you have to accept them where they are. If I've learned anything in teaching, it's that you have to realize that you make incremental changes that you may never see. When anyone goes in expecting to make tremendous changes immediately, they're going to be disappointed. You have to be positive; focus on the successes, not on the failures, both for your own sake and that of the kids.

**Angela:** I took a break from teaching for a few years to work with adults with mental retardation. Though I found it to be challenging and rewarding, I really missed working with children. Every holiday would come and I would want to be with my kids, so I realized I had to go back. So many people say to me, "It's time for you to move on." I've been approached by the district office to take an administrative job. They say that I could reach more children. I feel that's not true. . . . I know what I provide for my children and what they provide for me.

**Anthony:** It's difficult for some of those people to understand that you *want* to be in the classroom. That's where you want to be! That's where you find joy—not working with other teachers or working at the district office, but being with children.

**Donna:** One of the nicest things about teaching is the relationship with the students—I really get to know the children and they know me. That whole part of the job is such a wonderful thing. I can't say enough about that.

Without exception, studies carried out prior to Bracey's criticisms concluded that we need major changes in our educational system if the quality of education in the United States is to improve. The National Commission on Excellence in Education, for example, developed a curriculum for high schools that recommended the minimum number of years students should spend studying different subjects while in high school. It was found that only about 2 percent of high school seniors who graduated in 1982 had completed a curriculum that met all of the Commission's recommendations. Figure 1.2 shows the percentage of 1982 graduates who completed the recommended number of years studying various subjects at the high school level.

The findings of these studies led to the conclusion that our educational practices are failing to prepare students to succeed in the twenty-first century. In particular, students are not learning enough in areas such as mathematics and science, which are necessary to function in a modern, technological society. The recommendations of the task forces and commissions have resulted in reports like *America 2000* (U.S. Department of Education, 1991), which outlines how the United States can improve the quality of education its citizens receive by the end of this century.

*Annual* **Edition**

unit *1*

## Figure 1.2

Percentage of 1982 high school graduates who met curricular recommendations of the National Commission on Excellence in Education.

Source: U.S. Department of Education, National Center for Education Statistics (1984). *Condition of Education,* 1984.

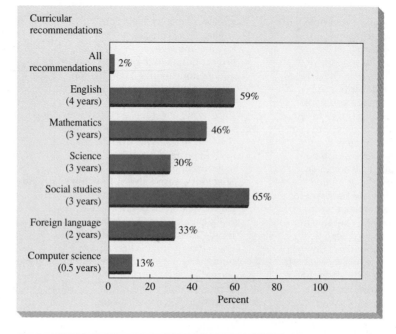

## Figure 1.3

Percentage of high school graduates who took selected mathematics and science courses.

Source: U.S. Department of Education. (1995). *High School Students Ten Years After "A Nation at Risk."* Office of Educational Research and Improvement.

| Courses | 1982 | 1987 | 1990 | 1992 |
|---|---|---|---|---|
| Geometry | 48.4 | 61.5 | 64.7 | 70.4 |
| Algebra II | 36.9 | 47.1 | 49.2 | 56.1 |
| Trigonometry | 12.2 | 19.0 | 18.4 | 21.1 |
| Calculus | 4.3 | 6.2 | 6.6 | 10.1 |
| Algebra II and geometry | 29.1 | 42.4 | 44.0 | 50.1 |
| Biology | 78.7 | 88.3 | 91.6 | 93.0 |
| Chemistry | 31.6 | 44.8 | 49.6 | 55.5 |
| Physics | 13.5 | 19.5 | 21.5 | 24.7 |
| Biology and chemistry | 28.6 | 43.0 | 48.2 | 53.9 |
| Biology, chemistry, and physics | 9.8 | 16.8 | 18.9 | 21.6 |

## Figure 1.4

Percentage of high school graduates who earned foreign language course credits.

Source: U.S. Department of Education. (1995). *High School Students Ten Years After "A Nation at Risk."* Office of Educational Research and Improvement.

| Year of graduation | 1 or more credits | 2 or more credits | 3 or more credits | 4 or more credits |
|---|---|---|---|---|
| All graduates | | | | |
| 1982 | 49.8 | 33.7 | 14.4 | 5.2 |
| 1992 | 73.9 | 58.2 | 26.6 | 10.6 |
| Expecting to earn a bachelor's degree | | | | |
| 1982 | 72.5 | 55.0 | 25.2 | 9.4 |
| 1992 | 87.1 | 73.1 | 35.6 | 14.5 |
| Expecting to attend 2 years of college or less | | | | |
| 1982 | 31.9 | 17.1 | 5.3 | 1.6 |
| 1992 | 52.5 | 32.8 | 10.4 | 2.9 |

Also as a result of the recommendations, teachers, parents, and school administrators have forged partnerships to develop more effective methods of instruction (Murphy & Hallinger, 1993), and educators are investigating new arrangements for preparing teachers for these new efforts (Holmes, 1986). A look 10 years after the *A Nation at Risk* (National Commission on Excellence in Education, 1983) data reveals that students are taking more traditional academic courses in high school to meet revised and more rigorous graduation requirements in many states (U.S. Department of Education, 1995).

For example, figure 1.3 shows that more students in 1992 were studying geometry, algebra, trigonometry, calculus, biology, chemistry, physics, or combinations of sciences than in 1982; in some cases the percentages have *doubled.* In addition, more high school graduates earned foreign language course credits in 1992 than in 1982 (see figure 1.4).

National Assessment of Educational Progress reports indicate that 17-year-olds are achieving higher scores in both mathematics and science, although reading scores have not significantly changed (U.S. Department of Education, 1995). Although the performance of our top students remained similar over the 10-year period, our lowest achieving students have gained. As a whole, while U.S. students are beginning to meet the demands of more rigorous standards, they still fall below the achievement levels of students in other industrial countries (U.S. Department of Education, 1995).

## Criticisms of Teaching

Criticism of teaching is not new. The profession has struggled through many periods in which the nation has blamed its schools for failing to prepare our youth to meet the demands of modern life. When the Russians launched the first space satellite, Sputnik, in 1957, for example, a stunned United States quickly demanded that the schools seriously examine the current state of science instruction. Perhaps not surprisingly, it was rapidly concluded that science education had not kept up with scientific developments and that drastic changes were needed.

Russian successes in the space race in the 1950s led the United States to reevaluate science education.

© Superstock

The country looked to many of its leading scientists to provide answers concerning not only what should be taught in science courses but also how to teach it. To some extent, science courses were updated to incorporate knowledge relevant to the new space age. Also, traditional science instruction by lecture and minimal laboratory experimentation, mainly in the upper grades, gave way to the "discovery method" of teaching. Using this method, even very young children play and experiment with materials and discover on their own how various scientific principles work. The finding that children learn best by actively manipulating objects largely stems from the ideas of prominent educational philosophers and psychologists.

### Education and the Economy

The rapid and alarming decline the United States has experienced as the world's leading economic power is the most important factor underlying widespread alarm about the status of education in the country. Today's students are tomorrow's work force, and business leaders have expressed grave concern that our schools are not producing citizens who can compete effectively in a highly technological world market.

**1.3** ◎

*Identify factors that have contributed to criticism of education in the United States.*

### The Relationship Between School Conditions and Student Learning

As early as 1975, Lortie urged researchers to study teachers in the workplace and examine the relationship between conditions in schools and student learning. The failure to examine the possible effects of school conditions on student learning encourages people to conclude incorrectly that students fail either because they can't learn or because teachers can't teach (Weiner, 1993). The conditions under which learning takes place, however, may hinder student learning. Pressure to prepare students to pass standardized tests, for example, frequently prevents teachers from restructuring their lesson plans (Commins & Miramontes, 1989) or trying to look at the classroom from students' perspectives (Liston & Zeichner, 1991).

**1.4** ◎

*Summarize important social conditions that affect student achievement.*

Sato and McLaughlin (1995) caution that comparisons of the academic performance of students from different countries must take cultural differences into account. They claim, for example, that U.S. teachers focus primarily on improving students' cognitive skills, whereas Japanese teachers focus on a broader array of student outcomes, including students' ability to interact with others in ways that foster social cohesion and collective responsibility. Furthermore, in comparison with students in the United States, students in Japan spend more time in school each day and more days in school each year. Comparing test scores of students from different cultures or from different socioeconomic segments fails to uncover cultural factors that contribute to differences in academic performance.

**1.5** ◎

*Describe the importance of higher-order thinking skills.*

## Figure 1.5

Core standards of effective teachers identified by the National Board for Professional Teaching Standards.

Reprinted with permission of National Board for Professional Teaching Standards.

Effective teachers:

1. Are committed to students and their learning
2. Know the subjects they teach and how to teach them
3. Take responsibility for managing and monitoring student learning
4. Think systematically about their practice and learn from experience
5. Are members of learning communities

**1.6**

*Explain how the current educational reform movement differs from previous ones.*

The educational reform movement is not a single movement. Many different people are proposing a wide variety of solutions to educational problems in the United States. One characteristic unites them: their agreement that radical change must occur if our schools are to improve.

**1.7**

*List important requirements for professional development.*

*Annual* **Edition**

unit *1*

Notice, when you begin teaching, how "old habits," derived from your experience as a student, emerge in your own teaching. One day you may hear the words of your third-grade teacher issuing from your own mouth.

The disturbing results of studies of education in the United States have jolted the nation's business leaders and spawned a powerful reform movement to restructure schools to prepare students for life in a global economy based on information, not industry.

# The Current Educational Reform Movement

The current movement for educational reform differs from previous movements in at least one significant way. For the first time, teachers are directly involved in bringing about changes. Teachers are being asked to collaborate with their critics in making decisions about how to improve the schools.

The involvement of teachers in making fundamental decisions reflects the growth of teaching as a profession. It acknowledges that there is a legitimate body of knowledge about teaching that teachers know best. Some of that knowledge comes from experience, but much comes from scientific research as well. If teachers are to be recognized as professionals, they must make educationally sound decisions by combining scientific knowledge with clinical knowledge gained from classroom teaching experience.

## Teachers as Professionals

Professionals are distinguished from other workers in the degree to which they make independent decisions and judgments about their work (Carnegie Forum on Education and the Economy, 1986; Lieberman & Miller, 1984; Short & Greer, 1993). Professionals make key decisions about the services they provide, and their actions are guided by state and national boards made up of peers who oversee the practice of the profession. The National Board for Professional Teaching Standards, which is developing national certification requirements for teachers, has identified five core standards for effective teachers (see figure 1.5).

In addition to the need for peer-developed standards and autonomy, professionals generally need support and time to plan, reflect on, and examine the problems that are unique to their field. They also need opportunities to collaborate and communicate with other professionals to decide how to resolve these problems (Carnegie Forum on Education and the Economy, 1986; Short & Greer, 1993). In teaching, such opportunities will require changes in the organization of school time and the responsibilities of teachers. Several task forces studying U.S. education recommend the creation of different teaching levels within schools, so that support staff, interns, and novice and expert teachers can work together and thus encourage professional development (Carnegie Forum on Education and the Economy, 1986; Holmes Group, 1986; Louis & King, 1993; Short & Greer, 1993).

## Becoming a Professional

Professional development as a teacher is a self-directed process that requires teachers to analyze their effectiveness (Zumwalt, 1986). This process is not simple, especially because teachers frequently teach the way they themselves were taught (Zumwalt, 1986), and they rarely have opportunities to see new methods of teaching and to analyze the outcomes. To some extent, you will be able to observe how various teachers teach as you take courses and do student teaching. To develop as professionals, however, beginning and novice teachers must also have opportunities to explore and examine their *own* teaching behavior.

### Teaching: Art or Science?

Teaching has been variously defined as either an art or a science. Educational researchers and practitioners tend to view teaching from one perspective or the other in an attempt to explain what teaching is. These efforts suggest that the profession is struggling to find a definition of *good* teaching.

Some educators describe teaching from a scientific perspective, but others claim that teaching cannot be considered a science alone (Gage, 1978). Teaching does not consist of a fixed set of principles or laws, and currently there is no way to measure teaching performance with the consistency and precision associated with scientific work. As far back as 1968, one of the first educational researchers to study classrooms, Philip Jackson, cautioned that events in a classroom are spontaneous and develop in ways that are not always predictable. Teaching involves intuition, spontaneity, artistry, and feeling, characteristics not usually regarded as scientific (Dawe, 1984; Eisner, 1983; Peterson & Comeaux, 1989).

Leonardo da Vinci (1452–1519)
Northwind Picture Archives

### Good Teaching Skills

Good teachers probably use the same skills used by artists and scientists alike. Insight, for example, is based on seeing something in a new light. Frequently, scientific innovations stimulate new artistic expression. Scientists use intuition, insight, and fantasy to develop new theories. Similarly, teachers can use new ideas to think creatively. As in other professions, such as medicine or law, science and art work together in creating meaningful practice in teaching.

## Teachers as Decision Makers and Problem Solvers

You can acquire many of the skills needed for good teaching only by being aware of the findings of new research and being open to new ideas and thoughtful reflection. As you become more involved in teaching as a profession, you will have to acquire thinking skills that expand your ability to make informed decisions and find creative solutions to professional problems. Good teaching is multifaceted (Lowman, 1992); you will be a decision maker and a mediator, as well as a problem solver, a communicator, and a learner.

You will acquire these skills as you study educational psychology and apply the knowledge you learn to classrooms and learning situations. The thinking skills discussed in this book are not merely the skills your students need to cope effectively in tomorrow's world. They are precisely the skills *you* need to function effectively as a professional. As you prepare yourself for your professional role, the public's renewed attention to teaching as a profession will give you the advantage of receiving support from many others who wish to help teachers gain greater control over their professional lives.

*Annual* **Edition**

unit *1*

## The Cognitive Revolution

While changes in the field of education have influenced how we view teaching, a concurrent change was occurring in the field of psychology: the cognitive revolution. Although psychology is a relatively new field (compared to other sciences, such as physics or biology), for centuries people have been intrigued by the human mind and how it works. The scientific study of the mind began in Germany in 1879, with the establishment of the first psychology laboratory. The primary method of investigation in this early laboratory consisted of having people describe their mental images while participating in various psychological experiments.

1.8 ◎

*Describe how the cognitive revolution has affected education in U.S. schools.*

"Teach."

This method of psychological investigation lasted only about 25 years. At that point, John Watson, a U.S. psychologist, succeeded in convincing many psychologists that if psychology was to be a science, it had to focus on observable behavior rather than on unobservable self-reports of how the mind works. He argued that psychologists, like other scientists, should study objective, not subjective phenomena. Largely because of Watson, the primary goal of psychology shifted to the study of observable **behavior,** and issues concerning how the mind works were rejected as irrelevant and unscientific.

Watson's views dominated the field until the early 1960s, when psychologists returned to the fundamental question of how the mind works. In doing so, psychologists had to find ways to examine mental processes, which are not observable. Specifically, psychologists became interested in investigating **cognitive processes,** the term that refers to mental activity such as attending, perceiving, thinking, remembering, problem solving, decision making, and creativity. This dramatic return to the original goal of the early psychologists is generally referred to as the "cognitive revolution" (Baars, 1986). This revolution has redefined the basic purpose of psychology.

One major reason underlying the cognitive revolution was the work of Jean Piaget, a Swiss psychologist, who showed that children actively use their cognitive processes to construct their understanding of the world, and their initial cognitive processes differ from those of adults. Children acquire the ability to think like adults only gradually as they proceed through a series of stages consisting of different kinds of thinking.

In addition, the rapid development of computer science contributed to the cognitive revolution. Many psychologists saw parallels between how information is processed by computers and how it is processed by the human mind. "Computers accept information, manipulate symbols, store items in 'memory' and retrieve them again, classify inputs, recognize patterns and so on" in ways that seem similar to how our own cognitive processes work (Neisser, 1976, p. 5).

## The Explosion of Cognitive Research

The large number of new books and journals concerned with cognitive processes reflects the growing interest in cognitive research. These books and journals address many topics of critical importance to teachers, including thinking, concept formation, comprehension, and problem solving. The goal of many educational psychologists today is to apply the findings of cognitive research in ways that will help

Reprinted by permission Shetland Productions.

teachers teach more competently and students learn more effectively. A major purpose of this book is to help you become an effective teacher by approaching teaching and learning from a cognitive perspective.

## Curriculum Changes in U.S. Schools

Many educational psychologists look at how students learn in the classroom and, consequently, how teachers should teach. If you are going to become an effective teacher, it is important for you to also consider *what* you are teaching and *why*.

Right now, in school districts all over the country, significant changes are occurring in the school curriculum. Until recently, most people considered students' mastery of the "three Rs" to be a reasonable outcome of formal schooling. Now, however, educators, parents, and leaders in business and government are demanding that students acquire additional skills, such as computer literacy and higher-order thinking skills, to deal effectively with the complexities of life in the twenty-first century.

Another major change is a reconsideration of what is important for students to know. A curriculum represents the body of knowledge that a society deems valuable. The curriculum of schools in the United States has centered on traditional Western ideas. A growing movement advocates a multicultural perspective, particularly the ideas and contributions of minorities, women, and members of other cultures. Not all educators and citizens endorse a multicultural perspective, and even those who do support it disagree about what content is appropriate for a multicultural curriculum. Curriculum content has important ramifications because *what* students learn often determines *how well* they learn. Minority students, for example, may be more eager to learn if the curriculum covers the contributions of members of their ethnic group. Furthermore, a multicultural curriculum helps members of all groups to understand perspectives that may differ from their own (Gollnick & Chinn, 1990; Richard-Amato & Snow, 1992; Sleeter & Grant, 1988; Weiner, 1993).

The future success of our students depends on our ability to broaden our perspective of education. Throughout the country numerous groups and organizations are urging schools to forge cooperative relationships with businesses, libraries, museums, adult education agencies, and other health and social services organizations

School-age children often play computer games at home and use a variety of media-based equipment. How has this change in home entertainment affected schooling? How can teachers capture students' interest in school subjects?

1.9 ◎

*Explain why educators in the United States are rethinking the curriculum.*

so that students can acquire the full range of experiences, information, and skills they will need in the future. The failure of education in the United States stems from weaknesses in the system, not weaknesses in our students.

Providing an excellent and equitable education is a particularly difficult challenge in a society that is as diverse and dynamic as ours. Changes occur so rapidly in the United States that no school can claim to be successful unless it can transform students into educated citizens who have acquired the thinking skills necessary to accommodate to a society in continual flux. Schools must equip students with skills that are generalizable to novel situations, some of which may not yet have been conceived.

Fantini (1986) has suggested that the following principles should govern our restructuring of the U.S. educational system: (a) all students can learn under the right conditions, (b) students must have choices among educationally sound options, (c) students possess various kinds of intelligences and talents, and (d) students' motivation is increased if they have some control over their own fate.

This book primarily takes a cognitive approach to the field of educational psychology. Cognitive theories focus on the processes of comprehension, problem solving, decision making, and creativity, and consequently help us to understand how students think and how teachers can help students learn. Independent thinking skills enable students to contribute productively to society and instill in them for the rest of their lives the self-confident feeling of being intellectually capable of solving whatever problems they might encounter.

## KEY POINTS

1. Comparisons of the academic achievement of students in the United States with that of students in other industrialized nations have shown that U.S. students typically achieve less. Economic and technological changes have created the need to prepare students better academically.

2. The poor academic performance of U.S. students has led to a strong national movement to reform education. An important aspect of this movement involves reforming the way teachers themselves are educated.

3. Teachers are increasingly perceived as professionals. Being a professional involves independent decision making and problem solving.

4. Changes in the field of psychology are having an impact on educational goals and teaching methods. As a result of the "cognitive revolution," educators are focusing on the role that thought processes play in teaching students to become independent thinkers and learners.

## SELF-STUDY EXERCISES

1. Explain how the current movement to reform education in the United States began.

2. Describe the characteristics that differentiate professionals from other kinds of workers.

3. Explain what is meant by the term *cognitive revolution* and give two reasons that it occurred.

## FURTHER READINGS

Fantini, M. D. (1986). *Regaining excellence in education.* Columbus, OH: Merrill.

Weiner, L. (1993). *Preparing teachers for urban schools: Lessons from thirty years of school reform.* New York: Teachers College Press.

Zumwalt, K. K. (Ed.). (1986). *Improving teaching.* Alexandria, VA: ASCD.

## REFERENCES

Baars, B. J. (1986). *The cognitive revolution in psychology.* New York: The Guilford Press.

Bracey, G. W. (1996). International comparisons and the condition of American education. *Educational Researcher, 25* (1), 5–11.

Carnegie Forum on Education and the Economy. (1986). *A nation prepared: Teachers for the twenty-first century.* New York: Carnegie Corporation.

Commins, N. L., & Miramontes, O. B. (1989). Perceived and actual linguistic competence: A descriptive study of four low-achieving Hispanic bilingual students. *American Education Research Journal, 26,* 443–472.

Commission on Reading. (1985). *Becoming a nation of readers.* Washington, DC: National Institute of Education.

Dawe, W. A. (1984). Teaching: Social science or performing art? *Harvard Educational Review, 54,* 111–114.

Educational Testing Service. (1992). *The second international assessment of educational progress.* Princeton, NJ: Educational Testing Service.

Eisner, E. W. (1983). The art and craft of teaching. *Educational Leadership, 40,* 4–13.

Fantini, M. D. (1986). *Regaining excellence in education.* Columbus, OH: Merrill.

Gage, N. L. (1978). *The scientific basis of the art of teaching.* New York: Teachers College Press.

Gollnick, D. M., & Chinn, P. C. (1990). *Multicultural education in a pluralistic society.* New York: Macmillan.

Holmes Group. (1986). *Tomorrow's teachers: A report of the Holmes Group.* East Lansing, MI: Holmes Group, Inc.

Jackson, P. W. (1968). *Life in classrooms.* New York: Holt, Rinehart & Winston.

Lieberman, A., & Miller, L. (1984). *Teachers, their world and their work: Implications for school improvement.* Alexandria, VA: ASCD.

Liston, D. P., & Zeichner, K. M. (1991). *Teacher education and the social conditions of learning.* New York: Routledge.

Lortie, D. (1975). *Schoolteacher.* Chicago: University of Chicago Press.

Louis, K. S., & King, J. A. (1993). Professional cultures and reforming schools: Does the myth of Sisyphus apply? In J. Murphy & P. Hallinger (Eds.), *Restructuring schools: Learning from ongoing efforts* (pp. 216–250). Newbury Park, CA: Corwin Press.

Lowman, J. (1992). *Mastering the techniques of teaching.* San Francisco: Jossey-Bass.

Merseth, K. K. (1993). How old is the shepherd?: An essay about mathematics education. *Phi Delta Kappan, 74,* 548–554.

Murphy, J., & Hallinger, P. (Eds.). (1993). *Restructuring schooling: Learning from ongoing efforts.* Newbury Park, CA: Corwin Press.

National Board for Professional Teaching Standards. (1995). What teachers should know and be able to do. In K. Ryan & J. M. Cooper (Eds.), *Kaleidoscope: Readings in education* (pp. 20–22). Boston: Houghton Mifflin.

National Commission on Excellence in Education. (1983). *A nation at risk.* Washington, DC: U.S. Department of Education.

Neisser, U. (1976). *Cognition and reality.* San Francisco: W. H. Freeman.

Peterson, P. L., & Comeaux, M. A. (1989). Assessing the teacher as a reflective professional: New perspectives on teacher evaluation. In A. Woolfolk (Ed.), *Research perspectives on the graduate preparation of teachers* (pp. 132–152). Englewood Cliffs, NJ: Prentice Hall.

Richard-Amato, P., & Snow, M. A. (1992). *The multicultural classroom: Readings for content-area teachers.* White Plains, NY: Longman.

Sato, N., & McLaughlin, M. W. (1995). Context matters: Teaching in Japan and in the United States. In K. Ryan & J. M. Cooper (Eds.), *Kaleidoscope* (pp. 367–375). Boston: Houghton Mifflin.

Short, P. M., & Greer, J. T. (1993). Restructuring schools through empowerment. In J. Murphy & P. Hallinger (Eds.), *Restructuring schools: Learning from ongoing efforts* (pp. 165–187). Newbury Park, CA: Corwin Press.

Sleeter, C. E., & Grant, C. A. (1988). *Making choices for multicultural education: Five approaches to race, class, and gender.* New York: Macmillan.

Stevenson, H. W., Lee, S-y., & Stigler, J. W. (1986). Mathematics achievement of Chinese, Japanese, and American children. *Science, 231,* 693–699.

Stevenson, H. W., & Stigler, J. W. (1992). *The learning gap.* New York: Summit Books.

U.S. Department of Education. (1991). *America 2000: An education strategy.* Washington, DC: U.S. Department of Education.

U.S. Department of Education, National Center for Education Statistics. (1984). *Conditions of education.* Washington, DC: U.S. Department of Education.

U.S. Department of Education, National Center for Education Statistics. (1985). *Second international mathematics study.* Washington, DC: U.S. Department of Education.

U.S. Department of Education, National Center for Education Statistics. (1995). *High school students ten years after "A nation at risk."* Washington, DC: U.S. Department of Education.

Weiner, L. (1993). *Preparing teachers for urban schools: Lessons from thirty years of school reform.* New York: Teachers College Press.

Zumwalt, K. K. (Ed.). (1986). *Improving teaching.* Alexandria, VA: ASCD.

# TEACHERS ROUNDTABLE

# "Educational Issues Are Multifaceted Issues"

**SK:** One of the things about teaching as a profession is that teachers walk into their classroom, close the door, and they're isolated. Of course, they're with a group of children for six hours a day. But with regard to other adults, they're pretty isolated. How do you "un-isolate" yourself?

**Anthony:** In some ways, the isolation is good. You may be isolated, but you're also in control of what's happening in your classroom.

**Angela:** It's a double-edged sword.

**Mary:** Yes, but it's also a lonely job sometimes. That's why many teachers love having student teachers. But I'm concerned about new teachers because they are thrown into their classrooms and no one pays attention to them.

**Anthony:** If they are fortunate enough to be near someone who has the experience and is willing to share, then they learn.

**Mary:** Unfortunately, some teachers don't share.

**Angela:** You are right, but I get the sense in my particular school that teachers are very overwhelmed with all that they have to do. They don't even have the time to work with a new teacher. For instance, we have a new speech service provider who is overwhelmed and has come to me for help, which I am happy to give. But it has gotten to the point where she has so many questions that I can't get my work done. So, even if you want to be supportive, it is an overwhelming job to guide another person and still do your own job. But part of it is also our history of being isolated. It's very difficult for us to even socialize together.

**Irwin:** Some teachers love the isolation because it's the most powerful position you can be in. You're a teacher, perhaps a tenured teacher; you can close that door and do whatever you want to do. And no one can tell you what to do. On the other hand, for new teachers the isolation can be detrimental, or even terrifying. In my school, we try to support the new teachers through curriculum committees. In every curriculum committee, there is a senior teacher. And each one is

responsible for particular files. If you came to my high school and taught global studies, you'd open a file, where you'd find a homework list, a term project list, 35 to 40 different motivational tools to use for your lessons. And at least you'd have a start. And when we meet, the teachers who are teaching the same thing ask each other about what they're doing, and many try what the others have done. But you have to be careful to teach your own personality. You can't be somebody else in the classroom. You have to be yourself, but you can learn from lots of people.

**DMP:** If you could change schools, if they put you in charge tomorrow, what would you want to change?

**Anthony:** I'd like to see fewer children in the classroom. I was teaching a fifth-grade class with 33, and the following year I moved to a third-grade class and had 25 children. What a difference!

**Irwin:** I don't think that makes much of a difference, unless the way you teach changes. I know we always say that we could reach more kids individually; I don't know if that's entirely true. I think you have to adjust the way you operate within the classroom with fewer kids. While I'm in favor of them, I don't know if a smaller class is magic.

**Angela:** But I feel it would help.

**Donna:** I think educational issues are multifaceted issues, so you cannot bring one solution to a complex problem. I agree with Tony that there are some lessons that I will do with a particular class that has even five fewer children because I can provide individual assistance if they need it. With other classes, I can't—the class size is just too large, so I'll do something different.

**SK:** How do you cope with large class size?

**Angela:** One thing I can say—children want to help other children. They are eager. If you ask, "Who wants to help?" they come running. You would really be amazed at how kids who can also be mean to each other at times can also be very kind and very helpful to each other.

**Irwin:** If I had to change one thing, I think what I would do is to

empower teachers. I would end the isolation of teachers. We need teachers to group together and help each other and work together. The core of education is appropriate-size classrooms with competent teachers who have assistance from other professionals that are available. Also, I think that having only 180 days of school should be reconsidered. Japanese kids are not smarter than American kids. In Japan, by the time kids reach the eighth grade, they have had 2½ more years of school than our eighth graders have had. Logically, why wouldn't they be ahead of us? Finally, I think we have to see schools as more than a place for education only. For many kids, the school is the safest place they know. I'm a high school teacher, but my wife is an elementary school teacher— elementary school teachers are unbelievable because you create such a safety net for these kids. They want to hug you. They want to come in. You provide the only kind word and the only nice touch some kids have in a day.

**Donna:** Another thing that needs to be changed is the communication between teachers. As a new teacher, I sometimes feel lost. I hear that there used to be a mentor program for new teachers, but it was cut out in one of the budget crises. I feel, boy, that's bad timing for me. I need someone to answer the questions I have every day. How do I deal with these disruptive behaviors? How do I make this lesson work? I know general practices, but I really need some fine tuning. . . . I need the guidance of someone. Another problem is communication between teachers and administrators. For example, a child was almost hurt, and I asked different people what we should have done had he been hurt. No one had any answers for me. I was absolutely astonished. Every day I find instances like this; I think it's the product of the schools being part of a bureaucracy. I think we could improve communication. It really bothers me and I think we could improve if we tried.

2

© Steve Skjold

# Learning:
# The Major Focus of
# Educational Psychology

# Chapter Outline

# Learning Objectives

2.1 Define the term *learning*.
2.2 Describe the philosophical roots of behavioral and cognitive approaches to learning.
2.3 Summarize the behavioral approach and distinguish between classical and operant conditioning.

2.4 Apply behaviorism to educational settings.
2.5 Describe the cognitive approach to learning and differentiate the cognitive-developmental from the information-processing model.

2.6 Discuss the principles of social learning theory and explain how models can influence learning.
2.7 Explain the ideas inherent in a humanist approach to learning and give examples of educational applications of humanism.

# Preview

Although the field of educational psychology is concerned with all psychological aspects of the educational process, its primary goal is to discover how people learn. Over the years, educational psychologists have used a variety of approaches in trying to describe and explain learning. In this chapter, we describe two approaches that have had the greatest impact on our understanding of learning: the *behavioral* and the *cognitive* approaches; in addition, we describe the *humanist* and *social learning* approaches.

   Both the behavioral and cognitive approaches have had more influence on educational practice than have the social learning or humanist approaches. The behavioral approach

has been around the longest, but more and more educational psychologists are shifting to the cognitive approach.

   Followers of the behavioral approach attempt to explain learning by studying behavior that is observable; behaviorists believe that internal mental processes are unobservable and consequently unknowable. Behaviorists use two types of conditioning to explain learning: *classical conditioning,* in which a response originally linked to one stimulus becomes linked to a different stimulus; and *operant conditioning,* in which the use of reinforcers leads to increases or decreases in the occurrence of a response.

   The cognitive approach tries to explain learning by examining the thought processes that underlie it. Cognitivists differ from behaviorists in a very fundamental way: Behaviorists do not address how the mind works, which is precisely the focus of cognitivists. There are two major models within the cognitive approach: (a) the *cognitive-developmental model,* which focuses on how individuals construct their own understanding and the stages that people go through in their cognitive development, and (b) the *information-processing model,* which examines the workings of the human mind as if it were a computer.

   According to the social learning approach, people learn by imitating the behavior exhibited by others. The social learning approach incorporates aspects of both the behavioral and the cognitive approaches by distinguishing between *learning* and *performance.* People may learn behavior they observe without being reinforced for doing so. The use of reinforcement, however, greatly increases the probability that they will actually perform the behavior. Social learning occurs in four sequential phases: attention, retention, reproduction, and motivation, each of which involves cognitive processes. Self-regulation of behavior occurs when people observe their own behavior.

The humanist approach is less concerned with how learning occurs than with the kinds of feelings and attitudes students acquire toward learning. Humanist education encourages students to become independent learners who determine for themselves how and what they learn. Humanists argue that *what* students learn in school is less important than learning *how* to learn. They emphasize the development of self-esteem and try to help students become fulfilled individuals. The open classroom movement represented an attempt to put the humanist philosophy of education into practice. ◉

# The Study of Learning

Psychology is the branch of knowledge devoted to the scientific study of behavior. It should therefore come as no surprise that psychology's most fundamental challenge is to explain how *changes* in behavior occur. Ever since psychology emerged as a separate field of study in the late nineteenth century, psychologists have been struggling to find the answer. Despite the enormous amount of time and energy psychologists have devoted to solving the puzzle, no completely adequate explanation has yet emerged. On the other hand, psychologists now know much more than they once did about how changes in behavior occur.

## Changes in Behavior as a Function of Learning

Ms. Harris is a second-grade teacher who works hard to make sure her students are learning. Throughout the second grade, she is teaching them addition and subtraction, spelling words, and reading; it can sometimes be a difficult task. Next door, Ms. Beecroft is also teaching second-graders, but Ms. Harris notes that her colleague has poorly structured her classroom, teaches ineffective lessons, and doesn't give her all to her teaching. In June, Ms. Beecroft comments, "I am so pleased with how much my students have learned since September!" Ms. Harris thinks about it and realizes that Ms. Beecroft's students *have* progressed, even though the quality of teaching was poor. She contemplates how such learning occurs in the absence of good teaching.

One answer is that some changes occur as a result of **maturation,** or normal growth. For example, we learn to sit up, crawl, walk, and speak simply because of getting older; we are not formally taught to do any of these things. Maturation accounts for some changes in humans, but other changes are attributable to **learning.** Learning refers to changes in an individual due to experience (Mazur, 1990). Psychologists try to explain *how* learning occurs. However, not all psychologists agree on how to approach the topic. Different psychologists have different theories about how learning takes place. Some theories are better than others in explaining particular types of learning, but to date, no single theory adequately explains how *all* learning takes place.

**2.1** ◉
*Define the term* learning.

Changes in physical qualities, such as height and weight, are due to maturation. Tying your shoelace or addressing an envelope are learned behaviors.

## Approaches to the Study of Learning

Certainly not all learning occurs in schools. Just think of how much children have learned before they ever enter a classroom. They know how to understand and use language, they can perform many motor skills, and they often understand a wide variety of concepts. Nevertheless, the purpose of schools is to promote learning, and as a teacher, your primary responsibility is to help students learn.

To further complicate our understanding of learning, students learn in different ways and at different rates. Can you recall, as a student, lessons in which some classmates were "getting it" but you didn't understand the concept? Or, can you recall lessons that bored you because you already understood the material? The term **individual differences** means that different people learn differently. Understanding how learning occurs will enable you to determine what conditions promote student learning, what methods and materials facilitate learning, and how to accommodate students' individual differences.

We will now explore in some detail four schools of thought concerning how people learn. Each approach accounts fairly well for some kinds of learning, but not very well for other kinds. Some approaches overlap in their assumptions about learning processes; others have nothing in common. The approaches differ with respect to their contribution to our understanding of how learning occurs because they vary in focus. Some look at learning quite broadly, others more narrowly.

Differences also exist in the depth of the research base on which each approach rests. Some approaches have engaged the interest of numerous educational researchers for a long time. Others have either existed for briefer periods or have captured the interest of a more limited number of researchers.

*Annual* **Edition**

unit *4*

How might Jamal have been reinforced for giving the correct answer?

# Behavioral and Cognitive Approaches: Contrasting Views

Jamal is a third-grader who is studying multiplication. When asked to solve $3 \times 4$ on Monday, he couldn't, but when asked again on Thursday, he could. Between Monday and Thursday, Jamal had learned to solve the problem, but behaviorists and cognitivists offer different explanations about how he learned.

**Behaviorism** and **cognitivism** are diametrically opposed in their underlying philosophies. Behaviorists attempt to explain learning in terms of how events in the environment affect behavior. Cognitivists attempt to explain learning in terms of how people think. Behaviorists would claim that Jamal learned to give the correct answer because he had been positively reinforced for doing so. Cognitivists, however, would claim that Jamal learned because he had actively placed the correct response in his memory.

## Philosophical Differences Between Behaviorism and Cognitivism

Behavioral and cognitive theories of learning have developed within two different philosophical frameworks: *empiricism* and *rationalism*. Each of these two philosophies makes different assumptions about the nature of human beings and the way in which we learn.

### Empiricism

Long before psychology developed as a science, philosophers had been debating the question of *how* we know *what* we know. Some philosophers argued that knowledge is based on experience. This kind of philosophy is called **empiricism**. Empiricists believe that a person can acquire knowledge only about things that can be experienced by means of the senses of sight, touch, hearing, smell, and taste; then, the individual verifies knowledge through observation and experiment. According to empiricists, a person acquires knowledge by forming various associations among different aspects of the environment that one can experience through one's senses (Bower & Hilgard, 1981). For example, a person acquires knowledge of what a flower is on the basis of having had sensory experiences with flowers. In other words, a person acquires knowledge of what a flower is by forming associations among the shape, color, fragrance, and perhaps the feel of different flowers the person has previously encountered.

Aristotle
(384–322 B.C.)

Behavioral theories depend on the philosophy of empiricism. Behaviorists attempt to explain how learning occurs by explaining how associations are formed between events occurring in the environment and the behaviors individuals exhibit when these events occur. In psychology, an event occurring in the environment is called a **stimulus** (the plural of which is *stimuli*). The behavior an individual exhibits when the stimulus occurs is called a **response.**

Behaviorists investigate the conditions under which individuals learn to make various kinds of responses when they encounter various kinds of stimuli in the environment. For example, suppose that while driving a car you approach a traffic light that is turning red and you respond by stepping on the brake pedal. The red light is an example of a stimulus, and for psychologists interested in learning theory, the issue is to explain how you have learned to stop your car when you see a red light.

Some drivers, however, respond to a light that is turning red by stepping on the gas to try to beat it. For a learning theorist, the issue is how did you learn to apply the brake, while others learned to step on the gas? Another issue for a learning theorist is how a person who has learned to step on the gas in response to a light that is turning red can learn to apply the brakes instead.

Numerous issues crop up when one begins to consider how stimuli and responses become associated. As in the example, one might be interested in explaining not only how an original response has become associated with a stimulus but also in figuring out how to substitute a different response to that stimulus. As a teacher, for example, you need to be concerned with how a student learns to make the response "North America" when you ask "What continent is the United States in?" And you need to be concerned about how best to help a student who responds "Canada" learn that the correct response is "North America."

## Rationalism

Other philosophers argue that knowledge is based on reasoning. This kind of philosophy is called **rationalism.** Rationalists believe that we learn because of our ability to interpret events occurring in the environment. Rationalists believe that human beings are born with an innate need to find meaning in the world and that what we perceive is determined as much by how our minds interpret the stimuli we encounter as by the nature of the stimuli themselves. Cognitive theories of learning are based on the philosophy of rationalism and attempt to explain how learning occurs by describing and explaining the nature of our internal mental activity. The primary goal of cognitive learning theorists is to determine how our minds work.

Cognitivists would approach the question of how one learns to respond to a red light by trying to determine how people perceive a particular situation. Similarly, a cognitivist would try to help a student who believes the United States is in Canada by trying to help the student understand the concepts of "continent" and "country" and show the location of each on the globe. A cognitivist would try to help the student understand concepts involved in geography so that he or she could understand *why* North America is the right answer.

Although this textbook approaches educational psychology primarily from a cognitive perspective, it is important that you understand fully the behavioral approach to learning so that you can appreciate the contributions behaviorists have made and recognize classroom situations in which a behavioral approach to learning may be useful.

# The Behavioral Approach to Learning

Behaviorism is the most ambitious approach to learning in that it tries to account for how all learning occurs. Its principal flaw is that its attempt to account for all learning leads to a rather simplistic definition of learning that omits many important kinds of human behavior. Behaviorists refuse to consider intervening mental processes, such as paying attention, that are not directly observable.

**2.2**

*Describe the philosophical roots of behavioral and cognitive approaches to learning.*

To what extent do you believe humans have an innate need to find meaning in the world?

**2.3**

*Summarize the behavioral approach and distinguish between classical and operant conditioning.*

Behaviorists often study the behavior of animals in a controlled laboratory setting.

© Hank Morgan/Photo Researchers

Just as physicists or chemists attempt to uncover universal scientific laws that explain various physical or chemical phenomena, behaviorists attempt to uncover universal scientific laws that explain how all organisms learn, regardless of whether the organism is a human being or an animal.

Behaviorists often prefer to study animals rather than people because an animal's environment can be rigorously controlled. Much behavioral research has focused on explaining how pigeons or white rats learn various tasks in a laboratory setting, with the assumption that these findings can explain how people learn in the real world.

## The Emergence of Psychology as a Scientific Discipline

As noted above, psychology can trace its historical roots to philosophy. In 1879, Wilhelm Wundt established the first experimental psychology laboratory in Leipzig, Germany, and students from around the world, particularly from England and the United States, flocked to Germany to learn psychology first from Wundt and then later from his students. The methods of conducting psychological research that were pioneered in Germany set the standard for psychologists throughout the world.

### Introspection

The principal method used by the early experimental psychologists is called **introspection,** a method in which persons participating in a psychological experiment attempt to analyze their own thought processes while they complete various experimental tasks. For example, much of the early psychological research focused on describing how people perceive various visual and auditory stimuli. People were shown different colors or were presented sounds of varying pitch and asked to describe whether they perceived, for instance, one shade of red as darker or lighter than another or one tone as being higher or lower in pitch than another.

People's reported perceptions, of course, were internal mental events that the experimenters themselves could neither observe nor measure. Psychologists were simply relying on subjective verbal reports given by persons who participated in the experiments. Some psychologists, particularly John B. Watson in the United States, began to protest the use of introspection as a means of scientific investigation on the grounds that one of the major characteristics of scientific inquiry is objectivity. Verbal reports based on subjective interpretation could never provide the kind of objective evidence that was needed for psychology to become a science.

### Watson's Contribution

Watson insisted that psychology could achieve the scientific status equivalent to that of physics, chemistry, or biology, only if psychologists restricted their focus to the study of *observable* behavior and rejected the study of unobservable mental processes. He argued strongly that it would be impossible to develop scientific theories of learning without first devising a means to observe and record changes in behavior in an objective way.

Watson turned to an unlikely source for such a means: the work of a Russian physiologist (not psychologist) whose investigations of the salivation response of dogs accidentally led to the discovery of conditioning. Watson thought that the process of conditioning provided the key to studying behavior objectively; as a result, the behavioral approach to learning, known as behaviorism, was born.

Watson argued the case for behaviorism with force and with flair. His startling claims quickly attracted the attention and support of many psychologists. Watson cloaked the potential power of behaviorism with drama by proclaiming in 1926:

> Give me a dozen healthy infants, well-formed and my own specified world to bring them up in and I'll guarantee to take any one at random and train him to become any type of specialist I might select—doctor, lawyer, artist,

merchant, chief, and yes, even beggarman and thief, regardless of his talents, penchants, tendencies, abilities, vocations, and race of his ancestors. (p. 18)

This argument ran counter to the prevailing notion that we inherit many of our traits, including our intelligence and our moral character.

Largely because of Watson's efforts, behaviorism became one of the major schools of thought in psychology and indeed dominated the study of learning in the United States from the 1920s to the 1960s (Horowitz, 1992). Although behaviorism's influence has diminished, it is still popular among many psychologists and educators probably because it is so easy to apply its principles. **Behavior modification** refers to the application of behavioral principles to change an individual's behavior. In the United States, teachers use this method frequently, sometimes informally (e.g., praising students for their effort), sometimes systematically (e.g., measuring and charting students' behavior and testing the impact of various reinforcers on student behavior). The systematic use of behavior modification occurs often in special education classes, particularly those in which student behavior is a significant problem.

# Conditioning

Behaviorists use the concept of **conditioning** to explain how learning occurs. Conditioning is the process by which an organism's behavior becomes associated with some stimulus in the environment, so that when the stimulus is presented, the behavior occurs. Behaviorists rely on two kinds of conditioning to account for learning: *classical conditioning* and *operant conditioning*. Historically, classical conditioning was the first form of conditioning psychologists focused on. Behavioral theory today relies on both forms of conditioning to explain learning, although operant rather than classical conditioning has achieved the predominant role.

## Classical Conditioning

Alexander is a 10-year-old who refuses to go to school. His parents have persuaded, cajoled, and threatened him to get dressed and get on the school bus, but Alexander consistently refuses. When his parents offer to drive him, he tells them he gets nauseous when he even thinks of school. With a great deal of effort, they convince Alexander to see a guidance counselor. After exploring the issue in detail, the guidance counselor discovers that Alexander gets carsick while riding the school bus; the association of carsickness and going to school has made Alexander nauseous simply at the mention of school.

The story of Alexander exemplifies **classical conditioning.** The Russian physiologist, Ivan Pavlov, discovered the process of classical conditioning while carrying out his well-known studies of the salivation response of dogs. The discovery of classical conditioning was an accident, for Pavlov's interest focused on physiological aspects of the salivation response, not on psychological aspects of learning. Pavlov was interested in determining if the amount of saliva produced by a dog would increase if the amount of food presented to the dog were increased. As he varied the amount of food presented to the dog and measured the amount of salivation, however, Pavlov noticed that after having presented food to the dog several times, the dog began to salivate as soon as it heard the footsteps of the attendant or as soon as it saw the food dish (Pavlov, 1927).

It is important to note that initially the dog salivated only when presented food, not in response to the attendant's footsteps or the sight of the food dish. Only after the dog had received food at the same time it heard the attendant's footsteps and saw the food dish, did the dog begin to salivate before actually being presented the food. It is also important to note that the response of salivating was a response the dog was already capable of making, although initially only in response to the presence of food.

Pavlov then began to present food in the presence of various stimuli, including the sound of a bell, and discovered that the dog learned to salivate in response to any new stimulus as long as the new stimulus was introduced at the same time food was presented. Pavlov noted that after the bell and the food had been presented several times together, the dog would salivate in response to the sound of the bell alone. It was no longer necessary to follow the sound of the bell with the presentation of food to make the dog salivate. In other words, the dog had learned to make a familiar response (salivation) to a new stimulus (the sound of the bell). The process by which one learns to make a familiar response to a new stimulus is known as classical conditioning (Pavlov, 1955).

In classical conditioning, the stimulus to which a response naturally occurs is called the **unconditioned stimulus.** The response is either called the **unconditioned response** (if it occurs in the presence of the unconditioned stimulus) or the **conditioned response** (if it occurs in the presence of the conditioned stimulus). In terms of Pavlov's study, salivation (the unconditioned response) at first occurred in the presence of food (the unconditioned stimulus), but after the food was paired with the bell, salivation (now the conditioned response) occurred in the presence of the sound of the bell (the **conditioned stimulus**). Note that a response is called unconditioned or conditioned, depending on whether it is made in response to an unconditioned or conditioned stimulus. The response remains the same. It is the stimulus that changes (Pavlov, 1957). To relate these concepts to our example of Alexander, riding in the school bus is the unconditioned stimulus; it automatically causes Alexander to feel nauseous, the unconditioned response. The pairing of riding in the school bus and going to school has resulted in going to school becoming a conditioned stimulus; the nausea is therefore a conditioned response.

## Classical Conditioning and Behaviorism

Watson quickly adopted Pavlov's model of classical conditioning to explain how all learning occurs, including that of human beings. In the now-classic study involving an eleven-month-old boy named Albert, Watson and Rayner (1920) used the process of classical conditioning to demonstrate how the child learned to become frightened by a number of different objects that he initially did not fear.

The study began by showing Albert a white rat and noting that the child showed no fear of the animal. After the rat had been removed, Watson and Rayner then banged a metal bar (the unconditioned stimulus) and noted that Albert was frightened (the unconditioned response) by the loud noise. After repeatedly showing Albert the rat while at the same time banging the metal bar, Albert eventually learned to be frightened (the conditioned response) by the sight of the rat (the conditioned stimulus).

Eventually Albert became frightened when he saw the rat, even if Watson and Rayner did not bang the metal bar. Just as Pavlov's dog had learned to salivate at the sound of a bell, Albert had learned to become frightened at the sight of a white rat. Watson and Rayner also demonstrated that once Albert had acquired a fear response to the presence of the white rat, he also showed the same response to stimuli similar to the white rat, such as a Santa Claus mask, a white rabbit, and a wad of white raw cotton.

## Classical Conditioning and Classroom Learning

Ultimately, classical conditioning has had no significant impact on educational practice, largely because in classical conditioning, the person must already be able to make the response to one stimulus before it can be conditioned to another stimulus. Education typically focuses on having students learn new responses, not on learning to make old responses to new stimuli.

Teachers, however, need to know how classical conditioning works for one important reason: Many emotional responses are learned by means of classical conditioning. Students, for example, may naturally exhibit signs of anxiety when an adult yells at them. So if a teacher yells at a student for not handing in a homework assignment or for not paying attention in class, the student's anxiety reaction may be conditioned to that teacher and perhaps generalized to all teachers, or to doing homework, or to merely being present in any classroom. On a more positive note, a teacher can use classical conditioning to help students develop good feelings about school, about learning, and about themselves.

## Environmental Control of Behavior

Even though the limitations of classical conditioning were apparent to many psychologists who adopted Watson's behavioristic approach, Watson nevertheless had a profound impact on the development of learning theory in the United States. He became a powerful influence on the course of U.S. psychology, not so much because of his studies of conditioning, but rather because of his arguments that the environment controls behavior and ultimately shapes each person's personality and character.

Watson (1924) argued that what people learn is a function of what environmental stimuli they are exposed to. He stressed that inborn characteristics play no role in a person's development and, as a result, convinced many psychologists that it was important to study how changes in the environment influenced what was learned.

## E. L. Thorndike and the Law of Effect

Another psychologist who was influenced by Pavlov's ideas was E. L. Thorndike, the "father" of educational psychology. Thorndike believed that some behavior is attributable to reflexes (the salivation of Pavlov's dog; a knee jerking when tapped among humans). But other behavior, he believed, was controlled by stimuli occurring in the environment *after* the occurrence of a behavior. Thorndike placed cats in boxes and studied their efforts to escape to obtain food. Over time, the cats became more adept at escaping from the box; they learned to repeat behaviors that had worked in previous attempts. They also learned to abandon behaviors that had not been effective (Thorndike, 1911).

Thorndike (1913) used these observations to create the **law of effect**, which states that if an organism encounters a pleasant or satisfying stimulus after first demonstrating an act, it will repeat the act. By obtaining food (a satisfying stimulus) after successful escape behaviors, Thorndike's cats were more likely to repeat the successful escape behaviors. Originally, Thorndike believed that the converse also holds true: If an action is followed by an unpleasant change in the environment, that action will be unlikely to recur. Later, however, he found that unpleasant outcomes did not always diminish the incidence of specific behaviors.

Can you think of instances where the law of effect has governed your behavior?

## Operant Conditioning

Wanda is a 16-year-old who consistently shows up late for biology class if she attends at all. Her teacher, Ms. Singletary, is frustrated because she feels Wanda has potential in science, but doesn't care about the class and, by missing so much of the class, is falling further and further behind. Although Wanda likes to take care of the animals in the biology lab, she hates to attend class, participate in experiments, and take notes. To encourage Wanda to attend biology and to do so on time, Ms. Singletary starts to award Wanda 1 point each time she comes to class and 2 points for arriving on time. Wanda can redeem her points later for time spent looking after the animals in the biology lab; for every 10 points Wanda earns, she can spend a free period with the animals. As a result, Wanda's attendance and on-time attendance improve markedly.

In the example of Wanda, learning occurred and her behavior changed. However, this change cannot be attributed to classical conditioning. It can be explained, however, by **operant conditioning,** an approach advocated most rigorously by B. F. Skinner.

Although strongly influenced by Watson's ideas, Skinner recognized that classical conditioning explains only how behavior that has already been acquired can occur in the presence of a new stimulus (Iversen, 1992). Most learning, however, consists of acquiring new behaviors, a process that classical conditioning does not address (Vargas, 1993). Unlike Watson, Skinner acknowledged that physiology and genetics influence human learning, but felt that they could not be modified (Debell

Ivan Pavlov (1849–1936)

Bettmann Archive

John B. Watson (1878–1958)

Archives of the History of American Psychology

Edward L. Thorndike (1874–1949)

Archives of the History of American Psychology

B. F. Skinner (1904–1990)

© Christopher Johnson/Stock Boston

& Harless, 1992). Skinner agreed, however, that psychologists should study observable behavior. Skinner developed operant conditioning to account for how *new* behaviors are learned.

Operant conditioning assumes that behavioral responses become connected to environmental stimuli largely as a result of what happens *after* the response occurs (Skinner, 1938). If you respond in a particular way to a particular stimulus and the consequences are pleasant, you are likely to respond the same way the next time you encounter that stimulus. In the case of Wanda the points she earned, redeemable for an activity she enjoyed, were given when she showed the desired behavior (attending class on time). As a result, the frequency of the desired behavior increased. Another example might be when a teacher compliments a student for handing in an assignment on time. It is likely that the next time the teacher gives a homework assignment, the student will complete it on time. Later we will consider what happens when a response is followed by unpleasant consequences.

From John McPherson, *Life at McPherson High*.
Copyright © 1991 by John McPherson. Reprinted by permission.

"Very good, Kathy. That is the correct spelling of 'carrot.' Don, would you please spell 'pseudoparenchyma.' "

Note that the teacher's praise represents a change in the environment, or a stimulus, that occurs after the student has made the response of completing the homework assignment on time. In operant conditioning, responses are controlled by stimuli that occur *after* the response is made; in classical conditioning, responses are controlled by stimuli that occur *before* the response is made.

## Laboratory Studies of Animal Behavior

Like Watson (1913), Skinner (1951, 1953) believed that universal laws govern how animals and human beings learn. To gain greater control of the environment, Skinner carried out most of his research with pigeons and white rats in laboratory situations. He believed that laws of learning discovered through the study of animals would explain equally well how human beings learn (Nevins, 1993).

To what extent do you believe that there are universal laws of learning?

## Reinforcers

Stimuli occurring after a response are called **reinforcers.** A reinforcer may be perceived as pleasant or unpleasant by the learner. Usually, receiving a compliment, getting a piece of candy, or being given time to play a computer game is considered pleasant by students. Being given extra homework or receiving a harshly worded criticism is often perceived as being unpleasant. Whether a reinforcer is pleasant, unpleasant, or neutral is in the eye of the beholder. Do not assume that what is pleasant or desirable to one student will be desirable to another. For some students, criticism is unpleasant, but for those who are seeking attention, it may be pleasant.

Reinforcers can be pleasant or unpleasant; also, they can be presented or removed. Figure 2.1 shows the four combinations of presenting and removing stimuli that may be pleasant or unpleasant, and the outcome of each combination.

## Positive Reinforcement

**Positive reinforcement** is the presentation of a "pleasant" stimulus following the occurrence of a response. For example, when a student waits to be called on to speak, a teacher may compliment the student for waiting. Or when a student spontaneously offers help to another student, a teacher may reinforce the student with a special task (e.g., being plant monitor). In both cases, receiving the pleasant stimulus *increases* the likelihood that the behavior (waiting to be called on; helping another student) will occur again.

## Punishment

**Punishment** is the presentation of an "unpleasant" stimulus following a response. For example, when a student calls out without being called on, the teacher may give

**Figure 2.1**
Outcomes resulting from presenting or removing pleasant and unpleasant stimuli.

| Type of stimulus | Action | |
|---|---|---|
| | Presented | Removed |
| Pleasant | Positive reinforcement | Extinction |
| Unpleasant | Punishment | Negative reinforcement |

the student an extra assignment, which the student perceives as undesirable. As a result, the calling-out behavior is likely to *decrease* in frequency. The use of punishment and its consequences are controversial, and many advocates of a behavioral approach to learning argue that it is preferable to positively reinforce desirable behaviors than to punish undesirable ones (see, for example, Sulzer-Azaroff & Mayer, 1977). Critics note that punishment can hurt students' self-esteem, cause them to perceive school and the classroom negatively, and associate learning with punishment. Some forms of punishment, such as physical punishment, are not appropriate in schools, and some teachers may have difficulty discriminating between appropriate and inappropriate types of punishment.

## Extinction

Another way to *decrease* the frequency of a response is through **extinction**, which involves removing a pleasant stimulus that previously followed a response. For example, a teacher may have been inadvertently rewarding students for calling out by allowing them to speak in the class discussion. After realizing this, the teacher may ignore calling out and recognize only students who raise their hand. As a result, the calling-out behavior can be expected to decrease.

## Negative Reinforcement

People sometimes confuse negative reinforcement with punishment. **Negative reinforcement** refers to a method of *increasing* behavior through the removal of an unpleasant stimulus following a response. For example, a student with a speech difficulty may not speak in class because the speech difficulty causes other students to laugh. In this case, the other students' laughter is an unpleasant stimulus. If the teacher explains the inhibiting effect of their laughter and persuades them to stop, the student may speak in class. The removal of the unpleasant stimulus (the other students' laughter) will increase the frequency of the student's response (speaking in class).

Extinction and negative reinforcement involve removing stimuli to change behavior. Positive reinforcement and punishment involve introducing stimuli to change behavior.

## Stimulus Discrimination and Stimulus Generalization

**Stimulus discrimination** is the process by which individuals learn that a particular response is appropriate in the presence of some stimuli, but not in the presence of others. Being reinforced after making a response to a correct stimulus and not receiving reinforcement after making the response to an incorrect stimulus helps an individual learn to discriminate between the stimuli and to identify the stimulus to which the response should be made.

Give some examples of when you have used stimulus discrimination.

Young children who are just beginning to learn to read, for example, frequently fail to discriminate between letters that look alike, such as "b" and "d." By reinforcing a child with a smile or praise for correctly identifying a letter and by ignoring or correcting the child when an incorrect response is given, a teacher can help the child to discriminate between the two stimuli. Students may learn to raise their hands, for example, in a history class, which the teacher runs in a formal manner, but not in an English class, where the teacher encourages informal discussion. By being reinforced in one setting and not the other, the student learns to discriminate between the two settings (stimuli).

Handwriting is among the skills learned through shaping.

© T. Rosenthal/Superstock

**Stimulus generalization,** the exact opposite of stimulus discrimination, is the process by which people learn to make the same response in the presence of more than one stimulus, such as when a kindergartner gives the same response to "B" and "b." A teacher can help the child learn to give the same response to a letter whether it is capitalized or not by positively reinforcing the child's correct responses to both stimuli. Stimulus generalization has occurred when a student learns that "10" is the correct response to "2 × 5" and to "5 × 2."

The process of generalization has important educational implications. One of the goals of all school learning is that students will be able to generalize what they have learned in school to similar situations outside the classroom. We teach students in school that 4 times 10 is 40 with the hope that when they go to a store to buy four items that cost 10 cents apiece, they will generalize and figure out that the total cost is 40 cents.

Give some examples of when you have used stimulus generalization.

## Shaping

Sometimes teachers want to increase the frequency of a behavior that a student is not yet able to produce. If you wanted to teach a young child how to print, for example, you could use the method of **shaping,** which is the process of teaching a new behavior by reinforcing behaviors that become closer and closer approximations of the desired behavior. At first you would reinforce the child for any attempt to print, but then you would withhold reinforcement until the child's efforts look a bit more like letters, and finally you would reinforce the child only for printing completely correct letters.

Shaping is sometimes called the method of "successive approximations." Skinner (1938, 1953) and his followers have demonstrated that shaping can be successfully used to teach pigeons and white rats to exhibit behaviors that these animals normally would never exhibit. Basically, shaping involves the use of reinforcers for behaviors that initially only approximate the desired behavior, but as the learning takes place, the individual must exhibit ever closer approximations of the desired behavior in order to be reinforced.

For example, shaping can be used to teach a white rat completely novel responses, such as turning twice completely around in a circle and climbing the side of the cage. Initially, one reinforces the rat merely for beginning to make a turn of perhaps 5 or 10 degrees. As the rat begins to learn to make this response, one then withholds the reinforcement until the turn increases perhaps to 15 degrees. After the rat has successfully learned to make a turn of 15 degrees, the reinforcement is withheld until the rat increases the turn to 20 or 25 degrees.

By gradually making greater and greater demands on the rat's behavior before introducing the reinforcement, one can shape the behavior of the rat until the animal eventually learns to make two 360-degree turns and then climb the side of the cage or to carry out practically any other sequence of behaviors one desires. In a remarkable instance of demonstrating the effectiveness of shaping, Skinner once even taught two pigeons to play a form of Ping Pong!

There are many ways in which teachers can use shaping to help students learn. For example, a foreign language teacher may initially praise students for speaking the foreign language with a heavy accent and then gradually demand more accurate pronunciation before rewarding the student. Or physical education teachers may use the process of shaping to help students learn new sports or physical activities by rewarding behaviors that at first only grossly approximate the desired behaviors and then gradually increasing the demand for more accuracy before giving rewards.

## Educational Applications of Behaviorism

**2.4**

*Apply behaviorism to educational settings.*

Behavioral learning theory has probably found its most widespread educational application in the form of behavior modification (Alberto & Troutman, 1990; Kaplan, 1991). Numerous classroom management techniques are based on principles of behaviorism. In addition to classroom management techniques, however, there are other educational applications of the principles of behavioral learning theory: programmed instruction and computer-assisted instruction.

### Programmed Instruction

One of the direct applications of behaviorism to educational practice is **programmed instruction.** Programmed instruction is closely related to the process of shaping in that instruction begins by having people answer questions with responses that they have already acquired. New information is introduced in exceedingly small steps and is followed by questions that are worded in such a way that it is difficult for the person to answer the question incorrectly. Programs may be either *linear,* in which all learners encounter a fixed sequence of instructional objectives, or *branched,* in which learners take brief tests that determine whether they should continue working on the same learning objective or move on to the next objective.

One of the assumptions underlying the use of programmed instruction is that by answering questions correctly, people receive positive reinforcement and are therefore more likely to repeat the learned behavior. By gradually adding new material and following the material with questions that people can answer correctly, a vast amount of new material can eventually be learned. Programmed instructional materials are usually in the form of workbooks, software programs, or videodiscs. It is assumed that because the materials are carefully structured and the sequence of presentation so carefully controlled, people can learn new material without the necessity of having a teacher. Programmed instruction is largely a method of self-instruction that gives the learner control. It is also private, which can help learners concentrate on what they are learning.

Programmed instruction has been used, for example, in teaching subjects that many students find difficult, such as statistics. Such programs typically begin with questions that require the student to respond with simple mathematical operations, such as addition or subtraction, and then gradually introduce information on statistical concepts. Mathematics is particularly suitable for programmed instruction because it is relatively easy to establish the sequence in which various behaviors need to be learned. For the most part, mathematics is a sequential, cumulative subject area. Programmed instruction, however, has been applied to other academic areas as well, as, for example, in introductory psychology courses.

Research indicates that programmed instruction is either no better or only slightly better than more traditional methods (Bangert, Kulik, & Kulik, 1983). Generally, programmed instruction has failed to gain much of a foothold in schools. Students often react negatively to programmed instruction because its extremely slow pace causes them to lose interest and become bored before they have progressed very far in the program.

### Computer-Assisted Instruction (CAI)

Many educational software programs follow the same design as programmed instruction. Students receive some instructional material, followed by a "probe" (a small test); if they respond correctly, they move on to the next lesson; if they do not, they repeat the lesson or receive a different lesson covering the same material. This approach is called **computer-assisted instruction (CAI)**.

CAI suffers from some of the same problems as programmed instruction. It is often repetitive, and it reduces learning to discrete units that sometimes obscure the relationships between ideas. CAI is better suited for drill and practice than for building concepts and promoting comprehension. Research has shown that when used in addition to regular instruction, CAI improves students' attitudes, motivation, and academic achievement (Lepper & Gurtner, 1989; Roblyer, Castine, & King, 1988).

## Controversial Issues Concerning Behaviorism

Although behaviorism explains reasonably well some human learning, an increasing body of evidence suggests that behavioral principles fail to explain adequately much human learning. Cognitive psychologists argue that behaviorism does not fully address a number of critical issues concerning human learning.

### Qualitative Changes in Learning

Psychological studies of human growth and development have produced convincing evidence that certain *qualitative* changes occur in the way individuals learn as they age. The work of Piaget demonstrates that adults and older children learn in ways that are remarkably different from the ways in which younger children learn. Nevertheless, behaviorists insist that a 5-year-old child, for example, learns in exactly the same way as a teenager does, except that the 5-year-old has had less experience in the world and consequently has accumulated less learning.

## Differences Between Animal and Human Learning

Many psychologists question whether laws of animal learning offer much help in understanding human learning. There are many reasons to doubt the assumption that universal laws of learning apply equally well to animals and human beings, particularly because human beings have the ability to use language and exhibit a far greater degree of judgment and reasoning than pigeons and rats.

## Extrinsic Versus Intrinsic Motivation

Some critics argue that the use of rewards to motivate students (extrinsic motivation) may dampen students' intrinsic motivation (Deci et al., 1991; Kohn, 1993). If students act in certain ways to receive rewards, they will not engage in the behavior for its own sake or because they know it to be the right thing to do (intrinsic motivation). Most educators want students to be self-motivated individuals who seek knowledge to satisfy their curiosity or because they love learning. If using rewards reduces students' intrinsic motivation, it may be a bad idea in the long run. Chance (1992; 1993) argues that both types of rewards have a place in educational settings and teachers need to strike a balance regarding use of extrinsic and intrinsic forms of motivation.

## Individual Differences

Teachers are well aware that what students learn may vary from student to student, even when students have been exposed to the same environment. Behaviorists claim that students who are placed in the same learning situation may respond differently because each student has a different set of previous experiences. As a result of these different experiences, some students have learned to make different responses than other students to the same stimuli, so that in any given situation, not all students will necessarily respond in the same way.

Cognitivists, however, argue that previous experiences are stored in memory and that even the same event is remembered differently by different people. The way in which a person remembers an experience is determined by how the person perceives the experience and thinks about it. According to cognitivists, a person's prior experience is not simply an accumulation of prior learning, but rather a body of knowledge that the person has created. How a person responds in a given situation is at least partially determined by the body of knowledge the person brings to the situation.

# The Cognitive Approach to Learning

2.5 ◎

*Describe the cognitive approach to learning and differentiate the cognitive-developmental from the information-processing model.*

The fundamental difference between behavioral and cognitive approaches to learning is the role that thinking plays. Thinking plays no role whatsoever in behavioral theories. In cognitive theories, however, thinking plays the central role (Schwartz & Reisberg, 1991).

**Cognition** is a term used to describe all of our mental processes, such as perception, memory, and judgment. The most important mental process is thinking, and cognitivists focus most of their attention on studying how people think. There are two major approaches to the study of thinking: the cognitive-developmental model and the information-processing model. A brief overview of these two approaches should help you grasp more clearly the theoretical contrast between cognitive and behavioral approaches to the study of learning.

## The Cognitive-Developmental Model

The **cognitive-developmental model** focuses on changes that occur in how people think as they progress from infancy though childhood and adolescence and ultimately into adulthood. The best-known cognitive-developmental psychologist is Jean Piaget, who revolutionized our understanding of how children think and construct knowledge.

Piaget viewed children as active learners who behave like "little scientists" who develop their own "theories" about how the world works and set out to confirm these hunches. Such a view of the fundamental nature of children contrasts markedly with the view of behaviorists, who see the child as a passive learner who merely reacts to environmental stimuli.

Piaget's primary concern was to discover how people acquire knowledge, which is often called the "epistemological question." Piaget considered himself less a psychologist than a "genetic epistemologist," studying the source, or genesis, of knowledge. His studies have shown that throughout the lifespan, people go through a sequence of four qualitatively different stages of thinking.

Briefly, infants acquire knowledge based on the sensory experiences of sight, hearing, touch, taste, and smell. Preschoolers progress to the stage of acquiring knowledge of the world though their perceptions of their own experiences in the world. Older children begin to apply the rules of logic to understand how the world works. And, finally, adolescents and adults progress to the stage where they can apply logic to hypothetical as well as to real situations.

Piaget believed that people are constantly trying to make sense of the world by comparing their internal understanding of how the world works with external evidence. Learning occurs when people periodically alter their internal understanding of the world as they encounter evidence that conflicts with their previous understanding. According to Piaget, even young students constantly create their own knowledge of the world by comparing external evidence with internal understandings. Given Piaget's theory, it seems clear that an important role of a teacher is to provide students with experiences that will help them develop a more accurate understanding of how the world works.

## The Information-Processing Model

The **information-processing model** uses the way a computer works as a way of understanding how the human mind works. Just as a computer takes in input, processes it, and produces output, the human mind takes in information (sensory experience), processes it (thinks), and produces output (behavior).

Information-processing theorists are concerned with the nature of the cognitive processes rather than with the developmental stages through which thinking evolves. These theorists agree with Piaget, however, that people are active learners and that a person's prior knowledge is a critical component of new learning. According to information-processing theory, students learn most effectively when they can relate new knowledge to what they already know. Information-processing theory has made its greatest contribution in explaining how human memory works, that is, how we take in information (encoding), organize it in our minds (storage), and gain access to it when needed (retrieval).

# The Social Learning Approach

**Social learning theory,** which is also called observational learning, focuses on how we learn by observing the behavior of others (Miller & Dollard, 1941). Conceptually, social learning theory provides a link between the behavioral and cognitive approaches. To understand the linkage, however, it is first necessary to distinguish the concepts of **learning** and **performance**.

## Learning and Performance

People can learn to do many things without actually doing them. Perhaps you have been on an airplane and learned how to put on a life jacket by observing the flight attendant's demonstration. You didn't have to put on the jacket to learn how to do so. The only way to verify that you have learned how to put on a life jacket would be to have you perform the behavior.

**2.6** ◎

*Discuss the principles of social learning theory and explain how models can influence learning.*

Give some examples of things you have learned by observing a model.

According to social learning theory, people may learn simply by observing a model. Consider the following illustration. Students in a keyboarding class may learn how to type capital letters by observing how the teacher strikes a letter key while simultaneously holding down the shift key. It is not necessary for students themselves to type capital letters to learn how to do so. In all likelihood, of course, the teacher would have students type capital letters to demonstrate by their performance that they have learned correctly.

The important point is that learning may take place without any observable response and without any reinforcement. In other words, even though the students may not do any typing at all or receive any form of reinforcement or reward from the teacher, they still may learn. The fact that people may learn without making an observable response and without being reinforced is a dominant principle in social learning theory.

Note that this principle is completely contrary to the view of behaviorists, who claim that a response can be learned only if it is observable and reinforced. On the other hand, note that this principle is consistent with the cognitive approach to learning. Cognitivists could easily account for students having learned to type capital letters without actually typing. They would argue that changes occurred in the students' mental images and thinking about typing as a result of having observed the teacher type. The cognitive approach and social learning theory both account for learning in terms of cognitive changes.

### The Role of Reinforcement in Social Learning Theory

Social learning theory, however, is related to the behavioral approach in that both approaches take reinforcement into account, although in different ways. Behavioral theory claims that behavior must be reinforced if learning is to occur. Social learning theory claims that although reinforcement is not *necessary* for learning to occur, the use of reinforcement increases the likelihood that what has been learned will actually be performed.

In social learning theory, reinforcement serves a motivational role. A person is more likely to perform a newly learned response if the response has been reinforced than if it has not been. Furthermore, if the person modeling a particular kind of behavior is reinforced, chances are increased that the observer will also perform the behavior. This kind of reinforcement is called **vicarious reinforcement.** People are more likely to perform the behavior carried out by the model if they see the model being reinforced. Reinforcing the model serves the same function as reinforcing the learner in terms of increasing the probability that the learner will perform the observed behavior.

Just as reinforcing the model *increases* the chances that the learner will engage in the observed behavior, punishing the model *decreases* the chances. The consequences following a response determine whether the response is likely to occur in the future or not.

## Effective Models

Effective models may be real people, such as teachers, classmates, entertainment celebrities, political leaders, or great athletes, but they don't have to be. Fictional characters appearing in television shows, stories, novels, or cartoons can also be effective models (Hill, 1990). As a matter of fact, much of the pioneering research on observational learning investigated the effects of the behavior of cartoon characters on the behavior of children (see, for example, Bandura, 1963). Individuals tend to imitate models who are perceived as competent, powerful, and attractive, as well as those whose behavior is relevant to the observer (Bandura, 1977, 1986). Models with whom learners identify can be particularly effective, but to a large extent, a model's effectiveness depends on the degree to which the learner is motivated to learn.

## Teachers as Models

Students learn much in the classroom by observing how their teachers behave, and students whose teachers have been trained in modeling techniques perform better academically than students whose teachers have not received such training (Swanson & Henderson, 1977). By observing teachers, students learn not only academic skills, such as how to solve algebraic equations or how to pronounce words in a foreign language, but also many important nonacademic behaviors. Students may learn interpersonal skills by observing how teachers interact with students and with other teachers. They may also adopt teachers' attitudes toward a variety of topics, ranging from those related to education and schooling to those extending well beyond the classroom. Students may even imitate mannerisms their teachers exhibit.

Good teachers are not only effective models; they also constantly keep in mind that their behavior, both intentional and unintentional, can profoundly affect what students learn. Above all, good teachers know how to motivate students to learn. A teacher's responsibility goes beyond just presenting lessons; the teacher is a model for students and can have a profound effect on students' attitudes, beliefs, and behavior.

Name some real people or fictional characters you have used as models. Who are models for elementary, junior high, and high school students today?

## The Phases of Social Learning

According to social learning theory, learning by observation occurs in four sequential phases: attention, retention, reproduction, and motivation. Learners must first pay attention to the model's behavior, remember the behavior, practice it, and be motivated to perform. A breakdown in any one of the phases prevents the learner from performing the behavior.

### Attention Phase

Obviously, learners cannot learn from a model unless they pay attention to what the model is doing. The attention phase consists of two parts: getting the learner's attention and maintaining it.

In most classrooms students may be attending to many different stimuli at any given moment. They may be attending to things they are doing at their desks, to distracting noises in the hall, to what they plan to do after school, or to other students. To get students' attention, provide a stimulus that is more noticeable than the other stimuli in the classroom.

There is no simple definition of an attention-getting stimulus. Various stimuli may signal to pay attention, depending on the circumstances. If you are teaching a class in which students engage in lots of individual or group activities, such as a science laboratory, a kindergarten, or a gym class, you should establish prearranged signals for paying attention, such as flicking the overhead lights, playing a chord on a piano, or ringing a bell. On the other hand, if you are instructing an entire class of students, you can get their attention simply by saying, "Now I'm going to show you how to . . . ."

One effective way to get students' attention is to use vicarious reinforcement. By praising students who are paying attention, other students who are *not* attending may be motivated to do so. Although this technique works particularly well with younger students, it may not work with older ones. Older students may regard teacher praise for paying attention as childish and taunt students who pay attention for being "teachers' pets."

To maintain students' attention, you need to provide them with sufficient incentive to attend. There is no simple way to describe what constitutes a sufficient incentive. Different students are motivated by different incentives. Ideally, students should be motivated to learn for the sake of learning, and for some students this is the case. Other students, however, require other incentives, such as being told that the next examination will cover the material about to be presented.

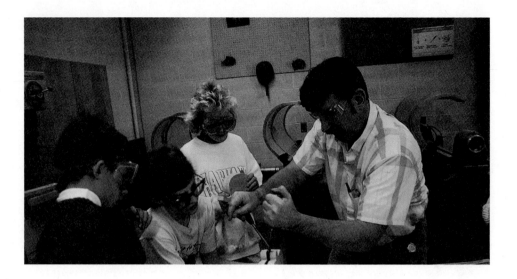

## Retention Phase

During the retention phase, learners encode the observed behavior in memory using verbal cues, mental images, or a combination of both. People can improve their memories by intentionally trying to encode the newly observed behavior, rehearsing the behavior mentally, or actually acting out the behavior.

You will help students learn better if you emphasize important aspects of the behavior you are demonstrating. In the keyboarding class example described earlier, the teacher should highlight the important steps in typing capital letters. It is easier to highlight behaviors comprised primarily of motor skills, such as typing capital letters, than behaviors comprised primarily of cognitive skills, such as solving a long division problem. When demonstrating behaviors consisting of cognitive skills, it is especially important to highlight the critical components. For example, in teaching students to divide 75 into 1,436, solve the problem on the chalkboard and talk through the steps involved. Your verbalization of the steps provides students with a model they can later imitate.

## Reproduction Phase

During the reproduction phase, learners actually attempt to perform the behavior. If the behavior is relatively complex, the reproduction phase may last for some time, as learners attempt to produce more and more refined performances. Help students during the reproduction phase by providing corrective feedback. Draw students' attention to components of the behavior they are performing incorrectly and demonstrate the correct performance.

Suppose a student who is learning to type capital letters has difficulty in finding the "home" keys (a-s-d-f on the left hand, and j-k-l on the right hand) after pressing the shift key. The keyboarding teacher should provide corrective feedback by pointing out that when pressing the shift key, only the little finger should be removed from its home key. All of the other fingers should remain on their respective home keys.

Give corrective feedback as early as possible to reduce the chances that students will learn incorrect behaviors. Assume that a student who is attempting to divide 1,436 by 75 correctly decides that 75 goes into 143 once, but then writes 75 under 36 instead of under 43. The student's answer will be incorrect. An effective teacher would not only point out that the student's answer is incorrect, but more importantly, strive to find out how the student arrived at the wrong answer and demonstrate the correct procedure for solving the problem.

 **Applying Social Learning Theory**

■■ Here are examples of how teachers use social learning theory in a variety of situations:

Ms. Simmonds notices that one of her fifth-graders is shy and does not belong to any of the circles of friends that have emerged through the school year. The student seems to want to make friends but doesn't know how. Ms. Simmonds pairs the student with more socially successful children in a variety of activities (e.g., collecting information from the encyclopedia on an assigned country or doing science experiments) with the hope that the student will learn more appropriate social skills by imitating the more successful students.

Mr. Dougherty's school is having a "Drug Awareness Week." For his group of fourth-graders, Mr. Dougherty decides to use a videotape with famous athletes from baseball, football, gymnastics, and basketball discussing the dangers of drug use. He notices that students seem more attentive when their favorite athletes appear on the tape.

Ms. Costner teaches students with limited proficiency in English whose native language is Spanish. She teaches them language arts, science, and mathematics in Spanish. She teaches social studies in English. She notices that, when students hand in papers written in English, they tend to write *wanna* for *want to* and *gonna* for *going to*. After she corrects their papers, one of her students says, "But Ms. Costner, that's what you always say!" Ms. Costner becomes more conscious of her speech, realizing that her use of English serves as a model for her students.

## Motivation Phase

The motivation phase is the final phase in observational learning. During this phase learners decide whether or not to perform the behavior they have learned. Of the four phases, the motivation phase is the most important one for you to take into account, because the only way you can determine if your students have learned is to have them perform. If students are unwilling to perform, you simply have no way of knowing whether or not they have learned. Furthermore, unless students have sufficient motivation to perform, trying to lead them through the preceding three phases is likely to be an exercise in futility.

Reinforcement is the key to motivation in social learning theory. Students are more apt to perform if their performance leads to a reward, such as a good grade, a favorable comment by you, or free time in the classroom. Reinforcing some students for performing is also likely to cause others to perform as a result of vicarious reinforcement.

Students may also perform if they are given opportunities to reward themselves for their behavior (Bandura, 1978). Help students establish realistic goals in terms of the quantity and quality of their performance. Allowing students to reward themselves for attaining goals they have set encourages them to become independent learners. Students who learn how to reward themselves for behaving in desirable ways are likely to generalize the process to situations other than the classroom and improve their performance in many areas.

Self-reward positively affects students' behavior in numerous circumstances. Think for a moment about the many students who would like to play a musical instrument, but who resist practicing. Such students are more likely to practice if they reward themselves by looking at a favorite TV program or phoning a friend after practicing for a given amount of time. Students can learn to reward themselves for helping with chores around the house, keeping their rooms neat, or reading books during their leisure time, to give but a few examples.

# The Humanist Approach to Learning

All of the approaches to learning discussed so far in this chapter have dealt with how people acquire various skills and knowledge. The **humanist approach** to learning differs from the others in that it focuses on the affective or emotional components of

2.7

*Explain the ideas inherent in a humanist approach to learning and give examples of educational applications of humanism.*

Can you think of instances in which your teachers have encouraged you to express yourself creatively?

learning (Kohn, 1991). The goals of the humanist approach are to enable students to express themselves creatively, to understand and cope with their feelings, and to become independent learners (Scotti, 1993). From a humanist perspective, teachers should be less concerned with *what* students learn than that they learn *how* to learn and develop positive attitudes toward learning and self-esteem.

Critics have frequently attacked schools for the rigid way in which instruction often takes place. (See, for example, Goodman, 1964; Holt, 1964; Kozol, 1967.) They argue that teachers typically control all learning that takes place in the classroom and prevent students from expressing themselves in creative ways. As a result, many students form negative attitudes toward learning and fail to learn very much. More importantly, the critics claim, many students never really learn *how* to learn, so that after they leave school, they are ill equipped to cope with new situations.

How would you define the terms *self-actualization* and *congruence*?

The principal educational goals of the humanist approach to learning are that students become independent learners and develop into emotionally healthy individuals. Humanists believe teachers should help students achieve "self-actualization" (Maslow, 1968) and "congruence" (Rogers & Freiberg, 1994). According to humanists, people are constantly seeking to fulfill their potential; the role of teachers is to remove obstacles that prevent students from reaching their potential and to help students feel a sense of self-determination (Deci et al., 1991).

The most radical aspect of the humanist approach is the central role students play in deciding for themselves what they will learn (Combs, 1984), which is often called **student-centered teaching.** The teacher's role shifts from that of *instructor* to that of *facilitator*. Teachers suggest various activities that students might want to engage in and provide assorted materials for them to use. The student, however, not the teacher, makes the final choice. Self-regulation of learning has a powerful effect on students' motivation to learn (Campbell, 1964).

## Open Education

The humanist approach to learning formed the basis for the open education movement, which was especially popular in the 1960s. (You may have noticed that most of the publications cited above about humanism were from the 1960s, the heyday of this approach.) **Open education** is a term that is somewhat loosely applied to educational settings in which students largely take charge of their own learning and where creativity and emotional growth are emphasized.

The best-known example of open education occurred at Summerhill, an English school established by A. S. Neill (1960). At Summerhill, teachers and students enjoyed equal rights. Summerhill constituted a nonthreatening environment in which students were never forced to learn or study. Creativity of expression was stressed, and there were no report cards or grades. As with most attempts at open education, there is no solid research evidence concerning the effects of Summerhill on its students.

Open education found its way to the United States in the form of the **open classroom,** in which elementary classrooms were designed with numerous activity centers, sometimes called "learning stations," where students could choose to work. Despite the desirability of focusing on the emotional aspects of learning, the open classroom has not achieved a secure place in our schools. One problem has been the lack of a precise definition. The term *open classroom* has been applied to educational settings that may be nontraditional, but that nevertheless differ markedly (Crowl, 1975).

Research has shown that open education does not improve student learning, but it does seem to have a beneficial effect on affective outcomes (e.g., self-esteem, attitude toward school, and social adjustment) and on creativity (Giacona & Hedges, 1982; Rothenberg, 1989).

## Using a Variety of Approaches

Billy is a five-year-old who has been diagnosed as having both emotional disturbance and mental retardation. He attends a special program for preschoolers with emotional and cognitive problems. Although his retardation is mild compared to that of his classmates, his behavioral problems are highly disruptive. Specifically, he often ignores teachers' instructions and is destructive and violent toward the teachers and the other students, particularly when the class is engaged in activities that don't interest him. His home life is very difficult, because his parents fight often and are frustrated by Billy's problems. Because of their inability to cope with him, they often ignore him until he does something so destructive that they are forced to pay attention.

The teachers in this program use a combination of social learning, behavioral, and humanist approaches. When Billy begins to act out, the teachers are quick to praise those children who are cooperating and from time to time give edible reinforcers, such as raisins. They do this to encourage Billy to imitate these students. According to social learning theory, Billy is more likely to imitate them if he sees them being reinforced. The teachers also use a behavioral approach by rewarding Billy with praise and sometimes a raisin when he spontaneously cooperates. When Billy joins the group after seeing the other students being rewarded, the teachers require him to cooperate for a period of time before rewarding him. In addition, using a humanist approach, the teachers work with Billy individually, giving him the opportunity to select the toys to play with and allowing him to govern the activity. The teachers encourage Billy to act out his feelings through his toys and games. Not surprisingly, Billy's games tend to be somewhat violent (making buildings with blocks and then knocking them down), but he sometimes chooses to play with puppets and acts out family stories with himself, his parents, and sister as the characters.

## Building Self-Esteem

One of the most important ideas underlying the humanist approach is that education should promote students' self-esteem (Purkey & Novak, 1984). Humanists believe that positive self-esteem is not only a worthwhile and important goal in itself, but also that students with strong self-esteem are likely to be more motivated to learn (Maslow, 1968). You are unlikely to see "building students' self-esteem" as part of the formal curricular goals of education in the United States, where we place greater emphasis on students' acquisition of knowledge and development of critical thinking skills. Many teachers, however, make the development of their students' self-esteem a goal in their own classroom.

## Values Clarification

Humanist education also emphasizes the development of student values (Glasser, 1969; Rogers & Freiberg, 1994), not by teaching specific values, but by encouraging students to reflectively formulate their own values. The teacher functions as a facilitator, not as an authority. Some teachers use an approach called **values clarification** (Simon, Howe, & Kirschenbaum, 1972), in which teachers engage students in discussion of problems in an effort to help them explore different values and select those they feel comfortable with.

## Teaching Without Grading

Many humanists also advocate teaching without grading, arguing that students should value learning for its own sake, not because they want a good grade (Kirschenbaum, Simon, & Napier, 1971). Advocates claim that poor grades cause students to have negative attitudes toward school and learning, and high grades make them focus on grades, not on learning. Humanists believe that students vary in their ability to learn and that students with less ability should not be penalized with low grades. Some evidence supports the idea that abolishing grades has a beneficial effect on students' achievement (Gutiérrez & Slavin, 1992).

## Criticisms of the Humanist Approach

Critics argue that the humanist approach is too unstructured (Beane, 1986). They contend that concepts such as "self-actualization" are too poorly defined to be useful for actual classroom planning, and it is doubtful whether programs can actually modify these characteristics in students. Humanists view students as unique individuals who should not be tested and measured. As a result, many humanist programs have not been evaluated properly to determine their effectiveness.

## KEY POINTS

1. There are four theoretical approaches to learning: behavioral, cognitive, social learning, and humanist. The behavioral and cognitive approaches have had more impact on educational practice than the other two.

2. Behaviorism tries to account for how all learning occurs by uncovering laws governing observable behavior.

3. Behaviorists use two kinds of conditioning to explain learning: classical conditioning, where responses become associated with new stimuli, and operant conditioning, in which new responses are acquired by means of reinforcement.

4. Positive reinforcement involves increasing the frequency of a behavior through the presentation of a pleasant stimulus; punishment decreases the frequency of a behavior through the presentation of an unpleasant stimulus.

5. Extinction reduces behavior through the removal of a pleasant stimulus; negative reinforcement increases behavior through the removal of an unpleasant stimulus.

6. Shaping is the process by which complex behaviors are learned through reinforcement of successive approximations of the desired behavior.

7. Programmed instruction and computer-assisted instruction are educational applications of behaviorism in which positive reinforcement is used to teach new behavior.

8. The behavioral approach has been criticized for failing to explain qualitative differences in learning and individual differences among learners and for its dependence on animal research.

9. The cognitive approach, which focuses on how the mind works, uses the cognitive-developmental and information-processing models.

10. According to the social learning approach, people learn by observing and modeling the behavior of others. Vicarious learning occurs when people learn as a result of observing someone else being reinforced.

11. The humanist approach emphasizes the affective components of learning; its goal is to help students develop as independent learners and emotionally healthy individuals.

12. Humanist educators attempt to build students' self-esteem by using values clarification and teaching without grading.

## SELF-STUDY EXERCISES

1. List four approaches to learning and describe their underlying philosophies.

2. Describe the difference between empiricism and rationalism.

3. What were the main contributions of behaviorism? What are the major drawbacks?

4. Consider your own experiences in education in elementary, junior high school, high school, and college. What approach or approaches did your instructors take regarding learning? Think of specific instances in which these approaches were used.

5. List three "pros" and three "cons" of each of the four approaches to learning presented in this chapter. What does each approach contribute to education and how is each limited?

6. What are the qualities that are most likely to result in a model being imitated? Why do you think people tend to imitate models possessing these qualities?

## FURTHER READINGS

Bandura, A. (1986). *Social foundations of thought and action: A social cognitive theory.* Englewood Cliffs, NJ: Prentice Hall.

Bower, G. H., & Hilgard, E. R. (1981). *Theories of learning* (5th ed.). Englewood Cliffs, NJ: Prentice Hall.

Gagné, E. D., Yekovich, C. W., & Yekovich, F. R. (1993). *The cognitive psychology of school learning* (2nd ed.). Boston: Little, Brown.

Patterson, C. H. (1973). *Humanistic education.* Englewood Cliffs, NJ: Prentice Hall.

Rogers, C., & Freiberg, H. J. (1994). *Freedom to learn* (3rd ed.). Columbus, OH: Merrill.

## REFERENCES

Alberto, P., & Troutman, A. C. (1990). *Applied behavior analysis for teachers: Influencing student performance* (3rd ed.). Columbus, OH: Merrill.

Bandura, A. (1963). The role of imitation in personality development. *Journal of Nursery Education, 18,* 207–215.

Bandura, A. (1977). *Social learning theory.* Englewood Cliffs, NJ: Prentice Hall.

Bandura, A. (1978). The self system in reciprocal determinism. *American Psychologist, 33,* 344–358.

Bandura, A. (1986). *Social foundations of thought and action: A social cognitive theory.* Englewood Cliffs, NJ: Prentice Hall.

Bangert, R., Kulik, J., & Kulik, C. (1983). Individualized systems of instruction in secondary schools. *Review of Educational Research, 53,* 143–158.

Beane, J. R. (1986). The continuing controversy over affective education. *Educational Leadership, 43,* 26–31.

Bower, G. H., & Hilgard, E. R. (1981). *Theories of learning* (5th ed.). Englewood Cliffs, NJ: Prentice Hall.

Campbell, V. N. (1964). Self-direction and programmed instruction for five different types of learning objectives. *Psychology in the Schools, 1,* 348–359.

Chance, P. (1992). The rewards of learning. *Phi Delta Kappan, 73,* 200–207.

Chance, P. (1993). Sticking up for rewards. *Phi Delta Kappan, 74,* 787–790.

Combs, A. W. (1984). *A personal approach to teaching: Beliefs that make a difference.* Boston: Allyn & Bacon.

Crowl, T. K. (1975). Examination and evaluation of the conceptual basis for the open classroom. *Education, 96,* 54–56.

Debell, C. S., & Harless, D. K. (1992). B. F. Skinner: Myth and misperception. *Teaching of Psychology, 19,* 68–73.

Deci, E., Vallerand, R. J., Pelletier, L. G., & Ryan, R. M. (1991). Motivation and education: The self-determination perspective. *Educational Psychologist, 26,* 325–346.

Giacona, R. M., & Hedges, L. V. (1982). Identifying features of effective open education. *Review of Educational Research, 52,* 579–602.

Glasser, W. (1969). *Schools without failure.* New York: Harper & Row.

Goodman, P. (1964). *Compulsory miseducation.* New York: Horizon Press.

Gutiérrez, R., & Slavin, R. E. (1992). Achievement effects of the nongraded elementary school: A best evidence synthesis. *Review of Educational Research, 62,* 333–376.

Hill, W. E. (1990). *Learning: A survey of psychological interpretations* (5th ed.). New York: Harper & Row.

Holt, J. (1964). *How children fail.* New York: Pittman.

Horowitz, F. D. (1992). John B. Watson's legacy: Learning and environment. *Developmental Psychology, 28,* 360–367.

Iversen, I. H. (1992). Skinner's early research: From reflexology to operant conditioning. *American Psychologist, 47,* 1318–1328.

Kaplan, J. S. (1991). *Beyond behavior modification* (2nd ed.). Austin, TX: Pro-Ed.

Kirschenbaum, H., Simon, S. B., & Napier, R. W. (1971). *Wad-Ja-Get? The grading game in American education.* New York: Hart.

Kohn, A. (1991). Caring kids: The role of the schools. *Phi Delta Kappan, 72,* 496–506.

Kohn, A. (1993). Rewards versus learning: A response to Paul Chance. *Phi Delta Kappan, 74,* 783–787.

Kozol, J. (1967). *Death at an early age.* Boston: Houghton Mifflin.

Lepper, M. R., & Gurtner, J. (1989). Children and computers: Approaching the twenty-first century. *American Psychologist, 44,* 170–178.

Maslow, A. H. (1968). *Toward a psychology of being* (2nd ed.). New York: Van Nostrand.

Mazur, J. (1990). *Learning and behavior* (2nd ed.). Englewood Cliffs, NJ: Prentice Hall.

Miller, N. E., & Dollard, J. C. (1941). *Social learning and imitation.* New Haven, CT: Yale University Press.

Neill, A. S. (1960). *Summerhill: A radical approach to child rearing.* New York: Hart.

Nevins, J. A. (1993). Why pigeons? *Educational Technology, 33*(10), 34–39.

Pavlov, I. P. (1927). *Conditioned reflexes.* London: Clarendon Press.

Pavlov, I. P. (1955). *Selected works.* Moscow: Foreign Languages Publishing House.

Pavlov, I. P. (1957). *Experimental psychology and other essays.* New York: Philosophical Library.

Purkey, W. W., & Novak, J. M. (1984). *Inviting school success: A self-concept approach to teaching and learning.* Belmont, CA: Wadsworth.

Roblyer, M. D., Castine, W. H., & King, F. J. (1988). *Assessing the impact of computer-based instruction: A review of recent research.* New York: Haworth.

Rogers, C., & Freiberg, H. J. (1994). *Freedom to learn* (3rd ed.). Columbus, OH: Merrill.

Rothenberg, J. (1989). The open classroom reconsidered. *Elementary School Journal, 90,* 68–86.

Schwartz, B., & Reisberg, D. (1991). *Learning and memory.* New York: Norton.

Scotti, W. H. (1993). School and classroom reform: Humanistic principles to consider. *Reading Improvement, 30,* 49–55.

Simon, S. B., Howe, L. W., & Kirschenbaum, H. (1972). *Values clarification: A handbook of practical strategies for teachers and students.* New York: Hart.

Skinner, B. F. (1938). *The behavior of organisms.* New York: Appleton-Century-Crofts.

Skinner, B. F. (1951). How to teach animals. *Scientific American, 185,* 26–29.

Skinner, B. F. (1953). *Science and human behavior.* New York: Macmillan.

Sulzer-Azaroff, B., & Mayer, G. R. (1977). *Applying behavior analysis procedures with children and youth.* New York: Holt, Rinehart & Winston.

Swanson, R. A., & Henderson, R. W. (1977). Effects of televised modeling and active participation on rule-governed question production among Native American preschool children. *Contemporary Educational Psychology, 2,* 345–352.

Thorndike, E. L. (1911). *Animal intelligence: Experimental studies.* New York: Macmillan.

Thorndike, E. L. (1913). *Educational psychology: The psychology of learning* (Vol. 2). New York: Teachers College.

Vargas, E. A. (1993). From behaviorism to selectionism. *Educational Technology, 33*(10), 46–51.

Watson, J. B. (1913). Psychology as the behaviorist views it. *Psychological Review, 20,* 158–177.

Watson, J. B. (1924). *Behaviorism.* New York: Norton.

Watson, J. B. (1926). What the nursery has to say about instincts. In C. Murchison (Ed.), *Psychologies of 1925* (p. 10). Worcester, MA: Clark University Press.

Watson, J. B., & Rayner, R. (1920). Conditioned emotional responses. *Journal of Experimental Psychology, 3,* 1–14.

© R.A. Lee/Superstock

# II

# Cognitive Processes

© T. Rosenthal/Superstock

# The Cognitive-
# Developmental Model

# Chapter Outline

# Learning Objectives

3.1 Describe the cognitive-developmental model and the concepts of development and developmental stages.

3.2 Describe Piaget's cognitive-developmental theory and the four developmental stages.

3.3 Explain how to apply Piaget's theory to help students construct knowledge.

3.4 Describe Vygotsky's theory of learning.

3.5 Explain how to apply Vygotsky's ideas in the classroom.

3.6 Summarize Bruner's ideas.

3.7 Describe the constructivist approach to learning.

# Preview

An infant says her first meaningful word; a first-grader learns to write his name; a college student studies educational psychology. Human beings spend their lives learning—but exactly how do they learn?

Among the theoretical approaches to learning illustrated in figure 3.1, the cognitive approach has gained increasing support among educational psychologists. Consequently, it is useful to examine the cognitive approach in more detail to help you better understand the thrust of current research on learning.

The *cognitive approach* encompasses two different ways of looking at learning: the cognitive-developmental model and the information-processing model. Although the goal of both models is to describe and explain cognitive processes, the ways in which they

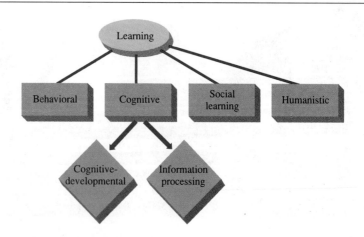

**Figure 3.1**
Theoretical approaches to learning.

attempt to do so differ markedly. Whereas the information-processing model looks at the mind as if it functions like a computer, the cognitive-developmental model looks at the

developmental changes that occur in our thinking as a function of maturation and experience. This chapter focuses on the cognitive-developmental model.

This chapter examines the influential work of three cognitive-developmental psychologists: Jean Piaget, Lev Vygotsky, and Jerome Bruner. Unlike behaviorism, in which virtually all of the leading figures lived in the United States, the cognitive-developmental model has a decidedly international flavor: Piaget was from Switzerland, Vygotsky from Russia, and Bruner lives in the United States. The work of Piaget and Vygotsky initially did not appear in English, so the cognitive-developmental approach failed to gain much attention in the United States for some time.

The fact that Piaget focused primarily on the psychological aspects of his work, not on the educational implications of his findings, also contributed to his failure to capture the attention of educators in the United States. Piaget gained enormous popularity in the United States, however, after his works appeared in English and researchers began to demonstrate the relevance of his findings to educational practice.

Vygotsky and Bruner focused not only on the psychological aspects of cognitive development, but also on the educational aspects. Educators in the United States quickly acknowledged Bruner's ideas, no doubt in part because he lives here, writes in English, and addresses educational issues. Increasing numbers of educators in the United States are taking Vygotsky's ideas seriously now that more of his work is available in English. ◉

# Developmental Stages

Before we examine the cognitive-developmental model, let us focus on what the term **development** means. In psychology, development refers to changes in behavior that occur over time. Consequently, age is a critical factor in developmental theories, which view human growth as a progression from one developmental stage to another. Behavior changes as people get older and, according to developmental theories, all people go through exactly the same stages in exactly the same order. Although this chapter focuses on theories of *cognitive* development, that is, the development of thought, other developmental theories focus on other areas, such as social, emotional and moral behavior.

**3.1** ◉

*Describe the cognitive-developmental model and the concepts of development and developmental stages.*

Stages are sequential, invariant, and universal to all individuals.

## Qualitative Changes in Behavior

The cognitive-developmental model's focus on changes in behavior as a function of age contrasts sharply with the behavioral approach to learning, in which the learner's age is irrelevant. It is therefore not surprising that the cognitive-developmental model and the behavioral approach ask different questions about the learning process. The focus on behavioral changes over time has an important consequence: Developmental theories examine *qualitative*, not just quantitative, differences in behavior. The cognitive-developmental model describes changes in learning, thinking, and reasoning that differ in kind, not merely in degree.

# Piaget's Approach to Cognitive Development

The best-known cognitive-developmental psychologist is Jean Piaget. His work on how people acquire knowledge provoked numerous psychologists to focus on the cognitive processes and to rethink how human learning occurs.

Piaget was a child prodigy who was interested in biology. His first studies looked at how various lower-order species adapt to their environments. Eventually, however, his interests shifted to the study of how human beings adapt to their environments and the role that cognitive growth plays in the process.

To pursue these interests, Piaget traveled to Paris to study with Alfred Binet, who had developed the first intelligence tests. Working in Binet's laboratory, Piaget administered many intelligence tests and soon concluded that intelligence testing was an inadequate method for studying the human mind. Although testing may reveal how much knowledge a person has, Piaget found that it sheds no light on *how* people acquire knowledge.

**3.2** ◉

*Describe Piaget's cognitive-developmental theory and the four developmental stages.*

Piaget revolutionized psychology by looking at *how* children acquire knowledge.

Jean Piaget (1896–1980)
© Yves De Braine/Black Star

Piaget discovered that children's *incorrect* answers provided more insight than their *correct* answers about how their minds work. He discovered that children's answers were not random. On the contrary, children frequently apply a systematic, though faulty, pattern of reasoning. Five- and six-year-old children, for example, consistently told Piaget that the sun and the moon are alive. If the responses were random, we would expect only half of the children to believe the sun and moon are alive. Piaget's major breakthrough came when he realized that not only were children's answers to individual test questions incorrect, but that the reasoning process underlying their answers differed from adult reasoning.

## Piaget's Method: The Clinical Interview

Piaget returned to Switzerland to begin his own investigation. As his primary method of collecting data, Piaget used the **semi-structured** or **clinical interview,** in which he would ask all his subjects the same initial question. Subsequent questions, however, would vary, depending on the subject's responses. Piaget's goal was to discover how children think by analyzing their responses to his questions. He also studied the cognitive growth of infants, including his own children, by presenting them with various tasks in a variety of situations and analyzing their reactions.

## Piaget's Philosophy

Piaget's philosophy rests on the belief that humans are inherently rational and seek to make sense of the world around them. The belief that human beings actively and rationally attempt to learn differed markedly from the psychological views of human behavior that prevailed in the 1920s, when Piaget began his research. Freudian psychologists believed that human beings are inherently irrational and that unconscious needs and drives determine human behavior. For behaviorists, the question of whether or not human beings are rational was irrelevant: they believed that people are passive learners and that various elements in the environment control behavior. Piaget viewed children as active learners who construct their own knowledge. To Piaget, children were like little scientists who test their own hypotheses to discover how the world works.

### Genetic Epistemology

Piaget never considered himself a psychologist. Rather, he called himself a **genetic epistemologist.** *Epistemology* is the branch of philosophy concerned with the origin, nature, and limits of knowledge. In this case *genetic* refers to "the genesis"—or origin—of knowledge, rather than to genes. Piaget's goal was to uncover the genesis of human knowledge—how people acquire knowledge.

### The Active Construction of Knowledge

Have you ever seen a year-old child sitting in a high chair drop a toy to the floor? Often, the parent picks up the toy and gives it back to the baby, only to have the child drop it again. If the parent keeps returning the toy to the child, the child will continue to drop it again and again.

Behaviorists would claim that the parent is reinforcing the child every time he or she returns the toy. Consequently, the child is more likely to drop it again. From a Piagetian perspective, however, the child repeatedly drops the toy to test the hypothesis that every time the toy is dropped it will fall to the floor.

Piaget's idea that children *construct* their own knowledge led to the use of the term *constructivism.*

Piaget would argue that children do not enter the world understanding that objects, when released, fall to the ground; they obtain this understanding through experience. The child, as a "little scientist," has discovered a pattern of events: By repeatedly dropping the toy the child is making sure that there is a predictable consequence when the toy is dropped. In effect, the child is studying the principles of gravity.

Piaget's idea about how children acquire new knowledge is often referred to as **constructivism** (Lauritzen, 1992; Yager, 1991). According to constructivists, people construct knowledge on the basis of their experiences. People need opportunities to explore and experiment, just as the child continually dropping the toy is experimenting with the predictability of gravity. Students also need opportunities in the classroom to learn through experience and experimentation. In science classes, for example, teachers can explain concepts to students, but it is better to have students carry out experiments so they can discover these concepts for themselves.

### Intrinsic Motivation

You might be wondering why a baby in a high chair would begin investigating the principles of gravity. The answer is that the child has an inborn curiosity to find out how things work. According to Piaget (1952), humans have **intrinsic motivation;** that is, they act because of an internal desire to understand and satisfy their curiosity. Piaget's belief that children are intrinsically motivated rests on Darwin's notion that a species adapts to its environment. The human species uses its mind to adapt. To survive, human beings use their minds to discover how the world works and to predict events.

Piaget viewed the child as a "little scientist" who explores the way the world works.
© Superstock

## Components of Piaget's Model of Cognitive Development

Piaget believed children construct knowledge by actively interacting with their environment and trying to make sense of their experiences. What kinds of events occur, as children actively interact with their environment, that cause them to construct knowledge? Are some characteristics of the child or of the environment especially effective in promoting children's cognitive development? Do all children in all environments construct knowledge in the same way?

You will find the answers to these questions in the remainder of this section on Piaget's theory. You will also learn how to use Piaget's model of cognitive development to create a classroom environment that enhances students' cognitive growth.

The idea that we are motivated by a desire to understand how the world works, a form of intrinsic motivation, differs from the behaviorists' idea that we are motivated by the desire to gain rewards and avoid punishment, a form of extrinsic motivation.

According to Piaget, children construct their own knowledge through experience and experimentation.
© David Frazier

# Using Piaget's Ideas About Motivation

If students are motivated intrinsically to learn and understand, what role do teachers play? According to Elkind (1971),

> intrinsic motivation resides in the child and not in [educational] methods and procedures. It is the child who must, at any given point in time, choose the method of learning and the materials that are reinforcing to *him.* Without the opportunity for student choice and the provision of large blocks of time, in which the child can totally engross himself in an activity, the values of intrinsic motivation will not be realized . . . [T]he education practice which would best foster intrinsically motivated children . . . would be the production of "interest areas" where children could go on their own and for long periods of time. (pp. 25–26)

Teachers must create a variety of learning environments in which students can choose areas of investigation and have access to the appropriate materials. Students also need opportunities to explore at their own pace. Wadsworth (1989) recommends that students be encouraged to explore their spontaneous interests. These interests, unique to each child, frequently reflect topics the student is struggling to comprehend. "We all know that when we can concentrate on things we are really interested in, our efforts are more intense and more productive than when we work on things that are of lesser interest . . . It is reasonable for educators to view time spent on spontaneous interests as valid for intellectual development and knowledge acquisition" (Wadsworth, 1989, p. 159).

## How We Construct Knowledge

Piaget identified four factors that determine cognitive growth (Wadsworth, 1989):

1. *Maturation,* growth due to hereditary factors, defines our potential for cognitive development.
2. *Active experiences,* such as the manipulation of objects, or even mental manipulation (thinking), allow us to develop and refine our understanding.
3. *Social interaction* with others (including teachers) enables us to share ideas and acquire new understandings.
4. *Equilibration,* the process by which we try to make sense of our experiences, enables us to reconcile how we expect the world to behave with how it actually functions.

The last of these, equilibration, is unique to Piaget's theory. **Equilibration** is the pursuit of an equilibrium or a balance. Specifically, the individual is seeking to balance his or her ways of understanding the world (schemata) with evidence of how the world actually functions.

*Schemata, Assimilation, and Accommodation*   **Schemata** is the term Piaget uses to refer to our existing understandings. (The singular form of *schemata* is *schema.*) Suppose a child's initial schema of where babies come from is that a stork brings them. Eventually the child will encounter experiences that challenge the accuracy of this schema. Perhaps the child learns that babies come home from the hospital, or sees a pregnant woman and is told that a baby is growing inside her, or learns from older children what they know (or think they know) about the origins of babies, or learns about human reproduction from his or her parents or in a sex education class in school. Such experiences challenge the child's current schema (let's call it the stork theory) and create a disequilibrium. How does the child resolve the inconsistencies and restore a state of equilibrium?

According to Piaget, people have a natural tendency to retain an existing schema and to try to force conflicting evidence to fit into it. Piaget refers to this process as **assimilation.** Think for a moment about small children's beliefs about how presents arrive on Christmas morning. Often a child in a family that celebrates Christmas initially believes that Santa brings the presents during the night.

We have a wide variety of schemata that we use to understand events. For example, you may have a schema that people are basically honest; when you realize that someone has lied to you, you face disequilibrium. Young children may have a schema that teachers live in the school; encountering a teacher in the street creates disequilibrium.

Conflicting evidence, however, may create a disequilibrium. The child may observe many Santas, big and small, black and white, male and female, fat and thin, standing on street corners during the holiday season. This evidence may conflict with the child's image of Santa Claus. Usually this evidence is forced to conform to the child's existing schema; the child is often told or decides that these are really Santa's helpers, and not the real Santa. The existing schema is retained—that is, the child assimilates the evidence into his or her existing schema. Further evidence may challenge the child's existing understanding, but assimilation continues. Other children deny Santa's existence, but the child may decide the other children are just jealous or spiteful; the child wonders how Santa makes so many stops in one night, or manages to get into homes without chimneys, but accepts the explanation that "Santa is magic."

Inevitably, however, the child encounters more conflicting evidence (perhaps the child finds the presents in the closet prior to Christmas morning or catches the parents wrapping them). Consequently, the child must reject the "Santa Claus theory" and develop a new schema. Piaget calls this step **accommodation;** new evidence surfaces that the existing schema cannot explain and, as a result, the child revises the existing schema to accommodate the new evidence. Whereas in assimilation, new evidence is forced to conform to the existing schema, in accommodation, the existing schema is revised to conform to the new evidence.

**Equilibration** is the process by which all human beings (not just children) use assimilation and accommodation to construct and refine their schemata, or their understandings of the world they live in. Our knowledge exists in the form of schemata, or mental representations, that undergo periodic revision based on new experiences.

> Equilibration, assimilation, and accommodation are not unique to children. Adults are constantly engaging in these activities, as well.

Think of instances when you have "kicked yourself" for not realizing something staring you in the face. You had at last accommodated and were kicking yourself for having previously assimilated. Some of our students have described humorous instances of assimilation and accommodation. One student believed for some time that all dogs were male and all cats were female! She finally rejected the idea when she learned about reproduction. Another student, who crossed the Hudson River to get from New York to New Jersey, believed that states were always separated by a body of water. Finally, the third author's nephew (at age three) had three uncles, all of whom had mustaches; when asked if he thought one of his uncles should shave off his mustache, he replied, "No, then you wouldn't be an uncle anymore"!

## Stages in Piaget's Theory of Cognitive Development

According to Piaget (1954), people progress through four sequential stages of cognitive development: sensorimotor, preoperations, concrete operations, and formal operations. Each stage is characterized by *qualitative* changes in behavior, an idea that contradicts the behaviorists' belief that changes in human growth are quantitative and cumulative. Figure 3.2 illustrates this difference. The graph on the left depicts human growth according to the behaviorists; the graph on the right illustrates the idea of stages of development.

The four stages of cognitive development coincide with approximate age ranges, as shown in figure 3.3. Note that the transition from one stage to another does not occur in the form of an abrupt change in behavior. On the contrary, transitions between stages occur in an uneven manner. During transitional phases, children typically exhibit some behaviors characteristic of the stage they are entering and other behaviors characteristic of the stage they are leaving. During a transitional phase, children often carry out a task at a higher stage on one occasion and at a lower stage on another occasion.

> Children may be in one cognitive stage, or they may show signs of two stages as they move from one stage to the other.

## Encouraging Disequilibrium

Strange as this may sound, one of your most important responsibilities is to create *disequilibrium* for your students. Much classroom teaching involves encouraging students to revise and improve their schemata. By providing experiences that cause students to question existing beliefs, or upsetting the students' mental "apple carts," you can help students revise schemata to accommodate new information. Creating disequilibrium also keeps students motivated by turning the classroom into an exciting place full of surprises instead of a boring place of monotonous routine.

The following guidelines will help you help your students to accommodate new information successfully:

1. Try to understand the nature of each student's existing schema of a phenomenon. You cannot decide how best to challenge a student's existing understanding unless you have an accurate idea of the student's schema. The process of challenging students' beliefs varies from student to student. If you were teaching the difference between rivers and lakes, you might ask students to list the names of rivers and lakes they have visited and describe how they can tell the difference between a river and a lake. Such an approach works fine for students who have visited many rivers and lakes, but for students who have not, a different approach is needed. You might show a series of videos depicting various rivers and lakes, and ask the students to try to identify what characteristics distinguish a river from a lake.

2. Make sure you have identified the concepts your students are supposed to learn from the curriculum. How do the concepts relate to one another, and which concepts depend on previously acquired ideas? For example, the scientific concepts of mass, volume, and weight are related in that they all describe physical characteristics of objects. It is likely, however, that students will learn the concept of mass more easily if they have already acquired the concept of weight.

3. Before beginning a lesson, decide what sorts of activities are likely to challenge your students' existing schemata. Selecting appropriate activities requires imagination and resourcefulness. As you gain more teaching experience, the process becomes easier because you can rely on your knowledge of what has and has not worked with previous groups of students. Your goal is to create situations that evoke students' curiosity, cause them to question themselves, and lead them to a more accurate or comprehensive understanding. For example, you might have students learn about important historical figures or events by designating one student (or a small group of students) to think of a figure or event and have other members of the class try to identify the figure or the event by asking questions about the figure or event that can be answered by "yes" or "no." If you are teaching older students, you could have them generate their own questions. If you are teaching younger students, you might have them randomly select questions from a previously prepared list.

4. Another way to create disequilibrium is through surprise (Wadsworth, 1989). By structuring situations in which the outcome is not easily predicted, you cause students to struggle with their own ideas about a phenomenon. As Wadsworth states, "The unknown and the unpredictable can generate both interest and cognitive conflict" (p. 159).

5. Do not forget that students construct their own knowledge; it is therefore critical that they have opportunities to be *active learners* and to learn through their own firsthand *experience*. Suppose your goal is to teach students the difference between sedimentary, igneous, and metamorphic rocks. Instead of explaining the differences, bring in samples of each and give students opportunities to examine the rocks. Let them generate a list of differences that could be the basis of your subsequent activities.

6. Above all, *listen* to your students, *pay attention* to the clues they give regarding how they are understanding events, and *look* closely at their behavior. Students' words and actions usually indicate how they are comprehending a situation. Remember that students' wrong answers often provide the most useful information for restructuring their existing schemata. Explore students' reasons for giving incorrect answers. Their explanations often provide just what you need to know to create disequilibrium.

**Figure 3.2**
Human growth: Two perspectives.

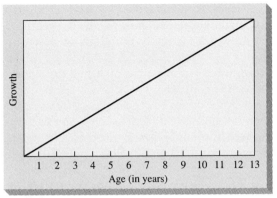

(a) Quantitative model of growth

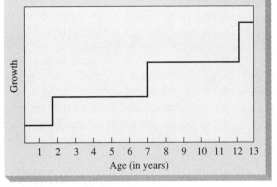

(b) Qualitative model of growth

**Figure 3.3**
Stages of cognitive development.

| Stage | Approximate age range | Major characteristics |
|---|---|---|
| Sensorimotor | Birth to 1½ or 2 | Increasing goal-directed behavior<br>Object permanence |
| Preoperations | 1½ or 2 to 6 or 7 | Egocentrism<br>Collective monologues<br>Magical thinking<br>Parallel play<br>Dramatic play<br>Centration |
| Concrete operations | 6 or 7 to 11 or 12 | Classification<br>Seriation<br>Transitivity<br>Conservation<br>Class inclusion<br>Decentration |
| Formal operations | 11 or 12 and older | Abstract thinking<br>Scientific reasoning<br>Hypothesis testing<br>Adolescent egocentrism<br>  (belief in the personal fable and the<br>  imaginary audience)<br>Adolescent disenchantment |

## Sensorimotor Stage

During the **sensorimotor stage,** infants explore their environments, seeing, hearing, touching, tasting, and smelling the objects around them. These sensory and motor experiences allow them to acquire skills and develop schemata. Toward the end of this stage, children start to use symbols, including language (Piaget & Inhelder, 1969). Consequently, infants' initial understandings of objects and events are necessarily restricted by the limited direct ways in which they are able to obtain information: the use of body movements and the senses.

Children are born with no internal representation of the outside world and have no conceptual understanding of their experiences with the world. As a result of their sensorimotor experiences, however, infants gradually learn how to adapt to their environments. They learn to integrate and coordinate information coming from different sources, such as guiding their movements in coordination with auditory or visual stimuli. They also develop goal-directed behavior and learn to satisfy their needs by combining a series of actions.

Piaget's ideas about the sensorimotor stage were largely based on his observations of his own three children as infants.

The discovery that objects exist even when unseen (object permanence) is an example of accommodation.

Infants exhibit goal-directed behavior when they grasp for a toy that is out of reach, making eye contact with parents and vocalizing to communicate to parents that they want the toy. As they progress through the sensorimotor stage, children develop more complex goal-directed behavior by combining their growing repertoire of schemata. For example, an older infant might understand how to crawl to get the toy or grasp an object (such as a blanket) on which the toy rests and pull it closer, thus obtaining the toy.

A very young infant does not realize that an object has an actual existence; to that infant, a ball exists only when he or she is playing with it and it ceases to exist when it is out of sight. Gradually, however, the infant has experiences that lead to the conclusion that the ball exists whether it is visible or not. Perhaps the infant sees a ball roll on the floor and stop at a point where it is half hidden by the couch, or perhaps the ball rolls completely behind the couch, but the infant comes upon it later when crawling there.

As a result of such experiences, infants at the sensorimotor stage learn that the world is a permanent place, not merely a temporary set of sensory stimuli that change from moment to moment. Infants develop the concept of **object permanence,** or the understanding that objects continue to exist even though they may not be visible at the moment. Children who are in the process of acquiring the concept of object permanence invariably enjoy "peek-a-boo" games; each time the adult's face is revealed, to the delight of the child, the notion of object permanence is supported.

## Preoperations Stage

The **preoperations stage** lasts approximately from the age of 2 to the age of 6 or 7. During this stage, children become better and better at using language to represent objects and events symbolically. Children use language not only to communicate with others but also to communicate with themselves, talking aloud or silently (that is, thinking). The child's rapid expansion of language during this stage facilitates thought. Although the child has a new capacity to think symbolically, there is an absence of adult-like logic in the thinking of a preoperational child. The following conversation illustrates the absence of adult forms of logic in the way children think during the preoperations stage:

> **Miriam (age 3) on the telephone:** Uncle Dave, this is my favorite book. Read it to me.
> **Uncle Dave:** Miriam, I can't see the book, so I can't read it to you.
> **Miriam:** But I want you to read it to me!
> **Uncle Dave:** But I'm in New York and you're in Massachusetts. You can see the book, but I can't.
> **Miriam:** But I want you to read it to me!

Miriam's comments in this conversation not only exemplify the nature of preoperational thought, but they also exemplify one of the foremost characteristics of preoperational thought: egocentrism. The term **egocentrism** refers to the preoperational child's inability to see the world from anyone else's perspective. Preoperational children see themselves as the focal point of all about them. They are able to see the world only from their own perspective and do not yet realize that others may see the world differently.

Note the egocentric thinking—the idea that even the sun and moon move in response to the child—in the following interview with a preoperational child (Piaget, 1979):

Notice how children's incorrect ideas about the sun and the moon reveal their underlying thinking.

> **Piaget:** Does the sun move?
> **Child:** Yes, when one walks, it follows. When one turns round it turns round too. Doesn't it ever follow you too?
> **Piaget:** Why does it go?

Peanuts reprinted by permission of United Feature Syndicate, Inc.

**Child:** To hear what we say.

**Piaget:** Is it alive?

**Child:** Of course, otherwise it couldn't follow us, it couldn't shine.

**Piaget:** Does the moon move?

**Child:** Yes, when one walks too, more than the sun, because if you run the moon goes as fast as running, but when you run with the sun it only goes as fast as walking. Because the moon is stronger than the sun, it goes faster. The sun can't ever catch it up. (p. 215)

**Piaget:** Does it follow you or does it not really move?

**Child:** It follows me. It stops if I stop.

**Piaget:** If I were to walk too, which of us would it follow?

**Child:** Me. (p. 217)

Piaget uncovered numerous characteristics of preoperational thinking, including children's tendency to engage in collective monologues, parallel play, dramatic play, and magical thinking.

The egocentric thinking of preoperational children affects the way they interact socially. Preoperational children often engage in **collective monologues,** in which they may take turns speaking, but what one child is saying has nothing to do with what the other child is saying. On the surface it may appear that the children are conversing with one another, but in reality each child is talking to him- or herself. Here is an example of a collective monologue between two 4-year-olds. The egocentrism of the two children is evident in their inability to interact meaningfully with one another.

**Elena:** We're having hot dogs for lunch today.

**Sean:** I've got more pens than you have.

**Elena:** Hot dogs is my favorite lunch.

**Sean:** I've got green and black, but you only have black.

Egocentric thinking also affects the way in which preoperational children play. Often children in the preoperational stage engage in **parallel play,** in which two children appear to be playing the same game or with the same toys, when in fact each child is engaging in his or her own activity. The children's egocentric thinking prevents them from engaging in the same game simultaneously. During this stage, children also commonly engage in **dramatic play** in which objects take on imaginary qualities. Have you ever bought an expensive toy only to find that the child prefers to play with the box the toy came in? Preoperational children often prefer the box because it is plain and they can easily invest it with any number of qualities through the use of imagination and fantasy.

This manner of thinking is consistent with a pattern of **magical thinking** common in preoperations. Children in this stage often enjoy stories with magical situations in them, but, lacking adult-like logic, they cannot easily differentiate fantasy from reality. For example, after watching the film *Mary Poppins,* a 3-year-old has her family act out the story, with her mother playing the part of Mary Poppins. When the time comes for Mary Poppins to fly away, the child says, "Okay, Mommy, now fly!" and is very distressed when her mother doesn't.

**Figure 3.4**
Logical operations in the concrete operations stage.

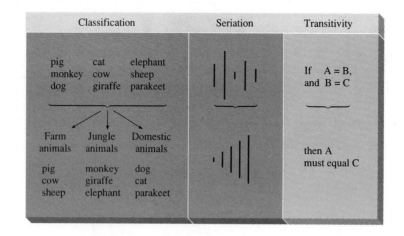

Because of their egocentrism, preoperational children have difficulty differentiating between their dreams and reality. They believe their dreams have physical properties. Similarly, children in this stage feel that words are somehow an intrinsic part of the object or event they represent—ask a preoperational child named "Felicia" if she could have been given some other name, and she will probably reply "no." Preoperational children frequently do not understand that words are arbitrary labels and therefore interchangeable. Bilingual children, who have more experience with language, learn earlier than monolingual children that words are symbols and not intrinsically bound to their referents (Diaz, 1983; Ianoc-Worrall, 1972).

Preoperational children also often believe that nonliving things are alive. The child in the interview concerning the sun and the moon, for example, believed the sun is alive.

The most striking characteristic of preoperational thinking is the absence of adult forms of logic. Children begin to use adult logic when they progress to the concrete operations stage.

## Concrete Operations Stage

The stage of **concrete operations** begins when children are 6 or 7 years old and lasts until they are about 11 or 12. Consequently, children remain at the concrete operational stage of cognitive development during most of elementary school.

Elementary school students begin to use adult forms of logic, but they can apply their new-found logic only to concrete situations. In other words, they can think logically about things they can experience, but not about hypothetical situations. Children at the concrete operations stage look at the world and interpret situations literally. For example, upon hearing the expression "pouring cold water" on an idea, a child in concrete operations might say, "Why do you want to get it wet?"

Children in concrete operations can classify objects according to various abstract characteristics. For example, as shown in figure 3.4, they can classify animals by where they are found (farm animals, jungle animals, domestic animals, and so on) or books by type of reading material (fiction, nonfiction). In contrast, preoperational children can classify objects only on the basis of physical properties (size, shape, and color), not on the basis of more abstract properties.

Children in concrete operations can engage in **seriation**, that is, arranging objects in a logical order. When given a set of sticks of varying lengths, concrete operational children can arrange them from shortest to longest, or vice versa, even without instruction. In contrast, a preoperational child would rearrange them in a random sequence, even when asked to put them in order.

The logical operations that children acquire in the concrete operations stage allow them to understand mathematical concepts, such as the commutative property, A + B = B + A, and associative property (A + B) + C = A + (B + C).

Concrete operational children also understand **transitivity**, the idea that if A equals B and B equals C, then A must equal C. The same holds true for "less than" or "greater than" relationships. For example, suppose you tell a child that "Albert is shorter than Bill, and Bill is shorter than Charles." If asked who is shorter, Albert or

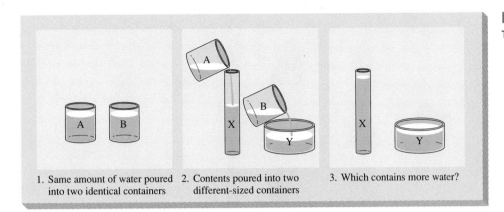

1. Same amount of water poured into two identical containers
2. Contents poured into two different-sized containers
3. Which contains more water?

**Figure 3.5**
The conservation of water task.

Charles, a concrete operational child would have no difficulty recognizing that the correct answer is "Albert." A preoperational child, however, could reach this conclusion only after first visually comparing Albert and Charles.

**Conservation** is probably the most famous of all the logical operations associated with the stage of concrete operations. In what has become a classical demonstration of conservation (see figure 3.5), Piaget poured water into two identical glasses until both held exactly the same amount. He showed a child the glasses, and the child agreed that both glasses contained exactly the same amount of water. Then Piaget poured the water from one glass into a long narrow glass and the water from the second glass into a short wide glass. Of course, the narrow glass would fill up to a higher point. He asked the child which of the two new glasses contained more water.

The responses of the children differed, depending on the child's level of cognitive development. Children in the concrete operations stage reported that the two new glasses contained the same amount, realizing that even though the two new glasses had different shapes, the amount of water remained unchanged. Concrete operational children understand the notion of **reversibility;** they know that if the water in either new glass were poured back into the original glass, it would rise to the same point as before.

Preoperational children did not understand the property of reversibility and thought the narrow glass contained more because the water level was higher, even though they saw that Piaget had poured the water without adding or removing any. They attended to only one dimension—the height of the water, but not to the width.

Other examples of conservation are the "ball of clay" and "row of coins" problems. If a ball of clay is flattened into a big pancake, preoperational children believe the pancake contains more clay than the ball. Concrete operational children, however, can simultaneously attend to more than one dimension and realize that although the form of the clay has changed, the amount has not. Similarly, if the same number of coins are placed close together in one row but spread far apart in a second row, preoperational children think the second row has more coins.

Preoperational children are **centered** and focus only on one dimension in the problem. They depend on their immediate perceptions and fail to use logic. Concrete operational children can **decenter** and attend to multiple dimensions of the problem simultaneously.

Whether students can successfully complete academic tasks depends on their stage of cognitive development. Students at the concrete operational stage can calculate the area of a rectangle, but preoperational students cannot because they can't focus on the rectangle's width and length simultaneously (Lautrey, Mullet, & Paques, 1989).

It is possible to teach preoperational children to give the correct response to a conservation problem, but they can't explain their answer and, when given a different conservation problem, they can't solve it. They also forget the answers they previously learned after a while and give typical preoperational responses to problems they

When Piaget's theory first became popular in the United States, some behaviorists tried to refute it by demonstrating that correct responses to the conservation task could be taught by systematically rewarding children for giving the correct answer.

**Figure 3.6**
Class inclusion task.

once could solve. Teaching preoperational students to perform logical operations associated with the stage of concrete operations has no lasting effect. Children can learn logical operations only when they are developmentally ready.

Casey (1990), for example, compared the performance of preschoolers attending an experimental preschool designed to "promote planning and problem-solving abilities" with the performance of similar children attending conventional preschools. After one year in their respective schools, children in the experimental program performed better on planning and problem-solving tasks than children in the conventional program, but the groups did not differ in their ability to conserve.

**Class inclusion,** the ability to classify objects according to more than one category simultaneously, is another operation that concrete operational children can perform but preoperational children can't. Preoperational children have difficulty determining if there are more shaded figures than triangles in figure 3.6 because they can't classify objects by color and shape simultaneously. Concrete operational children can easily give the correct answer.

## Formal Operations Stage

Concrete operational children can apply logic only to "here and now" situations. People in the **formal operations stage,** which begins around age 11 or 12 and continues through adulthood, can apply logic to abstract and hypothetical situations. At this stage, students can answer questions such as, "What would have happened if the Germans and Japanese had won World War II?" or "What might happen if we did not vote by secret ballot?" Concrete operational children cannot generate meaningful responses to these questions, but formal operational adolescents can.

Formal thinking requires the ability to think abstractly. Works of literature and art can take on abstract meaning only to someone in formal operations. Concrete operational children look at such works literally. Formal operational thinkers can also engage in hypothesis testing, or scientific thinking.

Suppose you ask students what controls the speed at which a pendulum moves back and forth. Some students may suggest that the weight at the end of the pendulum controls speed; others may believe that the length of the string is the important factor. To help the students experimentally determine the correct answer, you give them two weights, one weighing 1 gram and the other 2 grams, and two pieces of string, one 5 centimeters and the other 10 centimeters in length.

Concrete operational thinkers would try various combinations of weights and lengths of string haphazardly. They might stumble upon the correct answer, but they would not solve the problem efficiently and systematically. Formal operational thinkers, however, would test hypotheses: First, they might test the hypothesis that the weight controls speed. As shown in figure 3.7, testing this hypothesis involves two steps:

Works of art take on abstract meaning only for people in formal operations. (Senecio, Paul Klee)

© Offentliche Kunstsammlung, Basie/Bridgeman Art Library, London/Superstock

**Figure 3.7**
The pendulum problem.

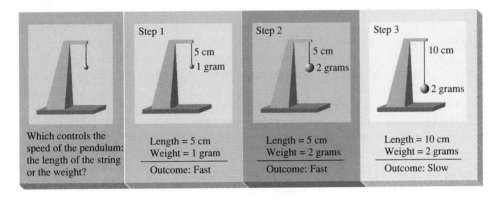

|  | Weight | Length | Outcome |
|---|---|---|---|
| Step 1: | 1 gram | 5 centimeters | Fast |
| Step 2: | 2 grams | 5 centimeters | Fast |

Note that the weight is varied, but the length is not. Since the outcome stayed the same, the students conclude that weight has no impact on speed.

Next, they might test the hypothesis that length controls speed by adding a third step:

|  | Weight | Length | Outcome |
|---|---|---|---|
| Step 3: | 2 grams | 10 centimeters | Slow |

A comparison of the outcomes of steps 2 and 3 shows that the longer the string, the slower the pendulum moves.

Formal operational thinkers do not need to carry out the fourth possible combination (1 gram and 10 centimeters) to know that lengthening the string slows the pendulum's speed. Concrete operational thinkers, however, can't extrapolate the results of the first three tests to predict that the 1-gram, 10-centimeter combination would move as slowly as the 2-gram, 10-centimeter combination. Only students in the stage of formal operations can carry out this kind of efficient, scientific thinking. Wavering (1989) found that students in the stage of formal operations (grades 9 through 12) performed significantly better than students in the stage of concrete operations (grades 6 through 8) in drawing line graphs that have positive and negative slopes and an exponentially increasing curve.

People sometimes use formal operations with some concepts but not with others. A student, for example, may think abstractly about literature and art, but not about physics. People are most likely to apply formal operations in areas in which they have experience and formal instruction (Rogoff, 1990; Tulviste, 1991). The lack of uniform application of formal operations demonstrates the distinction between cognitive competence (*having* the ability to perform a cognitive task) and cognitive performance (*using* the ability).

When adolescents first enter the formal operations stage, they develop a new kind of egocentrism that Elkind (1967) calls **adolescent egocentrism.** Adolescent egocentrism has two major characteristics: the **imaginary audience** and the **personal fable.** Adolescents often act as though they are performing before an imaginary audience. They feel that everyone is watching what they do, what they say, and what they look like. As a result of becoming highly self-conscious and sometimes inhibited, adolescents frequently begin to pay more attention to their appearance and to worry about how others perceive them.

Teenagers are typically self-conscious as a result of adolescent egocentrism.

© Steve Skjold

Adolescents also often have the erroneous belief (or personal fable) that they are indestructible. As a result, they sometimes engage in risk-taking behavior. When told of possible harmful outcomes, they think "That will never happen to *me*"! The belief that somehow they live a charmed life and cannot be hurt may account for why adolescents sometimes engage in dangerous activities. The belief of indestructibility can have serious consequences if it causes adolescents to drink and drive, mix drugs and alcohol, or expose themselves to AIDS and other sexually transmitted diseases or pregnancy. Group discussions help students overcome personal fables as they discover other students think the same way and consequently learn that their experience is not unique.

During the early phase of formal operations, adolescents often become disgruntled with society. Formal operational thinkers often ask, "Why isn't the world a better place?" Disenchantment with the "real world," as compared to their "utopian" idea of how the world should be, sometimes leads them to explore different religions, political beliefs, or unusual lifestyles. This aspect of formal operations is similar to the "identity crisis" of adolescence that the famous psychologist Erik Erikson described.

## Piaget's Influence on Educational Thinking in the United States

Piaget's accounts of his observations of and interviews with children leave little doubt that children and adults think in completely different ways. Piaget's theoretical explanations are difficult to read and comprehend, in part because of the dense and technical nature of his writing, and in part because of problems inherent in translating his works from French into English. Fortunately, many useful books written in English are available in which psychologists and educators have "digested" Piaget's work for interested students. (See the end of this chapter for a list of some of these works.)

Piaget's first books describing his theory appeared in the 1920s and early 1930s and were well received in Europe. They made little impression on psychologists in the United States primarily because his work did not fit into the behaviorist approach that dominated at the time.

Piaget's work began to attract attention in the United States because of an accident of history. When the Soviet Union successfully launched the Sputnik satellite in 1957, many in the United States recognized with considerable alarm that we were losing the space race. Anxiously struggling to find a solution that would permit the United States to regain its lead, people quickly turned to the schools for answers.

In their efforts to improve science and math education in the United States, educators "rediscovered" Piaget, whose work had particular relevance to the development of students' logical and scientific thinking. Piaget's ideas flourished in the United States during the 1960s and 1970s.

Piaget's pioneering work laid the groundwork for approaching educational psychology from a cognitive perspective and has provided important guidelines for teaching students at various stages of cognitive development. Most importantly, Piaget focused attention on the importance of *action* in learning and the need for students to have opportunities to explore and construct their own knowledge (DeVries & Kohlberg, 1987). Educational psychologists, however, began to shift from a cognitive-developmental model to an information-processing model in the 1980s and 1990s.

## Criticisms and Controversies

Psychologists began to lose interest in Piaget's theory because of some valid criticisms. Some critics argue that although Piaget has described the stages of cognitive development, his theoretical model provides no explanation of how people move from stage to stage. Clearly, a child does not go to sleep one night in preoperations and wake up the next day in concrete operations. The transition from one stage to another is gradual, but how gradual is it? What causes the transition to occur, and why do some people make the transition at an earlier age than others?

Children's increased ability to pay attention probably causes them to move from the stage of preoperations to that of concrete operations (Chapman & Lindenberger, 1989). Riley (1989), for example, found that the performance of fourth- and fifth-grade students with learning disabilities, who typically have difficulty paying attention, performed at a significantly lower level than nondisabled students did.

Other critics have observed that people seem to be in transition longer than they are in the stages (Flavell, 1982; Rohwer, Ammon, & Cramer, 1974; Siegler, 1991). Consequently, the usefulness of describing cognitive development in terms of stages seems limited. It might be more useful to describe the processes involved in the transitions between stages.

Piaget's ideas encouraged more use of active learning.

© Steve Skjold

It is well known that individuals vary in terms of how rapidly they develop cognitively, yet Piaget's theory does not account for such individual differences. Why does one child, for example, move into concrete operations at age 5 and another at age 8? Or, what accounts for the fact that some people are intellectually gifted and others have mental retardation?

When adults with mental retardation were matched for mental age with nonretarded children, both groups performed similarly on Piagetian tasks (Hore & Tryon, 1989). Piaget's theory, however, sheds no light on why some adults fail to continue to develop cognitively. Although Piaget describes the stages of cognitive development applicable to human beings as a species, he fails to explain cognitive differences among individuals.

Some parents and educators, particularly in the United States, were disappointed that Piaget's theory failed to provide guidelines for accelerating children's cognitive development. Piaget had no interest in trying to accelerate children's cognitive growth. He believed they would move to higher stages when they were developmentally ready. A number of educators in the United States, such as Elkind (1991), wholeheartedly agree. Teachers and parents should allow children to develop at a normal pace. Pressure to accelerate development only causes children needless stress.

According to Piaget, the best way to help children develop cognitively is to provide experiences that facilitate their cognitive growth, such as creating disequilibrium. It is simply impossible to push children into higher stages before they are ready; in fact, research appears to bear out his conclusion (Kuhn, 1974).

Another weakness of Piaget's theory is that it does not take into account that individuals in formal operations do not always use formal operational thinking (Rohwer, Ammon, & Cramer, 1974). A physicist, for example, may think abstractly about physics but concretely about other fields. People use formal operations inconsistently (Kamii, 1984). We tend to think abstractly in the areas in which we are trained or in which we work.

## Applying Piaget's Ideas

Piaget's theory suggests that creating *disequilibrium* is a useful instructional technique. Creating disequilibrium causes students to reconsider their existing schemata and perhaps to revise them to be more accurate.

To create disequilibrium, you have to understand the thinking that underlies students' mistakes. Students themselves are frequently the source of this information (Confrey, 1990). One common student error, for example, is the belief that in subtraction, like addition, order doesn't matter. When students are faced with a problem such as this:

$$\begin{array}{r} 143 \\ -25 \\ \hline \end{array}$$

they often figure that since they cannot subtract five from three they should subtract three from five, yielding the erroneous answer 122. Given that students know that 3 + 5 = 5 + 3, this misunderstanding is not surprising. Disequilibrium can challenge this way of thinking by demonstrating with manipulatives that 143 minus 25 is *not* 122.

In addition to creating disequilibrium, tailor *what* and *how* you teach in accordance with your students' stage of cognitive development. In mathematics, for example, use songs and rhymes to teach preoperational students to count. Use manipulative materials to teach preoperational students numerical quantities and concrete operational students how to apply the basic mathematical operations of addition, subtraction, multiplication, and division.

Students in the stage of concrete operations can perform multistep operations and deal with concepts such as fractions and decimals. Only after students have advanced to formal operations can they comprehend abstract mathematical topics such as algebra and calculus.

Finally, students must be *active* to learn. They must engage in activity that leads to construction and revision of their knowledge. Involve students in active forms of learning. Rather than telling them the procedures used to regroup in subtraction, for example, have them use manipulatives to see how regrouping makes sense.

3.3 ◎

*Explain how to apply Piaget's theory to help students construct knowledge.*

*Annual* **Edition**

unit *2*

Some researchers have also questioned whether cognitive development stops at the stage of formal operations (Kitchener et al., 1993). Is the thinking of a 13-year-old qualitatively the same as that of a 40-year-old? Arlin (1986) suggests there may be a stage beyond formal operations in which adults engage in problem solving and problem *finding*.

Perhaps the most damage to Piaget's theory comes from psychologists who criticize him for not carrying out rigorously controlled experiments (Larsen, 1977). His clinical interview method resulted in interviews that technically are not comparable because each individual was not asked identical questions. Furthermore, Piaget may have unintentionally led children to make statements supporting his beliefs. Others feel that children's responses may have reflected a failure to understand Piaget's questions, rather than a lack of knowledge of what was being discussed (Siegel, 1978).

Studies that are rigorously controlled have found that children perform certain tasks earlier than Piaget claimed (e.g., Gelman, 1985; Schiff, 1983). Although these findings challenge some aspects of Piaget's theory, most psychologists agree that learners construct their own knowledge and progress through a series of stages of cognitive development. There is also little doubt that Piaget's ideas have profoundly affected the ways today's teachers teach. Piaget has contributed to educational practice by demonstrating that learners

1. *construct* their own knowledge
2. must be *active*
3. go through a process of *equilibration* and
4. go through distinct *stages* of cognitive development

In addition, Piaget's theory has focused attention on the goals of education in the United States. Is the goal to have students learn a body of facts or to promote students' cognitive development? Those taking the latter view (e.g., Kohlberg & Mayer, 1972) argue that when students attain higher cognitive stages, they acquire

Some current researchers are exploring whether there is a postformal stage of cognitive development among adults.

If children in the United States now enter cognitive stages earlier than Swiss children of the 1920s did, are there problems with the methods Piaget used or are there differences in the two societies?

## DIVERSITY MAKES A DIFFERENCE

### Where Do Stereotypes Come From?

Piaget's concepts of equilibration, assimilation, and accommodation help us understand how people develop stereotypes. A *stereotype* is a generalization on which prejudices are based. Often stereotypes are beliefs individuals hold about a group of people. You are no doubt familiar with common stereotypes people hold about men, women, African Americans, Asians, Hispanics, Jews, WASPs, teenagers, elderly people, homosexuals, librarians, lawyers, athletes, short people, fat people, and so forth. Clearly, not all members of each group have the same traits, but we cling to our stereotypes.

According to Piagetian theory, stereotypes represent schemata we have developed, either from our own experience or more likely from hearing or observing others' attitudes. Children may see librarians portrayed on television as middle-aged women who are quiet and timid and who wear glasses hanging around their neck. When visiting the library, children may notice some librarians who fit this image, thereby reinforcing the schema for "librarian."

Not every librarian fits this image, of course, so children eventually encounter librarians who are young, outspoken, male, or not wearing glasses. According to Piaget's theory, children reconcile their image of librarians who don't fit the stereotype by assimilating, that is, by regarding the librarian who doesn't fit the stereotype as simply an exception. When faced with a challenge to schemata, people tend to assimilate, not accommodate, frequently maintaining rigid stereotypes in the presence of contradictory evidence (Hamilton, 1981; Hamilton & Rose, 1980).

Stereotypes may cause people to behave in certain ways toward an individual simply because the individual belongs to a stereotyped group. Although Piaget's theory explains how stereotypes develop, we should treat others fairly and without bias, especially in schools, where teachers, students, and parents may come from a variety of ethnic, cultural, and language groups.

Peanuts reprinted by permission of United Feature Syndicate, Inc.

skills and knowledge more efficiently; in other words, helping students learn to *think* allows them to learn more facts and skills than teaching them those facts and skills directly. Research tends to support this view (e.g., DeVries & Kohlberg, 1987).

# Vygotsky's Approach to Cognitive Development

Lev Semenovich Vygotsky was a pioneering Russian cognitive psychologist who made an enormous contribution to our understanding of language and thinking even though he was only 38 years old when he died. Because of his genius and creativity, he has been called the "Mozart of psychology" (Toulmin, 1978). Vygotsky's work did not attract much attention in the United States until the 1980s, even though his work had been known for some time. The cognitive revolution led to the rediscovery of Piaget long before the rediscovery of Vygotsky, perhaps because Vygotsky's work was done in the Communist Soviet Union. As better translations of Vygotsky's work appeared, however, Vygotsky's genius has become recognized in the United States.

Lev Semenovich Vygotsky (1896–1934).

© James Wertsch/Washington University in St. Louis

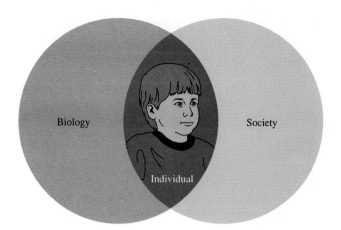

**Figure 3.8**
Vygotsky's view of cognitive development emphasizes societal as well as biological factors.

## Vygotsky's Basic Ideas

To understand the basic ideas of Vygotsky's approach, it is useful to compare his views with those of Piaget.

### Development and Learning

The theories of Vygotsky and Piaget have some significant similarities as well as important differences. Both were interested in development, but whereas Piaget believed that development must precede learning, Vygotsky believed that development and learning influence each other. Piaget claimed that a person must be in a particular developmental stage to grasp certain concepts. Vygotsky, on the other hand, argued that when children learn a specific skill, they also perceive the principles that underlie the new skill. For example, as children learn to write their names, they begin to associate the sounds that make up the name with the letters in the name. Cognitive development progresses as children learn (Vygotsky, 1987).

**3.4** ◎

*Describe Vygotsky's theory of learning.*

### The Role of Society in Cognitive Development

Both Piaget and Vygotsky believed that children construct their own knowledge and that maturation, experience, and social interaction play a role in children's cognitive growth. They differed strongly, however, in the degree to which they emphasized each of these areas in their theories. Piaget placed greater emphasis on maturation and experience than on the role of society. According to Piaget, children's development is due primarily to biological growth and their efforts to make sense of their experiences. Bruner (1987) notes that Piaget, the greatest Western child developmental psychologist, minimizes the role of the teacher. From Piaget's viewpoint, children have the job of trying to understand the world by themselves.

Vygotsky, on the other hand, believed that humans are biological beings living in a society, as illustrated in figure 3.8. Vygotsky emphasized the importance of social interaction and viewed the child's culture as the critical factor that determines cognitive growth. Teachers thus play an important role in a child's learning and cognitive development.

### Elementary Processes and Higher Mental Functions

Vygotsky believed that biological maturation accounts for **elementary processes** in cognitive development. Elementary processes are those that are automatic, immediate, and usually necessary for survival. If someone pops a balloon with a pin, the loud noise automatically attracts your attention; you can't help but be aware of the loud "pop." Social interactions have no influence over such processes.

**Figure 3.9**
Development of inner
speech.

Child reaches for silverware and parent says, "uh-uh." (No) | Child reaches for silverware and looks at parent who says, "uh-uh." (No) | Child looks at silverware and thinks "uh-uh." (No)

By contrast, society contributes to the development of **higher mental functions.** These functions are purposeful; we exercise our own will when we engage in higher mental functions. If someone asks you to look at a picture, you may choose to look at it or not. Unlike your reaction to the balloon pop, you control whether you'll look at the picture.

According to Vygotsky, children develop higher mental functions by internalizing the values and knowledge of their culture. For example, as illustrated in figure 3.9, a baby is crawling around the kitchen and happens upon the open dishwasher. Seeing the baby reach for the silverware, the parent says "uh-uh" (a common utterance meaning "don't do that!" in our culture); the child looks at the parent and notes the disapproval. In other words, the parent's speech has regulated the child's behavior. On another occasion, the child may crawl by the dishwasher and, while reaching for the silverware, say "uh-uh" aloud. At this point, the child is regulating its own behavior through speech. At yet a later date, the child may crawl by the dishwasher and *think* "uh-uh." Now, the child is regulating its own behavior internally, through **inner speech.**

From Vygotsky's perspective, cognitive development is intrinsically bound with one's culture.

Piaget believed that when children talk to themselves, they are demonstrating egocentrism. Vygotsky believed that children's self-talk, or inner speech, is part of the process of building higher mental functions. He believed that children use language not only to communicate with others, but also to regulate and monitor their own behavior. Vygotsky also believed that social interaction with oneself is the foundation of consciousness. Children often use this type of "private" speech when they are struggling with a difficult problem (Bivens & Berk, 1990). Vygotsky's notion of inner speech is crucial because the development of higher mental functions depends on the internalization of social ideas through inner speech, and this internalization depends on interactions among human beings.

Significant people in the lives of young children, such as parents, siblings, teachers, and peers, provide the social context in which a child's higher mental functions develop (Vygotsky, 1981). To understand an individual's cognitive development, you must understand the social environment and culture in which the individual lives (Rogoff & Wertsch, 1984; Wertsch, 1991). Vygotsky believed that teachers and school, along with the family, play a pivotal role in children's cognitive development.

## Vygotsky's Theory and Education

Let us look at some specific ways in which you can promote students' cognitive development.

3.5 ◉

*Explain how to apply Vygotsky's ideas in the classroom.*

### Zone of Proximal Development

Have you ever noticed that students seem to perform better when working with the teacher or in a group than when working on their own? Vygotsky claimed this phenomenon occurs because people's cognitive processes function differently at the individual and group levels. As figure 3.10 shows, the level of *actual* development is the

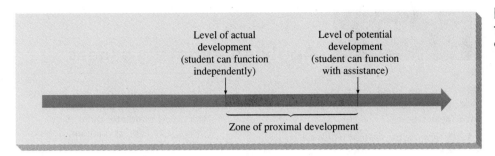

**Figure 3.10**
The zone of proximal development.

level at which an individual can function independently, whereas the level of *potential* development is the level at which the person can perform when working with a teacher or a group of students. As Vygotsky explains:

> Imagine that we have examined two children . . . [both of whom can] solve tasks accessible to seven-year-olds. However, when we attempt to push these children further in carrying out the tests, there turns out to be an essential difference between them. With the help of leading questions, examples, and demonstrations, one of them easily solves test items taken from two years above his level of [actual] development. The other solves test items that are only a half year above his level of [actual] development. (Vygotsky, 1956, pp. 446–447)

Vygotsky (1978) used the term **zone of proximal development** to refer to "the distance between the actual development level as determined by independent problem solving and the level of potential development as determined through problem solving under adult guidance or in collaboration with more capable peers" (p. 86). The zone of proximal development varies from individual to individual and from situation to situation. It defines functions that "will mature tomorrow, but are currently in an embryonic state. These functions could be termed the 'buds' or 'flowers' of development rather than the 'fruits' of development" (Vygotsky, 1978, p. 86).

Vygotsky's theory addresses individual differences among learners; Piaget's theory does not.

Try to determine the zone of proximal development for each of your students. As you work individually with students, ask questions or give suggestions that move students toward their potential levels of development. Create collaborative learning situations in which students guide each other.

## Scaffolding

Painters working high under the eaves of a building rely on scaffolding to reach higher levels. In educational psychology, the term **scaffolding** refers to the support and guidance adults give as a child attempts to solve problems beyond his or her current knowledge (Rogoff, 1990; Rogoff, Malkin, & Gilbride, 1984). Provide scaffolding for students by structuring problems and giving hints. Help students improve their ability to solve problems by asking questions that direct students' attention to important aspects of the problem. As Rogoff, Malkin, and Gilbride (1984) point out:

> Both adult and child are thus actively involved in solving the problem. The adult does not solve the problem while the child passively observes and spontaneously extracts the information. Rather, in [scaffolding], the adult guides the child through the process of solving the problem, with the child participating at a comfortable but slightly challenging level. (p. 33)

Engage students in active learning by presenting information in an implicit rather than explicit way (Reid & Stone, 1991). For example, after explaining that $6^2$ represents $6 \times 6$, let students try to figure out what $6^3$ represents. Help students actively find the correct answer on their own instead of sitting passively while you tell them what the answer is.

## Applying Vygotsky's Ideas

Here are some ways you can use Vygotsky's ideas to improve your teaching effectiveness:

1. *Determine the level at which each student can work effectively independently and the level at which he or she can work effectively with your guidance.* Knowing your students' zones of proximal development will help you to plan instructional activities that move students toward their potential. If you know, for example, that students can independently add fractions with unlike denominators, it is likely that with your help they will be able to subtract such fractions, and soon they will be able to do so without your help.

2. *Periodically, work individually with each student on scaffolded problems.* When you present students with new tasks, be nearby to give verbal guidance and to demonstrate the new skill. Arrange for students to work in groups so they can learn from one another. Peer learning motivates students, and social interaction stimulates them to use language to express opinions, defend positions, formulate pertinent questions, and answer other students' questions. Group work also teaches students to work cooperatively, agree and disagree, and look at things from different points of view.

3. *Encourage students to use inner speech when solving problems.* "Talking to yourself" or "saying the steps out loud" helps students recognize the critical aspects of a problem, judge possible solutions, and recognize flaws or inconsistencies in their reasoning.

4. *Make your classroom a community of learners* (Au & Kawakami, 1991). You can guide students, but students can also guide one another. Encourage students to support one another's learning in pairs or small groups.

## Language

Vygotsky claimed that language plays a crucial role in children's cognitive development (Wertsch, 1985, 1991). He believed that people with highly developed language skills can perform complex tasks that nonliterate people can't because literate people use language as a tool to **mediate** between a task and the performer of a task. According to Frauenglass and Diaz (1985), thinking is identical to inner speech.

The mediational role of language underlies the popular technique of cognitive behavior modification in which students learn to internalize adults' self-instructional speech and thereby control their own behavior. Teachers, for example, may teach students to verbalize self-monitoring and self-instructional rules during transitions between classroom activities. Students learn to ask themselves, "What should I be doing now? What do we do after social studies? Is there material I should be putting away from social studies, or material I should get together for the next subject?"

Rogoff (1990) has shown that parents and teachers play an important role in helping children learn to use language as a mediational process. Parents of gifted 3- and 4-year-old children encouraged their children to use language to predict, monitor, and check themselves, whereas the parents of nongifted children of the same age did not (Moss, 1990). The parents of gifted children asked questions, such as "What do you think will happen next in the story?" or "What do we do after Barney is over?" Similarly, you can help students develop higher-level thinking skills by encouraging them to verbalize when they are predicting, self-monitoring, and self-correcting (Braten, 1992).

The higher-level thinking skills of predicting, self-monitoring, and self-correcting are referred to as *metacognitive* skills.

## Vygotsky's Contribution to Educational Thinking in the United States

Vygotsky's theory has particular appeal to educators because it stresses the active role adults play in guiding children's cognitive growth and the potentially powerful contribution teachers can make in helping students become more sophisticated thinkers. By

# DIVERSITY MAKES A DIFFERENCE

## Culture, Learning, and Teaching

Vygotsky's theory highlights the importance of culture in students' learning. Unlike Piaget, who described cognitive development largely in terms of universal stages that all individuals go through, Vygotsky believed that development occurs in a cultural context. Culture profoundly influences *how* we think and *what* we think about, which suggests that patterns of cognitive growth may vary from culture to culture. The potential educational implications of this suggestion are staggering, given the immigration laws enacted by the United States Congress in the 1990s. These laws will greatly increase the number of foreigners seeking United States citizenship. Teachers in many urban settings are already familiar with this diversity, but in years to come, our classrooms will contain an even greater number of students from a vast variety of cultures.

*Cultural diversity* is the term commonly used to describe the variability of cultures within a single population. To educate students effectively, it is necessary to recognize and affirm their cultural backgrounds within the context of the classroom, demonstrating respect for their homes and families, and for the students themselves.

Language, which is crucial to human development, is deeply interwoven with culture. We use language to describe concepts that are part of our experience and our fund of knowledge (Blanck, 1990). Comedian Lily Tomlin once asked, "Why do Eskimos have twenty different words for snow, while we have twenty different words for beef?" The answer is that Eskimos need words to differentiate new snow from icy snow from wet snow. In our society, where we consume large amounts of beef, we need to differentiate different cuts of beef. Each culture develops its vocabulary to reflect its cultural values and experiences. Similarly, if you have ever studied a foreign language, you know that there are words or phrases in that language that have no English equivalent and vice versa. Terms such as *laissez-faire* and *esprit de corps* in French or *Gestalt* in German do not have direct equivalents in English.

We live in environments shaped by previous generations, and our ways of thinking reflect that background (Cole, 1990). Therefore, in a culturally diverse classroom, teachers have to educate students whose ways of thinking differ, sometimes in subtle and complex ways. Teachers will have to become as knowledgeable as possible about the cultural backgrounds of their students by *studying* the cultures their students represent.

Studying another culture is no simple feat. Given the complexity and subtlety of cultures, a superficial study of a culture will yield a superficial understanding. To understand individuals as members of a culture, we need to examine their ideas and philosophies, find out what events in their history have meaning to them, explore their values, and try to grasp how they look at the world by talking with them and reading the literature of the culture. People spend years trying to familiarize themselves with another culture, and there is no shortcut. As a teacher, you are always a student, and to be an effective teacher in a culturally diverse setting, you will have to learn the cultural values of your students.

---

applying Vygotsky's ideas, researchers are gaining new insights about creativity and play (Smolucha, 1989), writing (Bullock, 1983), science education (Glasson & Lalik, 1993), interdisciplinary teaching (Hedegaard, 1990), critical thinking (Brandt, 1989; Smolucha & Smolucha, 1989), second language learning (Roy, 1989), intelligence testing (Campione, et al., 1984), and mental handicaps (Holowinsky, 1988).

Vygotsky tells us that learners *internalize* knowledge most efficiently when others, such as teachers, parents, or peers guide and assist them. Gallimore and Tharp (1990) have identified six ways you can help students learn:

1. Model a behavior so that students can imitate it.
2. Reward students for behaving in desired ways.
3. Give students feedback about their performance and allow them to revise or improve it.
4. Provide students with information they need to learn.
5. Ask questions that require students to actively formulate a response.
6. Provide students with a cognitive structure for organizing and understanding new knowledge. A structure may be grand, such as a theory, a worldview, or a philosophy, or simple, such as labeling a concept (for example, plants and animals are both "kingdoms").

In both Piaget's and Vygotsky's approaches, the role of the teacher is to facilitate learning, not to transmit information.

**Figure 3.11**
Bruner's stages of cognitive development.

Enactive stage     Iconic stage     Symbolic stage

3.6

*Summarize Bruner's ideas.*

Jerome Bruner revolutionized educational psychology by introducing contributions from cognitive psychology.

Photo courtesy of Jerome Bruner

# Bruner's Approach to Cognitive Development

Jerome Bruner is a psychologist who developed a theory of cognitive development to help teachers promote student learning and thinking. Bruner (1961a, 1961b, 1966, 1983), one of the first to advocate approaching educational psychology from a cognitive perspective, laid the groundwork for the "rediscovery" of Piaget's work in America in the 1960s and 1970s.

## Stages of Development

Bruner believes that people go through three stages of cognitive development: the enactive stage, the iconic stage, and the symbolic stage, as illustrated in figure 3.11. These developmental stages, however, are not irreversible. As people get older, they typically use all three stages in acquiring knowledge.

### Enactive Stage

Infants are in the **enactive stage** and acquire knowledge by actively engaging in activities. Bruner's enactive stage is similar to Piaget's sensorimotor stage. Young children need lots of opportunities to engage in "hands-on" activities with a variety of objects if they are to learn effectively.

### Iconic Stage

In the **iconic stage,** children learn through visual stimuli (the word *icon* means "picture"). At this stage, roughly equivalent to the preoperational stage of Piaget's theory, children rely on visual representations to aid their thinking. Students' visual perceptions determine how they understand the world. Teachers of students in the early grades should use many pictures and visual aids to promote learning. For example, in a lesson on animals, use pictures of different species to illustrate the differences among them. In a lesson on different countries, show pictures of people in different countries to illustrate differences in styles of dress or appearance.

### Symbolic Stage

In the **symbolic stage,** children can understand symbols, including words and mathematical and scientific notations. Bruner's symbolic stage overlaps Piaget's stages of concrete and formal operations. Once students have reached the symbolic stage, they are able to take in large amounts and varied types of information. Symbolic material includes written passages, scientific and mathematical formulas, and abstract charts. If students at this stage are studying a particular country, you could show a bar graph illustrating the pattern of population growth or a pie chart showing the religious or ethnic distribution of the population.

## Discovery Learning

Suppose you have already taught about nouns, verbs, and adjectives, and your present lesson concerns adverbs. One way to approach this lesson is to say, "Adverbs modify verbs, similar to the way adjectives modify nouns. Here are some examples: "The doctor *strongly* recommended that the patient see a specialist." "The wind *quickly* shifted to the west, spreading the fire." "The defendant *slowly* turned to face the jury." You could also present the examples *first*. You might say, "As you read these three sentences, ask yourself what the function of the underlined word is." The students then read "The doctor <u>strongly</u> recommended that the patient see a specialist." "The wind <u>quickly</u> shifted to the west, spreading the fire." "The defendant <u>slowly</u> turned to face the jury."

Students learn best by **discovery** (Bruner, 1966), that is, when they have the "aha!" experience of suddenly understanding something. Encourage students to discover the *structure* of the material they are learning by focusing on ideas and their relationships to one another, not on specific details. Students learn best when they grasp the structure of material instead of memorizing details.

Give students numerous examples of general principles so they can learn to use **inductive reasoning.** A high school history teacher, for example, might use examples of Napoleon's rule after the French Revolution and Stalin's rule after the Russian Revolution so students can induce the general principle that dictators take over countries in the wake of revolutions.

The opposite of inductive reasoning is deductive reasoning, in which learners use rules to generate specific examples.

To foster the discovery of structures, encourage students to make intelligent guesses based on available evidence. Create an accepting atmosphere so students will risk making guesses even though they may be wrong. Make sure students understand that *wrong* answers are not *bad* and that intellectual gambles are worth taking.

Use the technique of **guided discovery,** in which you create situations that help students induce ideas and uncover relationships. Give feedback that lets students know how they are doing. You set the stage for students to explore and have the "aha!" experience. A high school history teacher, for example, might have students discuss the similarities between the aftermaths of the French and Russian Revolutions and give them feedback during the discussion.

## The Spiral Curriculum

Bruner (1971) also advocates the use of a **spiral curriculum** in which learners return periodically to a previously covered topic to study it within the context of information they have learned in the meantime. A social studies teacher, for example, might begin a unit by identifying the oceans and explaining how oceans differ from rivers and seas. The teacher might return to the topic of oceans during a unit on transportation, integrating knowledge about transportation by water with knowledge of oceans and again during a unit on preventing pollution. Each return provides an opportunity to link new knowledge with existing knowledge.

The discovery approach to learning requires teachers to use their imaginations to create hands-on activities for students and discourage them from using published worksheets that often accompany textbooks.

## Motivation

Like Piaget, Bruner emphasizes *active learning*. Students learn best by doing. Although **extrinsic motivation,** the use of rewards and reinforcers, may be useful when starting to teach an idea, Bruner stresses that in the long run, meaningful learning depends on students' **intrinsic motivation** to know and understand. He therefore recommends that teachers encourage students' curiosity and desire to explore. It is only through this exploration that students will have the "aha!" experience and "own" the knowledge they have acquired.

## Applying Bruner's Ideas

 Here are ways you can use Bruner's ideas to improve your teaching:

1. *Have students actively explore situations and discover things for themselves.*
2. *Help students discover the structure of material.* Place less emphasis on details and greater emphasis on overall organization or underlying principles. Let students know that it is more important to understand the "bigger picture."
3. *Encourage students to think intuitively.* Make sure students know that it is all right to make incorrect guesses. Urge them to be creative and to try an "off-the-wall" answer.
4. *Don't tell students everything: Let them figure it out for themselves.* Allow them to have the "aha!" experience.
5. *Use the spiral curriculum approach. Return periodically to the same topic.* When you do, introduce it on a more advanced level than before and tie it in with ideas students have learned from the previous presentation.
6. *Cultivate students' intrinsic motivation.* Excite their interest and curiosity by creating open-ended situations in which students ask "why?" and want to know what happens next.

# The Constructivist Approach

**3.7** ◎

*Describe the constructivist approach to learning.*

The term **constructivism,** which takes the position that learners actively construct their own knowledge, has been increasingly applied to the theories of Piaget, Vygotsky, and Bruner, and the constructivist approach has gained in popularity. Although the three theories vary with regard to the relative role of the individual learner and the social context, they have in common the notion that the learner actively makes sense of the world.

Constructivism not only provides an accurate picture of how learners learn, but it also offers a powerful tool for combatting one of the most difficult problems in schools today: boredom.

## Making School Learning Relevant

Students' chief complaint about school is that it is BORING! Too often their complaint is justified. Students frequently complain that what they learn in school is irrelevant and that they will never use what teachers force them to learn. As a result, too many drop out of school as soon as possible. Others decide they will "play the game" until they receive their diploma and can safely forget everything they learned in school. Only a few grasp the relevance of school learning to the rest of their lives.

The object of the getting-through-school game is to do whatever teachers demand so that you will pass. Students often play the game by figuring out what the teacher is seeking and meeting the minimum requirements to pass ("Do we need to know this for the test?"). Learning something becomes incidental to the whole process of getting through school.

If you base your teaching on the cognitive-developmental model of how people construct knowledge, two things will happen: (a) you will change your idea of what it means to be a teacher, and (b) students will find your classes interesting and relevant.

Watson and Konicek (1990) describe the experiences of a fourth-grade teacher who began a unit on heat by asking students what they already knew about the topic. They knew that the sun contains heat. They also "knew" that hats and sweaters contain heat. Rather than simply correcting the students, the teacher had them carry out a series of experiments in which they tucked thermometers into sweaters and hats for various lengths of time and under various conditions. When they discovered that the thermometer showed no changes in temperature, some (not all) of the students changed their ideas about whether hats and sweaters contain heat.

Had the teacher not uncovered students' erroneous beliefs, the students would have learned some superficial information about heat. But the information would be irrelevant to what they think they know about the real world—that hats and sweaters generate heat. Unless students grasp the relevance of what they are learning, they are apt to store "school knowledge" separately from "real knowledge" and conclude that school is a boring place.

Changing students' preexisting beliefs takes time. A single piece of evidence that contradicts a student's belief is not likely to result in a change of thinking. Students are apt to struggle to hold on to their beliefs, which, as far as they are concerned, have been repeatedly confirmed by past experiences. By giving students opportunities to test new knowledge within the context of their existing knowledge and by challenging their misconceptions, you can make school learning relevant and interesting. Students will find school a lot less boring if you connect the material they are learning to their lives, encourage them to make predictions, and challenge inconsistencies in their beliefs (Watson & Konicek, 1990).

> To demonstrate the relevance of the material to students, you must know the relevance of it yourself. If you are unsure, ask more experienced teachers.

## KEY POINTS

1. The cognitive approach, which is gaining popularity among psychologists who study learning, consists of (a) the cognitive-developmental model and (b) the information-processing model.

2. Developmental stages are sequential, qualitatively different periods individuals go through during the life sequence.

3. Equilibration is the process by which people try to reconcile how they expect the world to behave with how it actually does.

4. According to Piaget, people actively construct their own knowledge through the processes of assimilation and accommodation.

5. Piaget's model of cognitive development consists of four stages: (a) sensorimotor, (b) preoperations, (c) concrete operations, and (d) formal operations.

6. Vygotsky believed that learning occurs in a social context in which more proficient learners (parents, teachers, and others) support the learning of the novice (the student).

7. The zone of proximal development is the range from the level at which one can learn independently to the level at which one can learn with full assistance from a teacher.

8. Bruner advocates the use of guided discovery, in which the teacher guides students to induce the underlying structure of the material that they are studying.

9. Bruner also believes in the importance of the spiral curriculum, in which the teacher returns periodically to previously taught topics, integrating them with newly learned information.

## SELF-STUDY EXERCISES

1. Below is a list of various academic subjects and the stages of cognitive development exhibited by elementary and secondary school students. For each academic subject, write an example of what and how you would teach students at each level of cognitive development

**Science**
Preoperations:
_____
_____
_____

Concrete Operations:
_____
_____
_____

Formal Operations:
_____
_____
_____

**Social Studies**
Preoperations:
_____
_____
_____

Concrete Operations:
_____
_____
_____

Formal Operations:
_____
_____
_____

**Literature**
Preoperations:
_____
_____
_____

Concrete Operations:

_____

_____

_____

Formal Operations:

_____

_____

_____

**Music and Art**
Preoperations:

_____

_____

_____

Concrete Operations:

_____

_____

_____

Formal Operations:

_____

_____

_____

2. In what ways are the theories of Piaget, Vygotsky, and Bruner similar? How are they different?

3. Find two children between the ages of 4 and 9. Try to use Piaget's clinical method to discover whether they believe their dreams are real. Ask probing questions to elicit the reasoning underlying their responses.

4. With the children in problem 3, present the conservation of number and conservation of volume tasks. In the conservation of number task, present the children with two identically spaced rows of coins, each row having the same number of coins, as shown below:

  0  0  0  0  0
  0  0  0  0  0

Ask the children whether the two rows contain the same number of coins or whether one has more. Then, rearrange the coins so that they look like this:

  0  0  0  0  0
 0   0    0    0     0

Ask the same question. Are the responses of the children different? Can you determine the children's cognitive stage on the basis of their responses?

  In the conservation of volume task, present the children with two identical containers filled with the same amount of water. Then ask, "Is the amount of water in each container the same, or is there more or less in one container?" Then, pour the water from each container into another—one tall and thin, the other short and wide. Ask the question again. Are the children aware that the two containers hold the same amount of water? What can you determine about the cognitive stage of each child?

5. Both Vygotsky and Bruner emphasize the role of the adult in guiding the learner. Using their ideas, describe a learning activity you would use to teach fifth-graders about the concept of "democracy."

## FURTHER READINGS

Bringuier, J. C. (1977). *Conversations with Jean Piaget.* Chicago: University of Chicago Press.

Bruner, J. S. (1983). *In search of mind: Essays in autobiography.* New York: Harper & Row.

Bybee, R. W., & Sund, R. B. (1982). *Piaget for educators.* Columbus, OH: Charles E. Merrill.

Flavell, J. F. (1977). *Cognitive development.* Englewood Cliffs, NJ: Prentice Hall.

Ginsburg, H., & Opper, S. (1988). *Piaget's theory of intellectual development* (3rd ed.). Englewood Cliffs, NJ: Prentice Hall.

Pulaski, M. A. S. (1980). *Understanding Piaget: An introduction to children's cognitive development* (rev. ed.). New York: Harper & Row.

Rogoff, B., & Wertsch, J. V. (Eds.). (1984). *Children's learning in the "Zone of proximal development."* San Francisco: Jossey-Bass.

Vygotsky, L. S. (1978). *Mind in society: The development of higher psychological processes.* Cambridge, MA: Harvard University Press.

Wadsworth, B. J. (1989). *Piaget's theory of cognitive and affective development* (4th ed.). New York: Longman.

Wertsch, J. V. (1985). *Vygotsky and the social formation of mind.* Cambridge, MA: Harvard University Press.

## REFERENCES

Arlin, P. (1986). Problem finding and young adult cognition. In R. Mines & K. Kitchener (Eds.), *Adult cognitive development: Methods and models* (pp. 22–32). New York: Praeger.

Au, K. H., & Kawakami, A. J. (1991). Culture and ownership: Schooling of minority students. *Childhood Education, 67,* 280–284.

Bivens, J. A., & Berk, L. E. (1990). A longitudinal study of elementary school children's private speech. *Merrill-Palmer Quarterly, 36,* 443–463.

Blanck, G. (1990). Vygotsky: The man and his cause. In L. C. Moll (Ed.), *Vygotsky and education: Instructional implications and applications of sociohistorical psychology* (pp. 31–58). Cambridge: Cambridge University Press.

Brandt, M. E. (1989). Getting social about critical thinking: Power and constraints of apprenticeship. Paper presented at the Annual Meeting of the American Educational Research Association. ERIC Document ED 311 033.

Braten, I. (1992). Vygotsky as precursor to metacognitive theory: III. Recent metacognitive research within a Vygotskian framework. *Scandinavian Journal of Educational Research, 36*(1), 3–19.

Bruner, J. S. (1961a). The act of discovery. *Harvard Educational Review, 31,* 21–32.

Bruner, J. S. (1961b). *The process of education.* Cambridge, MA: Harvard University Press.

Bruner, J. S. (1966). *Toward a theory of instruction.* Cambridge, MA: Harvard University Press.

Bruner, J. S. (1971). *The relevance of education.* New York: Norton.

Bruner, J. S. (1983). *In search of mind: Essays in autobiography.* New York: Harper & Row.

Bruner, J. S. (1987). Prologue. In L. S. Vygotsky, *The collected works of L. S. Vygotsky, Volume 1: Problems of general psychology.* New York: Plenum Press.

Bullock, C. (1983). Using theory in the classroom: Vygotsky and the teaching of composition. *English Quarterly, 16,* 14–20.

Campione, J. C., Brown, A. L., Ferrara, R. A., & Bryant, N. R. (1984). The zone of proximal development: Implications for individual differences and learning. In B. Rogoff & J. V. Wertsch (Eds.), *Children's learning in the "Zone of proximal development"* (pp. 77–91). San Francisco: Jossey-Bass.

Casey, M. B. (1990). A planning and problem-solving preschool model: The methodology of being a good learner. *Early Childhood Research Quarterly, 5,* 53–67.

Chapman, M., & Lindenberger, U. (1989). Concrete operations and attentional capacity. *Journal of Experimental Child Psychology, 47,* 236–258.

Cole, M. (1990). Cognitive development and formal schooling: The evidence from cross-cultural research. In L. C. Moll (Ed.), *Vygotsky and education: Instructional implications and applications of sociohistorical psychology* (pp. 89–110). Cambridge: Cambridge University Press.

Confrey, J. (1990). A review of the research on students' conceptions in mathematics, science, and programming. *Review of Research in Education, 16,* 3–56.

DeVries, R., & Kohlberg, L. (1987). *Programs of early education: The constructivist view.* New York: Longman.

Diaz, R. M. (1983). Thought and two languages: The impact of bilingualism on cognitive development. In E. W. Gordon (Ed.), *Review of Research in Education* (Vol. 10, pp. 23–54). Washington, DC: American Education Research Association.

Elkind, D. (1967). Egocentrism in adolescence. *Child Development, 38,* 1025–1034.

Elkind, D. (1971). Two approaches to intelligence: Piagetian and psychometric. In P. Green, M. Ford, & G. Flamer (Eds.), *Measurement and Piaget.* New York: McGraw-Hill.

Elkind, D. (1991). Formal education and early childhood education: An essential difference. In K. M. Cauley, F. Linder, & J. H. MacMillan (Eds.), *Annual Editions: Educational Psychology 91/92* (pp. 27–37). Guilford, CT: Dushkin.

Flavell, J. H. (1982). On cognitive development. *Child Development, 53,* 1–10.

Frauenglass, M. H., & Diaz, R. M. (1985). Self-regulatory functions of children's private speech: A critical analysis of recent challenges to Vygotsky's theory. *Developmental Psychology, 21,* 357–364.

Gallimore, R., & Tharp, R. (1990). Teaching *Mind in society: Teaching, schooling, and literate discourse.* In L. C. Moll (Ed.), *Vygotsky and education: Instructional implications and applications of sociohistorical psychology* (pp. 175–205). Cambridge: Cambridge University Press.

Gelman, R. (1985). The developmental perspective on the problem of knowledge acquisition: A discussion. In S. F. Chipman, J. W. Segal, & R. Glaser (Eds.), *Thinking and learning skills* (Vol. 2, pp. 537–544). Hillsdale, NJ: Erlbaum.

Glasson, G. E., & Lalik, R. V. (1993). Reinterpreting the learning cycle from a social constructivist perspective: A qualitative study of teachers' beliefs and practices. *Journal of Research in Science Teaching, 30,* 187–207.

Hamilton, D. L. (1981). Cognitive representation of persons. In E. T. Higgins, C. P. Herman, & M. P. Zanna (Eds.), *Social cognition: The Ontario Symposium* (Vol. 1, pp. 135–160). Hillsdale, NJ: Erlbaum.

Hamilton, D. L., & Rose, T. (1980). Illusory correlation and the maintenance of stereotypic beliefs. *Journal of Personality and Social Psychology, 39,* 832–845.

Hedegaard, M. (1990). The zone of proximal development as basis for instruction. In L. C. Moll (Ed.), *Vygotsky and education: Instructional implications and applications of sociohistorical psychology* (pp. 349–371). Cambridge: Cambridge University Press.

Holowinsky, I. Z. (1988). Developmental psychology in the Soviet Union and its relevance for special education. *International Journal of Special Education, 3,* 141–148.

Hore, A. P., & Tryon, W. W. (1989). Study of the similar structure hypothesis with mentally retarded adults and nonretarded children of comparable mental age. *American Journal on Mental Retardation, 94*(2), 182–188.

Ianoc-Worrall, A. D. (1972). Bilingualism and cognitive development. *Child Development, 43,* 1390–1400.

Kamii, C. (1984). Autonomy: The aim of education envisioned by Piaget. *Phi Delta Kappan, 65*(6), 410–415.

Kitchener, K., Lynch, C., Fischer, K., & Wood, P. (1993). Developmental range of reflective judgment: The effect of contextual support and practice on developmental stage. *Developmental Psychology, 29,* 893–906.

Kohlberg, L., & Mayer, R. (1972). Development as the aim of education. *Harvard Educational Review, 42,* 449–496.

Kuhn, D. (1974). Inducing development experimentally. *Developmental Psychology, 10,* 590–600.

Larsen, G. Y. (1977). Methodology in developmental psychology: An examination of research on Piagetian theory. *Child Development, 48,* 1160–1166.

Lauritzen, P. (1992). Facilitating integrated teaching and learning in the preschool setting: A process approach. *Early Childhood Research Quarterly, 7,* 531–550.

Lautrey, J., Mullet, E., & Paques, P. (1989). Judgments of quantity and conservation of quantity: The area of a rectangle. *Journal of Experimental Child Psychology, 47,* 193–209.

Moss, E. (1990). Social interaction and metacognitive development in gifted preschoolers. *Gifted Child Quarterly, 34,* 16–20.

Piaget, J. (1952). *The origin of intelligence in children.* New York: Basic Books.

Piaget, J. (1954). *The construction of reality.* New York: Basic Books.

Piaget, J. (1971). *Biology and knowledge.* Chicago: University of Chicago Press.

Piaget, J. (1979). *The child's conception of the world.* Totowa, NJ: Littlefield, Adams.

Piaget, J., & Inhelder, B. (1969). *The psychology of the child.* New York: Basic Books.

Reid, K. K., & Stone, C. A. (1991). Why is cognitive instruction effective? Underlying learning mechanisms. *Remedial and Special Education, 12*(3), 8–19.

Riley, N. J. (1989). Piagetian cognitive functioning in students with learning disabilities. *Journal of Learning Disabilities, 22*(7), 444–451.

Rogoff, B. (1990). *Apprenticeship in thinking: Cognitive development in social context.* New York: Oxford University Press.

Rogoff, B., Malkin, C., & Gilbride, K. (1984). Interaction with babies as guidance in development. In B. Rogoff & J. V. Wertsch (Eds.), *Children's learning in the "Zone of proximal development"* (pp. 31–44). San Francisco: Jossey-Bass.

Rogoff, B., & Wertsch, J. V. (Eds.). (1984). *Children's learning in the "Zone of proximal development."* San Francisco: Jossey-Bass.

Rohwer, W. D., Jr., Ammon, P. R., & Cramer, P. (1974). *Understanding intellectual development: Three approaches to theory and practice.* Hinsdale, IL: Dryden Press.

Roy, A. M. (1989). Developing second language literacy: A Vygotskyan perspective. *Journal of Teaching Writing, 8,* 81–98.

Schiff, W. S. (1983). Conservation of length redux: A perceptual-linguistic phenomenon. *Child Development, 54,* 1497–1506.

Siegel, L. S. (1978). The relationship of language and thought in the preoperational child: A reconsideration of nonverbal alternatives in Piagetian tasks. In L. S. Siegel & C. J. Brainerd (Eds.), *Alternatives to Piaget: Critical essays on the theory* (pp. 43–67). New York: Academic Press.

Siegler, R. S. (1991). *Children's thinking* (2nd ed.). Englewood Cliffs, NJ: Prentice Hall.

Smolucha, F. (1989). The relevance of Vygotsky's theory of creative imagination for contemporary research on play. Paper presented at the National Biennial Meeting of the Society for Research in Child Development, Kansas City, MO. ERIC Document ED 314 168.

Smolucha, L., & Smolucha, F. (1989). A Vygotskian perspective on critical thinking. Paper presented at the Conference on Science and Technology for Education in the 1980s: Soviet and American Perspectives. ERIC Document ED 314 770.

Toulmin, S. (1978, September 28). The Mozart of psychology. *New York Review of Books.*

Tulviste, P. (1991). *The cultural-historical development of verbal thinking.* Commack, NY: Nova Science Publishers.

Vygotsky, L. S. (1956). *Selected psychological investigations.* Moscow: Izdstel'sto Akademii Pedagogicheskikh Nauk SSSR.

Vygotsky, L. S. (1978). *Mind in society: The development of higher psychological processes.* Cambridge, MA: Harvard University Press.

Vygotsky, L. S. (1981). The genesis of higher mental functions. In J. V. Wertsch (Ed.), *The concept of activity in Soviet psychology* (pp. 144–188). Armonk, NY: Sharpe.

Vygotsky, L. S. (1987). *The collected works of L. S. Vygotsky, Volume 1: Problems of general psychology.* New York: Plenum Press.

Wadsworth, B. J. (1989). *Piaget's theory of cognitive and affective development* (4th ed.). New York: Longman.

Watson, B., & Konicek, R. (1990). Teaching for conceptual change: Confronting children's experience. *Phi Delta Kappan, 71*(9), 680–685.

Wavering, M. J. (1989). Logical reasoning necessary to make line graphs. *Journal of Research in Science Teaching, 26*(5), 373–379.

Wertsch, J. V. (1985). *Vygotsky and the social formation of mind.* Cambridge, MA: Harvard University Press.

Wertsch, J. V. (1991). *Voices of the mind: A sociocultural approach to mediated action.* Cambridge, MA: Harvard University Press.

Yager, R. E. (1991, September). The constructivist learning model. *The Science Teacher,* 52–57.

© Steve Skjold

# Information-Processing Theory

# Chapter Outline

# Learning Objectives

4.1 Describe the linear model of information processing.
4.2 Describe methods you can use to get students' attention.

4.3 Define short-term and long-term memory and explain how information is stored in long-term memory.
4.4 Describe activities you can use to help students retain information.

4.5 Define metacognition.
4.6 Summarize the role of schema theory in students' learning.
4.7 Explain the generative model of learning.

# Preview

Cognitive psychology consists of cognitive-developmental theory and information-processing theory. This chapter examines **information-processing** theory. In the 1960s, information processing, a branch of computer science attracted the attention of psychologists interested in understanding how people think. Some psychologists realized that the way computer scientists use information-processing theory to describe how computers process information could provide a powerful model for explaining how human beings process information.

Using the computer as a model, psychologists initially formulated a

linear model of human information processing to explain how people encode, store, and retrieve information. Later they added psychological models to explain how information is organized when it gets into memory (Martindale, 1991; Schunk, 1991).

Different people process information in different ways. People have different cognitive styles that determine how they process new information, and their success in processing new information to a large extent depends on what kinds of information they already have. Although computers do not have emotions, people do, which raises the

important question of what role emotions play in how people process information.

The information-processing model is especially important for educators because it helps us understand how learning occurs in school. Current teaching methods barely begin to reflect the knowledge about learning and thinking that information-processing theory provides. The major goal of this chapter is to "translate" some of this knowledge into a form that you can use as a teacher. ◉

# The Computer as a Model of How People Think

Psychologists began to apply information-processing theory to the study of cognitive processes in the 1960s as they learned more about how computers process information (Siegler, 1991). Human information-processing theorists (e.g., Posner, 1989; Stillings et al., 1987) use the computer as a model for understanding how humans think.

Although psychologists have been studying aspects of cognition since the late nineteenth century, the information-processing model has generated an exceptionally large amount of research since the 1970s.

# Linear Model of Information Processing

Information processing is called a "linear model" because information progresses through the system along a direct path (see figure 4.1). According to Atkinson and Shiffrin (1968), the linear model consists of a series of **structural features,** which are static and not amenable to change, and **control processes,** which are dynamic and under the individual's control. The structural features include the sensory register, short-term memory, and long-term memory. The control processes are attention and rehearsal.

## Encoding, Storage, and Retrieval

The linear model describes encoding (how we take in and make sense of information); storage (how we save information for later use); and retrieval (how we "call up" stored information when we need it), which are the same processes that computers perform. Computers receive incoming information through a variety of mechanisms: keyboards, telephones, pressure-sensitive and heat-sensitive monitors, tapes, and others. This information is encoded in a form the computer can "understand." The computer stores the incoming information by placing it on a hard disk, a floppy disk, or in another type of "memory." Finally, the computer can retrieve the information when it is needed.

## The Sensory Register

**Sensation** is the process of receiving stimuli from the environment through our various senses (Goldstein, 1989). Just as the computer takes in information through keyboards and tapes, we take in information by seeing, hearing, smelling, tasting, and touching. According to information-processing theorists, information we take in through our senses first reaches our **sensory register,** a very, very short-term store of memory where an exact image of each sensory experience is housed. Information lasts in the sensory register for less than one second, giving us just enough time to move the information to the next step. If we don't, the information quickly disappears from the sensory register. Information that decays in the sensory register is lost forever.

## Perception

Whereas sensation concerns receiving stimuli, **perception** concerns making sense of incoming stimuli by attaching meaning to them (Rock, 1984; Sekuler & Blake, 1985). Sensations are not meaningful until we attribute meaning to them. If you hear two

**4.1** ◉

*Describe the linear model of information processing.*

Ironically, computer science uses the human mind as a model for designing computers, and psychologists use computers as a model for understanding the human mind.

**Figure 4.1**
The Atkinson and Shiffrin model of information processing.

people converse in a foreign language, you cannot attribute meaning to their words unless you know the language they are speaking.

The same is true for visual stimuli (Hoffman & Richards, 1985; Paivio, 1986). A student who is unfamiliar with a division sign may assume that it is an incomplete plus sign or an oddly printed subtraction sign. In the early twentieth century, behaviorists in the United States believed that perceptions could be broken down into individual stimuli. **Gestalt psychologists** in Germany argued that we tend to perceive things as wholes. Evidence seems to support their argument. For example, when we look at a painting, we see the whole work of art, not the individual brush strokes. When we remember a conversation, we recall the gist but seldom individual sentences. We will see later how the Gestalt position influenced schema theory and our understanding of various cognitive processes, such as reading.

### Factors Affecting Perception

We don't perceive all stimuli in the same way. Various factors affect how we perceive things. First, we are influenced if a new stimulus is similar to a familiar one. Second, we fill in gaps in new stimuli to make a whole. Third, proximity, or physical closeness, helps us interpret information. If you looked at five pairs of pennies, you would be aware you were seeing five pairs of pennies before you realized you had 10 pennies. Fourth, we use context to make sense of new information. Past experience is a fifth factor—we interpret new information in ways we have previously learned. Finally, our expectations influence our perceptions. Say, for example, you are reading *Hamlet* and come across the line "To be or not to be, that is the questior." Did you notice that the last word was *questior* and not *question?* If you didn't, your expectations were driving your perceptions.

## Attention

**Attention** is the control process that governs the flow of information from the sensory register to short-term memory (Parasuraman & Davies, 1984; Triesman & Gelade, 1980). Sensory impressions to which we attend move on to short-term memory; information to which we do not attend "dies" in the sensory register. We can attend to only so much information at a time. Think of instances when you are watching television and your best friend phones. Despite your efforts, you can't attend to both sources of incoming information. You may quickly switch back and forth between them, but you can't simultaneously attend to both.

Students often overestimate their attentional capacities and try to attend to more than one stimulus at a time.

Doing homework while watching television requires switching attention from one to the other.

© Martha McBride/Unicorn Stock Photos

Experiments presenting different information through each earphone showed that children can attend to only one earphone at a time.

© T. Rosenthal Superstock

## Dichotic Listening Experiments

A series of experiments called "dichotic listening" tasks (e.g., Cherry, 1953; Triesman, 1960) have demonstrated our inability to pay attention to more than one thing at a time. In these experiments, a set of earphones is placed on participants and two different types of stimuli are played in the left and right speakers. Participants are asked to ignore, or "shadow," the information from one speaker and to attend only to the information from the other. To ensure that participants truly attend to the appropriate speakers, they are tested on the information to which they were told to pay attention.

The critical issue is how much information participants process from the other ear, the "shadowed" information. Participants can describe the type of input (e.g., music, speech) but can't tell what the specific information was. This finding suggests that we have limited attention and typically can attend to only one input channel at a time.

Subjects who did not "pass" the test on the information were excluded from the study because they may have been attending to the information that should have been shadowed.

## 4.2

*Describe methods you can use to get students' attention.*

## Short-Term Memory (STM)

Once information has been identified (perceived) and attended to, it flows into the next structural feature, **short-term memory,** or **STM.** Sometimes described as the "workbench" of memory, STM is where we do our current thinking (Baddeley, 1992). Have you ever had a great idea and forgotten it a minute later? Chances are your great idea lived and died in STM. Did you ever enter a room to look for

## 4.3

*Define short-term and long-term memory and explain how information is stored in long-term memory.*

## The Role of Attention in School Learning

People cannot learn and retain anything to which they do not attend. *Attention is the precursor to learning.* You can help students learn more effectively by encouraging them to focus their attention effectively.

1. Reduce the number of stimuli that may distract students' attention. Seat students away from the window, for example, to minimize the impact of competing stimuli.
2. Visually highlight the written material you want students to attend to by using arrows, boxes, or highlighters; draw their attention to the exact information they should be looking at.
3. Use verbal cues regarding what to attend to and give verbal encouragement to sustain attention; let students know what they should be paying attention to and periodically check to keep them on-task.
4. Use interesting and new material. Present lessons dynamically to attract

and sustain students' attention. Variety in *how* and *where* you teach reduces boredom and increases attention.

5. Use stimuli that are unexpected, out of their typical context, slightly bizarre, or even somewhat shocking to attract attention.
6. Draw on students' personal interests; students pay attention to information that interests them (Gibson, 1992). When possible, relate classroom learning to students' interests, such as the newest rock bands, the most recent scientific discoveries, or the latest hit TV show.

Attention-getting techniques are particularly important if you are teaching students with learning disabilities. Such students have difficulty narrowing their attention or processing information as quickly as students without learning disabilities, even though they can sustain attention and inhibit impulsive behavior as well as non-learning disabled students can (Richards, 1990).

---

Many students assume that they have "learned" information when in reality it is only temporarily residing in short-term memory and will soon be lost.

something only to realize you had forgotten what you were looking for? Once again, your thought of the item you were seeking "died" in STM. STM is rather limited in its capacity because of time and size restrictions.

### Time Limitations

Information in STM lasts only about 20 seconds unless you act on it (Ellis & Hunt, 1993; Shiffrin & Cook, 1978). Have you ever looked up a phone number, only to have someone interrupt you before you had a chance to dial it? If the interruption lasted more than about 20 seconds, you probably forgot the number.

### Size Limitations

Additionally, we can hold only about seven chunks of information in STM at one time. Try this experiment: Read a list of random single-digit numbers to a friend and have your friend repeat them in order without writing them down. Start with a three-digit sequence (e.g., 3 8 5) and then increase to a four-digit sequence (e.g., 7 2 4 1). Keep increasing the number of digits and see when your friend can no longer repeat the sequence perfectly. Our short-term memory capacity varies from five to nine chunks of information, although most people can remember seven, which is often referred to as the "Magical Number Seven, plus or minus two" (Miller, 1956).

### Chunking

When discussing STM, we use the term *chunk* because people can hold more than seven items of information in STM if they "chunk" or combine them effectively. Suppose, for example, you had to remember the following sequence of letters: F B I C I A K G B. If you regarded each letter individually, you would have to remember nine items.

However, if you chunk them as "FBI," "CIA," and "KGB," you would have to remember only three items. Of course, chunking is effective only if the chunks have meaning for you. For example, one of the authors tried this experiment using the letter sequence: F D R J F K L B J. Only older students were able to remember them; younger students did not see a meaningful combination of the letters that allowed them to remember the letters easily. (The chunks are "FDR," "JFK," and "LBJ," initials of Franklin D. Roosevelt, John F. Kennedy, and Lyndon B. Johnson.)

We hold our current thoughts in STM. Over time, our ability to retrieve these thoughts depends on how well we have rehearsed them (Gillund & Shiffrin, 1984; Hintzman, 1986; Ratcliff & McKoon, 1989).

## Rehearsal

STM is limited in terms of time unless we act on the information being "held" in it. **Rehearsal** is the term that describes the various activities we can engage in to retain information for more than the 20-second limit of STM (Baddeley, 1992).

There are two types of rehearsal. **Maintenance rehearsal,** which helps us maintain information in STM beyond the 20-second limit, involves repetition of the new information. When you call directory assistance to find out a telephone number, you probably repeat it a few times to remember it long enough to make the call. Repetition keeps information "alive" in short-term memory long enough for us to act on it.

**Elaborative rehearsal,** which helps us store information that is currently in STM into long-term memory (LTM), involves associating new information with existing knowledge. Sometimes, students try to memorize information using repetition. If you've ever performed in a play, you may have repeated your lines many times to help you recall them. Teachers often encourage students to repeat certain types of information, such as the alphabet or addition and multiplication tables, to enhance later recall. While repetition may help retention in long-term memory, information that is memorized without being related to existing knowledge may be difficult to retrieve later. Some students think that memorization is all that learning involves. They use repetition when studying and, consequently, learn the new information at a superficial level (Iran-Nejad, 1990).

To be effective, rehearsal techniques must involve making new information meaningful. When rehearsing, students must engage in some kind of mental activity. Information can't enter long-term memory passively. You may recall attending lectures or reading chapters believing that you were "learning" the information, but until you actively do something with the information, it is unlikely to enter long-term memory.

Here are some things students can do to improve their memories. One is **verbal elaboration,** in which students use words to elaborate on new information. For example, a student can create sentences that contain the words to be remembered (Pressley et al., 1987). Suppose you were trying to learn a new vocabulary word: *postern.* A postern is a door or gate at the back of a house. To help you remember the word, you might create a sentence such as, "Before leaving the house, I closed and locked the postern."

Students may also use **visual imagery,** which involves creating a picture in their head of something to be remembered (Richardson, 1980; Shepard & Cooper, 1983; Yuille, 1983). To recall the word *postern,* you might visualize your back door; creating that picture will help you remember the word. It is easier to remember concrete information than abstract information because concrete information can be visualized (Sadoski, Goetz, & Fritz, 1993).

A popular rehearsal technique that helps students remember is the use of **mnemonic devices.** Typically, the student creates an acronym or a sentence that is easy to remember to help later recall of information that is difficult to remember. A commonly used acronym is "HOMES" for the Great Lakes (Huron, Ontario, Michigan, Erie, and Superior). A sentence such as "My very educated mother just served us

Note that the learner must be active for true learning to occur; that is, the learner must attend to and engage in an activity that will place information in LTM.

Young children need time to process information.

© David Frazier

nice peaches" can help students remember the order of the planets based on their distance from the sun. (The first letter of each word in the sentence is the first letter of a planet, that is, <u>M</u>ercury, <u>V</u>enus, <u>E</u>arth, <u>M</u>ars, etc.).

By far the most effective way to place new information in long-term memory is to relate the new information to already-known information (Ross, 1987). This will make the new information meaningful, and meaningfulness is at the heart of long-term memory effectiveness. Help students make associations between new and known information. Imposing associations will not work if they are based on *your* background knowledge, not the *student's* (Wang, Thomas, & Ouellette, 1992).

This is known as the new-to-known phenomenon.

### Age Differences in Rehearsal Usage

There are age differences associated with the ability to process information. For example, adults can process information through STM faster (Kail, 1988) than children can. Consequently, if you are teaching young children, allow them more time to process information than *you* need.

Here, we see the relationship between developmental theory and information-processing theory.

There are dramatic age differences in the use of rehearsal strategies (Kail, 1990). Children younger than 7 seldom use any rehearsal strategies, although they can learn to use them (Michalowitz, 1989; Pressley & Levin, 1983). Older children use rehearsal strategies spontaneously and get better at doing so as they get older. If you are planning to teach young children, teach them various rehearsal techniques. If you are planning to teach older students, remind them to use rehearsal strategies if they don't do so spontaneously.

## Long-Term Memory (LTM)

The structural feature in which information is permanently stored is called **long-term memory (LTM)**. Through rehearsal processes, information is stored in LTM for what appears an indefinite period. Information housed in LTM, however, may be difficult to retrieve. We have all experienced having a sense of "knowing" something even though we can't recall it at a given moment ("I can't think of her name right now, but I'll remember it suddenly in the middle of the night"). One of the most common reasons we sometimes have difficulty retrieving information from LTM is that the information was poorly stored to begin with.

### The Importance of Rehearsal

If a library book is misshelved, it is physically *in* the library, but no one can find it in a systematic search (e.g., by the author's last name or the Library of Congress call number). Similarly, information poorly stored in LTM will be inaccessible when you need it, which emphasizes the importance of using effective rehearsal techniques. Information that is well integrated with a rich body of already-known information in LTM will be more easily accessible later.

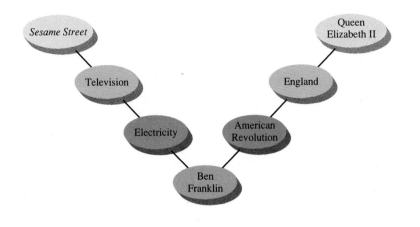

**Figure 4.2**
A network model of long-term memory.

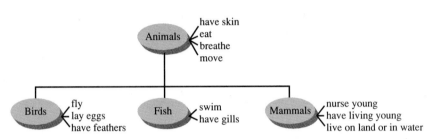

**Figure 4.3**
An example of a hierarchical model (Quillan, 1969).

## Semantic and Episodic LTM

Some cognitive psychologists believe we have two kinds of LTM for storing different types of information: **semantic LTM** and **episodic LTM** (Paivio, 1979; Tulving, 1983; 1985). Semantic memory contains information related to language and verbal concepts. For example, knowing what a "chair" is, what its functions are, and where one is likely to find one are types of information stored in semantic LTM. However, the memory that your cousin Harold pulled your chair out from under you at your eighth birthday party would be housed in episodic memory. Think of episodic memory as your autobiography—it contains a record of episodes that have occurred so far in your life.

## The Organization of LTM

Many cognitive psychologists believe that memories are associated in LTM by means of various networks (Ellis & Hunt, 1993; Raaijmakers & Shiffrin, 1992). Figure 4.2 shows an example of a network of ideas in LTM. Notice how each idea has a relationship with the others with which it is connected. One could travel from one end (Queen Elizabeth II) to the other (*Sesame Street*), two concepts that have nothing to do with each other, but they are related via the other concepts.

One network model views memory as a vast network of hierarchical associations between concepts (Quillan, 1969). In this model, the types of associations vary. Take, for example, the concept "animals." As shown in figure 4.3, some of the associations of "animals" are its subgroups, such as birds, fish, and mammals. Other associations pertain to its properties; animals, for example, have skin, eat, move, and breathe.

A somewhat different network model views LTM as a network of "propositions" (Anderson, 1983, 1990). The propositions pertain to a specific type of relationship between ideas. Take, for example, the sentence "Jennifer's job, which she enjoys, is difficult." We could have broken this sentence into three simple propositions: "Jennifer has a job." "She enjoys it." "It is difficult." Figure 4.4 shows each of these three propositions. The three propositions, however, can be combined into a single propositional network that encompasses all three relationships, as shown in figure 4.5.

The way information is organized in LTM has implications for how we should present new information to students.

**Figure 4.4**
A propositional network.

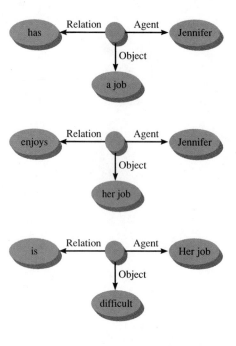

**Figure 4.5**
An elaborated propositional network.

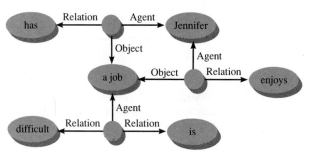

Another type of model, called the "feature model" (Smith, Shoben, & Rips, 1974), views semantic memory, not as a network, but as a collection of features. "Dog," for example, is associated with the features "has a wet nose," "wags its tail when happy," and "barks."

The feature model does not link concepts in a hierarchical manner as the network model does. The feature model takes into account that many semantic categories are rather "fuzzy" and their hierarchical relationships are sometimes ambiguous. For example, is a simple word processor a computer? Is it a typewriter?

## Theories of Forgetting

We now turn to three theories about how information in LTM is forgotten: interference, decay, and cue-dependent forgetting.

### Interference

Proactive interference sometimes inhibits the learning of a new language. The vocabulary and grammar of a previously learned language interferes with the learning of the new language.

**Interference** refers to the idea that people can't remember information because of other learning. New learning can cause the loss of the old knowledge (**retroactive interference**), or existing knowledge can prevent the learning of new information (**proactive interference**). For example, try to remember old telephone numbers of friends who now have new numbers. You may have forgotten the old numbers because they have been displaced by the new ones; this is an example of retroactive interference. Sometimes, however, the opposite occurs. You may have difficulty learning a new phone number, for example, and find yourself repeatedly dialing the old number. This is an instance of proactive interference. Problems of interference occur in the

People remember information more easily if it is related to existing knowledge.

© Eric R. Berndt/Unicorn Stock Photos

classroom when new learning is similar to existing knowledge; the more similar the information is, the more likely interference is to occur (Dempster, 1985).

Identify and highlight differences between new and existing knowledge and encourage students to remember both. While teaching reading, teachers often find that, having taught a word such as *house*, students may have difficulty when learning the word *horse* (proactive interference); or, having learned that 3 × 4 = 12, students may have difficulty remembering that 3 + 4 = 7.

## Decay as a Function of Time

Other information-processing theorists believe that forgetting is due to physical "decay" of the memory over time. That is, information is not lost because of subsequent learning, but because of natural processes occurring in the nervous system (Bahrick, 1984; Bahrick & Phelps, 1987). This position, however, does not explain why some memories are lost but others are not.

## Cue-Dependent Forgetting

Others believe that information is lost from LTM because of cue-dependent forgetting. According to this position, information enters LTM but is inadequately associated with related ideas. The new information is "adrift" in LTM and, with no links to other ideas, is inaccessible. Information that is adrift is very much like the misshelved library book described earlier.

Teachers have the greatest opportunity to overcome this type of forgetting.

## Semantic and Episodic Forgetting

Semantic and episodic memory differ with regard to how easily information is lost. We easily forget information in episodic memory, probably because so much new information is arriving. Try to remember what you had for dinner last night and then try to remember what you had a week ago. It is easy to remember information in semantic memory, probably because information enters far more slowly. We are unlikely to forget the concept "Thanksgiving," for example, because we rarely learn new concepts that might "dislodge" Thanksgiving from our memory.

## Effective Memory Strategies

You can use the following techniques to help students retain information in LTM:

1. Begin lessons with activities that require students to draw upon existing knowledge. For example, begin a lesson on the Reconstruction period with a question such as: "Who remembers what we discussed yesterday about how the Civil War ended? What else was happening in the United States at that time?" Such questions encourage students to bring information stored in LTM into working memory. Most importantly, encourage students to *link new information with existing knowledge.*

2. For certain types of information, have students engage in repetition to encourage long-term retention. Have students frequently repeat information such as basic facts in addition and multiplication to ensure the information

remains firmly fixed in LTM. Also, show students how to use acronyms and other mnemonic devices to remember various kinds of information. Note, however, that rote learning, while at times helpful, is far less important to students than meaningful learning.

3. Make sure you clarify the relationships between concepts. For example, consider the following relationships:
   • An eagle *is an example of* a bird.
   • Instinct *causes* birds to build nests.
   • Laying eggs *is a characteristic of* birds.
   If students understand how concepts are related, they can conceptualize information in meaningful ways and do not have to rely on rote memorization.

4. Review previously taught topics often to ensure that students haven't forgotten what they previously learned. When appropriate, integrate the previously learned material with ideas presented more recently.

---

**4.4** ◎

*Describe activities you can use to help students retain information.*

# Metacognition

The linear model of information processing, described earlier, gave a new focus to research on memory and other mental processes. However, the model does not account for the process by which people monitor their thinking. Brown (1987) and Flavell and Wellman (1978) noted that, people not only use the control processes of attention and rehearsal, but they also supervise and organize their use (see Weinert & Kluwe, 1987). In other words, people monitor their thinking and make certain "executive" decisions (Brown, 1987). This awareness of our own thinking, often called **metacognition,** is at work when students ask themselves if they have understood what the teacher is saying.

**4.5** ◎

*Define metacognition.*

## Monitoring One's Own Thinking

Metacognition is one of the most important abilities students develop.

You are using metacognition as you read this book if you ask yourself, "Am I paying attention?" or "Do I understand what I just read?" If the answer is no, you may skip back a few paragraphs and reread or you may turn the page and read on. No matter how you respond, the fact that you asked yourself if you were paying attention indicates that your metacognition was at work. When balancing your checkbook, you may remind yourself to double-check your subtraction through addition. Once again, metacognition is at work. In both cases, you are consciously monitoring and evaluating your own performance.

Some psychologists use the term *executive processes* rather than *metacognition* and, in some ways, the term is apt (Brown, 1987). Think of the mind as a factory with a limited number of workers, some of whom work in the loading dock, some on the production line, and others in quality control. In addition to the workers, one individual sits in the executive office and makes executive decisions.

The executive may say, "We are expecting a big delivery—we'd better move some workers from the production line to the loading dock." In our minds, the workers are analogous to the mental resources we devote to attention and rehearsal; the executive processes oversee how we use our resources and may decide to reallocate resources when needed.

## Metacognition as a Function of Age

As people get older their metacognitive abilities improve (Flavell, 1985). Young children have little metacognitive awareness and do not apply metacognitive strategies spontaneously, even though they are able to do so when reminded (Garner, 1990). You can teach elementary school students to use metacognitive strategies to improve their learning (Cross & Paris, 1988; Ghatala et al., 1985). Ormrod (1990) notes that, in general, as students get older, they

- become more realistic about their memory abilities
- are better able to develop and use effective learning strategies and
- are more accurate in knowing that they know something

A student who approaches learning passively may not engage in the metacognitive activities necessary for successful performance.

Not all students improve their metacognitive abilities as they get older. In fact, a surprising number of older students are unaware of techniques they can use to check their knowledge and performance. You may sometimes have to encourage your students to learn self-checking techniques; indeed, programs such as Meichenbaum's "cognitive behavior modification" method (1986) have been designed to help students learn how to monitor their thinking.

# Other Models of Information Processing

Have you ever been heavily engaged in a conversation and, although you are aware that a nearby group is having another conversation, you have no knowledge of what that group is talking about? The linear model of information processing easily explains this phenomenon: Your limited capacity of attention is focused on your own conversation and does not permit the neighboring conversation to enter STM. However, if your name is mentioned in the neighboring conversation, you would be instantly aware of it!

Have you ever been engaged in a conversation and, although you are aware that another conversation is occurring nearby, you have no knowledge of what the other group is talking about?

© Uniphoto, Inc.

**Figure 4.6**
An adaptation of Cowan's (1988) model of information processing.

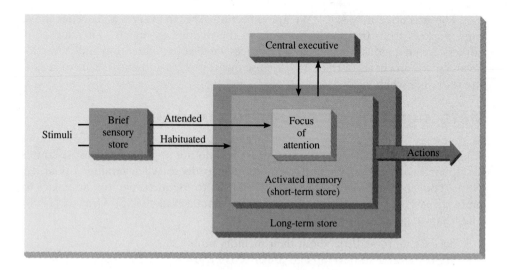

More recent models of information processing recognize the role of LTM at an earlier stage in the information-processing sequence.

The linear information-processing model (figure 4.1) does not explain this phenomenon. According to the linear model, if you are not attending to the neighboring conversation, you should not be aware that your name was spoken. To account for phenomena such as the one just described, researchers have begun to modify the model.

## Cowan's Model

A simplified version of a model proposed by Cowan (1988) appears in figure 4.6. In this model, the focus of attention is a subset of the information in STM, and STM itself exists within LTM under the new label "activated memory." Metacognition, now labeled the "central executive," supervises attention, activated memory, and long-term memory.

Cowan's model accounts for the phenomenon of detecting your name spoken in a nearby conversation. If the focus of attention exists within activated memory, which, in turn, exists within LTM, then an awareness that one's own name has been spoken outside the focus of attention is more easily understood.

## The Depth-of-Processing Model

The **depth-of-processing** model looks at the **levels of processing** in memory rather than at the linear sequence of structures and processes. According to this model, developed by Craik and Lockhart (1972), we hold information temporarily in a central processor; how well we remember information depends on how deeply and how completely we have processed it. If we process the information at a shallow level and integrate it poorly with existing knowledge, it will not last long in memory. We retain information better when we integrate new information with existing knowledge; the more thoroughly we do this, the more likely we will be able to retrieve the information later (Reed, 1992; Schwartz & Reisberg, 1991).

The depth-of-processing model explains why we remember some information, such as the temperature at which water freezes, longer than other information, such as the telephone number of the local theater. We do not process the theater's phone number on a deep level and consequently easily forget it. On the other hand, we process the temperature at which water freezes on a deeper level and remember it for an indefinite period. Students remember information better when they use several ways to learn it (McDaniel, Einstein, & Lollis, 1988; Walker, 1986).

# Automatic Processing

According to the linear model, we process all information in the same manner. Other theorists (Hasher & Zacks, 1984; Logan, 1988; Neves & Anderson, 1981), however, claim there are at least two ways in which we process information: **effortful** and **automatic processing.** We use effortful processing when first learning a task, such as when we first learned to read or first learned basic skills in mathematics. Recall how much effort it took when you were first learning to drive a car.

Effortful processing is slow and rather error-prone. Effortful processing demands concentration and, consequently, takes up a great deal of our limited resources in attention and memory. Very little is left to devote to other activities. When you first learned to drive, you probably had to concentrate to such an extent that you couldn't drive and simultaneously carry on a conversation or listen to the radio. After you became a proficient driver, you probably had little difficulty listening or talking while driving. By that time, your driving skills had become automatic.

Once we have sufficient practice and reach the level of automatic processing, we process information rapidly, accurately, and sometimes even without intention or awareness. You probably use automatic processing when you read. As a proficient reader, you read quickly, you seldom have to stop and think what a word means, and you sometimes read even when you are unaware of doing so. After reaching the level of automatic processing, further practice usually leads to little or no improvement.

## The Importance of Automatic Processing to Students

Automatic processing concerns the memory of facts and execution of skills. When people are automatic at a skill or know facts automatically, they don't have to rely on time-consuming and error-prone effortful processing (Bloom, 1986; Siegler & Jenkins, 1989). When students are automatic at certain skills, they can more efficiently perform higher-level skills. For example, students who do not automatically know that $3 \times 4 = 12$ have to use finger-counting strategies or other methods to figure out the answer; when they need to know the solution of $3 \times 4$ in a larger problem, such as a multidigit problem or a word problem, their inability to automatically know that the answer is 12 will slow them down.

We noted earlier that attention and STM have limited capacities. Effortfully solving the problem $3 \times 4$ will use up those capacities and leave the student with insufficient resources to deal with the larger problems in which $3 \times 4$ is embedded. Also, a student who uses a finger-counting method is more likely to make an error. When $3 \times 4 = 12$ is automatized, the student will not suddenly think that $3 \times 4 = 11$.

Students should become automatic at recognizing words when they read. Initially, all students struggle with identifying words. Teachers often use a phonics approach to help beginning readers decode printed words. Decoding is an effortful process and makes large demands on the reader's resources, leaving little for important tasks such as comprehension of a sentence or paragraph. It is important that students learn to recognize whole words automatically so they can devote their attention and memory to the important task of comprehension. Similarly, students who do not automatically know the spellings of words must struggle with spelling when trying to write, and consequently have less memory and attention to devote to the overall organization and content of their writing.

The ability to process information automatically is one of the characteristics that separates novices from experts (Chi, Glaser, & Farr, 1988; Lesgold, 1984). Expert pianists execute their hand motions automatically. Similarly, expert athletes coordinate the movements of their legs and upper body automatically. But one doesn't have to be an expert musician or athlete to need automatic skills. There are countless skills in which students should become automatic. For example, they should automatically know many of the basic facts in the content areas of science and social studies. Also, they should automatically know many study and research skills, such as how to use a card catalog, encyclopedia, or dictionary.

Although we often must start by processing effortfully, effortful processing tends to be inefficient.

Did you ever drive home and then realize you were paying very little attention to the driving? Driving home has become so automatic for you that it demands little of your attention.

If we do not ensure that students have become automatic at a skill, we may impede their success at subsequent skills.

Experts have automatized the basic skills of their craft.

© Sygma

## Automatic Processing and Practice

Have you ever heard the joke, "Excuse me, could you tell me how to get to Carnegie Hall?" The punchline is "Practice, practice, practice." Processes become automatic through practice (Logan, 1988; Shiffrin & Schneider, 1977). Just as musicians and athletes become automatic at their skills through hours and hours of practice, students become automatic at academic skills through extended practice. Many teachers use flashcards, classroom routines, and innovative games to "drill" students and give them practice. Although you may want students to develop higher-level thinking skills, it is sometimes important to first give them many opportunities to practice basic skills so that effortful processes can become automatic.

Automatizing basic skills is not at end in itself; after skills have become automatic, they should be used in higher-level skills. Vladimir Horowitz was not a great pianist simply because he had become automatic at playing the piano, nor was Jackie Joyner-Kersee a great athlete simply because she has become automatic at running and jumping. Automatic skills are simply the necessary precursors of performing the more complex and sophisticated tasks that lie ahead.

## Schema Theory

4.6

*Summarize the role of schema theory in students' learning.*

The development of a schema that is accurate and rich in detail improves the quality of students' thinking.

So far, we have described how information enters and is used by the memory system. Other theories focus on how information is organized within the information system rather than on how information enters and is processed. One such theory is **schema theory**. A schema (plural, *schemata*) is an abstract representation of information that contains a variety of details, such as characteristics and examples (Alba & Hasher, 1983; Anderson, 1984; Bauer, 1993). The term *schema* is being used somewhat differently here than in Piaget's theory of cognitive development. Piaget used the term *schema* to refer to an organized system of thoughts or actions we use to represent the outside world within our minds. In the present context, however, a schema is a system of relationships between concepts; it is a body of information related to a specific concept.

For example, in our own minds, the schema (or mental representation) of the idea "dog" contains characteristics (four legs, wet nose, barks) and examples (German shepherd, collie, poodle). Schemata that are rich in this kind of information facilitate understanding; when a student's schema lacks detailed information, the student will have limited comprehension of later incoming information. More complete and detailed schemata help students to engage effectively in higher-level thinking, such as problem solving and decision making (Lewis & Anderson, 1985).

Schemata fulfill a number of important functions (Anderson, 1984). Specifically, we use schemata to help us assimilate new information, make inferences about new information, attend to important components, perform systematic memory searches, summarize information, and make inferences needed to reconstruct ideas whose details may have been forgotten.

## Schema Theory and Reading Comprehension

Schema theory has had a profound impact on reading comprehension research. Reading theorists quickly recognized the importance of schema theory to their area of concern. The following story illustrates the importance of schema theory to reading comprehension:

> Paul looked down at the poor, helpless old lady lying unconscious below him. Her very life was in his hands. He looked at the cold, steel blade of the knife in his hand. He had never done this before. He looked around at the faces staring at him and wondered, "Can I do it? What will they think of me if I can't?" He didn't want to be a failure in their eyes; they were the toughest group he had ever known. Then he heard someone say "Go ahead. What are you waiting for?"

What is going on in the story? Did you think that Paul was a mugger who was afraid to slash his victim while his friends goaded him on, or did you think that Paul was a surgeon who was nervously about to perform his first operation? If you had known Paul was a mugger or a surgeon from the outset, the entire story would have had a different meaning for you.

People's prior knowledge influences their recall and interpretation of written material (for example, Anderson, 1984; Just & Carpenter, 1987; Spires, Gallini, & Riggsbee, 1992). Prior knowledge pertains not only to the *content* of a written passage but also to the *form*. According to Mandler and Johnson (1977), Tierney and Cunningham (1984) and Whaley (1981), people use **story grammars** to make sense of prose. Experienced readers know the structure and rules that govern stories. Experienced readers know, for example, that a story has a setting and at least one episode. They know that each episode has a beginning and then is developed. Most well-written children's stories follow a recognizable structure, so children have expectations about the organization of a story and can use these expectations to predict what will happen next.

Brown, Campione, and Day (1981) claim that readers use three kinds of knowledge to comprehend written material: (a) content, or background, knowledge about the subject presented, (b) strategic knowledge, or knowledge about how to learn effectively, and (c) metacognitive knowledge, or monitoring one's own comprehension (Baker & Brown, 1985; Markman, 1981), checking one's performance (Andre & Anderson, 1978; Brown, Campione, & Barclay, 1979; Cross & Paris, 1988), and awareness of one's performance relative to task demands (Myers & Paris, 1978). To help students learn to monitor their reading comprehension, Markman (1985) makes these recommendations:

1. Students should read well-written prose that has simple logical, causal, and temporal relations.
2. Teachers should ask students to make predictions about a story, to infer a character's motives or the causes of an event.
3. Students should ask themselves self-monitoring questions while reading, including "Do I understand?" and "What is the main point?"
4. Teachers should model self-monitoring techniques.
5. Students should practice evaluating text and discerning inconsistencies.

# Schema Theory and Teaching

Schema theory explains how people represent knowledge. Here are some ways to help students make the association between new and known information.

Make sure students recall old information before teaching them related new information. For example, before teaching a lesson on how airplanes and helicopters work, ask questions such as, "Do you remember the discussion we had yesterday about how transportation has changed over time? What different modes of transportation did we discuss?" These questions activate students' existing schemata. It is a good idea to begin a lesson by activating existing schemata. To ensure that students continue to relate new information to what they already know, ask questions throughout the lesson and, if necessary, point out the relationships between new and known information.

Do not assume that students already have sufficient background information; don't assume that they will make the connection between the new and the known on their own. Monitor yourself as you teach to ensure that you are providing students with appropriate background knowledge and encouraging them to activate their existing schemata.

One of the most effective ways to encourage students to relate new to known is to use **advance organizers** (Ausubel, 1980). An advance organizer is a general introduction of new information that is provided before the new information is actually presented (the "Previews" at the beginning of each chapter serve this purpose). In classrooms, give students a one-paragraph overview of the chapter they are about to read before they read the chapter. Advance organizers activate students' existing schemata related to the topic and promote new linkages between the new and the known (Derry, 1984).

Careful study of advance organizers helps people remember the content of written passages later (Corkill et al., 1989; Dinnel & Glover, 1985; Spires, Gallini, & Riggsbee, 1992). Advance organizers need not be verbal; diagrams can also be effective advance organizers (Mayer, 1983, 1984). Sadoski, Goetz, and Fritz (1993) have demonstrated that new information that is both verbal and easily visualized is best remembered.

According to Mayer (1987), advance organizers are most effective when students are dealing with unfamiliar text, the task requires transfer of learning to new situations, and the advance organizer provides concrete models.

## Educational Implications of Schema Theory

The quote by Bransford et al. (1989) is critical; it highlights the crucial role of background knowledge in academic success and failure.

"One clear implication of schema theory is that some students may appear to be poor learners *not* because they have some inherent comprehension or memory 'deficits,' but because they lack, or fail to activate, the background knowledge that was presupposed by a message or text" (Bransford et al., 1989, p. 209).

A second major implication is that new information is best learned when it is related to known information. This conclusion, which has been reached by many theorists (Ausubel, 1968; Gagné, 1985; Piaget, 1952), is perhaps the most important message cognitive theory has for teachers.

A third implication concerns the accuracy of memory. Experience and information are not actually stored in memory, but instead exist as schemata (Di Vesta, 1989); thus, how one person has "learned" information may differ from how another has "learned" it. This difference is partially explained by cultural background; the ideas and beliefs that we bring with us when we learn greatly affect how we understand new information (Erwin, 1991).

Schemata vary among different individuals and within the same individual at different times (Gerrig, 1988). For example, developmental changes, the experiences you encounter, and your personal growth as an individual, will make how you "know" the idea "education" ten years from now different from how you "know" the idea "education" now.

## Script Theory

An approach closely related to schema theory is **script theory.** This view of information organization relies on the idea that, in LTM, we house various scripts that we use in appropriate situations (Abelson, 1981; Schank & Abelson, 1977). A script is a sequence of steps used in a specific situation. For example, when you enter a fast-food restaurant, you don't have to think about the correct procedure for obtaining your food—you have a script in your mind. You get in line, order your food, pay, take your tray, sit down, eat, throw away your trash, and leave. But individuals who have had no experience in a fast-food restaurant must observe how others behave and figure out the correct procedure. Scripts appear to provide us with a shortcut for thinking. We don't have to analyze and judge each situation; rather, we can rely on a script to guide us in familiar situations.

Even preschoolers have accurate scripts of highly familiar events (Nelson, 1978), although they tend to be rigid in their notion of the proper sequence (Nelson, 1986). As they get older, children become more flexible in their scripts, and develop more complex scripts (Mandler, 1984).

Script knowledge influences how we understand and remember stories. Children know, for example, when a story is out of order, varies from the expected sequence, or is missing information, and they make corrections when retelling it (Chi & Glaser, 1985; Nelson, 1986). Script knowledge also influences how we draw inferences from information we are given. We often embellish a story using our existing knowledge, usually without realizing that we are doing so (Salomon, 1983).

# A Generative Model of Learning

Earlier, we discussed the notion that information is organized in LTM in a hierarchical network (Quillan, 1969) or in a propositional network (Anderson, 1990). A related but somewhat different approach, proposed by Wittrock (1978, 1984), is a **generative model of learning.** According to Wittrock, people learn by generating meaning from the information presented to them and actively generating relationships among ideas.

These self-generated relationships can be both visual and verbal. Linden and Wittrock (1981) instructed two groups of fifth-graders in elaboration activities. One group received instructions to draw a picture of what they had read, followed the next day by instructions to write one- or two-sentence summaries about the story, and, finally, to create an analogy or metaphor about the story they had read. This group was called the *imaginal to verbal* group because they performed first image elaboration and then verbal elaboration.

The second group was instructed in reverse order: from *verbal to imaginal.* Two other groups received no instruction in elaboration. The elaboration instruction resulted in higher scores in reading comprehension. In both experimental groups the students created appropriate and relevant elaborations; the more elaborations the student had created, the higher the student's score on the reading comprehension test (more so for the group who moved from images to verbalization).

# Cognitive Styles

Not all individuals process information the same way. Individuals often have different **cognitive styles** that influence how they process information. Cognitive styles "reflect individual variations in modes of attending, perceiving, remembering, and thinking . . . [they are an] interface between cognition and personality" (Kogan, 1980, p. 64). Cognitive styles are patterns that govern our way of processing information; they tend to be stable, although not necessarily unchangeable (Holland, 1982).

Most cognitive styles that have been investigated exist along a continuum, with most people falling somewhere between the two poles. While various cognitive styles have been investigated (see Blackman & Goldstein, 1982), field independence-dependence and conceptual tempo have evoked the greatest interest among educators.

**4.7** ◎

*Explain the generative model of learning.*

Two learners may generate very different meaning from the same information, based on differences in prior knowledge and experience.

*Annual*  **Edition**

unit *4*

## Using a Generative Model of Learning in Teaching

■■ Activities that cause students to respond
■■ actively enhance intentional learning (Rothkopf, 1970). Here are some activities you can use. Encourage students to engage in a variety of activities to help them generate meaning from information presented in class:

1. *Note taking* is effective for this purpose. The act of taking in new spoken or written information and transforming it into short notes helps students understand the information and retain it in the long-term (Irwin, 1991; Peper & Mayer, 1978).
2. *Summarizing* requires students to consider the most important aspects of a body of information and reiterate them (Doctorow, Wittrock, & Marks, 1978).
3. *Underlining* forces students to judge the importance of a given sentence or sentence fragment. Making judgments forces students to consider the relationship between the information presented in the sentence and other related ideas (Irwin, 1991).
4. *Outlining* compels students to organize incoming information in a hierarchical manner and consider the relationships between ideas: Is idea Y a subordinate idea to idea X? Is idea Y distinct and separate from idea X? Outlining imposes an organization on a body of information.
5. *Adjunct questions* are used to signal important information to readers: They can be used as prereading questions, inserted questions, or postreading

questions. Students who use adjunct questions retain more information than students who do not (Reynolds & Anderson, 1982). Postquestions are most valuable because they encourage students to review material to clarify their understanding (Sagerman & Mayer, 1987). However, prequestions help students focus immediately on the most important or the most general ideas (Klauer, 1984).

According to Mayer (1987, 1992), activities generate meaning only if they are designed to generate meaning. Such activities should:

1. *Direct attention.* They should guide students to the important or relevant information to help them more easily grasp the meaningfulness.
2. *Build internal connections.* They should demonstrate how information is related (how new idea X is related to new idea Y).
3. *Build external connections.* They should show the relationship between new and existing knowledge (how new idea X is related to known idea Y).

Note that in all of these methods (note taking, summarizing, underlining, outlining, and adjunct questions), the learner must act *upon* the information presented. Transforming, reiterating, judging, and imposing organization on information are other active processes that enhance comprehension and retention.

## Field Dependence and Independence

Have you ever known individuals who "can't see the forest for the trees"? That is, they are particularly good at seeing specific details but may miss the larger picture. Have you known others who see only the forest and seem unable to focus on the specific trees? This phenomenon is best explained by one of the best-documented cognitive styles, namely the field independent-field dependent continuum.

**Field independence** refers to the tendency to "use internal, independent factors as . . . guides in processing information" (Kaplan, 1990, p. 134). Individuals with a high degree of field independence perceive components of stimuli without depending on external frames of reference. **Field dependence,** on the other hand, refers to the tendency to look outside and rely on external sources of information. Individuals with a high degree of field dependence tend to perceive the whole, resulting in dependence on outside structure and organization. Much of the field-independence/ dependence research has focused on people's ability to perceive an image embedded within a more complex picture, with the premise that field-independent people would be better at detecting the embedded picture, being less influenced by external forces (Witkin et al., 1977).

Field-independent people tend to perform better when working in unstructured situations and are efficient working alone (Shuell, 1981). In general, their school performance is better than that of field-dependent students,

Use instructional methods that match students' learning styles.

but field-dependent students appear to have a greater social orientation (Blackman & Goldstein, 1982; Kogan, 1983). Academically, they may require greater structure and clarity to perform well in school tasks.

As with all cognitive styles, neither end of the continuum is inherently better than the other: There are strengths and weaknesses associated with both field independence and field dependence. In certain ways, field independence is more valued in our society, however, in that this style appears to enhance analytic thinking ability and academic achievement. Field-dependent people, on the other hand, may be better suited for cooperative work with other individuals. Field independence and field dependence are not amenable to change; therefore, teachers should attend to the cognitive style of individual students and foster an environment that takes advantage of their particular strengths.

## Conceptual Tempo

Another cognitive style that has received much attention is the dimension of conceptual tempo. The two ends of the continuum are **reflectivity** and **impulsivity** (Kagan, 1965; Stuart & Pumfrey, 1987). This style has to do with how rapidly individuals make decisions: Do they sit back and think about their response before acting (the reflective style), or do they act immediately, without pausing to think (the impulsive style)? Neither end of the conceptual tempo continuum is inherently good or bad; rather, each has its advantages and disadvantages, depending on the situation.

At times, it is useful to act reflectively, as when you are making a decision that has long-range implications, such as choosing a career or a mate. However, there are times when you would not want someone to act reflectively, such as in the case of an emergency. In classroom settings, a reflective style is often desired, except in situations where speed is particularly important, such as on timed tests.

Impulsive students are more error-prone than reflective students (Borkowski et al., 1983). Also, underachieving students tend to be more impulsive than average students (Blackman & Goldstein, 1982). Students who are in the middle of the reflectivity-impulsivity continuum do better on problem-solving tasks than those at the reflective or impulsive extremes (Duemler & Mayer, 1988).

Unlike the field independence-dependence cognitive style, the conceptual tempo cognitive style is amenable to change. Kogan (1983) found that impulsive students can be taught to be more reflective. One approach, which effectively used a self-monitoring strategy, is called "cognitive behavior modification" (Meichenbaum, 1986).

Reflective people think and consider before acting.

© Robert W. Ginn/Unicorn Stock Photos

## Hemispherality

A related topic that has intrigued educators is **hemispherality,** which is the idea that one side of the brain or the other is dominant in any individual. The left hemisphere, which is dominant in most people, is responsible for language and verbal concepts and sequential, logical thinking (Mannies, 1986), whereas the right side is responsible for visual, musical, and spatial thinking. The left hemisphere seems to address details, while the right is more concerned with the whole (Kinsbourne, 1983).

Educators have wondered whether teachers should take into account students' cerebral dominance and the nature of the specific school tasks. Art, music, and movement would be considered right hemisphere tasks, whereas writing, reading, and mathematics would be left hemisphere tasks. According to Davidson (1992), the left hemisphere governs logic, and the right hemisphere governs creativity, intuitive thinking, and emotions.

The two hemispheres have a high degree of interaction via the "corpus collosum," the material that connects the two. Any given task makes demands on both the right and left hemispheres, which work in an integrated fashion (Springer & Deutsch, 1981). When a student reads a story, the demands are visual, verbal, conceptual, emotional, and logical; when a student draws a picture, the student uses verbal labels to describe what he or she is drawing, as well

The right hemisphere of the brain governs musical activity.

© A. Ramey/Unicorn Stock Photos

as visual and spatial ideas. Nevertheless, individuals do seem to have a preference for left or right brain activities.

# New Directions of Research

Cognitive psychology has grown immeasurably in the past two decades, and many of its applications to education have already been noted. Newer branches, however, continue to grow. One branch of cognitive psychology concerns artificial intelligence (Charniak & McDermott, 1985; Winston, 1984). Another area (although not new) generating increased interest is neuropsychology, in which researchers examine activity occurring in a person's brain as the person engages in various cognitive tasks.

## Artificial Intelligence

The field of **artificial intelligence** concerns the overlap between human and computer information processing. Artificial intelligence researchers study language processing, pattern recognition, game-playing, vision, speech recognition, theorem proving, and robotics (Dehn & Schank, 1982; Schank, 1982). Specifically, artificial intelligence experts are trying to design "intelligent" computer programs (Hayes-Roth, Waterman, & Lenta, 1983; Marcus, 1988; Schunk, 1991; Wenger, 1987).

Optimally, one use of such programs could be to act as intelligent tutors to enhance human learning (Clancey, 1987; Corbett & Anderson, 1989; Polson & Richardson, 1988; Sleeman & Brown, 1982). But the primary goal of artificial intelligence research is to create programs that replicate as closely as possible human intelligence (e.g, Johnson-Laird, 1983; Langley et al., 1987). The attempt to create such programs may shed light on human intelligence itself (Fodor & Pylyshyn, 1988; Pylyshyn, 1986).

Some of the attempts to replicate human information processing have resulted in striking demonstrations, such as chess programs that can beat even the most expert of chess players. A computer's huge memory and speed account for this extraordinary performance; however, it is clear that computers at the present time cannot reproduce some of the uniquely human qualities of the mind, such as improving performance with practice, distinguishing between relevant and irrelevant information, responding appropriately within different contexts (adapting when necessary), and using partial information to create new ideas (Gagné, Yekovich, & Yekovich, 1993).

## Neuropsychology

Another growing area related to cognitive psychology is **neuropsychology** (Crick & Asanuma, 1986; Lynch & Baudry, 1984; Squire, 1987). Medical researchers are rapidly obtaining a more comprehensive understanding of how the brain works. To a large extent, this progress is due to the more precise measures we now have of brain activity. Previously, X rays and electroencephalographic readings (EEGs) were the primary ways of "seeing" what was going on inside the brain.

Today, researchers can use two far more powerful tools: CAT scans and MRI. The CAT scan (computerized axial tomography) is, in effect, a three-dimensional X-ray. The CAT sends X ray beams through the brain and the picture is transmitted to a computer monitor, revealing the inside of the brain in three-dimensional slices. The MRI (magnetic resonance imaging) uses magnetic fields and radio waves to analyze brain activity more precisely; it, too, provides three-dimensional pictures, but more precisely and without the risks associated with X rays.

Neuropsychological growth occurs developmentally (Goldman-Rakic, 1987). Many researchers have investigated localization of functions of the brain, that is, the areas specifically responsible for activities such as thinking (Roland & Friberg, 1985) and reading (Posner et al., 1988). Recent research is contributing to an understanding of where the various information-processing constructs (such as STM and LTM) may be housed in the brain (Goldman-Rakic, 1992; Kandel & Hawkins, 1992). The contribution of future research in neuropsychology to our understanding of learning holds much promise (see, for example, Grossberg, 1987).

# Controversial Issues

Despite the contributions of cognitive psychology and the promise of future contributions (Roediger & Craik, 1989), there are controversial issues in the field.

## Research Methods

One controversy pertains to the methods used in cognitive research (see Richardson-Klavehn & Bjork, 1988). Behaviorists choose to study behavior exclusively because they feel that a science of the human mind should have as its data observable, measurable phenomena (namely, behavior). Cognitive researchers feel that internal mental processes, while unobservable, can nevertheless be measured and investigated.

Cognitive researchers find it difficult to develop suitable measures of the hypothetical constructs they wish to explore. Constructs such as "automatic processing," "short-term memory," and "schemata" are interesting and useful but have no tangible existence. We look at behavior that we believe reflects these constructs, and we use them to develop theories and hypotheses that we hope will give us insight about the workings of the mind.

But cognitive psychologists must clearly define the constructs, create inventive ways to measure them, and carefully implement experiments to study them. Because of these problems, many cognitive researchers seek converging evidence of a phenomenon; that is, if evidence of a phenomenon or a relationship is found across studies using different measures, then we can be more confident of our findings. According to cognitivists, the difficulties of defining and measuring constructs are present but not insurmountable.

The difficulties in defining and measuring hypothetical constructs can lead to debate and disagreement among researchers.

## Cognition and Emotion

A second issue relating to cognitive psychology lies in the relationship between cognition and emotion. Increasingly, psychologists are noting that cognition, emotion and personality are not entirely independent. Earlier, we looked at cognitive styles, which may be a function of personality but which very much affect cognition. Clearly, emotion and cognition are related. Cognition can influence emotion. Sometimes, thinking clearly can ease emotional problems. In addition, emotion can influence thinking. In a peak emotional state, you may think more clearly. Of course, the opposite is also true. Emotions sometimes inhibit thinking ability.

### The Effects of Anxiety

**Anxiety** refers to a feeling of tension and foreboding that can obstruct clear thinking. We have probably all experienced anxiety related to taking tests; a little anxiety may help keep us alert and make the adrenaline flow, but too much anxiety prevents us from doing our best. If students experience anxiety not only while taking tests but also in all their school activities, school will become a highly unpleasant place for them, and their academic performance will suffer.

## Eyewitness Testimony

Another concern relevant to the study of cognitive psychology is how reliable our memories actually are. A good body of evidence supports the idea that memory involves reconstruction rather than exact recollection of events and ideas (Loftus, 1979). This fact has considerable bearing on how reliable memory is when individuals are giving **eyewitness testimony.** The testimony of children, who are increasingly involved in criminal cases either as witnesses or as victims (Straus, Gelles, & Steinmetz, 1980), is viewed by many as less credible than that of adults (Goodman et al., 1987), perhaps because children are viewed as being more suggestible or having poorer memories.

Actually, the research literature on the relative suggestibility of children and adults is equivocal (Duncan, Whitney, & Kunen, 1982; Goodman & Reed, 1986; Kaliski, 1983) and, while there are developmental patterns in short-term memory capacity and retrieval strategies, children can perform as well as adults when background knowledge is equated (Lindberg, 1980). Further research in this important area is clearly needed.

# Learning and Thinking: More Than Just Memory

The major concern of this chapter has been information processing, and the major focus of information-processing theories is memory. But, learning involves more than just memory. We engage in many higher-level mental processes, including comprehension, concept formation, problem solving, decision making, and critical thinking. Perhaps we can think of memory as the foundation of these higher processes. You cannot comprehend, form concepts, solve problems, make decisions, or think critically until you first have the memory of an idea to work with. Memory is the foundation for learning and thinking, but it is just the beginning.

## KEY POINTS

1. Human information-processing theorists believe that the analogy of the computer is a useful model for understanding how humans think.

2. Information processing has been viewed by means of a "linear model" in which information flows through three structural features: the sensory register, short-term memory, and long-term memory. Control processes of attention and rehearsal determine the flow of information between the structural features.

3. We have limited capacities in attention, and only that information to which we attend flows into short-term memory. Attention is a necessary precursor for learning.

4. Short-term memory holds seven plus or minus two "chunks" of information and can retain that information for only about 20 seconds, unless the learner engages in maintenance rehearsal.

5. Elaborative rehearsal stores information in long-term memory. Rehearsal strategies include repetition, verbal elaboration, visual imagery, and use of mnemonic devices such as acronyms.

6. Rehearsed information is placed in long-term memory, where it can be easily accessible if it is integrated with other related ideas. Network, proposition, and feature models have been developed to describe how we organize information in long-term memory.

7. Three explanations have been offered for forgetting from long-term memory. The memories themselves decay over time, new learning interferes with old learning (or vice versa), and information is poorly associated with related knowledge.

8. Metacognition refers to our awareness of our known mental activities. We monitor and evaluate our performance and "supervise" our use of mental resources.

9. According to the depth-of-processing model, memory is a function of the meaningfulness of new information. A model of automatic and effortful processing suggests that, while some processes are effortful, highly practiced activities are automatic. Automatic processes occur rapidly, accurately, and sometimes unconsciously.

10. Schema theory is another way to explain how information is stored in long-term memory. A schema is an abstract representation of information that contains a variety of details, such as characteristics and examples. When a student's schema lacks detail, the student will have limited comprehension of later incoming information.

11. An *advance organizer* is a brief general overview of new information that is provided before the material is actually presented. Advance organizers activate students' existing schemata related to the topic and promote new linkages between the new and the known.

12. A related explanation of how information is organized in long-term memory is script theory, which relies on the idea that we house in LTM various *scripts* that we use in appropriate situations.

13. A generative model of learning suggests that learners generate their own meaning and make their own connections between new and known information. This model highlights the importance of activities such as note taking, underlining, summarizing, outlining, and the use of adjunct questions.

14. Researchers have noted that individuals vary in their cognitive styles. One style, field independence-field dependence, pertains to the degree to which one can differentiate a stimulus from the context in which it is seen. Another style, conceptual tempo, suggests that some individuals are reflective, while others are impulsive.

15. Recent areas of interest related to cognitive psychology have included artificial intelligence, in which computer programs are written to emulate the activities of the human brain, and neuropsychology, in which researchers investigate how brain activity relates directly to mental processes such as learning and reading.

16. Current issues in cognitive psychology include controversies concerning the methods used in cognitive research, the relationship between cognition and emotion, and the accuracy of memory, in particular, the reliability of eyewitness testimony.

## SELF-STUDY EXERCISES

1. Is information processed in a linear manner? What evidence do we have one way or the other?

2. What tasks do you perform in everyday life that are automatic for you? What tasks are effortful?

3. How does information get into LTM? How is it forgotten?

4. What are the major implications of schema theory for reading instruction? What are the implications for instruction in the content areas of social studies and science?

5. Describe the two cognitive styles discussed in this chapter. What are the advantages and disadvantages of each extreme? What is the relationship between cognitive style and personality?

6. How can teachers encourage long-term retention of new information?

## FURTHER READINGS

Anderson, J. R. (1990). *Cognitive psychology and its applications* (3rd ed.). New York: W. H. Freeman.

Baine, D. (1986). *Memory and instruction.* Englewood Cliffs, NJ: Educational Technology Publications.

Ellis, H. C., & Hunt, R. R. (1993). *Fundamentals of cognitive psychology* (5th ed.). Madison, WI: Brown & Benchmark.

Kail, R. (1990). *The development of memory in children* (3rd ed.). New York: W. H. Freeman.

Klatzky, R. L. (1980). *Human memory: Structures and processes* (2nd ed.). San Francisco: W. H. Freeman.

Pearson, P. D. (Ed.). (1984). *Handbook on research in reading.* New York: Longman.

## REFERENCES

Abelson, R. P. (1981). Psychological status of the script concept. *American Psychologist, 36,* 715–729.

Alba, J. W., & Hasher, L. (1983). Is memory schematic? *Psychological Bulletin, 93,* 203–231.

Anderson, J. R. (1983). *The architecture of cognition.* Cambridge, MA: Harvard University Press.

Anderson, J. R. (1990). *Cognitive psychology and its implications* (3rd ed.). New York: W. H. Freeman.

Anderson, R. C. (1984). Some reflections on the acquisition of knowledge. *Educational Researcher, 13*(9), 5–10.

Andre, M. D. A., & Anderson, T. H. (1978). The development and evaluation of a self-questioning study technique. *Reading Research Quarterly, 14,* 605–623.

Atkinson, R. C., & Shiffrin, R. M. (1968). Human memory: A proposed system and its control processes. In K. W. Spence & J. T. Spence (Eds.), *The psychology of learning and motivation: Advances in research and theory* (Vol. 2, pp. 89–195). New York: Academic Press.

Ausubel, D. P. (1968). *Educational psychology: A cognitive view.* New York: Holt, Rinehart & Winston.

Ausubel, D. P. (1980). Schemata, cognitive structure, and advance organizers: A reply to Anderson, Piro, and Anderson. *American Educational Research Journal, 17,* 400–404.

Baddeley, A. D. (1992). Working memory. *Science, 255,* 556–559.

Bahrick, H. P. (1984). Semantic memory content in permastore: Fifty years of memory for Spanish learned in school. *Journal of Experimental Psychology: General, 113,* 1–24.

Bahrick, H. P., & Phelps, E. (1987). Retention of Spanish vocabulary over 8 years. *Journal of Experimental Psychology: Learning, Memory, and Cognition, 13,* 344–349.

Baker, L., & Brown, A. (1985). Metacognitive skills of reading. In D. Pearson (Ed.), *Handbook of reading research* (pp. 231–272). New York: Longman.

Bauer, P. J. (1993). Memory for gender-consistent and gender inconsistent event sequences by 25-month-old children. *Child Development, 64,* 285–297.

Blackman, S., & Goldstein, K. (1982). Cognitive styles and learning disabilities. *Journal of Learning Disabilities, 15,* 106–115.

Bloom, B. S. (1986). Automaticity: The hands and feet of genius. *Educational Leadership, 43,* 70–86.

Borkowski, J. G., Peck, V. A., Reid, M. K., & Kurtz, B. E. (1983). Impulsivity and strategy transfer: Metamemory as mediator. *Child Development, 54,* 459–473.

Bransford, J. D., Vye, N. J., Adams, L. T., & Perfetto, G. A. (1989). Learning skills and the acquisition of knowledge. In A. Lesgold & R. Glaser (Eds.), *Foundations for a psychology of education* (pp. 199–249). Hillsdale, NJ: Erlbaum.

Brown, A. (1987). Metacognition, executive control, self-regulation and other more mysterious mechanisms. In F. E. Weinert & R. N. Kluwe (Eds.), *Metacognition, motivation, and understanding* (pp. 41–54). Hillsdale, NJ: Erlbaum.

Brown, A. L., Campione, J. C., & Barclay, C. R. (1979). Training self-checking routines for estimating test readiness: Generalization from list learning to prose recall. *Child Development, 50,* 501–512.

Brown, A. L., Campione, J. C., & Day, J. D. (1981). Learning to learn: On training students to learn from texts. *Educational Researcher, 10,* 14–21.

Charniak, E., & McDermott, D. (1985). *Introduction to artificial intelligence.* Reading, MA: Addison-Wesley.

Cherry, E. C. (1953). Some experiments on the recognition of speech with one and two ears. *Journal of the Acoustical Society of America, 25,* 975–979.

Chi, M. T. H., & Glaser, R. (1985). Problem-solving ability. In R. J. Sternberg (Ed.), *Human abilities: An information-processing approach.* New York: W. H. Freeman.

Chi, M. T. H., Glaser, R., & Farr, M. (Eds.). (1988). *The nature of expertise.* Hillsdale, NJ: Erlbaum.

Clancey, W. J. (1987). *Knowledge-based tutoring: The GUIDON program.* Cambridge, MA: MIT Press.

Corbett, A. T., & Anderson, J. R. (1989). The LISP intelligent tutoring system: Research in skill acquisition. In *Proceedings of the Fourth International Conference in Artificial Intelligence in Education,* 64–72.

Corkill, A. J., Glover, J. A., Bruning, R. H., & Krug, D. (1989). Advance organizers: Retrieval hypotheses. *Journal of Educational Psychology, 81,* 43–51.

Cowan, N. (1988). Evolving conceptions of memory storage, selective attention, and their mutual constraints within the human information-processing system. *Psychological Bulletin, 104,* 163–191.

Craik, F. I. M., & Lockhart, R. S. (1972). Levels of processing: A framework for memory research. *Journal of Verbal Learning and Verbal Behavior, 11,* 671–684.

Crick, F. H. C., & Asanuma, C. (1986). Certain aspects of the anatomy and physiology of the cerebral cortex. In J. L. McClelland & D. E. Rumelhart (Eds.), *Parallel distributed processing: Explorations in the microstructure of cognition* (Vol. 2). Cambridge, MA: MIT Press/Bradford Books.

Cross, D. R., & Paris, S. G. (1988). Developmental and instructional analyses of children's metacognition and reading comprehension. *Journal of Educational Psychology, 80,* 131–142.

Davidson, R. J. (1992). Emotion and affective style: Hemispheric substrates. *Psychological Science, 3,* 39–43.

Dehn, N., & Schank, R. (1982). Artificial and human intelligence. In R. J. Sternberg (Ed.), *Handbook of human intelligence* (pp. 352–391). Cambridge: Cambridge University Press.

Dempster, F. N. (1985). Proactive interference in sentence recall: Topic-similarity effects and individual differences. *Memory & Cognition, 13,* 81–89.

Derry, S. (1984). Effects of an organizer on memory for prose. *Journal of Educational Psychology, 76,* 98–107.

Dinnel, D., & Glover, J. A. (1985). Advance organizers: Encoding manipulations. *Journal of Educational Psychology, 77,* 514–521.

Di Vesta, F. J. (1989). Applications of cognitive psychology to education. In M. C. Wittrock & F. Farley (Eds.), *The future of educational psychology* (pp. 37–73). Hillsdale, NJ: Erlbaum.

Doctorow, M., Wittrock, M. C., & Marks, C. (1978). Generative processes in reading comprehension. *Journal of Educational Psychology, 70,* 109–118.

Duemler, D., & Mayer, R. E. (1988). Hidden costs of reflectiveness: Aspects of successful scientific reasoning. *Journal of Educational Psychology, 80,* 419–423.

Duncan, E. M., Whitney, P., & Kunen, S. (1982). Integration of visual and verbal information in children's memories. *Child Development, 53,* 1215–1223.

Ellis, H. C., & Hunt, R. R. (1993). *Fundamentals of cognitive psychology* (5th ed.). Madison, WI: Brown & Benchmark.

Erwin, B. (1991). The relationship between background experience and students' comprehension: A cross-cultural study. *Reading Psychology, 12,* 43–61.

Flavell, J. H. (1985). *Cognitive development.* Englewood Cliffs, NJ: Prentice Hall.

Flavell, J. H., & Wellman, H. M. (1978). Metamemory. In R. V. Kail, Jr., & J. W. Hagen (Eds.), *Perspectives on the development of memory and cognition* (pp. 3–33). Hillsdale, NJ: Erlbaum.

Fodor, J. A., & Pylyshyn, Z. W. (1988). Connectionism and cognitive architecture: A critical analysis. *Cognition, 28,* 3–71.

Gagné, E. D., Yekovich, C. W., & Yekovich, F. R. (1993). *The cognitive psychology of school learning* (2nd ed.). New York: Harper Collins.

Gagné, R. M. (1985). *The conditions of learning and theory of instruction* (4th ed.). New York: Holt, Rinehart & Winston.

Garner, R. (1990). When children and adults do not use learning strategies: Toward a theory of settings. *Review of Educational Research, 60,* 517–530.

Gerrig, R. J. (1988). Text comprehension. In R. J. Sternberg & E. E. Smith (Eds.), *The psychology of human thought* (pp. 242–266). Cambridge: Cambridge University Press.

Ghatala, E. S., Levin, J. R., Pressley, M., & Lodico, M. G. (1985). Training cognitive strategy monitoring in children. *American Educational Research Journal, 22,* 199–216.

Gibson, E. J. (1992). How to think about perceptual learning: Twenty-five years later. In J. L. Pick, P. Van Den Brock, & D. C. Knoll (Eds.), *Cognitive psychology: Conceptual & methodological issues.* Washington, DC: American Psychological Association.

Gillund, G., & Shiffrin, R. M. (1984). A retrieval model for both recognition and recall. *Psychological Review, 91,* 1–67.

Goldman-Rakic, P. S. (1987). Development of cortical circuitry and cognitive function. *Child Development, 58,* 601–622.

Goldman-Rakic, P. S. (1992). Working memory and the mind. *Scientific American, 267,* 111–117.

Goldstein, E. B. (1989). *Sensation and perception* (3rd ed.). Belmont, CA: Wadsworth.

Goodman, G. S., Golding, J. M., Helgeson, V. S., Haith, M. M., & Michelli, J. (1987). When a child takes the stand: Jurors' perception of a child's eyewitness testimony. *Law and Human Behavior, 11,* 27–40.

Goodman, G. S., & Reed, R. S. (1986). Age differences in eyewitness testimony. *Law and Human Behavior, 13,* 530–538.

Grossberg, S. (1987). *The adaptive brain, I: Cognition, learning, reinforcement and rhythm.* Amsterdam: North-Holland Elsevier.

Hasher, L., & Zacks, R. T. (1984). Automatic processing of fundamental information. *American Psychologist, 39,* 1372–1388.

Hayes-Roth, F., Waterman, D. A., & Lenta, D. B. (1983). *Building expert systems.* Reading, MA: Addison-Wesley.

Hintzman, D. L. (1986). "Schema abstraction" in a multiple-trace memory model. *Psychological Review, 93,* 411–428.

Hoffman, D. D., & Richards, W. (1985). Parts of recognition. *Cognition, 18,* 65–96.

Holland, R. P. (1982). Learner characteristics and learner performance: Implications for instructional placement decisions. *Journal of Special Education, 15,* 7–10.

Iran-Nejad, A. (1990). Active and dynamic self-regulation of learning processes. *Review of Educational Research, 60,* 573–602.

Irwin, J. W. (1991). *Teaching reading comprehension* (2nd ed.). Boston: Allyn & Bacon.

Johnson-Laird, P. N. (1983). *Mental models.* Cambridge, MA: Harvard University Press.

Just, M. A., & Carpenter, P. A. (1987). *The psychology of reading and language comprehension.* Boston: Allyn & Bacon.

Kagan, J. (1965). Reflection-impulsivity and reading ability in primary grade children. *Child Development, 36,* 609–628.

Kail, R. (1988). Developmental functions for speeds of cognitive processes. *Journal of Experimental Child Psychology, 45,* 339–364.

Kail, R. (1990). *The development of memory in children* (3rd ed.). New York: W. H. Freeman.

Kaliski, V. A. (1983). The effect of suggestive questions and age on the eyewitness reliability of children's reports. *Dissertation Abstracts International, 43,* 4127-B.

Kandel, E. R., & Hawkins, R. D. (1992). The biological basis of learning and individuality. *Scientific American, 267,* 79–86.

Kaplan, P. S. (1990). *Educational psychology for tomorrow's teacher.* St. Paul, MN: West Publishing Company.

Kinsbourne, M. (1983). Do learning disabled children lack functional hemispheric lateralization? *Topics in Learning and Learning Disabilities, 3,* 14–28.

Klauer, K. (1984). Intentional and incidental learning with instructional texts: A meta-analysis for 1970–1980. *American Educational Research Journal, 21,* 232–339.

Kogan, N. (1980). Cognitive styles and reading performance. *Bulletin of the Orton Society, 39,* 63–77.

Kogan, N. (1983). Stylistic variation in childhood and adolescence: Creativity, metaphor, and cognitive style. In P. Mussen (Ed.), *Handbook of child psychology* (4th ed., Vol. 3, pp. 630–706). New York: Wiley.

Langley, P. W., Simon, H. A., Bradshaw, G. L., & Zytkow, J. (1987). *Scientific discovery: Computational explorations of the cognitive processes.* Cambridge, MA: MIT Press.

Lesgold, A. M. (1984). Acquiring expertise. In J. R. Anderson & S. M. Kosslyn (Eds.), *Tutorials in learning and memory* (pp. 31–61). New York: W. H. Freeman.

Lewis, M. W., & Anderson, J. R. (1985). Discrimination of operator schemata in problem solving: Learning from examples. *Cognitive Psychology, 17,* 26–65.

Lindberg, M. (1980). Is knowledge base development a necessary and sufficient condition for memory development? *Journal of Experimental Psychology, 30,* 401–410.

Linden, M., & Wittrock, M. C. (1981). The teaching of reading comprehension according to the model of generative learning. *Reading Research Quarterly, 17,* 44–57.

Loftus, E. F. (1979). *Eyewitness testimony.* Cambridge, MA: Harvard University Press.

Logan, G. D. (1988). Toward an instance theory of automatization. *Psychological Review, 95,* 492–527.

Lynch, G., & Baudry, M. (1984). The biochemistry of memory: A new and specific hypothesis. *Science, 224,* 1057–1063.

Mandler, J. M. (1984). *Stories, scripts, and scenes: Aspects of schema theory.* Hillsdale, NJ: Erlbaum.

Mandler, J. M., & Johnson, N. S. (1977). Remembrance of things passed: Story structure and recall. *Cognitive Psychology, 9,* 111–151.

Mannies, N. (1986). Brain theory and learning. *Clearinghouse, 60,* 127–130.

Marcus, S. (1988). *Automating knowledge acquisition for expert systems.* Boston, MA: Klaver.

Markman, E. M. (1981). Comprehension monitoring. In P. Dickson (Ed.), *Children's oral communication skills* (pp. 61–84). New York: Academic Press.

Markman, E. M. (1985). Comprehension monitoring: Developmental and educational issues. In S. F. Chipman, J. W. Segal, & R. Glaser (Eds.), *Thinking and learning skills: Volume 2, Research and open questions* (pp. 275–291). Hillsdale, NJ: Erlbaum.

Martindale, C. (1991). *Cognitive psychology: A neural-network approach.* Pacific Grove, CA: Brooks/Cole.

Mayer, R. E. (1983). Can you repeat that? Qualitative and quantitative effects of repetition and advance organizers on learning from science prose. *Journal of Educational Psychology, 75,* 40–49.

Mayer, R. E. (1984). Twenty-five years of research on advance organizers. *Instructional Science, 8,* 133–169.

Mayer, R. E. (1987). *Educational psychology: A cognitive approach.* Boston: Little, Brown.

Mayer, R. E. (1992). *Thinking, problem solving, cognition* (2nd ed.). New York: W. H. Freeman.

McDaniel, M. A., Einstein, G. O., & Lollis, T. (1988). Qualitative and quantitative considerations in encoding difficulty effects. *Memory and Cognition, 16,* 455–458.

Meichenbaum, D. (1986). Cognitive behavior modification. In F. Kanfer & A. Goldstein (Eds.), *Helping people change: A textbook of methods* (3rd ed., pp. 346–380). New York: Pergamon.

Michalowitz, R. (1989). *The development and cultivation of imagination and logical operations in young children.* International Conference on Early Education and Development, Hong Kong. ERIC Document ED313134.

Miller, G. A. (1956). The magical number seven, plus or minus two: Some limits on our capacity for processing information. *Psychological Review, 63,* 81–97.

Myers, M., & Paris, S. B. (1978). Children's metacognitive knowledge about reading. *Journal of Educational Psychology, 70,* 680–690.

Nelson, K. (1978). How children represent knowledge of their world in and out of language: A preliminary report. In R. S. Siegler (Ed.), *Children's thinking: What develops* (pp. 255–273). Hillsdale, NJ: Erlbaum.

Nelson, K. (1986). *Event knowledge.* Hillsdale, NJ: Erlbaum.

Neves, D. M., & Anderson, J. R. (1981). Knowledge compilation: Mechanisms for the automatization of cognitive skills. In J. R. Anderson (Ed.), *Cognitive skills and their acquisition* (pp. 57–84). Hillsdale, NJ: Erlbaum.

Ormrod, J. E. (1990). *Human learning: Principles, theories, and educational applications.* Columbus, OH: Merrill.

Paivio, A. (1979). *Imagery and verbal processes.* New York: Holt, Rinehart & Winston.

Paivio, A. (1986). *Mental representations: A dual coding approach.* New York: Oxford University Press.

Parasuraman, R., & Davies, D. R. (1984). *Variables of attention.* New York: Academic Press.

Peper, R., & Mayer, R. E. (1978). Note taking as a generative activity. *Journal of Educational Psychology, 70,* 514–522.

Piaget, J. (1952). *The origins of intelligence in children.* New York: International Universities Press.

Polson, M. C., & Richardson, J. J. (1988). *Foundations of intelligent tutoring systems.* Hillsdale, NJ: Erlbaum.

Posner, M. I. (1989). *Foundations of cognitive science.* Cambridge, MA: MIT Press.

Posner, M. I., Peterson, S. E., Fox, P. T., & Raichle, M. E. (1988). Localization of cognitive operations in the human brain. *Science, 240,* 1627–1631.

Pressley, M., & Levin, J. R. (Eds.). (1983). *Cognitive strategy research: Psychological foundations.* New York: Springer-Verlag.

Pressley, M., McDaniel, M. A., Turnure, J. E., Wood, E., & Ahman, M. (1987). Generation and precision of elaboration: Effects on intentional and incidental learning. *Journal of Experimental Psychology: Learning, Memory and Cognition, 13,* 291–300.

Pylyshyn, Z. W. (1986). *Computation and cognition: Toward a foundation for cognitive science.* Cambridge, MA: MIT Press.

Quillan, M. R. (1969). The teaching language comprehender: A simulation program and theory of language. *Communications of the Association for Computing Machinery, 12,* 459–476.

Raaijmakers, J. G. W., & Shiffrin, R. M. (1992). Models for recall and recognition. *Annual Review of Psychology, 43,* 205–234.

Ratcliff, R. A., & McKoon, G. (1989). Memory models, text processing, and cue-dependent retrieval. In J. L. Roediger & F. I. M. Craik (Eds.), *Varieties of memory and consciousness.* Hillsdale, NJ: Erlbaum.

Reed, S. K. (1992). *Cognition* (3rd ed.). Pacific Grove, CA: Brooks/Cole.

Reynolds, R., & Anderson, R. (1982). Influence of questions on the allocation of attention during reading. *Journal of Educational Psychology, 74,* 623–632.

Richards, G. P. (1990). Sustained and selective attention in children with learning disabilities. *Journal of Learning Disabilities, 23*(2), 29–36.

Richardson, J. T. E. (1980). *Mental imagery and human memory.* London: Macmillan.

Richardson-Klavehn, A., & Bjork, R. A. (1988). Measures of memory. *Annual Review of Psychology, 39,* 475–543.

Rock, I. (1984). *Perception.* New York: W. H. Freeman.

Roediger, H. L., & Craik, F. I. M. (1989). *Varieties of memory and consciousness.* Hillsdale, NJ: Erlbaum.

Roland, P. E., & Friberg, L. (1985). Localization of cortical areas activated by thinking. *Journal of Neurophysiology, 53,* 1219–1243.

Ross, B. H. (1987). This is just like that: The use of earlier problems and the separation of similarity effects. *Journal of Experimental Psychology: Learning, Memory, and Cognition, 13,* 629–639.

Rothkopf, E. (1970). The concept of mathemagenic activities. *Review of Educational Research, 40,* 315–336.

Sadoski, M., Goetz, E. T., & Fritz, J. B. (1993). Impact of concreteness on comprehensibility, interest, and memory for text: Implications for dual coding theory and text design. *Journal of Educational Psychology, 85,* 291–304.

Sagerman, N., & Mayer, R. (1987). Forward transfer of different reading strategies evoked by adjunct questions in science text. *Journal of Educational Psychology, 79,* 189–191.

Salomon, G. (1983). Television watching and mental effort: A social psychological view. In J. Bryant & D. R. Anderson (Eds.), *Children's understanding of television* (pp. 181–196). New York: Academic Press.

Schank, R. C. (1982). *Dynamic memory: A theory of reminding and learning in computers and people.* New York: Cambridge University Press.

Schank, R. C., & Abelson, R. P. (1977). *Scripts, plans, goals, and understanding.* Hillsdale, NJ: Erlbaum.

Schunk, D. H. (1991). *Learning theories: An educational perspective.* New York: Merrill.

Schwartz, B., & Reisberg, D. (1991). *Learning and memory.* New York: Norton.

Sekuler, R., & Blake, R. (1985). *Perception.* New York: Knopf.

Shepard, R. N., & Cooper, L. A. (1983). *Mental images and their transformations.* Cambridge, MA: MIT Press.

Shiffrin, R. M., & Cook, J. R. (1978). Short-term forgetting of item and order information. *Journal of Verbal Learning and Verbal Behavior, 6,* 156–163.

Shiffrin, R. M., & Schneider, W. (1977). Controlled and automatic human information processing: II. Perceptual learning, automatic attending, and a general theory. *Psychological Review, 84,* 127–190.

Shuell, T. J. (1981). Dimensions of individual differences. In F. H. Harley & N. J. Gordon (Eds.), *Psychology and education: The state of the union* (pp. 32–59). Berkeley, CA: McCutchan.

Siegler, R. S. (1991). *Children's thinking* (2nd ed.). Englewood Cliffs, NJ: Prentice Hall.

Siegler, R. S., & Jenkins, E. (1989). *How children discover new strategies.* Hillsdale, NJ: Erlbaum.

Sleeman, D., & Brown, J. S. (Eds.). (1982). *Intelligent tutoring systems.* New York: Academic Press.

Smith, E. E., Shoben, E. J., & Rips, L. J. (1974). Structure and process in semantic memory: A featural model for semantic decision. *Psychological Review, 81,* 214–241.

Spires, H. A., Gallini, J., & Riggsbee, J. (1992). Effects of schema-based and text structure-based cues on expository prose comprehension in fourth graders. *Journal of Experimental Education, 60,* 307–320.

Springer, S. P., & Deutsch, G. (1981). *Left brain, right brain.* San Francisco: W. H. Freeman.

Squire, L. R. (1987). *Memory and brain.* New York: Oxford University Press.

Stillings, N. A., Feinstein, M. H., Garfield, J. L., Rissland, E. L., Rosenbaum, D. A., Weisler, S. E., & Baker-Ward, L. (1987). *Cognitive science: An introduction.* Cambridge, MA: MIT Press.

Straus, M. A., Gelles, R. J., & Steinmetz, S. K. (1980). *Behind closed doors: Violence in the American family.* Garden City, NY: Anchor/Doubleday.

Stuart, A., & Pumfrey, P. D. (1987). Reflectivity-impulsivity and problem solving by primary school children. *Research in Education, 38,* 27–50.

Tierney, R. J., & Cunningham, J. W. (1984). Research on teaching reading comprehension. In P. D. Pearson (Ed.), *Handbook of reading research* (pp. 609–655). New York: Longman.

Triesman, A. M. (1960). Contextual cues in selective listening. *Quarterly Journal of Experimental Psychology, 12,* 242–248.

Triesman, A. M., & Gelade, G. (1980). A feature-integration theory of attention. *Cognitive Psychology, 12,* 97–136.

Tulving, E. (1983). *Elements of episodic memory.* London: Oxford University Press.

Tulving, E. (1985). On the classification problem in learning and memory. In L. Nilsson & T. Archer (Eds.), *Perspectives on learning and memory* (pp. 73–101). Hillsdale, NJ: Erlbaum.

Walker, N. (1986). Direct retrieval from elaborated memory. *Memory and Cognition, 14,* 321–328.

Wang, A. Y., Thomas, M. H., & Ouellette, J. A. (1992). Keyword mnemonic and retention of second-language vocabulary words. *Journal of Educational Psychology, 84,* 520–528.

Weinert, F. E., & Kluwe, R. H. (Eds.). (1987). *Metacognition, motivation and understanding.* Hillsdale, NJ: Erlbaum.

Wenger, E. (1987). *Artificial intelligence and tutoring systems.* Los Altos, CA: Morgan Kaufmann.

Whaley, J. F. (1981). Story grammars and reading instruction. *The Reading Teacher, 34,* 762–771.

Winston, P. H. (1984). *Artificial intelligence.* Reading, MA: Addison-Wesley.

Witkin, H. A., Moore, C. A., Goodenough, D. R., & Cox, P. W. (1977). Field-dependent and field-independent cognitive styles and their educational implications. *Review of Educational Research, 47,* 1–64.

Wittrock, M. C. (1978). The cognitive movement in instruction. *Educational Psychologist, 13,* 15–29.

Wittrock, M. C. (1984). Learning as a generative activity. *Educational Psychologist, 11,* 87–95.

Yuille, J. C. (1983). *Imagery, memory, and cognition: Essays in honor of Allan Paivio.* Hillsdale, NJ: Erlbaum.

© Superstock

# Culture and Language

# Chapter Outline

# Learning Objectives

5.1 Identify aspects of culture that create diversity among students.

5.2 Describe three approaches to multiculturalism.

5.3 Explain how teachers' expectations of students of different cultures can influence school achievement.

5.4 Identify the main components of language.

5.5 List the assumptions underlying four theoretical explanations of language acquisition.

5.6 Describe the stages of language acquisition.

5.7 Describe how the family helps children become literate.

5.8 Explain how teachers can help students develop language.

5.9 Describe the effects of bilingualism, dialects, and social class differences on language development.

# Preview

This chapter examines how the relationship between culture and language influences students' experiences in school. Cultural diversity has important implications for educational reform because the cultural group to which an individual belongs plays a critical role in learning and achievement. We integrate some of the latest theories about language and learning as they relate to cultural differences and explain how cultural diversity influences teaching. We also examine aspects of cultural diversity that create conflict or misunderstanding for teachers and students and discuss how teachers can help students of different cultural backgrounds learn more effectively.

In this chapter we also examine the stages of language acquisition, the relationship between language, literacy, and thought, and the role of communication in the classroom. The chapter concludes with an examination of the controversy surrounding bilingual education and teaching English as a second language. ◉

# Culture

**Culture** is something human beings make, not something that occurs in nature (Cushner, McClelland, & Safford, 1992). It is a system of shared beliefs, values, and customs that people in a social group collectively construct. Children learn the values of their culture from adults in subtle ways through example and modeling.

Cultures contain many subcultures, which are sometimes defined by ethnicity, age, gender, sexual preference, or disability. On a broader scale, language groups (Native Americans, Hispanics, and Asians to name a few) or racial distinctions differentiate cultures. Cultural differences also arise from differences in socioeconomic or educational backgrounds.

The need to know how to teach diverse groups has become more acute as more varied subcultural groups enter our schools. Until recently educators believed that teachers should teach the same curriculum to all students in the United States in the same way. Educators, however, are now challenging the belief that a clearly defined majority culture exists in the United States, thus questioning the assumptions underlying the unified approach to education (Banks, 1994; Banks & Banks, 1993; Hernandez, 1989; Sleeter & Grant, 1994).

## Cultural Diversity and Minority Status

In recent decades, the population of the United States has increased in racial and ethnic diversity. In 1990 12.1 percent of the population was African American, 9.0 percent Hispanic, 2.9 percent Asian, 71.2 percent non-Hispanic White, .8 percent Native Americans, and 3.9 percent others. Many of the immigrants of the last two decades came from non-European countries (Sleeter & Grant, 1994). According to Sleeter and Grant (1994), separation of individuals based on socioeconomic status dominates our society.

The entrance of many diverse groups into the United States has enriched our cultural resources, but it has also caused misunderstandings and confusion. Social perceptions of minority groups have become more favorable, but African Americans, Hispanics, and Native Americans remain outside the economic and political mainstream. In 1990, for example, African Americans attained an educational level only slightly below that of whites, but the median income of African American families was 60 percent of the median income of white families. Statistics show similar findings for Hispanic families and even more disastrous results for Native Americans.

Despite the perception that sexism, racism, and bias against people who are different from the majority have diminished in recent years, progress to eliminate prejudice has been slow and, in many instances, ineffective. Discrimination against people of color continues despite national efforts to eliminate bias in the workplace. Children of color are more likely to be poor (National Commission on Children, 1991) and live in homes with one parent or with adults who are unemployed. Persistent racial inequality continues to affect adversely a whole new generation. Children tend to grow up to occupy the same social class position as their parents.

Women and persons with disabilities also suffer from similar bias in the workplace. Adults with disabilities are overrepresented in low socioeconomic groups, often working only part-time or for low wages (Sleeter & Grant, 1994). Although women are increasingly assuming roles as heads of households, their salaries continue to lag behind those of males.

## Membership in Subcultural Groups: The Development of Several Selves

Most people in our society belong to more than one cultural group; individuals identify in varying degrees with several subgroups, depending on their experiences and their family's general orientation. Suppose you were a U.S.-born female member of the middle class with parents of Italian descent, and that you grew up in an

**5.1** ◎

*Identify aspects of culture that create diversity among students.*

Identify the groups that make up your own cultural identity. Include gender, social class, ethnicity, religion, education, or any other affiliation that forms a cultural description of you.

Why do you think this reconsideration of the curriculum has occurred in recent years?

**Figure 5.1**
Factors influencing students'
sense of self.

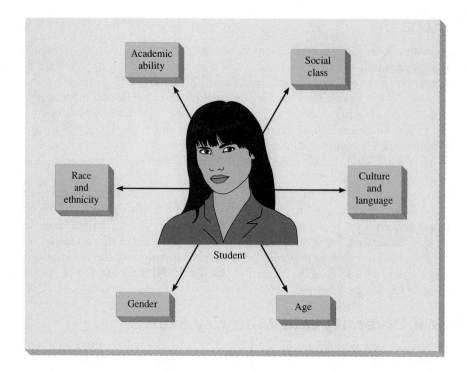

urban community and attended a local community college. How would you rank your affiliations with the majority cultural group and the subgroups defined by ethnicity, social class, education, and gender?

Suppose you were male, had been born in Italy, had parents who had immigrated to this country in recent years, and had no more than a high school education. Would your alliances change? In all likelihood, the amount of time your family had to assimilate into the majority culture would influence how strongly you felt attached to your ethnic background. Also, the extent to which your economic situation differs from your family's may alter your response. In addition, your educational attainment, your family's expectations, or society's emphasis might affect the expectations of your role as a female or male. How would you rank your affiliations with cultural subgroups if you were African American, male, from an economically poor family living in Alabama, and were college educated with advanced degrees in business or law? The roles we assume as members of several subgroups become complex in an intricate society such as ours.

Students' sense of belonging to a cultural group depends on how schools, families, media, and other relevant sources transmit that culture to them. Multicultural education addresses the complex issues of teaching students with varying backgrounds, differing cultural values, and multidimensional connections to various cultural subgroups.

## Multicultural Education: Reshaping Our Schools

*Describe three approaches to multiculturalism.*

Contemporary educational reform emphasizes **multicultural education** as a viable curriculum for *all* students (Banks, 1994; Banks & Banks, 1993; Nieto, 1992). A multicultural approach is a way to address cultural diversity effectively. While definitions of multiculturalism may differ, the general premise underscores the rights of individuals to be respected for their differences, yet simultaneously recognizing the similarities among individuals (Banks, 1994; Nieto, 1992). The multicultural movement rests on the belief that all cultures have values, beliefs, customs, language, knowledge, and world views that are valid and viable, and that these characteristics reflect the synthesized experiences of a cultural group

Contemporary educational reform emphasizes multicultural education as a viable curriculum for all students.

© Steve Skjold

over time. These beliefs and ideals become part of the culture because a group of individuals value and share them; all cultural groups develop common understandings that benefit the group as a whole.

Advocates of multicultural education base their assumptions on theories of cultural pluralism and cultural transmission. One theory holds that when minority cultural groups come into contact with a majority cultural group, over time the values of the majority group displace the values and beliefs of the minority group. This theory emphasizes the process of **assimilation,** and many of the assumptions underlying our educational system validate this process as natural and appropriate. Although there is some support for this theory (e.g., the social and economic integration of second-generation immigrants), assimilation is not a general rule in the United States (Sleeter & Grant, 1994). The United States does not have one language, one set of values, one set of beliefs, or one set of customs. Much of the tension between those who advocate education exclusively in English and those who advocate bilingual education results from different viewpoints about the theory of assimilation (Cushner, McClelland, & Safford, 1992; Sleeter & Grant, 1994).

Another theory proposes that minority groups enter the majority culture through a process of **amalgamation,** or a synthesis of the minority and majority cultures. Although amalgamation is apt to occur over long periods of time, the fact that minority groups have a low status in the society thwarts this process. Some researchers suggest that members of low socioeconomic groups may resist acculturation with the majority culture due to differing historical roots (Bennett, 1995; Ogbu, 1992).

**Cultural pluralism** is the theory that different cultural groups maintain their own culture while participating in the majority culture. This theory does not account for the development of a changing majority culture.

In a **modified cultural pluralism** approach, theorists attempt to explain group life in terms of cultural pluralism with a shared culture among all groups. According to this theory, educators should incorporate ideas from many cultural groups for all students and give the shared culture a prominent role in the education of all.

## Sociocultural and Psychological Aspects of Cognition

In addition to integrating cultural diversity into the curriculum, educators must attend to the role culture plays in the social and cognitive behavior of their students. Cole (1985) has called Vygotsky's zone of proximal development the place where "culture and cognition create each other" (p. 146). Culture creates cognition by defining what constitutes appropriate interactions for adults to have with children, so that the cognitive growth of the child is steered toward a set of goals specified by the culture. In our culture, for example, children learn by playing "peek-a-boo" that people exist even when not seen. Wertsch (1991) provides another example by describing how children learn through reciprocal conversation. For show-and-tell, a child brings in a rock. Other children ask questions about the rock: Do you like it? Where did you get it? Gradually, the child learns that certain questions, such as those about the characteristics of the rock, are more important. Children learn this by hearing the kinds of questions the teacher asks: Is it hard? Is it heavy? Will it sink in water? As a result, the child begins to use the language of the classroom without being formally told to do so (Wertsch, 1991). Palinscar and Brown (1984) emphasize the complementary interaction between student and teacher in their discussion of reciprocal teaching.

Cognition creates culture by structuring the social interactions between adult and child. People generate new practices, and ideas are generated that fit into the culture's ideals and mores. Storytelling in the classroom, for example, is particularly effective with children whose culture has a strong tradition of storytelling, such as Hawaiian and Native American cultures. Recent literacy efforts have emphasized the power of storytelling in transmitting knowledge. Au and Kawakami (1991) describe reading lessons in a Hawaiian classroom that consist of "talk-story narrative events," in which teachers and children produce a joint narration in a reading lesson. One child begins and another continues, adding details or another event. As children randomly add to the narration, the teacher encourages them not only to tell the story but also to talk about it (Diamond & Moore, 1995). Children learn through rich narrative performances of the teacher and their classmates in much the same way they learn by interacting with adults at home. These interactions contrast markedly with the rule-making, turn-taking interactions typical of most classrooms.

How has your culture influenced how *you* think? It may be difficult to answer this question unless you have examined other cultures and considered their perspective of the world.

Recent literacy efforts have emphasized the power of story-telling in transmitting knowledge.
© Tami Dawson/Photo Resource Hawaii

## DIVERSITY MAKES A DIFFERENCE

### Incongruity Between the Student's Culture and the Culture of the Classroom

Cultures determine appropriate social interactions that do not always coincide with school expectations for social behavior. Several Native American communities, for example, emphasize group cooperative effort. Children in these cultures are often confused and embarrassed in a classroom that stresses competition. Asking them to act individually creates conflict between the values of their culture and those of the school. Although Native American children might not be able to explain their perceptions, they often withdraw from competition and fail to behave the way teachers expect.

Teachers can avoid this dilemma by using cooperative learning arrangements, such as group projects, and involving students in planning. This approach conforms better to Native American values than individualistic or competitive organizations (Hernandez, 1989). Setting up classrooms to foster cultural differences permits students to learn in familiar and comfortable ways.

*Annual* **Edition**

unit *4*

**Socialization** refers to the explicit and implicit processes by which children acquire the values and beliefs of their culture and learn how others expect them to behave (Diamond & Moore, 1995). People frequently believe that the socialized forms of behavior they have learned represent the "correct" way. This tendency to hold a viewpoint determined by the perspective of one's own group is called **ethnocentrism.**

Sometimes the customs of one culture are obvious to members of another culture. It is easy, for example, to recognize that the social behavior Asians use to denote deference and respect stems from their set of cultural mores and customs. Cushner, McClelland, and Safford (1992) point out, however, that there are "hidden recurring patterns of behavior and thought" (p. 27) that people find difficult to recognize and explain, and that sometimes lead to misunderstandings and breakdowns in communication between members of different cultures.

People learn the subtle rules of conduct informally by observation and trial and error, and they acquire cultural knowledge through interactions with others. Before entering school, children have mastered a complex set of rules and norms about behavior, language, ideals, and customs. Frequently, these norms differ from those in the schools.

## Teachers' Expectations and Students' Success in School

Teachers' expectations play a significant role in students' success in school. Cazden (1986) warns teachers to distinguish between differential treatment that *individualizes favorably* and differential treatment *based on bias*. If a student has specific needs, it is appropriate to provide differential treatment. Otherwise, differential treatment is biased.

Teachers often communicate expectations in subtle, implicit ways. They may differentiate between boys and girls (Sadker & Sadker, 1985; Sadker, Sadker, & Klein, 1991), students of lower- and middle-class membership (Podell & Soodak, 1993), and students from minority and majority cultures (Hernandez, 1989).

Teachers commonly assume that boys outperform girls in mathematics. Although boys still show a slight advantage, the difference has diminished (Linn & Hyde, 1989; Mills, Ablard, & Stumpf, 1993). Among African Americans, however, girls outperform boys, and among Asian Americans, boys and girls perform at the same level (Grossman & Grossman, 1994; Yee, 1992).

When teachers treat students differently, two things happen: (a) Teachers' expectations become self-fulfilling, and (b) students develop a self-image that perpetuates the differential treatment, particularly when applied to high and low achievers

5.3
*Explain how teachers' expectations of students of different cultures can influence school achievement.*

*Annual* **Edition**

unit *5*

Can you recall instances when a teacher treated you differently from other students? Was the differential treatment due to your needs or due to the teacher's bias?

*A*+

(Good & Brophy, 1991). Good and Brophy (1991) found that teachers usually have accurate expectations about their students and adjust inaccurate expectations when given additional information.

Teachers who *do* discriminate often form their expectations about individual students early in the school year, sometimes based on information about achievement levels, race, socioeconomic status, ethnicity, gender, speech characteristics, or labels (Good & Brophy, 1991).

In the case of low achievers, teachers communicate their expectations by waiting less time for low achievers to respond to questions, giving them answers, criticizing them for failure, rarely praising them for success, asking them simple questions, and seating them further from the teacher. In contrast, teachers give high achievers more time to respond and to think about their answers and usually encourage them to elaborate. Teachers allow high achievers more opportunity to perform publicly, give them more assignments that encourage high levels of thinking, and give them more feedback. These same teacher behaviors occur regardless of students' gender (Sadker & Sadker, 1985). Teachers interact more with boys than with girls and give boys more approval, more attention, more detailed instructions, and ask boys more questions. Low-achieving boys, however, often receive criticism and reprimands. Some students come to believe that teachers' expectations accurately describe their ability.

Knowledge of cultural differences can improve teachers' attitudes toward students and change their expectations. Hernandez (1989) urges teachers to integrate the curriculum both *inside* and *outside* the classroom, by making connections between students' "real life" experiences and their classroom experiences.

Be careful not to let your knowledge of cultural differences influence your judgments about individual students. There is as much variation of behavior *within* as *between* cultural groups (Banks & Banks, 1993; Cushner, McClelland, & Safford, 1992). Native American or Hispanic individuals can be competitive, for example, even though their cultures encourage cooperation. Individual female students will excel in mathematics even though males on the average score higher on mathematics tests. Similarly, not all Asian students excel in mathematics and science, nor are they all hardworking or passive (Yee, 1992). Teachers must understand their students' cultural backgrounds, but at the same time remain sensitive to students as unique individuals.

# Language

5.4 ◎

*Identify the main components of language.*

By the time children enter kindergarten, most of them have already mastered one of the most demanding tasks they will encounter in their entire lifetimes. They have learned to speak the language of their culture well enough to communicate their needs to others easily and effectively. And they have learned to do so without any formal instruction.

As children mature, they increase their vocabulary and their understanding of how their language is structured, but the astonishing fact remains that they have acquired a large portion of their knowledge of language by the time they have reached the age of 5. Kindergartners already have a sense of the basic structure of their language and have acquired a vocabulary of a thousand words or more. This remarkable feat should be apparent to any adult who has tried to learn the meanings of even a dozen new words or who has tried to learn a second language. Major changes, however, in language competence occur throughout the school years as well.

An important transition occurs between the ages of 6 and 9 (Wood, 1992), when children begin to develop an awareness of language apart from their own immediate experiences. Furthermore, language, and in particular written language, continues to develop throughout later childhood and adolescence.

## TEACHERS ROUNDTABLE

# "I Teach Awareness, Respect, and Tolerance of Other Cultures"

**SK:** How does the cultural diversity of your students affect your teaching?

**Donna:** Cultural diversity is a big issue for me every day, because my school is culturally diverse in the truest sense of the word. I have [native-born American] children from a variety of ethnic backgrounds, as well as children who have recently arrived in the United States as immigrants. Among my students are Albanian children, Hispanic children, and African American children. I feel it's one of my responsibilities to provide culturally diverse materials every day. On a regular basis, I look for culturally diverse materials. When I go to the library to pick out books for my students, my students' diversity is central to my selections. This is a topic that I would get on top of a mountain and shout about: Children need for school to reflect their culture. Let them see and hear about their culture—the artists or authors of their cultures; it's really important for children to identify with role models.

**Mary:** I emphasize respecting one another. We don't have the usual classroom "rules." Our classroom rule is "hurt no living thing." I find this rule—as opposed to "raise your hand," "don't call out," all that nonsense—is beautiful.

**Angela:** In my curriculum, I teach awareness, respect, and tolerance of other cultures. When we have holidays, my students know all about it—all of the holidays are discussed, but particularly those of the groups that exist within our school. I do a great deal of traveling, and I make sure the students know where I'm going and why I'm going there. When I come back, I share things with them, and they become aware of other places in the world.

**Anthony:** An administrator once told me that, in a classroom, you have to be like a family. I learned this was true. When those children come into my room in September, they become my family. We live and work together as a family for 10 months.

**Angela:** I agree. I am fortunate enough to be able to work with the same children for many years. I'm also able to work with their families and I know their siblings. As a family, we developed the idea and practice of always treating each other with respect.

**Irwin:** The variety of students makes you look at things in a much more global way. I think the things we teach today and the way I approach things are a lot different than when I started. It would be naive to teach a class, as I'm doing in American history now, saying that the westward movement in the United States was simply a glorified bunch of Americans going west, and neglect the fact that a Northern Mexican empire was destroyed. And that there were Sioux and Crow nations that existed before. So I think the diversity in our schools has made us much more aware and has encouraged us to search for

material we hope is accurate. You can't change history, but you have to incorporate more inclusive material than when I first started. This requires a great deal of searching—we have acquired a large number of textbooks, but as soon as we get them, they are out of date. You really have to develop files. I work with many other social studies teachers, and we make material available in files for our social studies department so everyone can use and share them.

**SK:** Of course, diversity has many aspects. How do you deal with the diversity in abilities among the students you teach?

**Mary:** My school groups homogeneously, which I don't like. I don't think the school administrators should say, "Okay, all the bright students are here, and we'll put all the 'slow' children there." I think that no matter what kind of children you have, they teach one another. We are not the only teacher in the classroom. I have 25 children and I have 25 teachers.

**Irwin:** I've taught high school students who could barely read, and I've taught students who are reading Hobbes' *Leviathan*. My belief is that ability level very much affects the way you teach.

## Psychological Aspects of Language Acquisition

Theories about how children initially acquire language rely heavily on prevailing psychological theories and, therefore, reflect more general points of view about how children learn. Since children in all cultures learn language, it is not surprising that language acquisition has long been the object of much study and fascination. Reports from as early as the fifth century B.C. have confirmed this interest (Dale, 1976).

Rather than memorize language, children *construct* language from their experiences in interacting with others.

Two premises underlie language acquisition. First, children do not merely speak a simplified version of adult language; they speak a language they construct themselves. Second, when confronted with language in their environment, they try to make sense of the language so they can use it. These two premises form the basis for the way much learning occurs.

### Hypothesis Testing

Learning language involves hypothesis testing and forces the child to interact actively with the environment. According to Piaget, language development occurs in much the same way that children's thinking develops. Most student learning occurs gradually as students make approximations to what they are learning and increase their understanding by receiving confirming feedback. Other language processes, such as reading and writing, require the same kind of interaction between the learner and print or text (Rice, 1993; Santrock, 1995).

## The Universality of Language Acquisition

One of the most fascinating characteristics of language is its universality (Howe, 1992). All people go through almost exactly the same phases in acquiring language regardless of what language they are learning and regardless of the nature of the culture in which the learning takes place. Thus, a child in Tennessee learning English goes through the same sequence of language development as a child in Tokyo learning Japanese, or a child in Moscow learning Russian.

Children in all cultures appear predisposed to acquire language and in fact may be born with an innate mechanism that is "programmed" to learn language. Considerable evidence suggests that the ability to learn language is grounded in the biological makeup of human beings (Coltheart, 1987; Lenneberg, 1967).

## Language: A Uniquely Human Ability

The most compelling evidence supporting the idea that we have an innate mechanism for learning language is that human beings are the only species capable of learning language. Periodic media coverage of "talking apes" may appeal to the general public, but there is no scientific proof that any animal other than humans has the capacity for speech. Success in training some primates to use sign language has generated interest, but so far there is not enough evidence to conclude that primates have the capacity for language (Seidenberg, 1986).

## The Components of Language

Before discussing how language develops, let us define some basic terms to describe various aspects of language. All languages, despite their differences, have common aspects: sound, structure, and meaning.

### Phonemes

The smallest units of sound in a language are called **phonemes.** Although the English alphabet contains only 26 letters, one must be able to produce approximately 44 different phonemes or sounds in order to speak English.

English differs from some other languages, such as Russian, in which every sound is represented by a single letter. English also differs from languages such as Italian or Spanish, which are phonetic languages; that is, the same combination of letters always represents the same sound. Although it may be harder to learn to speak English as a second language than some other languages, there is little evidence that English is more difficult to learn to read than any other language.

## Morphemes

**Morphemes** are the most basic units of meaning in a language. A word (e.g., *book*) is a morpheme because it conveys a single unit of meaning ("a set of bound pages"). However, *s* at the ending of a noun is also a morpheme because it conveys the meaning that there are more than one. Thus, the word *books* contains two morphemes, *book* and *s*.

## Syntax

**Syntax** refers to ways in which words are organized and sequenced to produce meaningful sentences. Because we understand the syntax of English, we know that in the sentence, "Fran ate the cheeseburger," Fran did the eating (that is, the cheeseburger did not eat Fran). Different languages have different rules governing word order, which sometimes makes second language learning difficult. People learning a foreign language sometimes make the mistake of using the vocabulary of the second language but the syntax of their native language.

Sometimes word order follows custom, not rules; for example, in English we say "What are you looking for" rather than "For what are you looking?" not because of rules, but because of custom.

## Semantics

**Semantics** refers to the system of meanings of words within a context. When we say "Karen flew down the street in her new car," we know that *flew* has a different meaning than it does in the sentence "The pilot flew to Toronto and back in the same day." Note that both semantics and morphemes are linguistic concepts dealing with meaning. Semantics, however, focuses on units of meaning associated with the relationships among words, whereas morphemes are units of meaning associated with the components that make up a single word.

## Pragmatics

**Pragmatics** pertains to social aspects of language, that is, the relationship of language to the situation in which it is used, the intentions of the speaker, and the needs and background knowledge of the listener. Suppose you were to speak at a PTA meeting and had difficulty getting the attention of your audience. The language you would use to get the audience's attention would probably differ markedly from the language you would use to get the attention of disruptive students in your classroom. Researchers have begun to focus on language usage within various social contexts and the notion of communicative competence, a topic described later in this chapter.

How does your use of language vary in different contexts? Do you speak differently to friends than you would in a job interview? Specify how you would use language differently.

# Theoretical Approaches to Language Acquisition

The various theories about language acquisition can be categorized to help clarify their differences. Menyuk (1977) suggests four categories representing different explanations for language learning: biological, cognitive, sociocultural, and behavioral.

5.5 ◎

*List the assumptions underlying four theoretical explanations of language acquisition.*

## Biological Basis for Language Acquisition

Some evidence suggests that the structure of the brain plays a role in the development of language (Lenneberg, 1967; Munsell, 1988). It is not clear, however, whether these structures are present at birth for specific language development or whether they take on unique features for language learning as the infant grows within a specific language environment. Gleitman (1986) has uncovered much evidence that supports the biological predisposition theory.

Three of her findings are particularly compelling: (a) language learning appears to proceed in a uniform manner regardless of the language being learned or the culture in which the learning takes place, (b) people do not simply imitate the language they hear, but, rather, they construct their own language, which gradually approximates with increasing accuracy the language of their culture, and (c) people learn to generalize language rules and construct grammatically correct sentences they have never heard or read before.

Additional evidence of the critical period of language acquisition comes from individuals who have had brain injuries affecting language. When children and adults have similar injuries, children regain greater language usage and do so faster.

More evidence for the biological approach is the fact that there appears to be a **critical period** of language acquisition (Lenneberg, 1967). It is easier for people to learn language during their first decade than during the remainder of the life span. Compare how quickly a young child learns vocabulary and grammatical rules without formal instruction with your efforts to learn a second language in adolescence or adulthood.

## Cognitive Basis for Language Acquisition

In contrast to a biological theory of language acquisition, cognitive theory attempts to describe and explain language acquisition by examining how individuals comprehend the meaning inherent in language (Bruner, 1975) and how children develop knowledge of morphemes (units of meaning) and semantics (meanings of words in context). Cognitivists believe that language acquisition depends on nonlinguistic aspects of cognitive development and cannot be separated from more general cognitive growth.

From a cognitive perspective, language acquisition occurs as children actively seek ways to express themselves. A child who wishes to express hunger, for example, searches for aspects of the language, such as the words *eat* or *cookie* as a way of conveying "I'm hungry." The invariant sequence of cognitive development, as described by Piaget, supports the cognitive/language relationship that is central to cognitive theories of language development (Slobin, 1973). Chomsky (1969) claims that certain types of operational thought are required to use language.

Research on concept formation and language development suggests that children infer the meanings of words by hearing how they are used (Keil, 1989). Children represent the meaning of a word in terms of their mental concept of that word. Cognitive theorists argue that children must use induction to acquire language.

Children also overgeneralize rules when they form concepts, so that a "dog" can be all animals (donkeys, horses, etc.). As they begin to notice features of different animals, they begin to attach other names (lions, tigers, giraffes). Sometimes, children *undergeneralize;* they use a word or name too narrowly, as, for example, when they believe two people cannot have the same name or when they think "kitty" refers only to their own cat whose name is Kitty (Santrock, 1995).

Evidence supporting the cognitive approach to language acquisition comes from the **overgeneralizations** that children use (Goodluck, 1986). Overgeneralization is the application of rules to situations beyond those for which the rules are appropriate. English is replete with *irregulars,* or words that are exceptions to the usual grammatical rules (e.g., the plural of *mouse* is *mice,* not *mouses*—unless you are talking about computer peripherals and not small animals).

As a result of hearing adults use language, children infer various language rules, such as adding *ed* to a verb to change it to the past tense. The child then applies this rule to all verbs. So, typically, children will spontaneously say, "We runned to the park," even though they have probably never heard an adult use the word *runned.* In other words, the child is testing a hypothesis. After discovering the rule, the child uses it, overgeneralizes it, and gradually becomes aware that *runned* sounds funny and that adults don't use it. Finally, the child starts to understand that in English some verbs are irregular and adjusts the rule accordingly.

## Sociocultural Basis for Language Acquisition

Theorists who rely on sociocultural ideas consider language primarily a vehicle for communication. Vygotsky (1986) believed that children acquire language mainly as a result of communicating with adults. This position maintains that children need to determine the rules for using language in *particular* contexts or situations. Therefore, children may develop more than one grammar. These theorists examine linguistic *variability* rather than linguistic *universality.* They see language as having many uses and consequently analyze it within various situational contexts (Labov, 1970).

## Behavioral and Social Learning Bases for Language Acquisition

Behaviorists, such as Skinner (1957), regard language acquisition as just one more example of how learning occurs as a result of connecting responses to stimuli. They do not believe that language learning differs from other kinds of learning. From a

## Stages of Language Development in the Classroom

■■ Knowledge of how children acquire lan-
■■ guage will help you determine what
characteristics the learning environment
should have to help students learn language
in informal ways. It can also guide you in developing classroom activities appropriate for
students at various stages of language development (Cook, 1989; Stark, 1989).

Students in the early grades are still developing the basic elements of language, including phonemes, morphemes, and syntax.
If you become an early childhood teacher,
provide students with experiences that encourage language use and with good models
of language use in your own speech. As an
elementary school teacher, you may have to
help students refine grammatical rules for
more complex language structures (e.g., the
conditional tense and embedded sentences
even though most of them already know
the basic rules of grammar). Help students
build their vocabulary and improve their
writing. If you become a high school teacher,
help students develop a more technical vocabulary in the specific fields they are studying and learn the formal rules of written
language.

How you provide explanations, ask questions, and deliver feedback gives students information about language use. Be sure that
your language use is appropriate; use a wide
variety of vocabulary, use a more precise
word rather than a more general one and use
varied sentence structure. Tailor your language to the developmental level of your students so that they can model you.

---

behavioral perspective, children acquire language through the processes of discrimination and generalization. In other words, children learn to speak because they are
reinforced for doing so.

Similarly, social learning theorists, such as Bandura (1986), argue that language learning is a result of imitation of models and vicarious reinforcement.
Clearly, much of language learning does involve imitation, as any parent knows.
How many times does a child imitate a word or expression that the parents have
used, sometimes to the parents' shock and embarrassment?

## Stages of Language Acquisition

In the following sections, we describe the stages that all individuals go through as
they acquire language.

### Early Communication and Babbling

Almost from birth, infants and the adults in their lives communicate with one another (Golinkoff & Hirsch-Pasek, 1990; Molfese, Molfese, & Carroll, 1982). The
communication between infants and adults occurs when babies cry, when adults
and babies exchange eye contact, when an adult hugs a baby, and when an infant
frowns, to give only a few examples.

One of the earliest forms of communication occurs when the infant smiles in
response to the mother's smile (Spitz & Wolf, 1946). Mothers talk to their infants
as if they were trying to engage the infant in conversation, and they often ask questions and give infants a chance to respond, even though they know their child cannot yet speak (Snow, 1988).

From about the age of 3 months, babies begin **babbling** (Brown, 1973). As the
infant matures, babbling takes on specific characteristics and represents different
functions for the baby. Some sounds signal basic needs, such as distress, irritation,
or hunger. Others, such as cooing, represent pleasure and finally, some begin to re-
semble real words. Near the age of 6 months, speech-like words increase and general babbling decreases.

5.6 ◎
*Describe the stages of language
acquisition.*

Babbling tends to follow a pattern,
beginning with front-of-the-mouth
sounds, such as *ba* and *ma*,
followed by *da* and *ta*, and then
more difficult-to-produce sounds.

Almost from birth, infants and the adults in their lives communicate with one another.

© Laura Dwight/Corbis Media

Even infants who are born with hearing impairment engage in babbling, despite their inability to hear the sounds they make—a fact that supports the biological theory of early language acquisition. On the other hand, their babbling declines over time, a fact that supports behavioral and social learning theories of language development.

## First Words and Holophrases

As children with normal hearing approach their first birthday, they use speech sounds heard in the environment instead of babbling. Children typically say their first words between the ages of 1 year and 15 months. A child's first words usually consist of one- or two-syllable consonant-vowel sounds, such as *dada* or *mama*. When children utter these words, they begin attaching them to persons or things and start developing a vocabulary of many isolated words. Children use one-word speech, called **holophrases,** as a substitute for whole phrases or sentences to convey their thoughts.

## Telegraphic Speech

From about 1½ to 2 years of age, children use two-word phrases, generally consisting of a noun and a verb or adjective. These two-word and, later, three-word phrases are called **telegraphic speech** (Brown, 1973) and represent whole thoughts or sentences.

At this point children rapidly increase their use of words to communicate thoughts. Two-word utterances, such as "Daddy hat" and "Mommy go," can represent a host of ideas or requests, such as "I want Daddy's hat" or "I'm wearing Daddy's hat" and "I want to go with Mommy" or "Mommy can go." By the time children have reached the age of 2 to 2½, they are adding more grammatical structure to their sentences and are becoming more precise.

Children now begin to follow the rules of the language and often overgeneralize (Goodluck, 1986). Children may attach an *s* to nouns to indicate that the noun is plural, overregularizing by saying such things as *gooses* instead of *geese,* or *mouses* instead of *mice.* These overgeneralizations indicate that the child has grasped the essential rules of the language but has yet to learn the exceptions. By age 5, children are competent conversationalists. During the middle and later childhood years, children meet the language demands for reading and writing.

**Figure 5.2**
Milestones of language acquisition.

| Age range | Milestones |
|---|---|
| 3 to 6 months | Interested in sounds and voices |
| 5 to 6 months | Babbles; communicates needs through crying and body language |
| 6 to 9 months | Begins to understand words (receptive language) |
| 9 to 12 months | Begins to understand simple directions and questions ("Where's Daddy?") |
| 10 to 15 months | Begins to produce first words |
| 15 to 24 months | Begins to produce two-word utterances; understanding of words continues to grow |

**Figure 5.3**
Early vocabulary development.

| Age range | Skills |
|---|---|
| 12 to 26 months | Child produces utterances that follow adult noun-verb sequencing |
| 27 to 30 months | Child begins to produce plurals, past tense, some simple prepositions (e.g., *in* and *on*) |
| 31 to 36 months | Child produces pronouns, yes-no questions, negatives, imperatives, wh— questions |
| 36 months and above | Child produces more grammatically complex sentences with correct syntax |

© Glenn Bernhardt.

"No, Timmy, not 'I sawed the chair'; it's 'I saw the chair' or 'I have seen the chair.'"

## Language Development in Middle and Later Childhood

As children mature, they add clauses and compound sentences and, during middle childhood, master some of the more elusive constructions in English, such as passive voice, embedded clauses, and directives (Chomsky, 1969; Liebling, 1988). Reading and writing, rather than just oral language, exert an increasing influence on children's language learning during their school years.

Between the ages of 5 and 7, children discover that language is independent of experience and can be used to tell others what they themselves think or feel. At about the age of 7, children begin to use language for a wide range of purposes and to understand the subtle relationships signaled by such words as *although, however, if,* and *since.* They also use language to explain, question, and explore relationships.

Language development continues into adulthood. By the time children reach the middle grades, they begin to think about language beyond their most immediate experiences. They no longer tie language to only their actions and perceptions but become more analytical of words and their meanings (Santrock, 1995). You can capitalize on children's growing ability to understand abstract language when you teach social studies and science, which require that students understand concepts outside of their particular background.

Students in middle and later childhood also use more complex syntax, such as subjunctives ("If I were king"), comparatives (*bigger, smaller*) and passives (Chomsky, 1969; Santrock, 1995). Wood (1992) proposes that between the ages of 6 and 9 children's language development advances from skill in conversation, which is collaborative, to skill in the use of linguistic devices, such as narration, exposition, or other autonomous speech. Students' implicit knowledge of language also occurs at this time. For example, at this point the ability to tell a story (narrate) requires an awareness that a context must be developed for the listener or audience.

### Adolescence and Adulthood

Between the ages of 13 and 17, students' competence in written language exceeds their competence in spoken language. Vocabulary usage and understanding improve as adolescents become more competent writers, particularly if they are given opportunities to explore the subtle variations of language meaning and syntax. Adolescence is a critical period for students to increase their ability to formulate more complex concepts, to construct new meanings, and to deal in more abstract ideas (Santrock, 1995). Thought and language consolidate as individuals learn specific bodies of knowledge that rely on precise vocabularies and ways of thinking.

## Language and Thought

The relationship between language and thinking remains unclear. Although there is general agreement that language ability can positively affect one's thinking ability, the specific role that language plays in cognitive processes remains a mystery. We do not know if language is a necessary component of thinking or merely helpful. Nor do we know the extent to which cognitive development underlies language acquisition.

### Which Comes First?

Much philosophical and psychological debate has centered on the question of which comes first, language or thought. The debate resembles the age-old question of which came first, the chicken or the egg. Just as it is clear that there is a connection between the chicken and the egg, it is clear that there is a connection between language and thought. It is the nature of the connection that has prompted so much speculation.

Some (e.g., Piaget & Inhelder, 1969) argue that thought precedes language and that if people couldn't think, they would never acquire language. According to Piaget, thought can occur without language. Children can conceptualize even if they don't know the precise language of the concepts they are conceptualizing. On the other hand, Piaget acknowledges that at an early point in the child's development, language and thought become closely allied.

Vygotsky (1986) believed language precedes thought. He too acknowledged that language and thought are closely tied, but maintained that thinking cannot occur without some form of language.

The riddle of which comes first may never be solved, but everybody agrees that language *facilitates* thought. Semantic knowledge (knowledge of the meaning of words in specific contexts) is strongly related to thinking. When children begin to learn the meanings of words, they also begin to understand the concepts the words represent.

## Language and Literacy

Let us now focus on language in its written form. Oral language involves speaking and listening. Written language involves writing and reading. Written language forces the communicator to create a context rather than assume a shared context as in conversation.

A major goal of schooling is to produce educated citizens who are competent readers and writers. The term **literacy** refers to the ability to read and write. We define people as literate or illiterate depending on their ability to read and write at a level acceptable to members of their culture. The foundation for becoming literate, however, occurs long before students enter school.

How do you think the meaning of the term *literacy* has changed in recent years? What requirements for reading and writing will be necessary for practical use in the next century?

### Emergent Literacy

**Emergent literacy** refers to the knowledge that children develop about reading and writing through experience with books and other printed matter before they receive formal instruction. Before entering school, children discover that written materials, such as books, magazines, and newspapers, contain printed symbols corresponding to the words they speak and hear in the environment around them (Sulzby & Teale, 1991). In literate societies, young children develop hypotheses about the meaning of written language because they are surrounded naturally by print (Ferreiro & Teborosky, 1982).

The more exposure children receive to printed matter before starting school, the more likely they will profit from the formal reading instruction. The frequency and types of contacts children have with written language before they enter school directly affect their success as students. The literacy events in which the child's family engages are particularly important. The family's actual literacy practices play an instrumental role in determining the ease with which school-age children become literate (Diamond & Moore, 1995).

### The Role of Family Literacy Practices

Children who come from families where reading is a prominent daily activity start school with a "literacy advantage." When parents place their young child on their laps and read aloud to the child, important informal learning occurs. The child begins to acquire essential concepts, such as *reading* and *book*. By the time children with a literacy advantage enter school, they already know that books contain pages filled with print and pictures. They also know that print corresponds to spoken words and pictures depict the meaning of the words. The extent to which children grasp the relationship between print and school learning influences how successful they are in learning to read.

Learning to read and write are important components of the more general acquisition of language in a literate society. You can foster the development of literacy by recognizing the linguistic and cognitive tools students possess and by providing experiences that enhance their growth (Diamond & Moore, 1995; Hennings, 1990).

5.7 ◎

*Describe how the family helps children become literate.*

## Building Linguistic Knowledge

**5.8** ◎

*Explain how teachers can help students develop language.*

■■ You can use many activities to encour-
■■ age students' language development.
Although children have developed the basis
for oral language by the time they enter
school, you can nevertheless have a major impact on increasing students' language competency and linguistic knowledge.

1. Give students many opportunities to
   learn the meaning of words through
   reading, speaking, listening, and writing.
   Students begin to understand the
   different meanings some words have by
   encountering the words in various
   contexts.

2. Have students read and write language
   in various forms, including fiction,
   nonfiction (e.g., biographies), poetry,
   and drama.
3. Read aloud to your students and
   encourage them to read the books you
   have read to them.
4. Students who have difficulty reading
   may benefit from reading their own
   writing. Have students dictate stories to
   you, and then have them read the story
   back. This practice encourages students
   to see the relationship between spoken
   and written words.

Language is a major vehicle for social interaction.

© Alon Reininger/Unicorn Stock Photos

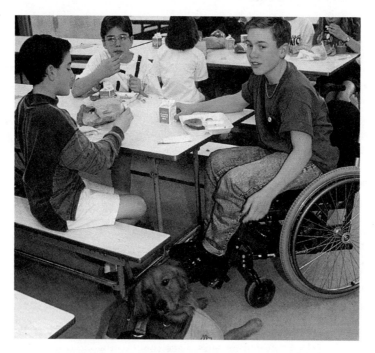

## Language and Communication

The primary function of language is to communicate. People communicate by sending
verbal messages to one another, using language in both its oral and written forms.
Nonverbal signals, such as frowns, smiles, or gestures, may also convey information
(Neill, 1989), but the dominant form of communication is verbal. Numerous factors
determine how we use verbal communication, such as the kind of information to be
conveyed, the social context in which the communication is to take place, and the
nature of the relationship among the persons who are communicating.

### Verbal and Nonverbal Aspects of Communication

Sometimes verbal and nonverbal cues transmit unintentional messages. Although
you would undoubtedly understand the intended meaning of a parent who says,
"There ain't nothing I can do to get my kid to study," you would also probably
note the faulty grammar and conclude that the parent has not had much formal
education. Further, you would likely interpret the message as an indication that the

parent is concerned about the child's future. Nonverbal cues, such as vocal qualities, pronunciation, and intonation sometimes provide information about the speaker's personal characteristics. For example, if you hear an unfamiliar voice when you answer the telephone, you instantly know the speaker's gender, approximate age level, and the likelihood that the person's native language is English.

## Communicative and Linguistic Competence

The term **linguistic competence** refers to how well one knows the structure of a language. A person who is linguistically competent in English knows how to speak and write English in a form that is grammatically and syntactically correct.

**Communicative competence,** a term broader than linguistic competence, consists not only of being able to use grammar correctly but also of knowing when to speak and when not to, where and with whom to speak, what to talk about, and in what manner (Hymes, 1972). Communicative competence is the ability to use and understand language appropriately in a variety of situations.

To communicate competently, one must understand various rules that apply to the act of communicating, such as the rule that people take turns speaking or that certain speech styles are appropriate only in certain social settings. Communicative competence is a dynamic process through which two or more people negotiate meaning, and it applies to written as well as oral language (Savignon, 1983).

### Students' Communicative Competence

Students exhibit varying levels of communicative competence for a number of reasons. The rules for communicating in school often differ from those for communicating at home or in other community settings, especially for students who come from different cultures (Woolfolk, 1985). Schools, however, are ideal places for students to increase their communicative competence. By interacting with teachers and classmates who come from different backgrounds and use language in a variety of ways for a variety of purposes, students acquire a fuller understanding of the process of communication.

One of the most important ideas students learn in school is that communication is a process they can use for numerous purposes, such as explaining, informing, relating experiences, or expressing feelings. Help your students become more competent communicators by designing activities that require them to use language in a variety of ways.

*A*⁺

## Communication in the Classroom

Although teachers use various instructional techniques, including hands-on formats, discovery experiences, audiovisual presentations, and computer-assisted instruction, most learning in the classroom takes place through oral language interactions between teachers and students and among students. The use of language in recitations, lectures, reports, and discussions occurs routinely in most classrooms.

The most common form of communication between teacher and student is recitation, in which the teacher asks questions and students respond (Wood, 1992). Recitation remains the most frequent form of classroom communication regardless of the classroom's organization. It makes no difference if students are seated in desks arranged in straight rows, in small groups or in a large circle, teachers overwhelmingly do most of the talking.

When one examines the differences between talk at home and talk at school, one is struck by the differences in the interactions between adults and children. At home, the child initiates most verbal interactions, but in school the teacher initiates most interactions. In addition, teachers determine the theme or topic that they maintain through the questions they ask (Wood, 1992).

What are the implications of this difference in talk at home and in school? How does the culture of the school differ from the culture of the home?

The purposes of asking questions are different when school and home are compared. In ordinary conversation children ask questions to clarify something in which they are interested. In school, teachers usually ask questions about something that they already know and the child is supposed to answer in a particular way. Teacher questions and conversation questions differ because the aims are different. Teachers can ask questions that provoke thinking or generate reflection. Most teachers, however, ask questions concerned with facts and simple recall (Wood, 1992).

It is possible to learn without verbal communication, but it is difficult to learn without some form of language. Students' competency in using language significantly affects their level of academic achievement (Tough, 1981). Your verbal interactions with students can serve as a model for examining and reflecting upon ideas. Your verbal interactions with students will improve if you are aware of the implicit differences in question asking and conversation that children experience at home and at school.

## Variety of Language Usage

5.9 ◎

*Describe the effects of bilingualism, dialects, and social class differences on language development.*

In classrooms, students vary in their use of language for a variety of reasons, including social class differences, use of dialects, and the language of the home being other than English.

### Social Class Differences

The way in which adults communicate with children at home exerts a powerful influence on children's development of language. The way parents use language depends to a large extent on the family's social class. Parents in different social classes have different views about their children's needs and what skills are important for children to acquire. Consequently, parents from different social classes use language differently in communicating with their children.

Parents of both low and middle social classes use an abbreviated, simple form of language with their children in their daily encounters. Middle-class parents, however, tend to use language that is more consistent with the standard English language used in the schools.

Some researchers argue that the two forms of language usage reflect only slight variations in style of talking and have little connection to intellectual development (Arntson, 1982; Labov, 1970). Among researchers who believe language usage is related to cognitive development, some concede that differences in everyday experiences between lower- and middle-class children have more impact on school success than differences in language usage (Wells, 1986; Wood, 1992).

A study by Wells (1986), known as the Bristol study, found little evidence that *initial* language development differs appreciably as a function of whether children come from lower- or middle-class families. Language differences associated with social class first occurred when children entered school, particularly in test situations, where middle-class students performed better than lower-class students.

Lower-class students may have been unfamiliar with the rules of tests or test situations. Teachers may have perceived lower-class students as having less linguistic ability than their middle-class counterparts and consequently may have interacted with the two groups differently. In any event, by age 10, children's oral language ability bore no relationship to social class, but their academic achievement levels did.

Academically, middle-class children in the Bristol study outperformed lower-class students. Students' success in school, particularly in learning to read and write, was significantly related to the value their families placed on literacy. Since reading and writing skills are important to school success, children whose families valued literacy achieved better in school. Also, students' vocabulary test scores are positively related to social class and to school achievement (Ferreiro & Teborosky, 1982).

## Bilingualism

There are approximately 5,000 languages used in the world today, and bilingual individuals outnumber monolingual individuals. In addition, more people speak English as a second, not a first, language. By the year 2000, 39.5 million people in the United States will have native languages other than English, with most of these people between the ages of 5 and 14 (Hernandez, 1989).

Despite the large number of people in the United States whose first language is not English, our schools do not use this rich language source to encourage all students to learn another language. As of 1980, only 15 percent of all high school students studied a second language. There are fewer *students* of Russian in the United States than there are *teachers* of English in the former Soviet Union (Hernandez, 1989).

## Dialects

**Dialects** are normal variations of speech that evolve within subgroups in most language communities. They are generally tied to specific groups differing in socioeconomic status as well as ethnic or racial membership. Dialects arise as people within a subgroup communicate with one another, sharing commonly held beliefs and perceptions.

Dialects may develop within age groups, professions, regional groups, or ethnic groups. Geography and social class, however, are the main factors that determine dialect. People in some regions of the country speak with such a distinctive accent that listeners can immediately identify where the speakers come from. Consider the difference between a "Southern accent" and a "Western drawl." Or, consider the typical speech of New York ("New Yawk") versus Boston ("Paak your caa in Haavaad Yaad").

Vocabulary may also vary from region to region. People in some parts of the country, for example, say *pancakes* while others say *hotcakes* or *griddle cakes*. A *submarine sandwich* to some is a *grinder* or a *hoagie* to others. Words sometimes take on different meanings, depending on who uses them. The word *bad* means one thing when a college professor says "This paper is bad," but another thing when a teenager says "This record is bad."

Although regional variations are usually tolerated in the schools, social class language differences are not, perhaps because of the attitudes associated with them. Lower-class dialects are often viewed as *deviations* rather than *differences* and are frequently unacceptable in school (Eller, 1989).

All dialects are coherent systems of communication. When people speak a dialect, they have mastered a set of language rules that make up that system. Dialects are subsets of the more generally accepted dialect, which in the United States is known as standard American English, and have more in common with the standard form than not. For the most part, dialects are merely variations or alternatives of the standard form of a language (Torrey, 1983).

The language used in schools usually approximates standard American English. Generally, teachers speak standard American English in the classroom, and authors write textbooks in standard American English. We also expect students to learn to read and write standard American English because one mission of schools is to transmit the generally held standards and beliefs of the overall culture. Difficulties may arise when students fail to shift to the dominant standard dialect at school or when teachers reject the validity of the language the child brings from home (Brice-Heath, 1988; Leibowicz, 1984; Weller & Levi, 1981; Wright, 1983).

## Bilingual and Multilingual Language Learners

In the United States, an increasing number of students come to school speaking English as a second language or speaking no English at all. Students not only vary in their competence in English but also in their competence in their native language. Many students who have recently arrived in the United States have difficulty adjusting to the new culture and trying to learn a new language at the same time. Their adjustment is often complicated by the divergent school backgrounds they bring from their native countries.

The term **limited English proficient** refers to students whose competence in English as a second language is minimal. Students who have limited English proficiency need to learn both the content of the school curriculum and how to speak, read, and write English. Federal law mandates that students with limited English proficiency receive bilingual education, in which instruction in academic subjects takes place partially in English and partially in the student's native language.

In addition to bilingual education programs, some schools have English as a second language (ESL) programs (Cushner, McClelland, & Safford, 1992; Nieto, 1992). ESL programs differ from bilingual education programs in that students in ESL programs receive instruction on how to speak, read, and write English several periods a week in a setting other than their regular classroom; it is therefore considered a "pull-out" program. Whereas bilingual education programs provide students instruction in academic subject areas, ESL programs do not. Students in ESL programs receive their academic instruction in regular English-speaking classes.

## Bilingual Education and Political Controversy

Increasingly, arguments about the value of bilingual education have entered not only the educational domain but also the political arena. Proponents of bilingual education argue that students should be taught subject matter in their native language while learning English as a second language (Cushner, McClelland, & Safford, 1992; Hudelson, 1987; Willig, 1987).

Opponents argue that all students should become competent in English and that this should take precedence over any other academic goal. Several instructional formats have attempted to bridge both arguments, including intensive second language instruction along with some subject matter instruction (such as mathematics) conducted in the first language. Some schools attempt to teach beginning reading in both languages, whereas others focus on reading acquisition in only one (Lado, 1981).

The simultaneous acquisition of two languages does not adversely affect proficiency in either language nor harm cognitive development (Genesee, 1989). If anything, there may be cognitive advantages to bilingualism (Hakuta & Garcia, 1989), unless a child is language disabled or is having difficulty in his or her first language.

The lack of bilingual teachers in many school systems makes it difficult to deliver bilingual instruction to all non-English-speaking students. All teachers need to be sensitive to students' language differences and provide students valid instruction (Cummins, 1981; Dolson, 1985). As students progress in school and become more proficient in English, they should not conclude that their native language and culture are inferior.

## Promoting Language Development Among First and Second Language Learners

You can use several techniques to promote students' language development. Some pertain to all students and some pertain to students for whom English is not a first language.

1. Children acquire language without formal instruction. As they mature, their language learning is enhanced through contact with teachers, books, and ideas. Give students opportunities to interact with ideas and discover meanings without immediate teacher intervention or control. Students learn better in an environment that encourages experimentation and hypothesis testing. Support discovery learning by providing materials that students can manipulate on their own. Allow students to make errors or to approximate accuracy as they explore ideas before you provide "correct" answers. To help students learn by discovery, be *flexible, patient,* and *knowledgeable.*

2. Children's language grows as they interact with adults. One of the most satisfying forms of oral language is *conversation* in which children learn to alternate speaking and listening by imitating the teacher in this form of interaction. Use opportunities in the classroom to interact with individual students, allowing them to converse with you about something that is important to them. All children need to be listened to and to have an adult's attention and feedback. Also encourage students to demonstrate their understanding of classroom lessons through oral reports, discussions, and peer interaction.

3. Students often learn to use language more precisely if they write down their ideas so others can read them. Since written language usually demands that language be explicit to help the reader comprehend, writing can become a framework through which students develop vocabulary and more complex sentence structure. Assign different kinds of writing tasks, including logs or diaries. Some teachers ask students to keep written logs that record what they understand and what they need for more complete understanding. Others use logs as a starting point for more structured writing assignments, such as writing descriptive or explanatory compositions. Have students use their interests as a basis for narrative or creative writing.

4. Respect students' native languages while providing opportunities for them to become proficient in standard American English.

5. Be a model for your students by speaking and conversing in appropriate standard language. Encourage students to read well-written books and to imitate written language both orally and in writing.

6. Students who are bilingual or who lack proficiency in English need to practice English as well as maintain their knowledge of their first language. Consider the variability in your students' language competence and help them develop a rich vocabulary and language proficiency so they can expand their potential for learning.

7. Convey to students from different cultural backgrounds that their use of language is not wrong, but simply different. At the same time, make sure they know that they need to master the standard form of spoken English.

## KEY POINTS

1. Culture is a system of beliefs, values, and customs that are shared by a group of people; all cultures socialize children into their system of beliefs and values.

2. Teachers' expectations of their students, based on knowledge of their cultural or socioeconomic background, can adversely affect students' achievement in school.

3. Some recent efforts to reshape schools have focused on multicultural education as an effective approach for all students.

4. Most language learning occurs before children enter school; children have an inborn mechanism that is "programmed" to make language learning possible.

5. The sequence of language learning appears to be universal; children learn language in the same sequence regardless of their culture.

6. Children learn to construct grammatically correct sentences they have never heard before by generalizing about language. They also overgeneralize grammatical rules, which supports a cognitive view of language acquisition.

7. The fact that it is easier for people to learn language prior to the age of 10 supports a biological view of language acquisition.

8. Language acquisition occurs in increasingly complex stages: babbling, first words, holophrases, telegraphic speech, and finally adult-like speech.

9. Everyone agrees that thought and language are related, but the nature of the relationship remains controversial. Most psychologists believe that language facilitates thought.

10. Literacy refers to one's ability to read and write at a level of competence acceptable in one's culture; emergent literacy refers to the process by which children learn about reading and writing as a result of exposure to printed materials occurring naturally in the environment.

11. Linguistic competence refers to the ability to use language in a grammatically correct form; communicative competence refers to the ability to vary one's use of language so that it is appropriate to the social setting in which communication takes place.

12. Students come to school with varying levels of communicative competence because rules for communicating at home or in the community differ from those in school. Students from minority cultures may find the transition to the rules for communicating in school particularly difficult.

## SELF-STUDY EXERCISES

1. Define and describe culture and explain how most people are members of several subcultural groups.

2. Describe four theories of cultural plurality used by multicultural education proponents.

3. Describe how teachers' beliefs about students can affect student achievement in school.

4. Describe how the acquisition of language reflects more general principles of learning.

5. Compare the biological and cognitive bases for language acquisition and describe the evidence supporting each.

6. Describe how the sociocultural basis for language acquisition differs from a social learning approach.

7. What aspects of language acquisition cannot be accounted for by a behavioral approach?

8. List the major characteristics of the stages of language development.

9. Explain how language facilitates concept formation.

10. Some uses of dialect are likely to be accepted and others rejected in school. Give an example of each.

11. Compare the educational and political implications of bilingual education versus an ESL approach.

## FURTHER READINGS

Calkins, L. M. (1983). *Lessons from a child: On the teaching and learning of writing.* Portsmouth, NH: Heinemann.
Cushner, K., McClelland, A., & Safford, P. (1992). *Human diversity in education.* New York: McGraw-Hill.
Downing, J., & Valtin, R. (1984). *Language awareness and learning to read.* New York: Springer-Verlag.
Heath, S. B. (1983). *Ways with words: Language, life and work in communities and classrooms.* New York: Cambridge University Press.
Lindfors, J. W. (1987). *Children's language and learning* (2nd ed.). Englewood Cliffs, NJ: Prentice Hall.

Nieto, S. (1992). *Affirming diversity: The sociopolitical context of multicultural education.* New York: Longman.
Sleeter, C. E., & Grant, C. A. (1994). *Making choices for multicultural education: Five approaches to race, class, and gender.* New York: Merrill.
Taylor, E., & Dorsey-Gaines, C. (1988). *Growing up literate: Learning from inner-city families.* Portsmouth, NH: Heinemann.
Weaver, C. (1988). *Reading process and practice.* Portsmouth, NH: Heinemann.

## REFERENCES

Arntson, P. (1982). Testing Basil Bernstein's sociolinguistic theories. *Human Communication Research, 8*(1), 33–48.
Athey, I. (1983). Language development factors related to reading development. *Journal of Educational Research, 76*(4), 197–203.
Au, K. H., & Kawakami, A. J. (1991). Culture and ownership: Schooling of minority students. *Childhood Education, 67,* 280–284.

Bandura, A. (1986). *Social foundations of thought and action: A social cognitive theory.* Englewood Cliffs, NJ: Prentice Hall.
Banks, J. A. (1994). *Multiethnic education: Theory and practice.* Boston: Allyn & Bacon.
Banks, J. A., & Banks, C. M. (1993). *Multicultural education: Issues and perspectives.* Boston: Allyn & Bacon.

Bennett, C. (1995). Preparing teachers for cultural diversity and national standards of academic excellence. *Journal of Teacher Education, 46,* 259–265.

Brice-Heath, S. (1988). Language socialization. *New Directions, 42,* 28–41.

Brown, R. (1973). *A first language: The early stages.* Cambridge, MA: Harvard University Press.

Bruner, J. (1975). From communication to language: A psychological perspective. *Cognition, 3,* 255–287.

Cazden, C. B. (1986). Classroom discourse. In M. C. Wittrock (Ed.), *Handbook of research on teaching* (3rd ed., pp. 432–463). New York: Macmillan.

Cazden, C. B. (1988). *Classroom discourse: The language of teaching and learning.* Portsmouth, NH: Heinemann.

Chomsky, C. (1969). *The acquisition of syntax in children 5 to 10.* Cambridge, MA: MIT Press.

Cole, M. (1985). The zone of proximal development: Where culture and cognition create each other. In J. V. Wertsch (Ed.), *Culture, communication and cognition: Vygotskian perspectives* (pp. 146–161). Cambridge: Cambridge University Press.

Coltheart, M. (1987). Functional architecture of the language-processing system. In M. Coltheart, R. Job, & G. Sartori (Eds.), *The neuropsychology of language* (pp. 3–26). Hillsdale, NJ: Erlbaum.

Cook, V. (1989). Universal grammar theory and the classroom. *System, 17,* 169–181.

Cummins, J. (1981). Empirical and theoretical underpinnings of bilingual education. *Journal of Education, 163,* (l), 16–29.

Cushner, K., McClelland, A., & Safford, P. (1992). *Human diversity in education.* New York: McGraw-Hill.

Dale, P. S. (1976). *Language development: Structure and function* (2nd ed.). New York: Holt, Rinehart & Winston.

Diamond, B. J., & Moore, M. A. (1995). *Multicultural literacy: Mirroring the reality of the classroom.* New York: Longman.

Dolson, D. P. (1985). Bilingualism and scholastic performance: The literature revisited. *NABE Journal, 10*(1), 1–36.

Eller, R. G. (1989). Johnny can't talk, either: The perpetuation of the deficit theory in classrooms. *Reading Teacher, 42*(8), 70–74.

Ferreiro, E., & Teborosky, A. (1982). *Literacy before schooling.* Portsmouth, NH: Heinemann.

Genesee, F. (1989). Early bilingual development: One language or two? *Journal of Child Language, 16,* 161–178.

Gleitman, L. R. (1986). Biological dispositions to learn language. In W. Demopoulos & M. Ausonio (Eds.), *Language learning and concept acquisition: Foundational issues* (pp. 3–28). Norwood, NJ: Ablex.

Golinkoff, R. M., & Hirsch-Pasek, K. (1990). Let the mute speak: What infants can tell us about language acquisition. *Merrill-Palmer Quarterly, 36,* 67–92.

Good, T. L., & Brophy, J. E. (1991). *Looking in classrooms.* New York: Harper Collins.

Goodluck, H. (1986). Language acquisition and linguistic theory. In P. Fletcher & M. Garman (Eds.), *Language acquisition* (2nd ed., pp. 44–49). London: Cambridge University Press.

Grossman H., & Grossman, S. H. (1994). *Gender issues in education.* Boston: Allyn & Bacon.

Hakuta, K., & Garcia, E. (1989). Bilingualism and education. *American Psychologist, 44*(2), 374–379.

Hennings, D. G. (1990). *Communication in action: Teaching the language arts* (4th ed.). Boston: Houghton Mifflin.

Hernandez, H. (1989). *Multicultural education: A teacher's guide to content and process.* Columbus, OH: Merrill.

Howe, C. J. (1992). *Language learning.* Hillsdale, NJ: Erlbaum.

Hudelson, S. (1987). The role of native language literacy in the education of language minority students. *Language Arts, 64,* 827–841.

Hymes, D. (1972). *Towards communicative competence.* Philadelphia: University of Pennsylvania Press.

Jencks, C., Smith, M., Acland, H. J., Bane, M. J., Coehn, D., Gintis, H., Heyns, B., & Michelson, S. (1972). *Inequality: A reassessment of the effect of family and schooling in America.* New York: Harper & Row.

Keil, F. C. (1989). *Concepts, kinds, and cognitive development.* Cambridge, MA: MIT Press.

Labov, W. (1970). The logic of non-standard English. In F. Williams (Ed.), *Language and poverty* (pp. 153–189). New York: Markham Press.

Lado, R. (1981). Aula/The classroom: Developmental reading in two languages. *NABE: The Journal for the National Association for Bilingual Education, 6* (2–3), 98–110.

Leibowicz, J. (1984). ERIC/RCS Report: Classrooms, teachers and nonstandard speakers. *Language Arts, 61*(1), 88–91.

Lenneberg, E. (1967). *Biological foundations of language.* New York: Wiley.

Liebling, C. R. (1988). Means to an end: Children's knowledge of directives during the elementary school years. *Discourse Processes, 11*(1), 78–88.

Linn, M. C., & Hyde, J. S. (1989). Gender, mathematics and science. *Educational Researcher, 18,* 17–27.

Menyuk, P. (1977). *Language and maturation.* Cambridge, MA: MIT Press.

Mills, C. J., Ablard, K. E., & Stumpf, H. (1993). Gender differences in academically talented young students' mathematical reasoning: Patterns across age and subskills. *Journal of Educational Psychology, 82,* 410–419.

Molfese, D. L., Molfese, V. J., & Carroll, P. L. (1982). Early language development. In B. B. Wolman (Ed.), *Handbook of developmental psychology* (pp. 301–323). Englewood Cliffs, NJ: Prentice Hall.

Munsell, P. E. (1988). Language learning and the brain: A comprehensive survey of recent conclusions. *Language Learning, 38,* 261–278.

National Commission of Children. (1991). *Beyond rhetoric.* Washington, DC: U.S. Government Printing Office.

Neill, S. R. St J. (1989). The effects of facial expression and posture on children's reported responses to teacher nonverbal communication. *British Educational Research Journal, 15*(2), 195–204.

Nieto, S. (1992). *Affirming diversity: The sociopolitical context of multicultural education.* New York: Longman.

Ogbu, J. (1992). Understanding cultural diversity and learning. *Educational Researcher, 21*(8), 5–14.

Palinscar, A. S., & Brown, A. L. (1984). Reciprocal teaching of comprehension-fostering and monitoring activities. *Cognition and Instruction, 1,* 117–175.

Piaget, J., & Inhelder, B. (1969). *The psychology of the child.* New York: Basic Books.

Podell, D. M., & Soodak, L. C. (1993). Teacher efficacy and bias in special education referrals. *Journal of Educational Research, 86*, 247–253.

Rice, M. (1993). *Review of child development* (6th ed). Madison, WI: Brown & Benchmark.

Sadker, M., & Sadker, D. (1985, March). Sexism in the schoolroom of the 80s. *Psychology Today, 19*, 54–57.

Sadker, M., Sadker, D., & Klein, S. (1991). The issue of gender in elementary and secondary education. *Review of Research in Education, 17*, 269–334.

Santrock, J. W. (1995). *Children.* Madison, WI: Brown & Benchmark.

Savignon, S. J. (1983). *Communicative competence: Theory and classroom practice.* Reading, MA: Addison-Wesley.

Seidenberg, M. S. (1986). Evidence from great apes concerning the biological bases of language. In W. Demopoulos & M. Ausonio (Eds.), *Language learning and concept acquisition: Foundational issues* (pp. 29–53). Norwood, NJ: Ablex.

Skinner, B. F. (1957). *Verbal behavior.* New York: Appleton-Century-Crofts.

Sleeter, C. E., & Grant, C. A. (1994). *Making choices for multicultural education: Five approaches to race, class, and gender.* New York: Merrill.

Slobin, D. (1973). Cognitive prerequisites for the development of grammar. In C. Ferguson & D. Slobin (Eds.), *Studies of child language development.* New York: Holt, Rinehart & Winston.

Snow, C. E. (1988). The development of conversation between mothers and babies. In M. B. Franklin & S. S. Barten (Eds.), *Child language: A reader* (pp. 20–35). New York: Oxford University Press.

Spitz, R., & Wolf, K. (1946). The smiling response. *Genetic Psychology Monographs, 34*, 57–125.

Stark, R. E. (1989). Early language intervention: When, why, how? *Infants and Young Children, 1*, 44–53.

Sulzby, E., & Teale, W. (1991). Emergent literacy. In R. Barr, M. L. Kamil, P. Moselthal, & P. D. Pearson (Eds.), *Handbook of reading research* (Vol. II, pp. 727–757). New York: Longman.

Torrey, J. W. (1983). Black children's knowledge of standard English. *American Educational Research Journal, 20* (4), 627–643.

Tough, J. (1981). *A place for talk.* London: Ward Lock Educational.

Vygotsky, L. S. (1986). *Language and thought.* Cambridge, MA: MIT Press.

Weller, L., & Levi, S. (1981). Social class, IQ, self-concept and teachers' evaluations in Israel. *Adolescence, 16*(63), 569–576.

Wells, G. (1986). *The meaning makers: Children learning language and using language to learn.* Portsmouth, NH: Heinemann.

Wertsch, J. V. (1991). *Voices of the mind: A sociocultural approach to mediated action.* Cambridge, MA: Harvard University Press.

Willig, A. C. (1987). Examining bilingual education research through meta-analysis and narrative review: A response to Baker. *Review of Educational Research, 57*(3), 363–376.

Wood, D. (1992). Culture, language and child development. *Language and Education* 6(2), 123–140.

Woolfolk, A. E. (1985). Research perspectives on communication in classrooms. *Theory into Practice, 24*(1), 3–7.

Wright, R. L. (1983). Functional language, socialization, and academic achievement. *Journal of Negro Education, 51*(1), 3–14.

Yee, A. H. (1992). Asians as stereotypes and students: Misperceptions that persist. *Educational Psychology Review, 4*, 95–132.

6

© David Frazier

# Knowledge and Comprehension

# Chapter Outline

# Learning Objectives

6.1 Describe three kinds of knowledge.

6.2 Explain how declarative knowledge is best learned.

6.3 Describe the relationship between declarative knowledge and higher-level tasks.

6.4 Define procedural knowledge.

6.5 Define conceptual knowledge and describe dimensions along which concepts vary.

6.6 Demonstrate four methods of teaching concepts.

6.7 Describe the role of schemata in students' comprehension of new material.

6.8 Describe five methods of helping students comprehend.

# Preview

This chapter focuses on the kinds of knowledge we acquire and the cognitive processes we use in comprehending. There are three kinds of knowledge: (a) declarative knowledge, or "knowing *that,*" which involves memorizing factual information; (b) procedural knowledge, or "knowing *how,*" which involves knowing the steps needed to complete a specific task; and (c) conceptual knowledge, or "knowing *about,*" which involves understanding the relationships among ideas.

Concepts differ in terms of abstractness, generality, and complexity. You can teach concepts effectively by using attributes, prototypes, examples, and nonexamples. Concepts linked together by rules are called principles.

Students' prior understanding determines how they comprehend new information. You can help students comprehend better by using paraphrasing, summarizing, questioning, note taking, and graphic organizers. ◉

# Types of Knowledge

The most fundamental principle of cognitive psychology is that learners *construct* knowledge (Leinhardt, 1992). To help students construct knowledge, you must understand (a) what types of knowledge there are, and (b) how different types of knowledge are best learned.

Psychologists divide knowledge into three different types: declarative, procedural, and conceptual, which overlap and are interrelated in many ways. By examining each separately, you will better understand what role each plays in school learning and how you can help students learn.

**6.1** ◎

*Describe three kinds of knowledge.*

## Declarative Knowledge ("Knowing *That*")

**Declarative knowledge** involves memorizing factual information. Typical instances include word recognition, number facts, basic facts from different fields of study (e.g, the Declaration of Independence was signed in 1776, or $H_2O$ is the symbol for water), and generalizations (e.g, leap year falls every four years). Declarative knowledge is sometimes called *verbal information* (Gagné, 1985).

**6.2** ◎

*Explain how declarative knowledge is best learned.*

### Practice and Overlearning

*A*⁺

Students learn factual information best by practicing, and they retain it longer if they overlearn it. Overlearning involves continuing to practice even though you can recite newly learned information perfectly. Suppose, for example, students have to learn the definitions of 20 words in a foreign language. Students overlearn the list if they continue to practice until they can correctly define all 20 words the same number of times it took them to learn to define them correctly once. Students who take 6 attempts to define all 20 words correctly once, for example, should continue practicing until they can define them correctly 6 times in a row. Similarly, students who take 10 times to learn all 20 definitions should continue practicing until they can define the words correctly 10 times in a row.

Students often learn factual information easily, but forget it just as easily. Students retain information for a long time only if they internalize it to the point that its retrieval becomes automatic (Sywlester, 1985). Help students acquire and retain new information by reviewing it frequently and integrating it with things they already know (Bruner, 1966).

Students need factual information to be able to solve problems rapidly and accurately. By knowing the sum of 8 + 7, for example, students can more easily solve the problem of 58 + 47. Similarly, when students recognize words without having to decode them by sounding them out, they are more likely to read a passage fluently and comprehend it.

Many students use a massed practice approach, cramming their studying into the period just before a test. However, even when the same amount of study time is used, the distributed practice approach is more effective.

**Rote learning** involves remembering through repetition. Although it lacks meaning, rote learning helps students who are just beginning to learn a body of information. We want students to understand conceptually what 8 + 7 means, for example, but they also need to know the answer rapidly and accurately.

**Distributed practice,** with breaks between study periods, is more effective than **massed practice,** with no breaks (Dempster, 1989). Students learn more, for example, if they spend three 30-minute periods studying than if they study for one 90-minute period. The amount of study time is the same, but breaking it into smaller units increases its effectiveness.

### Automatic Accessibility

Once learned, declarative knowledge is automatically accessible and permits learners to attend to other aspects of the learning situation. As noted earlier, students can concentrate on reading for meaning if they can automatically decode all the words. Similarly, students who know basic historical names and dates can focus more easily on more complex issues, such as the development of social movements or the causes and effects of political events.

**6.3** ◎

*Describe the relationship between declarative knowledge and higher-level tasks.*

Typical classroom interactions involve "recitations" in which teachers ask questions that require specific and brief answers involving declarative knowledge. Most questions tend to be fact-finding. Despite the recent emphasis on higher-level thinking to prepare students for a future complex society, the use of recitation persists in many classrooms today.

**6.4** ◎

*Define procedural knowledge.*

Can you think of other instances of procedural knowledge? Others include knowing how to operate a specific software package, keep score in tennis, tie your shoelace, and research a topic to write a report.

Knowing when *not* to apply a procedure is very important. For example, you need to find a common denominator when adding fractions with unlike denominators, but you don't need to do so when multiplying fractions with unlike denominators.

Declarative knowledge provides the foundation on which to build more complex information. Students often have difficulty understanding and remembering complex information because they have not learned sufficiently well the declarative knowledge on which the information is based. As a result, they cannot concentrate on the meaning of the complex information because they are too busy trying to recall factual information.

Much of what we expect students to learn in school involves the acquisition of declarative knowledge, which is reflected in the large number of factual questions on many academic achievement tests. Students need to have a mastery of facts, but it is *not* desirable to place such heavy emphasis on memorized information that students have little opportunity to acquire other types of knowledge.

## Procedural Knowledge ("Knowing *How*")

The knowledge of rules and their application is called **procedural knowledge.** Typical instances include knowing how to multiply fractions, how to decode unfamiliar words, or how to use a dictionary.

Procedural knowledge is more general than declarative knowledge. Whereas declarative knowledge involves learning specific facts, procedural knowledge involves learning rules that apply to a wide array of situations. The rules of multiplication or division, for example, apply to an infinite number of problems. In addition to knowing rules, students need to know when, and when not, to apply them.

### Transformation of Information

We use rules to *transform* information. Students may intuitively understand that one-half of two-thirds equals one-third. They may have more trouble understanding that two-thirds of one-half also equals one-third. Knowing how to multiply fractions, however, permits students to discover that $\frac{2}{3} \times \frac{1}{2} = \frac{1}{3}$. Similarly, when students decode a word, they transform a set of printed letters into a meaningful entity. The purpose of transforming information is to make it meaningful.

Procedural knowledge is more difficult to learn than declarative knowledge because it involves both mastering a sequence of steps and knowing when to use them. Once students have learned procedural knowledge, they don't forget it (Sywlester, 1985). You can probably still ride a bicycle, play a musical instrument, or speak a foreign language even though you may not have practiced these skills for years. Psychologists don't yet know the extent to which various kinds of procedural knowledge are retained or the processes by which retention takes place.

 **WINDOWS on TEACHING**

## Familiar and Interesting Contexts

▪▪ Students learn factual information best when teachers introduce it in a familiar and interesting context (Bransford & Johnson, 1972). Some students, for example, are familiar with and interested in sports. Introducing basic number facts or fundamental principles of physics by using illustrations from various sports helps such students learn information more quickly and remember it more easily.

Different students have different interests, so you need to find out what your students are interested in and use these interests as a context for introducing new factual information. Good teachers introduce declarative knowledge in a variety of different contexts to accommodate students whose interests differ.

Help students memorize by presenting new information in ways that connect to what they already know (Anderson, 1976). If students already know that $2 + 2 + 2 = 6$, for example, they can learn more easily that $3 \times 2 = 6$. Repeating information in different contexts helps students see the broader use of factual information. For example, encourage beginning readers to read the same story more than once and to read other stories that contain many of the same words.

## Steps in Acquiring Procedural Knowledge

Acquiring procedural knowledge involves three sequential steps:

1.  Identify the type of situation or problem.
2.  Choose the appropriate strategy to address it.
3.  Proceed through the steps of the strategy.

Procedural knowledge has been mastered when the learner can execute the three steps automatically and without errors. Like declarative knowledge, procedural knowledge permits the learner to execute the procedures without awareness while attending to other information. Consequently, mastery of procedural knowledge contributes importantly to independent and efficient problem solving.

Students typically use procedural knowledge to solve word problems that require the use of mathematics. Students must first identify the type of problem and then select an appropriate strategy, and, finally, apply the strategy.

Consider the following word problem:

> *A student had $29 to spend on CDs. If each CD costs $9 and the student buys as many as possible, how much money will be left over?*

Solving this problem involves (a) identifying the problem as a division problem where the correct answer is the *remainder,* (b) selecting the strategy of dividing 29 by 9, and (c) carrying out the division: 29 divided by 9 = 3 with a remainder of 2, the answer to the problem.

> Declarative and procedural knowledge are often interrelated. Embedded in procedural knowledge may be facts that facilitate the use of the procedure. Young children can learn to identify unknown words by using the context, using a word that "fits" (use of syntax), or using the sound of the initial letter in the word. These procedural strategies require declarative knowledge.

## Incorrect Generalizations

Sometimes you may have to teach students when a procedure is *not* appropriate. Students achieve true mastery when they can generalize the procedures. Some students, however, may generalize to situations where the procedure is not appropriate. Point out to these students the critical aspects that distinguish situations in which a strategy is appropriate from those in which it is not. When students understand the *purpose* of the procedure they are using, they are more likely to generalize correctly.

> It is important to teach not only *how* to implement a procedure, but also *when* and *why* one should do so.

## Independent Acquisition of Procedural Knowledge

Students can acquire procedural knowledge independently or with limited teacher guidance. Self-discovery of procedural knowledge makes learning more meaningful (Bruner, 1966). Some students acquire procedural knowledge on their own by means of trial and error. Others use the more sophisticated method of testing self-generated hypotheses. Regardless of method, however, students who acquire procedural knowledge on their own often learn the important additional lesson of "debugging" and refining their own procedures.

Because students periodically develop inefficient strategies that Resnick (1987) calls "buggy algorithms" or "malrules," you must monitor students' independent efforts and correct erroneous strategies before students learn them too well.

## Teaching Procedural Knowledge

Procedural knowledge involves learning rules, not just facts. Students also need to learn how and when to apply the rules. Teach procedural knowledge by following this four-step sequence:

1.  Explain the goal of using the procedure and define the set of problems for which the procedure is appropriate.

2.  Demonstrate the procedure step by step.
3.  Have students practice choosing the appropriate procedure and carrying out the steps.
4.  Give students feedback about their performance.

Concepts, such as "plant," are classifications of a set of related ideas or events.

© Richard Heinzen/Superstock

### General Versus Domain-Specific Procedural Knowledge

Knowledge can be general or domain-specific (Alexander, 1992; Farnham-Diggory, 1992). We use **general knowledge** in a broad range of situations. Knowing how to use the index of a book, knowing how to write, and knowing what is meant by "seven" are examples of general knowledge. We use **domain-specific knowledge** in a narrow domain. Knowing how to solve an algebra problem, to program a computer, and to tune a violin are examples of domain-specific knowledge. Experts typically have a rich collection of domain-specific knowledge that allows them to achieve a high level of performance in their field. Expert teachers, for example, know domain-specific procedures concerning how to manage student outbursts, how to motivate an unmotivated student, and how to present material in ways that promote comprehension (Gagné, Yekovich, & Yekovich, 1993).

### Conceptual Knowledge ("Knowing *About*")

**6.5** ◎

*Define conceptual knowledge and describe dimensions along which concepts vary.*

Knowledge that involves categorizing related information into an organized idea is called **conceptual knowledge** (or "knowing *about*"). **Concepts** are classifications of a set of related ideas or events. For example, the concept of "plant" includes trees, flowers, shrubs, and weeds. The concept of "revolution" includes specific events, such as the American or French Revolution or any kind of large and dramatic change, such as when millions of people suddenly bought television sets in the 1950s.

Bruner (1957, 1966) notes that concepts are valuable because they:

1. Allow people to reduce a large amount of information into smaller, more manageable units.
2. Help people make sense of new situations by generalizing characteristics of a known concept.
3. Permit people to understand abstract ideas without referring to all of an idea's tangible characteristics.
4. Amplify thinking by reducing a body of information to a single concept, thereby freeing people's memory and attention for processing additional information.
5. Can relate to other concepts that permit higher-level thought processes, such as analysis and synthesis.

Take a typical concept, such as "dog." "Dog" is a category that applies not to just one specific dog but to all dogs. To acquire the concept of "dog," one must have factual information about dogs in general and understand how this information relates in an organized way that distinguishes "dog" from some other concept, such as "wolf" or "cat."

Such information may consist of knowing that a dog is a four-legged animal often kept as a pet. This information, of course, also applies to a cat. It is therefore necessary to acquire information that pertains to dogs, but not to cats, such as "dogs bark" but cats don't. Children often acquire these concepts gradually. Young children may initially call all animals *dogs,* or call all men *dada.* People *construct* their understanding of concepts (Mayer, 1992) and may periodically revise their understanding as a result of new experiences and encounters with new information.

Words and concepts are related, but they are not identical. The word *newspaper,* for example, is the name given to the concept "newspaper." Words function as labels that permit us to distinguish among various concepts. Different people, however, may use the same word when referring to different concepts. One person may use the word *reading* to describe the process of pronouncing printed words, but someone else might use it to refer to the process of understanding what the printed words mean.

Sometimes we need several words to describe concepts, such as "freedom of the press" or "representational art." Periodically, we borrow words and phrases from other languages, such as "modus operandi" or "laissez-faire" to designate concepts for which no English words exist. Of course, other languages borrow from English to label concepts, such as "le micro-chip" or "le cheeseburger."

This phenomenon is not unique to children; adults also gradually refine their understandings of new concepts as a result of experiences with the concept. Can you think of concepts that you gradually refined as you learned more about them?

## Relationships Among Concepts

When students learn a concept, they do not simply remember factual information; they understand the relationships among ideas and associations with concepts (Cameron, 1994; Schwartz & Reisberg, 1991). Students form concepts by integrating meaningful factual information within a larger network of information. Students may know that the United States gained its independence from England by means of the American Revolution. When they can relate the American Revolution to other revolutions, such as the French Revolution or the Russian Revolution, and recognize that all revolutions have a common purpose, they have a fuller understanding of the concept "revolution." When they have learned how "revolution" differs from other concepts, such as "evolution" or "rebellion" they have an even more complete understanding of the concept.

## Factual Information and Concept Acquisition

Factual information differs from concept acquisition. Facts are only verbal labels for ideas. Concepts involve understanding how the facts comprising a concept are organized and how the concept relates to other concepts. You can determine if students have acquired a concept or merely have mastered factual information by having them describe the concept in their own words.

## Variation Among Concepts

Concepts vary in terms of their level of abstraction, generality, and complexity. Concepts range from **concrete** to **abstract.** Concrete concepts are those we can see and touch, such as the concept "dog." Abstract concepts do not have a physical existence; "species" is an example of an abstract concept. Students learn concrete concepts more easily than abstract ones, largely because students can have experiences with tangible objects. Whether a concept is perceived as concrete or abstract depends on how the learner understands it. Thinking of "home" as the place where one lives is a concrete idea, whereas thinking of it as a place of comfort and security is more abstract. Older students may perceive concepts abstractly that younger students may perceive concretely (Kossan, 1981).

**Figure 6.1**

Two dimensions of concepts: Level of abstraction and level of specificity.

| | Concrete | Abstract |
|---|---|---|
| General | Animals | Kingdom |
| | Chordata | Phylum |
| | Vertebrates | Sub-phylum |
| | Carnivores | Order |
| | Canidae (includes dogs, coyotes, wolves, and foxes) | Family |
| | Canis (includes dogs, wolves, and coyotes) | Genus |
| | Canis Familiaris (dogs) | Species |
| Specific | German shepherd | Breed |

**Figure 6.2**

Concepts with low and high degrees of complexity.

Chair

| | |
|---|---|
| Function: | To sit on |
| Appearance: | Has three or four legs, sometimes wheels |
| Made of: | Wood, metal, plastic |

Microcomputer

| | |
|---|---|
| Functions: | Word processing, games, statistical analyses, record keeping, graphics, research, communications |
| Appearance: | Like a typewriter with a screen |
| Components: | Monitor, CPU, disk drives |
| Capabilities: | Dependent on level of memory, storage capacity, microprocessor speed |
| Energy source: | Electricity |
| Input sources: | Diskettes, keyboard, pressure-sensitive screen, modem |
| Output sources: | Screen, printer |
| Output types: | Letters, symbols, sounds |

Concepts also range from general to specific. "Mode of transportation" is a general concept, but "train" is specific. "Great Dane" is specific, "dog" is general. At the same time, "dog" is specific relative to "mammal," which is more general.

Concepts can vary in terms of generality and abstraction at the same time. Figure 6.1 demonstrates how general concepts may be concrete (e.g., "animals") or abstract (e.g., "kingdom") and also how specific concepts may be concrete (e.g., "German shepherd") or abstract (e.g., "breed").

Concepts range from simple to complex, depending on the type and number of relationships they have with other concepts. As the number of relationships increases and the nature of the relationships becomes more varied, a concept becomes more complex. As illustrated in figure 6.2, "chair" is a comparatively simple concept because it has only simple relationships to a few other concepts. To acquire the concept "chair," one needs to know only its function ("something to sit on"), its general appearance ("usually has four legs"), and its similarity to other concepts ("like a bench or stool").

On the other hand, the concept "microcomputer" has numerous and varied relationships with many other concepts, such as its functions (to process information, to play games on, to keep records, etc.), its components (the central processing unit, the monitor, the disk drives, etc.), its use (how and when to use it), and its capabilities. People who have lots of knowledge about technology may perceive the concept "microcomputer" as simple, but people who know little about technology may perceive it as complex.

Concepts, such as political and economic philosophies ("capitalism," "socialism," "communism," "feudalism") are the most difficult to grasp because they are both complex and abstract.

## Ways to Teach Concepts

Let us focus on ways to teach concepts effectively. By having students explain concepts in their own words, you can uncover the nature of problems they may be having and select teaching strategies accordingly.

### Attributes

The characteristics of a concept are called **attributes.** Consider the concrete concept "piano." Its attributes include wires of varying lengths, comes with a bench, makes sounds when keys are struck, made of wood and ivory, has pedals, and so forth. Attributes that are essential to the concept, such as "makes sounds when keys are struck," are called *defining features*. Nonessential attributes, such as "has keys made of ivory," or "comes with a bench," are called *correlational features* (Ormrod, 1990).

Present students a list of attributes associated with a concept and attributes that are not. Have students identify correct attributes and classify each correct attribute as a defining or correlational feature.

It is difficult to identify the attributes of abstract concepts such as "humor" (Benjafield, 1992). Is one of the attributes "something that makes you laugh"? What about a situation that makes one person laugh but not another? Or what about something humorous that doesn't cause laughter?

**6.6** ◎
*Demonstrate four methods of teaching concepts.*

Try to identify the defining and correlational features of these concepts: "culture," "love," "freedom," "life," "democracy." You may find that it is not so easy.

### Examples and Nonexamples

One of the best ways to teach concepts is to present students with numerous **examples** (Tennyson & Park, 1980). Examples of the concept "continent" are South America and Africa; examples of "fascism" are Germany under Hitler and Italy under Mussolini.

If you don't present enough examples, students may come to an erroneous understanding. Suppose, for example, in teaching the concept "vehicle," you use only examples such as bicycles, wagons, and skateboards. Students may conclude that a "vehicle" is something children ride. Additional examples, such as train, automobile, ship, or airplane, permit students to form an accurate meaning.

It is particularly helpful to present **nonexamples** and compare them with examples. Nonexamples of "continent" are the Atlantic Ocean and the United States; nonexamples of "fascism" include the United States under Franklin Roosevelt and Great Britain under Winston Churchill.

The most helpful nonexamples share some of the properties of the concept to be learned. A good nonexample of "vehicle" is bathtub. One can sit in a bathtub just as one can sit in a wagon or in a car, but a bathtub does not move. Another good nonexample is bird. Birds move about like airplanes, but you can't ride on a bird. Such nonexamples help students focus on the concept's defining features. Comparing examples and nonexamples helps students understand the critical "limits" of the concept.

Here is a set of examples and nonexamples of the concept "novel":

| Examples | Nonexamples |
| --- | --- |
| *To Kill a Mockingbird* | *Romeo and Juliet* |
| *Catcher in the Rye* | "The Raven" |
| *Winds of War* | "The Far Side" |
| *War and Peace* | *Profiles in Courage* |
| *Little Women* | *A Streetcar Named Desire* |

The examples and nonexamples share the attribute of "written work," but only the examples are novels. The nonexamples include plays, poems, cartoon strips, and nonfiction. Contrasting nonexamples with examples makes it clear that not all written works are novels. "Novel" refers only to book-length written works of fiction.

Examples are items that belong in the category defined by the concept, whereas attributes are characteristics of the concept. *War and Peace* is an example of the concept "novel," but "tells an invented story" is an attribute.

## Building Concepts Through Discovery Learning

You can help students acquire concepts by designing situations that encourage exploration, questioning, testing hypotheses, and drawing conclusions. This instructional approach is called **discovery learning,** and is especially well suited to concept learning (Bruner, 1966; Neale, Smith, & Johnson, 1990).

To teach students about the difference between the concepts "fiction" and "nonfiction," you might bring in a dozen books, half of which are fiction and half nonfiction. Have students examine the books and sort them into two categories. Students may *discover* the two basic types of books. Some students may classify the books in a different way, finding a different but adequate set of categories. Explore and discuss their alternative approach.

---

Sometimes it helps to present both typical and atypical examples of a concept. "Whales," for instance, is an atypical example of the concept "mammal." Including "whale" in the list of examples helps learners identify critical features (for example, "mothers suckle their young") and drop erroneous ideas, such as "mammals live on land."

Having students produce their own examples of a concept helps them relate their existing understanding of the concept to other ideas (Ellis & Hunt, 1983), provides you an opportunity to give feedback, and helps students to recall the concept later (Watts & Anderson, 1971).

**Generate examples and nonexamples that you feel would help a naive learner understand the concepts of "season," "communication," "compound," and "entertainment."**

Another way to help students grasp a concept is to have them classify new examples into different concepts (Wilson, 1988). For example, having taught the concepts "reptile," "insect," "amphibian," "fish," and "mammal," give students examples that you did *not* use in previous instruction. If students truly grasp the concepts, their classifications should be accurate; if not, you will gain insight regarding their misconceptions and be able to provide clarification.

### Prototypes

Psychologists, such as Rosch (1978), believe that people use **prototypes,** or models, to understand concepts whose parameters are vague and difficult to define. Prototypes are the first instances of a concept that come to mind and possess the concept's most characteristic attributes. For many people, the prototype of "school principal," for example, might be a stern man who makes announcements over a loudspeaker.

Students can compare an object to their prototype to see if the object belongs. Although prototypes can help students learn concepts, strict adherence to the prototype can lead to stereotyping.

### Concepts and Procedural Knowledge

A firm grasp of concepts helps students acquire more complex ideas, perceive new relationships, and become more flexible in their thinking. Conceptual knowledge is particularly helpful in enabling students to use procedures effectively because it provides an understanding of *why* a procedure is used and therefore encourages its appropriate use.

For example, when students first confront a subtraction problem, such as 40 – 25, many subtract the smaller from the larger number in the ones column, instead of subtracting the bottom from the top number. Once students have learned the concept "place value," however, they are more likely to subtract correctly because they understand what the 0 in 40 stands for.

## Concept Acquisition and Learner Characteristics

Characteristics of the learner sometimes influence how students understand a particular concept. Young children, for example, tend to understand all concepts in a concrete manner, whereas older learners, who have more advanced cognitive abilities, are more likely to differentiate between concrete and abstract concepts (Kossan, 1981). Teachers often rely on concrete examples to teach the meaning of abstract concepts. This practice, while useful, may affect the learning of young and older students differently. Older students may use the concrete examples to construct an understanding of an abstract concept, whereas young students may understand only the concrete examples. For instance, the concept "brave" may be understood by younger students as meaning "the way Batman is," whereas older students may understand that "brave" is an abstract concept meaning "having courage."

## Concept Formation

Klausmeier and Sipple (1980) have developed a hierarchical model of concept formation consisting of four levels:

> *Level 1:* Concrete. The concrete level of concept formation is the lowest level. At this level, concept formation involves attending to an object, discriminating it from other objects, and recognizing it when it is encountered again in the same situation.
>
> *Level 2:* Identity. The next highest level is the identity level, in which the learner can recognize the object when it is encountered in a new situation.
>
> *Level 3:* Classificatory. The next highest level is the classificatory level, in which the learner knows two or more examples of the concept at the identity level.
>
> *Level 4:* Formal. The highest level of concept formation is the formal level. Students have reached the formal level when they can attach a verbal label to the concept, describe its inherent characteristics, and distinguish examples of the concept from nonexamples.

When you design lessons, remember the various levels of concept development and help the students move from the concrete level to the identity, classification, and formal levels. Keep in mind that young children and older children conceptualize at different levels.

Klausmeier (1985) gives detailed information about how to teach concepts at each level. When deciding which concepts to teach, select those that are most easily learned, most frequently used, most precisely defined, most inclusive, and most likely to help students with subsequent learning (Klausmeier, 1985, 1990).

 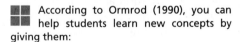

## Ways to Teach Conceptual Knowledge

According to Ormrod (1990), you can help students learn new concepts by giving them:

1. A definition of a concept
2. Many and varied examples
3. Nonexamples
4. Examples and nonexamples simultaneously
5. Opportunities to classify new examples into a set of concepts
6. Opportunities to generate their own examples of a concept
7. Skills that are prerequisite to understanding concepts

Here is an example of how you might use each strategy to teach the concept "element."

1. A definition of the word *element* is "one of the basic substances that exist that cannot be broken down into any further substances."
2–4. Examples of elements are oxygen, hydrogen, gold, silver, and calcium. Nonexamples are water ($H_2O$), salt (NaCl), atoms, and electrons.
5. Ask students whether the following are or are not elements: radium, nitroglycerine, baking soda, and copper.
6. Ask students to generate their own list of elements and nonelements.
7. Prerequisite skills to understanding the concept "element" may be using a dictionary (to look up terms such as *radium*), reading the periodic chart, and understanding what is meant by related terms such as *compound* and *mixture*.

## The Problem of Inert Knowledge

Even though students have learned information, they sometimes fail to "know" it when asked. Psychologists refer to this phenomenon as "inert knowledge" (Gagné, Yekovich, & Yekovich, 1993). Students often have inert knowledge because instead of developing a thorough, conceptual understanding of the knowledge, students simply memorize information. The knowledge may be inaccessible, or accessible only for tests of rote memory but not for solving actual problems.

Here are some things you can do to help students overcome the problem of inert knowledge (Bransford et al., 1989; Cooper & Sweller, 1987):

1. Make sure students comprehend rather than just memorize information by having them describe the information in their own words and having them explain why the information is relevant.
2. Encourage students to describe a variety of situations in which the information may be applied.
3. Give students sufficient opportunity to review and practice using new information so that they learn to use it automatically.
4. Have groups of students engage in problem-solving activities. Have them identify the *type* of problem they are trying to solve to activate knowledge they have that relates to the problem.

## Principles: Relationships Among Concepts

Concepts provide students an entry point from which they can broaden their knowledge of the world by building relationships among different concepts. Concepts may relate to each other in various ways, and "generalizations that describe relationships between or among concepts" are called **principles** (Marzano et al., 1988, p. 37).

Katz (1976) has identified four major types of principles that describe different kinds of relationships among concepts:

1. *Cause and effect principles* describe a causal relationship between concepts, such as:

   *If water is heated to 212 degrees Fahrenheit, it will boil.*

   or

   *If the demand for gasoline increases or the supply decreases, the price of gasoline will rise.*

2. *Correlational principles* describe how two concepts are related in quantity or degree, such as:

   *People who read more tend to have large vocabularies.*

   Note that correlational principles provide no information about causation. In the example above, one cannot conclude that reading causes people to have large vocabularies. It may be that having large vocabularies causes people to read more. Or, there may be other factors, such as the amount of formal education one has, that cause the concepts of amount of reading and vocabulary size to be related.

   As a test of your knowledge of these principles, try to generate an example of each.

3. *Probability principles* describe the chance that some event may occur, such as:

   *There is a 50 percent chance that one might guess the correct answer to a true-false question.*

4. *Axiomatic principles* express universally accepted beliefs regarding society, philosophy, or science, such as:

   *People who commit crimes should be punished.*

   or

   *All people are entitled to life, liberty, and the pursuit of happiness.*

Teach principles either by the method of deduction or induction. Using a deductive method, first describe the principle and then ask students to give examples of it. Using an inductive method, first give students examples and then ask them to figure out the principle.

# Comprehension

**Comprehension** is the process by which we construct meaning from incoming information. Concept formation, which helps us structure and organize information in meaningful ways, makes comprehension easier. Although we may transmit information by various means, such as signs, symbols, or graphics, we most often use words. Research on comprehension has focused primarily on how students comprehend what they read because of the central role reading plays in the process of educating students.

## The Role of Schemata

The term **schema** (the plural of which is *schemata*) refers to an individual's existing organization of knowledge about a topic (Anderson, 1990; Kintsch, 1994), and many researchers have examined the role schemata play in comprehension (e.g., Kuhara-Kojima & Hatano, 1991).

Schemata about a particular topic may vary from person to person, depending on their prior experiences, so that different people will not always comprehend in the same way. You may teach a lesson to an entire class and find that different students have understood the lesson in different ways (Pressley et al., 1992). Students' existing schemata determine the meanings they construct from your presentations.

**6.7** ◎

*Describe the role of schemata in students' comprehension of new material.*

### Students' Existing Schemata and Comprehension

Suppose a teacher says, "A revolution takes place when a government is overthrown and a new government is created. Often, this involves creation of a new form of government. For instance, an absolute monarchy may be replaced by a democratic form of government." Here are some examples of different meanings different students may attach to what the teacher has said.

- A student who has no schema for the concept "revolution" would probably be unable to make any sense of the teacher's words.
- A student who is familiar only with the American Revolution has a narrow schema for "revolution" and might interpret the teacher's statements to mean that a revolution occurs when colonists overthrow the domination of the mother country and, in doing so, create a new government.
- A student who is familiar with the American, Russian, and French Revolutions has a broad understanding of "revolution" and might interpret the teacher's words to mean that a revolution occurs when a government is overthrown by people over whom the government has control. The people may be citizens of the country whose government is overthrown, as in the French and Russian Revolutions, or they may be citizens of the country's colonies, as in the American Revolution.

Schemata are mental structures that represent bodies of knowledge people have accumulated and stored in memory. Existing schemata determine how people process and understand new information. Since students construct their own schemata, their ability to interpret new information will also vary.

Sometimes new information contradicts a person's existing understandings. Many people resist new knowledge that does not conform to existing schemata. In such cases, major cognitive reorganization is necessary so that the new information can be integrated. You can help students restructure their schemata when necessary by (a) providing them with a wide range of examples and nonexamples, (b) having them discuss and write about their understandings, (c) confronting them with richer and more powerful ideas, and (d) giving them opportunities for hands-on, experiential learning.

# Eight Steps of Teaching New Schemata

Hyde and Bizar (1989) applied the following eight phases of teaching to science instruction. You may find this sequence of steps useful in developing complex schemata among your students in other areas as well.

1. Diagnosing existing schemata. Ask probing questions to examine students' existing conceptions and misconceptions.
2. Confronting schemata. Challenge preexisting ideas by presenting situations that students are unable to explain.
3. Exploring phenomena. Provide opportunities for hands-on exploration, "messing around," to give students raw data they can use in generating new explanations.
4. Generating opinions. Ask students to formulate and verbalize their

hypotheses, speculate on consequences, guess, and brainstorm.
5. Conducting systematic inquiry. Encourage students to become more focused and systematic; this kind of guidance allows students to think independently yet prevents them from pursuing dead ends and simplistic answers.
6. Debriefing explanations and concepts. Encourage students to reflect on their experiences and attempt to integrate their new findings with their previously existing ideas.
7. Debriefing cognitive processes. Ask students to consider the process that they engaged in and verbalize it.
8. Broadening schemata. You and your students relate the new understandings to other concepts.

Students typically try to make sense of new information by constructing and generating their own meanings (Driscoll, 1994; Perkins, Jay, & Tishman, 1993; Wittrock, 1974). The more actively and intentionally they go about generating new meanings, the better they will comprehend (von Glaserfeld, 1991).

# Activities for Strengthening Student Comprehension

**6.8** ◎

*Describe five methods of helping students comprehend.*

The following strategies can help increase your comprehension of material you are studying and help your students increase their comprehension.

## Paraphrasing and Summarizing

One of the simplest yet most effective methods to increase your comprehension is to paraphrase, or "tell in your own words," something you have just learned. Recalling and reconstructing recently learned material forces you to attend not only to various components of the material but also to ways in which the components are related to one another. Having to focus on relevant aspects of recently acquired information inevitably leads to better comprehension.

Summarizing, a more specific activity than paraphrasing, requires you to reconstruct material and condense it to its most important elements (van Dijk & Kintsch, 1983; Wittrock & Alesandrini, 1990). You have to identify and make judgments about ideas to isolate the most important ones.

## Questioning

Asking yourself questions is a valuable strategy because it forces you to evaluate your knowledge and examine your ideas in an effort to answer the question (King, 1992). Questioning yourself causes you to test your own understanding. Formulating questions aids comprehension (Palinscar & Brown, 1984), but students need to learn to ask questions that require higher-order thinking (Duell, 1978; Frase & Schwartz, 1975).

A variation on this involves **reciprocal questioning,** in which students in pairs or groups of three ask each other questions about material they have learned (King, 1990). A teacher may provide examples of good questions or helpful stems of questions (for example, "What are the strengths and weaknesses of . . . ?"). By developing questions and finding answers, students develop a more integrated understanding of new material.

*Continued on next page.*

## PQ4R

PQ4R, which stands for Preview, Question, Read, Reflect, Recite, and Review, is a well-known method for increasing reading comprehension that combines paraphrasing and questioning (Adams, Carnine, & Gersten, 1982; Anderson, 1990). Using this method, students first *preview* a passage to determine its length and how it is organized by headings and subheadings. Previewing allows people to see how the new information may relate to what they already know and provides them with a structure in which the new information can be placed.

The second step, *question,* calls for the student to use the organization of the passage to formulate questions. For example, using the subheading for the section of the chapter you are now reading, "Activities for Strengthening Student Comprehension," one might ask: "What are the activities for strengthening student comprehension?"

Next, students *read* the passage and *reflect* on the material presented to consider how it relates to existing knowledge, how the facts presented relate to one another, whether the information is consistent, and how the information will be useful in the future. Immediately afterward they should *recite* answers to the questions they developed earlier. They should be able to answer the questions without depending on the passage itself. If not, they should go back and begin the process again. Finally, they should *review* the material to make sure they will remember what they have learned.

## Note Taking

Note taking is another effective way to enhance comprehension (Kiewra, 1985, 1991; McWhorter, 1992). The process of writing down a set of ideas, either from spoken or written material, helps people remember and understand the material. Note taking is most effective when people take notes in their own words.

## Graphic Organizers

The use of graphic organizers, which are various kinds of charts and graphs, helps people analyze the structure of information,

organize information in a meaningful way, and comprehend it better (Mayer & Gallini, 1990; Winn, 1991).

The easiest kind of chart to make is a **linear array,** which is simply a line on which events are sequenced according to the time they took place. Consider the following passage:

> Our modern computers represent the fourth generation of computers; they are differentiated from previous computers because of their use of integrated circuits on a minute silicon chip, a method developed in the mid-1970s. Makers of the first generation of computers, back in 1946, had no idea of these developments, however. Their machine, called the ENIAC, weighed over 30 tons and relied on vacuum tubes. By the late 1950s, transistors had replaced vacuum tubes, heralding the beginning of the second generation of computers. The third generation of computers began in 1964 when transistors were replaced by integrated circuits.

Below is an example of a linear array based on information contained in the passage above:

I - 1946      1st generation: vacuum tubes
I
I - late 50s  2nd generation: transistors
I
I - 1964      3rd generation: integrated circuits
I
I - mid 70s   4th generation: integrated circuits on silicon chip

Creating a linear array forces the learner to reorganize information and place it in sequential order.

Frequently, the sequence of information is less important than its structure. The creation of **hierarchies** (or trees) helps people to examine the relationships between ideas to detect subordinate (lower) and superordinate (higher) categories (Van Patten, Chao, & Reigeluth, 1986). The chart depicted in figure 6.3 illustrates a hierarchy of information about living things. People who use hierarchies remember more information than those who do not (Bower, 1970).

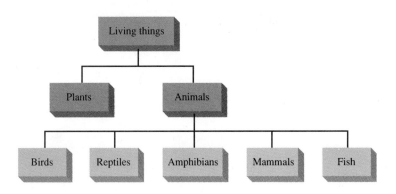

**Figure 6.3**
A hierarchy of information.

*Continued on next page.*

Although a hierarchy is more complex than a linear array, there are relationships among concepts that even the hierarchy cannot capture. Creating **networks** that depict the links among various ideas is an effective way to organize more complex information (Derry, 1990; Rafoth, Leal, & De Fabo, 1993). Consider the following passage:

> The Protestant Reformation in sixteenth-century Europe was to the church what the development of the nation-state was to politics. The various branches, such as the Lutheran, Calvinist, and Anglican churches, had their own identity and philosophies. At the same time, they had certain beliefs in common, such as the importance of Scripture. And, together with the Roman Catholic church, they shared certain intrinsically Christian beliefs. However, differences in interpretation of Scripture led to the development of substantially different sects. It was not until recently that this pattern was reversed; many sects nowadays seek greater cooperation and eventual unity, as demonstrated by the ecumenical movement of the present century.

The passage contains numerous ideas that are related in complex ways. Neither a linear array nor a hierarchy is adequate for graphically portraying the relationships among these ideas.

A network, however, allows even these complex ideas to be charted (Holley et al., 1979). Dansereau and his associates (e.g., Holley and Dansereau, 1984) have noted six types of links between ideas:

1. *Part of link,* in which one idea is part of another. In the passage, the Protestant church is *part of* Christianity. "Part of" links are frequently demonstrated by phrases such as "is a part of" or "is a type of."

2. *Type of/example of link,* in which one idea is an example of another. In the passage, the Lutheran, Calvinist, and Anglican churches are *examples of* Protestant churches. "Type of/example of" links are often indicated by phrases such as "is a kind of" or "is an example of."

3. *Leads to link,* in which one idea results in another. In the passage, "differences in interpretation of Scripture" *leads to* the development of different Protestant sects. This relationship is indicated by phrases such as "causes" or "results in."

4. *Analogy link,* in which one idea is analogous to another. In the passage, the development of Protestant churches was *analogous to* the development of nation-states. Analogies are indicated by phrases, such as "is similar to" or "corresponds to."

5. *Characteristic link,* in which one idea is a characteristic or trait of another idea. In the passage, "belief in the importance of Scripture" is a *characteristic of* Protestant sects. This relationship is often indicated by the phrases "is a feature of" or "is an aspect of."

6. *Evidence link,* in which one idea is presented as evidence of another. In the passage, "the ecumenical movement of the present century" is *evidence of* the reversal of the trend for the sects to have their separate identities.

These six different relationships are depicted by different graphic devices, as shown in figure 6.4. Once students have mastered this system, they can use it to improve their comprehension of a body of new material.

**Figure 6.4**
A network of information.

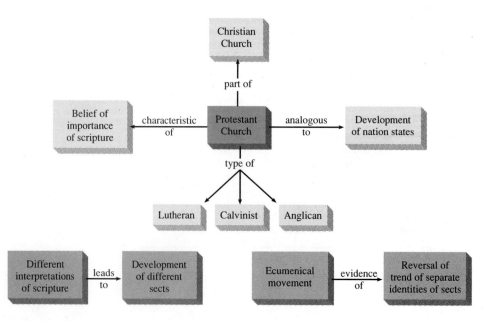

*Continued on next page.*

| Philosophy | Psychology | Education |
|---|---|---|
| Romanticism | Humanistic; client-centered therapy (C. Rogers) | Humanistic; open education movement; Summerhill (A. S. Neill) |
| Empiricism | Behaviorism (J. Watson, B. F. Skinner) | Social or cultural transmission; back-to-basics movement |
| Rationalism | Cognitivism; constructivism (J. Piaget, L. Vygotsky, information processing) | Progressive approach (J. Piaget, J. Dewey, J. Bruner) |

**Figure 6.5**
A matrix of information.

Comparisons of several topics along multiple dimensions can be graphed using a **matrix** (plural *matrices*). Suppose one wanted to organize three different philosophies with related approaches in psychology and education. Figure 6.5 depicts a matrix of these relationships.

## KEY POINTS

1. The three kinds of knowledge are declarative ("knowing *that*"), procedural ("knowing *how*"), and conceptual ("knowing *about*").

2. To help remember declarative knowledge, students should practice, overlearn, and review material frequently, so that it becomes automatically accessible.

3. Procedural knowledge differs from declarative knowledge in that procedures and rules are often used to transform information.

4. Procedural knowledge is best taught by explaining the purpose of the procedure and what kinds of problems the procedure is designed for, then by demonstrating the procedure, and finally by giving students feedback while they practice the procedure.

5. Students who acquire procedural knowledge on their own often learn how to debug and refine their procedures.

6. Conceptual knowledge involves categorizing a set of related information into an organized idea.

7. Young children acquire conceptual knowledge only gradually and may initially overgeneralize the concept; they also may understand an abstract concept in a concrete fashion.

8. Concepts may vary in terms of abstraction, generality, and complexity.

9. Concepts are best taught by pointing out their attributes and by using examples, nonexamples, and prototypes.

10. Conceptual knowledge is particularly helpful in enabling students to use procedures effectively because it provides an understanding of why a procedure is used.

11. To avoid inert knowledge, make sure students comprehend, not merely memorize, material and grasp the significance of it. Provide examples of numerous situations in which the material can be used and give students sufficient practice to automatize the material.

12. Four major kinds of relationships among concepts are cause and effect, correlational, probability, and axiomatic.

13. Comprehension is the process by which we construct meaning from incoming information; it is affected by peoples' schemata, or existing knowledge.

14. Activities for strengthening student comprehension include paraphrasing, summarizing, questioning, PQ4R (Preview, Question, Read, Reflect, Recite, and Review), note taking, and graphic organizers, such as linear arrays, hierarchies, networks, or matrices.

## SELF-STUDY EXERCISES

1. Contrast the three types of knowledge.

2. Describe procedures you would use to help students automatize information.

3. Define the term *concept* and give examples at varying levels of abstraction, generality, and complexity.

4. Select a concrete and an abstract concept and list their attributes.

5. Name some nonexamples you could use to teach the concept "profession" and describe attributes of the nonexamples that are and are not shared by the concept.

6. Of the following scientific concepts, select the one you think should be taught first and explain why: magnetism, temperature, and radioactivity.

7. Explain what schemata are and describe the role they play in the acquisition of new knowledge.

## FURTHER READINGS

Anderson, J. R. (1990). *Cognitive psychology and its implications* (3rd ed.). New York: W. H. Freeman.

Bruner, J. S. (1957). On going beyond the information given. In J. S. Bruner (Ed.), *Contemporary approaches to cognition* (pp. 41–69). Cambridge, MA: Harvard University Press.

Bruner, J. S. (1966). *Toward a theory of instruction.* New York: Norton.

Gagné, E. D., Yekovich, C. W., & Yekovich, F. R. (1993). *The cognitive psychology of school learning* (2nd ed.). New York: Harper Collins.

Marzano, R. J., Brandt, R. S., Hughes, C. S., Jones, B. F., Presseisen, B. Z., Rankin, S. C., & Suhor, C. (1988). *Dimensions of thinking: A framework for curriculum and instruction.* Alexandria, VA: ASCD.

## REFERENCES

Adams, A., Carnine, D., & Gersten, R. (1982). Instructional strategies for studying content area texts in the intermediate grades. *Reading Research Quarterly, 18,* 27–55.

Alexander, P. A. (1992). Domain knowledge: Evolving themes and emerging concerns. *Educational Psychologist, 27,* 33–51.

Anderson, J. R. (1976). *Language, memory, and thought.* Hillsdale, NJ: Erlbaum.

Anderson, J. R. (1990). *Cognitive psychology and its implications* (3rd ed.). New York: W. H. Freeman.

Benjafield, J. G. (1992). *Cognition.* Englewood Cliffs, NJ: Prentice Hall.

Bower, G. H. (1970). Organizational factors in memory. *Cognitive Psychology, 1,* 18–46.

Bransford, J. D., & Johnson, M. K. (1972). Contextual prerequisites for understanding: Some investigations of comprehension and recall. *Journal of Verbal Learning and Verbal Behavior, 11,* 717–726.

Bransford, J. D., Vye, N. J., Adams, L. T., & Perfetto, G. A. (1989). Learning skills and the acquisition of knowledge. In A. Lesgold & R. Glaser (Eds.), *Foundations for a psychology of education* (pp. 199–249). Hillsdale, NJ: Erlbaum.

Bruner, J. S. (1957). On going beyond the information given. In J. S. Bruner (Ed.), *Contemporary approaches to cognition* (pp. 41–69). Cambridge, MA: Harvard University Press.

Bruner, J. S. (1966). *The process of education.* Cambridge, MA: Harvard University Press.

Cameron, L. (1994). Organizing the world: Children's concepts and categories and implications for the teaching of English. *ELT Journal, 48,* 28–39.

Cooper, G., & Sweller, J. (1987). Effects of schema acquisition and rule automation on mathematical problem-solving transfer. *Journal of Educational Psychology, 79,* 347–362.

Dempster, F. N. (1989). Spacing effects and their implications for theory and practice. *Educational Psychology Review, 1,* 309–330.

Derry, S. J. (1990). Learning strategies for acquiring useful knowledge. In B. L. Jones & L. Idol (Eds.), *Dimensions of thinking and cognitive instruction.* Hillsdale, NJ: Erlbaum.

Driscoll, M. P. (1994). *Psychology of learning for instruction.* Boston: Allyn & Bacon.

Duell, O. K. (1978). Overt and covert use of objectives of different cognitive levels. *Contemporary Educational Psychology, 3,* 239–245.

Ellis, H. C., & Hunt, R. R. (1983). *Fundamentals of human memory and cognition* (3rd ed.). Dubuque, IA: William C. Brown.

Farnham-Diggory, S. (1992). *Cognitive processes in education* (2nd ed.). New York: Harper Collins.

Frase, L. T., & Schwartz, B. J. (1975). Effect of question production and answering on prose recall. *Journal of Educational Psychology, 67,* 628–635.

Gagné, E. D., Yekovich, C. W., & Yekovich, F. R. (1993). *The cognitive psychology of school learning* (2nd ed.). New York: Harper Collins.

Gagné, R. M. (1985). *The conditions of learning and theory of instruction* (4th ed.). New York: Holt, Rinehart & Winston.

Holley, C. D., & Dansereau, D. F. (1984). Networking: The technique and the empirical evidence. In C. D. Holley & D. F. Dansereau (Eds.), *Spatial learning strategies: Techniques, applications, and related issues* (pp. 81–108). New York: Academic Press.

Holley, C. D., Dansereau, D. F., McDonald, B. A., Garland, J. D., & Collins, K. W. (1979). Evaluation of a hierarchical mapping technique as an aid to prose processing. *Contemporary Educational Psychology, 4,* 227–237.

Hyde, A. A., & Bizar, M. (1989). *Thinking in context: Teaching cognitive processes across the elementary school curriculum.* New York: Longman.

Katz, S. E. (1976). *The effect of each of four instructional treatments on the learning of principles by children.* Madison, WI: Wisconsin Research and Development Center for Cognition and Learning, University of Wisconsin.

Kiewra, K. A. (1985). Investigating notetaking and review: A depth of processing alternative. *Educational Psychologist, 20,* 23–32.

Kiewra, K. A. (1991). Aids to lecture learning. *Educational Psychologist, 26,* 37–53.

King, A. (1990). Enhancing peer interaction and learning in the classroom through reciprocal questioning. *American Educational Research Journal, 27,* 664–687.

King, A. (1992). Facilitating elaborative learning through guided student-generated questioning. *Educational Psychologist, 27,* 111–126.

Kintsch, W. (1994). Text comprehension, memory, and learning. *American Psychologist, 49,* 294–303.

Klausmeier, H. J. (1985). *Educational psychology* (5th ed.). New York: Harper & Row.

Klausmeier, H. J. (1990). Conceptualizing. In B. Jones & L. Idol (Eds.), *Dimensions of thinking and cognitive instruction* (pp. 93–138). Hillsdale, NJ: Erlbaum.

Klausmeier, H. J., & Sipple, T. (1980). *Learning and teaching concepts.* New York: Academic Press.

Kossan, N. E. (1981). Developmental differences in concept acquisition strategies. *Child Development, 52,* 290–298.

Kuhara-Kojima, K., & Hatano, G. (1991). Contribution of content knowledge and learning ability to the learning of facts. *Journal of Educational Psychology, 83,* 253–263.

Leinhardt, G. (1992). What research on learning tells us about teaching. *Educational Leadership, 49*(7), 20–25.

Marzano, R. J., Brandt, R. S., Hughes, C. S., Jones, B. F., Presseisen, B. Z., Rankin, S. C., & Suhor, C. (1988). *Dimensions of thinking: A framework for curriculum and instruction.* Alexandria, VA: ASCD.

Mayer, R. E. (1992). Cognition and instruction: Their historical meeting within educational psychology. *Journal of Educational Psychology, 84,* 405–412.

Mayer, R. E., & Gallini, J. K. (1990). When is an illustration worth ten thousand words? *Journal of Educational Psychology, 82,* 715–726.

McWhorter, K. T. (1992). *Study and thinking skills in college* (2nd ed.). New York: Harper Collins.

Neale, D. C., Smith, D., & Johnson, V. G. (1990). Implementing conceptual change teaching in primary science. *Elementary School Journal, 91,* 109–131.

Ormrod, J. E. (1990). *Human learning: Principles, theories, and educational applications.* Columbus, OH: Merrill.

Palinscar, A. S., & Brown, A. L. (1984). Reciprocal teaching of comprehension-fostering and comprehension-monitoring activities. *Cognition and Instruction, 1,* 117–175.

Perkins, D., Jay, E., & Tishman, S. (1993). New conceptions of thinking: From ontology to education. *Educational Psychologist, 28,* 67–85.

Pressley, M., Wood, E., Woloshyn, V. E., Martin, V., King, A., & Menke, D. (1992). Encouraging mindful use of prior knowledge: Attempting to construct explanatory answers facilitates learning. *Educational Psychologist, 27,* 91–109.

Rafoth, M. A., Leal, L., & De Fabo, L. (1993). *Strategies for learning and remembering: Study skills across the curriculum.* Washington, DC: National Education Association Professional Library.

Resnick, L. B. (1987). Constructing knowledge in school. In L. S. Liben (Ed.), *Development and learning: Conflict or congruence?* (pp. 19–50). Hillsdale, NJ: Erlbaum.

Rosch, E. H. (1978). Principles of categorization. In E. Rosch & B. Lloyd (Eds.), *Cognition and categorization.* Hillsdale, NJ: Erlbaum.

Schwartz, B., & Reisberg, D. (1991). *Learning and memory.* New York: Norton.

Sywlester, R. (1985). Research on memory: Major discoveries, major educational challenges. *Educational Leadership, 42,* 69–75.

Tennyson, R. D., & Park, O. (1980). The teaching of concepts: A review of instructional design literature. *Review of Educational Research, 50,* 55–70.

van Dijk, T. A., & Kintsch, W. (1983). *Strategies in discourse comprehension.* New York: Academic Press.

Van Patten, J., Chao, C.-I., & Reigeluth, C. M. (1986). A review of strategies for sequencing and synthesizing instruction. *Review of Educational Research, 56,* 437–471.

von Glaserfeld, E. (1991). *Radical constructivism in mathematics education.* Boston: Kluwer.

Watts, G. H., & Anderson, R. C. (1971). Effects of three types of inserted questions on learning from prose. *Journal of Educational Psychology, 62,* 387–394.

Wilson, P. S. (1988, April). The relationship of students' definitions and example choices in geometry. Annual meeting of the American Educational Research Association, New Orleans, LA.

Winn, W. (1991). Learning from maps and diagrams. *Educational Psychology Review, 3,* 211–247.

Wittrock, M. C. (1974). Learning as a generative process. *Educational Psychologist, 11,* 87–95.

Wittrock, M. C., & Alesandrini, K. (1990). Generation of summaries and analogies and analytic and holistic abilities. *American Educational Research Journal, 92,* 169–184.

7

© Carol Petrachenko/NASA/Corbis Media

# Problem Solving, Decision Making, and Critical Thinking

# Chapter Outline

# Learning Objectives

7.1 Define higher-order thinking skills and explain their role in school learning.

7.2 Describe the process of problem solving.

7.3 Describe ten problem-solving strategies.

7.4 Describe five ways to teach problem solving.

7.5 Define *critical thinking* and explain its role in school learning.

# Preview

We now turn to the most important goal of the entire educational process: the transformation of students into individuals who can engage effectively in higher-order thinking. Higher-order thinking, or complex thinking, as it is sometimes called, includes the processes people use to solve problems, make decisions, and think critically.

The terms researchers use to study higher-order thinking are sometimes vague or overlapping. The three processes described in this chapter share properties related to the concept of creative thinking. To further complicate matters, the three processes also share elements with one another. To help you understand the processes better, we discuss each separately, but in practice people often engage in aspects of all three processes at the same time.

The material in this chapter will help you help students improve their higher-order thinking skills and, equally importantly, help *you* become a more effective thinker. Consider some typical problems teachers face: Should I refer a student for possible placement in a special education class? Should I move on to teach fractions or spend more time on basic number facts? How can I enlist the support of a student's parents? How can I help a fifth-grader who reads at the third-grade level learn social studies? What are the consequences of failing a student for a full academic year? Do I have sufficient grounds for notifying the authorities that a student may be a victim of child abuse?

These are only a few problems that teachers face every day. To solve any of them you need to use higher-order thinking skills. You need to

(a) critically evaluate the problem,
(b) devise possible solutions, and
(c) decide on the appropriate course of action.

Before examining the nature of higher-order thinking, let us raise a controversial question: Are there general higher-order thinking skills that apply across the board, or do various situations demand different kinds of specific thinking skills? The way we answer this question determines the strategies we will select to improve students' thinking.

If there are general higher-order thinking skills, we should develop courses to teach students how to think, and these courses should become as much a part of the school's curriculum as courses for teaching biology, history, or any other academic discipline.

On the other hand, if higher-order thinking skills vary from one discipline to another, creating courses to teach thinking seems pointless. Instead, teachers of different disciplines must help students learn different types of higher-order thinking.

It is, of course, possible that both interpretations have merit, in which case it would be necessary to teach general as well as domain-specific thinking skills. The remainder of this chapter focuses on the psychological properties of higher-order thinking as they relate to educational and instructional issues. ◉

# Higher-Order Thinking Skills

Higher-order thinking skills, such as solving problems, making decisions, and thinking critically, involve more complex ways of thinking than the lower-order cognitive processes, such as perceiving, remembering, or comprehending (Lewis & Smith, 1993; Underbakke, Borg, & Peterson, 1993). People cannot engage in effective higher-order thinking, however, unless they have already mastered the less complex cognitive skills. If people can't comprehend and remember what they hear, read, and see, they would never be able to solve problems, make decisions, or think critically about any issue.

What is your interpretation of higher-order thinking?

## Higher-Order Thinking in Schools

Critics frequently complain that teachers spend too much time teaching factual information and fail to challenge students in ways that lead them to develop higher-order thinking skills. Many educators and business leaders believe that because schools devote so little attention to these skills, numerous high school graduates leave school unprepared to deal effectively with the complexities of modern life.

**7.1** ◉

*Define higher-order thinking skills and explain their role in school learning.*

## Higher-Order Thinking Skills and Modern Life

Technological advancements increasingly dominate life in the United States and other industrialized countries. Consequently, today's students will face more complicated problems on a far larger scale than those previous generations faced. To cope effectively in the future, students will have to apply the skills of higher-order thinking. Consider the implications of just a few of the technological achievements

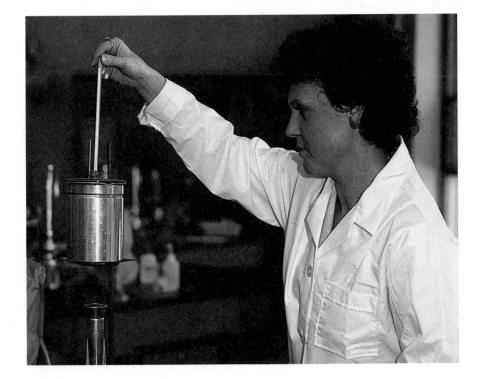

Higher-order thinking skills are necessary in modern life.

© Martha McBride/Unicorn Stock Photos

**Figure 7.1**

Sequential steps in solving a problem.

| |
|---|
| 1. Recognize that a problem exists. |
| 2. Form a mental representation of the problem by carrying out the steps below. |
| 3. Determine the goal(s) to be reached. |
| 4. Determine the givens at the start of the problem. |
| 5. Tentatively choose or devise a plan to achieve the goal(s). |
| 6. Determine if obstacles stand in the way of achieving the goal(s) according to the plan made in Step 5. If there are obstacles, return to Step 5 and devise another plan. If there are no obstacles, proceed to Step 7. |
| 7. Carry out the plan in Step 5. |
| 8. Evaluate the results of Step 7. If the problem is solved, stop. If not, begin again at Step 2. |

**Figure 7.2**

Characteristics of well- and ill-structured problems.

| Component | Well-structured | Ill-structured |
|---|---|---|
| Goal | Usually one concrete goal | One or more abstract goals |
| Givens | Clearly recognizable | Poorly recognizable or nonexistent |
| Solution | Usually one clear method that can be tested | Several methods that are untestable |

in such diverse areas as science, medicine, and communication. Scientific discoveries have already led to the ability to create nuclear energy or to carry out genetic engineering. It is certain that future discoveries will enable us to control the environment in ways not yet known. All people, scientists and nonscientists alike, will need to understand the nature of the potential problems associated with scientific breakthroughs.

Advances in medicine have increased people's lifespans, so today's students will have to decide how to deal with the physical, psychological, and economic well-being of an aging population. Global communications systems have made the concept of a world community a reality. Millions of people hear of major events as soon as they occur. Students will need to think critically about varied interpretations of such events to decide what to believe.

These examples are not hypothetical issues. They are merely a few illustrations of the complex realities students will confront. Let us now turn to the nature of higher-order thinking and what you can do to make yourself and your students more effective thinkers.

# Problem Solving

A problem is typically defined as "a situation in which the individual wants to do something but does not know the course of action needed to get what he or she wants" (Newell & Simon, 1972). Although various researchers define problem solving in slightly different ways (e.g., Anderson, 1993; André, 1986; Beyer, 1987; Halpern, 1989), all basically agree on the sequence of events that occurs. Figure 7.1 shows the commonly accepted sequential steps in solving a problem.

## The Structure of Problems

7.2

*Describe the process of problem solving.*

Problems consist of three components: **goal(s)**, **givens**, and **method of solution** (Ormrod, 1990). The more precisely one can define these components, the more clearly structured the problem is. Problems range along a continuum from those that are well-structured to those that are ill-structured. Figure 7.2 shows the ways in which well- and ill-structured problems differ.

## The IDEAL Approach to Problem Solving

Students can remember the basic steps involved in problem solving if they associate each step with the letters making up the word *IDEAL*, a mnemonic device proposed by Bransford and Stein (1984).

| | |
|---|---|
| I | Identify the problem. |
| D | Define and represent the problem. |
| E | Explore possible strategies. |
| A | Act on the strategies. |
| L | Look back and evaluate the effects of your activities. |

Suppose a teacher asks students to find the West African country of Benin on the globe. After failing to find Benin on the globe, the students suspect that Benin may be a new name for the country. How can they find Benin on the globe if it is called something else?

Using the IDEAL strategy, they first *identify* the problem. ("We can't locate Benin on the globe.") Next, they *define* and *represent* the problem. ("Benin is not shown on the globe; we need to find some other way to find its location beside looking at the globe.") Then, the students *explore* possible strategies ("We could go to the library and try to find a more up-to-date map or globe, but there's no guarantee that the library material is more up-to-date; we could call the embassy from Benin and ask them the country's location or its former name—a bit complex because we have to call Washington, DC, but it could work; or, we could look up Benin in the encyclopedia and see if Benin was previously called something else"). Next, the students *act* on the strategy of looking up Benin in the encyclopedia. Finally, they *look* back to see if their strategy worked. From the encyclopedia, they learn that Benin was previously called Dahomey. The students return to the globe and look for Dahomey.

## Well-Structured Problems

The major characteristic of well-structured problems is the possibility of objectively testing the correctness of the solution. The kinds of problems students must solve in school frequently fall at the well-structured end of the continuum. Often the student's task is to identify the givens and goal(s) and then apply the "correct" method of solution.

Math problems are classic examples of well-structured problems. If the problem is to determine how much carpeting it will take to cover the floor of a 12- by 15-foot room, the only correct answer is 180 square feet. Apart from reasoning the problem out, one could find out if the answer is correct by actually seeing if 180 square feet of carpeting cover the floor.

## Ill-Structured Problems

Many problems people encounter outside of school fall at the ill-structured end of the continuum. The problem of carving out a successful career is an example of an ill-structured problem. The definition of *career* has countless possibilities: teacher, travel agent, bank teller, and so on. Furthermore, the abstract goal of *successful* career is subject to numerous interpretations.

It is also difficult to establish clearly what the numerous givens in the problem are. They might include, among other things, a person's personality and talents, the cost of preparing for a career, and future economic or social conditions that might alter the nature of the career. Similarly, there are numerous solutions for achieving a successful career.

In an ill-defined problem, it is virtually impossible to verify whether the solution is correct. One could argue that the only thing that counts is whether the person who pursues a career finds it "successful." The point, however, is that we can't test the solution in the same objective way we can determine if the amount of carpeting covers the floor.

"The best way to approach ill-defined problems is to specify multiple goals in objective terms so that a variety of solution paths can be considered" (Halpern, 1989, p. 355). A person trying to carve out a successful career might define

Give examples of ill-structured problems that students at the elementary, junior, and senior high school levels probably encounter.

"successful" in terms of more objective criteria. In other words, although different people have different notions of what constitutes success, the person seeking a successful career must define his or her idea of success in more objective or concrete terms, such as amount of income, prestige, or degree of interest in the career.

Having defined success in more objective terms, the person can focus on careers that lead to those goals. Using objective terms also makes it easier to specify the method of solution and to determine whether the necessary givens are present.

### Problems Encountered by Teachers

In contrast to nonprofessionals, professionals typically confront ill-structured problems. As a teacher, you will have to impose structure on the many ill-structured problems you will encounter.

Take, for example, the problem of introducing a new unit in a way that captures students' interest. You could define the relatively abstract goal of capturing students' interest in more objective terms, such as the amount of on-task behavior students exhibit. Although some of the givens in the problem may be clear, such as the content of the unit or the amount of time available for instruction, other givens, such as students' current knowledge and level of interest in the topic, may not be evident.

As with most ill-structured problems, there are numerous possible solutions: presenting a film, taking the class on a field trip, or asking students to predict what they think the unit will cover, to name just a few possibilities. After defining the goals and the givens of the problem as objectively as possible, make a professional judgment as to which solution is most likely to achieve the goals.

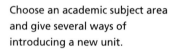

Choose an academic subject area and give several ways of introducing a new unit.

This problem with ill-structured components is typical of those facing classroom teachers. Notice, however, that the problem has one critically important characteristic of well-structured problems: the possibility of objectively testing the correctness of the solution.

In other words, you could determine the amount of on-task behavior students exhibited during your lesson. If you are satisfied with the results, you may decide to use the same method again with future classes. If not, you might decide to try another form of presentation the next time you teach the unit. By analyzing problems in the classroom, experienced teachers gradually add to their store of effective teaching strategies.

## Problem Representation

One of the biggest obstacles to solving problems is the failure to represent the problem accurately (e.g., Resnick, 1989). An accurate representation of a problem includes a clear, objective definition of the goals and an accurate assessment of the relevant givens. Many people, including teachers, often fail to achieve their goals because the goals themselves are not defined objectively. Another frequent stumbling block to achieving goals is the failure to use all relevant information or to pay attention to irrelevant information.

## Representing Problems in Written Form

Often, the best way to represent a problem accurately is simply to write it down. Some problems lend themselves to pictorial representation. If possible, have students draw a diagram of the problem. If a problem does not lend itself to pictorial representation, have students write down the goals, the givens, and the connections between them. Representing problems in written form helps to clarify what the goals are and what relevant information is available. It also frees up students' working memory to focus on possible solutions without having to keep the nature of the problem in mind.

Students use different strategies to solve a problem.

© Martin R. Jones/Unicorn Stock Photos

## General Problem-Solving Strategies

Here are some descriptions of **heuristics**, or rules of thumb, that you and your students may use to solve various kinds of problems. Note that not all heuristics are equally helpful for all types of problems. The nature of the components of a problem determine which heuristics are likely to be most helpful. The strategies described in the following sections appear in André (1986), Gagné, Yekovich, and Yekovich (1993), and Halpern (1989). If you wish more information about them, refer to the original sources.

### Means-Ends Analysis

Means-ends analysis consists of identifying obstacles that stand in the way of solving a problem and then creating subgoals whose objectives are to overcome each of the obstacles. This approach is a general problem-solving strategy that applies to many kinds of problems. Halpern (1989) uses the example of a chess game, in which the goal of winning the game is achieved by subgoals, such as putting the opposing king in check, which might require further reduction by determining the steps needed to accomplish it.

Suppose you assign a group of students to make a class presentation on how a bill becomes law. Tell them to analyze the obstacles preventing them from completing the task, which might be not knowing where to get information on the subject in the library, not knowing how to divide the labor among members of the group, or not knowing how to develop an interesting and easily understood presentation.

Having identified the obstacles, the group should then define appropriate subgoals (find out where to get information in the library, decide how to divide the labor and how to design the presentation) and start considering possible solutions. Reaching the final goal now becomes easier.

### Working Backward

The strategy of working backward consists of trying to define the goal in terms of the givens. Young children often intuitively use this strategy when they solve a maze problem; by working backward from the end of the maze, they are often able to quickly draw the correct path to its origin. You may remember using this approach in high school geometry; you started with the theorem and worked backwards to the postulates.

7.3 ◎

*Describe ten problem-solving strategies.*

Novices often select the method of working backward because it helps them limit the search to relevant areas and avoid blind alleys. On the other hand, working backward is usually the last approach experts use (Gagné, Yekovich, & Yekovich, 1993). Experts don't need to avoid blind alleys because they know where they're going.

## Simplification

When trying to solve complex problems, it sometimes helps to focus initially on major components of the problem, temporarily ignoring less important information. Of course, this method is risky. Information that appears to be less important may in fact be crucial, and its omission may prevent students from solving the problem. Nevertheless, when the given information overwhelms students, simplification may be an effective strategy.

Suppose students are trying to determine the causes of the American Civil War. Instead of having them look at the political, social, and economic conditions, have them focus more narrowly on political factors or on social or economic factors. Of course, simplification can mislead because students may omit important information (e.g., the economic basis of slavery). However, having investigated the problem after simplifying it, they can then focus on other aspects to gain a broader and more comprehensive understanding.

## Generalization and Specialization

Generalization is the process of viewing a problem as a particular example of a broader problem. Specialization is the process of viewing the problem narrowly and identifying its unique components. This strategy involves categorizing the problem as a subset of a larger problem. For example, air pollution is a subset of environmental pollution. Once the broader category is identified, identify commonalities and differences between the larger category and the subset. In addition, further categorization can identify acid rain and chemicals emitted from factories as subsets of air pollution. You can then approach a problem from both a broad and a narrow point of view.

## Trial and Error

Trial and error often works well when the problem is well structured and there are relatively few possible solutions. Although this strategy may help students during initial exploration of a problem, you should intervene if they begin activities that will lead to misconceptions or incorrect conclusions. Trial-and-error approaches are most likely to be effective when the problem solver has some background about the concepts involved; for example, persons familiar with computers use "hacking" as a way to expand their knowledge about what computers can do. "Hacking" won't help people who don't understand how computers work.

## Rules

It is possible to solve many well-structured problems, particularly those in mathematics and science, by applying rules. One may discover possible rules in other kinds of problems by paying attention to patterns that occur among subgoals or givens. Rules in other areas, such as the social sciences are not as hard-and-fast as those in science or mathematics. For example, the rule "after a war, the victor goes through a period of economic growth" may be generally correct but not universally true.

## Brainstorming

The objective of brainstorming is to produce as many novel or uncommon solutions to a problem as possible, regardless of how off-beat they may seem. Group brainstorming sessions may not only trigger a possible solution, but they may also spark

**THE FAR SIDE** By GARY LARSON

"Maybe we should write that spot down."

lively interest in the problem. You need not confine brainstorming to group settings; individuals may also brainstorm on their own.

Brainstorming is used successfully in a variety of areas in the curriculum, from planning a science project to comprehending a difficult text or writing a play. For example, Beck (1989) urges students to use a prereading brainstorming strategy known as PrEP to help them use their current knowledge to comprehend new concepts. PrEP requires students to (a) free-associate about a concept that will be important in the upcoming text, (b) determine how they arrived at their free associations, and (c) discuss new ideas that have developed as a result of this activity.

In brainstorming, being "wild and crazy" is desirable. The goal is to generate as many solutions as possible. Encourage students to think "around the problem" and to come up with imaginative and unusual ideas. To promote creative thinking, withhold judgments about the value of the ideas until after final decisions are made. Criticism may make students anxious and dampen creativity.

Form a small group and brainstorm about how to learn as much as possible in your educational psychology course.

## Contradiction

Contradiction, which uses the process of elimination to find the correct solution, works best with problems having only a few, mutually exclusive solutions. If you can show that all but one of the possible solutions are incorrect, the remaining solution must be correct. Suppose, for example, that you were asked this question:

Which of the following is *not* part of Great Britain?

a. England

b. Scotland

c. Ireland

d. Wales

You may not know that Ireland is not part of Great Britain, but if you know that England, Scotland, and Wales are, then Ireland must be the correct answer.

### Restate the Problem

Rewording an ill-structured problem by formulating a new goal that is broader than the original goal generally leads to more possible solutions. Students might restate the problem of "How can I pass the upcoming test?" to "How can I learn more about this subject?" resulting in finding a new approach to studying.

### Analogies and Metaphors

Sometimes it is possible to uncover a solution to a problem by applying strategies used to solve similar problems dealing with different content (Glynn, 1991). For example, a group of sixth-graders charged with writing a "class constitution" that outlines the rules for classroom behavior might use the process of drafting the U.S. Constitution as an analogy. What processes did the authors engage in, what laws did they include, and how did they ratify the document?

## Domain-Specific Problem Solving

The kinds of heuristics described so far are general problem-solving strategies because they apply to a wide range of situations. Their usefulness depends on the structure, not the content of the problem.

**Why do you think there is little evidence that general problem-solving strategies are effective?**

There is little evidence that people trained in general problem-solving strategies become more competent in solving problems in various domains such as science, medicine, or teaching. Expert problem solvers in various disciplines have good problem-solving strategies, but they also have a great deal of knowledge about their discipline (Mayer, 1987; Perkins & Solomon, 1989).

To become an expert teacher, you have to acquire a lot of knowledge about the field. Your study of educational psychology will increase your knowledge of teaching and enable you to solve more effectively problems you will encounter as a teacher.

## Expert and Novice Problem-Solving Strategies

Experts in a field are more competent than novices at solving problems related to that field because experts have had years of experience in that particular discipline. The superior performance of experts, however, does not result simply because they have spent more time in a field and have accumulated more knowledge. It also comes from how they organize knowledge. Experts organize knowledge in a hierarchical manner, ranging from the most general to the most specific (Gagné, Yekovich, & Yekovich, 1993). Novices tend to view problems as consisting of discrete pieces of information, but experts perceive problems as consisting of organized clusters of related information. As a result, experts solve problems more rapidly and effectively than novices do.

Regardless of the discipline, experts and novices exhibit similar differences in problem-solving behavior. Experts spend more time than novices in analyzing problems and exploring various ways of representing them before attempting a solution (Kurfiss, 1988). They also actively search for connections between the problem and their existing knowledge. Novices often jump rapidly to the solution phase and fail to include all of the relevant information (Schoenfield, 1985).

Even though experts in different disciplines use similar problem-solving strategies, experts in one discipline are no better than novices in solving problems related to another discipline. Experts also learn things related to their discipline more rapidly than they learn unrelated things (Resnick & Klopfer, 1989). These findings underscore the important role that knowledge plays in the problem-solving process. Cognitive psychology has shown that the amount of knowledge in a person's organized schema often accurately predicts how well and how rapidly the person will

*Annual* **Edition**

unit *4*

learn new information. It is the amount of knowledge experts have that increases their ability to comprehend new information about their field. These findings suggest that problem-solving strategies are domain-specific, not general in nature.

### Problem Solving by Expert and Novice Teachers

Just as in other fields, expert teachers represent teaching-related problems in cognitively more complex ways than novices do (Chi, Glaser, & Farr, 1988; Livingston & Borko, 1989). In comparison to novices, expert teachers integrate and use more information and are more sensitive to students' behavioral cues that signal the need to change the instructional approach to maintain a smoothly flowing lesson (Westerman, 1990). For example, expert teachers can more accurately interpret nonverbal cues indicating students' lack of comprehension than novices can (Stader, 1990). Experience alone, however, does not constitute expertise; that is, teachers do not become expert simply by teaching for many years. Expertise in teaching is a function of how teachers organize their experience and knowledge, such as the kinds of questions they ask about the process of teaching and learning or the way in which some teachers analyze their own teaching behavior.

Effective problem solving relies heavily on being knowledgeable about the problem.

## The Nature of Generative Knowledge

Your ability to think effectively about a topic depends on your knowledge of the topic (Walker, 1987). The more knowledgeable you are, the more likely you can think effectively. Building an appropriate knowledge base as support for higher-order thinking must begin in the early grades and continue throughout your school years.

Knowledge is sometimes used as a synonym for information. Such a view creates the false impression that students are receptacles into which teachers should pour information. However, research in cognitive psychology has consistently demonstrated that students are active learners who seek to make sense of the world in which they live.

**Generative knowledge** is the term applied to "knowledge that can be used to interpret new situations, to solve problems, to think and reason, and to learn . . . [in order to acquire such knowledge] students must elaborate and question what they are told, examine the new information in relation to other information, and build new knowledge structures" (Resnick & Klopfer, 1989, p. 5). You cannot give students generative knowledge. Having students learn things by rote merely equips them with a certain amount of information, not knowledge. Students acquire generative knowledge only by constructing it themselves.

## The Role of Practice in Learning to Solve Problems

In school students typically solve problems within the framework of an academic discipline. How you solve problems in one discipline as opposed to another depends on the generative knowledge associated with the discipline. Solving a math problem, for example, demands different skills than solving a problem in social studies.

Learning how to solve problems within an academic discipline takes time and practice (Delclos & Harrington, 1991). Initially, students' understanding of a particular class of problems is at the level of declarative knowledge, so they must keep in mind the steps they are using to solve a problem. To become proficient problem solvers, students must learn to carry out these steps automatically.

Repeated practice leads to automatic performance, but it requires lots of time. Teachers sometimes face the dilemma of whether they should have students continue practicing or move on to other concepts so they can cover the entire curriculum in the time allotted. Teachers often find it difficult to achieve a balance between practicing and moving on because of the pressure to have their students pass standardized tests that cover the entire curriculum (Delclos & Harrington, 1991).

## Helping Students Become Better Problem Solvers

**7.4** 

*Describe five ways to teach problem solving.*

Here are some ways you can help students become better solvers of discipline-related problems.

### Demonstrating Problem-Solving Behavior

When introducing problem-solving strategies to students, demonstrate to the class how *you* go about solving the problem. Model techniques of problem solving; point out the goal and the givens of the problem and explain step-by-step how you devise the solution. Consider the following problem:

What is the value of *x* if the area of the triangle is 20 percent of the area of the rectangle?

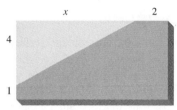

You may say to the class, "Well, I could try to solve this through trial and error by trying different values of *x* to find the value that makes the triangle 20 percent of the rectangle. Or, I could try to solve it by using what I know about areas of rectangles and triangles. The area of the rectangle would be (4 + 1) times (*x* + 2). The area of the triangle would be 1/2 times *x* times 4. Since I want the triangle to be 20 percent of the rectangle, I set the problem up as follows:

$$.20 \times (4 + 1) \times (x + 2) = 1/2 \times x \times 4$$

Now, I simplify terms and solve for *x:*

$$.20 \times (5) \times (x + 2) = 4x/2$$
$$1 \times (x + 2) = 2x$$
$$x + 2 = 2x$$
$$2 = x$$

And I arrive at my solution.

Having modeled the process, have students solve similar problems. You could also follow this problem with another: "Now, try to find the value of *x* if the triangle is 30 percent of the rectangle."

### Cognitive Apprenticeship

A cognitive apprenticeship approach involves having groups of students (the apprentices) work with you (the expert). The apprenticeship consists of (a) modeling the problem-solving behavior for students, (b) coaching students, (c) gradually removing teacher support, (d) articulating reasoning processes with knowledge, (e) comparing students' behavior with yours, and (f) encouraging students to establish their own goals and subgoals within a task (Collins, Brown, & Newman, 1986; Farnham-Diggory, 1992).

Make sure students understand what the problem is by having them explain it in their own words. Have students think through a problem aloud to help them focus on what they are doing and monitor their progress. Having students verbalize aloud is particularly effective when problems are abstract (Stinessen, 1975). Gradually increase the difficulty of problems. Show students how to solve problems that include irrelevant information to help them focus more clearly on relevant information.

Have small groups of students work on problems. Students can learn a lot about solving problems from each other (Webb, 1982, 1983). A small-group setting also signals that problem solving is a socially valued activity. Working in a group makes problem solving more fun and may help motivate students (Resnick & Klopfer, 1989).

In problem-solving groups, students can learn from feedback and explanations from their peers.

© CLEO Photography

### Reciprocal Teaching

An effective way to promote learning is to have pairs of students teach one another. Such teaching, which is called reciprocal teaching, benefits students because they have to form a more clearly organized structure of the problem. King (1990) found that reciprocal teaching is better than discussion groups for improving student performance. Students who study for the purpose of teaching the material to another student can solve problems better than students who merely study the material (Benware & Deci, 1984).

## Transfer of Problem-Solving Skills

The major purpose of teaching problem-solving skills is not to enable students to solve individual problems, but rather to enable them to solve various types of problems. Numerous problems within an academic discipline share the same structure. One of the best ways to help students learn to transfer their problem-solving skills is to have them solve numerous problems of the same type.

### Diagrams and Pictorial Models

The use of labeled diagrams and pictorial models is particularly helpful for less-able students. A review of twenty studies comparing the performance of students taught with and without diagrammatic models found that less-able students taught with diagrams consistently performed better on transfer problems than students not taught with diagrams (Mayer, 1989). The same results occurred regardless of whether the teacher presented the model before or during instruction. The use of models had no effect on the performance of higher-ability students.

# Decision Making

"A decision always involves two or more competing alternatives of action. Usually, each alternative has several pros and cons associated with it" (Halpern, 1989, p. 308). Decision making is intimately related to problem solving. Only well-structured problems that have a single goal and a single method of solution do not require a decision. Solving most problems, however, requires a series of successive decisions, each of which depends on the outcomes of those that precede it.

## Teachers as Decision Makers

Most of the problems you will confront as a teacher involve decision making. You will have to make decisions about what and how to teach and how to manage student behavior: What should I teach today? How can I make the material understandable and interesting? What do I do about students who already know the material? What do I do about students who aren't ready for this material? How do I handle disruptive students? How do I respond to the parent who complains that I assign too much homework?

Conceptualizing classroom teaching within the framework of problem solving and decision making will help you organize classroom activities so that instruction will proceed smoothly. If you regard the act of teaching within the framework of decision making, the first decision you must make involves problem selection. Often there are several choices regarding problem selection; for example, you must sometimes decide whether to continue work on a particular topic or move on to another one. Another example of decision making involving problem selection is deciding how to present a new unit in a way that captures students' interest. Deciding to attack the problem of student interest means you have decided to work on that problem instead of some other one.

Having made the decision to solve a particular problem, your next step is to decide which goal or goals you wish to achieve. Having decided on the goal(s), you must decide what solution to apply and how to evaluate its effectiveness.

### Seeking Disconfirming Evidence

Teachers take actions to produce results. It is helpful if research evidence confirms that certain actions lead to certain results, as, for example, in the case of increasing lower-ability students' performance on transfer problems through the use of diagrammatic models (Mayer, 1989). It is not uncommon, however, for teachers to take actions whose results are not clearly documented by research findings. For example, a teacher who pairs students of the same gender to work cooperatively on a project may decide that the cause of their improved performance is that each student is the same gender.

Students learn best when they actively participate in the learning process.

Formulate a problem and list the series of decisions you would have to make to reach a solution.

**Students working in pairs reinforce each other's learning.**

© Martha McBride/Unicorn Stock Photos

This conclusion, however, may be incorrect. Improved student performance may result from the fact that pairs worked cooperatively, not from the fact that they were the same gender. One way to confirm the soundness of a decision such as forming student pairs of the same gender is to seek disconfirming evidence (Halpern, 1989) by forming pairs of opposite genders to observe the effects on academic performance. If performance continues to improve, the cause of the improvement is more likely to be cooperative learning, not pairing students of the same gender.

# Critical Thinking

7.5

*Define* critical thinking *and explain its role in school learning.*

Many people believe individuals have different opinions that are all equally valid. People are, of course, entitled to have their own opinions, but some opinions are supported by stronger evidence than others. We use **critical thinking** when we analyze arguments and opinions and try to justify, refute, and evaluate them.

Critical thinking is an ambiguous concept (Hudgins & Edelman, 1988; Lewis & Smith, 1993) that is used in a number of different ways. Part of the ambiguity of critical thinking stems from the fact that the processes involved in critical thinking frequently overlap those involved in other forms of higher-order thinking. The boundaries separating the forms of complex thinking are sometimes blurred and somewhat artificial, often reflecting the particular interest of individual investigators. It is difficult to summarize research findings dealing with critical thinking because different researchers use the term in different ways. Furthermore, some researchers use other terms such as *thinking skills* or *reasoning* to refer to *critical thinking,* and these terms also vary in meaning.

Some researchers (e.g., Udall & High, 1989) use the term *critical thinking* loosely as a synonym for higher-order thinking. Others define critical thinking as "directed thinking," that is, "thinking that is purposeful, reasoned, and goal directed" (Halpern, 1989, p. 5) or as "a rational response to questions that cannot be answered definitively and for which all the relevant information may not be available" (Kurfiss, 1988, p. 2).

Many researchers believe critical thinking includes the thinker's conscious process of monitoring and evaluating his or her own thinking (e.g., Covington, 1985; Halpern, 1989) and regard critical thinking as "*reflective* [emphasis added] and reasonable thinking that is focused on deciding what to believe or do" (Ennis, 1985, p. 45). In addition, some believe that the ability to recognize when it is appropriate to think critically (Hudgins & Edelman, 1988) and the ability to engage in critical thinking without having to be told to do so (Hudgins et al., 1989) are important components of critical thinking.

Definitions of critical thinking vary in terms of precision. Defining critical thinking as higher-order thinking is much less precise than defining it as reflective, reasoned thinking directed at achieving some goal. Probably the most precise definition of *critical thinking* emerges when it is used in conjunction with the concept of *problem solving*.

## Critical Thinking and Problem Solving

According to Kurfiss (1988, p. 29), "critical thinking is a form of problem solving, but a major difference between the two is that critical thinking involves reasoning about open-ended or 'ill-structured' problems, while problem solving is usually considered narrower in scope." The result of critical thinking is not a testable solution, but rather a conclusion that is justified on the basis of a reasoned argument. But conclusions cannot be tested, placing the responsibility on the individual to provide supporting arguments.

Critical thinking involves the process of seeking and evaluating the *evidence* of an argument before accepting its conclusion. An argument's conclusion may be that a particular belief or a certain course of action is justified. You can use critical thinking to examine the soundness of your own conclusions or those of someone else.

Arguments that allegedly justify beliefs and actions take many forms in everyday life. Politicians running for office spend much time and energy presenting arguments as to why they should be elected. Newspaper editorials present arguments justifying the paper's belief or call for action. Television bombards us with commercials, which are really arguments that try to justify the conclusion that one brand is better than all others and that we should buy it. Critical thinking skills help us decide whether the conclusions an argument leads to are justified.

> Explain how you can think critically about your performance as a teacher.

## Critical Thinking Skills: General or Domain-Specific?

As with other forms of higher-order thinking, there is debate about whether critical thinking skills apply to all disciplines or whether they differ from discipline to discipline.

There is little doubt that people can learn the general skills of analyzing weaknesses in arguments, such as drawing conclusions from too little evidence or on the basis of one's limited experience rather than on the basis of knowledge (Kurfiss, 1988). McPeck (1981), however, dismisses the idea that there are general critical thinking skills on the grounds that what constitutes sound evidence varies from discipline to discipline. A counterargument, however, is that regardless of the discipline, students may approach a problem critically by applying such skills as first identifying what they already know and then determining what they need to know before beginning to gather more information (Stasz & Associates, 1981).

> Do you think critical thinking skills are general or domain-specific? Why?

### General Critical Thinking Courses

The belief that critical thinking skills are generalizable has led to the development of courses and textbooks on critical thinking (e.g., Copi, 1986; Kelly, 1988; Ruggiero, 1984), particularly at the college level. Some evidence suggests that such courses are effective, but this evidence is limited largely to self-reports given by the professors who teach the courses and by students who have taken such courses (Nickerson, Perkins, & Smith, 1985; Resnick, 1987). Paul (1982) claims that courses in critical thinking only teach students how to rationalize their existing beliefs.

Debating requires analyzing weaknesses in your opponent's arguments.

© Sygma

### Critical Thinking Courses in Teacher Education

Several efforts have been made to teach students in teacher education programs how to think critically about education. Zeuli and Buchmann (1986) found that, after completing a social foundations course designed to increase students' use of reflective thinking, students still failed to grasp the limitations of employing teaching practices based on their own experiences as students.

In another study, student teachers participated in a program that included attending a seminar to promote reflective thinking. One of the program's major goals was to increase students' respect for cultural diversity and enable them to identify and modify curricular materials containing cultural bias. At the end of the program, students regarded teaching with a less custodial view than student teachers typically develop. In general, however, students retained views they had prior to the program and became more articulate about them. The report notes, however, that it may be too early in the students' careers to determine the full effectiveness of the program (Zeichner & Liston, 1987).

## Critical Thinking in the Schools

Critical thinking has received less systematic attention from researchers than problem solving. It seems clear, however, from the existing evidence that people typically do not naturally engage in critical thinking. Although strategies to improve critical thinking remain largely speculative, two major obstacles to thinking critically are apparent: the failure to think reflectively and the powerful resistance we have to change existing beliefs.

Encouraging students to monitor and challenge their own thinking and the thinking of others helps to promote critical thinking. In one study, teachers taught groups of four fourth- and fifth-graders how to think critically by having the groups work on a series of tasks. The teacher assigned children to the roles of task definer, strategist, monitor, and challenger, with students rotating in these roles in successive group meetings. When given individual tasks similar to those used in the group settings, students who had been trained in self-directed critical thinking applied more thinking skills and found higher-quality solutions than students without the training (Hudgins & Edelman, 1988).

Let students know that it is desirable for them to think reflectively about their beliefs and to question *why* they believe *what* they believe. Encourage students to justify their beliefs in terms of evidence. Often, the process of trying to justify a position helps students realize its strengths and weaknesses.

It is important for you to understand the nature of critical thinking not only so you can help students become more effective thinkers, but also so that you yourself can learn to think more critically. Thinking reflectively about your role as a teacher will help you teach more effectively by forcing you to justify why you are doing what you are doing. Reflective thinking will also help uncover biases you may have and alert you to make sure those biases do not interfere with your teaching.

# Thinking Skills Programs

The inability of many students to think effectively has caused elementary and secondary schools throughout the country to use **thinking skills programs** to teach students how to think. Collectively, the number of skills that these programs allegedly teach is overwhelming. Various programs focus on various skills, with the result that the programs do not share a set of central and unifying themes.

Thinking programs are popular in many countries, including the United States, where in 1991, 1,700 school districts were using the "Cognitive Research Trust Thinking" program, 5,000 schools were using the "Philosophy for Children" program, and 70,000 teachers were using the "Tactics for Thinking" program (DePalma, 1991).

The CoRT (Cognitive Research Trust) Thinking program (de Bono, 1985), consists of six units of 63 lessons, each taking about 35 minutes. Among other methods, CoRT uses mnemonics to help students reason about a problem. For example, *CAF* stands for "consider all factors," that is, examining a situation and listing the factors that might influence it. Another device is *PNI,* which stands for "positive, negative, and interesting"; "doing a PNI" means making a list of the positive, negative, and interesting aspects of a situation. According to de Bono, the developer of CoRT, the various operations taught in the CoRT program enhance students' thinking. The skills taught in the curriculum are presumably generalizable to students' real-life critical thinking, but unfortunately, research studies of CoRT have either been poorly designed or have failed to demonstrate that CoRT skills generalized to other situations (Halpern, 1993).

# An Alternative View of Higher-Order Thinking

We know less about generalized higher-order thinking (both critical and creative) than about how students think when performing specific tasks, especially school tasks in science and mathematics (Resnick, 1989; Riley & Greeno, 1988). As a result, theorists have begun to create new concepts to study general thinking abilities.

Greeno (1989) points out that researchers have conceptualized thinking as something that arises in the individual's mind. They have also assumed that thinking processes are more or less uniform among individuals and that the resources for thinking are school-learned knowledge and skills. Greeno suggests that progress in understanding thinking will result by reconceptualizing the nature of thinking.

Greeno's suggestion for a new approach to thinking consists of three components: (a) **situated cognition,** or thinking that takes place within a physical and social context; (b) **personal and social epistemologies,** or thinking that is conceptualized differently by different individuals and by different social groups; and (c) **conceptual competence,** or the ability to apply what you know, reorganize your knowledge, and embellish what you know and understand.

## Situated Cognition

The way people use higher-order thinking to solve problems varies as a function of the context in which the problem occurs (Scribner, 1984). Lave and Wenger (1991), for example, found that people in a dieting program chose their daily food allotments by selecting appropriate amounts of different kinds of food instead of calculating amounts of protein, carbohydrates and fats the way they had learned in the program.

Give examples of when you have used situated cognition.

## Personal and Social Epistemologies

Different people have different ideas about the nature of thinking, and their ideas often influence how they learn. For example, researchers who asked children to explain what *intelligence* means found that some children believe intelligence is a fixed entity over which they have no control, whereas other children believe that the more they learn, the more their intelligence increases (Dweck & Bempechat, 1983; Dweck & Leggett, 1988). Children who believe their capacity to learn is fixed regard situations that require them to learn as situations that will expose their weaknesses. On the other hand, children who believe their capacity to learn is not fixed regard new learning tasks as opportunities to get smarter.

What are your beliefs about the nature of knowledge?

Teachers' beliefs about the nature of knowledge probably also affect the way they use instructional approaches in their classrooms. Teachers who believe students learn passively are more likely to lecture or control a class discussion than teachers who believe that students learn by engaging in intellectual tasks. Creating classroom settings where students can try various options, evaluate the merits of their efforts, and draw conclusions produces different kinds of learning and different kinds of knowledge.

## Conceptual Competence

Some studies suggest that children have implicit understandings of principles needed to learn important concepts and procedures (Carey, 1985; Gelman & Gallistel, 1986). Children may have inherent knowledge structures, and what they learn enables them to elaborate, modify, alter, or reorganize these structures. Studies of infants (Carey, 1985) indicate that these knowledge structures are present at birth. Consequently, children approach learning with implicit understandings of basic concepts.

## Implications for Developing Thinking Abilities

Greeno's (1989) ideas of situated cognition, personal epistemology, and conceptual competence have important implications for teaching critical thinking. Situated cognition implies that learning is the ability to *think with and about* the information or procedures in a given knowledge domain, rather than simply acquiring information and procedures. Personal epistemology implies that students hold different notions about the nature of intelligence and learning. Teachers need to take students' notions into account when constructing learning environments. Finally, the notion of conceptual competence suggests that teachers need to build the curriculum on children's intuitions about knowledge.

## A Three-Story Approach to Teaching Thinking Skills

Fogarty and McTighe (1993) focus on one approach to addressing the problem of transferring higher-order thinking skills called the "thoughtful classroom/mindful school." Students engage in *metacognitive reflection* in which they think about their own thinking, assess themselves, and make adjustments as needed. Because students initially find metacognitive reflection difficult, Fogarty and McTighe recommend starting with "three stories of intellect" (see figure 7.3):

### The First Story

At this level, teachers teach students specific creative and critical thinking skills, such as those shown in figure 7.4, by:

- Providing names and definitions for each skill
- Asking students for synonyms for these skills and examples of using them
- Modeling the steps needed to use the skill
- Discussing the context in which a skill is appropriate
- Providing opportunities for guided practice

| Level | Focus | Processes | Description |
|---|---|---|---|
| Third story | Thoughtfulness | Applying the skills and processes in diverse academic and personal settings | Creative use and transfer of skills and processes through metacognitive reflection |
| Second story | Thinking | Processing skills through articulation and visualization | Intense student involvement to think and reason using cooperative learning and graphic organizers |
| First story | Thinking skills | Gathering information and acquiring skills | Direct instruction in explicit thinking skills |

**Figure 7.3**

Teaching thinking using a three-story intellect model.

From R. Fogarty and J. McTighe, "Educating Teachers for Higher-Order Thinking: The Three-Story Intellect" in *Theory Into Practice,* 32,(3), 161–169. (Theme issue on "Teaching for Higher-Order Thinking") Copyright 1993, College of Education, The Ohio State University. Reprinted with permission.

| Creative thinking skills | Critical thinking skills |
|---|---|
| Brainstorming | Attributing |
| Visualizing | Comparing/contrasting |
| Personifying | Classifying |
| Inventing | Sequencing |
| Associating relationships | Prioritizing |
| Inferring | Drawing conclusions |
| Generalizing | Determining cause/effect |
| Predicting | Analyzing for bias |
| Hypothesizing | Analyzing for assumptions |
| Making analogies | Solving for analogies |
| Dealing with ambiguity and paradox | Evaluating |

**Figure 7.4**

Creative and critical thinking skills.

From R. Fogarty and J. McTighe, "Educating Teachers for Higher-Order Thinking: The Three-Story Intellect" in *Theory Into Practice,* 32,(3), 161–169. (Theme issue on "Teaching for Higher-Order Thinking") Copyright 1993, College of Education, The Ohio State University. Reprinted with permission.

## The Second Story

At this level, the teacher creates situations that require students to use creative and critical thinking skills, preferably in cooperative learning groups of three or four students. Having students interact with others in a critical thinking task gives the teacher an opportunity to *hear* students using their critical thinking skills. Bellanca and Fogarty (1991) also recommend graphic organizers which allow teachers to *see* how students approach a critical thinking task.

## The Third Story

At the third level, students engage in metacognitive reflection. Fogarty and McTighe (1993) describe a classroom at this level as "a place where students can develop productive problem-solving strategies, mindful decision-making tactics, and creative, innovative thinking . . . where, as capable apprentices, students gradually accept responsibility for their own learning" (p. 165).

As an example of the "thoughtful classroom/mindful school," Fogarty and McTighe (1993) describe students meeting in small groups to discuss their math homework; their goal is to examine the problems for which different students have different answers and to trace their problem-solving steps to find out how they differed. In this type of environment, teachers ask questions that have more than one answer, encourage students to inquire and experiment, value different points of view, and accept unconventional thinking styles.

Most importantly, this way of teaching thinking emphasizes *continuous reflection;* students examine their beliefs, reflect on their problem-solving methods, and evaluate the effectiveness of their thinking. The goal is to produce students who are better thinkers and who can apply their learning in new situations.

# KEY POINTS

1. Higher-order thinking skills involve more complex ways of thinking, such as solving problems, making decisions, and thinking critically. They rely on basic skills such as memory and comprehension.

2. Problem solving is necessary when one encounters a situation in which the course of action is not immediately apparent; problems consist of goals, givens, and the method of solution.

3. One can objectively test the accuracy of solutions to well-structured problems, but it is impossible to verify whether the solution to an ill-structured problem is indeed correct.

4. A critical factor in finding solutions to a problem is representing the problem's goals and givens accurately.

5. Heuristics are general strategies used to solve problems; they include means-ends analysis, working backward, simplification, generalization and specialization, trial and error, applying rules, brainstorming, using contradiction, restating the problem, and using analogies and metaphors.

6. Expert problem solvers have a great deal of knowledge about a discipline and represent problems as clusters of related information rather than many discrete units of information.

7. Decision making involves evaluating and choosing the best from among a set of solutions; teachers make many decisions every day.

8. Critical thinking refers to analyzing arguments and opinions and trying to justify, refute, and evaluate them; some people use the term to include reflective thinking.

9. There is a debate whether critical thinking skills are general or domain-specific.

10. Students should reflect on their beliefs and try to validate them with evidence.

11. New ways of looking at critical thinking recognize the importance of the social and personal context in which thinking takes place and that, by thinking, children elaborate on and reorganize their understanding.

# SELF-STUDY EXERCISES

1. How are problem solving, decision making, and critical thinking different? How are they related?

2. Differentiate between well-structured and ill-structured problems. Give an example of each. How does this distinction influence teaching?

3. How do novices differ from experts in their problem-solving approaches? How can novices become experts?

4. You are assigned to a group of six students and asked to develop a presentation to the class on how education in the United States compares to that of other countries. In your first meeting, everyone speaks at the same time, and it becomes clear in 10 minutes that you are making no progress. How should you organize the group and its activities to complete the assignment?

   a. Describe possible ways of gathering information needed for the presentation.

   b. Describe ways of presenting the information to the class.

   c. What strategies did you use in answering *a* and *b*?

5. You are a fifth-grade teacher with a child who speaks no English in your class. You want to give the child the best opportunity to learn English.

   a. What approaches might you take?

   b. On what grounds would you select one of these approaches? What are the pros and cons of each?

6. Within an elementary school content area (e.g., social studies, science), choose a topic you know well (e.g., the United States Constitution, plants) and give two examples of how you would teach problem solving, decision making, or critical thinking.

# FURTHER READINGS

Baron, J., & Sternberg, R. (Eds.). (1987). *Teaching thinking skills: Theory and practice.* New York: W. H. Freeman.

Chance, P. (1986). *Thinking in the classroom: A survey of programs.* New York: Teachers College Press.

Halpern, D. F. (1989). *Thought and knowledge: An introduction to critical thinking* (2nd ed.). Hillsdale, NJ: Erlbaum.

Hyde, A. A., & Bizar, M. (1989). *Thinking in context: Teaching cognitive processes across the elementary school curriculum.* New York: Longman.

# REFERENCES

Anderson, J. R. (1993). Problem solving and learning. *American Psychologist, 48,* 35–44.

André, T. (1986). Problem solving and education. In G. D. Phye & T. André (Eds.). *Cognitive classroom learning: Understanding, thinking and problem solving* (pp. 169–204). New York: Academic Press.

Beck, I. L. (1989). Improving practice through understanding reading. In L. B. Resnick & L. E. Klopfer (Eds.), *Toward the thinking curriculum: Current cognitive research* (pp. 40–58). Washington, DC: ASCD.

Bellanca, J., & Fogarty, R. (1991). *Blueprints for thinking in the cooperative classroom* (2nd ed.). Palatine, IL: Skylight Publishing.

Benware, C. A., & Deci, E. L. (1984). Quality of learning with an active versus passive motivations set. *American Educational Research Journal, 21,* 757–765.

Beyer, B. K. (1987). *Practical strategies for the teaching of thinking.* Boston: Allyn & Bacon.

Bransford, J. D., & Stein, B. S. (1984). *The IDEAL problem solver: A guide for improving thinking, learning and creativity.* New York: W. H. Freeman.

Carey, S. (1985). *Conceptual change in childhood.* Cambridge, MA: MIT Press/Bradford Books.

Chi, M. T. H., Glaser, R., & Farr, M. (Eds.). (1988). *The nature of expertise.* Hillsdale, NJ: Erlbaum.

Collins, A., Brown, J. S., & Newman, S. E. (1986). Cognitive apprenticeship: Teaching the craft of reading, writing, and mathematics. In L. B. Resnick (Ed.), *Cognition and instruction: Issues and agendas* (pp. 453–494). Hillsdale, NJ: Erlbaum.

Copi, I. M. (1986). *Informal logic.* New York: Macmillan.

Covington, M. V. (1985). Strategic thinking and the fear of failure. In J. W. Segal, S. F. Chipman, & R. Glaser (Eds.), *Thinking and learning skills: Vol. 1. Relating instruction to research* (pp. 389–416). Hillsdale, NJ: Erlbaum.

de Bono, E. (1985). The CoRT thinking program. In J. Segal, S. Chipman, & R. Glaser (Eds.), *Thinking and learning skills: Volume 1: Relating instruction to research* (pp. 363–388). Hillsdale, NJ: Erlbaum.

Delclos, V. R., & Harrington, C. (1991). Effects of strategy monitoring and proactive instruction on children's problem-solving performance. *Journal of Educational Psychology, 83,* 35–42.

DePalma, A. (1991, Jan. 6). Winning game plans. *New York Times,* Education Life, Section 4A, p. 24.

Dweck, C. S., & Bempechat, J. (1983). Children's theories of intelligence. In S. G. Paris, G. M. Olson, & H. W. Stevenson (Eds.), *Learning and motivation in the classroom* (pp. 239–256). Hillsdale, NJ: Erlbaum.

Dweck, C. S., & Leggett, E. L. (1988). A social-cognitive approach to motivation and personality. *Psychological Review, 95,* 256–273.

Ennis, R. H. (1985). A logical basis for measuring critical thinking skills. *Educational Leadership, 42,* 44–48.

Farnham-Diggory, S. (1992). *Cognitive processes in education* (2nd ed.). New York: Harper Collins.

Fogarty, R., & McTighe, J. (1993). Educating teachers for higher-order thinking: The three-story intellect. *Theory Into Practice, 32,* 161–169.

Gagné, E. D., Yekovich, C. W., & Yekovich, F. R. (1993). *The cognitive psychology of school learning* (2nd ed.). New York: Harper Collins.

Gelman, R., & Gallistel, C. (1986). *The child's understanding of number* (2nd ed.). Hillsdale, NJ: Erlbaum.

Glynn, S. M. (1991). Explaining science concepts: A teaching-with-analogies model. In S. M. Glynn, R. H. Yeany, & B. K. Britton (Eds.), *The psychology of learning science* (pp. 219–240). Hillsdale, NJ: Erlbaum.

Greeno, J. G. (1989). A perspective on thinking. *American Psychologist, 44,* 134–141.

Halpern, D. F. (1989). *Thought and knowledge: An introduction to critical thinking* (2nd ed.). Hillsdale, NJ: Erlbaum.

Halpern, D. F. (1993). Teaching thinking: An anecdotal, atheoretical, antiempirical approach. *Contemporary Psychology, 38,* 380–381.

Hudgins, B. B., & Edelman, S. (1988). Children's self-directed critical thinking. *Journal of Educational Research, 81,* 262–273.

Hudgins, B. B., Riesenmy, M., Ebel, D., & Edelman, S. (1989). Children's critical thinking: A model for its analysis and two examples. *Journal of Educational Research, 82,* 327–338.

Hyde, A. A., & Bizar, M. (1989). *Thinking in context: Teaching cognitive processes across the elementary school curriculum.* New York: Longman.

Kelly, D. (1988). *The art of reasoning.* New York: W. W. Norton.

King, A. (1990). Enhancing peer interaction and learning in the classroom through reciprocal questioning. *American Educational Research Journal, 27,* 664–687.

Kurfiss, J. G. (1988). *Critical thinking: Theory, research, practice, and possibilities.* ASHE-ERIC Higher Education Report No. 2, Washington, DC: Association for the Study of Higher Education.

Lave, J., & Wenger, E. (1991). *Situated cognition: Legitimate peripheral participation.* Cambridge: Cambridge University Press.

Lewis, A., & Smith, D. (1993). Defining higher-order thinking. *Theory Into Practice, 32,* 131–137.

Livingston, C., & Borko, H. (1989). Cognition and improvisation: Differences in mathematics instruction by expert and novice teachers. *American Educational Research Journal, 26,* 473–498.

Mayer, R. E. (1987). *Educational psychology: A cognitive approach.* Boston: Little, Brown.

Mayer, R. E. (1989). Models for understanding. *Review of Educational Research, 59,* 43–64.

McPeck, J. (1981). *Critical thinking and education.* New York: St. Martin's Press.

Newell, A., & Simon, H. (1972). *Human problem solving.* Englewood Cliffs, NJ: Prentice Hall.

Nickerson, R. S., Perkins, D. N., & Smith, E. E. (1985). *The teaching of thinking.* Hillsdale, NJ: Erlbaum.

Ormrod, J. E. (1990). *Human learning: Principles, theories, and educational applications.* Columbus, OH: Merrill.

Paul, R. (1982). Teaching critical thinking in the "strong" sense: A focus on self-deception, world views, and a dialectical mode of analysis. *Informal Logic, 4,* 3–7.

Perkins, D., Jay, E., & Tishman, S. (1993). New conceptions of thinking: From ontology to education. *Educational Psychologist, 28,* 67–85.

Perkins, D., & Solomon, G. (1989). Are cognitive skills context-bound? *Educational Researcher, 18,* 16–25.

Resnick, L. B. (1987). *Education and learning to think.* Washington, DC: National Academy Press.

Resnick, L. B. (1989). Developing mathematical knowledge. *American Psychologist, 44,* 162–169.

Resnick, L. B., & Klopfer, L. E. (1989). Toward the thinking curriculum: An overview. In L. B. Resnick & L. E. Klopfer (Eds.), *Toward the thinking curriculum: Current cognitive research* (pp. 1–18). Alexandria, VA: ASCD.

Riley, M. S., & Greeno, J. G. (1988). Developmental analysis of understanding language about quantities and of solving problems. *Cognition and Instruction, 5,* 49–101.

Ruggierio, V. R. (1984). *The art of thinking: A guide to critical and creative thought.* New York: Harper & Row.

Schoenfield, A. H. (1985). *Mathematical problem solving.* New York: Academic Press.

Scribner, S. (1984). Studying working intelligence. In B. Rogoff & J. Lave (Eds.), *Everyday cognition: Its development in social context* (pp. 9–40). Cambridge, MA: Harvard University Press.

Stader, E. (1990, April). *Expert and novice teachers' ability to judge student understanding.* Paper presented at the meeting of the American Educational Research Association, New Orleans, LA.

Stasz, B. B., & Associates. (1985). A problem-solving model for teaching reading proficiency. *Forum for Reading, 16*(2), 56–60.

Stinessen, L. (1975). Conditions which influence acquisition and application of verbal representations in problem solving. *Psychological Reports, 36,* 335–342.

Udall, A. J., & High, M. H. (1989). What are they thinking when we're teaching critical thinking? *Gifted Child Quarterly, 33,* 156–160.

Underbakke, M., Borg, J. M., & Peterson, D. (1993). Researching and developing the knowledge base for understanding higher-order thinking. *Theory Into Practice, 32,* 138–146.

Walker, C. H. (1987). Relative importance of domain knowledge and overall aptitude on acquisition of domain-related information. *Cognition and Instruction, 4,* 25–42.

Webb, N. M. (1982). Peer interaction and learning in small groups. *Journal of Educational Psychology, 74,* 642–656.

Webb, N. M. (1983). Predicting learning from student interaction: Defining the interaction variables. *Educational Psychologist, 18,* 33–41.

Westerman, D. A. (1990). *A study of expert and novice teacher decision making: An integrated approach.* (ERIC Reproduction Service Number ED 322 128).

Zeichner, K. M., & Liston, D. P. (1987). Teaching student teachers to reflect. *Harvard Educational Review, 57*(1), 23–48.

Zeuli, J. S., & Buchmann, M. (1986). *Implementation of teacher thinking research as curriculum deliberation.* (Occasional Paper No. 107). East Lansing, MI: Michigan State University, Institute for Research on Teaching. (ERIC Reproduction Service Number ED 275 644).

## PART III

© Jeffry W. Myers/Corbis Media

# Learner Characteristics

8

# Intelligence and Creativity

# Chapter Outline

# Learning Objectives

8.1 Explain how your beliefs and your students' beliefs about intelligence influence classroom activity.

8.2 Describe six theories of human intelligence.

8.3 Identify the methods used to measure intelligence and the issues surrounding intelligence testing.

8.4 Explain how the nature/nurture issue pertains to the development of intelligence.

8.5 Describe the various definitions of creativity.

8.6 Summarize how creativity has been explored as a function of personality, cognition, and as a product of the social psychological environment.

8.7 Describe the problems associated with measuring creativity.

8.8 Identify methods of developing creativity in the classroom.

# Preview

This chapter examines various theories of intelligence, beginning with the early psychometric theories and concluding with descriptions of two of the most popular current theories: Gardner's theory of multiple intelligences and Sternberg's triarchic theory. We also explain how to apply current theories of intelligence to classroom teaching and how students' beliefs about the nature of intelligence relates to their motivation in school.

You will learn about the two most widely used intelligence tests and how to calculate an IQ score. You will also learn about culture-fair intelligence testing and how ethnic and socioeconomic factors relate to intelligence test scores. We explain how the findings of studies of fraternal and identical twins help clarify the relative impact of genetic factors (nature) and environmental factors (nurture) on people's intelligence.

We then focus on the nature of creativity and examine its relationship to intelligence, personality, social psychological environment, motivation, knowledge, and problem solving. We describe problems associated with measuring creativity and explain how you can help students become more creative.

# Intelligence

Intelligence has been variously defined as the ability to (a) learn, (b) adjust to the environment, (c) adapt to new situations, or (d) profit from experience (Sternberg, 1981). The lack of a single definition often results in confusion and disagreement about how we understand, explain, and measure intelligence. Nevertheless, we often rely on the concept of intelligence in making decisions about students and how to educate them. In this chapter we use Wechsler's (1958) definition of intelligence: "the aggregate or global capacity of the individual to act purposefully, to think rationally, and to deal effectively with [the] environment" (p. 7).

Most of us would probably agree that people vary in terms of intelligence. You will find far less agreement, however, about *how much* people vary, how static or dynamic intelligence is, and where intelligence comes from because there are different theories of intelligence. Let us now examine the major theories and compare them.

## Psychometric Models

In the early part of the twentieth century, educational psychology focused mainly on ways of measuring intelligence. **Psychometrics** refers to the process of measuring psychological traits. The early models of intelligence, called psychometric models, rely heavily on statistical research methods.

### Spearman's *g* and *s* Factors

Spearman developed a psychometric model in which intelligence consists of a general (or *g*) factor and a set of specific (or *s*) factors. Intelligence reflects a combination of general and specific abilities. People use the *g* factor when performing any kind of task, but different *s* factors, depending on the nature of the task they are performing. For example, people use the *g* factor whether they are solving geometry problems or learning a foreign language. They use the mathematics *s* factor, however, when solving geometry problems and the verbal *s* factor when learning a foreign language. People differ in terms of their general ability as well as the relative strength of their various specific abilities.

People's scores on a wide variety of tests tend to be positively correlated. Some people score well on almost all tests, others score moderately, and others score poorly. This consistency in test performance provides evidence of a *g* factor. On the other hand, the fact that the same person scores better on some tests than on others provides evidence of *s* factors. Sternberg (1981) believes there are so many factors that the influence of each individual factor is too small to measure accurately. Consequently, the *g* factor is of more interest in understanding intelligence.

A positive correlation means that people who score high in one area tend to score high in the other, and people who score low in one tend to score low in the other.

### Crystallized and Fluid Intelligence

Some psychologists, however, argue that a single *g* factor fails to provide a comprehensive enough explanation of intelligence. Cattell (1971) and Horn (1968), for example, divide intelligence into two types: **crystallized** and **fluid.** Crystallized intelligence involves learning things a given culture considers important, which vary from one culture to another. Fluid intelligence involves thinking and reasoning abilities that are independent of any given culture. Although aging and health factors can affect fluid intelligence (Anastasi, 1988; Havighurst, 1981), crystallized intelligence remains stable (Horn, 1985).

Knowledge of the particular symbols of our mathematical system (1, 2, 3, +, =) is a type of crystallized intelligence; an understanding of the concepts of numbers and mathematical operations is a type of fluid intelligence.

### Thurstone's Primary Mental Abilities

Thurstone (1938) proposed a model in which intelligence consists of seven factors: verbal comprehension, word fluency, number, space, associative reasoning, perceptual speech, and general reasoning. Thurstone's theory that there are different types of intelligence is an early forerunner of newer theories of multiple intelligences (Gardner, 1983, 1993b) and supports the belief that students can be weak in some types of intelligence and strong in others (Mann & Sabatino, 1985).

**Figure 8.1**
Guilford's Structure of Intellect
Model.

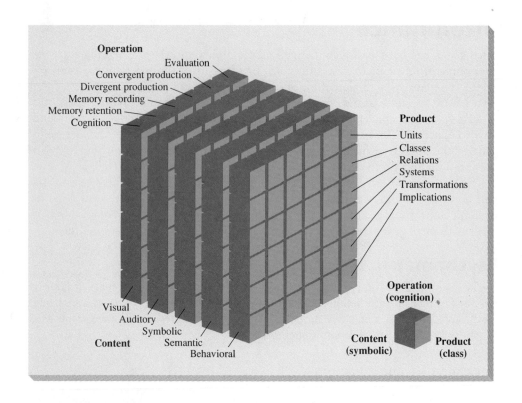

## Your Beliefs About Intelligence

*Explain how your beliefs and your
students' beliefs about intelligence
influence classroom activity.*

■■ Your views about intelligence may affect
■■ the way you deal with students. If you
believe intelligence is a single entity, you may
expect a student's academic performance in all
subjects to be comparable. On the other hand,
if you believe intelligence is multifaceted, you
may expect students' performance levels to

vary from one subject to another. Your beliefs about intelligence may also affect decisions you make about grouping students,
designing lessons, and deciding the appropriate level of difficulty of assigned academic tasks.

### Guilford's Structure of Intellect Model

Of all the psychometric models, Guilford's Structure of Intellect (Guilford, 1988)
has generated the most interest (see figure 8.1). Guilford's model contains 120
unique types of intelligence within a three-dimensional system. The first dimension
is *operation,* or types of the mental processes; the second is *content,* or the types of
information to which mental processes are applied; and the third is *product,* or the
types of outcomes of mental processes. The model is difficult to apply in practical
situations because it has so many different types of intelligence.

## Current Theories of Intelligence

Current theories, which regard intelligence as multidimensional, stem from cognitive
psychology and neuropsychology, not from psychometrics. The leading theorists
are Howard Gardner and Robert Sternberg.

8.2 ◉

*Describe six theories of human
intelligence.*

### Gardner's Theory of Multiple Intelligences

Gardner (1983, 1993b) believes that people have seven kinds of intelligence, with
high ability in some and low ability in others. These intelligences, shown in figure
8.2, are independent of one another.

| Type of intelligence | Abilities |
|---|---|
| 1. Linguistic-verbal | To use language and have awareness of its functions |
| 2. Logical-mathematical | To manipulate numbers and reason through a series of logical statements |
| 3. Spatial | To perceive the physical world and transform one's perceptions |
| 4. Musical | To have appreciation for the qualities of music (e.g., pitch, rhythm); to produce these qualities |
| 5. Bodily-kinesthetic | To control the body's movements; to manipulate objects |
| 6. Interpersonal | To be sensitive to the needs, moods, personalities, and motivations of others |
| 7. Intrapersonal | To be aware of one's own needs, feelings, motivations, strengths, and weaknesses, and to use this awareness as a basis for one's behavior |

**Figure 8.2**
The seven intelligences comprising Gardner's Theory of Multiple Intelligences.

## Students' Beliefs About Intelligence

Students' beliefs about intelligence affect their motivation in school (Dweck & Bempechat, 1983). Students who believe intelligence is fixed and cannot change tend to set educational goals in terms of a specific level of performance. For example, a student may say, "I want to get 16 out of the 20 vocabulary words right." Such students are motivated by a desire to obtain rewards and avoid negative judgments.

Students who believe they can increase their intelligence seek challenging tasks. This type of student may say, "I want to learn the words to increase my vocabulary."

Gardner believes that the early emphasis on intelligence testing diverted attention from studying the mental abilities people use in typical circumstances. For example, he found that the abilities teachers, surgeons, athletic coaches, dancers, artists, or psychotherapists need to be successful vary widely from job to job.

Gardner studied child prodigies, children with learning disabilities, people with brain damage who have lost one or more of their intelligences, and people with **savant syndromes** (people who show exceptional talent in a narrow, specific area but who otherwise have mental retardation) and concluded that the seven intelligences are independent of one another and account for the varying abilities of these diverse populations.

Gardner believes that our society and our schools emphasize linguistic and mathematical intelligence and deemphasize the other types of intelligence (Gardner & Hatch, 1989). Some people have used Gardner's theory to encourage schools to address all types of intelligence. Gardner, however, maintains that schools simply reflect the larger society's emphasis on verbal and mathematical intelligence, but that schools should use the other forms of intelligence to motivate students and to give them additional opportunities to succeed. Schools should develop curriculum and use teaching methods that match the abilities and talents of individual students.

In which of Gardner's types of intelligence do you excel? Which are your weaker areas? Has your schooling developed the areas in which you are strongest?

### Sternberg's Triarchic Theory

Focusing on *situations* in which people solve problems and the *processes* by which they solve them, Sternberg (1988, 1990) developed a *triarchic theory* that conceptualizes intelligence as consisting of three major aspects: (a) the *componential* (the mental processes or components of problem solving), (b) the *experiential* (the management of new experiences), and (c) the *contextual* (the application of cognition to the environment). Each aspect requires different mental strategies. His theory is more complex than Gardner's or the psychometric theories because it attempts to explain how intelligence and cognition are related. An outline of Sternberg's theory appears in figure 8.3.

**Figure 8.3**
Sternberg's Triarchic Theory of Intelligence.

1. Componential aspect
   a. Metacomponents (the ability to organize and monitor one's thinking)
   b. Performance components (recognizing and carrying out those operations needed to complete a task)
   c. Knowledge-acquisition (organizing incoming information to comprehend it)

2. Experiential aspect
   a. The best indicator of intelligence is how a person confronts new and unfamiliar situations
   b. Intelligence tests fail to measure how people cope with novel or unfamiliar situations
   c. Automatization of behaviors needed to execute familiar tasks quickly and accurately so that the demands on one's mental capacity are minimal

3. Contextual aspect  (a person's ability to adapt, select, or shape the environment in order to succeed)

These strategies have been termed by others as **metacognition,** the ability to observe one's own thinking behavior in action.

The *componential* aspect consists of metacomponents, performance components, and knowledge-acquisition components, which are not necessarily carried out in sequence, but collectively enable people to solve a problem.

Metacomponents involve recognizing the existence of a problem, defining its nature, generating a set of steps to solve it, putting the steps in the best sequence, allocating mental resources to solve the problem, and monitoring the solution (Sternberg, 1988). Suppose, for example, your history instructor assigned you to write a research paper on the industrial revolution in the United States. You might first consider what kind of paper you wish to write, plan how to do your research, organize the paper with an outline, and monitor the quality of your paper periodically. Finally, you might look at the final product and judge whether it satisfies the requirements of the assignment.

Performance components involve operations required to carry out a task. Sternberg (1988) notes that there are innumerable performance components and cites, as examples, drawing inferences and perceiving relationships between concepts. Performance components of writing a research paper would include looking in the library book catalog or computerized index for books on the topic, finding the books, taking notes, drawing conclusions about the topic, and writing the paper.

Knowledge-acquisition components are the ways in which people organize incoming information to comprehend it; in other words, knowledge-acquisition components refer to understanding what information is relevant for solving a problem, grasping *how* it is relevant, combining and reorganizing information, and comparing the problem at hand with previously encountered problems. In the example of the research paper above, these components would include choosing the information in your readings that pertains to the industrial revolution, understanding how this information contributes to your understanding, and recognizing how writing this paper is similar to or different from previous papers you may have written.

Sternberg's inclusion of the *experiential* aspect distinguishes his work from that of others. Sternberg argues that intelligence tests fail to measure people's ability to cope with novel or unfamiliar situations and that the best indicator of intelligence is how a person confronts new and unfamiliar situations.

Performance on familiar tasks in *familiar* settings demonstrates nothing about how a person would deal with a *new* challenge. However, presenting the same or a similar task in a new setting tests the person's ability to cope. For example, someone who is highly successful in school may not succeed in a job where the demands, similar to those in school, may occur in a less nurturing environment.

The experiential aspect of intelligence includes how well one automatizes behaviors needed in a highly familiar situation. Automatizing means executing a task quickly and accurately, making minimal demands on your mental capacity. Tasks we engage in frequently, such as reading, are automatized. People who fail to become automatic at frequently encountered tasks perform poorly, slowly, and inconsistently. Becoming automatic allows people to attend more carefully to unfamiliar aspects of novel situations.

# Applying the Ideas of Gardner and Sternberg

Gardner's and Sternberg's theories apply directly to school learning. Gardner's theory is particularly exciting because it suggests that teachers can create opportunities for students to excel by finding out their students' strengths and devising activities that develop these strengths. If students succeed in at least one area, they often develop a more positive attitude toward school and apply themselves in other areas.

Educators also use Gardner's theory to decide how to present lessons. Teachers can create lessons that use the various types of intelligence in classroom activities. This work, of course, requires much ingenuity and creativity on the part of the teacher, particularly since most curricula emphasize the verbal and logical-mathematical types of intelligence.

Sternberg's triarchic theory should also help you understand that the way students solve novel problems or solve familiar problems in novel situations reveals their ability to cope intelligently. You can help students automatize their responses and develop new ways of managing new situations by giving them novel problems to solve.

---

The *contextual aspect* of Sternberg's theory emphasizes the ability of people to adapt, select, or shape their environments so they can succeed. Human behavior occurs in a context, and the ability to work within that context is related to success. As Sternberg (1988) notes, "Successful people are able not only to adapt to fit their environments but actually to modify them so as to maximize the fit" (p. 66). Sternberg sees this area as culturally influenced and regards success in career and social decisions as aspects of this part of his theory.

## Intelligence Testing

The most frequently used intelligence tests are the Stanford-Binet and the series of tests developed by David Wechsler. These tests are individually administered by qualified psychologists. Individual intelligence tests are generally given in schools only when a student is having significant academic problems or when a school is considering placing a student in a program for gifted students.

**8.3** ◎

*Identify the methods used to measure intelligence and the issues surrounding intelligence testing.*

### The Stanford-Binet Test

In 1905, the French government asked Theodore Simon and Alfred Binet to develop a test to identify children who were likely to fail first grade and need remedial education. Simon and Binet's test measured intelligence as if it were a single characteristic that we all have in varying degrees, much like height or weight.

The test items measured memory of words and numbers, knowledge of basic facts, and vocabulary. In 1915, Lewis Terman, a psychologist at Stanford University, translated Simon and Binet's test into English and adapted it for use with U.S. school children. This test became known as the Stanford-Binet Intelligence Test and for a long time was the most frequently used intelligence test in the United States.

The original Stanford-Binet yielded a single score called **mental age**. Mental age is the average score achieved on the test by children of a given **chronological age** (actual age). For example, if a 10-year-old student answered correctly the same number of items that the average 12-year-old answered, the 10-year-old would have a mental age of 12. A major drawback in using mental age as a measure of intelligence is that it can be interpreted meaningfully only in relation to current chronological age, which is always changing.

To express intelligence in a more stable form, revised versions of the Stanford-Binet reported intelligence in terms of **intelligence quotient (IQ)**. An IQ is the ratio of students' mental age to their chronological age. To avoid decimals, this ratio is multiplied by 100. Thus, the formula for IQ is:

$$IQ = MA/CA \times 100$$

(where MA = Mental Age and CA = Chronological Age).

Wechsler tests, like many other intelligence tests, are administered individually by a psychologist.
© 1996 Laura Dwight

Using this formula, what is the IQ of an 8-year-old whose score is typical of the average 6-year-old? What is the IQ of a 6-year-old whose score is typical of the average 8-year-old?

Using this formula, a child whose mental age and chronological age are equivalent would have an IQ of 100. Consequently, 100 is the average IQ. A 10-year-old with a mental age of 12 would have an IQ of 120. A 10-year-old with a mental age of 8 would have an IQ of 80. This formula is no longer used, but it describes how the concept of IQ score was originally developed.

The most recent version of the Stanford-Binet, the fourth edition published in 1985, differs significantly from previous versions. It yields a composite score (which is similar to IQ) and scores in verbal reasoning, quantitative reasoning, abstract/visual reasoning, and short-term memory.

### The Wechsler Tests

David Wechsler developed a well-known series of individual intelligence tests that measure people's intelligence at three different age ranges:

WPPSI: Wechsler Preschool and Primary Scales of Intelligence
(3 years to 7 years, 3 months)
WISC:  Wechsler Intelligence Scale for Children (6 to 16 years)
WAIS:  Wechsler Adult Intelligence Scale (16 to adult)

The current versions of the Wechsler tests are the WPSSI-R (revised), the WISC-III (3rd edition), and the WAIS-R. The Wechsler tests yield a verbal IQ, a performance (nonverbal) IQ, and a full-scale IQ.

All three Wechsler tests have a similar design. Half the subtests are verbal and half nonverbal. On the WISC-III, the verbal half consists of:

- *Vocabulary.* Tests knowledge of words (e.g., "What does *obtuse* mean?")
- *Similarities.* Tests the ability to discern abstract verbal concepts (e.g., "How are a flower and a bee alike?")
- *Information.* Tests general knowledge (e.g., "At what temperature does water freeze?")
- *Comprehension.* Tests practical knowledge (e.g., "Why do we have speed limits?")
- *Arithmetic.* Tests arithmetic knowledge (e.g., "If four students want to share 28 pencils evenly, how many should each get?")
- *Digit Span.* Tests memory of number sequences (e.g., "Repeat these numbers: 7 4 6 1")

The verbal questions are similar to those on the Stanford-Binet, but the nonverbal or performance portion evaluates a distinctly different aspect of intelligence. The nonverbal subtests consist of:

- *Picture Completion.* Students examine a series of pictures of objects with important pieces missing, such as a dog without a tail, and must identify the missing piece. This measures attention to detail and practical knowledge.
- *Picture Arrangement.* Students must rearrange a series of cartoon-like frames that are out of sequence so that the pictures make sense. This measures sequencing ability and the ability to understand causal relationships.
- *Object Assembly.* Students must assemble a set of unattached pieces to make an object, such as a horse. This measures awareness of part/whole relations and problem-solving ability.
- *Block Design.* Students must create various designs with a set of red and white blocks. This measures abstract nonverbal reasoning.
- *Coding.* Students examine symbols, for example, = and ×, that are paired with numbers and then must write the matching symbol to a series of random numbers. This measures the ability to learn new information.
- *Symbol Search.* After examining an array of symbols, students look at symbols one at a time and must indicate which appear among the original array. This measures attention, short-term memory, concentration, and perceptual discrimination.
- *Mazes.* Students must find a route from the center of the maze to an exit. This subtest measures the ability to plan and follow a visual pattern.

Digit Span is an optional subtest in the Verbal portion; Mazes and Symbol Search are optional subtests in the Performance portion.

The Wechsler tests, and in particular the WISC-III, are now the most frequently used individual intelligence tests in the United States.

In what ways did the Wechsler tests improve upon the Stanford-Binet? What drawbacks do they have in common?

## Nature or Nurture?

Perhaps the most controversial issue in the field of psychology is how human beings develop intelligence. The main issue is whether the primary source of our intelligence is genetic (nature) or environmental (nurture). This issue is especially important to educators who must decide what students can and should learn. If intelligence is genetic, then a student's ability to learn is fixed. If the environment determines intelligence, then we can improve students' ability to learn by altering the environment.

Most psychologists believe that both genetics and the environment determine intelligence. People are born with genetically determined capacities that various environmental factors may affect. Scarr (1993) argues that heredity dominates the development of intelligence although she concedes that the environment has an impact in extreme instances, such as child abuse. Baumrind (1993), however, criticizes Scarr for failing to provide clear definitions of acceptable and unacceptable environments. Ceci (1991) claims that environmental factors such as schooling positively affect IQ scores, and some evidence suggests that infant stimulation or early preschool intervention leads to higher IQ scores (Garber, 1988; Santrock, 1995).

8.4

*Explain how the nature/nurture issue pertains to the development of intelligence.*

### Differences Among Ethnic Groups

Jensen (1980, 1985) claims that genetic factors cause differences in the IQ scores of various ethnic and racial groups. Others (e.g., Horn, 1968; Loehlin, Lindzey, & Spuhler, 1975) contend that cultural and environmental factors cause these differences, and some (e.g., Snyderman & Rothman, 1987) believe it is impossible to distinguish between genetic and environmental effects.

## Culture-Fair Testing

Many factors confound the arguments on both sides of the nature-nurture issue. One confounding factor is how intelligence is measured. Widely used intelligence tests, such as the Stanford-Binet and the Wechsler tests, do not claim to measure individuals' innate abilities. It is impossible to create such a test since the environment influences us from birth. It is also impossible to create a "culture-free" test. Human abilities manifest themselves within the context of a culture; test questions necessarily reflect the culture. It is impossible to tease apart innate ability and cultural influences. The challenge is to create intelligence tests that are "culture-fair" and discriminate by levels of intelligence, not by cultural background.

*If you were creating a culture-fair test, what would be the content? How would you design the test so that it does not discriminate against students' cultural background?*

**Scorer bias** is another problem in individual intelligence testing. Various student characteristics may bias psychologists who administer individual intelligence tests. Although scoring bias does not occur often (Sattler, 1992), factors such as a student's gender, physical appearance, or ethnicity may influence the score a psychologist assigns.

Students score higher if they are familiar with the examiner or the class of people the examiner represents. We don't know if familiarity causes students to behave differently in the testing situation or causes the examiner to interpret and score the student's test performance differently. We do know, however, that the "familiarity effect" is greater for students of low socioeconomic status (Fuchs & Fuchs, 1986).

## Ethnicity and Socioeconomic Factors

Ethnicity and socioeconomic status are closely linked in our society. The relative disparity in economic conditions experienced by ethnic and racial groups may explain the IQ differences found among different groups. Poverty affects the performance of many children in both urban and rural areas. When economic conditions are held constant, members of different ethnic groups have similar IQs (Nichols & Anderson, 1973).

If students whose native language is not English are tested in English, their IQ scores are not valid. If students are given an IQ test translated from English into their native language, their scores are still questionable because translated words sometimes do not have precisely the same meaning as the original.

The variability of IQ scores is greater within different racial and cultural groups than between them. Absolutely no predictions can be made about any individual's IQ based on that person's ethnicity or racial membership.

## IQ Scores and Achievement

*Despite the limitations of intelligence tests, they are commonly used and furnish important information about individuals. When interpreted by well-trained psychologists, IQ tests tell us about an individual's general ability and, when used with other tests, help us place students in special programs. An IQ test should not, however, be the sole determinant of a student's placement.*

The relationship between IQ scores and school achievement is far from perfect. Sattler (1992), for example, notes that almost 58 percent of the variability in students' levels of academic achievement is accounted for by factors other than IQ scores. Similarly, McClelland found that IQ scores fail to predict accurately the job success of college graduates, which may be more significantly determined by other factors, such as motivation (Sternberg & Wagner, 1993).

## Twin Studies

Studies of identical and fraternal twins offer insight into the role of heredity in the development of intelligence (Bouchard et al., 1990). Identical twins grow from one fertilized egg; fraternal twins grow from two separately fertilized eggs. Fraternal twins differ genetically from one another as much as they differ from any sibling. Identical twins, on the other hand, are genetically identical. By comparing fraternal twins with identical twins, we can separate genetic effects from environmental ones. Both kinds of twins may have common environments, but only identical twins have a common genetic makeup (Santrock, 1995).

# *The Bell Curve* Controversy

The long-standing debate regarding the degree to which intelligence is inherited resurfaced in 1994 with the publication of *The Bell Curve: Intelligence and Class Structure in American Life* by Richard J. Herrnstein and Charles Murray. The authors believe that the research finding that, on average, African Americans score 15 points lower on traditional IQ tests than do whites is primarily due to genetic differences and that this difference cannot be altered.

Many assumptions underlying Herrnstein and Murray's argument can be challenged. First, do IQ tests accurately measure intelligence? Alfred Binet, the author of the test that became the antecedent of current intelligence tests, did not believe so (Binet & Simon, 1905, p. 40). Second, is intelligence a fixed, stable characteristic, or is it a fluid ability that changes over time? Evidence indicates that IQ *can* change over time, depending on a number of variables, such as physical state, emotional state, and changes in students' motivation (Sattler, 1992).

The conclusion drawn by Herrnstein and Murray, that compensatory programs (such as Head Start) are essentially pointless, can also be refuted. Ramey, Bryant, and Suarez (1985) examined 18 well-designed studies of preschool enrichment projects and found that increases in IQ *did* occur and were greatest for year-round and full-day programs and for those with family education training as well as education of preschool children.

The authors of *The Bell Curve* argue that IQ tests are not biased against any socioeconomic, ethnic, or racial group. Lehman (1994) points out, however, that research demonstrates the opposite. Recognizing the bias, most school districts do not use IQ test scores alone to place students in classes for students with mental retardation.

By studying identical twins, we are able to understand better how heredity and environment influence development because they have identical genes.
© David Frazier

By studying identical twins who have grown up apart, researchers can determine how much of the difference between the twins is attributed to the environment because identical twins have the same **genotype,** or genetic makeup.

About three sets of twins are reared apart per million population, with only one set per million population knowing of each other's existence (Farber, 1981). Separation from birth, of course, is not a frequent occurrence and may vary from country to country, often as a result of war, poverty, or cultural attitudes.

Early studies of reared-apart twins consistently demonstrated the powerful effect of heredity on intelligence and personality (Newman, Freeman, & Holzinger, 1937). The IQs of identical twins reared apart were less similar than IQs of identical twins reared together and more similar than fraternal twins reared together (Newman, Freeman, & Holzinger, 1937).

Twins in these early studies were more often females than males, mostly born to lower-class parents in desperate situations, and were often premature at birth; thus, they were not a representative sample and the findings could not be generalized.

Later studies using more representative samples (Bouchard et al., 1990; Farber, 1981; Scarr & Weinberg, 1983; Segal, 1990) support the findings of prior studies that, despite having been reared apart, twins show remarkable similarities in physical characteristics and some physical disorders, such as dental problems, cardiovascular disease, and musculoskeletal disorders. Researchers of separated twins, however, have consistently found that "personality is more affected by environment than any other area of human functioning" (Farber, 1981, p. 269). Although the data on IQ suggest a strong genetic component, flaws in collecting the data led Farber to conclude that more reliable studies are needed.

# Creativity

### 8.5 ◎
*Describe the various definitions of creativity.*

Many people think of a "creative person" as eccentric and out-of-the-mainstream—the kind of person who "goes it alone." And to some extent, this stereotype may be true. More often than not, however, creative people are neither strange nor unconventional but have worked hard to invent fresh ways of looking at problems. Society perceives such people as creative because they have solved a problem in a novel, yet appropriate, way.

The label of creativity also requires durability; the Pablo Picassos and the Marie Curies of the world have gained their reputations through enduring works. Given the products that have received the status of greatness throughout the centuries, we have clearly had creative people among us for as long as history has been recorded. Yet we seem to know little about creativity. What is it and where does it come from? Why do some people seem to have it and others don't?

Brown (1989) points out that psychologists have been interested in creativity for a long time. Binet, for example, attempted to measure creativity by including open-ended items on his intelligence test. He later discarded these items, however, because they could not be scored reliably (Freeman, 1924). Guilford (1967) and Torrance (1974), however, later succeeded in developing reliable tests of creativity. Psychologists have explored the cognitive and personality dimensions of creativity (e.g., Gardner, 1993a; Perkins, 1988; Simonton, 1988; Sternberg, 1988) and examined the role that insight, dreams (Feldman, 1988), and the social environment (Hennessey & Amabile, 1988) might play in the creative process.

## Defining Creativity

Defining creativity may be even more difficult than defining intelligence. More people agree on what represents the outcome of intelligent behavior than on what represents the outcome of creative behavior. Our judgments of creativity are highly subjective.

Creativity is variously defined as a *characteristic* that a person possesses, a *product* or outcome that is regarded as original, and a *process* by which an unusual outcome is obtained. For a solution to be creative, it must be both novel and suitable. A definition of creativity is further complicated because the criteria used to judge creativity vary within specific time frames and differ over time, as well. Also, what people in one culture might call creative, people in another culture might not. Creativity is not something people do or do not have; individuals have varying degrees of creativity. However difficult it may be to define creativity, over time people within a culture reach consensus about who the most creative people are.

### Different Ways of Thinking

Some people define creativity as a different way of thinking. DeBono (1976) suggests two forms of thinking: "vertical thinking," which focuses on refinement of existing ideas, and "lateral thinking," which goes around a problem, or reformulates a problem.

Halpern (1989) characterizes Sherlock Holmes as a lateral thinker who sees something new or different in the obvious. Others have defined creativity as **divergent thinking,** as compared to **convergent thinking** (Guilford, 1967). Convergent thinking is similar to vertical thinking; it is systematic and focused, and tends to elaborate or improve upon existing knowledge. Divergent thinking is similar to lateral thinking; it involves thinking "around" (or tangentially from) a central problem. Answering the question "How did the early explorers cross the Mississippi River?" requires convergent thinking because there is only one correct answer. Answering the question "What might have happened if the early explorers had not crossed the Mississippi River?" requires divergent thinking because there is more than one possible answer.

## Creativity as Insight

Many of us believe that a creative act comes about suddenly, analogous to the proverbial light bulb going on inside someone's head. We imagine unusual individuals who act alone under the spell of a passionate drive. Some of us believe that great works result from the intervention of a divine spirit or from a mysterious vision, and that these ideas occur outside of the consciousness of the inventor. Creative persons' accounts of the creative process sometimes confirm this belief. Samuel Taylor Coleridge, for example, reported that while in an opium daze he wrote "Kubla Khan" exactly as it was published. Later reports suggest, however, that the final version of this great poem resulted from many revisions (see Perkins, 1988). Many creative people claim their most creative works have developed without consciousness, sometimes when they have stepped away from a problem, abandoning it until they "discover" a solution (Weisberg, 1993). These sudden insights are no doubt real to the person who describes them, but such descriptions do not explain how creativity occurs or why some individuals create and others do not.

## The Accidental or Coincidental Nature of Creativity

Serendipity is a chance occurrence, sometimes the coincidental fusion of two unrelated ideas, or an accident that is recognized as having some special importance. Scientists sometimes report that serendipity played an important role in major scientific discoveries, such as the relationship of the pancreas to diabetes, the anesthetic effects of ether, the connection between electricity and magnetism, or the discovery of penicillin to name just a few (Rosenmann, 1988). The critical aspect of all these discoveries, however, is the scientist's ability to make sense out of the "accident" (Weisberg, 1993). Pasteur keenly observed that "chance favors only the prepared mind" (Rosenmann, 1988, p. 135). Only a trained mind can make connections between unrelated events and recognize meaning in a serendipitous event. Furthermore, after the initial "discovery," the scientist must persevere to create a useful solution from the accidental observation.

## Creativity as a Function of Personality

Personality theorists view creativity as a personal attribute, and they hypothesize that certain characteristics converge in some individuals leading to creative behavior. Some (Gardner, 1993a; Gruber, 1981) have approached creativity by studying the characteristics of well-known creative people. Creative people appear to be independent, intuitive, self-confident, and able to live with conflicting traits in their concept of themselves (Barron & Harrington, 1981). According to Guilford (1950), creative people see problems where others do not; that is, they are not only good problem solvers, they are problem finders. Guilford also believed that creativity stems from a set of stable traits that can be measured. Several studies have found that creative persons have significant energy, high tolerance for risk, believe in their own effectiveness to control outcomes, and when necessary, are able to sustain periods of isolation, despite their need for eventual approval of others (Barron & Harrington, 1981; Solomon, 1985).

**8.6** ◎

*Summarize how creativity has been explored as a function of personality, cognition, and as a product of the social psychological environment.*

"Nothing yet. . . . How about you, Newton?"

Although there is no relationship between giftedness and emotional distress (Santrock, 1995), many people associate the two conditions, perhaps because of the incidence of these two conditions among some famous artists, such as Sylvia Plath, poet, Virginia Woolf, novelist, and Vincent Van Gogh, artist , to name a few. Gifted individuals actually tend to be more mature and have fewer emotional problems than others.

Although creativity appears to be a stable trait, there is some evidence that it has peak periods in peoples' lives (Dacey, 1989). Age and creativity have a curvilinear relationship; that is, creativity is low at very young ages, peaks in young adulthood, and then declines. Most creative work is accomplished at a fairly early age, although this phenomenon varies in different domains (Martindale, 1989).

## Creativity as a Function of Cognition

Creativity involves three facets: the person, the process, and the product. While cognitive psychologists focus primarily on the mental processes involved in creating, they recognize the importance of all three aspects when they try to define and analyze creativity (see Gardner, 1993a; Sternberg, 1988, 1990).

### Creativity and Intelligence

Gardner (1988, 1993a) suggests that creativity can evolve within each of the seven intelligences, and that individuals can be creative in one domain but not in others. He does not believe that creative people have a set of characteristics that can be observed across a wide array of behaviors.

Gardner (1988) analyzed the life and work of Freud, an individual who has been judged creative by many standards, but whose creativity is clearly evident in a very specific knowledge domain. One of the first outcomes of this analysis is the recognition that Freud was extremely intelligent. Some prior work has implied that creativity and intelligence, although related, are not necessarily highly related (see Torrance, 1974). Gardner, however, views Freud's exceptionally high intelligence as central to his ability to create. For example, Freud's memory was close to photographic; he lectured without notes and appeared to need little preparation. In Gardner's view, Freud was gifted in linguistic intelligence; he learned foreign languages with ease and read extensively in them. He was also an excellent writer who wrote profound essays on metapsychology. Freud also had talent in science, although he did not perceive his own abilities in that area. From a personality viewpoint, Freud was curious, persistent, and had good work habits. In addition he had what Simonton (1988) regards as a critical talent: leadership, or the ability to influence others.

Gruber and Davis (1988) examined the mental processes of creative persons across broad fields of endeavor, such as art, literature, and science. They examined several case studies of famous creative people (e.g., Charles Darwin and Benjamin Franklin) trying to identify the mental processes in creative people working in different disciplines. The case study approach permitted the researchers to scrutinize each individual without the assumption that all creative people think similarly. Instead, the investigators sought some consistency within the life work of each creative person. Darwin, for example, consistently relied on the concept of gradualism. Benjamin Franklin used the ideas of conservation and equilibrium in his early and later scientific work.

## Creativity and Divergent Thinking

Some interpretations of Guilford's Structure of Intellect model suggest that divergent thinking is analogous to creativity; Guilford (1950), however, believed that creativity extends beyond the domain of intelligence and that fluency of ideas and flexibility in idea production are fundamental to divergent thinking. Although he was unable to establish a positive relationship between creativity and intelligence using traditional IQ tests, it is clear that fluent and flexible ideas require a sufficient store of concepts in memory and an ability to extract a variety of plausible relationships. Individuals of low intelligence may have difficulty storing or accessing a sufficient number of ideas to be both fluent and flexible; thus, people must have at least average intelligence before they can demonstrate creativity.

## Creativity and Convergent Thinking

Some theorists propose that creative people often demonstrate convergent and systematic thinking, working within a clear focus, setting their own agenda, and striving for originality (Hayes, 1989; Wishbow, 1988). Hayes found that the cognitive processes of creative people in various fields had commonalities, including long periods of preparation and conscious goal setting. Creative persons choose good problems, evaluate their own shortcomings accurately, and take effective action to remedy those weaknesses.

## Creativity as a Function of the Social Psychological Environment

Social psychologists contend that social and environmental factors play a major role in creative production (Hennessey & Amabile, 1988). They focus on the relationship between motivation and creativity and on factors in the environment that can constrain creative work.

Some famous creative persons were not identified as gifted when they were students in school. Thomas Edison, for example, was considered slow-witted by one of his teachers. Walt Disney was criticized for not having good ideas, and Winston Churchill failed one year of secondary school (Santrock, 1995). In today's schools, students who are gifted in art or music are frequently overlooked in the selection process of classes for the gifted.

### Creativity and Motivation

Researchers in creativity and motivation find that extrinsic rewards decrease creativity (see Deci & Ryan, 1985, for a review of this literature). Amabile, Hennessey, and Grossman (1986), finding similar results, propose that children are less creative when they perceive a task as the means to an extrinsic end.

### The Influence of Choice and Evaluation on Creativity

When children are given the choice of materials or theme, they perform more creatively (Amabile & Gitomer, 1984). When choice and reward were examined together, researchers found that extrinsic rewards undermined the positive effect of choice (Amabile, Hennessey, & Grossman, 1986). Researchers have also found that the expectation of evaluation curtailed creative performance (Amabile, Hennessey, & Grossman, 1986).

## Creativity and Knowledge

People cannot be creative unless they are steeped in their area of expertise and have worked hard to develop the skills and insight necessary for creative production. Picasso's famous mural "Guernica" resulted from numerous sketches and modifications. Picasso spent years constructing the overarching theme he wished to convey (Weisberg, 1993). Other enduring creative works grounded in a deep knowledge base include Edison's invention of the kinetoscope (Jenkins, 1983), and Watson and Crick's discovery of DNA (Watson, 1968).

## Creativity and Problem Solving

According to Sternberg and Davidson (1982, 1983; Davidson & Sternberg, 1984), three cognitive abilities are involved in solving problems creatively: selective encoding, selective combination, and selective comparison. When using **selective encoding,** creative persons select the relevant aspects of a problem and ignore the irrelevant; they determine which information is valuable in the long run. **Selective combination** involves putting pieces of relevant information together in the right combination; creative thinkers can create a coherent system from disparate bits of information. Finally, **selective comparison** allows the individual to integrate new information with what the person already knows.

## Problems in Assessing Creativity

Measures of creativity include tests of divergent thinking, attitude and interest inventories, personality scales, biographies, nominations by teachers and peers, judgments of the products of creativity, and self-reports (Hocevar & Bachelor, 1989). Of these, the most widely used are tests of divergent thinking, based primarily on Guilford's identification of specific abilities: fluency, flexibility, originality, redefinition, and elaboration. These measures, as well as the interest and attitude scales and personality measures, meet the basic requirements of internal consistency and interjudge reliability moderately well; that is, the scoring procedures yield fairly consistent results (Hocevar & Bachelor, 1989). Ratings, self-reports, and studies of eminent persons are less reliable.

However, the validity of these measurements (that is, whether they measure what creativity is) is a problem in psychometrics. Most studies indicate that creativity overlaps with other characteristics, such as intelligence, academic ability, dependability, adaptiveness, and independence (Hocevar & Bachelor, 1989). Consequently, tests that claim to measure creativity may really measure other characteristics related to creativity. In addition, there is some question about whether the various dimensions of creativity differ from one another. Studies have found that judges have difficulty distinguishing among the attributes, such as flexibility, fluency, and originality (Hocevar & Bachelor, 1989).

8.7
*Describe the problems associated with measuring creativity.*

Arroyo and Sternberg (1993) discuss the importance of recognizing and supporting disadvantaged children who are gifted. Frequently these children are overlooked because they are assessed too narrowly—often in the one dimension of intellectual ability. Such children can be identified by personality measures, their clear motivation and self-confidence, and their individualism.

 **Promoting Creativity in the Classroom**

■■ Here are some ways to encourage cre-
■■ ativity in the classroom:

1. Students find their own capacity for creativity by experimenting and developing tentative solutions to a variety of problems, including "artistic" enterprises, such as painting, music, and story writing, as well as scientific and mathematical undertakings that allow for divergent solutions. In fact, you can use all areas of the curriculum to encourage creative thinking, helping students not only to seek solutions, but also to find new problems.
2. Minimize the use of extrinsic rewards for creative production; stimulate students to find intrinsic satisfaction in their efforts. This form of reward, while difficult to establish, can be achieved only when students pursue activities that capture their imaginations and interests.
3. When possible, allow students choices. In writing stories, for example, give students opportunities to create their own themes. In science projects, encourage students to identify an area of interest that they can pursue.

Students become problem finders when you give them freedom to make their own choices.

4. Students can learn to be creative when they experience success. The ability to create depends on their belief in their own competence. Helping students develop self-esteem and a sense of their own ability is an ongoing responsibility in teaching.
5. Where possible, involve students in the evaluation of their own work. Instead of students accepting a teacher-imposed assessment of their efforts, students can benefit from self-evaluation and peer evaluations. Brainstorming, honest critiques, and small-group discussions help students perceive their own work accurately.
6. Provide opportunities for students to solve problems through brainstorming, the use of analogy, and other strategies. Encourage students to think "around" the problem and give them time to produce "divergent" or "lateral thinking" solutions. Make sure students understand that unusual or original solutions must pertain to the problem at hand.

**8.8** ◎

*Identify methods of developing creativity in the classroom.*

## KEY POINTS

1. Intelligence has been conceptualized as both a single entity and a combination of several entities. How teachers think about intelligence influences what expectations they hold for students' performance.
2. Spearman introduced the idea of two factors of intelligence: the *g* factor (a general mental ability) and the *s* factors (specific abilities).
3. Intelligence has been identified as both crystallized and fluid. Crystallized intelligence includes general knowledge and comprehension, and fluid intelligence involves thinking and problem-solving abilities.

4. The concept of a general mental ability was challenged by Thurstone's theory of Primary Mental Abilities in which he advanced a seven-factor model that included verbal comprehension, word fluency, number, space, associative reasoning, perceptual speed, and general reasoning.
5. Guilford's Structure of Intellect model included many components and addressed the ideas of convergent and divergent thinking, concepts that played an important role in the development of theories about creativity.
6. Recent theories of intelligence are best exemplified in the work of Gardner and Sternberg. Gardner's theory of multiple intelligences

postulates at least seven different intelligences: linguistic-verbal, logical-mathematical, spatial, musical, bodily-kinesthetic, interpersonal, and intrapersonal.

7. Sternberg's triarchic theory proposes three separate constructs for intelligence: componential (components of problem solving), experiential (the ways in which humans use their experience to solve novel and familiar problems), and contextual (the context in which thinking occurs).
8. Intelligence testing has been developed by two major theorists: Binet and Wechsler. Originally designed as a single-entity test, the most recent Stanford-Binet Test (Thorndike, Hagen, & Sattler,

1986) differs significantly from previous versions in that, in addition to a composite score (similar to IQ), it yields scores in four specific domains: verbal reasoning, quantitative reasoning, abstract/visual reasoning, and short-term memory.

9. The Wechsler tests yield two main scores: a Verbal IQ and a Performance or nonverbal IQ score. While both areas are tested separately, they are believed to be related, and the tests produce a composite IQ score based on this assumption.

10. Theorists of human intelligence continue to debate whether nature (genes) or nurture (environment) contributes more to the development of intelligence. Twin studies attempt to illuminate the contributions of nature and nurture to the formation of intelligence.

11. Creativity has been considered as a product of personality, cognition, or the social psychological environment. Several theorists have found that both divergent and convergent thinking are involved in the creative process. The ability to maintain fluency of ideas and flexibility in thinking also appears to be important.

12. Social psychologists have found that creativity requires a positive self-concept, the sense that one can control one's effectiveness, and strong intrinsic motivation. Extrinsic motivation, restraint on choice, and the pressure of outside evaluation undermine creative expression.

13. Knowledge in a domain is necessary for creative production. Most creative individuals are, or have been, heavily involved in their area of expertise.

14. Good problem solving and creativity are related; most creative individuals find unique or unusual solutions to accepted problems.

## SELF-STUDY EXERCISES

1. Describe four psychometric models of intelligence and describe their differences.

2. What are some implications of Gardner's theory of multiple intelligences for classroom tasks and student performance? Describe some ways that teachers can account for differences in intelligence based on Gardner's theory.

3. Compare the Stanford-Binet and the Wechsler IQ tests. In what ways are these tests similar and different?

4. What are the arguments given by both sides in the nature/nurture debate? What are the implications of each position for education?

5. Why do some theorists claim that a threshold of intelligence is necessary to produce creative behavior? How does knowledge play a part in the creative act?

6. How can a teacher use the social-psychological approach to creativity to promote creative behavior in the classroom. Name at least four conditions that appear to be necessary to foster creativity.

7. Describe the problems involved in assessing creativity. How are these problems similar to those in assessing intelligence?

## FURTHER READINGS

Gardner, H. (1983). *Frames of mind: The theory of multiple intelligences.* New York: Basic Books.

Gardner, H. (1993a). *Creating minds: An anatomy of creativity through the lives of Freud, Einstein, Picasso, Stravinsky, Eliot, Graham, and Gandhi.* New York: Basic Books.

Gardner, H. (1993b). *Multiple intelligences: Theory in practice.* New York: Basic Books.

Glover, J. A., Ronning, R. R., & Reynolds, C. R. (Eds.). (1989). *Handbook of creativity.* New York: Plenum.

*The Journal of Creative Behavior,* published by the Creative Education Foundation, is dedicated to publishing research and theory on creativity.

Sternberg, R. J. (1988). *The triarchic mind: A new theory of human intelligence.* New York: Viking.

## REFERENCES

Amabile, T. M., & Gitomer, J. (1984). Children's artistic creativity: Effects of choice in task materials. *Personality and Social Psychology Bulletin, 10,* 209–215.

Amabile, T. M, Hennessey, B. A., & Grossman, B. S. (1986). Social influences on creativity: The effects of contracted-for reward. *Journal of Personality and Social Psychology, 50,* 14–23.

Anastasi, A. (1988). *Psychological testing* (6th ed.). New York: Macmillan.

Arroyo, C. G., & Sternberg, R. J. (1993). *Against all odds: A view of the gifted disadvantaged.* New Haven, CT: Yale University Department of Psychology.

Barron, F., & Harrington, D. M. (1981). Creativity, intelligence, and personality. *Annual Review of Psychology, 32,* 439–476.

Baumrind, D. (1993). The average expectable environment is not good enough: A response to Scarr. *Child Development, 64,* 1299–1317.

Binet, A., & Simon, T. (1905). Méthodes nouvelles pour le diagnostic du niveau intellectuel des anormaux. *L' année psychologique, 11,* 245–336.

Bolen, L. M., & Torrance, E. P. (1978). The influence on creative thinking of locus of control, cooperation, and sex. *Journal of Clinical Psychology, 34,* 903–907.

Bouchard, T. J., Lykken, D. T., McGue, M., Segal, N. L., & Tellegen, S. (1990). Sources of human psychological differences: The Minnesota study of twins reared apart. *Science, 250,* 223–228.

Brown, R. T. (1989). Creativity: What are we to measure? In J. A. Glover, R. R. Ronning, & C. R. Reynolds (Eds.), *Handbook of creativity* (pp. 3–32). New York: Plenum.

Cattell, R. B. (1971). *Abilities: Their structure, growth and action.* Boston: Houghton Mifflin.

Ceci, S. J. (1991). How much does schooling influence general intelligence and its cognitive components? A reassessment of the evidence. *Developmental Psychology, 23,* 703–722.

Dacey, J. S. (1989). Peak periods of creative growth across the lifespan. *Journal of Creative Behavior, 23,* 224–241.

Davidson, J. E., & Sternberg, R. J. (1984). The role of insight in intellectual giftedness. *Gifted Child Quarterly, 28,* 58–64.

de Bono, E. (1976). *Teaching thinking.* London: Temple Smith.

Deci, E., & Ryan, R. (1985). *Intrinsic motivation and self-determinism in human behavior.* New York: Plenum.

Dweck, C. S., & Bempechat, J. (1983). Children's theories of intelligence: Impact on learning. In S. Paris, G. Olson, & W. Stevenson (Eds.), *Learning and motivation in the classroom* (pp. 239–256). Hillsdale, NJ: Erlbaum.

Farber, S. L. (1981). *Identical twins reared apart: A reanalysis.* New York: Basic Books.

Feldman, D. H. (1988). Creativity: Dreams, insights, and transformations. In R. J. Sternberg (Ed.), *The nature of creativity* (pp. 271–297). New York: Cambridge University Press.

Freeman, F. N. (1924). *Mental tests.* New York: Houghton Mifflin.

Fuchs, D., & Fuchs, L. S. (1986). Test procedure bias: A meta-analysis of examiner familiarity effects. *Review of Educational Research, 56,* 243–262.

Garber, H. L. (1988). *The Milwaukee project: Preventing mental retardation in children at risk.* Washington, DC: American Association on Mental Retardation.

Gardner, H. (1983). *Frames of mind: The theory of multiple intelligences.* New York: Basic Books.

Gardner, H. (1988). Creative lives and creative works: A synthetic scientific approach. In R. J. Sternberg (Ed.), *The nature of creativity* (pp. 298–321). New York: Cambridge University Press.

Gardner, H. (1993a). *Creating minds: An anatomy of creativity through the lives of Freud, Einstein, Picasso, Stravinsky, Eliot, Graham and Gandhi.* New York: Basic Books.

Gardner, H. (1993b). *Multiple intelligences: Theory in practice.* New York: Basic Books.

Gardner, H., & Hatch, T. (1989). Multiple intelligences go to school. *Educational Researcher, 18*(8), 4–10.

Gruber, H. (1981). *Darwin on man: A psychological study of scientific creativity.* Chicago: University of Chicago Press.

Gruber, H. E., & Davis, S. N. (1988). Inching our way up Mount Olympus: The evolving-systems approach to creative thinking. In R. J. Sternberg (Ed.), *The nature of creativity* (pp. 243–270). New York: Cambridge University Press.

Guilford, J. P. (1950). Creativity. *American Psychologist, 5,* 444–454.

Guilford, J. P. (1967). *The nature of human intelligence.* New York: McGraw-Hill.

Guilford, J. P. (1981). Potentiality for creativity. In J. C. Gowan, J. Khatena, & E. P. Torrance (Eds.), *Creativity: Its educational implications* (pp. 83–88). Dubuque, IA: Kendall/Hunt.

Guilford, J. P. (1988). Some changes in the structure-of-intellect model. *Educational and Psychological Measurement, 48,* 1–4.

Halpern, D. (1989). *Thought and language: An introduction to critical thinking* (2nd ed.). Hillsdale, NJ: Erlbaum.

Havighurst, R. J. (1981). Life-span development and educational psychology. In F. H. Farley & N. J. Gordon (Eds.), *Psychology and education: The state of the union.* Berkeley, CA: McCutchan.

Hayes, J. R. (1989). Cognitive processes in creativity. In J. A. Glover, R. R. Ronning, & C. R. Reynolds (Eds.), *Handbook on creativity* (pp. 135–146). New York: Plenum.

Hennessey, B. A., & Amabile, T. M. (1988). The role of the environment in creativity. In R. J. Sternberg (Ed.), *The nature of creativity* (pp. 11–38). New York: Cambridge University Press.

Herrnstein, R. J., & Murray, C. (1994). *The bell curve: Intelligence and class structure in American life.* New York: Free Press.

Hocevar, D., & Bachelor, P. (1989). A taxonomy and critique of measurements used in the study of creativity. In J. A. Glover, R. R. Ronning, & C. R. Reynolds (Eds.), *Handbook of creativity* (pp. 53–76). New York: Plenum.

Horn, J. L. (1968). Organization of abilities and the development of intelligence. *Psychological Review, 75,* 242–259.

Horn, J. L. (1985). Remodeling old models of intelligence. In B. Wolman (Ed.), *Handbook of intelligence* (pp. 267–300). New York: Wiley.

Jenkins, R. V. (1983). Elements of style: Continuities in Edison's thinking. *Annals of the New York Academy of Sciences, 424,* 149–162.

Jensen, A. R. (1980). *Bias in mental testing.* New York: Free Press.

Jensen, A. R. (1985). The nature of the black-white difference on various psychometric tests: Spearman's hypothesis. *Behavioral and Brain Sciences, 8,* 193–219.

Lehman, L. R. (1994, December 5). Race, IQ, and lies. *Daily Challenge, 5.*

Loehlin, J. C., Lindzey, G., & Spuhler, J. N. (1975). *Race differences in intelligence.* San Francisco: Freeman.

Mann, L., & Sabatino, D. A. (1985). *Foundations of cognitive process in remedial and special education.* Rockville, MD: Aspen.

Martindale, C. (1989). Personality, situation, and creativity. In J. A. Glover, R. R. Ronning, & C. R. Reynolds (Eds.), *Handbook of creativity* (pp. 211–232). New York: Plenum.

Newman, H. H., Freeman, F. N., & Holzinger, K. J. (1937). *Twins: A study of heredity and environment.* Chicago: University of Chicago Press.

Nichols, P. L., & Anderson, V. E. (1973). Intellectual performance, race, and socioeconomic status. *Social Biology, 20,* 367–374.

Perkins, D. N. (1988). The possibility of invention. In R. J. Sternberg (Ed.), *The nature of creativity* (pp. 362–385). New York: Cambridge University Press.

Ramey, C. T., Bryant, D. M., & Suarez, T. M. (1985). Preschool compensatory education and the modifiability of intelligence: A critical review. In D. K. Detterman (Ed.), *Current topics in human intelligence: Volume 1, Research Methodology* (pp. 247–296). Norwood, NJ: Ablex.

Rosenmann, M. F. (1988). Serendipity and scientific discovery. *Journal of Creative Behavior, 22*(2), 132–138.

Santrock, J. W. (1995). *Children.* Madison, WI: Brown & Benchmark.

Sattler, J. M. (1992). *Assessment of children* (3rd ed.). San Diego: Jerome M. Sattler.

Scarr, S. (1993). Biological and cultural diversity: The legacy of Darwin for development. *Child Development, 64,* 1333–1353.

Scarr, S., & Weinberg, R. A. (1983). The Minnesota adoption studies: Genetic differences and malleability. *Child Development, 54,* 253–259.

Segal, N. L. (1990). The importance of twin studies for individual difference research. *Journal of Counseling and Development, 68*(6), 612–622.

Simonton, D. K. (1988). Creativity, leadership and chance. In R. J. Sternberg (Ed.), *The nature of creativity* (pp. 386–426). New York: Cambridge University Press.

Snyderman, M., & Rothman, S. (1987). Survey of expert opinion of intelligence and aptitude testing. *American Psychologist, 42,* 137–144.

Solomon, R. (1985). Creativity and normal narcissism. *Journal of Creative Behavior, 19,* 47–55.

Spearman, C. (1927). *The abilities of man: Their nature and measurement.* New York: Macmillan.

Sternberg, R. J. (1981). Intelligence and nonentrenchment. *Journal of Educational Psychology, 73,* 1–16.

Sternberg, R. J. (1988). *The triarchic mind: A new theory of human intelligence.* New York: Viking.

Sternberg, R. J. (1990). *Metaphors of mind: Conceptions of the nature of intelligence.* New York: Cambridge University Press.

Sternberg, R. J., & Davidson, J. E. (1982). The mind of the puzzler. *Psychology Today, 16,* 37–44.

Sternberg, R. J., & Davidson, J. E. (1983). Insight in the gifted. *Educational Psychologist, 18,* 51–57.

Sternberg, R. J., & Wagner, R. K. (1993). The g-ocentric view of intelligence and job performance is wrong. *Current Directions in Psychological Science, 2,* 1–5.

Thorndike, R. L., Hagen, E. P., & Sattler, J. M. (1986). *Guide for administering and scoring the Stanford-Binet Intelligence Scale: Fourth Edition.* Chicago: Riverside Publishing.

Thurstone, L. L. (1938). Primary mental abilities. *Psychometric Monographs,* No. 1.

Torrance, E. P. (1974). *Torrance tests of creative thinking.* Lexington, MA: Ginn.

Watson, J. (1968). *The double helix.* New York: Signet.

Wechsler, D. (1958). *The measurement of adult intelligence* (4th ed.). Baltimore: Williams & Wilkins.

Weisberg, R. W. (1993). *Creativity: Beyond the myth of genius.* New York: W. H. Freeman.

Wishbow, N. (1988). *Creativity in poets.* Unpublished doctoral dissertation, Carnegie-Mellon University, Pittsburgh, PA.

9

© David Frazier

# Social and Emotional Development

# Chapter Outline

# Learning Objectives

9.1 Define *personality* and identify where it comes from.

9.2 Describe Erikson's theory of psychosocial development and identify methods of promoting students' psychosocial development.

9.3 Summarize the social cognition approach to social development.

9.4 Compare the theories of moral development of Piaget, Kohlberg, and Gilligan.

9.5 Summarize the research concerning self-concept and its role in academic achievement.

9.6 Describe the role of parents and peers in students' social and emotional development.

9.7 Describe how stress and anxiety, child abuse and neglect, drug and alcohol abuse, and prejudice and discrimination affect students' social and emotional development.

# Preview

We now turn to the social and emotional side of students' development. After defining *personality,* we examine how it develops. We describe how people develop their sense of morality and their self-concepts and consider the role family and peers play in students' social and emotional development. We then look at factors that adversely affect social and emotional development: stress in school, child abuse and neglect, drug and alcohol abuse, prejudice, and discrimination. We conclude with a discussion of what you can do to enhance students' social and emotional development. ◉

Students bring diverse
personalities to the classroom.
© Tom McCarthy/Unicorn Stock Photos

Just as individuals differ in terms of intelligence and creativity, they also differ in terms of personality. Some students are shy and withdrawn, whereas others are outgoing and enjoy the company of others. Some students are conscientious and cooperative; others are rebellious and uncooperative. It is not just students, however, who exhibit diverse personality characteristics. Teachers do, too.

You probably remember having some teachers who were warm and supportive and who made school a fun place to be. Perhaps such a teacher inspired you to become a teacher yourself. Unfortunately, you probably also remember some teachers who handled the classroom like drill sergeants.

In this chapter we discuss the nature of personality, including factors affecting its development and explain how you can help students acquire healthy emotions and appropriate social behaviors. This chapter will give you a framework for examining your own social and emotional behavior and also give you guidelines for helping students develop positive attitudes toward school and learning.

*Annual* **Edition**

unit *2*

# Personality: Where Does It Come From?

Psychologists use the term **personality** to refer to "a broad collection of attributes—including temperament, attitudes, traits, values, and distinctive behavioral patterns (or habits)—that seem to characterize an individual" (Shaffer, 1988, p. 43). Various psychologists hold different views about how personality develops, depending on their philosophy about the nature of human beings and the relative importance of hereditary and environmental factors on personality development.

# Erikson's Theory of Psychosocial Development

Erik Erikson was one of the most distinguished students of Sigmund Freud, who believed that human beings are driven by *irrational* impulses. Erikson, however, believed human beings are inherently *rational* and that social aspects of culture, not instinctive biological drives, determine people's emotional and social behavior. Erikson also believed that despite cultural differences, all people progress through the same sequence of psychosocial development (Erikson, 1963).

**9.1**

*Define* personality *and identify where it comes from.*

How does the psychological definition differ from other definitions of personality?

**9.2** ◎

*Describe Erikson's theory of psychosocial development and identify methods of promoting students' psychosocial development.*

**Figure 9.1**
Erikson's eight life crises.

| Crises | Age ranges | Primary social agent |
|---|---|---|
| Trust vs. mistrust | Birth to 1 year | Family caregiver |
| Autonomy vs. shame and doubt | 1 to 3 years | Family caregiver |
| Initiative vs. guilt | 3 to 6 years | Family caregiver and teachers |
| Industry vs. inferiority | 6 to 12 years | Teachers and peers |
| Identity vs. role confusion | 12 to 20 years | Peers |
| Intimacy vs. isolation | 20 to 40 years | Close friends and spouse |
| Generativity vs. stagnation | 40 to 65 years | Spouse and cultural standards |
| Ego integrity vs. despair | Over 65 years | Earlier social experiences |

A universal sequence of cognitive development applies to people of all cultures.

Erikson's emphasis on the influence of social forces on people's emotional development offers more promise than Freudian theory in helping you to understand your students' personalities. Erikson's model of personality development can help you foster a positive social climate in your classroom so that students are more likely to develop healthy personalities.

According to Erikson (1980), people go through a sequence of eight age-related stages, each of which is characterized by a crisis in their psychosocial development (see figure 9.1). The effects of successfully resolving each crisis are cumulative. It is possible to resolve a crisis successfully only if each crisis earlier in the sequence has been successfully resolved. The cumulative nature of crisis resolution is important for two reasons: (a) your students' success in resolving each crisis depends on how they resolved earlier crises, and (b) their success in resolving future crises depends on how successfully they resolve their current crisis.

## Trust Versus Mistrust (Birth to 1 Year)

During the first year of life, infants view the world as consisting of people who either can or cannot be trusted. Which view the infant adopts depends on how adults (usually the infant's parents) take care of the infant's need for food, comfort, security, safety, and affection. If the caregiver is consistent and responsive to the infant's needs, the child will learn to trust people. If the caregiver is inconsistent, unresponsive, or perhaps even abusive, the child will learn to distrust people.

## Autonomy Versus Shame and Doubt (1 to 3 Years)

During the early years, children learn to view themselves as capable individuals who can function independently or to doubt their abilities and feel ashamed because of their inadequacies. Characteristically, children going through this stage of psychosocial development insist on doing things by themselves, often rejecting the assistance of others. Children who are permitted to do things on their own learn to see themselves as competent. Children who are not permitted to do things on their own or who are ridiculed for attempting to behave independently develop feelings of shame and self-doubt.

## Initiative Versus Guilt (3 to 6 Years)

As children approach school age, they sometimes extend their independence in ways that exceed their abilities or that infringe on the rights of others. Initially, the family caregiver, and later the teacher, can help the child learn to take the initiative without infringing on other people's rights. Children whose behavior leads to conflicts with other people may develop feelings of guilt.

## Industry Versus Inferiority (6 to 12 Years)

During the elementary school years, children begin to compare themselves with their peers in terms of academic performance and social behavior. Teachers can encourage students to be industrious and to achieve proficiency at both academic and social tasks, thereby gaining self-confidence. Children who do not become proficient begin to view themselves as inferior to others.

How might peer comparisons promote psychosocial development? How might they hinder it?

## Identity Versus Role Confusion (12 to 20 Years)

Teenagers wrestle with the question of establishing a personal identity. They need to define themselves socially and formulate career goals. The influence of peers peaks during this period, particularly in terms of development of the teenager's conception of a social self. Failure to establish a personal identity leads to confusion about what roles the teenager will play in society.

In an **identity crisis**, which is typical of this stage, adolescents struggle to formulate a set of beliefs, behaviors, and goals, often involving religious and political beliefs, and career goals. Marcia (1989) observed that adolescents tend to fall into one of four patterns of identity development:

*Annual* **Edition**

unit 2

1. *Identity Achievement.* After considering several sets of behaviors and beliefs, the adolescent settles on which behaviors to show and which beliefs to follow. This adolescent has had an identity crisis and has satisfactorily resolved it.
2. *Identity Foreclosure.* The adolescent accepts the behaviors and beliefs chosen by his or her parents and does not consider possible alternatives. This adolescent has never had an identity crisis.
3. *Identity Diffusion.* The adolescent is unable to decide on a set of behaviors and beliefs; the individual's identity is in constant flux. This adolescent has failed to resolve the identity crisis satisfactorily. This level is sometimes also called "identity confusion."
4. *Moratorium.* The adolescent has not yet resolved the identity crisis and, therefore, has not yet selected his or her behaviors and beliefs. The adolescent in the moratorium group is having an ongoing identity crisis.

Students in the identity achievement group are most likely to be autonomous and creative, have a stronger self-concept, demonstrate higher levels of moral reasoning, reject authoritarian values, be less self-conscious, and resist peer pressure (Adams, Abraham, & Markstrom, 1987; Bosma & Gerrits, 1985; Orlowsky & Ginsberg, 1981). Students in the identity foreclosure group tend to have the weakest self-concept, be the least autonomous, and believe in authoritarianism. Young people in this group have never gone through an identity crisis and don't know themselves. The identity crisis of adolescence, which can exasperate parents and teachers alike, serves an important purpose in adolescent development.

## Intimacy Versus Isolation (20 to 40 Years)

During early adulthood, people face the crisis of trying to share their identity with others in the form of close friendships or an intimate relationship with a partner for life. Failure to establish close relationships leads to a sense of isolation.

## Portraits of Adolescents

■■
■■ To help clarify the four categories of identity development, here are four "portraits" of adolescents. Can you determine which student is in which group?

1. Karen is a 17-year-old sophomore. Against her parents' wishes, she dropped out of school for a year to try to become an actress. She worked in a fast-food restaurant while trying to go to auditions. She returned to high school and, although she still dreams of acting professionally, she acknowledges that few people succeed in that field. Her friends encourage her to keep trying to break into acting, but she has decided to go to college after high school.

2. Alan is a 17-year-old who has been working in a bakery for the past two months. Prior to that, he had a series of jobs, none of which lasted long. He got these jobs by chance, not by actively seeking them out. He has had a series of short-term relationships, but each time he gets involved with a new girlfriend, he quickly becomes dissatisfied with the relationship. He has no plans for the future.

3. Maggie is a 16-year-old in her third year of high school where her favorite course is biology. After high school, she hopes to go to school to become a pharmacist. Her father is a pharmacist and encourages her to study this field. Her

parents say she is the model child because she never questions their authority and gladly follows their advice.

4. Michael is a 17-year-old who is unsure of his future. He is currently thinking of going to college after high school but has changed his mind about college twice in two years. He has also changed girlfriends twice in that time. He has recently been considering joining a new religion. His friends think he is still trying to "find himself."

Did you conclude that Karen is in the identity achievement group? Note that she has gone through a period of struggle, rejecting her parents' values as she attempts to define her own. She has selected specific career goals and is following them against the advice of her peer group. Alan, on the other hand, appears to be in the identity diffusion group. Although he has a job, he has no specific goals or plans. He appears to be drifting through life, without any idea of what he seeks from life. Maggie seems as goal-oriented as Karen, but her father, not Maggie, has defined her goals. She appears to be in the identity foreclosure group. Note that Maggie has deferred to her father's authority without questioning it. Michael appears to be in the moratorium group, going through the identity crisis, trying out new majors, new relationships, and new beliefs, much as one tries on clothing. He is struggling to find out what "fits" him.

## Generativity Versus Stagnation (40 to 65 Years)

During the latter part of adulthood, people face the crisis of trying to infuse their lives with meaning by becoming intensely involved in their work or by helping either their own or somebody else's children. Failure to contribute to the welfare of others leads to a sense of stagnation and self-centeredness.

## Ego Integrity Versus Despair (65 Years and Older)

During the final years, people face the crisis of evaluating the lives they have led. If their lives have been happy and meaningful, they feel a sense of self-fulfillment and accept death as the natural conclusion to their personal histories. People whose lives have been meaningless and full of disappointment fall into a state of despair and have difficulty accepting death.

# Social Cognition

**9.3**

*Summarize the social cognition approach to social development.*

We spend much of our waking time interacting with others. This section examines the factors that influence how we behave socially and how we interpret events occurring in a social context. **Social cognition** refers to "the manner in which individuals interpret, analyze, remember, and use information about the social world" (Baron & Byrne, 1991, p. 133). We also describe the reciprocal relationship between thinking and emotion, how students infer motives from the behavior of others, and factors that influence teachers' judgments about students.

## Promoting Psychosocial Development

It is helpful for teachers of preschoolers to keep in mind that children in this age group are resolving the crisis of initiative versus guilt. Generally, preschool is the first social experience children have with a relatively large group of peers, and some have trouble learning to respect the rights of others. Teachers should arrange activities so that children are less likely to interfere with one another. It is important, however, not to emphasize the rights of others to the point that children refrain from initiating activities. If possible, encourage children to take the initiative by suggesting alternate ways that do not interfere with other children's rights.

Elementary school teachers can encourage students to be industrious by presenting them with numerous and varied activities. Have students engage in challenging activities that are neither too difficult nor too easy. Students who successfully complete activities that require a certain amount of effort learn to see themselves as competent.

In addition to focusing on academic skills, teachers should involve elementary school students in activities that promote social skills. For example, in addition to having students write reports about a particular topic, have them present their reports orally to the class or work in groups on a collaborative report.

Junior and senior high school teachers confront one of the most difficult periods of personality development: adolescence. Developmentally, teenagers are trying to define who they are and rely heavily on peers in forming a definition. The important role that the peer group assumes during adolescence frequently leads to consequences that have educational significance. For example, some students tend to give in to pressure from peers and behave in ways counter to the teacher's wishes. Students may rebel against authority and lose interest in school.

Successful secondary teachers are sensitive to the need of many teenagers to conform to group norms and often acknowledge this need openly in an understanding way. At the same time, however, these teachers convey that classroom and school standards should be met.

One effective way to achieve this balance is to determine which students are regarded by other students (not necessarily by teachers or school administrators) as influential members of the peer group. Teachers can sometimes develop rapport with influential students and use these students' influence in constructive ways.

Teenagers sometimes also find it easier to talk with an understanding teacher than to a parent about their social or emotional problems. Teachers can provide support and information without, however, taking on counseling responsibilities that more appropriately belong to school counselors and psychologists.

Some students select unrealistic career goals, such as becoming a professional athlete, or they restrict their options to a relatively limited number of jobs they happen to know about, such as teacher, doctor, electrician, or hair stylist. Secondary school teachers can provide students with a wide array of career choices to consider.

Use Erikson's stages of psychosocial development to help yourself as well as your students. If you are like most beginning teachers, you will be entering the field during the stage of intimacy versus isolation (ages 20 to 40). Many beginning teachers are unprepared for one of teaching's occupational hazards: social isolation. In most occupations people routinely encounter others of their own age at the workplace. Teachers, however, do not. You will spend most of your day interacting with students, not with adults.

Although socializing occurs naturally as a part of many jobs, teachers almost never have the opportunity to socialize with colleagues for extended periods of time. Consequently, acknowledge your psychosocial need for interaction with peers and actively seek ways to meet and interact with other adults during your leisure time. In addition to participating in various group activities available in most communities, such as those sponsored by social, political, or religious organizations, you can involve yourself with local groups of educators, such as a county association of secondary science teachers or a local association of reading teachers.

*Why should teachers not enter into counseling relationships with students?*

*What careers other than teaching have you considered?*

## Thought in the Social Context

For thinking to occur in a social context, the individual has to realize that he or she is a distinct entity, separate from all other human beings in the world (Shaffer, 1988). Infants can distinguish between themselves and the rest of the world almost from the moment of birth (Stern, 1985). Furthermore, most infants demonstrate before they reach their first birthday that they understand the intentions of others (Klinnert et al.,

**Figure 9.2**
Barenboim's developmental model of person perception.

| Age range | Phase of person perception | Example |
|---|---|---|
| 6 to 8 years | Behavioral comparison | Judith is the best speller in our class. |
| 8 to 10 years | Psychological construct | Joey is a bully. |
| 11 or 12 years | Psychological comparison | Sharon is nicer than Rita. |

1983). For example, by the age of 9 months, most infants react differently to an adult's smiling or frowning face (Campos et al., 1983; Feinman, 1982).

## Forming Impressions of Others: Developmental Differences

As students become older, their thinking processes gradually shift from the concrete stages of preoperational and operational thought to the abstract stage of formal operational thought. This shift in thinking occurs not only in how students conceptualize the physical world, but also in how they form impressions of themselves and others.

Preschoolers typically describe themselves and others in concrete terms, such as physical characteristics, where they live, or the activities they engage in (Hayes, Gershman, & Bolin, 1980). In the early grades, however, students begin to use abstract, psychological characteristics in describing themselves and others. Figure 9.2 shows Barenboim's (1981) model of students' age-related progression from the use of concrete to abstract dimensions in perceiving themselves and others.

By first grade, students begin to describe others in comparative rather than in absolute terms. For example, instead of describing Judith simply as a good speller, 6-year-olds are more apt to describe her as the best speller in the class. By about 8 years old, students focus on psychological traits rather than concrete behaviors, but not until students are about 11 or 12 years old do they compare other people in terms of psychological characteristics.

Barenboim's developmental model of person perception coincides remarkably well with Piaget's model of cognitive development (Shaffer, 1988). Students replace behavioral comparisons with psychological constructs at about the same age they advance from preoperational to concrete operational thinking. Similarly, students replace psychological constructs with the psychological comparisons at about the same age they advance from concrete to formal operational thinking.

## Selman's Developmental Levels of Social Perspectives

To understand social behavior, children must realize not only that people can cause things to happen but that people may *intentionally* cause things to happen. Furthermore, they must realize that people frequently behave in consistent ways that reflect an underlying personality trait or predisposition (Peevers & Secord, 1973).

The development of students' social cognitive abilities depends on the extent to which they are able to look at the world from other people's perspectives (Selman, 1980). All students progress through the same age-related stages in developing their role-taking ability (Gurucharri & Selman, 1982). See figure 9.3 for a description of Selman's developmental levels of social perspectives.

# Moral Development

To live harmoniously in a social context, people need a sense of morality that governs how they act. Morality is "a set of principles or ideals that help the individual to distinguish right from wrong and to act on this distinction" (Shaffer, 1988, p. 314). Jean Piaget developed one of the earliest models of moral development and Lawrence Kohlberg expanded and refined many of Piaget's ideas.

*Annual* **Edition**
unit *2*

Piaget's stages of cognitive development apply to students' understanding of social behavior.

*Annual* **Edition**
unit *2*

9.4 ◉

*Compare the theories of moral development of Piaget, Kohlberg, and Gilligan.*

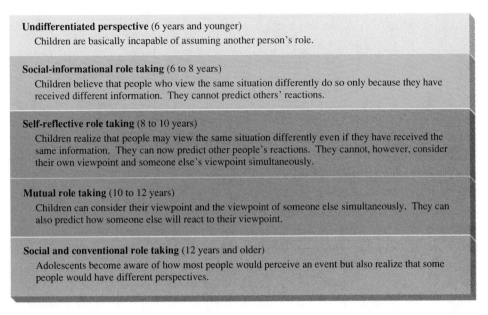

**Figure 9.3**
Selman's developmental levels of
social perspectives.

## Piaget's Theory

Piaget believed that moral reasoning develops in an invariant sequence of stages and that all people go through exactly the same stages in exactly the same order, which is the same idea underlying his theory of cognitive development. According to Piaget (1965), moral development occurs as a joint result of children's cognitive growth and their social interaction with others of the same age. As children move away from egocentric thinking and begin to see things from different perspectives, their concepts of morality mature.

Prior to the age of 4 or 5, children are in the premoral stage and are unaware that any rules exist. As they begin to socialize with other children, particularly during play activities, they gradually realize not only that there are rules, but that rules represent guidelines for behavior that are mutually agreed to by members of the group.

During the stage of *moral realism*, which occurs roughly between the ages of 6 and 10, children become almost fanatical in their belief that rules are sacred pronouncements governing people's behavior. At this stage, children believe everyone must obey rules at all times and at any cost. Children judge the morality of a person's behavior in terms of the physical consequences of the behavior rather than in terms of the person's intention. Children at the stage of moral realism are apt to believe that a child who accidentally bumps into a table and breaks six cups deserves more severe punishment than a child who purposely picks up a single cup and smashes it on the floor.

At about 11 years of age, children advance to the stage of *moral relativism*. They now understand not only that rules are arbitrary agreements among members of a group but also that members may agree to change the rules. Older children judge the morality of people's behavior in terms of the extent to which a person willfully breaks a rule and the extent to which circumstances justify breaking a rule. Children who have reached the stage of moral relativism, for example, find it justifiable for a driver to break the speed limit to get a critically ill person to the hospital.

Some studies have confirmed Piaget's claim that older children make moral judgments in relative rather than absolute terms and take into account people's intentions, not just the consequences of behavior (Hoffman, 1979; Lickona, 1976). Other studies, however, suggest Piaget's model of moral development is flawed. Several studies have found that children as young as 3 to 5 can distinguish between people's intentions and the consequences of their actions (Nelson, 1980; Nelson-Le Gall, 1985; Schickedanz, 1994; Schultz, Wright, & Schleifer, 1986; Surber, 1982), an ability that, according to Piaget, should not occur until children are about 11 years old.

*Annual* **Edition**

unit *4*

What factors might affect students' ideas about the kinds of rules teachers have a right to enforce?

Turiel (1983) has criticized Piaget's model for its failure to differentiate between *moral rules* that deal with the rights of others and *social conventional rules* that people follow in given social situations. Children as young as 2½ can distinguish between the two types of rules and regard moral rules as more important than social conventional ones (Smetana, 1981, 1985).

Children as young as 6 can determine who has the authority to enforce which kind of rule. For many children parents have the right to enforce moral rules, but not social conventional ones (Tisak, 1986). Children would probably agree that parents have the right to enforce a rule of not hitting a younger sibling but not a rule that one must complete homework before watching television.

## Kohlberg's Theory

Kohlberg (1981, 1984) elaborated on Piaget's work by examining in detail how people reason about moral issues. He became interested in this subject because after World War II and the Holocaust, each Nazi war criminal tried by an international tribunal claimed to be innocent because he was just following orders. Yet, many people in Germany and other countries did *not* follow orders during this period, and many paid dearly for their resistance.

Kohlberg wondered what caused some people to obey authority and others to defy it. He found that Piaget's theory of moral reasoning did not adequately resolve this issue. He began exploring the moral judgments of a small sample of men *longitudinally,* that is, across an extended period of time. He wanted to find out how these men judged moral issues and how their judgments changed over time.

Kohlberg presented his sample with hypothetical moral dilemmas, such as the one that follows:

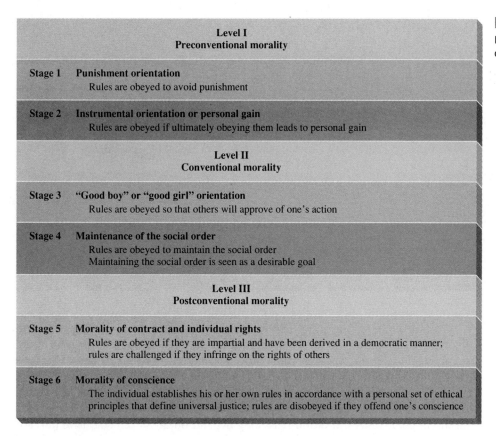

**Figure 9.4**
Kohlberg's levels of moral development.

*In Europe a woman was near death from cancer. One drug might save her, a form of radium that a druggist in the same town had recently discovered. The druggist was charging $2,000, 10 times what the drug cost him to make. The sick woman's husband, Heinz, went to everyone he knew to borrow the money but he could only get together about half of what it cost. He told the druggist that his wife was dying and asked him to sell it cheaper or let him pay later. But the druggist replied, "No." The husband got desperate and broke into the man's store to steal the drug for his wife.*
    *Should the husband have done that? Why? (Kohlberg, 1969, p. 379)*

Kohlberg was not interested in whether people agreed or not with what Heinz had done, but rather in the thinking processes underlying their answers. Kohlberg would ask probing questions: If someone said, "No, Heinz should not steal the drug, because stealing is bad," Kohlberg would ask "Why is stealing bad?"

Kohlberg agreed with Piaget that moral development occurs in an invariant sequence of stages. Kohlberg, however, proposed a different sequence consisting of three levels, each of which is comprised of two stages. Kohlberg discovered that younger children obey rules because they fear punishment, not because they respect the rules or the authority figures who impose them, as Piaget had suggested (Shaffer, 1988).

Most importantly, Kohlberg concluded that Piaget had erred in contending that moral development is complete by the time children reach the age of 10 to 12. Kohlberg found that people's sense of morality continues to mature until they reach early adulthood. Studies of people living in various foreign countries have confirmed Kohlberg's finding, thus supporting the notion that the stages of moral development are invariant and universal (See, for example, Parikh, 1980; Turiel, Edwards, & Kohlberg, 1978).

Figure 9.4 presents Kohlberg's levels of moral development. Up until the age of 10 most children function at the *preconventional level*. Between the ages of 10 and 18, people begin to shift to the *conventional level*, and by their early 20s, most have made the shift. Few people, however, reach the *postconventional level*.

**Figure 9.5**
Gilligan's model of the moral
development of women.

| **Level I**<br>**Orientation to self-survival** |
| --- |
| Initially, women are oriented toward protecting their own self-interests. To advance to Level II they must go through a transitional phase in which they recognize that sometimes there may be a conflict between doing what is good for themselves and doing what is the responsible thing to do. |

| **Level II**<br>**Goodness as self-sacrifice** |
| --- |
| At this level, women attempt to behave in a responsible manner, avoiding doing harm to others when possible, even though such behavior may involve self-sacrifice. To advance to Level III, they must go through a transitional phase in which they begin to consider not only their responsibility to avoid hurting others but also their responsibility to avoid hurting themselves. |

| **Level III**<br>**The morality of nonviolence** |
| --- |
| At this level, women accept the principle of nonviolence as the basic underlying rationale of all moral behavior. In making moral judgments they now consider avoiding harm to themselves just as important as avoiding harm to others. |

Kohlberg's levels of moral development correspond closely to Piaget's stages of cognitive development. Students who are at the preconventional level of moral development are at the stage of preoperational thinking, whereas students who have reached the conventional level of moral development have reached the stage of concrete operational thinking. Only people who are at the stage of formal operational thinking can advance to the postconventional levels of moral development. Note that although advances in moral reasoning depend on advanced cognitive development, there is no guarantee that students with advanced cognitive development will exhibit advanced moral reasoning (Kuhn et al., 1977; Tomlinson-Keasey & Keasey, 1974). Cognitive development is necessary but not sufficient for moral development to occur.

Cognitive development precedes moral development.

According to Kohlberg, advances in moral development also require challenges to one's current thinking. Confronting students with moral reasoning at one level higher than their current level generally leads to higher-order moral reasoning (Arbuthnot, 1975; Rest, 1986). Furthermore, adolescents who discussed moral issues with their peers to reach consensus achieved greater gains in moral reasoning than adolescents who made individual judgments without discussion (Berkowitz, Gibbs, & Broughton, 1980; Maitland & Goldman, 1974).

## Gilligan and the Moral Development of Women

Kohlberg studied the moral reasoning of males, but not females. Although most studies suggest that the process of moral development of boys and girls is the same (Walker, 1984, 1986), among adults, women tend to function at stage 3, whereas men tend to function at stage 4 (Holstein, 1976; Parikh, 1980). Gilligan (1977, 1982; Gilligan & Attanucci, 1988) argues that these differences occur because women and men have different orientations toward moral issues, not because men have a superior level of moral reasoning. Gilligan believes that males and females in our society have different orientations toward moral issues because they go through different socialization processes.

Males are encouraged to be independent and assertive, which causes them to perceive moral issues in terms of resolving conflicting interests by applying social rules concerning individuals' *rights*. Females, on the other hand, are encouraged to be nurturant, which causes them to perceive moral issues in terms of resolving conflicts in ways that concern individuals' *responsibilities*.

Kohlberg used hypothetical moral dilemmas in his studies, but Gilligan used a real-life moral dilemma. Based on the moral reasoning of a group of pregnant women concerning the issue of abortion, Gilligan developed the model shown in figure 9.5. Gilligan's model not only describes levels of moral development but also the changes that occur during the transition from one level to the next.

## Presenting a Moral Dilemma

Gilligan presented elementary school children with a moral dilemma: It is a cold, rainy night and a porcupine pokes its head into the home of a mole and asks to take shelter there. The mole then invites the porcupine in but soon discovers that sharing a small home with a porcupine can be extremely uncomfortable. The mole tells the porcupine to leave, but the porcupine says, "You invited me in and I'm going to stay." What should the porcupine do?

Consistent with her theory, Gilligan found that girls' responses concerned the responsibilities of the mole and the porcupine, but boys' responses concerned the rights of each. (It is important to note that some boys gave responses with a "responsibilities" orientation, some girls gave responses reflecting a "rights" orientation, and some children produced solutions that showed elements of both orientations.)

Now it's your turn: Read the "Mole and Porcupine" dilemma to some elementary school-age children and listen to their responses. Ask probing questions and see what orientation (or orientations) their responses reflect, and what stage they represent within the framework of Kohlberg's and Gilligan's theories.

# Self-Concept

**Self-concept,** or one's perception of oneself, probably develops at the moment the child is aware of his or her separateness (Stern, 1985). Early experiences with caregivers, parents, and family provide the backdrop from which attitudes about the self grow. Psychologists regard the early years as critical to the eventual sense of confidence, personal regard, and competence that an individual experiences (Markus & Wurf, 1987; Suls & Greenwald, 1986). Self-concept, however, is not simply an emotional response to experience; it is a complex cognitive schema that the individual creates from experience (Markus & Nurius, 1986).

Just as we develop schemata for other concepts, we develop a schema of the self. Our **self-schema** is a cognitive structure we construct as we receive information about ourselves (Markus & Nurius, 1986). Markus and Nurius contend that most self-concepts are **working self-concepts** that are open to change as we encounter new experiences that provide us new feedback. How we imagine ourselves now and in the future determines our self-concept. As a teacher you will be most concerned with the impact of students' self-concepts on their motivation to learn.

## Academic Self-Concept and Academic Achievement

Most students enter school expecting to learn (Entwhistle & Hayduk, 1981; Stipek, 1988), but negative school experiences often reverse their views. In particular, students who have learning difficulties begin to perceive themselves as unable to learn (Chapman, 1988).

Most people see themselves in several different roles. For example, students have varying beliefs about their athletic ability, their ability to make lasting friendships, their musical ability, and their academic ability. They also have a generalized self-concept, such as a propensity toward optimism or pessimism. General self-concept has only a small positive correlation with academic achievement. Some specific perceptions of self, such as athletic or social abilities, have no relationship to academic achievement (Hansford & Hattie, 1982; Marsh & Shavelson, 1985).

9.5 ◎

*Summarize the research concerning self-concept and its role in academic achievement.*

Students' self-concepts can change as a result of new experiences.

What are some school experiences that might negatively affect students at the elementary, junior high, and senior high school levels?

How we imagine ourselves now and in the future determines our self-concept.

© Superstock

Students' perception of their academic ability is the only aspect of self-concept that correlates moderately or highly with academic achievement (Marsh & Holmes, 1990). The strongest relationships are between specific academic self-concepts (such as believing one is good at math or not good in English) and achievement in those subject areas.

As students mature, this sense of self becomes more differentiated, and separate concepts of the self emerge. Students hold academic and nonacademic self-concepts of themselves and often differentiate these concepts more specifically (for example, "I'm good at baseball and bad at basketball"). As students evaluate themselves, they also compare themselves with others.

## Facilitating the Development of a Positive Self-Concept

Preschoolers begin to identify themselves in terms of gender, which becomes a principal source of identity. They also become aware of their distinct relationship to others, such as their parents, caretakers, siblings, and other children. They learn the social rules that define acceptable behavior toward others. At this age, children also begin to integrate the values and customs of their family into their own sense of identity. In addition, they judge themselves on the basis of their own accomplishments (Damon & Hart, 1982). Teachers can help preschoolers develop positive self-concepts by encouraging socially acceptable behavior with peers and by emphasizing the unique qualities of family life that each child experiences. Formation of a positive self-concept relies in part on individual achievement, so teachers should give young children tasks they can successfully complete and acknowledge their success.

Elementary school children meet new and more demanding social expectations as they become aware of their relative status in their peer-age group. Younger children do not focus on comparisons with others, but elementary school children do, and these comparative self-evaluations are crucial to self-concept development.

Since many classrooms emphasize competition, elementary school students' self-evaluations are further elaborated by evaluations from teachers and other students. As students move through the elementary and middle schools, these comparisons play an increasing role in determining their self-concepts (Eccles, Midgley, & Adler, 1984).

Elementary school teachers should balance independent and individual activities with opportunities for children to work cooperatively, where group effort is paramount. Teachers can also point out that there are many useful skills to learn and that individuals differ in which ones they do well; elementary students should learn that abilities vary and that all students are valuable learners (Cohen, 1986).

Adolescence is the most difficult period for a student's development of a sense of self. Adolescents are struggling to find out who they are and frequently must balance their need for independence with the continuing dependence on family and other adults. Teenagers' self-concepts rely heavily on their success with peers, who play an increasingly important role in their lives. This turbulent period is characterized by a need to know how others feel about them and by a need to experiment with a variety of roles (Slavin, 1994).

As adolescents struggle with self-identity through their relationships with family and peers, they are also developing a sense of their own identity through changes in cognitive growth. Adolescents recognize the inadequacy of their thinking as they struggle to solve complex problems that have no simple solutions. They become more concerned about the complexity of their roles as adults. As students get better at solving problems, their self-concepts become more positive. Teachers can help adolescents learn to think critically, use abstract thinking, and recognize the importance of experimentation, interpretation, and openmindedness.

Give examples of how you could help a teenager think critically.

## Patterns of Parenting

9.6 ◎

*Describe the role of parents and peers in students' social and emotional development.*

Warm, involved parents who enforce rules have children who succeed socially in school, whereas angry, rejecting, or uninvolved parents have less successful children (McDonald & Parke, 1984; Puttalaz, 1987). Parenting practices differ among individuals and groups because of family history, ethnic perceptions of family hierarchical relations, socioeconomic status, and education. How a parent interacts with a child is complex, socially and culturally determined, and often, idiosyncratic. The means by which parents and children communicate have strong effects on children's social and emotional development. Baumrind (1973) characterizes parent interactive styles as authoritarian, permissive, or authoritative. **Authoritarian** parents value conformity, are detached, and do not explain rules, but expect compliance from the child. The children of authoritarian parents frequently exhibit withdrawn and passive behavior and often are unwilling to take risks. **Permissive** parents give children total freedom and have few expectations or demands. Permissive parents foster dependence and immaturity, thereby creating anxiety and lack of self-control in their children. **Authoritative** parents are firm, but are also caring, explain the reasons for rules, and have high expectations of their children. Authoritative parents facilitate positive self-concepts in their children, who often become individuals secure enough to take risks.

# DIVERSITY MAKES A DIFFERENCE

## Self-Concept and Cultural Background

School achievement is not always linked directly to students' self-concept but rather, indirectly through students' cultural backgrounds. Ogbu (1992) believes that complex social, economic, historical, and cultural factors affect minority children's school learning and performance. He argues that, while society often denies minorities equal access to education and while schools may engage in discriminatory practices, differential cultural forces are also at work in determining students' perceptions regarding school achievement.

Ogbu believes it is useful to differentiate among three types of minority groups: (a) *autonomous*—minorities who are integrated in society but are minorities only in the numerical sense; (b) *immigrant or voluntary minorities*—those who have come to another country seeking economic opportunities or political freedom; and (c) *involuntary minorities*—those who were brought to another country against their will for slavery, colonization, or forced labor. Examples of the latter in the United States include African Americans and early Mexican Americans in the Southwest.

Minorities in the first two groups value the attitudes and behaviors needed for school success. Involuntary minorities, however, establish cultural norms for behavior that differ from those of the majority because they find behaviors of the majority inappropriate for themselves. Instead, they develop their own cultural values, events, and symbols as a cultural reaction to the values of the majority culture, known as *cultural inversion*.

Self-concept and achievement may be linked *as long as students' cultural groups value school achievement.* Some minority students have well-developed self-concepts, but their behaviors reflect cultural values that oppose school achievement. This attitude prevails within other groups, such as adolescents and, in particular, adolescent girls whose subculture may place greater value on social than academic success.

Parenting practices have a strong effect on children's development.

© Eric R. Berndt/Unicorn Stock Photos

## Parenting and Teaching Patterns That Foster Initiative

Teachers who use an authoritative style with students help them to learn to take risks and accept new challenges. Children of different ages need different forms of opportunities to express their opinions and carry out problem-solving activities. Although young children can work independently to gain skills, they also need support and guidance from an adult.

**Co-regulation,** in which adults (parents as well as teachers) give children more control as they demonstrate competence and responsibility, is an important phase in helping students move from dependent to independent learning. This interactive style is transitional and sensitive; that is, problems can occur when adults offer either too little or too much control.

# Calvin and Hobbes                     by Bill Watterson

Successful adults establish ground rules and procedures but also allow for experimentation and freedom within these boundaries (Grolnick & Ryan, 1989). There is an important link between parental interactive styles and students' self-regulatory behavior (Wentzel & Feldman, 1990) and achievement (Dornbusch et al., 1987). Students of authoritative parents are more considerate, more responsible, and higher achieving. The balance between clear expectations and freedom leads to confident and capable behavior.

## Working Parents

Working mothers, per se, do not constitute a problem for the developing child; more important than the mother's presence during the young child's day is the quality of care provided (Belsky, 1987). Some working mothers, however, may be divorced and experience lowered income and often poverty (Weinraub & Wolf, 1983). In these instances, the effects on children are confounded by the reasons that force these mothers to work (Cole & Cole, 1989; Milne et al., 1986). Girls and adolescents of working mothers often achieve more and have more positive self-concepts than their counterparts (Hoffman, 1984).

Whether one or both parents work is less important than the quality of the interaction that takes place in the home. How parents talk with a child, how they share time, and how much support they provide can affect a child's sense of security no matter what the structure of the family (Easterbrooks & Goldberg, 1985; Hoffman, 1984).

## Effects of Divorce and Single-Parent Families

The traditional family with two parents and children, where the father works and the mother stays home is now the exception. This "traditional" family structure exists in only 7 percent of households in the United States. Approximately 60 percent of mothers work, increasing to 68 percent for single-parent households (Hayghe, 1986; Mirga, 1986).

The effects of divorce on children depend on the child's age and gender (Wallerstein, 1987). Preschoolers may become anxious and tearful and sometimes believe they are the cause of their parents' problems. Children of elementary age often focus on the departure of one parent and fantasize that their parents will be reconciled. Adolescents tend to be angry but are more likely to understand the nature of the conflict between their parents.

Boys seem to be more vulnerable to divorce than girls (Block, Block, & Gjerde, 1986). They often display adjustment problems in school and recover more slowly from the effects of divorce. Boys have lower academic achievement, more incidents of discipline problems (Guidubaldi et al., 1983), and more absences and tardiness. They also are more likely to lack concentration, drop out of school, or become a "loner" (Cornacchia, Olsen, & Nickerson, 1988).

## Collaborating with Parents

Some educators believe that collaboration between the schools and parents is the key to improving students' social, emotional, and cognitive development. Epstein (1992) suggests six ways in which schools can collaborate with parents:

1. Help parents develop parenting skills by telling them what students need at various levels of development.
2. Inform parents about students' progress and school programs that may foster two-way communication.
3. Involve parents in the school as assistants, supporters of events, and audiences for student performances.
4. Guide parents in ways to help students at home.
5. Provide opportunities for parents to share in decision making in the schools.
6. Collaborate with community agencies, businesses, and cultural organizations where parents may have affiliations.

Teachers can help students who are suffering the effects of divorce by providing empathy and offering guidance and friendship. Teachers should refer students to the guidance counselor if the behavior becomes distressing. It sometimes helps children if they know they are not alone and that perhaps as many as half the students in their class are facing the same problem.

# Interactions with Peers

One of the most important goals of childhood is for children to learn how to get along with their peers (Hartup, 1989). No aspect of schooling has more impact on students' social and emotional behavior than their interactions with classmates. Think back to your own high school or elementary school days. If you are like most of us, many of your most vivid thoughts are about some of the students who were in your class. Such thoughts are understandable because your interactions with other students probably played a powerful role in shaping how you perceive yourself and how you now interact with others. We form a mental image of ourselves primarily by interacting and comparing ourselves with others.

The way students interact with their peers predicts remarkably well numerous important cognitive and emotional aspects of future student behavior, including attitudes toward school, academic performance (Ladd, 1990), self-concept (Buhrmester, 1990), disruptive and aggressive behavior (Coie, Dodge, & Coppotelli, 1982), and the likelihood of dropping out of school (Parker & Asher, 1987). Psychologists have begun to investigate how students interact with their peers in a variety of situations to try to discover what factors determine the nature of the interaction.

## Factors Influencing Peer Interaction

Students' perceptions of themselves result from comparing their performance to that of their peers. But how do students select the peers they will use for comparison? The answer depends, among other things, on students' ages. Meisel and Blumberg (1990) examined the peer comparison selections of black and white students in the second, third, fourth, and ninth grades. Students in the early elementary grades tended to compare themselves with peers of the same race and gender. They also tended to compare themselves with students who are popular, but who are not necessarily their friends. In contrast, ninth-graders frequently compared themselves with their best friends, although they also tended to restrict their comparisons to students of their own race and gender.

Students who participated in the study came from a wide range of socioeconomic levels. Consequently, it is not clear to what extent students of different races may also have come from different socioeconomic levels. Perhaps students selected peers from their own socioeconomic level for comparison, and the fact that they were also of the same race was merely coincidental.

Howes and Wu (1990) examined the social interactions of students in kindergarten and third-grade classrooms comprised of Euro-American (51 percent), African American (25 percent), Spanish American (16 percent), and Asian American (8 percent) students. In this study, students in each ethnic group came from comparable socioeconomic levels. Consequently, there was no systematic relationship between student ethnicity and socioeconomic level.

After considering the unequal numbers of students in the four ethnic groups, the researchers found that in general students interacted and made friends with students from other ethnic groups as well as from their own. Third graders tended to have more positive interactions and less conflict with peers of other ethnic groups than did kindergartners. Regardless of grade level, however, Euro-American students had fewer positive interactions and Asian American students had more positive interactions with students of other ethnic groups. Euro-American students also had fewer friends from other ethnic groups than did other students.

## Friendship and School Adjustment

The nature of social interaction among students can predict their future adjustment to school. One study found, for example, that among a group of predominantly white middle-class kindergartners, children who entered school with a large number of friends had more positive attitudes toward school than children with fewer friends, and the school attitudes of children who continued to maintain their friendships became even more positive over time (Ladd, 1990).

Children who made new friends during the course of the school year also exhibited increased levels of academic performance. On the other hand, children whose peers socially rejected them had less favorable attitudes toward school and exhibited decreased levels of academic performance as the school year progressed.

As students grow older, the nature of their friendships changes. Friendship among younger students typically involves shared play and acceptance by members of the play group. Among older students, however, the number of close friends decreases (Buhrmester, 1990), and friendship takes on the quality of intimacy, characterized by the mutual self-disclosure of personal feelings and reciprocated emotional support (Steinberg, 1989).

## Factors Affecting Changes in Friendship

Hallinan and Kubitschek (1990) examined changes in friendships during a school year among fourth-, fifth-, and sixth-graders as a function of students' gender, race, and social status in the classroom as measured by popularity. In general, students were likely to drop as friends classmates who were less popular than themselves. Changes in friendship patterns were similar for girls and boys, but not for whites and blacks. Blacks were initially more likely than whites to select a student from the other race as a friend but less likely than whites to maintain the friendship.

According to the researchers, "if whites have higher social status than blacks, whites may simply avoid choosing lower-status black peers as friends. Blacks, on the other hand, may be initially attracted to higher-status whites but, as a result either of the status differential or of other dissimilarities, find the relationship too difficult to maintain" (Hallinan & Kubitschek, 1990, pp. 517–518).

## Intimate Friendships

As students enter adolescence and struggle with the problem of validating their self-worth, the need for intimacy intensifies (Buhrmester, 1990). Adolescents who fail to establish intimate friendships often experience feelings of social alienation and insecurity. Additionally, they are deprived of emotional support from peers in coping with personal problems that may be difficult to discuss with parents, such as dating or changes in bodily functions (Buhrmester & Furman, 1987). Among adolescents, the desire to discuss emotional concerns with friends rather than parents increases with age and is particularly strong among students whose self-esteem is high (Papini et al., 1990).

The establishment of intimate friendships requires students to engage competently in complex and often subtle forms of interpersonal behaviors. A study of preadolescent and adolescent students (Buhrmester, 1990) found that students perceived themselves as more competent at interpersonal relations than their close friends did. Also, preadolescents perceived themselves as more competent than did adolescents, suggesting that as students mature, they begin to doubt their social competence. Girls rated their friendships as more intimate than boys did, but there was no difference between ratings of friendship intimacy given by younger and older students.

Both girls' and boys' ratings of friendship intimacy correlated positively with measures of social adjustment, such as sociability, self-esteem, lack of anxiety, and lack of hostility, although the relationship was stronger for adolescents than for preadolescents. Furthermore, self-reported ratings of intimacy were more similar to ratings given by friends among adolescents than among preadolescents, suggesting that friendships become closer as students become older.

## Play and Friendships in Early Childhood

Play activity is a central component in the social development of young children. Not only is it a source of pleasure, it is young children's "work"; play is what young children *do*. Although very young children play alone or with a caregiver, they begin as early as the toddler stage to comprehend what behavior is appropriate when interacting with other children.

Social play involves several stages, from *observer* play, in which the child merely watches other children play, to *parallel* play, when the child plays next to another with little or no interaction. Parallel play is typical of 2-year-olds, who are beginning to learn social rules but are not yet ready to implement them. Teachers can help youngsters by arranging activities that allow children to work side by side without requiring that they influence one another (Bakeman & Brownlee, 1980).

As preschoolers mature, they begin to associate more with one another, discussing what they are doing and copying, and borrowing and loaning materials to one another. This form of play, called *associative* play, has no formal rules. Once children are ready to attend to rules and share a common goal, they move toward *cooperative* play. Most children have reached the stage of cooperative play by the time they enter kindergarten.

The proliferation of day-care centers and nursery schools to accommodate the growing population of working mothers has put teachers in touch with increasingly younger children. Teachers, therefore, are playing key roles in helping very young children learn the social rules of play. They can use play to encourage friendships among children and to recognize those friendships that are already in place. Teachers can provide numerous small-group activities and arrange groups to include children who are already friends as well as children who do not yet know each other well. Encouraging children not only to make new friends but to maintain the friends they already have sends a strong message about the importance of friendship. Teachers of kindergarten-age and primary-grade students can reinforce these attitudes by providing opportunities for children to work together on classroom projects in small cooperative groups.

## Middle Childhood Friendship Patterns

In middle childhood, children develop an awareness of the needs and feelings of others. As they become less egocentric, they begin to perceive the point of view of others. Children in the early primary grades usually have no empathy for others, since they believe that people feel the same way they do. Children of middle childhood, however, can put themselves into the shoes of others. By age 8, children can identify the feelings or motives of their friends; by 10, many are quite sophisticated about interpreting another's feelings or thoughts (Selman, 1980).

In some schools, classrooms have as many as 30 or 35 students who spend the entire school day together. The classroom, therefore, becomes a place where friendships develop and grow. As parental influence recedes, children rely more and more on peer opinion. Middle childhood is the age of peer interaction. Although friendships often change rapidly, peer groups in the elementary school are very important.

In fact, peers usually shape a child's behavior to such an extent that delinquent behavior can often develop in middle childhood as a result of peer expectations. The popularity of some children is often determined by this age group and has consequences for the way in which others respond within the peer group. Popular children are dependable, friendly, intelligent, and caring (Green, Bjorklund, & Quinn-Cobb, 1988; Hartup, 1983). They have learned socially appropriate ways to interact with others and are often more adaptable than their unpopular peers (Asher, 1983). Teachers can encourage children to acquire more appropriate behaviors in play and study groups that use a cooperative approach in learning.

## Adolescent Friendship Patterns

You may have heard that opposites attract, but research suggests that the more alike people are, the more likely they will become friends. Attitude similarity is one of the main reasons people develop relationships with others (Byrne, Clore, & Smeaton, 1986; Park & Flink, 1989). When we meet someone who thinks about the world as we do, we receive confirmation or validation of our own beliefs. We develop positive feelings toward those who agree with us and negative feelings toward those who disagree (Goethals, 1986). Friendships are not based solely on similar attitudes, for in some instances openness to those we disagree with can lead to friendships forged by alternative viewpoints.

Similarity of attitude is only one basis for friendship; other similarities leading to friendship are age (Ellis, Rogoff, & Cramer, 1981), academic and nonacademic skills (Tesser, Campbell, & Smith, 1984), race, gender, and religion (Kandel, 1978).

Adolescence is a time of great change in peer relations. Students spend more time with peers than with adults. During a time when relationships can be strained at home, adolescents rely on peers to provide the support they need and to reflect their own values and beliefs. In addition, friendships become more intimate in adolescence and, therefore, afford opportunities for students to share feelings and ideas they may no longer share with their families.

Patterns in adolescent friendships change from early adolescent same-gender cliques, to mixed-gender groups and couples as students mature (Thornburg, 1982). Frequently, same-gender relationships persist into adulthood and act as a backdrop for the more volatile relationships with the opposite gender. Although adolescence is a period of identity crisis and identity formation, these concerns are not usually solved within this growth period. More often, college-age or postsecondary-age individuals continue their quest for identity (Waterman, 1985).

*To what extent does the basis for friendship vary from friend to friend?*

# Students at Risk
## Stress and Anxiety in Schools

As many of us know from personal experience, school can be a place of anxiety and pressure. What seem to be endless evaluations, comparisons, and examinations are commonplace occurrences. Even for high-achieving students, constant expectations to perform well in school can produce stress. For students who are underachieving, learning disabled, shy, or reluctant, the pressure can produce undue anxiety, furthering a cycle of failure. School-age children become sensitized to their ranking among their peers. Although comparisons among children cannot always be avoided, teachers can help students develop a balanced viewpoint about achievement and self-worth. To help reduce the stress and anxiety associated with school,

**9.7** ◎

*Describe how stress and anxiety, child abuse and neglect, drug and alcohol abuse, and prejudice and discrimination affect students' social and emotional development.*

# TEACHERS ROUNDTABLE

## "The Students Need to Bring Their Lives into the Classroom"

**DMP:** Have you observed that kids have changed over the time that you've been teaching?

**Anthony:** The attitudes of children and their parents have changed over the years. When I first started to teach, all parents and children expected the kids to be assigned a great deal of work from you. The more work you gave them, the more the parents enjoyed that. Over the years, that perception has changed. Parents don't want that any longer—they want their children happy. I think we are almost fighting the entertainment system. You have to be an entertainer in the classroom—you're fighting computers, you're fighting television.

**Mary:** And then, in a single-parent home or with both parents working, you have baby sitters. That's changed.

**Anthony:** The parents don't devote the large amounts of time that they once did to their children. With the latch-key program, we're keeping children in school from 8:00 in the morning until after 6:00 at night—they spend 10 hours in school.

**Irwin:** The population in public school has changed radically. Nowadays, if it's not single-family homes, it's two parents with both parents working. The days are over when Mom had lunch at home and you walked back to school. You have young kids having kids. You're dealing with kids no longer coming to school with basic socialization skills. I think one of the problems we have at the high school level is that kids have already begun to "dis-identify" with school. They don't see high schools as vehicles for success. They don't see that if I finish this program, something good is going to happen to me. When I was a kid, you had to go to school; you had to go to college; you worked hard. You prayed that you made it into a good public college so it wouldn't cost you anything—we saw that as a way out of our tenement. I don't know if kids see that today. I don't know if they are so clouded with the terrible conditions and lack of success that they see around them.

**Mary:** We also have to allow students to bring their lives into the classroom. Their concerns are AIDS and drugs, and those things should be talked about. Our job is twice as hard because, sometimes, they have no one to talk to about these things where they're living and they need answers. They need security, and their life in school should be predictable; it should be a safe environment where they bring their problems, not just reading, writing, and arithmetic.

**Angela:** In my school, I'm starting to see more and more children who are very, very needy, to the point where, when you walk into a class, they cling to you. They want hugs. Also, I don't see more children with academic problems—we've always had that—but more emotional and social issues are seen. And many of my fellow teachers don't know what to do with them; I find that a lot of my time is taken talking with the teachers, giving them suggestions and strategies for dealing with these children. The problem is that so many of these children are being referred to special education—and it's gotten to the point that the whole school cannot be referred. So we need to do more within our particular school to address those needs.

*Annual* **Edition**

unit 2

teachers can group students based on friendship, interest, or choice, use alternative ways to evaluate performance, and provide activities that interest students.

## Child Abuse and Neglect

Child abuse is a complicated issue that does not discriminate by age, gender, race, or socioeconomic status. It reaches all segments of our society either directly or indirectly and can result in enormous cost to our nation, both financially and socially. Without prevention, children of abuse often become potential abusers, thus perpetuating the cycle of devastation.

Public awareness of the physical and sexual abuse of children has increased considerably in the last decade with scores of reported deaths of children at the hands of abusing parents or other adults. As a result of this awareness, teachers and other school personnel are *required* to report suspected child abuse cases to appropriate agencies. Indicators for both physical and sexual abuse are described in figures 9.6 and 9.7.

1. Unusually aggressive, disruptive, or destructive behavior
2. Unusually shy, withdrawn, or passive behavior, or overly compliant behavior
3. Unusual apprehension and an atypical curiosity when other children cry
4. Unusual apprehension when adults approach a crying child
5. Consistent alertness for danger
6. Frequent, severe mood changes
7. Excessive passive, withdrawn behavior
8. A neglected appearance, indicating malnutrition, or the child is inadequately clothed
9. Overneatness, especially when criticism brings about signs of fear

**Figure 9.6**

Behavioral signs of physical abuse.

Source: J. Wilson, D. Thomas, and L. Schuette, "The Silent Scream: Recognizing Abused Children" in L. W. Barber, (Ed.), *Child Abuse*, 1987: Chula Vista, California, Project Innovation.

1. Difficulty in walking or sitting
2. Torn or stained underclothing
3. Complaints of pain or itching in the genital area
4. Bruises or bleeding in external genitalia, vaginal, or anal area
5. Venereal disease, particularly in children under age 13
6. Poor peer relationships
7. Behavior typical of a younger child such as bed-wetting or infantile, withdrawn, or even retarded behavior
8. A change in appetite or sleeping patterns
9. Need for an unusual degree of reassurance from a parent and excessive clinging, particularly when the offender is around
10. Unwillingness to change for gym or participate in physical activities
11. Fear or anxiety regarding the opposite gender
12. Bizarre, sophisticated, or unusual sexual knowledge or behavior
13. Indiscriminant hugging, kissing, or seductive behavior with children or adults

**Figure 9.7**

Signs of sexual abuse.

Source: M. R. Brassard, A. Tyler, and T. Kehle, "Sexually Abused Children: Identification and Suggestions for Intervention." 1983: *School Psychology Review,* 12:94.

## Physical Abuse

Symptoms of physical injuries that may be labeled abuse include the evidence of repeated injuries, such as burns, welts, cuts, and bruises, as well as internal injuries that are not always apparent to the observer. Teachers, therefore, must know the behavioral signals of physical abuse that arise from both repeated internal and external injury. (See figure 9.6.)

## Sexual Abuse

Sexual abuse is less likely to be recognized, since overt signs are often not present. While the trauma may send some children to a teacher or counselor for help, more often the abused child is embarrassed and hides or denies the problem. Overt behavior is often the only way in which teachers can decide that sexual abuse is likely taking place. Figure 9.7 indicates some overt behaviors.

## Neglect

Since children are unable to provide themselves with the care and attention necessary for health and safety, the responsibility of such care resides with the parent or caretaker who is guardian of underage children. When this care is not provided, children are considered to be neglected. **Neglect** includes the failure to furnish adequate food, shelter, medical care, guidance, or nurturance necessary for children to grow normally and optimally. Signs of neglect are malnutrition, untreated medical problems, inadequate clothing, and lack of cleanliness.

## Reporting Suspected Abuse and Neglect

*In all cases of suspected child abuse or neglect, teachers are responsible for reporting their suspicions;* the method of reporting and the legal definitions of abuse, however, differ from state to state. All fifty states have regulations *that require teachers to report suspected cases of abuse or neglect to child protection agencies.* You must learn your state's reporting procedures.

In addition to recognizing and reporting suspected child abuse, your responsibility lies directly with the student. Show extra care, sensitivity, and concern for neglected or abused students. Provide a classroom environment that allows the student to feel safe, to develop normal status with peers, to develop a positive self-concept within the context of academic and social parameters of the classroom, and to cultivate modes of self-expression that facilitate healthful emotional behaviors (Roscoe, 1984). In addition, establish and maintain close contact with professionals who are specially trained to work with sexually and physically abused children, such as social workers, police, or psychologists.

## Drug and Alcohol Abuse

Drug and alcohol abuse has become a national problem; recent studies report that high school students' use of drugs and alcohol, although not increasing, remains at a high level (U.S. Department of Health & Human Services, 1991). More than 50 percent of high school seniors reported using marijuana at some time and almost 90 percent reported using alcohol within the past year. Over half the students studied began using drugs in intermediate school.

### Characteristics of Drug and Alcohol Abusers

One study reported that among high school boys, those who are shy tended to use more illicit drugs than those who are not. Although in general there was no relationship between students' use of illicit drugs and their need to socialize with others, students who were both shy and had a high need to socialize with others were especially likely to use hallucinogens (Page, 1990). The consequences of drug and alcohol abuse are many; among the most serious are the effects on adolescent health, motivation, and learning (Papalia & Wendkos-Olds, 1989). For society as a whole, the most startling consequence is the increase in violence and aggression to others, particularly in urban areas.

# Prejudice and Discrimination

We often think of prejudice as the irrational emotional feelings some people have toward others who happen to be members of a particular group. In addition to emotional feelings, however, there are important cognitive aspects of prejudice in terms of how people perceive, process, and recall information. When prejudice is operating, people tend to notice more readily information that is consistent, rather than inconsistent, with their prejudicial beliefs (Bodenhausen, 1988).

Prejudice may lead to overt discrimination toward members of a particular group that ranges from simply avoiding them to excluding them from enjoying opportunities available to others or, in extreme cases, even to violent assaults on them (Baron & Byrne, 1991). Cognitive theorists believe that prejudice is a natural part of the development of schemata. From this viewpoint, prejudices are simply beliefs that an individual develops from information and experience to deal with classes (or categories) of people (or things) rather than each individually. This kind of processing facilitates mental processing, but is risky if the individual stops attending to the unique attributes of each individual and generalizes from one individual to many. Teachers should help students examine prejudices and dispel myths about groups.

## KEY POINTS

1. *Personality* refers to an individual's temperament, attitudes, traits, values, and behavior patterns.

2. Erikson believed human beings are inherently *rational,* that the social aspects of their culture determine individuals' emotional and social behavior and that all individuals go through a sequence of eight life crises. The best-known crisis is the *identity crisis* in which adolescents struggle to establish a sense of who they are.

3. Adolescents who successfully resolve their identity crisis are more likely to have positive self-concepts and trust their own judgment than adolescents who fail to resolve the crisis or never go through one.

4. Social cognition refers to how individuals interpret, analyze, remember, and use information about the social world. Children's social cognition follows a distinct developmental sequence.

5. Kohlberg's theory of moral development describes a sequence of stages in individuals' judgments of morality. Kohlberg believed that individuals go from a preconventional level (morality is based on selfish need) to a conventional level (morality is based on social rules and laws). Some

individuals achieve the postconventional level (morality is based on the greatest good for the greatest number).

6. Gilligan's theory of moral development pertains primarily to women; in her approach, a person defines right and wrong from a responsibilities perspective rather than a rights perspective as in Kohlberg's theory.

7. An individual's self-concept is a complex cognitive schema that the individual constructs about who he or she is. Parents, teachers, and friends strongly influence an individual's self-concept.

8. Parenting styles strongly influence social and emotional development. Authoritative parents enforce rules but encourage open discussion of them and have children who take risks, solve problems, and are open to new challenges. Teachers who use an authoritative form of interaction with students can help students learn these forms of behaviors.

9. The effects of working or divorced parents on students' development are complex and vary as a function of many factors, including the student's age and gender.

10. Children's peer group and friends strongly influence their social and emotional development. Friendship among younger students typically involves shared play and acceptance by members of the play group; among older students, however, the number of close friends decreases and friendship takes on the quality of intimacy, characterized by the mutual self-disclosure of personal feelings and reciprocated emotional support.

11. Child abuse does not discriminate by age, gender, race, or socioeconomic status. Teachers must recognize the behavioral signals of physical abuse, sexual abuse, and neglect. Teachers are required by law to report their suspicions to appropriate authorities.

12. Drug and alcohol abuse among young people continues to be a national problem with negative effects on students' health, motivation, and learning.

13. Prejudice and discrimination are serious problems in schools. Teachers should help students examine prejudices and dispel myths about groups.

## SELF-STUDY EXERCISES

1. What is personality and how does it develop?

2. Describe Erikson's eight stages of psychosocial development and give the age range associated with each.

3. What is the responsibility of schools in general and teachers in particular in promoting students' social and emotional development? What can schools and teachers do toward this end?

4. Describe four patterns teenagers typically follow during their identity crisis.

5. Describe Selman's developmental levels of social perspectives.

6. How are the theories of Piaget, Kohlberg, and Gilligan regarding students' moral development similar? How do they differ?

7. Describe the relationship between self-concept and academic performance.

8. What are three different parenting styles, according to Baumrind? How do these parenting styles relate to child behavior?

9. Describe how friendships change as students pass from early childhood through middle childhood to adolescence.

10. What are a teacher's responsibilities regarding suspected child abuse?

## FURTHER READINGS

Baron, R. A., & Byrne, D. (1991). *Social psychology: Understanding human interaction* (6th ed.). Boston: Allyn & Bacon.

Gilligan, C. (1982). *In a different voice: Psychological theory and women's development*. Cambridge, MA: Harvard University Press.

Kohlberg, L. (1984). *Essays on moral development. Vol. 2: The psychology of moral development*. New York: Harper & Row.

Piaget, J. (1965). *The moral judgment of the child*. New York: Free Press. (Original work published 1932).

Shaffer, D. R. (1988). *Social and personality development* (2nd ed.). Pacific Grove, CA: Brooks/Cole.

## REFERENCES

Adams, G., Abraham, K., & Markstrom, C. (1987). The relations among identity development, self-consciousness, and self-focusing during middle and late adolescence. *Developmental Psychology, 23*, 292–297.

Arbuthnot, J. (1975). Modification of moral judgment through role-playing. *Developmental Psychology, 11*, 319–324.

Asher, S. R. (1983). Social competence and peer status: Recent advances and future directions. *Child Development, 54*, 1427–1433.

Bakeman, R., & Brownlee, J. R. (1980). The strategic use of parallel play: A sequential analysis. *Child Development, 51*, 873–878.

Barenboim, C. (1981). The development of person perception in childhood and adolescence: From behavioral comparisons to psychological constructs to psychological comparisons. *Child Development, 52*, 129–144.

Baron, R. A., & Byrne, D. (1991). *Social psychology: Understanding human interaction* (6th ed.). Boston: Allyn & Bacon.

Baumrind, D. (1973). The development of instrumental competence through socialization. In A. Peck (Ed.), *Minnesota symposium on child psychology* (Vol. 7, pp. 3–46). Minneapolis: University of Minnesota Press.

Belsky, J. (1987). *Mother care, other care and infant-parent attachment*. New York: American Psychological Association.

Berkowitz, M. W., Gibbs, J. C., & Broughton, J. M. (1980). The relation of moral judgment stage disparity to developmental effects of peer dialogues. *Merrill-Palmer Quarterly, 26*, 341–357.

Block, J. H., Block, J., & Gjerde, P. (1986). The personality of children prior to divorce: A prospective study. *Child Development, 57*, 827–840.

Bodenhausen, G. V. (1988). Stereotypic biases in social decision making and memory: Testing process models of stereotype use. *Journal of Personality and Social Psychology, 55*, 716–737.

Bosma, H., & Gerrits, R. (1985). Family functioning and identity status in adolescence. *Journal of Early Adolescence, 5*, 69–80.

Brassard, M. R., Tyler, A., & Kehle, T. (1983). Sexually abused children: Identification and suggestions for intervention. *School Psychology Review, 12*, 94.

Buhrmester, D. (1990). Intimacy of friendship, interpersonal competence, and adjustment during preadolescence and adolescence. *Child Development, 61*, 1101–1111.

Buhrmester, D., & Furman, W. (1987). The development of companionship and intimacy. *Child Development, 58*, 1101–1113.

Byrne, D., Clore, G. I., & Smeaton, G. (1986). The attraction hypothesis: Do similar attitudes affect anything? *Journal of Personality and Social Psychology, 51*, 1167–1170.

Campos, J. J., Barrett, K. C., Lamb, M. E., Goldsmith, H. H., & Sternberg, C. (1983). Socioemotional development. In P. H. Mussen (Ed.), *Handbook of child psychology, Vol 2: Infancy and developmental psychobiology* (4th ed., pp. 783–916). New York: Wiley.

Chapman, J. (1988). Learning disabled children's self-concept. *Review of Educational Research, 58*, 347–371.

Cohen, E. G. (1986). *Designing group work: Strategies for the heterogeneous classroom*. New York: Teachers College Press.

Coie, J. D., Dodge, K. A., & Coppotelli, H. (1982). Dimensions of social status: A cross age perspective. *Developmental Psychology, 17*, 557–570.

Cole, M., & Cole, S. R. (1989). *The development of children*. New York: Scientific American Books.

Cornacchia, H. J., Olsen, L. K., & Nickerson, C. J. (1988). *Health in elementary schools* (4th ed.). St. Louis: Times Mirror/Mosby College.

Damon, W., & Hart, D. (1982). The development of self-understanding from infancy through adolescence. *Child Development, 53*, 841–864.

Dornbusch, S., Ritter, P., Leiderman, H., Roberts, D., & Fraleigh, M. (1987). The relationship of parenting style to adolescent school performance. *Child Development, 58*, 1244–1257.

Easterbrooks, M. A., & Goldberg, W. A. (1985). Effects of early maternal employment on toddlers, mothers, and fathers. *Developmental Psychology, 21*, 774–783.

Eccles, J., Midgley, C., & Adler, T. (1984). Grade-related changes in the school environment: Effects on achievement motivation. In J. Nicholls (Ed.), *Advances in motivation and achievement* (Vol. 3, pp. 283–331). Greenwich, CT: JAI Press.

Ellis, S., Rogoff, B., & Cramer, C. C. (1981). Age segregation in children's social interactions. *Developmental Psychology, 17*, 399–407.

Entwhistle, D., & Hayduk, L. (1981). Academic expectations and the school achievement of young children. *Sociology of Education, 54*, 34–50.

Epstein, J. L. (1992). School and family partnerships. In M. Alkin (Ed.), *Encyclopedia of educational research* (pp. 1139–1151). New York: Macmillan.

Erikson, E. H. (1963). *Childhood and society* (2nd ed.). New York: Norton.

Erikson, E. H. (1980). *Identity and the life cycle* (2nd ed.). New York: Norton.

Feinman, S. (1982). Social referencing in infancy. *Merrill-Palmer Quarterly, 28,* 445–470.

Gilligan, C. (1977). In a different voice: Women's conceptions of self and morality. *Harvard Educational Review, 47,* 481–517.

Gilligan, C. (1982). *In a different voice: Psychological theory and women's development.* Cambridge, MA: Harvard University Press.

Gilligan, C., & Attanucci, J. (1988). Two moral orientations: Gender differences and similarities. *Merrill-Palmer Quarterly, 34,* 223–237.

Goethals, G. R. (1986). Social comparison theory: Psychology from the lost and found. *Personality and Social Psychology Bulletin, 12,* 261–278.

Green, B. L., Bjorklund, D. F., & Quinn-Cobb, C. (1988, March). *Development of metaimitation.* Paper presented at the meeting of the Conference on Human Development, Charleston, SC.

Grolnick, W., & Ryan, R. (1989). Parent styles associated with children's self-regulation and competence in school. *Journal of Educational Psychology, 81,* 143–154.

Guidubaldi, J., Perry, J. D., Cleminshaw, H. K., & McLoughlin, C. S. (1983). The impact of parental divorce on children: Report of the Nationwide NASSP study. *School Psychology Review, 12,* 300–323.

Gurucharri, C., & Selman, R. L. (1982). The development of interpersonal understanding during childhood, preadolescence, and adolescence: A longitudinal follow-up study. *Child Development, 53,* 924–927.

Hallinan, M. T., & Kubitschek, W. N. (1990). The formation of intransitive friendships. *Social Forces, 69,* 505–519.

Hansford, B., & Hattie, J. (1982). The relationship between self and achievement/performance measures. *Review of Educational Research, 52,* 123–142.

Hartup, W. W. (1983). Peer relations. In P. H. Mussen (Ed.), *Handbook of child psychology. Vol. 4: Socialization, personality, and social development* (pp. 103–196). New York: Wiley.

Hartup, W. W. (1989). Social relationships and their developmental significance. *American Psychologist, 44,* 120–126.

Hayes, D. S., Gershman, E., & Bolin, L. J. (1980). Friends and enemies: Cognitive bases for preschool children's unilateral and reciprocal relationships. *Child Development, 51,* 1276–1279.

Hayghe, H. (1986). Rise in mother's labor force activity includes those with infants. *Monthly Labor Review, 109,* 43–45.

Hoffman, L. W. (1984). Work, family, and the socialization of the child. In R. C. Parke (Ed.), *Review of child development research* (Vol. 7, pp. 223–282). Chicago: University of Chicago Press.

Hoffman, M. L. (1979). Development of moral thought, feeling, and behavior. *American Psychologist, 34,* 958–966.

Holstein, C. (1976). Irreversible, stepwise sequence in the development of moral judgment: A longitudinal study of males and females. *Child Development, 47,* 51–61.

Howes, C., & Wu, F. (1990). Peer interactions and friendships in an ethnically diverse school setting. *Child Development, 61,* 537–541.

Kandel, D. B. (1978). Similarity in real-life adolescent friendship pairs. *Journal of Personality and Social Psychology, 36,* 306–312.

Klinnert, M. D., Campos, J. J., Sorce, J. F., Emde, R. N., & Svejda, M. (1983). Emotions as behavior regulators: Social referencing in infancy. In R. Plutchik & H. Kellerman (Eds.), *The emotions. Vol. 2: Emotions in early development* (pp. 57–86). New York: Academic Press.

Kohlberg, L. (1969). Stage and sequence: The cognitive-developmental approach to socialization. In D. A. Goslin (Ed.), *Handbook of socialization theory and research* (pp. 347–380). Skokie, IL: Rand McNally.

Kohlberg, L. (1981). *Essays on moral development. Vol. 1: The philosophy of moral development.* New York: Harper & Row.

Kohlberg, L. (1984). *Essays on moral development. Vol. 2: The psychology of moral development.* New York: Harper & Row.

Kuhn, D., Kohlberg, L., Langer, J., & Haan, N. (1977). The development of formal operations in logical and moral judgment. *Genetic Psychology Monographs, 95,* 97–188.

Ladd, G. W. (1990). Having friends, keeping friends, making friends, and being liked by peers in the classroom: Predictors of children's early school adjustment? *Child Development, 61,* 1081–1100.

Lickona, T. (1976). *Moral development and behavior.* New York: Holt, Rinehart & Winston.

Maitland, K. A., & Goldman, J. R. (1974). Moral judgment as a function of peer group interaction. *Journal of Personality and Social Psychology, 30,* 699–704.

Marcia, J. E. (1989). Identity and intervention. *Journal of Adolescence, 12,* 401–410.

Markus, H., & Nurius, P. (1986). Possible selves. *American Psychologist, 41,* 954–969.

Markus, H., & Wurf, E. (1987). The dynamic self-concept: A social psychological perspective. *Annual Review of Psychology, 38,* 299–377.

Marsh, H., & Holmes, I. (1990). Multidimensional self-concepts: Construct validation of responses by children. *American Educational Research Journal, 27,* 89–117.

Marsh, H., & Shavelson, R. (1985). Self-concept: Its multifaceted hierarchical structure. *Educational Psychologist, 20,* 107–123.

McDonald, K. B., & Parke, R. D. (1984). Bridging the gap: Parent-child play interaction and interactive competence. *Child Development, 55,* 1265–1277.

Meisel, C. J., & Blumberg, C. J. (1990). The social comparison choices of elementary and secondary school students: The influence of gender, race, and friendship. *Contemporary Educational Psychology, 15,* 170–182.

Milne, A., Myers, D., Rosenthal, A., & Ginsburg, A. (1986). Single parents, working mothers and the educational achievement of school children. *Sociology of Education, 59,* 125–139.

Mirga, T. (1986). Today's numbers, tomorrow's nation. *Education Week, 4,* 14–22.

Nelson, S. A. (1980). Factors influencing young children's use of motives and outcomes as moral criteria. *Child Development, 51,* 823–829.

Nelson-Le Gall, S. A. (1985). Motive-outcome matching and outcome foreseeability: Effects on attribution of intentionality and moral judgments. *Developmental Psychology, 21,* 332–337.

Ogbu, J. U. (1992). Understanding cultural diversity and learning. *Educational Researcher, 21*(8), 5–14.

Orlowsky, J., & Ginsburg, S. (1981). Intimacy status: Relationship to affect cognition. *Adolescence, 16,* 91–100.

Page, R. M. (1990). Shyness and sociability: A dangerous combination for illicit substance use in adolescent males? *Adolescence, 25,* 803–806.

Papalia, D., & Wendkos-Olds, S. (1989). *Human development* (4th ed.). New York: McGraw-Hill.

Papini, D. R., Farmer, F. F., Clark, S. M., Micka, J. C., & Barnett, J. K. (1990). Early adolescent age and gender differences in patterns of emotional self-disclosure to parents and friends. *Adolescence, 25,* 959–976.

Parikh, B. (1980). Moral judgment development and its relation to family factors in Indian and American families. *Child Development, 51,* 1030–1039.

Park, B., & Flink, C. (1989). A social relations analysis of agreement in liking judgments. *Journal of Personality and Social Psychology, 56,* 506–518.

Parker, J. G., & Asher, S. R. (1987). Peer relations and later personal adjustment: Are low-accepted children "at risk"? *Psychological Bulletin, 102,* 357–389.

Peevers, B. H., & Secord, P. F. (1973). Developmental changes in attribution of descriptive concepts to persons. *Journal of Personality and Social Psychology, 27,* 120–128.

Piaget, J. (1965). *The moral judgment of the child.* New York: Free Press. (Original work published 1932).

Puttalaz, M. (1987). Maternal behavior and children's sociometric status. *Child Development, 58,* 324–340.

Rest, J. R. (1986). *Moral development: Advances in theory and research.* New York: Praeger.

Roscoe, B. (1984). Sexual abuse: The educator's role in identification and interaction with abuse victims. *Education, 105,* 82–86.

Schickedanz, J. A. (1994). Helping children develop self-control. *Childhood Education, 70,* 274–278.

Schultz, T. R., Wright, K., & Schleifer, M. (1986). Assignment of moral responsibility and punishment. *Child Development, 57,* 177–184.

Selman, R. L. (1980). *The growth of interpersonal understanding.* Orlando, FL: Academic Press.

Shaffer, D. R. (1988). *Social and personality development* (2nd ed.). Pacific Grove, CA: Brooks/Cole.

Slavin, R. E. (1994). *Educational psychology* (4th ed.). Englewood Cliffs, NJ: Prentice Hall.

Smetana, J. G. (1981). Preschool children's conceptions of moral and social rules. *Child Development, 52,* 1333–1336.

Smetana, J. G. (1985). Preschool children's conceptions of transgressions: Effects of varying moral and conventional domain-related attributes. *Developmental Psychology, 21,* 18–29.

Steinberg, L. (1989). *Adolescence.* New York: Alfred A. Knopf.

Stern, D. N. (1985). *The interpersonal world of the infant.* New York: Basic Books.

Stipek, D. (1988). *Motivation to learn.* Englewood Cliffs, NJ: Prentice Hall.

Suls, J., & Greenwald, A. G. (Eds.). (1986). *Psychological perspectives on the self* (Vol. 3). Hillsdale, NJ: Erlbaum.

Surber, C. F. (1982). Separable effects of motives, consequences, and presentation order on children's moral judgments. *Developmental Psychology, 18,* 257–266.

Tesser, A., Campbell, J., & Smith, M. (1984). Friendship choice and performance: Self-evaluation maintenance in children. *Journal of Personality and Social Psychology, 46,* 561–574.

Thornburg, H. (1982). *Development in adolescence* (2nd ed.). Monterey, CA: Brooks/Cole.

Tisak, M. S. (1986). Children's conceptions of parental authority. *Child Development, 57,* 166–176.

Tomlinson-Keasey, C., & Keasey, C. B. (1974). The mediating role of cognitive development in moral judgment. *Child Development, 45,* 291–298.

Turiel, E. (1973). Stage transitions in moral development. In R. Travers (Ed.), *Second handbook of research on teaching* (pp. 732–758). Chicago: Rand McNally.

Turiel, E. (1983). *The development of social knowledge: Morality and convention.* Cambridge: Cambridge University Press.

Turiel, E., Edwards, C. P., & Kohlberg, L. (1978). Moral development in Turkish children, adolescents, and young adults. *Journal of Cross-Cultural Psychology, 9,* 75–86.

U.S. Department of Health & Human Services. (1991). *Drug use among American high school students and young adults, 1975–1990.* Washington, DC: Author.

Walker, L. J. (1984). Sex differences in the development of moral reasoning: A critical review. *Child Development, 55,* 677–691.

Walker, L. J. (1986). Sex differences in the development of moral reasoning: A rejoinder to Baumrind. *Child Development, 57,* 522–526.

Wallerstein, J. S. (1987). Children of divorce: Report of a ten-year follow-up of early latency-age children. *American Journal of Orthopsychiatry, 57*(2), 199–211.

Waterman, A. (1985). Identity in the context of adolescent psychology. *New Directions for Child Development, 30,* 5–24.

Weinraub, M., & Wolf, B. M. (1983). Effects of stress and social supports on mother-child interactions in single- and two-parent families. *Child Development, 54,* 1297–1311.

Wentzel, K., & Feldman, S. (1990, April). *The relationship between family interaction patterns, classroom self-restraint and academic achievement.* Paper presented at the annual meeting of the American Educational Research Association, Boston.

Wilson, J., Thomas, D., & Schuette, L. (1987). The silent scream: Recognizing abused children. In L. W. Barber (Ed.). *Child abuse.* Chula Vista, CA: Project Innovation.

© David Frazier

# Motivation

# Chapter Outline

# Learning Objectives

10.1 Describe two ways of viewing motivation.

10.2 Describe four factors that affect students' motivation.

10.3 Distinguish between performance and mastery goals and describe how each affects students' motivation.

10.4 List nine ways to motivate students in the classroom.

10.5 Describe Maslow's hierarchy of needs, achievement motivation, locus of control, attribution theory, and efficacy expectation.

10.6 Describe how teacher expectation and motivation affect student motivation and performance.

10.7 Describe how to use praise, set goals, determine a reward structure, and evaluate students' performance in ways that maximize student motivation.

# Preview

This chapter examines the nature of student motivation and presents techniques you can use to motivate students to perform well. Almost all children in the United States enter kindergarten eager to learn. As they progress through school, however, many lose their enthusiasm. Why do our students, who are as bright as any in the world, perform worse academically than students in other industrialized countries? Part of the reason is their lack of motivation.

This chapter describes the relationship between motivation and self-confidence, reward, task difficulty, and task value. We describe various theories of motivation and the role that motivation plays in distinguishing between performance and mastery goals. We explain how to create a motivating classroom environment, how to use praise effectively, and how to establish realistic short- and long-term learning goals. ◉

# The Nature of Motivation

**Motivation** is an internal state that activates and gives direction to our thoughts, feelings, and actions (Lahey, 1995). We sometimes make incorrect assumptions about the motivation of others. For example, a French teacher may assume that a student who can't conjugate *être* lacks the motivation to do so, when in fact the student may simply lack knowledge about general principles of grammar or misunderstand the teacher.

The most salient characteristics of motivation are persistence and focused behavior. Motivated people engage in goal-directed behavior and persist until they have achieved the goal. As a personality **trait,** motivation represents a relatively stable predisposition to engage in focused and persistent behavior. Different people exhibit different levels of motivation regardless of the task they are pursuing.

On the other hand, motivation may also represent a specific **state** or temporary condition that depends on a particular situation. People may be highly motivated to act in one situation yet completely unmotivated in another.

For example, a student may engage in highly motivated behavior to become a member of a varsity team, yet remain completely unmotivated to perform well in algebra. Another student, however, may be highly motivated to perform well in algebra, yet lack the motivation to compete for a spot on a varsity team.

Motivation doesn't work the same way for everybody. For example, Adam, a 10-year-old who is intelligent and gets goods grades in school, usually spends one and a half to two hours a day on homework. He occasionally asks his parents a question, but much of the time works on his own. He displays no excitement about doing his homework.

After completing his homework, Adam generally gets together with friends or speaks with them on the phone. Their talk is animated and enthusiastic. Adam and his friends collect baseball cards. They can easily rattle off statistics for every player on every team in each league. They challenge each other with questions that demand detailed knowledge of little-known facts about various players. They also know which cards are most valuable and swap cards with the confident knowledge of what constitutes a good trade.

**10.1** *Describe two ways of viewing motivation.*

The individual nature of motivation presents challenges to teachers, who have to motivate students with different interests to apply themselves in learning the same curriculum.

## Effortful and Effortless Task Performance

How can we explain the *effortless* involvement of Adam and his friends with baseball cards, an activity that demands the acquisition of much detailed information, the application of mathematical skills, and judgments about abstract concepts? How does such activity compare with the *effortful* behavior Adam displays while completing homework?

Adam and his friends have learned about baseball players and teams because of a strong interest they share. In fact, their level of interest might be secondary to their involvement with one another. Peer interaction occupies much of the activity of collecting baseball cards. The desire to make good trades, develop a comprehensive collection, and be a part of a peer group may be motivation enough to learn about statistics and biographies of baseball players.

Adam completes his homework by expending only a small amount of effort probably because he finds homework assignments easy. We don't know how motivated Adam would be if confronted with a task he finds both difficult and dull. We know that Adam will complete a difficult task that is interesting and involves interacting with others. He will also complete an easy task if it requires little effort.

## Possible Reasons Underlying Effortful Task Performance

Janice, a 14-year-old with a poor academic record, is a gifted basketball player. She likes the praise and attention she receives from friends when she shoots baskets, and she fantasizes about being the star player on the school team. Janice learns, however, that she is not eligible for the team because her grades fall below the standard set for varsity athletes.

# TEACHERS ROUNDTABLE

## "Provide Students with the Freedom to Respond Without Fear"

**SK:** Can you talk a little about trying to motivate your students and the problems you encounter in your efforts?

**Anthony:** Motivation is really the most exciting part of the lesson. It's a part where you get the children involved in your topic. I guess if I could motivate all day I would.

**Angela:** For me, by virtue of working with children who have so many deficits [in special education], it's frustrating because you work hard and teach good lessons and you still see so many things that they don't know. So what I do is go home and I think about what I'm doing and I think about what I can do differently to help motivate the children, or how I can present the information in a different way to address their particular needs.

**Irwin:** Sometimes it's frustrating beyond words. You give it your best shot and you think the kids are really getting it. You call on them, and they comment intelligently. And then you give a test and you check your answer key because you're not quite sure that the answer key is correct because the marks are so

out of synch with what you expected. So, you ask yourself "What's going on here?" One thing I've learned is that if you've done something and it hasn't worked, repeating it a second time and a third time is not going to work. What you really have to do is try something else, a different approach. And that may not work either and then you analyze why it's not working.

We did that recently; we analyzed why some social studies lessons weren't working and we found out that the problem was vocabulary; the kids simply didn't understand the words that we assumed they knew. While you believe they understand the material, they see the word *tyranny* and they have no idea what it means. Or they see the word *justified* and they have no concept of what it means. So you have to say to yourself, well, this is what the problem is. We have to go back and incorporate explanations of the words into the lessons. But, I have to say, no matter how carefully you've

designed your lessons or how terrific you think you are, you are not going to reach every kid in the classroom. It just doesn't happen. That's the real frustration.

You have to try to motivate kids based on their own life experience. Try to make them part of the lesson. For example, instead of teaching specific facts, such as climatic zones, I would say to a kid, "Okay, you have the option to take five things with you to survive in a particular place. What would you take?" The kid can't be wrong. He takes what he wants to take and then he explains it. And the kid feels good about himself.

**Donna:** I try to personalize the lesson. I have a child who is math phobic and he couldn't do word problems. But now, he has no difficulty because I know what his interests are, and the word problems that I write have to do with him and his interests. Also, to motivate students, I present the topic and ask the kids, "Why do you think we need to learn that? What are we going to do with that?" And that always gets them thinking and talking.

---

Janice, determined to make the team, starts to study harder. She begins to study several hours each day after school and consults with teachers when assignments cause her trouble. Janice persists at improving her academic performance and recognizes that school learning does not come easily to her. Eventually, her grades improve and she makes the team.

The example of Janice illustrates how motivation directed toward one goal may lead simultaneously to achieving another goal. Janice's motivation to learn school subjects reflects no inherent interest in academic material. She simply decided to make an effortful attempt to achieve a goal of little interest to accomplish a goal of genuine interest.

## Factors Related to Motivational Level

**10.2**

*Describe four factors that affect students' motivation.*

*Annual* **Edition**

_____

unit *5*

These examples represent typical instances in which students' motivation may arise from different needs. They also highlight a critical issue: In what ways does a person's motivation depend on how difficult the task is? For example, can tasks that are too easy or too difficult lead to boredom and low motivation? Is it possible for a task to be so easy that it requires no motivation to accomplish?

Might a person's motivation to accomplish an easy task mask other motives the person might have? Could a person's motivation to succeed at an easy task, for example, conceal an underlying desire to build sufficient self-confidence to risk

**Irwin:** That's a dangerous question!

**Donna:** I've never had a problem with it. It gets them thinking, because they feel that they'll never use a lot of the things that they learn.

**Irwin:** And they are right.

**Angela:** The freedom to respond without fear is something you need to provide in your classroom. Otherwise you are simply not going to get responses. I've done things that I thought were going to be wonderfully motivating that turned out to be incredibly flat. To some extent, it helps to be a ham. One of my biggest joys is reading a story and using different voices and hand motions; that's been effective in motivating students. It works to put that extra effort in and to put your personality into it. That's part of the motivation, but it's also part of the fun.

**Mary:** I taught for years using basal readers. When I taught that way, I remember always wishing that some day I could teach and not have those children looking bored in front of me. Now, I've moved to a whole language approach. I find that the kids are excited about being in school, and that makes me excited.

**Angela:** I believe that if they're involved, they're motivated, and they are in charge of their own learning.

**Anthony:** And in the elementary schools, they simply tell you. They are open, and they say, "I want to be here. I like to come here."

**Mary:** There was an article in the newspaper last week about one of the schools that the school district wants to close because students' scores are so low. There was one sentence that really struck me: It said that schools fail not because the books are old, but because the children are not engaged.

**Irwin:** One good way to evaluate a class at the high school level is to look in a classroom and see how many students are actually involved with the learning. The more you involve kids, the more they respond in a positive way. You are reaching kids because there is some kind of interaction between them and you, or between them and the material. And you don't just ask simple questions. You ask them to *think* before they respond. "Do you agree or disagree with what this student just said? Why?" If a kid doesn't answer, I say, "Hey, that's not a problem . . . I'll get back to you." And I do get back to them, sometimes with a different or easier question. And you keep getting back until the kid thinks, "He's going to ask, so I better answer." Before you know it, they're answering.

**Angela:** Because my students come to my resource room, they spend the rest of their school day in the regular classroom. Many of them try in the resource room, but don't try back in the classroom. The teachers say they just don't participate or volunteer. I encourage them to believe that simply *trying* is the challenge; it doesn't matter if their answer is correct. The fact that they even attempted it is important. But you see, also, that whether or not students try relates not only to the teacher but to the group of students in the class.

**SK:** Do you think we should pay more attention to effort than to achievement?

**Donna:** I think I recognize both. The process is important, but the product is rewarded also. When students finish a lesson, I always tell them they did a great job. What I'm really telling them is that I recognize that they tried. I compliment them whether they "succeeded" or not because I want them to keep trying.

tackling more difficult tasks? Or might individuals who successfully complete easy tasks learn to engage only in tasks that lie clearly within the range of their abilities and avoid more difficult tasks?

Why will some people engage only in tasks that are easy, yet other people purposely search out difficult ones that challenge their abilities? What role does interest in a task play in guiding the individual's behavior? Must people possess a certain amount of self-confidence before they are willing to persist at a task? To what extent might people's success or failure at one task influence their behavior on subsequent tasks? And the central question for teachers: What are the characteristics of "ideal" tasks that maximize students' motivation to learn?

## Self-Confidence and Motivation

As a rule, people who feel they cannot succeed at a task do not make the effort to do so. Conversely, people who feel they can succeed usually expend the necessary effort. Janice clearly felt she could improve her grades if she tried. Her success in improving her grades encouraged her to exert even more effort. On the other hand, Adam never gave much thought to the effort required to complete his homework assignments. Did Adam ignore the effort he was expending because he knew that the work was within easy reach, or did hidden factors motivate him?

Despite different reasons, both Janice and Adam exhibited sufficient self-confidence to enable them to complete their respective tasks successfully. Unless students have enough self-confidence in their ability to succeed, they typically won't exert the necessary effort. Motivation requires at least some degree of self-confidence.

## Rewards and Motivation

Self-confidence is only one prerequisite for motivation. Another prerequisite is the likelihood that reward will follow motivated behavior. Janice's reward for achieving higher grades was a place on the school basketball team. We don't know if achieving higher grades became a reward in itself. Do you think Janice will continue to study hard after the basketball season is over? It seems reasonable that competence would encourage confidence, in which case achieving good grades may be sufficient to motivate her to continue to work hard.

In Adam's case, the rewards are largely social, and the give and take among peers is maintained by trading baseball cards. These rewards seem to be highly motivating. Adam's academic rewards, however, are not clear-cut; he does what is required, but doesn't appear to get much personal satisfaction from it. Yet, further examination might reveal that the feedback he receives from school for good homework is sufficiently motivating for him to continue performing well.

Janice's and Adam's rewards differ in another important respect. In Janice's case, both the **intrinsic** (internally satisfying) rewards and **extrinsic** (externally determined) rewards are obvious. Her academic accomplishment is initially secondary to her athletic fulfillment; at a certain point, however, she may experience both intrinsically, that is, enjoy each for its own sake. The extrinsic rewards for Adam's involvement with his peers are balanced by his intrinsic interest in baseball cards. New hobbies involving interactions with friends will probably create the same rewarding experience.

The rewards for completing homework assignments do not seem to be tied to an increase in motivation. The relatively low level of task difficulty associated with completing homework assignments may reduce the need for much incentive. Reward is not the only factor that motivates people. The difficulty of a task and the value that one attaches to successfully mastering it modify the effect of rewards.

Gottfried, Fleming, and Gottfried (1994) found that students whose parents emphasize intrinsic rather than extrinsic value of tasks excel in school-related tasks. Structuring classrooms to encourage intrinsic rewards also increases students' levels of school-related motivation (Ames, 1992; Craven, Marsh, & Debus, 1991; Graham & Golan, 1991).

### Choosing Intrinsic or Extrinsic Rewards

Intrinsic and extrinsic rewards have different effects on the behavior of students (Deci & Ryan, 1985). Differences among individual students' perception of control and outcome all contribute to the relative effectiveness of extrinsic or intrinsic incentives. Although extrinsic incentives may encourage student involvement in tasks for which students have no interest, such incentives tend to undermine intrinsic motivation and continuing motivation (Deci & Ryan, 1985).

Rewards play an important role in helping students gain information about how they are progressing. When rewards are used as a way to control student behavior, however, students lose confidence in their competence. Students also respond to classroom environments. For example, students exhibit higher levels of intrinsic motivation if teachers emphasize the development of curiosity and the desire to learn and do not attempt to control the classroom by teacher approval. Cameron and Pierce (1994) concluded that (a) rewards do not necessarily reduce intrinsic motivation, (b) verbal praise can increase or maintain intrinsic motivation, and (c) rewarding students simply for engaging in a task has a negative impact on motivation.

Researchers who study intrinsically motivated behavior try to explain why people experience some activities as rewarding. According to Deci and Ryan (1985), intrinsically motivated behavior leads to feelings of self-confidence and competence. Intrinsic motivation arises from a belief that one's behavior is internally determined. Extrinsic rewards may control behavior but they likely reduce intrinsic motivation. To feel competent, humans need to experience activity that is internally satisfying.

Intrinsic motivation cannot sustain all activities. Extrinsic rewards are often an important part of people's persistence. Many of us would not work if we didn't get paid, although both extrinsic and intrinsic rewards are probably necessary for most people to maintain their efforts. On the other hand, many people perform valuable services for others without getting paid; in fact, the reward for helping others is intrinsic. Teachers must balance intrinsic and extrinsic rewards for students when there is little immediate satisfaction in the learning situation.

### Student Interest and Types of Rewards

The level of student interest determines what kinds of rewards teachers use. Uninteresting material needs external encouragement to motivate students to carry out the assignment. Rewards are valuable and perhaps necessary to motivate students in most classrooms (Slavin, 1991). Although some research suggests that extrinsic rewards undermine intrinsic motivation (Deci & Ryan, 1985; Lepper, 1988), there are equally compelling findings that extrinsic rewards *increase* motivation when students have little interest in a task or would not do the work without rewards (Lepper, 1988).

When students are internally satisfied by their work, both teachers and students benefit; intrinsic motivation goes a long way toward aiding the learning process. Teachers can use extrinsic rewards, however, to celebrate good work. Extrinsic rewards tangibly demonstrate teachers' pride and satisfaction with students' performance or group effort (Slavin, 1991).

## Task Difficulty and Motivation

According to the "arousal theory" of motivation (see Weiner, 1980, 1992), the extent to which people pay attention to a task varies as a function of task difficulty. Generally, humans strive for an optimal level of arousal by seeking neither too much nor too little stimulation from the environment.

People who are bored tend to seek more stimulation. A student who daydreams in class, for example, no doubt finds the daydream more stimulating than the instructor's lecture. If a stimulus is too intense, one may simply withdraw. Some students, for example, find the stimulation generated by taking a test so overwhelming they become anxious and lose their ability to concentrate.

Effective task performance depends not only on how attentive the individual is, but also on task difficulty. Easy tasks, such as collating copies of a 10-page paper, for example, require so little attention that most people could easily collate and at the same time engage in conversation. On the other hand, difficult tasks may demand so much attention that people can concentrate only on the task at hand.

### Emotional Reactions to Difficult Tasks

Emotional reactions to difficult tasks vary among individuals. Some people react more emotionally than others, but almost everyone has had the experience of "freezing" when confronted with an exacting and difficult task. Even the most seasoned actors, for example, occasionally experience stage fright, and writers sometimes develop writer's block. Emotions, such as fear or stress, prevent people from coping with difficult tasks.

### Arousal Theory and Classroom Motivation

Attention and task difficulty have particular relevance for motivation in the classroom. Academic tasks that are too complex may cause students to become so anxious that they are unable to learn. Correspondingly, tasks that are too simple may

*Annual* **Edition**

unit *8*

Arousal theory indicates that performance is a function of an individual's level of arousal or anxiety; both low and high levels of arousal lead to low levels of performance. Only at a moderate level of arousal is performance optimal.

result in student apathy and boredom. To enable students to achieve at an optimal level, present meaningful and interesting tasks whose level of difficulty matches students' abilities.

A major criticism of arousal theory is its narrow focus on the duration and intensity of task involvement, which are less important than the *quality* of task engagement. Arousal theory does not address qualitative aspects of motivated behavior (Ames, 1990). Students' time-on-task does not inform us about what they are learning, how they are processing information, or the importance they assign to the task. Our appraisal of motivation and learning should include the *value* that students place on a task.

## Task Value and Motivation

No matter what teachers may do, some students may reject a task because they see no value in doing it. Some students accept school learning without questioning its value; others need to see the value in concrete terms. Similarly, some teachers believe the tasks they assign students have intrinsic merit; others doubt the value of the school curriculum.

The value of a school assignment relates to teachers' and students' goals. The most successful lessons are those teachers endorse and whose value students can clearly see. According to Ames (1990), students' self-esteem is tied not only to their belief in their ability to succeed at a task but also to their perception that the task is important.

## Performance Goals and Mastery Goals

Several researchers have looked at achievement and motivation in terms of **mastery goals** or **performance goals** (Dweck, 1986; Dweck & Elliot, 1983). Some individuals perceive the purpose of a task in terms of mastery; they believe their work in school, for example, will make them competent in a variety of areas, and they work toward attaining those goals (Dweck, 1989). Such students often find that learning in and of itself is rewarding; good teachers communicate the satisfaction inherent in accomplishing mastery of a skill or idea.

Students who are performance- rather than mastery-oriented believe the purpose of mastering a task in school is to gain the teacher's approval. Such students will work hard and long if they receive encouraging feedback. They also select tasks they feel they can master and avoid those they may fail.

Students who focus on performance goals can be as intelligent as students who focus on mastery goals. Mastery-oriented students, however, persist at difficult tasks, whereas performance-oriented students give up (Dweck, 1986). In comparison with students with performance goals, students with mastery goals select more difficult courses in school and enjoy attacking challenging obstacles.

Even mastery-oriented students who believe their ability is low perceive tasks differently than performance-oriented students do. Figure 10.1 illustrates the effects of goal orientation and confidence on the kinds of goals students seek and the likelihood of their persistence. Note that students with low

Junior and senior high school teachers often face the question, "Why do we need to learn this?" The "relevance" question is not always easy to answer: It is useful to give some thought to the question, even when it is not asked

10.3
*Distinguish between performance and mastery goals and describe how each affects students' motivation.*

**Figure 10.1**
Achievement goals and behavior.

Source: C. Dweck, "Motivation" in A. Lesgold and R. Glaser (Eds), "Foundations for a Psychology of Education." 1989: Hillsdale, NJ, Lawrence Erlbaum Associates.

| Goal orientation | Confidence in present ability | Task difficulty choice | Persistence |
|---|---|---|---|
| Performance | Low | Avoid challenge | Low |
| | High | Seek challenge | High |
| Mastery | Low | Seek challenge (which fosters learning) | High |
| | High | | High |

## Creating a Classroom That Emphasizes Mastery Goals

Stipek (1993) makes the following suggestions for motivating students:

1. Make sure students get the message that making mistakes is okay; in fact, it is an important part of learning.
2. Ensure that tasks are neither too easy nor too difficult. Successful completion of easy tasks does not lead to a sense of competence; tasks that are too difficult discourage sustained effort.
3. Individualize activities and assignments whenever possible to accommodate students of varying abilities and learning styles. Many schools discourage teaching material outside the established curriculum. Many teachers also develop a habit of teaching in one way to all students. Varying *what* material is presented and *how* it is presented to meet individual needs helps keep students motivated. In some cultures, a form of individualization is common: Chinese teachers, for example, often present a range of tasks, but students

are expected to solve only some of them (Stevenson & Sigler, 1992).
4. Use learning centers to create meaningful small-group activities.
5. Vary tasks. Stimulate students' interest with novel, complex, or surprising activities. Ask questions that require solving a paradox, speculating on an outcome, or thinking divergently.
6. Give students opportunities to offer opinions; have them back up opinions with reasons.
7. Be enthusiastic. Your enthusiasm will generate enthusiasm in the students.
8. Evaluate students in several ways, not just by tests. Let students evaluate themselves and each other, and let the evaluative tasks vary (e.g., in science, rather than give a test, have students perform an experiment and then discuss their effectiveness).
9. Have as a goal *autonomy* in learning. Students who become self-regulated learners rely more on intrinsic than extrinsic motivation.

**10.4** ◎

*List nine ways to motivate students in the classroom.*

## A Classroom Observation

Observe a classroom and analyze the activities in terms of the value each task has for students. Does the instructor motivate the students? If so, how? Observe an elementary or high school classroom, or simply observe an activity in one of your own college classes. Use the following questions to guide your observation:

1. Do the activities promote student interest and curiosity? Can students understand and attain the goals? What changes in instruction can you suggest on the basis of your knowledge or suspicions concerning the students' interests? For example, might the students' involvement increase by giving them opportunities to select assignments and choose peers to work with?

2. Was the difficulty level of the activity appropriate for the students? Did the instructor attempt to maintain a challenging level and discourage anxiety and stress? Did the activity appear too easy for some students and result in boredom? What clues did students' behavior give you about the relationship between task difficulty and task involvement?
3. What kinds of tasks might the instructor have assigned to help students shift their emphasis from performance goals to mastery goals? How might the students experience a sense of personal satisfaction that is necessary to pursue mastery goals?

confidence who focus on performance goals fall into a pattern of helplessness, but those with mastery goals persevere (Ames, 1992; Craven, Marsh & Debus, 1991; Dweck, 1989).

# Theories of Motivation

10.5 ◎

*Describe Maslow's hierarchy of needs, achievement motivation, locus of control, attribution theory, and efficacy expectation.*

Theories of motivation include Maslow's hierarchy of needs, achievement motivation, locus of control, attribution theory, and efficacy expectation.

## Maslow's Hierarchy of Needs

Abraham Maslow (1987) believed that human beings have a variety of needs that are hierarchically organized so that individuals cannot satisfy higher needs until they have satisfied more basic needs. The most basic needs are *biological* (for example, the need for air, water, and food). When we satisfy our biological needs, we can satisfy the need for *safety*. After we feel safe, we can seek *love* and *belongingness*, and after we feel loved, we can seek to satisfy our *self-esteem* needs. Next, we seek to satisfy our *intellectual* needs, then our *aesthetic* needs, and, finally, our need for *self-actualization*.

In schools with a high level of violence, both students and teachers are concerned for their physical safety, interfering with the teaching/learning process.

Don't take for granted that students' basic biological and safety needs are met; some students feel threatened in school, which could explain their lack of academic or intellectual growth. Maslow's theory highlights the importance that schools be safe, comfortable places for students and teachers.

Maslow's theory highlights the importance of developing students' self-esteem not only as a goal of its own, but as a necessary precursor of learning.

To satisfy intellectual needs, students must first feel loved and a sense of belonging in a social circle, and they must have adequate self-esteem. Schools are most effective when they help students feel socially accepted and valued and when they build students' sense of self.

## Achievement Motivation

Human beings have basic needs that are part of their personalities (McClelland et al., 1953). **Achievement motivation** is the product of two conflicting needs: the need to achieve success and the need to avoid failure. Some students strive to succeed; others worry less about achieving success than avoiding failure. Students motivated by the need to succeed pursue attainable goals of moderate difficulty (Atkinson & Feather, 1966). In contrast, students motivated by the need to avoid failure set goals that are either very easy or very difficult, enabling them to avoid failure by succeeding at easy tasks or by blaming their failure on the fact that the task is difficult.

## DIVERSITY MAKES A DIFFERENCE
### Cross-Cultural Studies

Many studies report that students from various Pacific Rim countries outperform students in the United States (Stevneson, 1992; Stevenson, Chen, & Lee, 1993), particularly in mathematics, suggesting that Asian students are more motivated to learn. Many students in the Asian studies, however, were middle class and members of professional families (Santrock, 1995), and some researchers argue that social class has more impact on achievement and motivation than ethnicity does. Graham (1994; Graham & Long, 1986), for example, found that middle-class minority students are similar to white middle-class students in their expectations of success. Asian immigrants from repressed societies display problems similar to those of other minorities, such as difficulty in learning English and trouble adjusting to school (Santrock, 1995).

Cultural differences can affect motivation among various groups. Stevenson and his colleagues (1993) observed Asian classrooms and conducted interviews with American and Asian parents, students, and teachers. American parents had low expectations of their children and were highly satisfied with their children's achievement. Asian parents believed their children's achievement was largely a result of effort, and they encouraged their children to persist; many American parents believed that achievement was related to ability. Classrooms in Asian countries reflected the same values as classrooms in the United States: encouragement for effort and opportunities for students to represent knowledge in their own ways. The researchers found no evidence that Asian students are under undue stress. Clearly, cross-cultural studies provide us with information that can help us improve our schools.

Many people perform valuable services for others as volunteers; their motivation is intrinsic because they receive no tangible reward.

© Kevin Morris/Corbis Media

## Locus of Control

Some theorists look at motivation as a cognitive phenomenon. Rotter's (1966) theory of **locus of control,** for example, considers motivation to be a function of our beliefs. Locus of control refers to differences in individuals' beliefs about what controls the events in their lives. People who have an **external locus of control** believe that forces other than themselves control the outcomes of their actions (whether these be failures or successes). People who have an **internal locus of control** believe they control the outcomes of their actions.

Individuals with an external locus of control see no relationship between their actions and the consequences of those actions, nor do they perceive a strong link between effort and outcome. On the other hand, individuals with an internal locus of control believe they have direct control of the outcomes of their behavior. Most individuals' locus of control is neither completely external nor completely internal. The tendency to justify success and failure in terms of either external or internal forces reflects inherent differences in personality types.

Parents' behavior contributes to their children's development of locus of control (Katkovsky, Crandall, & Good, 1967) and teachers play an important role in confirming or disconfirming this attribute by approving students' efforts (Lefcourt, 1966; Strickland, 1989).

Students with an external locus of control score high on tests of anxiety and hostility; students with an internal locus of control tend to perceive themselves as more effective and often pursue more academic activities (Lefcourt, 1982). Students with an internal locus of control are more motivated to achieve than students with an external locus of control.

Do you believe outcomes are due to sources outside yourself (external locus of control) or to your own characteristics (internal locus of control)?

For an illuminating discussion of the role of achievement motivation among some minority students, read J. U. Ogbu's article "Understanding Cultural Diversity and Learning" in *Educational Researcher* (1992), vol. 21, no. 8, pp. 5–14.

## Attribution Theory

**Attribution theory** also explains motivation in cognitive terms. Attribution theory focuses on students' beliefs about the *causes* of their successes and failures. Weiner (1992) believes individuals attribute successes and failures to ability, effort, task difficulty, or luck; people's beliefs about the causes of their success and failure influence their motivation (Frieze, 1981).

The model in figure 10.2 defines attributions in terms of stability and locus of control. Ability and task difficulty are stable attributions; effort and luck are unstable. Ability and effort are internal, whereas task difficulty and luck are external. Effort is the only attribution that people control completely.

Because *effort* is the only attribution that students can control, it is important to highlight its importance to students.

**Figure 10.2**
Dimensions of attribution.

| | Stable | Unstable |
|---|---|---|
| **Internal** | Ability | Effort |
| **External** | Task difficulty | Luck |

## Forming Attributions

Individuals assign attributions in a variety of ways. Consider two students who got high scores on a mathematics test. One may attribute success to ability; the other may attribute it to effort. Both students provide internal explanations for their success; they perceive the attribution as something they govern. Students who attribute success to effort believe they can control the amount of effort to accomplish the goal; they are more likely to apply effort when next confronted with a similar task. Students who attribute success to ability may not need to exert much effort (remember Adam?). Reliance on ability may waiver when the individual is confronted by a very difficult task.

Students who attribute their high score on the math test to luck cannot count on continued good fortune because they can't control luck. Such students will likely rely on luck on future tests. Students who attribute success to the easiness of the test also cannot count on continued good fortune because difficulty level depends on the whim of the teacher or test examiner.

Attributions for failure are more complex (Weiner, 1994). Students who attribute failure to a lack of ability are likely to give up; students who attribute failure to lack of effort, however, may try harder. According to Weiner (1994), attributing failure to lack of ability results in less punishment from others and leads to poorer future performance than attributing failure to lack of effort. Students who attribute failure to luck may continue to believe their efforts cannot change the results. Students who attribute failure to task difficulty are likely to blame the teacher.

Perhaps the most unfortunate outcome is when a student attributes failure to a lack of ability. Such students may learn to expect failure and develop negative attitudes toward school (Ames, 1992), and they may be less likely to look for help (Ames & Lau, 1982).

Graham (1991) found that students attribute their failure to their lack of ability when teachers express pity or hollow praise ("That was a good try."). Also students made attributions to lack of ability when teachers gave them help even though they didn't ask for any. Students read an unstated message in teachers' expressions of pity, unearned praise, or unsolicited help: "I don't believe you are able to do this task."

## Learned Helplessness

Seligman developed his concept of learned helplessness by studying dogs whose behavior had no effect on whether or not they were punished. The dogs became listless and showed signs of depression.

Suppose you studied hard for an exam but nevertheless failed. You don't study at all for the next exam and again you fail. You may conclude that whether you study or not, you get the same grade. Students who have learned from experience that effort does not affect outcomes develop **learned helplessness** (Seligman, 1975). They stop trying.

John is a fourth grader who is having significant difficulty in math. When given a worksheet of subtraction problems involving regrouping (or "borrowing"), he hands the worksheet back to the teacher, saying "I can't do these kinds of problems." When a problem requiring regrouping is mixed with other subtraction problems, however, he correctly solves the regrouping problem. John's problem is not lack of knowledge or ability; it is motivational. He has learned a sense of helplessness and assumes he will fail.

Not all low-achieving students develop a sense of helplessness. Some believe that effort will ultimately pay off. Teachers can help such students by rewarding effort and individualizing goals for different learners, thereby making success possible for all students. Teachers who minimize the importance of grades and emphasize learning help students develop attitudes that will overcome problems of habitual failure (Ames, 1992).

## Efficacy Expectation

Rotter's (1966) theory of efficacy expectation consists of four concepts: behavior potential, expectancy, reinforcement value, and the psychological situation. Theoretically, the potential of any particular behavior is determined by the expectation that the behavior will lead to a reward (or reinforcement) and will be influenced by the value of the goal. According to the theory, expectancy is a personal belief that is determined in part by an individual's history in particular situations having subjective meaning.

Hypothetically, the four concepts can function independently of one another, although in actuality they usually do not. For example, failure to attain a goal may lead to a reduced reinforcement value. Similarly, it may be more rewarding to accomplish a difficult goal (that is, a more difficult goal has a higher value), but the potential for success may be low; in such cases, individuals tend to withdraw, thereby decreasing their chances of achieving similar goals in subsequent situations.

According to Bandura (1977), people are capable of (a) holding beliefs about their ability to reach a goal, (b) assessing the effort needed to reach it, and (c) persisting. This ability is called **efficacy expectation.**

Generally, if people perceive a task as moderately difficult and reachable in a reasonable amount of time, they will persist. Many students commit themselves to achieve goals that are challenging, specific, and attainable in the near future (Bandura & Schunk, 1981).

### Integrative Theories

Stipek (1981, 1993) found that as individuals mature, changes occur in self-perceptions of ability, perceptions of outcomes, and expectations of one's own performance.

Younger children are less concerned with outcomes than with the task itself and rarely compete against peers. As they mature (at least in a society such as ours) and begin to compete with others, they may recognize their own failure and begin to avoid tasks they can't do well. In extreme cases, this avoidance can lead to learned helplessness. Throughout elementary and junior high school, students' self-perceptions of competence decline (Butler, 1989; Eccles, 1987).

# Teacher Motivation

Teachers' perceptions of their *own teaching effectiveness* determine the amount of effort they expend on creating an environment that inspires learning. Similarly, teachers' beliefs about *students' learning ability* also affect their willingness to persist in finding ways to promote student learning. In short, teachers' attitudes play a significant role in motivating students.

Different people have different motives for becoming a teacher. Some select teaching as a career for their love of children, their interest in a particular subject area, or for teaching's convenience, hours, or status. Wanting to teach is not sufficient motivation to succeed in teaching. Successful teachers believe they can inspire students and that students can learn.

## Teacher Expectations of Student Achievement

As noted earlier, young children rarely experience the hopelessness of failure; they perceive ability as strongly related to effort and, therefore, expend effort in their school tasks, believing that such exertion will lead to success. If they fail, they simply try harder. As students grow older, however, they begin to interpret the

**10.6** ◎

*Describe how teacher expectation and motivation affect student motivation and performance.*

Students generally make accurate judgments about the sincerity of a teacher's praise. To ensure trust and confidence in your students, give praise only when appropriate.

**Figure 10.3**

Choosing to teach.

Source: Kevin Ryan and James M. Cooper. *Those Who Can, Teach,* 7th ed. 1995: Boston: Houghton Mifflin.

**Check the statements that best describe why you want to teach.**

_____ 1. I love children and want to be with them.
_____ 2. I like subject matter, such as social studies or science, and want to impart knowledge to younger people.
_____ 3. I think that a teacher can become one of the most important persons in a child's life.
_____ 4. I hope to contribute something important to society.
_____ 5. I think that the quality of my life will be enhanced by working with young people.
_____ 6. I like the daily/yearly schedule, which gives me time for myself.
_____ 7. I like to have the same work schedule as my children's school schedule.
_____ 8. I like long summer vacations.
_____ 9. I like to work independently and have control over my working day.
_____ 10. I like job security; teaching can give me this possibility.
_____ 11. I like the financial rewards given to teachers for their experience and extra training.
_____ 12. I like to be a member of a group and have colleagues with whom I can share my concerns and interests.
_____ 13. I dislike the highly competitive atmosphere present in most business enterprises.
_____ 14. I look forward to the respect and recognition that teachers get from the parents, other professionals, and members of the community.

classroom reward system and to separate ability and effort. In extreme cases, when students attempt to avoid failure, they compare their ability with classmates who receive rewards (often in the form of teacher approval). Such comparisons often intensify students' doubts about their ability and encourage them to concentrate on performance rather than learning. These feelings are further intensified because they realize their assessments are accurate.

Most classrooms are implicitly competitive, and students learn to compare their abilities with the abilities of others long before they reach the middle grades. Teachers often group students according to ability level and set up incentives for good grades and special rewards; these actions contribute to the sense that each student is measured in terms of others. Grouping students by ability level reveals that teachers lack confidence in the ability of some students to learn. Yet, confidence in students' ability is crucial to effective teaching.

Good and Brophy (1991) urge teachers to focus on instruction by establishing goals and to modify their expectations of individual students by carefully observing how each advances toward the goals.

Teachers tend to treat students differently, often to the disadvantage of low-achieving students (Good & Brophy, 1991; Rosenthal & Jacobson, 1968; Tollefson, Melvin, & Thippavajjala, 1990). Students' race, social class, previous academic achievement, and personality affect teachers' expectations (Graham & Long, 1986) and often lead to self-fulfilling prophecies: Students who are perceived as unsuccessful in fact become unsuccessful.

## Pygmalion in the Classroom

Rosenthal and Jacobson's study *Pygmalion in the Classroom* (1968) found that students perform academically in accordance with how their teachers expect them to perform. This finding highlighted the need to examine the effects of teacher expectation on student performance, even though other researchers criticized the study's research methods, and subsequent studies failed to confirm the original findings (Fleming & Anttonen, 1971).

Researchers in *Pygmalion in the Classroom* and subsequent studies attempted to *induce* teacher expectations by giving teachers false information about students academic ability. Good and Brophy (1991) used a more naturalistic approach and found that students respond to teacher expectations and that differential expectations lead to different patterns of interaction between teachers and students. Teachers' behavior toward low achievers includes less praise, less wait-time for their answers, calling on them less often, criticizing them more frequently, and interacting with them less often and in private. High achievers provide teachers with reasons for preferential treatment. They are more responsive, complete assignments, and are more cooperative.

## Teachers' Attributions Regarding Low Achievement

Teachers typically believe low-achieving students exert little effort and lack motivation; they rarely explain low achievement in terms of teacher behavior or classroom variables (Tollefson, Melvin, & Thippavajjala, 1990). Teachers most frequently blame poor academic performance on low student motivation and poor family attitudes. They believe that students who exert little effort are not likely to change. Although these teachers believe that with more effort, low-achieving students could achieve more, they do not expect such students to be any more successful in the future than they have been in the past.

This finding conflicts with attribution theory, which classifies effort as unstable and, therefore, changeable. If teachers regard effort as a stable trait, they will expect students who exert little effort to continue to fail. Similarly, if teachers believe lack of family involvement is a stable characteristic, they will also conclude that low achievers cannot change.

Teachers who attribute low achievement to unstable variables, such as teacher effort or classroom climate, believe that student performance can improve in the future by altering the factors affecting classroom achievement. In other words, teachers can alter their own behavior to help students expend more effort. Teachers who are aware that the classroom environment can influence student learning can create optimal learning environments.

## Teacher Efficacy

**Teacher efficacy** refers to teachers' beliefs about their ability to teach. People first entering the teaching profession typically believe they will succeed and have positive attitudes about students; indeed, most enter the field with much enthusiasm and are eager to help students learn. Some teachers, however, lose their initial positive attitude and begin to believe that low-achieving students are unteachable.

It is useful to try to understand this change in attitude by examining teachers' experiences in classrooms. Ashton and Webb (1986) describe changes that took place in a young teacher after six years of teaching. The teacher had entered teaching with glowing reports and recommendations from supervisors and cooperating teachers. Six years later, the researchers observed the same teacher teaching in a mechanical and subdued style and presenting lessons in a routine and boring manner.

After observing teachers and conducting interviews with them, the researchers concluded that teachers, particularly those who are teaching low-achieving students, make compromises from their original position of optimism out of a sense of frustration. These compromises eventually cause teachers to lose self-esteem, develop negative attitudes toward the profession, and regard poor student achievement and motivation as givens. Often these teachers attempt to maintain their sense of self-respect and professional accomplishment, but because they cannot account for their failure to motivate students to learn, they conclude that the students are unteachable. As a result, they lower their standards, routinize their teaching strategies, and become victims of hopelessness.

When teachers interact with low-achieving students, both may attempt to protect their self-esteem (Tollefson, Melvin, & Thippavajjala, 1990). Low-achieving students frequently blame their failure on external conditions; similarly, teachers sometimes blame students' poor academic performance on the students rather than on their own teaching efforts. Even when teachers expend great effort, student failure may still represent teacher failure.

Many teachers have difficulty maintaining a strong sense of professional competence (Ashton & Webb, 1986). Teachers with a low sense of efficacy are at greater risk for experiencing personal failure when teaching low-achieving students. Their inability to teach such students may eventually lead to a generalized sense of failure.

### Low and High Teacher Efficacy

Teachers with a high sense of efficacy acknowledge that teaching low-achieving students is difficult, but they also believe that such students are reachable and teachable. Teachers with low self-efficacy are similar to students at risk of learned helplessness; both groups believe external forces rather than their own efforts determine their successes and failures.

In addition to special education referral, teacher efficacy is related to how teachers use their time, ask questions, and manage the classroom.

Soodak and Podell (1993) presented teachers with vignettes about students with classroom problems and asked whether students should remain in regular classrooms or be referred to special education. Teachers who perceived themselves as effective believed that a regular classroom could meet the needs of students with problems. Teachers who perceived themselves as less effective believed the students required special education placement.

Podell and Soodak (1993) also found that teachers who perceive themselves as ineffective are more likely to refer underachieving students from families of low socioeconomic status (SES) to special education classes, while retaining similar students from high-SES families in regular classes. On the other hand, teachers who perceive themselves as effective do not differentiate students by SES.

New teachers can support one another and find mentors among more experienced colleagues.
© Dennis MacDonald/Unicorn Stock Photos

 **Supporting New Teachers in Their Work**

Many school systems are beginning to provide mentors to help entering teachers. Generally, mentors are experienced teachers who have a high sense of self-efficacy and can translate both their teaching skills and this important attitude to others.

New teachers can also form support groups made up of previous classmates, college faculty, or new colleagues. Look for opportunities to maintain relationships that will help you become effective. Teachers who work in isolation (perhaps because they are afraid of being judged as imperfect or incompetent) are more likely to become frustrated and rigid than those who share ideas and solve problems with colleagues and actively seek support.

# Classroom Environment and Motivation

The classroom environment influences the level of student motivation. Factors that contribute to classroom environment include how teachers reward student behavior, establish learning goals, select materials, group students, and evaluate classroom operating procedures.

## Teacher Use of Praise

Positive responses from the teacher help students maintain their efforts in school-related tasks. Teachers, however, walk a fine line between appropriate feedback and critical response to students' work. Teachers must recognize students' ability and base their feedback on realistic assessments of students' progress.

Both the *kind* and *amount* of praise teachers use are important in maintaining student motivation (Brophy, 1981). Although teacher praise has long been considered an important factor in teacher effectiveness (Flanders, 1970), some studies suggest that praise is effective only if students believe they have earned it (Brophy, 1981; Good & Brophy, 1991). Young children can thrive on positive feedback for their efforts because they do not always distinguish between effort and ability (Butler, 1989; Nicholls & Miller, 1983; Stipek, 1993), but older students recognize that effort is not the only factor leading to success.

### Effective Praise

Praise provides information about performance and lends support to feelings of self-worth. It tells us that we have done a good job, that we are competent, and that our efforts are appreciated. Many teachers do not use praise effectively; they often base their praise on what they believe students need rather than on what students have actually done. Brophy (1981) suggests that effective praise should (a) be based on students' specific behavior, (b) provide information for students to use in the future, and (c) focus on students' prior accomplishments as a context for describing present accomplishments.

When students believe they have not been successful, they interpret praise as an indication that the teacher lacks confidence that they can do better. If praise is given for actual accomplishment, students can assess their successes and failures realistically. Praise should not be used to elevate the teacher's authority but to focus students' attention on their own behavior and to instill in students an appreciation for achieving their learning goals.

## Long- and Short-Term Goals

One key to effective student involvement is the teacher's understanding and development of appropriate short- and long-term instructional goals (Locke & Latham,

**10.7** ◎

*Describe how to use praise, set goals, determine a reward structure, and evaluate students' performance in ways that maximize student motivation.*

Praise should be used to focus students' attention on their own behavior and instill in students an appreciation for achieving learning goals.

© Jim Whitmer

1990). Student motivation is enhanced when goals are specific, likely to be attained within a reasonable amount of time, and moderately challenging. Many students are able to set short-term goals for themselves, but have difficulty establishing long-term goals. Young students have difficulty perceiving the future and generally expect immediate gratification. Even older students often don't see the connections between school learning and their future lives.

## Setting Realistic Goals

Numerous demands influence the goals teachers establish for students in their classrooms. Teachers must tailor and apply school and state curriculum requirements to their particular classroom, taking into account their professional assessment of what students need to know. Teachers sometimes overlook *students'* goals, which are the most important factor in motivating students.

Ames (1990, 1992) urges teachers to redirect some attention away from institutional goals to those of students. After organizing classroom goals in terms of students' goals, teachers can easily set realistic objectives for learning.

Ames (1990) also recommends that teachers assess the success of classroom goals by analyzing the quality of students' task engagement, their reasons for learning, and their ability to adapt to the demands of the task, instead of measuring the intensity, direction, and duration of student goal-oriented behavior.

## Evaluation in the Classroom

Some teachers publicly compare students with one another, assuming that such comparisons motivate students. Procedures such as displaying students' grades, exhibiting student assignments, or sharing in other ways the accomplishments of successful students *decrease* rather than increase the motivation level of low-achieving students.

Excessive emphasis on teacher-approved performance interferes with students' development of self-created goals. When teachers assign grades for all classroom tasks or use the same criteria for evaluating all individuals, students begin to believe that all school-related effort is subject to teacher judgment. Excessive evaluation weakens intrinsic motivation and increases students' anxiety about subsequent learning.

## Anxiety in the Classroom

Although teacher behavior is not the only factor that affects student anxiety, a teacher's evaluation practices may produce anxiety in some students. Anxiety varies greatly among students and is related to many factors outside of schooling. For example, preschoolers and primary-grade children whose parents hold unrealistic expectations regarding academic achievement frequently experience test anxiety (Hill & Wigfield, 1984).

Many students develop various forms of school anxiety, ranging from fear of teachers or fear of specific subjects to a generalized fear of the school setting. The public nature of some classroom evaluation procedures may lead to anxiety and feelings of humiliation. Anxiety is the root of many undesirable student behaviors, such as inattention, avoidance of challenging tasks, lack of response to instructional methods that require student risk, and withdrawal. Reflecting on the kinds of classrooms you experienced as a young student will help you identify how various kinds of classroom climates promote anxiety.

## Self-Evaluation

Use a variety of instructional techniques that give students alternative ways to learn and at the same time permit a variety of forms of evaluation. **Cooperative learning** gives students the opportunity to interact and work with their peers to accomplish a goal. It also enables students to establish their own criteria for success and carry out projects in which every student has a chance to succeed (Johnson & Johnson, 1994).

Effective cooperative learning involves not only grouping by ability, which is the most common form of grouping, but also grouping by complementary skills and abilities. Students should be grouped so they can learn from one another. Students need to monitor each other's involvement because group accomplishment depends on everyone's input. Self-evaluation, peer evaluation, and group evaluation replace the teacher's assessment of individual students. Cooperative learning allows students to experience evaluation in a low-risk context and increases student involvement. In addition to cooperative learning, use individualized learning so students can work at their own pace and participate in self-evaluation along with your help.

## Goal Orientation in the Classroom

Teachers directly affect students' perceptions of learning by creating classrooms that emphasize either mastery or performance. Students in classrooms with a mastery orientation are likely to be intrinsically motivated and receive satisfaction from the learning itself. Students in classrooms with a performance orientation are likely to be extrinsically motivated and concerned by the feedback they receive, striving for teacher approval or commendation. For performance-oriented students, how the teacher regards them as learners is more important than what they are learning.

Ames and Archer (1988) demonstrated that student behavior depends in part on how students perceive the classroom to be organized. Junior and senior high school students who believed their classrooms emphasized mastery goals used more effective strategies and preferred more challenging tasks than students who believed their classrooms emphasized performance goals. Students who perceived their classrooms as mastery-oriented also attributed their academic success to the effort they exerted. Students who perceived their classrooms as performance-oriented focused on ability and attributed their failures to their lack of ability. Students used more and better learning strategies when classrooms were mastery-oriented, even when they believed that their classes were equally high in performance orientation. Mastery orientation sustained a way of thinking that encouraged student involvement and overrode feelings of perceived ability. Students who sense they have low ability still benefited from classrooms that stressed mastery rather than performance.

The findings of this study and others that have focused on student involvement (e.g., Jagacinski & Nicholls, 1987) indicate that when classrooms are mastery-oriented, social comparisons or public evaluations do not interfere with students'

 **Applying What We Know About Motivation**

Here are some techniques for motivating students:

1. Use praise wisely. Praise a student's work when it warrants commendation; help students develop their own standards for success.

2. Include student purpose and interest in the development of class learning goals; present materials in interesting and different ways, so that students can deal with ideas in analogous forms and can draw generalizations between what they are learning and what they are interested in. Always inform students about the purpose of a task; don't let "busy work" dominate your classroom.

3. Make sure that students know the best strategies for achieving their learning goals. Learning strategies, particularly for low-achieving students, will help them see accomplishment in incremental steps.

4. Design a variety of classroom arrangements for learning, such as cooperative, competitive, and individual activities, so that students experience several sources of evaluation and begin to examine their own competence in nonthreatening ways.

5. Provide opportunities for self- and peer-evaluations; allow students to develop criteria for success that they themselves can understand.

6. Explain to students the various levels of evaluation that operate in the classroom. Help them distinguish between absolute evaluative devices and more individual assessments that measure growth.

7. Minimize anxiety in your classroom. Give students many opportunities to perform tasks with no external evaluation.

8. Prompt curiosity in students by pointing out conflicts or contradictions and setting up problem-solving groups to work out solutions. Provide some problems that appear to have no solutions; ask students to brainstorm some ideas. Use other problem-solving techniques that you have learned to give students more control over how they are learning.

9. Recognize differences in student abilities and set standards for performance that are congruent with what students can accomplish. Reward effort but maintain standards for good work.

10. Minimize comparisons among students and make your critical responses to students' work both private and helpful. Don't criticize without teaching a good strategy that can help students overcome their learning problem.

self-evaluations. The conclusion of these studies underscores the need to help students focus on effort, use appropriate learning strategies, and develop a positive attitude toward learning. Students produce adaptive responses when they believe their classrooms foster mastery; a mastery orientation provides the framework for helping students develop learning strategies for long-term use.

# DIVERSITY MAKES A DIFFERENCE

## Motivating All Students

To motivate students to learn, you need to know about their concerns and interests. Students' interests vary enormously, so you have to motivate them on an individual basis.

To what extent are motivational differences due to race or ethnicity? Are some groups more motivated than others to achieve? Graham (1994) notes that many people believe that African American students perform poorly in school not because they lack skills or ability, but because they have low expectations of themselves or feel hopeless. She analyzed the results of 140 studies comparing the motivation of African American students to other groups and concluded:

1. African American students do not differ from others with regard to the personality traits associated with academic success.
2. African American students do not differ from others with regard to their attributions for success and failure.
3. Among African American students, expectation of success and self-concept were high, whether or not achievement was high.

Graham's conclusions support the notion that motivation is not related to group membership. Rather, differences in motivation are highly individual.

*Annual* **Edition**

unit *5*

© The 5th Wave, Rockport MA

## KEY POINTS

1. Motivation can be viewed from two perspectives: Some educators and psychologists stress the importance of extrinsic motivation (receiving rewards); others emphasize intrinsic motivation (people's desire to satisfy their curiosity and to feel able).

2. Students' self-confidence influences their motivation: Students who feel they cannot succeed at a task will probably display little or no effort; those who feel confident will put forth the effort needed.

3. Task difficulty also influences motivation: Easy tasks bore students while very hard tasks create anxiety. Tasks of moderate difficulty maintain student attention and motivation.

4. Students must sense that the tasks they are doing have value or importance. The value of a task can be related to students' goals.

5. Some students have a mastery orientation: They seek to learn concepts taught in school because learning itself is rewarding. Other students have a performance orientation and seek to obtain positive feedback from teachers. Orientation interacts with task difficulty: Students with a mastery orientation display effort whether or not they are succeeding; those with a performance orientation give up on difficult tasks or tasks they think are difficult.

6. Students who attribute outcomes to external factors are less likely to try, whereas those attributing outcomes to internal factors are more likely to try. Students' motivation to achieve is moderated by their need to avoid failure.

7. Students' sense of self-efficacy (their belief in their own competence) and their beliefs about whether intelligence is fixed influence their motivation as well.

8. Teachers' self-efficacy and their expectations about students affect students' motivation in the classroom. Teachers' praise and feedback, their methods of grouping and evaluation, and the nature of the goals they set send messages to students. Teacher behavior determines in part students' sense of self-worth.

9. The classroom environment is an important factor in motivating students to learn. How teachers use praise, how they help students determine and strive for realistic goals, and how they evaluate students' performance influence students' motivation in the classroom.

## SELF-STUDY EXERCISES

1. What problems are associated with the use of extrinsic rewards? How might the use of such rewards backfire?

2. How can you promote intrinsic motivation when it appears to be absent in a student? How can you make a topic interesting for a student who shows no apparent interest?

3. How does your choice of goals affect student motivation and learning? What types of goals appear to be effective in motivating students?

4. What factors do you think deaden students' innate curiosity to learn?

## FURTHER READINGS

Ames, C. (1990). Motivation: What teachers need to know. *Teachers College Record, 91,* 409–421.

Good, T., & Brophy, J. (1991). *Looking in classrooms* (5th ed.). New York: Harper & Row.

Stipek, D. J. (1993). *Motivation to learn.* Boston: Allyn & Bacon.

## REFERENCES

Ames, C. (1990). Motivation: What teachers need to know. *Teachers College Record, 91,* 409–421.

Ames, C. (1992). Classrooms: Goals, structures, and student motivation. *Journal of Educational Psychology, 84,* 261–271.

Ames, C., & Archer, J. (1988). Achievement goals in the classroom: Students' learning strategies and motivation processes. *Journal of Educational Psychology, 80,* 260–267.

Ames, R., & Lau, S. (1982). An attributional analysis of student help-seeking in academic settings. *Journal of Educational Psychology, 74,* 414–423.

Ashton, P. T., & Webb, R. B. (1986). *Making a difference: Teachers' sense of efficacy and student achievement.* New York: Longman.

Atkinson, J. W., & Feather, N. T. (1966). *A theory of achievement motivation.* New York: Wiley.

Bandura, A. (1977) *Social learning theory*. Englewood Cliffs, NJ: Prentice Hall.

Bandura, A., & Schunk, D. (1981). Cultivating competence, self-efficacy, and intrinsic interest through proximal self-motivation. *Journal of Personality and Social Psychology, 41*, 586–598.

Brophy, J. (1981) Teacher praise: A functional analysis. *Review of Educational Research, 51*, 5–32.

Butler, R. (1989). Interest in the task and interest in peers' work in competitive and noncompetitive conditions: A developmental study. *Child Development, 60*, 562–570.

Cameron, J., & Pierce, W. D. (1994) Reinforcement, reward, and intrinsic motivation: A metaanalysis. *Review of Education Research, 64*, 363–423.

Craven, R. G., Marsh, H. W., & Debus, R. L. (1991). Effects of internally focused feedback and attribution feedback on enhancement of academic self-concept. *Journal of Educational Psychology, 83*, 17–27.

Deci, E. L., & Ryan, R. M. (1985). *Intrinsic motivation and self-determination in human behavior*. New York: Plenum.

Dweck, C. (1986). Motivational processes affecting learning. *American Psychologist, 41*, 1040–1048.

Dweck, C. (1989) Motivation. In A. Lesgold & R. Glaser (Eds.), *Foundations for a psychology of education* (pp. 87–136). Hillsdale, NJ: Erlbaum.

Dweck, C., & Elliott, E. (1983). Achievement motivation. In P. Mussen & E. Hetherington (Eds.), *Handbook of child psychology: Vol. IV. Socialization, personality and social development* (pp. 643–691). New York: Wiley.

Eccles, J. (1987) Gender roles and women's achievement-related decisions. *Psychology of Women Quarterly, 11*, 135–172.

Flanders, N. A. (1970). *Analyzing classroom behavior*. Reading, MA: Addison-Wesley.

Fleming, E., & Anttonen, R. (1971). Teacher expectancy or My Fair Lady. *American Educational Research Journal, 8*, 241–252.

Frieze, I. H. (1981). Children's attributions for success and failure. In S. S. Brehm, S. M. Kassiim, & F. X. Gibbons (Eds.), *Developmental social psychology* (pp. 51–71). New York: Oxford University Press.

Good, T., & Brophy, J. (1991). *Looking in classrooms* (5th ed.). New York: Harper & Row.

Gottfried, A. E., Fleming, J. S., & Gottfried, A. W. (1994). Role of parental motivation practices in children's academic intrinsic motivation and achievement. *Journal of Educational Psychology, 86*, 104–113.

Graham, S. (1991). A review of attribution theory in achievement contexts. *Educational Psychology Review, 3*, 5–39.

Graham, S. (1994). Motivation in African-Americans. *Review of Educational Research, 64*, 55–117.

Graham, S., & Golan, S. (1991). Motivational influences on cognition: Task involvement, ego involvement, and depth of information processing. *Journal of Educational Psychology, 82*, 187–194.

Graham, S., & Long, A. (1986). Race, class and the attributional process. *Journal of Educational Psychology, 78*, 4–13.

Hill, K. T., & Wigfield, A. (1984). Test anxiety: A major educational problem and what can be done about it. *Elementary School Journal, 85*, 105–126.

Jagacinski, C. M., & Nicholls, J. (1987). Competence and affect in task involvement and ego involvement: The impact of social comparison information. *Journal of Educational Psychology, 79*, 107–114.

Johnson, D. & Johnson, R. (1994). *Learning together and alone: Cooperation, competition and individualization.* (4th ed.). Boston: Allyn & Bacon.

Katkovsky, W., Crandall, V. C., & Good, S. (1967). Parental antecedents of children's beliefs in internal-external control of reinforcements in intellectual achievement situations. *Child Development, 38*, 765–776.

Lahey, B. B. (1995). *Psychology: An introduction* (5th ed.). Madison, WI: Brown & Benchmark.

Lefcourt, H. M. (1966). Internal versus external control of reinforcement: A review. *Psychological Review, 65*, 206–220.

Lefcourt, H. M. (1982). *Locus of control: Current trends, theory and research* (2nd ed.). Hillsdale, NJ: Erlbaum.

Lepper, M. R. (1988). Motivational considerations in the study of instruction. *Cognition and Instruction, 5*, 289–309.

Locke, E. A., & Latham, G. P. (1990). *A theory of goal setting and task performance*. Englewood Cliffs, NJ: Prentice Hall.

Maslow, A. H. (1987) *Motivation and personality* (3rd ed.), New York: Harper & Row.

McClelland, D. C., Atkinson, J. W., Clark, R. W., & Lowell, E. L. (1953). *The achievement motive*. New York: Appleton-Century-Crofts.

Nicholls, J., & Miller, A. (1983). Conceptions of ability and achievement motivation. In R. Ames & C. Ames (Eds.), *Research on motivation in education* (Vol. 1, pp. 39–73). New York: Academic Press.

Podell, D. M., & Soodak, L. C. (1993). Teacher efficacy and bias in special education referrals. *Journal of Educational Research, 86*, 247–253.

Rosenthal, R., & Jacobson, L. (1968). *Pygmalion in the classroom: Teacher expectation and pupil's intellectual development*. New York: Holt, Rinehart & Winston.

Rotter, J. (1966). Generalized expectancies for internal versus external control of reinforcement. *Psychological Monographs, 80*, 1–28.

Ryan, K., & Cooper, J. M. (1995). *Those who can, teach* (7th ed.). Boston: Houghton Mifflin.

Santrock, J. W. (1995). *Children*. Madison, WI: Brown & Benchmark.

Seligman, M. E. P. (1975). *Helplessness: On depression, development, and death*. San Francisco: W. H. Freeman.

Slavin, R. E. (1991). Group rewards make groupwork work. *Educational Leadership, 48*, 89–91.

Soodak, L. C., & Podell, D. M. (1993). Teacher efficacy and student problems as factors in special education referral. *Journal of Special Education, 27*, 66–81.

Stevenson, H. W. (1992). Learning from Asian schools. *Scientific American, 267*(6), 70–76.

Stevenson, H. W., Chen, C., & Lee, S. Y. (1993). Mathematics achievement of Chinese, Japanese, and American children: Ten years later. *Science, 259*, 53–58.

Stevenson, H., & Sigler, J. (1992). *The learning gap*. New York: Summit Books.

Stipek, D. J. (1981). Children's perceptions of their own and their classmates' ability. *Journal of Educational Psychology, 73,* 404–410.

Stipek, D. J. (1993). *Motivation to learn*. Boston: Allyn & Bacon.

Strickland, B. R. (1989). Internal-external control expectancies: From contingency to creativity. *American Psychologist, 44,* 1–12.

Tollefson, N., Melvin, J., & Thippavajjala, C. (1990). Teachers' attributions for students' low achievement: A validation of Cooper and Good's attributional categories. *Psychology in the Schools, 27,* 75–83.

Weiner, B. (1980). *Human motivation*. New York: Holt, Rinehart & Winston.

Weiner, B. (1992). *Human motivation: Metaphors, theories, and research*. Newbury Park, CA: Sage.

Weiner, B. (1994). Integrating social and personal theories of achievement striving. *Review of Educational Research, 64,* 557–573.

© Dennis MacDonald/Unicorn Stock Photos

# Learning Difficulties: The Special Student

# Chapter Outline

# Learning Objectives

11.1 Describe the characteristics of students with learning disabilities, mental retardation, emotional disturbance, and physical disabilities.

11.2 Describe three methods of teaching students with learning disabilities.

11.3 Explain how disabilities are relative to the culture in which they occur.

11.4 Describe the legal background of special education and the major provisions of the Individuals with Disabilities Education Act.

11.5 Define *mainstreaming* and *inclusion* and describe the issues surrounding the inclusion movement.

11.6 Describe how to integrate students with disabilities in regular education classes.

11.7 Describe how low achievers differ from students with learning disabilities.

# Preview

You need to know about students with learning difficulties for three important reasons: (a) you will have to identify such students in your classroom, (b) you will have to develop instructional approaches to help them deal with the challenges they face, (c) and you must decide whether to refer a student for special services. The decision to refer has major consequences not only for the duration of the student's school career, but for the rest of the student's life. Once a student is labeled "special," it is almost impossible to reverse the classification, and unfortunately the label typically carries a stigma with it.

This chapter describes the characteristics of students who have mental retardation, learning disabilities, emotional disturbance or physical disabilities, and the challenges they face. It also discusses the field of special education, federal laws protecting the rights of students with special needs, the practice of integrating special needs students into regular classes, and your role in referring students for special education placement.

# Learning Disabilities

Students who have average or above-average intelligence but perform poorly in one or more specific academic areas rather than in all areas have **learning disabilities.** The specific nature of students' poor academic performance distinguishes them from underachievers, whose academic performance falls short of their potential in virtually every academic area.

Prior to 1962, when Kirk first coined the term *learning disabled*, people with learning disabilities were either incorrectly classified as having mental retardation or successfully disguised their disability and led relatively normal lives. Many professionals once used the term **minimal brain dysfunction (MBD)** to describe persons with learning disabilities. It is best to think of *learning disabled* and *minimal brain dysfunction* as terms that refer to some of the same behavioral characteristics: hyperactivity, perceptual-motor difficulties, emotional instability, attention problems, and impulsivity. MBD implies the existence of permanent physical damage to the brain, but there is no evidence that people labeled MBD have any brain damage. The behavior of people with proven brain damage resembles that of people labeled MBD, but similar behaviors don't necessarily stem from the same cause.

Learning disabled has no clear definition. Professionals agree that mental retardation, emotional disturbance, or poor teaching do *not* cause learning disabilities, but they cannot agree on what does. Various professional organizations and state departments of education define learning disabilities somewhat differently. The National Joint Committee for Learning Disabilities (NJCLD) in 1989 devised one of the most widely accepted definitions:

> *Learning disabilities is a generic term that refers to a heterogeneous group of disorders manifested by significant difficulties in the acquisition and use of listening, speaking, reading, writing, reasoning, or mathematical abilities. These disorders are intrinsic to the individual and* presumed *[emphasis added] to be due to central nervous system dysfunction, and may occur across the life span. . . . Although learning disabilities may occur concomitantly with other handicapping conditions (for example, sensory impairment, mental retardation, serious emotional disturbance) or extrinsic influences (such as cultural differences, insufficient or inappropriate instruction), they are not the result of these conditions or influences. (NJCLD, 1989, p. 1)*

**11.1**

*Describe the characteristics of students with learning disabilities, mental retardation, emotional disturbance, and physical disabilities.*

Educators cannot agree on a definition of learning disabilities.

Some students' learning disabilities go undetected when teachers focus too much on successful students.

© Superstock

## Significant Discrepancy Between Actual and Expected Achievement

The category of learning disabilities applies only to students whose actual academic performance is *significantly* worse than their expected academic performance, which raises two difficult questions: (a) how does one define expected achievement (e.g., based on IQ or based on grade level), and (b) how large must the discrepancy be to be considered significant?

The same student may or may not be classified as learning disabled, depending on the definition of "expected achievement." For example, if IQ defines expected academic performance, a student with an IQ above average might be considered learning disabled if the student's academic performance is only average. On the other hand, if grade level defines expected academic performance, a student with an above average IQ might not be considered learning disabled as long as the student performs academically as well as others at the same grade level.

Similarly, a student whose academic performance is one and one-half years below grade level would be considered learning disabled in schools that define "significant discrepancy" as at least one and one-half years below grade level, but not in schools that define "significant discrepancy" as at least two years below grade level. The lack of a clear definition of learning disabilities, therefore, makes it difficult to interpret information about learning disabilities because one cannot be sure to what kinds of students the information applies.

## How Many Students Are Learning Disabled?

Regardless of definition, learning disabilities is the fastest growing classification of special students. The U.S. Department of Education estimates that the percentage of students labeled learning disabled throughout the United States rose from 1.79 percent during the 1976–1977 school year to 4.57 percent during the 1983–1984 school year. The percentage has remained at about 4 percent since that time (U.S. Department of Education, 1993).

Looked at differently, in a single decade the percentage of *special* students classified as learning disabled doubled from 23 percent in 1976–1977 to 50 percent in 1990–1991 (U.S. Department of Education, 1993). Some educators believe this doubling does not reflect a dramatic increase in the number of students with learning disabilities. Instead it reflects the tendency to label students with any kind of academic difficulty as learning disabled. During the 1980s, the federal government argued that labeling students as learning disabled only increased educational costs and resulted in little educational improvement (General Accounting Office, 1981); however, the referral and labeling rates remain high.

## Likely Causes of Learning Disabilities

Actual causes of learning disabilities are unknown, but likely causes include disorders of the central nervous system (Duffy & McAnulty, 1985) and lack of a sufficiently stimulating and educational environment (Engelmann, 1977). There is no evidence that dietary substances, such as food additives, cause learning disabilities. Note that the NJCLD definition cautiously states that learning disabilities are "presumed to be due to central nervous dysfunction" because we are currently not able to detect central nervous system dysfunction in the vast majority of cases. Technological advances, however, may one day document neurological differences between students with and without learning disabilities.

In the meantime, it seems reasonable to accept the NJCLD definition of learning disabilities as a "heterogeneous group of disorders." Students with learning disabilities exhibit a wide array of problems and require much individualized instruction.

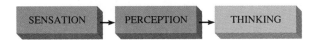

**Figure 11.1**
The precursors of thinking.

## Cognitive Theories of Learning Disabilities

Students with learning disabilities have average or above-average IQs, so lack of intelligence cannot be the cause. The three major theoretical approaches to learning disabilities focus on different kinds of cognitive deficit: perceptual, attention, and metacognitive.

### Perceptual Deficits

Note in figure 11.1 that sensation (the impact of stimuli on a person's senses) precedes perception (the person's recognition and interpretation of the stimuli), which in turn precedes thinking.

The perceptual deficit approach, which dominated during the 1960s and 70s, attributed learning disabilities to either errors in visual or auditory perception or a lack of perceptual-motor ability (e.g., hand-eye coordination). Thus, a student with a learning disability has no difficulty seeing, but may have difficultly interpreting what is seen. Because numerous studies have failed to support the perceptual deficit approach (Kavale & Mattson, 1983; Myers & Hammill, 1990), researchers are now focusing on deficits in the cognitive processes of attention, rehearsal, and meta-cognition.

Despite the lack of evidence, many educators and parents continue to believe that perceptual deficits cause most cases of learning disabilities.

### Attention Deficits

The most striking characteristic of students with learning disabilities is their inability to pay attention. Students with learning disabilities have difficulty attending to relevant stimuli and are easily distracted by irrelevant stimuli (Hallahan & Reeve, 1980; Krupski, 1986). Students who don't focus on relevant stimuli won't learn what they are supposed to.

unit *3*

### Rehearsal and Metacognitive Deficits

When processing new information, students with learning disabilities often don't use rehearsal and metacognitive strategies in the spontaneous way that nondisabled students do (Pressley et al., 1989). The rehearsal and metacognitive behavior of older students with learning disabilities resembles that of nondisabled children in the early elementary grades, who don't understand that they can take active measures to increase their learning. Students with learning disabilities don't understand that actively trying to learn increases learning or that they already have the ability to take active measures.

unit *3*

Attention is a necessary precursor for learning; inattention hinders learning.

© Jim Whitmer

# Helping Students with Learning Disabilities

11.2

*Describe three methods of teaching students with learning disabilities.*

Here are some ways to help students with learning disabilities.

## Increasing Attention

Students with learning disabilities learn best in an environment free of distractions. Classrooms equipped with opaque or translucent windows, carpeting, and sound-proofing make particularly good learning environments for such students. Even in an ordinary classroom you can reduce distracting sights and sounds by having students with learning disabilities work in cubicles or some other three-sided work area that shields them from distractions to the front and to the sides.

When preparing written material to hand out to students with learning disabilities, highlight relevant stimuli and eliminate competing irrelevant stimuli. For example, highlight important written information by using capital letters, underlining, or a different color. Do not decorate pages in ways that may have visual appeal to nondisabled students but may distract students who have learning disabilities. Use a clean and uncluttered design on written materials.

Similarly, when presenting lessons orally to students with learning disabilities, highlight important information and eliminate unnecessary talk. Tell students when you are about to give important information. Repeat the information, stress its importance, and explain how the new information relates to other aspects of the lesson or to what students already know.

## Direct Instruction

Thirty years ago it was common practice to remediate learning disabilities by strengthening students' underlying perceptual deficits. For example, during the 1960s, students with learning disabilities spent hours carrying out visual-motor tasks, such as connecting dots with a straight line, on the assumption that such practice would improve hand-eye coordination and ultimately enable such students to perform better at academic tasks. As noted earlier, numerous studies have shown that instructional practices based on a perceptual deficit approach do *not* help students with learning disabilities overcome their difficulties.

Instead, use **direct instruction** to help students with learning disabilities overcome deficiencies in specific academic skills (Lovitt, 1977). If, for example, a student has difficulty decoding printed words, teach the student how to decode words. Direct instruction emphasizes the mastery of specific academic skills, not the improvement of basic perceptual processes.

Direct instruction techniques typically follow highly structured formats that permit teachers little discretion in deviating from the instructional plan. Teachers using direct instruction usually follow a detailed written script of step-by-step instructions that emphasize repetition, student participation, and teacher feedback (Engelmann et al., 1989). Although direct instruction techniques effectively achieve both their short- and long-term goals (Tarver, 1986), some educators claim the goals are inappropriate. Critics argue that direct instruction techniques make no attempt to achieve the most important goal of all: correcting students' underlying cognitive deficits.

## Strategy Training

Many teachers also use **strategy training** (Ellis, Deshler, & Schumaker, 1989) to teach students learning strategies that apply in a variety of situations. One example of a learning strategy is the "multipass" method, which is used to improve reading comprehension (Schumaker et al., 1982). (See figure 11.2.) Students read written material three times; that is, they "pass" through written material three times. Each pass serves a different purpose.

| Pass 1. | Survey |
| Pass 2. | Size up |
| Pass 3. | Sort out |

**Figure 11.2**
The multipass method of reading.

*Pass 1 (Survey)*   Students use the first pass to get a general idea of what the material is about. They survey the material by reading only chapter titles and subtitles and introductory and summary paragraphs. They do not read the entire text. During the survey pass, they try to get a general idea of how chapters or other large segments of the text relate to one another.

*Pass 2 (Size Up)*   Students use the second pass to identify important points. Students "size up" the passage by actively searching for cues to information that might be important. During the size-up pass, the student functions much like a detective trying to solve the mystery of what important information the passage contains. For example, the word *except* in the following sentence signals an important piece of information: "The dictator succeeded in suppressing an armed rebellion, except in several villages along the coast."

During the size-up pass, students look for contextual cues to important information and they also ask themselves questions to try to elaborate on the information given. In the previous example, students might ask themselves why the dictator succeeded in areas other than villages along the seacoast. What permitted inhabitants of coastal villages to rebel? Was the rebellion successful in the villages? Did the dictator take further action against the villagers? After skimming the text for answers to their questions, students rephrase the answers in their own words.

*Pass 3 (Sort Out)*   During the final sort-out pass, students attempt to answer questions about the passage prepared by the textbook publisher or by the classroom teacher, skimming the text for answers only when necessary.

Learning strategies, such as "multipass," equip students with ways to learn, regardless of the nature of the content to be learned. Students can apply such strategies effectively to written materials as diverse as a description of the geological formation of continents or an anthropological account of family structures in various cultures.

## Attention Deficit/Hyperactivity Disorder

Some students have significant difficulty attending and concentrating and may be excessively restless. Such problems are often associated with learning disabilities; however, they may also occur independently or in association with emotional disturbance or mental retardation. Students with attentional problems have difficulty concentrating on a teacher's presentation, focusing on academic tasks, and following directions. They may also have difficulty making friends because of poor social skills and impulsiveness.

Students with sufficiently severe attention problems are classified as having **attention deficit/hyperactivity disorder (ADHD)**. There are three types of ADHD: (a) the predominantly inattentive type, where students find it very difficult to pay attention, are easily distracted, and are forgetful, (b) the predominantly hyperactive-impulsive type, where students can't sit still, talk frequently, and can't play quietly, and (c) the combined type. These difficulties must be present for at least six months before students are diagnosed as having ADHD to prevent misclassification of students whose inattention and restlessness may be due to transient stresses in their lives (Reeve, 1990).

The treatment of ADHD often involves the work of specialists from a variety of disciplines. Teachers often help students with ADHD by providing more structured instruction and opportunities for hands-on learning; they also frequently use behavior modification and cognitive behavior modification programs to promote on-task behavior (Nussbaum & Bigler, 1990). Psychologists may help students and their families cope with the social and emotional problems associated with ADHD, and medical personnel may recommend the use of stimulants, such as Ritalin and Cylert. The use of stimulants helps the majority of students with the hyperactive-impulsive type of ADHD (Reeve, 1990), and smaller doses help many students with the inattentive type of ADHD (Lahey & Carlson, 1991). There is no research evidence, however, that the use of stimulants leads to long-term gains in academic achievement or improvements in social behavior; in addition, there are possible undesirable side effects, such as sleeping and eating difficulties (Turnbull et al., 1995), and abuse of stimulant drugs.

# Mental Retardation

In 1992, the American Association on Mental Retardation, the leading organization for professionals working with persons who have mental retardation, defined **mental retardation** as follows (Luckasson et al., 1992):

> *Mental retardation refers to substantial limitations in present functioning. It is characterized by significantly subaverage intellectual functioning, existing concurrently with related limitations in two or more of the following applicable adaptive skill areas: communication, self-care, home living, social skills, community use, self-direction, health and safety, functional academics, leisure, and work. Mental retardation manifests before 18. (p. iii)*

To understand this definition more fully, it is necessary to interpret the phrases "subaverage intellectual functioning" and "adaptive skills."

## Subaverage Intellectual Functioning

The most common way to establish a person's level of intellectual functioning is to administer an intelligence test. The most widely used intelligence tests include the Stanford-Binet, the Wechsler Intelligence Scale for Children (WISC), and the Wechsler Adult Intelligence Scale (WAIS). A person's score on any of these tests represents that person's intelligence quotient, or IQ. The average score on any IQ test is 100. Technically, people with IQs above 100 have above-average IQs and people with IQs under 100 have below-average IQs, although obviously, small differences between IQ scores are meaningless. It would be silly, for example, to say that a student with an IQ of 99 has below average intelligence but one with an IQ of 101 has above average intelligence. In fact, both students have average intelligence.

Currently, "subaverage intellectual functioning" means IQs below the range of 70 to 75 on the Wechsler intelligence tests. According to this definition, approximately 2 percent of the population have mental retardation (Mercer, 1973; Tarjan et al., 1973). Although there is a cut-off score of 70 to 75, the American Association on Mental Retardation, *recognizing that all tests have some degree of measurement error*, urges psychologists to use clinical judgment in addition to the IQ score when diagnosing someone as having mental retardation (Grossman, 1983).

## Adaptive Skills

The term **adaptive skills** refers to the skills an individual uses to function in his or her environment. This criterion underscores that an individual's behavior must be interpreted within the context in which it occurs. Because contexts vary, a person might have difficulty meeting environmental demands in one context or on one occasion, but not in another context or on another occasion.

Psychologists sometimes administer IQ tests to students on an individual basis.

© 1996 Laura Dwight

Classifying people as having mental retardation solely on the basis of IQ scores can lead to the misclassification of persons whose learning problems have nothing to do with mental retardation. People from economically disadvantaged or culturally different environments, for example, may score poorly on an IQ test even though they do not have mental retardation (Dunn, 1968; President's Committee on Mental Retardation, 1969). Although most psychologists use standardized measuring instruments, such as the American Association on Mental Deficiency (AAMD) Adaptive Behavior Scale, to document deficits in this area, they also usually interview and observe the person to determine if the person's behavior is adaptive in the context in which the person lives and works.

## Causes of Mental Retardation

There are numerous causes of mental retardation. For example, mothers who have diseases such as German measles or syphilis or who use drugs (illegal or prescription) or alcohol while they are pregnant may give birth to children with mental retardation. Other possible causes include premature birth, brain damage due to the lack of oxygen, head injuries (most commonly caused by automobile accidents and child abuse), exposure to toxic substances, nutritional deficiencies, metabolic disorders, diseases of the brain, malformations of the brain, inherited diseases such as Tay-Sachs and phenyletonuria (PKU), and chromosomal abnormalities such as Down syndrome, which accounts for about 6 percent of the population with mental retardation (Morrison & Polloway, 1995).

In many cases, the precise cause of mental retardation cannot be determined authoritatively.

Other causes of mental retardation are the lack of a stimulating environment in the early years, insufficient variety of stimuli, poor language models and language stimulation, health complications, improper nutrition, and child abuse.

## Individuals with Mental Retardation

Contrary to popular belief, it is almost impossible to recognize people with mental retardation on the basis of physical appearance. Individuals who have mental retardation usually look like the rest of us and are a heterogeneous group who vary from one another in a number of other important ways.

Despite the common image of a person with mental retardation having Down syndrome, most individuals with mental retardation have no distinctive physical traits.

**Figure 11.3**
Classification of mental
retardation.

| Approximate IQ range | Classification |
|---|---|
| 50 to 69 | Mild mental retardation or Educable mental retardation (EMR) |
| 35 to 50 | Moderate mental retardation or Trainable mental retardation (TMR) |
| 20 to 35 | Severe mental retardation |
| Below 20 | Profound mental retardation |

One of the most important variations among persons with mental retardation is their degree of retardation. Although the IQs of all persons with mental retardation lie below the range of 70 to 75 on the Wechsler intelligence scales, the mental abilities of persons within this range vary markedly. For many years, mental retardation specialists divided the range into four levels, *mild, moderate, severe,* and *profound,* as shown in figure 11.3. Recently, however, the American Association on Mental Retardation eliminated the categories and conceptualized mental retardation as existing along a continuum (Luckasson et al., 1992).

## Contrasting Theories of Mental Retardation

The two major theories of mental retardation are the developmental theory and the difference theory. According to the developmental theory, individuals with mental retardation are developmentally delayed (Zigler & Balla, 1982). In other words, individuals with mental retardation go through exactly the same stages of development as individuals without mental retardation, but they develop at a slower rate. For example, a 14-year-old student with an IQ of 50 has an IQ that is one-half the average IQ of 100. Although the student's actual age is 14, the student's mental age is 7 and, according to developmental theory, the student should function mentally like a 7-year-old with an IQ of 100. According to the difference theory, the cognitive processes of persons with and without retardation differ qualitatively, not quantitatively.

The theoretical debate continues despite evidence that retarded and nonretarded persons who are matched on mental age do *not* function alike (Ellis & Cavalier, 1982). Most current research is based on the difference theory and relies heavily on cognitive psychology.

Mounting evidence suggests that most persons with mental retardation have cognitive problems because they have difficulty paying attention (Brooks & McCauley, 1984; Zeaman & House, 1963) or because they do not spontaneously use rehearsal strategies the way people without retardation do (Belmont & Butterfield, 1971; Ellis, 1970). Individuals with mental retardation who are trained to use rehearsal strategies frequently apply them successfully in the specific training situation (e.g., Glidden, 1979; Taylor & Turnure, 1979), but rarely generalize them to other situations (Campione, Brown, & Ferrara, 1982).

# Emotional Disturbance

Students whose behavior significantly disrupts the classroom are classified as having **emotional disturbance.** (Sometimes the terms *behaviorally disordered* or *socially maladjusted* are used.) Although students with emotional disturbance are generally intellectually competent, their academic performance may range from far above to far below average. Many perform poorly because of emotional difficulties (Kauffman, 1989). Although emotional difficulties can lead to learning problems,

Aggressive behavior is demonstrated by many students; only when it deviates greatly from the norm can we infer that a student has emotional disturbance.

© James L. Shaffer

it is always possible for learning problems to lead to emotional difficulties, in which case the student should be classified as learning disabled rather than emotionally disturbed. When both a learning and a behavior problem are present, it is not always easy to determine whether the learning problem is causing the behavior problem or vice versa.

The behavior of students classified as having emotional disturbance must *differ markedly from the norm*, which raises the question of how one defines *norm*. Norms vary from culture to culture, from one period of time to another, and even from one environment (e.g., the schoolyard) to another (e.g., the classroom). Consequently, behavior considered normal in one environment may be considered markedly different from the norm in another environment.

Students are not classified as having emotional disturbance unless their behavior deviates markedly from *what is normal in their environment.* Furthermore, students are not classified as having emotional disturbance unless their behavior is *continually* disruptive. The continual nature of disruptive behavior is what distinguishes true emotional disturbance from temporary adjustment difficulties.

Temporary adjustment difficulties sometimes arise when students experience serious personal problems (e.g., their parents are getting divorced or a family member dies). At such times a student's emotional burdens may trigger instances of disruptive classroom behavior. Compassionate teachers recognize such behavior as a symptom of the student's temporary difficulty in adjusting, not as a symptom of chronic emotional disturbance.

Teachers who have trouble coping with difficult but transient behaviors may erroneously refer students for placement in a class for those with emotional disturbance.

## Aggression and Withdrawal

The causes of emotional disturbance are many, and different theoretical approaches attribute the causes to different factors (Kauffman, 1989). Current popular theoretical approaches attribute emotional disturbance variously to biological, psychodynamic, family-systems, environmental, or social learning causes (see figure 11.4). Regardless of the cause, the most striking behavior of students with emotional disturbance is aggression. Forceful aggression of such students typically frustrates teachers and alienates classmates.

Withdrawal is another form of emotionally disturbed behavior, although it occurs less frequently than aggression. Withdrawn students often are immature; they daydream and fantasize, become depressed, show excessive concern with physical ailments, and fail to make friends. The emotional problems of withdrawn students are as serious as those of aggressive students. Withdrawn students need just as much help as aggressive students, but often teachers overlook them because their behavior rarely interferes with the functioning of the classroom. As a result, they do not always receive the help they need.

**Figure 11.4**
Theoretical causes of emotional disturbance.

| Theoretical approach | Presumed cause |
|---|---|
| Biological | Genetics or biochemistry |
| Psychodynamic | Internal psychological conflict |
| Family systems | Problems in the family |
| Environmental | Rewarding inappropriate behavior |
| Social learning | Role modeling |

Teachers often overlook withdrawn students whose behavior does not disrupt the classroom.

© Martin Jones/Unicorn Stock Photos

## Working with Students with Emotional Disturbance

Many teachers use behavior modification techniques to change the behavior of students with emotional disturbance; others teach appropriate social skills by having students model, role-play, and discuss and practice behaviors such as turn-taking and speaking politely.

Many teachers feel that they are poorly prepared to work with students with behavior problems.

Still others use counseling techniques to encourage students to overcome internal conflicts by recognizing and analyzing their feelings. The "Windows on Teaching" section that follows describes the "Rogerian approach," a popular counseling technique developed by the noted psychologist, Carl Rogers (1977).

Schools frequently employ counselors and psychologists to provide individual or group therapy for students with emotional disturbance (and occasionally for the families of such students) in an effort to complement teachers' attempts to improve students' classroom behavior. On the surface it makes sense to combine the efforts of professionals who approach behavior problems from different perspectives. The problems teachers perceive, however, are often quite different from those therapists perceive. Consequently, it is not unusual to find teachers and therapists striving to achieve different behavioral outcomes for the same student. Furthermore, therapists must protect student confidentiality, thereby limiting the information they may pass on to teachers (Kastner & Podell, 1991).

## Using the Rogerian Approach

Carl Rogers' book *Freedom to Learn* describes how his approach to counseling applies more generally to educating students. Although many teachers find the Rogerian approach particularly effective in stimulating the emotional growth of students who have emotional disturbance, it can be used to enhance any student's feeling of self-worth.

The goal of the Rogerian approach is to help people recognize and understand their feelings so they can devise their own ways of coping emotionally. It entails the following three principles:

1. *Demonstrating unconditional positive regard for students.* Merely telling students that you respect them won't work. You must convey *genuine* respect.

2. *Acknowledging students' feelings.* Let students know that you will accept their feelings and won't make any judgment about whether their feelings are justified or not.

3. *Showing students that you empathize with them.* Establish rapport by letting students know you are able to understand what they are feeling and that you can see things from their perspective.

The negative feelings students with emotional disturbance often have about themselves lead to a lack of self-esteem, which in turn adversely affects their ability to learn. It is particularly important for teachers to respect, accept, and understand students with emotional disturbance.

Signers help students with hearing impairment understand the lesson.
© NASA/Corbis Media

# Sensory and Physical Disabilities

Although most special needs students fall into one or more of the categories of mental retardation, learning disabilities, and emotional disturbance, not all do. A small number suffer from sensory impairments (partial or total loss of vision or hearing) or physical disabilities. Such students are as capable of learning as students without disabilities, but unless you alter your instruction to accommodate their needs, you may deprive them of opportunities to learn.

## Hearing Impairment

Audiologists determine hearing loss by testing a student's ability to hear sounds that vary in pitch and loudness. Students who have diminished or no hearing ability are classified as having **hearing impairment**. Test results show that approximately 1 in every 1,000 students in U.S. schools is partially or totally deaf (U.S. Department of Education, 1989).

Most students with physical disabilities can perform academically as well as other students, so academic expectations for them should be the same.

© Alon Reininger/Unicorn Stock Photos

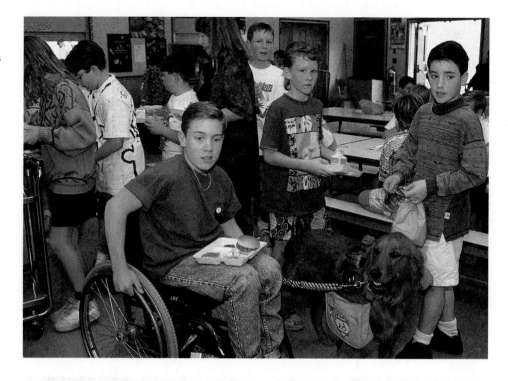

The age at which a student has lost the ability to hear is crucial. Children whose hearing loss occurs before they acquire language face enormous academic obstacles precisely because of their inability to use language. Students whose hearing loss occurs after they acquire language skills fare much better academically.

Hearing-impaired students learn to communicate either by using **American Sign Language (ASL)** or **total communication**, which combines manual signing and fingerspelling with speech and speech reading.

Sign language differs from country to country. Do not expect someone educated outside of the United States to speak ASL.

## Visual Impairment

Approximately 1 in every 2,000 students in U.S. schools has visual problems that cannot be corrected with glasses (U.S. Department of Education, 1989); such students are classified as having **visual impairment**. Students with visual impairment can learn by touching and hearing. Encourage students with visual impairment to use whatever sight they have and, if necessary, Braille. Visually impaired students must become skillful listeners and learn how to move about the environment.

## Physical Disabilities

Providing students who have **physical disabilities** with easier access to buildings, water faucets, and toilets has increased the number of disabled students attending regular classes with nondisabled peers. Neither physical disabilities nor disorders, such as cerebral palsy, spina bifida, paralysis, or muscular dystrophy, indicate anything about a student's intelligence or academic performance. Although some students with cerebral palsy have both intellectual and physical disabilities, most students with physical disabilities have no intellectual impairment.

## Human Immunodeficiency Virus (HIV) Infection

The vast majority of students who test positive for **human immunodeficiency virus (HIV)** are born to infected mothers who transmitted the disease during pregnancy. Not all children of infected mothers, however, are born with the disease, and some may test positive for HIV antibodies but may not have the virus in their bodies. The drug AZT can reduce the chances that mothers will transmit the infection during pregnancy.

HIV-infected students attend regular classes. Research evidence has not shown that the HIV infection in any way affects students' academic performance. HIV-infected students have the same academic and personal needs as other students. The chances of HIV-infected students infecting classmates or teachers are extremely remote; HIV infection spreads only through contact with blood or semen.

## Children of Addicted Parents

There has been a sharp rise in the number of students whose parents are addicted to drugs, particularly "crack," and it is likely that this is only the beginning of a trend. Typically, such students are immature, both cognitively and physically. Most also have severe social and emotional difficulties.

Children of crack-addicted mothers often have attention deficits.

Another group of students at risk for significant developmental delays and possible mental retardation are those suffering from **fetal alcohol syndrome (FAS)**. Mothers who drink alcohol during pregnancy are apt to have children afflicted with FAS.

# What Is a Disability?

Students with disabilities are like nondisabled students in most ways. They have the same basic needs and many of the same characteristics. However, they may have additional needs that must be met before they can learn.

**11.3** ◎

*Explain how disabilities are relative to the culture in which they occur.*

Consider a fourth-grader with a history of reading difficulty. Although he is near the end of fourth grade, he is reading on approximately a second-grade level. He has become so disillusioned that he seldom applies himself. To avoid embarrassment, he avoids reading aloud. His reading problems are starting to interfere with his performance in science and social studies. He reads so slowly that he rarely finishes tests and consequently fails.

Students who do not "fit" into our expectations are often considered disabled. As shown in figure 11.5, a student possesses cognitive, motivational, emotional, personality, social, and motor characteristics that, together, create the uniqueness of the individual. The school and the classroom, on the other hand, are usually designed with expectations for students based on a sense of what is typical or normal. When a student's characteristics are not easily met in the typical school or classroom, the student is usually considered disabled.

Educators often follow the "medical model" and see a disability as an inherent characteristic of a student.

The disability is not in the student but in the *gap between the student and the educational environment.* To what extent do we allow for differences among students and try to accommodate their varying characteristics? To what extent do we

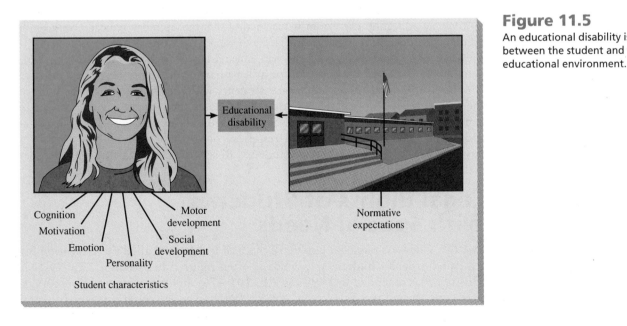

**Figure 11.5**
An educational disability is the gap between the student and the educational environment.

insist that students conform to our expectations? Accommodations such as glasses for a student with a visual impairment or a hearing aid for a student with a hearing impairment are easily accepted. What about having an interpreter in the classroom to sign for a student with profound deafness or having a paraprofessional work with a student with mental retardation in the regular classroom?

Several accommodations might help the fourth-grader described earlier. He might, for example, benefit from having someone read aloud to him the material in science and social studies. The teacher could also design lessons in which learning occurs more by exploration and discovery than by reading or that allow students to work in pairs or small groups so that their complementary skills aid each other's learning. He could also take tests on an untimed basis so he has enough time to complete them. All too often, educators view a disability as occurring *within* the student rather than in the interaction between the student and the learning environment.

Teachers in this study offered a wide range of solutions to the student's reading problem.

Soodak and Podell (1994) asked teachers to suggest solutions to a problem in which a student was failing in reading; the solutions most commonly offered by the teachers fell into two categories: teacher-based and nonteacher-based. Teacher based-suggestions included tutoring by the teacher or by a peer, using high-interest materials, using a whole language or literature-based approach, and involving the parent in the student's instruction. Nonteacher-based suggestions included assessment by the a multidisciplinary team or a reading specialist, counseling, and placement in a remedial reading class or a resource room. When asked which solutions they thought would be effective, the teachers strongly endorsed the nonteacher-based solutions. In other words, the teachers believed that solutions provided by others would be more effective than those they could provide themselves. This finding suggests that teachers tend to look to others rather than to themselves to solve the problems of difficult-to-teach students. Consequently, teachers may inappropriately refer students for placement in special education.

## Special Education

**Special education** is the branch of education designed for students whose needs cannot be met in regular educational settings. Special education teachers receive specialized training to deal with students who have mental retardation, learning disabilities, emotional disturbance, or physical disabilities.

The kind of extra help students with disabilities receive depends on their particular needs. Some spend the entire school day with a special education teacher in a self-contained classroom. Such students typically require a great deal of individualized instruction, so the special education teacher may be assisted by one or more teacher aides who work with students in small groups or individually. Also, the number of students in a special education classroom is far smaller than the number typically found in a regular classroom, making individualized and small-group instruction feasible.

Since the late 1970s, students with special needs have been increasingly educated in regular education settings for at least part of the school day. This practice is referred to as **mainstreaming**. Some students with disabilities spend the bulk of the day in self-contained special education classes, but attend regular classes in some subjects as well. Other students spend the bulk of the day in regular classrooms, but meet separately with a **resource room** teacher one or two periods a day in small groups of about five students. Resource room teachers are also special education teachers.

## Legal Rights of Students with Special Needs

**11.4** ◎

*Describe the legal background of special education and the major provisions of the Individuals with Disabilities Education Act.*

In 1975, Congress passed a landmark piece of legislation called the Education for All Handicapped Children Act, which is often referred to as **Public Law 94-142.** This law was amended in 1990 (as **P.L. 101-476**) and was renamed the Individuals with Disabilities Education Act, or IDEA. The law guarantees a free and appropriate education to all disabled children, *regardless of their disability*, thereby making access to public education a legal right of all students, not a privilege only for nondisabled students.

Previously, students with disabilities were *not* guaranteed a public education and could be denied educational services.

## Right to Due Process

An important provision of IDEA is the protection of students' right to due process. P.L. 94-142 insists that school systems follow procedures that protect the rights of students and their families. For example, parents have the legal right to refuse to have their children formally evaluated for special education placement. If parents permit their child to be formally evaluated but then disagree with the school district's decision, they have the right to a hearing by an impartial judge who then makes the final decision.

## Least Restrictive Environment and Individualized Education Plans

IDEA mandates that students be educated in the **least restrictive environment**. In other words, students with disabilities have the legal right to be educated in as normal an environment as possible, a provision that has led to the practice of mainstreaming.

The concept of least restrictive environment has been difficult to define.

IDEA also requires the development of an **individualized education plan (IEP)** for each student placed in special education. The IEP, which must be developed in consultation with the student's parents, is a document that contains long- and short-term instructional goals and a description of the instructional methods and materials to be used. Teachers must use the IEP as a blueprint to guide instruction. A sample IEP appears in figure 11.6.

## Multidisciplinary and Nondiscriminatory Evaluation

IDEA also requires that a **multidisciplinary team** evaluate students for placement to ensure input from professionals having different perspectives (e.g., an educator, a social worker, a psychologist). The evaluation team must take into account possible cultural and language differences when assessing a student, thus ensuring a **nondiscriminatory evaluation**.

## P.L. 99-457

Some federal laws enacted after the initial passage of P.L. 94-142 have extended the rights of students with disabilities. **P.L. 99-457** lowered the minimum age of those for whom special services are provided to 3 years and encourages states to develop early intervention programs for infants and toddlers with disabilities.

# Referral for Special Education Placement

Some students who have problems functioning in a regular classroom only require **support services**, such as speech therapy, physical therapy, or counseling. These students can function adequately in regular classrooms if they periodically receive specific kinds of help from professionals other than the classroom teacher. Students who have severe problems, however, may need to be educated in a more restrictive environment (e.g., a self-contained class or special school) to get the kind of help they need.

How is the decision made to place a student in a special education class? In most cases the regular classroom teacher starts the process by referring a student for evaluation for possible special education placement (Gottlieb, Gottlieb, & Trongone, 1991). Generally, teachers refer students for two reasons: learning problems and emotional problems. A team of professionals from various disciplines evaluates

## INDIVIDUALIZED EDUCATION PLAN

Student: *Carl MacArthur*                     Date: *10/1/95*

Birth date: *3/1/86*          IEP Period: From *10/1/95* To *6/30/96*

School: *Cleveland Elementary School*                Grade: *4*

**IEP Team Members:**

*Sara Thomas, LD Specialist*        *Malcolm Bishop, Reg. Ed. Tchr.*

*Juanita Lopez, Social Worker*       *Keesha Allen, Speech + Language*

| Area: | Present Level of Functioning | Annual Goals | Instructional Objectives | Objective Criteria and Evaluation |
|---|---|---|---|---|
| Reading | Carl recognizes words in isolation and in context. Carl comprehends text when read to him, but not when he reads aloud or silently. | Carl will demonstrate literal comprehension of text. | 1. Carl will correctly answer main idea questions when main idea is explicitly stated in text. | 75% accuracy (3 out of 4) teacher-prepared questions on class readings |
| | | | 2. Carl will correctly answer detail questions when information is explicitly stated in text. | 75% accuracy (3 out of 4) teacher-prepared questions on class readings |
| Mathematics | Carl performs math operations accurately. He has difficulty selecting the appropriate operation when responding to word problems. | Carl will answer word problems requiring a variety of math operations. | 1. Carl will correctly paraphrase word problems demonstrating comprehension of the problem. | 100% accuracy (5 out of 5) of teacher-prepared word problems |
| | | | 2. Carl will correctly identify the appropriate math operation for each word problem presented. | 80% accuracy (4 out of 5) of teacher-prepared word problems |
| | | | 3. Carl will select the appropriate operation and compute the answer in word problems presented. | 80% accuracy (4 out of 5) of teacher-prepared word problems |

**Services to be Provided:**

| Service | Duration | Frequency | Individual Responsible |
|---|---|---|---|
| *Resource Room* | *50 mins.* | *5x per week* | *Carol Meyers, Res. Rm. Tchr.* |

**Placement and Justification:**

Carl will continue in his fourth-grade regular education placement, but will receive resource room services one period per day, focusing on his reading comprehension skills. Regular education placement with resource room services is considered the least restrictive choice for Carl as it will allow him to maintain his social interaction with his same-age peers while providing him with instruction focusing on his specific needs.

**Parents:** Please check the appropriate statement and sign below:

___X___ I have had an opportunity to participate in the development of this individualized education plan.

_____ I have not had an opportunity to participate in the development of this individualized education plan.

___X___ I agree with the content of this individualized education plan.

_____ I do not agree with the content of this individualized education plan.

*Ann MacArthur*                          *William MacArthur*

Parent s signature                        Parent s signature

## Figure 11.6

An Individualized Education Plan (IEP).

Special education referral is sometimes a teacher's only way to get students the extra help they need.

the referred student and decides whether to recommend special education placement. Most referrals result in special education placement (Algozzine, Christenson, & Ysseldyke, 1982; Gottlieb, 1985).

Special education placement means that the student is removed from the roster of a regular classroom and assigned to a special education service. This may mean placement in (a) a smaller, self-contained class run by a special education teacher, (b) half-time special education and half-time regular education placement, or (c) placement in regular education for most of the school day with one or two

## DIVERSITY MAKES A DIFFERENCE

# Minority Students and Special Education

African American and Hispanic students are overrepresented in special education classes (Cummins, 1984). Several factors account for this overrepresentation:

1. A disproportionately large number of minority students grow up in poverty-stricken areas, and it is well known that economically disadvantaged students tend to perform poorly academically.
2. Teachers and psychologists may hold personal negative biases toward minority groups that lead to increased referrals and placements of minority students. In many cities in the United States, the majority of public school students are from minority groups, while the majority of teachers are white.
3. Teachers may incorrectly attribute the academic difficulties of students whose native language is not English to a learning disability rather than to the student's lack of English proficiency. A student may be able to communicate effectively in English on an interpersonal level yet not be able to understand the kind of English used in academic contexts. Such a student needs to acquire better language skills, not remediation of a "learning disability."
4. Tests used to evaluate students for special education placement may be culturally biased and place minority students at a testing disadvantage.

Educators must make sure that only students who truly have disabilities are placed in special education. We must make our assessment practices as free of bias as possible, monitor our own decision making, and be aware of our own biases.

---

# Deciding When to Refer

Before referring a student for possible special education placement, ask yourself the following questions:

1. *Have I exhausted all possibilities within my own classroom to improve the student's situation?* Can I use other instructional approaches, such as grouping students differently or designing different kinds of classroom activities?
2. *Have I sought help from colleagues and other professionals?* Professionals in all fields routinely consult with one another about difficult cases; however, many classroom teachers are reluctant to do so, perhaps fearing that they will be perceived as incompetent. Other teachers may be able to suggest instructional approaches that permit you to keep the student in your classroom. Seek help and advice from any source you can think of. Refer a student out of regular education only when all else fails.
3. *Does the regular education system already provide appropriate services for the student?* You may be able to use the services provided by guidance counselors, speech therapists, school psychologists, and other professionals. Consider using resource room services if they are available within regular education.
4. *Is a referral in the best interests of the student?* Hard-to-teach students frustrate even the best teachers, and it can be tempting to use special education placement as a way of "solving the problem" by getting the student out of the regular classroom. But the question is whose problem is being solved—yours or the student's?

---

periods per day in a resource room. Placing a student in special education carries its own risks. The student, the student's parents, and the student's teachers may lower their expectations of the student's ability to achieve.

Placement in special education is undoubtedly one of the most important events in a student's life. Your decision to refer a student is by far the most important step in the placement process, and it should not be made lightly. The possible negative outcomes may outweigh the benefits. Once students are referred, they are usually placed. And once placed, they rarely return to the status of regular student. Use referral as a last resort.

## Teacher Characteristics and the Decision to Refer

Special education referral is not only a function of a *student's* characteristics, but it is also related to the *teacher's* characteristics.

Some teachers are less prone than others to refer students for special education placement. For example, teachers who believe in their own effectiveness as teachers are less likely to refer students than those who feel ineffective (Podell & Soodak, 1993; Soodak & Podell, 1993). Teachers' biases also influence their decision to refer. For example, teachers are more likely to refer students from poor families than students with equivalent difficulties whose parents are well-off financially.

# Mainstreaming and Inclusion

11.5 ◎

*Define* mainstreaming *and* inclusion *and describe the issues surrounding the inclusion movement.*

The normalization principle underlies both mainstreaming and inclusion.

Historically, people with disabilities often spent their entire lives in hospitals or state institutions, segregated from the rest of the population. Segregation, however, often breeds contempt and fosters negative attitudes and stereotypes among the rest of the population toward those who are segregated. Society comes to devalue the lives of people who are disabled by regarding them as less human, less important, and less worthy of the respect and consideration afforded nondisabled people.

In the 1960s, Denmark embraced the philosophy of **normalization,** the idea that people with disabilities should live as normally as possible. This philosophy led the Danes to integrate people with disabilities into the larger society. The success of Denmark's pioneering efforts eventually led to changes in how the United States treats its citizens with disabilities. To a much greater extent than in the past, persons with disabilities in the United States now live, work, and attend school in the same environments in which nondisabled people function. As a result of interacting with people with disabilities in the community, at school, and on the job, the attitudes of nondisabled people toward people with disabilities are likely to improve.

The normalization movement in the United States led, among other things, to the deinstitutionalization of individuals with mental retardation. Adults with mental retardation now live in smaller community-based residences. It also led to the passage of P.L. 94-142.

## Mainstreaming

As noted earlier, the "least restrictive environment" clause of P.L. 94-142 led to mainstreaming as a way of making the academic lives of students with disabilities as similar as possible to the lives of their nondisabled peers. Mainstreaming occurs when students with disabilities are placed in regular education classes for

Inclusion of students with disabilities teaches students to respect and value one another.

© Betts Anderson/Unicorn Stock Photos

part of the school day. The decision to mainstream a student is usually based on whether the student's teachers believe the student can succeed academically in a regular education classroom (not necessarily the age-appropriate class). A student with a disability must, in a sense, "earn" the opportunity to enter the regular education class.

The academic performance of students with disabilities who are mainstreamed and given resource room assistance is about the same as that of similar students placed in self-contained special classes (Epps & Tindel, 1987). On the other hand, the effects of regular class placement on the social development and self-esteem of students with disabilities are unclear. Some evidence suggests the effect is positive because of the better social models students with disabilities have in a regular classroom. Other evidence suggests the effect is negative because nondisabled students may ridicule and reject students with disabilities (Pearl, Donahue, & Bryan, 1986). Despite the conflicting evidence, educators try to mainstream students with disabilities for one simple reason. The "least restrictive environment" clause of IDEA mandates that students with disabilities must be mainstreamed when possible.

Students with mild disabilities are usually mainstreamed in a regular classroom for part (if not most) of the school day. Consequently, many states now require regular education teachers to take coursework in special education to prepare them for mainstreamed students. Successful mainstreaming depends primarily on the regular classroom teacher's skill in working with students with disabilities. The major barriers to successful mainstreaming are the difficulty regular education teachers have in instructing mainstreamed students and the reluctance of nondisabled students to accept students with disabilities socially.

## Inclusion

Increasingly, school districts are implementing **inclusion** programs in which students with disabilities are provided appropriate support services and attend regular classes with nondisabled students of the same age.

In the late 1980s and 1990s, the "inclusion movement" grew out of dissatisfaction with special education and the tendency by school districts to place students with disabilities in self-contained special classes (Biklen, 1992; Gartner & Lipsky, 1989; Stainback & Stainback, 1992; Wang, Reynolds, & Walberg, 1989). Even when a student with a disability was placed in regular classes with one or two class periods in the resource room, the student's status was ambiguous: Did the student "belong" to the regular education or the special education system? Which teacher was responsible for the student's learning? Pulling out students for resource room or therapy often stigmatized them in the eyes of their peers.

Critics of the existing system also noted that the regular and special education systems were strictly separate entities, with little interaction between the personnel in each and duplication of services. And many inclusion advocates argue that students have an inherent right to participate in the regular class for their grade in the local school; otherwise, students are being discriminated against because of their disability.

However, critics of inclusion (Fuchs & Fuchs, 1994; Kauffman, 1991) are concerned that hard-won rights for the disabled will be lost and that students with disabilities will receive inappropriate education in regular classes. Nevertheless, successful inclusion programs have been implemented, and inclusion appears to be a trend that will continue. The debate over inclusion is also likely to continue.

Consider a sixth-grade student with cerebral palsy and mild mental retardation. Since kindergarten, she has been in special education classes but not in the school in her own neighborhood: That school did not have a special education program. Instead, she travels by bus each day to another school to attend class with other students with mental retardation. The teacher works on academic skills and practical, daily living skills, such as feeding and dressing. The class consists of eight students, the special education teacher, and a paraprofessional. The student also

The inclusion movement has been gaining momentum throughout the 1990s.

## Teaching Students with Disabilities in the Regular Classroom

**11.6**

*Describe how to integrate students with disabilities in regular education classes.*

■■ The widespread practice of mainstream-
■■ ing and the increasing practice of inclusion guarantee that almost all regular education teachers will have some students with disabilities in their classes. Here are some suggestions for successfully integrating students with disabilities:

1. *Have a positive attitude toward integrated students in your class.* If your attitude toward integrated students isn't positive, how can you expect the attitudes of the nondisabled students in your class to be? You set the tone of the classroom. If you resent having students with special needs placed in your classroom, all of the students in your class (including integrated students) will sense your resentment no matter how you try to conceal it. You may, for example, inadvertently ignore integrated students or, conversely, overcompensate by making too much of a fuss over them. It is helpful if you recognize that mainstreaming and inclusion can benefit both the nondisabled and the disabled students in your class. Both groups can learn from one another.

2. *Physically place integrated students in ways that facilitate their social acceptance and academic success.* Where you seat students can have important consequences. Seating a student with special needs in the back of the room or right next to your desk, for example, would probably doom the student to social rejection. Instead, seat the student next to popular students or near other students you feel will interact positively with the integrated student.

3. *When appropriate, prepare students in your class for the arrival of a student with special needs.* If a student has a physical or sensory disability or a chronic illness, discuss the student's disability with the class openly so that students can express their feelings and you can

dispel myths and promote social acceptance.

4. *Plan activities that require other students to work collaboratively with integrated students.* Nothing fosters positive social interaction more than working toward a shared goal. Students who work cooperatively in groups are far more likely to develop positive feelings toward one another and become friends.

5. *Design lessons that take into account the needs of the integrated student.* If you keep the student's particular needs in mind, you will be able to promote his or her learning.

6. *Consult special education teachers to learn new methods of working with students with disabilities.* Seek assistance from colleagues who have more experience than you have and whose backgrounds are different from yours.

7. *Cooperate with the special education teachers who work with your integrated students.* Effective mainstreaming requires coordination between the special and regular education teachers. When the two teachers interact and share knowledge, the student's opportunities for meaningful learning and social acceptance are heightened.

8. *Communicate frequently with integrated students' parents.* You may have to communicate more frequently with the parents of a mainstreamed student than with the parents of other students. Teachers often credit the success of mainstreaming to their success in getting parents to cooperate.

9. *Judge integrated students' abilities on the basis of your own observations and experiences, not on the basis of a student's "label."* Students often detect teachers' expectations and perform accordingly. Your expectation may therefore become a self-fulfilling prophecy.

leaves the class three times a week for speech, occupational, and physical therapy. The teacher would like her to achieve academically to the point where she could be mainstreamed for one or two subjects, but this has not yet occurred. When she returns home after school, she feels lonely and isolated because she doesn't know the other children in the neighborhood well and they sometimes make fun of her.

Some argue that this student has the right to be educated in her local community in a regular sixth-grade classroom in her neighborhood school, where the expectations will be higher and where she would have models with good academic skills and appropriate social behavior. Placement in the regular class would also allow her to get to know the other students and allow the other students to get to know her and her needs, which might prevent them from perceiving her as an object of ridicule.

Others maintain that the student is better served in the special education class, where the teacher is specially trained to work with students with special needs, class size is small, the curriculum is designed to teach both academic and daily-living skills, and the student can receive the various therapies she needs. Proponents of this position argue that she may not be socially accepted in the regular classroom and that she may lose the support and services she needs.

# Low Achievers

The term **low achiever** is used to describe students who are not disabled, but whose academic performance nevertheless is poor. There are numerous possible causes of low achievers' poor academic performance, but they do *not* include mental retardation, learning disabilities, emotional disturbance, or physical disabilities. Students with learning disabilities perform poorly in only some academic areas. Low achievers, however, tend to perform poorly in all academic areas.

## Causes of Low Achievement

Some low achievers lack the motivation to achieve in school. Others come from families that do not stress the value of schooling. Some fail to achieve because they have not acquired a sufficient academic background to build on. For example, they may be chronic truants. Or they may come from families whose frequent moves cause them to attend one school after another in rapid succession.

Every time a student changes schools, the continuity of instruction is disrupted. Disruptions in instruction result in poor academic performance. The cumulative effects of poor academic performance cause many students to fall further and further behind and to develop negative academic self-concepts.

Students who rarely spend a sustained amount of time in the same school never have the opportunity to become full-fledged members of the school community. Teachers barely get to know them even at a superficial level. Similarly, the students have insufficient time to develop any kind of in-depth relationship with teachers or classmates. As a result, these students frequently feel alienated.

## Helping Low Achievers Learn

Low achievers usually do not respond well to traditional forms of instruction, but they often benefit from techniques used with special education students, such as strategy training or direct instruction. Large-group instruction, the dominant form of instruction in most regular classrooms, may overwhelm low-achieving students. Low achievers learn best through individualized instruction or when working in pairs or small groups. Improving low achievers' academic performance has the additional advantage of increasing their self-esteem and self-confidence. Convey to students that you have confidence in their ability to learn. If you do not expect low achievers to learn, they may fall into the trap of a self-fulfilling prophecy.

**11.7** ◎

*Describe how low achievers differ from students with learning disabilities.*

*Annual* **Edition**

unit *5*

Low achievers are sometimes wrongly classified as learning disabled.

Low achievers can succeed when teachers adjust instruction to meet their individual needs.

Teachers use individual, paired, or small group assignments to address the differing needs of students.

© 1996 Laura Dwight

## KEY POINTS

1. Although students with learning disabilities are a heterogeneous group, their major characteristics include hyperactivity, perceptual-motor difficulties, emotional instability, attention problems, and impulsivity.

2. To help students with learning disabilities learn more effectively, place them in a nondistracting environment, use direct instruction, and teach them general learning strategies.

3. Mental retardation is defined as subaverage intellectual functioning (IQ less than 70) that occurs concurrently with deficits in adaptive behavior and has a variety of causes, including lack of a stimulating environment in the early years and improper nutrition.

4. Behavior classified as emotionally disturbed must differ markedly from the norm. Students with emotional disturbance are frequently either extremely aggressive or withdrawn.

5. Teachers of students with emotional disturbance use behavior modification techniques, direct instruction of appropriate behaviors, and the Rogerian counseling technique.

6. Special education is designed for students whose needs cannot be met in regular educational settings.

7. *Mainstreaming* is the term used when a student in a special education classroom attends a regular classroom for part of the day.

8. IDEA mandates that all students, regardless of their disability, have a right to a free and appropriate education in the least restrictive environment.

9. Regular classroom teachers should exhaust all possible remedies before referring a student for possible special education placement.

10. Students from ethnic minorities are overrepresented in special education classes for a number of reasons unrelated to their learning difficulties.

11. Inclusion is the practice of placing students with disabilities in age-appropriate classes with appropriate supportive services.

## SELF-STUDY EXERCISES

1. Why is the term *learning disabled* so difficult to define? Give one definition of the term.

2. Contrast the developmental and difference theories of mental retardation.

3. Define the term *adaptive behavior* and explain why it is an important aspect of mental retardation.

4. How do emotional disabilities interfere with learning? Describe a behavior modification approach and the Rogerian approach to teaching students with emotional disturbance.

5. Explain how the age at which hearing loss occurs affects student learning. Describe the role of American Sign Language or total communication in teaching students with hearing loss.

6. Name two important instructional goals for students with visual impairments.

7. What are the legal rights of the student with special needs? What is meant by *least restrictive environment?*

8. What is an IEP? How does mainstreaming affect the regular teacher's role in determining students' educational needs?

9. How do mainstreaming and inclusion differ? What are the pros and cons of each?

10. List specific measures you can take to assure that students with disabilities have sufficient opportunities to learn in a regular classroom.

11. What should you do before deciding to refer a student to special education?

12. How does cultural bias affect student referral for possible special education placement? What accounts for the overrepresentation of minorities in special education?

13. Discuss possible causes for low academic achievement among students who are not disabled. Describe effective instructional techniques for low-achieving students. How can you help low achievers improve their self-esteem?

## FURTHER READINGS

Gartner, A., & Joe, T. (1986). *Images of the disabled/disabling images.* New York: Praeger.

Hallahan, D. P., & Kauffman, J. M. (1991). *Exceptional children: Introduction to special education* (5th ed.). Englewood Cliffs, NJ: Prentice Hall.

Larivee, B. (1985). *Effective teaching for successful mainstreaming.* New York: Longman.

Rogers, C. (1977). *Freedom to learn.* Columbus, OH: Merrill.

## REFERENCES

Algozzine, B., Christenson, S., & Ysseldyke, J. E. (1982). Probabilities associated with the referral to placement process. *Teacher Education and Special Education, 5,* 19–23.

Belmont, J. M., & Butterfield, E. C. (1971). What the development of short-term memory is. *Human Development, 14,* 236–248.

Biklen, D. (1992). *Schools without labels: Parents, educators, and inclusive education.* Philadelphia: Temple University Press.

Brooks, P. H., & McCauley, C. (1984). Cognitive research in mental retardation. *American Journal of Mental Deficiency, 88,* 479–486.

Campione, J. C., Brown, A. L., & Ferrara, R. A. (1982). Mental retardation and intelligence. In R. J. Sternberg (Ed.), *Handbook of human intelligence* (pp. 392–490). Cambridge: Cambridge University Press.

Cummins, J. (1984). *Bilingualism and special education: Issues in assessment and pedagogy.* Cleveland, Avon, England: Multilingual Matters, Ltd.

Duffy, F. H., & McAnulty, G. B. (1985). Brain electrical activity mapping (BEAM): The search for a physiological signature of dyslexia. In F. H. Duffy & N. Geschwind (Eds.), *Dyslexia: A neuroscientific approach to clinical evaluation* (pp. 105–122). Boston: Little, Brown.

Dunn, L. M. (1968). Special education for the mildly retarded: Is much of it justifiable? *Exceptional Children, 35,* 5–22.

Ellis, E. S., Deshler, D. D., & Schumaker, J. B. (1989). Teaching adolescents with learning disabilities to generate and use task-specific strategies. *Journal of Learning Disabilities, 22,* 108–119, 130.

Ellis, N. R. (1970). Memory processes in retardates and normals. In N. R. Ellis (Ed.), *International review of research in mental retardation* (Vol. 4, pp. 1–32). New York: Academic Press.

Ellis, N. R., & Cavalier, A. R. (1982). Research perspectives in mental retardation. In E. Zigler & D. Balla (Eds.), *Mental retardation: The developmental-difference controversy* (pp. 121-152). Hillsdale, NJ: Erlbaum.

Engelmann, S., Carnine, L., Johnson, G., & Meyers, L. (1989). *Corrective reading: Comprehension.* Chicago: Science Research Associates.

Engelmann, S. E. (1977). Sequencing cognitive and academic tasks. In R. D. Kneedler & S. G. Tarver (Eds.), *Changing perspectives in special education* (pp. 46–61). Columbus, OH: Merrill.

Epps, S., & Tindel, G. (1987). The effectiveness of differential programming in serving students with mild handicaps: Placement options and instructional programming. In M. Wang, M. Reynolds, & H. Walberg (Eds.), *Handbook of special education: Research in practice* (Vol. 1, pp. 213–248).

Fuchs, D., & Fuchs, L. S. (1994). Inclusive schools movement and the radicalization of special education reform. *Exceptional Children, 60,* 294–309.

Gartner, A., & Lipsky, D. K. (1989). *The yoke of special education: How to break it.* Rochester, NY: National Center on Education and the Economy.

General Accounting Office. (1981). Disparities still exist in who gets special education. Report to the Chairman, Subcommittee on Select Education, Committee on Education and Labor, House of Representatives of the United States. Gaithersburg, MD: GAO.

Glidden, L. M. (1979). Training of learning and memory in retarded persons: Strategies, techniques, and teaching tools. In N. R. Ellis (Ed.), *Handbook of mental deficiency, psychological theory and research* (2nd ed., pp. 619–657). Hillsdale, NJ: Erlbaum.

Gottlieb, J. (1985). Report to the Mayor's Commission on Special Education on COH practices in New York City. In New York City Commission on Special Education, *Special education: A call for quality.* New York: Mayor's Commission on Special Education.

Gottlieb, J., Gottlieb, B. W., & Trongone, S. (1991). Parent and teacher referrals for a psychoeducational evaluation. *Journal of Special Education, 25,* 155–167.

Grossman, H. J. (1983). *Classification in mental retardation.* Washington, DC: American Association on Mental Deficiency.

Hallahan, D. P., & Reeve, R. E. (1980). Selective attention and distractibility. In B. K. Keogh (Ed.), *Advances in special education* (Vol. 1, pp. 141–181). Greenwich, CT: JAI Press.

Kastner, S., & Podell, D. M. (1991). Psychotherapy as an approach to special education prevention: Perceptions of student behavior. *American Journal of Orthopsychiatry, 61,* 563–566.

Kauffman, J. M. (1989). *Characteristics of children's behavior disorders* (4th ed.). Columbus, OH: Merrill.

Kauffman, J. M. (1991). Restructuring in sociopolitical context: Reservations about the effects of current reform proposals on students with disabilities. In J. W. Lloyd, N. N. Singh, & A. C. Repp (Eds.), *The regular education initiative: Alternative perspectives on concepts, issues, and models* (pp. 57–66). Sycamore, IL: Sycamore Publishing Co.

Kavale, K., & Mattson, P. D. (1983). One jumped off the balance beam: Meta-analysis of perceptual-motor training. *Journal of Learning Disabilities, 16,* 165–173.

Kirk, S. A. (1962). *Educating exceptional children.* Boston: Houghton Mifflin.

Krupski, A. (1986). Attention problems in youngsters with learning handicaps. In J. K. Torgesen & B. Y. L. Wong (Eds.), *Psychological and educational perspectives on learning disabilities* (pp. 161–192). Orlando: Academic Press.

Lahey, B. B., & Carlson, C. L. (1991). Validity of the diagnostic category of attention deficit disorder without hyperactivity: A review of the literature. *Journal of Learning Disabilities, 24,* 110–120.

Lovitt, T. C. (1977). *In spite of my resistance . . . I've learned from children.* Columbus, OH: Merrill.

Luckasson, R., Coulter, D. L., Polloway, E. A., Reiss, S., Schalock, R. L., Snell, M. E., Spitalnik, D. M., & Stark, J. A. (1992). *Mental retardation: Definition, classification, and systems of supports.* Washington, DC: American Association on Mental Retardation.

Mercer, J. R. (1973). *Labelling the mentally retarded.* Berkeley: University of California Press.

Morrison, G. M., & Polloway, E. A. (1995). Mental retardation. In E. L. Meyer & T. M. Skrtic (Eds.), *Special education and student disability* (4th ed., pp. 213–270). Denver, CO: Love Publishing Co.

Myers, P. I., & Hammill, D. D. (1990). *Learning disabilities: Basic concepts, assessment practices, and instructional strategies* (3rd ed.). Austin, TX: Pro-Ed.

National Joint Committee for Learning Disabilities. (1989). *Letter from NJCLD to member organizations.* Washington, DC: NJCLD.

Nussbaum, N., & Bigler, E. (1990). *Identification and treatment of attention deficit disorder.* Austin, TX: Pro-Ed.

Pearl, R., Donahue, M., & Bryan, T. (1986). Social relationships of learning-disabled children. In J. K. Torgesen & B. Y. L. Wong (Eds.), *Psychological and educational perspectives on learning disabilities* (pp. 193–224). Orlando: Academic Press.

Podell, D. M., & Soodak, L. C. (1993). Teacher efficacy and bias in special education referral decisions. *Journal of Educational Research, 86,* 247–253.

President's Committee on Mental Retardation. (1969). *The six-hour retarded child.* Washington, DC: U.S. Government Printing Office.

Pressley, M., Symons, S., Snyder, B. L., & Cariglia-Bull, T. (1989). Strategy instruction comes of age. *Learning Disabilities Quarterly, 12,* 16–30.

Reeve, R. E. (1990). ADHD: Facts and fallacies. *Intervention in School and Clinic, 26*(2), 70–78.

Rogers, C. (1977). *Freedom to learn.* Columbus, OH: Merrill.

Schumaker, J. B., Deshler, D. D., Alley, G. R., Warner, M. M., & Denton, P. H. (1982). Multipass: A learning strategy for improving reading comprehension. *Learning Disabilities Quarterly, 5,* 295–304.

Soodak, L. C., & Podell, D. M. (1993). Teacher efficacy and student problem as factors in special education referral. *Journal of Special Education, 27,* 66–81.

Soodak, L. C., & Podell, D. M. (1994). Teachers' thinking about difficult-to-teach students. *Journal of Educational Research, 88,* 44–51.

Stainback, S., & Stainback, W. (1992). Schools as inclusive communities. In W. Stainback & S. Stainback (Eds.), *Controversial issues confronting special education: Divergent perspectives* (pp. 29–44). Baltimore, MD: Paul H. Brooks.

Tarjan, G., Wright, S. W., Eyman, R. K., & Keernan, C. V. (1973). Natural history of mental retardation: Some aspects of epidemiology. *American Journal of Mental Deficiency, 77,* 369–379.

Tarver, F. G. (1986). Cognitive behavior modification, direct instruction, and holistic approaches to the education of students with learning disabilities. *Journal of Learning Disabilities, 19,* 368–375.

Taylor, A. M., & Turnure, J. E. (1979). Imagery and verbal elaboration with retarded children: Effects on learning and memory. In N. R. Ellis (Ed.), *Handbook of mental deficiency, psychological theory and research* (2nd ed., pp. 659–697). Hillsdale, NJ: Erlbaum.

Turnbull, A. P., Turnbull, H. R., Shank, M., & Leal, D. (1995). *Exceptional lives: Special education in today's schools.* Englewood Cliffs, NJ: Merrill.

U.S. Department of Education. (1989). *Eleventh annual report to Congress on implementation of P.L. 94-142.* Washington, DC: U.S. Government Printing Office.

U.S. Department of Education. (1993). *Fifteenth annual report to Congress on the implementation of the Individuals with Disabilities Education Act.* Washington, DC: U.S. Government Printing Office.

Wang, M. C., Reynolds, M. C., & Walberg, H. J. (1989). Who benefits from segregation and murky water? *Phi Delta Kappan, 71*(1), 64–67.

Zeaman, D., & House, B. J. (1963). The role of attention in retardate discrimination learning. In N. R. Ellis (Ed.), *Handbook of mental deficiency: Psychological theory and research* (pp. 159–223). New York: McGraw-Hill.

Zigler, E., & Balla, D. (1982). Introduction: The developmental approach to mental retardation. In E. Zigler & D. Balla (Eds.), *Mental retardation: The developmental-difference controversy* (pp. 3–8). Hillsdale, NJ: Erlbaum.

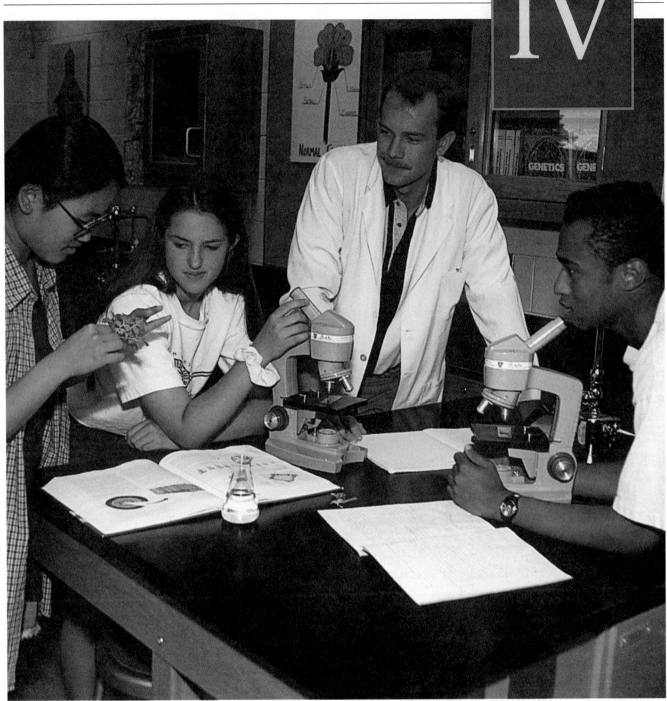

© Jim Whitmer

# Shaping the Learning Environment

© Martin R. Jones/Unicorn Stock Photos

# Planning for Instruction

# Chapter Outline

# Learning Objectives

12.1 Describe the ends-means and integrated ends-means approaches to planning.

12.2 Identify two types of learning objectives and create objectives of both types.

12.3 Explain how planning occurs before, during, and after instruction.

12.4 Describe the relationship between content and planning approaches.

12.5 Describe the impact of planned questions and identify the level of comprehension related to various questions.

12.6 Describe the instructional approaches of Ausubel, Bruner, and Gagné and apply their principles to instruction.

12.7 Identify ways to plan for transfer of learning and for individual differences among students.

# Preview

This chapter focuses on how to create an environment that facilitates learning. Using the curriculum goals set by your school district, your knowledge of your students' abilities, and the instructional materials available to you, you can design an instructional plan. You must first decide *what* to teach and then *how* to teach it.

Often, school districts determine what topics should be covered in different grades. But these are *minimal* goals; you can elect to teach more. Sometimes, major issues that challenge our society, such as social problems or world events, determine *what* to teach. Students are eager to understand topics of current interest.

Deciding *how* to teach depends on the availability of materials, the subject matter, and your knowledge of how students learn. The range of teaching methods is limited only by your imagination.

New technologies will probably influence the teaching methods you choose. Your classroom, for example, may contain VCRs, personal computers, and networked computer labs. Future technology will also influence you and your students, many of whom will be more comfortable with the latest technology than you are.

This chapter describes the ends-means and the integrated ends-means approaches to planning instruction and

discusses what research has uncovered about teachers' planning in real-life classrooms. Next, we explain how a general-to-specific planning approach helps you maintain focus on long-range goals as you develop day-to-day plans.

We then describe how to (a) initiate an instructional design, (b) ask questions that require students to demonstrate their ability to function at various levels of cognition, and (c) identify learning strategies that students can use. In addition, we describe how you can transfer learning outcomes from one situation to another. ◉

# Approaches to Planning

In the 1960s and 1970s, research on teaching focused primarily on teachers' overt behavior, such as the effects of teachers' praise, their use of rewards, and how they engage students in problem solving. In the last two decades, however, researchers have investigated teacher planning and decision making to understand how teachers' thinking influences the teaching process (e.g., Bullough, 1994; Clark & Peterson, 1986; Clark & Yinger, 1988; McCutcheon, 1980; Shavelson, 1983; Wolcott, 1994; Yinger, 1980).

Clark and Peterson (1986) characterize the teacher's thought processes as complex, multidimensional, and involving three stages: the **preactive stage**, the **interactive stage**, and the **postactive stage.** Most of teacher planning takes place in the preactive stage (i.e., before instruction begins), but teachers frequently revise their plans as instruction takes place (in the interactive stage) to accommodate unexpected events and new ideas. Even after instruction has occurred (the postactive stage), planning continues as teachers consider the last lesson and make decisions about the next lesson. They also consider how to improve the completed lesson in the future. These stages are not a linear process that moves from daily to weekly to yearly instructional units. Teacher planning is cyclical and often involves initiation, implementation, and reassessment of both short- and long-range goals, which occur at different times and for different lengths of time in the school year.

Teachers use many different types of planning that are not completely independent of one another. The curriculum, for example, is transformed from the form of a written teaching guide to a dynamic set of activities that teachers have added, deleted, and altered. Teachers allocate instructional time to various aspects of the curriculum according to their perceptions of students' needs, school schedules, or the requirements of the school system. Teachers arrange instructional materials, students' desks and their own desk depending on their beliefs about student learning and student behavior (Egeler, 1993; Kennedy, 1994). Teachers' decisions about grouping students and their choices of instructional materials set the "tone" or the climate of the classroom.

Teachers usually approach instructional planning by establishing (a) performance objectives or (b) instructional activities. These two major approaches result from teachers' training and their beliefs about instruction and student learning (Egeler, 1993; Kennedy, 1994).

The teacher must translate from the curriculum, as determined by the state or local school district, to the actual lessons presented to the class.

Teachers take different approaches to teaching.
© Jeff Greenberg/Unicorn Stock Photos

# Models of Planning

Although there are no hard and fast rules about planning instruction, many teachers use one of three models: ends-means planning, integrated ends-means planning, or planning based on content.

## Ends-Means Planning

*Describe the ends-means and integrated ends-means approaches to planning.*

**12.1**

In the **ends-means model of planning,** teachers first formulate objectives (ends) and then choose instructional methods (means) that appear to be appropriate. Teachers who follow this model generally organize tasks sequentially and evaluate student performance through observable and measurable behaviors. This "objectives-first" model (McCutcheon, 1980) is the most efficient and effective means of training teachers in instructional planning and is used in many colleges and universities that train teachers. The lesson plans written by student teachers usually follow the ends-means model and consist of (a) determining objectives, (b) selecting tasks and procedures, (c) initiating and maintaining student task involvement, and (d) specifying student outcomes and evaluation procedures.

The planning in the linear ends-means model (Yinger, 1980) progresses in a logical fashion. It is used in other fields, such as city planning, and sometimes in economic planning. The model is appealing because of its rational and scientific qualities and its reliable measurement of outcomes. Once the objectives have been precisely detailed, they can be evaluated in concrete and behavior-based testing.

Although this model can be used for any unit of time (daily, weekly, etc.), it is most often used for daily lesson planning. Teachers select the primary objective for a lesson and specify the behavior and outcomes they expect from students.

## Integrated Ends-Means Planning

An alternative method of planning is the **integrated ends-means approach,** which starts with the selection of activities that seem to be appropriate for students, and from which objectives evolve. In this model, ends and means become integrated. Advocates of this form of planning (Eisner, 1967; McDonald, 1965) believe that teachers should be more concerned with creating an environment that involves students in learning than with identifying and defining objectives.

## Choosing Learning Objectives

Arends (1988) summarizes the important ingredients of a good learning objective. He suggests that it should (a) identify what the student is supposed to learn, (b) define the testing situation, and (c) describe the acceptable level of performance. When writing objectives, the teacher must specify the learning component in measurable terms. Literal learning objectives, such as identifying the states in New England or solving a mathematical problem, can easily be specified. Higher-level thinking skills, such as creating something original, speculating, making judgments, and synthesizing research, are less amenable to precise definitions. When you encourage students to be creative and to think independently and divergently, you will find it more difficult to write objectives in observable, measurable terms.

Here is a set of objectives. Which are the easiest to observe and assess?

1. The student will identify methods the community uses for recycling.

2. The student will explain why recycling is important.
3. The student will describe how recycling benefits society.
4. The student will identify new ways the community could use to recycle.
5. The student will develop a plan to promote community involvement in recycling.

It is easier to assess the first three objectives than the last two. Generally, this information is part of a curriculum, and students will offer standard responses (e.g., Recycling is important so we do not waste our natural resources). However, objectives 4 and 5 ask students to be creative and inventive. How will you assess students' ideas for new ways of recycling or new plans to encourage recycling? Will you assess their usefulness, their practicality, or their originality?

## Two Types of Learning Objectives

 Compare these two learning objectives:

- Given a list of 20 countries and continents, the student will identify which is a country and which is a continent with 80 percent accuracy.
- The student will understand the difference between a country and a continent.

The first is a *behavioral* objective; it describes a behavior that you can observe a student carry out. The second is a *cognitive* objective; you cannot observe a person *understand* something, although you can observe behavior that suggests a person understands.

According to Mager (1975), behavioral objectives have three parts: (a) what the student is expected to do ("The student will identify which is a country and which is a continent"), (b) the conditions under which the student's behavior is to occur ("Given a list of 20 countries and continents"), and (c) what the acceptable level of performance is ("With 80 percent accuracy"). Behavioral objectives use verbs that describe observable behaviors, such as *define, list, add, explain,* and *demonstrate.*

Gronlund (1991, 1993) believes teachers should develop objectives by starting with general cognitive goals using verbs such as *comprehend, understand,* and *solve.* The teacher then specifies examples of appropriate student behavior, such as comparing two ideas or distinguishing between two opposing viewpoints.

**12.2** ◎

*Identify two types of learning objectives and create objectives of both types.*

---

Studies indicate that, although teachers may be trained to use the ends-means model, in fact most focus first on the type of learning activities they want and only later, determine learning objectives (Cleary & Groer, 1994; Egeler, 1993; Wolcott, 1994). Early studies (Zahorik, 1970) found that teachers who use the ends-means model are often not sensitive to students' needs, perhaps because they focus on instruction and do not consider students' interests or abilities.

Research about lesson-planning activities has found that teachers are most concerned about the learning activities within the lesson and the content of the lesson (Clark & Yinger, 1988; Yinger, 1980). Teachers also plan routines for regulating activities and other classroom events. Yinger found that once routines are in place, teachers become increasingly flexible and effective because they can focus on instruction rather than on monitoring behavior. Teachers use learning objectives as a framework for planning activities. Behavioral objectives in Yinger's study were customarily set by the school district and used by teachers to structure some of their decisions, but were not, in themselves, dominant in the planning process.

The routines you set up in the classroom allow students to know what to expect and to feel more secure. Well-designed routines also make transitions efficient and contribute to the students' sense of purpose.

### Planning Based on Content

Some teachers consider materials and resources before considering students' interests (Glidden, 1991; Roehler, 1988; Taylor, 1970; Zahorik, 1975). Zahorik (1975) found that when planning instruction, only 28 percent of teachers considered objectives or activities first; the majority began with content, materials, and resources. Peterson, Marx, and Clark (1978) also found that teachers focus first on content and then on activities and strategies, and finally on objectives. The content of a subject area is the most important factor in determining instructional activities. The more you know about a subject area, the easier you will find it to develop lesson plans.

## How Teachers Plan

You can examine planning processes in several ways. One way is to look at teacher planning in terms of various instructional time frames: yearly plans, term plans, unit plans, weekly plans, and daily plans. Another way is to examine the chronological sequence of preactive, active, and postactive planning. You can also think of planning more generally in terms of stages:

## Choosing Activities

When teachers select activities, they make decisions to select (a) a method of grouping students, (b) materials, and (c) the form of instruction, such as lecturing, discussion, student-directed activities, or independent work. Many teachers consider activities the basic units of planning (Arends, 1988; Clark & Yinger, 1988; Yinger, 1980) around which all classroom action occurs during instructional periods. The remaining time is devoted to preparing activities and detailing transitions from one activity to another.

The types of activities you select reflect the classroom climate you wish to establish. For example, classrooms built around whole-class instruction with teacher-directed discussions create a different environment from those whose main activities revolve around group work and cooperative endeavors. The choices you make also reveal your beliefs about how students best learn and how you can best maintain control over learning outcomes (Brickhouse, 1990; Glidden, 1991; Levin & Ammon, 1992). In the planning stage, you should consider activities that develop routines, develop group cohesion, and provide a flow of instruction that produces a variety of tasks throughout the day.

### Activities that Develop Routines

Establishing routines is necessary to create a learning environment that works (Arends, 1988). Teachers need to establish routines for tasks such as distributing materials, moving within the classroom, making assignments, collecting homework, and making transitions between activities. Arends provides six guidelines for routinizing these activities: (a) write detailed plans for routines, (b) inform students of these procedures the first time they are needed, (c) post plans on bulletin boards for easy reference, (d) train students to carry out the routines, (e) maintain a consistent attitude

toward the established routines, and (f) alter routines when more efficient or effective means are apparent.

Routines benefit both you and the students; by setting norms that are acceptable to both you and the students, students will accept the rules and take responsibility for them (Yorke, 1988).

### Activities that Create Group Cohesion

Many activities offer students an opportunity to work together and to solve problems. Pairing students for assignments or forming small groups in task-oriented arrangements are two ways that allow students to interact with one another and develop group cohesion and morale. These activities can be informal, such as meetings at the beginning of the day to plan activities, or formal, such as research groups or writing groups that carry out academic tasks. Group projects can be student-generated and can provide opportunities for students with different talents and abilities to interact. Allowing students to develop ideas, solve problems, and evaluate their own work increases their motivation.

### Activities that Vary Instruction

One of the best ways to stimulate and maintain student interest is to use a wide variety of instructional activities. Beginning teachers often find it difficult to decide how much material to cover, how long a lesson should last, how to modify a lesson when it fails to generate interest, and when to end a lesson. When you consider that you must determine the flow of activity within a lesson and from lesson-to-lesson on a daily, as well as a weekly basis and even over longer periods of time, it becomes apparent that careful planning is a critical ingredient of successful teaching.

---

Individual, small-group, and large-group activities should be varied, depending on the nature of a lesson and the students' needs.

problem finding; problem formulation, solution, and implementation; evaluation; and routinization (Yinger, 1980).

## Time Frames for Planning

**12.3**

*Explain how planning occurs before, during, and after instruction.*

In yearly planning, you establish general content, often dictated by school systems or individual schools (e.g., "Fifth-grade social studies will cover the colonists' revolt against the British and the establishment of the United States"). You also determine the general sequence of the curriculum and identify the materials and resources you will use to implement the program. Subsequent planning involves refining the year-long plans in terms of the specific content you intend to cover and defining instructional goals for your students. Select learning experiences that match your students' abilities and interests and establish large units of instruction centered on important concepts. Then select specific lessons for daily instruction.

Clark and Yinger (1988) found that teachers believe unit planning is the most important, followed by weekly and daily planning. Few teachers viewed individual lessons as important, a significant finding since so much instruction for teachers focuses on the lesson plan.

Many teachers nest smaller planning levels within larger ones (Morine-Dershimer, 1978–1979), producing a smooth flow of activity for the whole year. Elementary school teachers must plan for many subject areas. Similarly, secondary school and specialized teachers must plan for subtopics within their discipline. In terms of the planning process, teachers' cognitive functions are similar, whether they are involved in single-subject or multiple-subject teaching. All teachers must select content, identify problems, choose teaching methods, devise activities, and develop methods of evaluation.

Establishing routines and schedules is particularly important in planning, especially in the early part of the school year. Once established, routinized features persist throughout the year and sustain the flow of various activities. Psychologically, the organization of classroom structures and routines define the "problem space" (Newell & Simon, 1972) within which you and students operate.

*Teachers sometimes focus on a specific daily lesson plan and lose sight of how that lesson relates to a broader, long-term objective.*

## Models of Teacher Thought and Action

You will go through the same stages of planning regardless of the length of the instructional time frame you choose. In the preactive stage, you select activities and materials that you believe will help students reach the selected learning goals. During this phase you are becoming familiar with the students and developing the classroom climate that coincides with your beliefs about learning and teaching. In the interactive stage, you carry out your plan, observe how students respond, and make decisions (Schon, 1987), depending on how successful the instruction was. After you have completed the lesson or unit plan, you enter the postactive phase and should reflect on how the results of the last lesson should influence your next plan. Figure 12.1 presents a model of the relationship between teacher thought and action and student outcomes.

This model shows the relationship between teachers' observable behaviors and unobservable factors that influence how teachers behave. We can measure overt actions, but not thinking processes. Consequently, it is difficult for researchers to demonstrate how different kinds of thinking affect teaching performance. Teacher planning involves decision making, problem solving, and conceptualization, so it is clear that teacher planning and teacher thinking are linked (Isenberg, 1990a). Understanding the nature of this relationship is crucial for improving teaching.

### The Preactive Stage of Planning

In *Among Schoolchildren* (Kidder, 1989), a teacher describes how she begins to plan instruction in August, before the school year begins. Her first thoughts concern how she will organize her classroom and establish routines for the school year.

Research by Clark and Peterson (1986) shows that in the preactive stage teachers' thoughts about teaching and their beliefs about how students learn determine how they plan. Some information-processing theorists suggest that when confronted with a complex situation, people create a simplified model of the situation

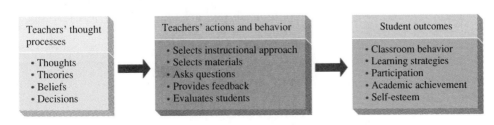

**Figure 12.1**
A model of teachers' thoughts, actions, and student outcomes.

and then behave rationally within that model (Simon, 1980). Teachers combine information from diverse sources with new, ongoing research findings, and their own beliefs and attitudes to develop a rational, comprehensive classroom curriculum.

### The Interactive Stage of Planning

Teachers make hundreds of decisions during their teaching day, as often as once every two minutes. Their most frequent thoughts are about students, followed by instructional procedures and learning objectives (Clark, 1988). Teachers improvise and make major changes if continual fine-tuning and adjusting their teaching fail to preserve the flow of a lesson. During the interactive stage, teachers move back and forth between implementing what they had planned in the preactive stage and modifying their teaching on the basis of feedback they receive while they are teaching. Some studies indicate that teachers become better at interactive decision making as they become successful and more experienced (Berliner, 1986; Clark & Lambert, 1986; Cleary & Groer, 1994).

### The Postactive Stage of Planning

Postactive planning is more similar to preactive than to interactive planning. In fact, the thinking involved is almost identical; that is, teachers reflect on the success of their plan, observe the outcomes of the interactive stage and make decisions about the next phase of their teaching. It is useful to conceptualize teaching as a series of cycles, in which the postactive planning of one cycle becomes preactive for the next.

Interactive planning also blurs with the other stages. We may separate the three stages of planning for the sake of clarity, but it is important to recognize their overlapping functions in actual planning and teaching. Similarly, teachers' thoughts, in all of these phases, are informed by teachers' actions, which have been previously determined by their belief system. Thus, the teachers' thoughts and actions influence each other.

*Annual* **Edition**

unit *8*

## Teachers' Beliefs and Theories

Teachers hold implicit theories about their students, their subject matter, and their own professional roles and responsibilities (Clark, 1988; Glidden, 1991; Isenberg, 1990a, 1990b; Levin & Ammon, 1992; McIntyre & Pape, 1993; McNamara, 1990). These theories are not always neatly organized or rational. Instead they often reflect biases, personal experiences, insights based on fragments of behavior, and incomplete experiences. In fact, they do not differ much from the kinds of theories most of us have about the world and its workings: some truth, combined with some bias, misconceptions, and faulty thinking. Teachers' implicit theories influence many aspects of their decision making. Teachers' beliefs in their own effectiveness, or self-efficacy, affect how they deal with difficult-to-teach students. Teachers with low self-efficacy sometimes develop faulty notions about student learning to justify the failure of their own teaching efforts. Instead of regarding their efforts as worthwhile but unsuccessful, which should encourage new approaches, low self-efficacy teachers sometimes blame the students or look to other educators to solve the students' problems (Soodak & Podell, 1994). Teachers with high self-efficacy, on the other hand, search within themselves for other solutions and often make imaginative and effective decisions about how to teach underachieving students. As Clark (1988) points out, while misconceptions, idiosyncracies, and incomplete experiences may be human, they do not help students learn. He recommends that teachers and students examine their ideas about teaching, schooling, and learning to clarify their own motives and actions.

## Planning as Problem Solving

■■ Planning is a form of problem solving.
■■ Teachers solve planning problems by developing activities, drawing on prior experience, altering the curriculum to fit their sense of what will work, and orienting instruction around themes or units (Arends, 1988; Brown, 1988; McCutcheon, 1980).

Expert teachers are better than novices at solving planning problems (Peterson & Comeaux, 1987; Shavelson, 1987) because their experience enables them to recognize and categorize types of problems. Much like expert chess players, expert teachers identify patterns that occur in classrooms with reasonable consistency and devise plans of action to deal with them.

Here are a few suggestions for becoming a better planner.

1. *Ask experienced teachers how they solve recurring classroom problems.* (Problems, incidentally, are not always bad. They may simply be events that need to be addressed, such as routinizing the collection of homework or grouping students according to the goals of a particular task.)
2. *Observe classrooms and identify problems for which the teacher has organized a plan of action.* If the teacher's plan seems ineffective, consider what other plans might address the problem.
3. *Organize your teaching around themes that are appropriate for your students.* Curriculum guides will help you identify appropriate content and concepts for any particular age group or grade level.

# Selecting an Approach to Planning

There is no single correct approach to plan instruction. The approach you select will depend on your personal preference or style and the nature of what you are going to teach.

The knowledge of some subject areas can be broken down into sequential steps and learned by moving from one level to another. Other subject areas have more diffuse goals, such as understanding the "gist" of a particular reading or synthesizing several ideas. The approach to planning and to teaching is often dictated by how structured the subject matter is.

**12.4** ◎

*Describe the relationship between content and planning approaches.*

## Structured Subject Areas

For most elementary and middle school students, there is much to learn in mathematics that is sequential, logical, and dependent on prior lessons. For this reason, an objectives-first approach to instruction is often suitable. On the other hand, if teachers believe that their long-range goals should include *comprehension* of mathematical concepts, it is better to allow students to "discover" these concepts through activity-centered experimentation. These two approaches are not mutually exclusive, and you can shift between the two to achieve different goals.

Other structured subject areas in elementary school are the routine skills of handwriting, spelling, and phonics. Similarly, some practical skills, such as using a computer or a dictionary, are highly structured. Skills within other subject areas, such as setting up a science experiment or preparing a social studies report, also often lend themselves to a structured approach. Once these skills become routinized and automatic, students can move on to higher-order thinking and concept development. An objectives-first approach can often help students acquire these skills efficiently.

## Less Structured Subject Areas

In content areas such as literature, social studies, and science, however, much of the material is not sequential or structured and requires a different approach to planning. Instruction in these areas usually anticipates higher-order thinking: why events occur, how they influence our behavior, how they relate to our lives, and how they can affect our decisions for the future, to name a few. It is better to plan subject areas of this sort through an activities-first approach, which allows students to investigate, reflect on, and solve problems. Exposure to a variety of experiences, such as experimentation and hands-on activities, may be necessary for students to learn to think about the concepts inherent in the disciplines.

# Planning Good Questions

Many teachers find it useful to develop key questions to ask students. These questions can be placed at various points: at the beginning of a lesson or unit to stimulate interest and focus student attention, during the implementation of the lesson to redirect student focus or elaborate on what is being learned, or at the end of a lesson to summarize and evaluate student learning. Although teachers may generate many questions "on the spot" or alter and abandon some as they observe whether students are learning, some planned questions are valuable in focusing on what students should be learning and at what levels of comprehension they are achieving the learning goals.

## Levels of Comprehension

The kind of cognitive skill required to answer a question depends on the nature of the question. Benjamin Bloom and his colleagues (1956) developed a taxonomy of educational objectives that arranges six levels of cognitive skills in hierarchical order, ranging from simple (i.e., knowledge and comprehension) to complex (i.e., synthesis and evaluation). By using Bloom's taxonomy, you can make sure you ask questions at every cognitive level. Bloom's levels and the types of questions associated with each are illustrated in figure 12.2.

Several studies that examined teachers' questions found that 85 percent of the questions teachers ask are factual and require simple recall (Goodlad, 1984). Also after observing 1,000 classrooms, Goodlad and his colleagues rarely found teachers asking questions that stimulated curiosity or demanded problem solving.

Some researchers have criticized Bloom's taxonomy, arguing that the classification system may not reflect a true hierarchy and that it is often difficult to classify all learning objectives reliably (Fairbrother, 1975; Seddon, 1978). When the taxonomy is viewed as a framework for cognitive skills, however, the classification scheme helps teachers formulate questions at different cognitive levels.

A simplified version of this categorization is often used to analyze reading comprehension on literal, inferential, or interpretive levels. Pearson and Johnson (1978) present a model that includes reading *on the lines, between the lines,* and *beyond the lines.* The literal level of comprehension deals with what is actually stated in print (i.e., on the lines), the inferential involves comprehension of the implications of what is printed (i.e., between the lines), and interpretive comprehension deals with the conclusions, comparisons, and predictions that readers can make about the reading material as it relates to other information (i.e., beyond the lines). You can use this classification to develop questions that require different levels of comprehension. Examples of questions in each level are shown in figure 12.3.

When you vary questions from simple recall to application problems, you help students see the relevance of what they are learning. To push beyond the literal level, ask questions that require students to use critical thinking. Examples include identifying a character's motive in a story or analyzing the evidence for a hypothesis. Similarly, divergent questions that ask students to speculate or originate a new plan or proposal compel students to think beyond the literal and engage in higher-order thinking. When asking questions that require evaluation, have students support their opinions with evidence or identify and apply standards.

## 12.5 ◎

*Describe the impact of planned questions and identify the level of comprehension related to various questions.*

In addition to planning good questions, you can have students generate their own questions about topics to help guide them as they learn new material.

To some extent, the level of a question depends on whether information has already been presented to students. The question "Why was the Civil War fought?" could require only recall if the information was previously given, but if it wasn't, the question may require higher-level thinking.

**Level 1:**

*Knowledge*: Remembering information presented to the learner.

Questions: In what city was the Declaration of Independence signed?
Who wrote most of the Declaration of Independence?

**Level 2:**

*Comprehension*: Understanding the information presented.

Questions: Why is the signing of the Declaration of Independence so important in American history?
What was the purpose of the Declaration of Independence?

**Level 3:**

*Application*: Using information in problem solving.

Questions: How did the Declaration of Independence address the issue of the right of the colonists to self-determination?
How did the Declaration of Independence address the issue of the slave trade?

**Level 4:**

*Analysis*: Breaking down information into its component parts.

Questions: What were the essential points of the Declaration of Independence?
How do the Declaration of Independence and the French Declaration of the Rights of Man differ?

**Level 5:**

*Synthesis*: Finding connections and relationships among different ideas.

Questions: How did the Declaration of Independence reflect the ideas of English philosopher John Locke?
How are the Declaration of Independence and the French Declaration of the Rights of Man similar?

**Level 6:**

*Evaluation*: Examining and judging ideas to determine how well they satisfy criteria.

Questions: How well did the Declaration of Independence address the issues that existed between the colonists and the British?
How well do the ideas expressed in the Declaration of Independence relate to issues in today's society?

**Figure 12.2**
Bloom's cognitive taxonomy and questions (1956).

Cognition does not occur in a vacuum. People's thoughts are influenced by their personalities, attitudes, and social and emotional development, which are collectively referred to as the *affective domain*. You can take the affective domain into account by planning activities that address students' interests and concerns and helping them express opinions and feelings. Bloom and his colleagues established a taxonomy of the affective domain, shown in figure 12.4, to identify the dimensions of affective behavior (Krathwohl, Bloom, & Masia, 1964). Although you may not specify these levels in your planning, you should be aware of the impact of student affect on learning.

# Planning Instructional Strategies

Often the most important decision a teacher makes is how to present new material, an area frequently referred to in lesson planning as *motivation*. In this section, we describe three approaches to developing instructional strategies. The first is Ausubel's use of **advance organizers,** or introductory statements or events that help prepare students for new learning and demonstrate a relationship between what they will learn and a broader concept or idea. The second is Bruner's model of **discovery learning** in which teachers present problems in ways that encourage students to investigate and discover the solutions. The third is Gagné's model of **events** within a lesson.

12.6 ◎

*Describe the instructional approaches of Ausubel, Bruner, and Gagné and apply their principles to instruction.*

## Figure 12.3

Pearson and Johnson's model
(1978).

Source: P. D. Pearson and D. D. Johnson, *Teaching
Reading Comprehension,* 1978. Orlando, Florida:
Holt, Rinehart & Winston College Publishing.

> Although the assassination of the heir to the Austrian throne, Archduke Franz Ferdinand, on June 28, 1914 triggered the outbreak of the First World War, the causes of the war were much more complex. For years, Germany had been building up its military. The death of the Archduke, at the hands of a Serbian nationalist, led Austria to declare war on Serbia on July 28, with the encouragement of Austria's ally, Germany. Soon thereafter, Russia mobilized its army to protect the Serbs, giving Germany an excuse to declare war on Russia on August 1. Russia, France, and Great Britain were allied to one another. Germany demanded that France declare itself neutral; when it did not, Germany declared war on France on August 3 and invaded Belgium in an effort to conquer France. With Germany so close to its doorstep and with its alliance with France and Russia, Great Britain entered the war on August 4. Thirty-eight days after the assassination of the Austrian Archduke, most of Europe was at war.

**Level 1:**   "On the lines"
*Questions:*   What are the two reasons Great Britain entered the war?
               What event triggered the First World War?

**Level 2:**   "Between the lines"
*Questions:*   Who does the author perceive as the aggressor in the outbreak of World War I?
               What does the author believe to be the real cause of World War I?

**Level 3:**   "Beyond the lines"
*Questions:*   What appears to be an underlying problem that caused the initial hostilities between
               Austria and Serbia to escalate into a world war?
               How might countries prevent a conflict between two nations from drawing in the allies
               of the two nations?

## Figure 12.4

Bloom's affective taxonomy
(Krathwohl, Bloom, & Masia, 1964).

Source: D. Krathwohl et al., *Taxonomy of
Educational Objectives: Handbook 2: Affective
Domain,* 1956. New York: David McKay Company.

**Level 1:**
*Receiving:* Being aware of events and conditions in the environment

**Level 2:**
*Responding:* Demonstrating a new behavior as a result of exposure to new stimuli

**Level 3:**
*Valuing:* Manifesting an involvement or commitment to the events or conditions

**Level 4:**
*Organization:* Internalizing a new value among one's existing values

**Level 5:**
*Characterization by value:* Showing behavior that is consistent with one's values

## Ausubel's Meaningful Verbal Learning

Ausubel (1960, 1977) advocates the use of active interaction between teachers and students in what he calls *meaningful verbal learning.* His model stresses **expository teaching,** in which teachers present material in an explicit and fully organized manner, thus allowing students to receive a well-ordered set of ideas in an efficient way.

Ausubel's model depends on deductive reasoning, in which people first learn principles and then learn to recognize specific instances of those principles. This approach assumes that people learn best when they understand general concepts and proceed *deductively* from rules or principles to examples.

Ausubel's *meaningful verbal learning* relies heavily on dynamic verbal interactions between teachers and students. He starts with an advance organizer to set the scene for subsequent teaching and learning and then develops a series of steps that the expository teacher uses to instruct.

Ausubel suggests that teachers give students the overarching structure of material to help them learn the specifics (a deductive approach). Bruner recommends giving student specifics and letting *them* discover the overarching structure (an inductive approach).

# TEACHERS ROUNDTABLE

## "The Kids Lead Us . . . They Tell Us"

**SK:** So what happens when you start a lesson and you can't finish it, or it goes the wrong way, or the kids don't get it? What do you do?

**Donna:** As a beginning teacher, I (luckily) learned to get good guidance. It's important to find a mentor or at least someone you can talk to. The first few weeks of school I was, I hate to use the expression, freaking out. Things were going wrong. So I did what I learned from my cooperating teacher from my student teaching days—I changed gears and tried something else. You might have to abandon the whole thing or go with the interests of the students. If you are reading something to them and they're not really interested, you may have to ask them, "What are you interested in?" You have to tap into their interests, and you have to be flexible.

**Mary:** The kids lead us . . . they tell us.

**Anthony:** Over the years, you keep adapting and changing your lessons. You find out what works with children, and then you use that approach. When a lesson is not good, you have to leave it. You have to reevaluate your methods and arrive at a method that works with children.

**Irwin:** At the high school level, there is a tension between completing the curriculum and moving in other directions. Whether people like to hear it or not, there are points where students have to take a test and pass it or they don't graduate from high school. It becomes very tense when you say, "Here's a lesson I would really like to teach," but there's material which, realistically, you have to cover. What's going to happen if the kids don't get to the Civil War?

**DMP:** As an experienced teacher, how has your role changed over the years?

**Irwin:** In the "good old days," you could just open a textbook, and that was what you taught in the classroom. I think that's inappropriate—a textbook is a *guide* to what you teach. If the teacher is just going to repeat the textbook, the teacher becomes an information presenter. And teachers are really not information presenters. I'm an old line teacher who has changed along the way. Originally, I saw myself as the information presenter: I have all the information; you [the students] just sit in your seats and I'm going to tell you what's important. When we taught separation of powers in U.S. history, we had charts and we'd say, "This is how separation of powers works." Now, I ask kids to tell me what would be logical if they were creating a government. Why would they separate powers? What's more difficult is, of course, as a teacher now, you give up control because you are not directing students as you once did. But, kids start to respond much more—they agree and they disagree. And then, you have to take their words and give meaning to what they say; then you come up with a list—which may not be the list that you had five years ago. But in the end, when the students generate their own list, they get the concept of what separation of powers is; they get the concept that it's more logical for an executive or a president to do one thing, a Congress to do another, and a court system to do something else. In the old days, you had to complete a lesson in one session. You had to do the "aim" in

five minutes, the "summary" in 20 minutes. What I think that I've learned about teaching is that it's more important that the kids leave the class with the idea that separation of powers is important.

**DMP:** But you mentioned that to some extent you have to give up control?

**Irwin:** Absolutely. That's very scary for young people when they first start. When you first start teaching, you have a lesson plan and you're afraid to put it down. And you were told to "Start out tough . . . Keep those kids in line at first, and then you can ease off."

**Mary:** We used to think that teachers were responsible for children's learning. Now, we know that it's the child's ultimate responsibility to learn. We set up the environment and then the child must take up the opportunity to learn.

**SK:** So you just let the knowledge float out there, and whatever the kids get, they get, and whatever they don't, they don't?

**Mary:** No, now you let the knowledge float, but then you are constantly checking their learning and changing your approach. The responsibility is shared. We do our best, but then the child has to take the learning on.

**Angela:** For me, I present my curriculum but the children know that they are responsible for finding out more information. If they are interested in a particular topic that we talked about, it is their responsibility to follow up on it. I will provide the materials; I will provide the time and structure. But it's their job to go out and to take an active part in learning.

## Advance Organizers

Read the following passage:

*In the early years of England's history, London quickly emerged as the capital city. Later, when England and Scotland were united as Great Britain, London was without question the capital of the united country. But London is not only the capital of Great Britain; over the years, it has been the center of countless important events, both historical and cultural, both wonderful and terrible, that have influenced not only the English-speaking world but the*

## Applying Ausubel's Ideas

These steps will help you apply Ausubel's ideas:

1. *Plan an advance organizer.* Suppose you are teaching a history class and wish to introduce the causes of World War II. Develop an advance organizer that taps students' prior knowledge about wars or conflicts. Select a broad concept that pertains to the upcoming lesson on World War II, such as the scarcity of resources, territoriality, or nationalism. Now plan an introduction that shows students how their prior knowledge relates to the concept. You might begin with a conflict that students have experienced or recently read about.

2. *Use examples.* Elicit examples from the students that relate to the concept. List some of the examples that you will offer if students do not respond, such as other wars, or other events in which nations have argued for territorial rights, such as the Arab-Israeli conflict. Plan questions that will lead students to other examples. These might include questions about their familiarity with Europe and Asia, maps and globes of different countries that were involved in the conflict, and changes that occur in the distribution of resources before and after wars.

3. *Prepare similarities and differences.* Write out some of the similarities and differences that you expect to encounter in your discussion with students. Use a chart to record similarities and differences so that students can see relationships among concepts.

---

*entire world. It is the birthplace of parliamentary government. It acted as the center of an empire that spread across the globe. It was the home to such giants as Shakespeare, Sir Isaac Newton, Milton, and Virginia Woolf, whose works have been translated into countless languages. It was the center of European resistance to Hitler.*

As a teacher, you could ask students to read this passage to comprehend the information it contains. You could focus the students' attention on the most essential aspects of the passage, however, by using an advance organizer. Consider the effect of giving students the following advance organizer prior to their reading the passage:

*The influence of some capital cities extends well beyond the countries in which they are located. Cities that achieve world-wide influence often have long histories, large populations, and geographic locations that make travel to and from foreign countries easy. Also, such cities frequently attract people who generate creative works and pioneering ideas.*

This advance organizer presents the idea of a world capital at an abstract, general, and inclusive level that makes it easier for the reader to understand and remember the information contained in the passage.

Teachers use advance organizers to activate students' schemata (their existing understandings), to remind students of what they already know, and to help them recognize the relevance of their existing knowledge. Advance organizers introduce new knowledge in a global way that students can use a framework for understanding details contained in the new information. You can use advance organizers to teach any subject matter.

### Steps in Expository Teaching

After presenting an advance organizer and using examples, the next step is to point out similarities and differences.

Teachers present the lesson and then ask students questions and help them understand the ideas subsumed under the broader concept and to reconcile differences between what they knew before and what they have learned. Ausubel's model incorporates Bruner's idea of active student involvement once the conceptual framework has been laid out.

# Bruner's Discovery Model

## Discovery Learning

Bruner's (1966) model of instruction assumes that students learn best when they discover information and concepts on their own. In the discovery model, students use inductive reasoning to derive principles underlying a set of examples. For example, a teacher may describe to students the invention of the light bulb, the camera, and the gramophone, and contrast these inventions with discoveries (e.g., electricity, nuclear fission, and gravity). The students may then derive for themselves what constitutes an invention and how it differs from a discovery.

In discovery learning, students "discover" the basic concept or overarching principle by engaging in activities that demonstrate the concept. Bruner believes that students "own" their knowledge when they discover it themselves and that giving students responsibility for their own learning increases their motivation to learn.

## Problem Solving

Discovery learning begins with the presentation of a problem. Teachers then guide students through a problem-solving process to generate their own questions or hypotheses. Students then test the hypotheses and draw conclusions from their experimentation. Discovery learning focuses on *process,* not *product* (Carin & Sund, 1985). The teacher stimulates inquiry and provides examples that students examine or manipulate to arrive at a general idea or principle.

## Guided Discovery

In a **guided discovery** approach, teachers give students some direction to help them avoid blind alleys. They ask stimulating questions or pose dilemmas that need solutions, furnish appropriate and interesting materials, and encourage students to generate and test hypotheses.

When have you most enjoyed learning? Was it when material was presented in an expository format (as Ausubel advocates) or when a discovery approach was followed (as recommended by Bruner)?

In discovery learning, students often benefit from making mistakes; wrong answers generate problem solving, which can help lead to the discovery of the right answer.

The guided discovery approach changes the role of the teacher from the provider of information to the facilitator of learning.

© Tom McCarthy/Unicorn Stock Photos

"Excuse me, Mrs. Neltik. We had a biology project get a little out of control next door.
Did you by any chance see a green and red snake, about 6 or 7 feet long . . .
Oh, there he is!"

## Applying Bruner's Ideas

Using Bruner's discovery learning model, you might teach the concept of "square root" in this way:

Start by presenting students with a series of examples of square roots.

- The square root of 49 is 7.
- The square root of 4 is 2.
- The square root of 100 is 10.

With these examples, most students will be able to generate for themselves what "square root" is (i.e., use inductive reasoning). You can test their understanding by asking them to describe "square root" in their own words or to generate examples of their own (e.g., use deductive reasoning). Many problems require both inductive and deductive reasoning; consequently, give students opportunities to use both types of reasoning.

When using Bruner's model, it is best to present both examples and nonexamples of the concepts you want students to learn. For example, if you are teaching a third-grade class how environmental factors determine how people live, you want them to discover the impact of the environment on the choices people make. You might carry out the following steps:

1. *Present students with a particular stimulus.* Begin by showing pictures of people living in various kinds of homes and asking what the pictures tell us about how people live.

2. *Provide data and materials for problem solving.* You might give students data about the climate in various geographic locations. Students will then select areas of the world to study and begin to gather information about the living conditions in various locations. They can then identify the homes that people build, the food they eat, and the clothes they wear.

3. *Ask guiding questions.* Eventually you will want to stimulate inquiry by asking some important questions, such as what kind of work do people do, how do they get their food, and finally how do various environmental conditions (climate, geography, etc.) determine how they live.

4. *Encourage intuitive thinking.* If students do not have ready answers, encourage them to make calculated guesses based on what they have read or discussed. At the end of the unit, students can share their information and conclude how environmental factors affect the way people live.

## Applying Gagné's Ideas

Here is an example using Gagné's nine "events" to teach a geography lesson on the continents:

1. Gain students' attention by bringing up a recent event in the news that occurred on another continent (e.g., a war, an earthquake) and ask students if they have heard about it.
2. Explain that the purpose of the lesson is to help students understand where these events are occurring relative to where they live by understanding the locations of different continents.
3. Have students retrieve prior knowledge by asking: "Who knows where Africa is? Where is Africa on this globe? What do you know about Africa?"
4. Introduce new information by showing students some of the continents, such as North America and South America, on the globe and naming them.
5. Ask students to define *continent* on the basis of the examples you have shown them. Ask students how a continent differs from a country or an island.

6. Ask: "What other continents do you see on the globe? Why isn't Canada a continent?"
7. If students identify Africa and Australia as continents, acknowledge their correct response, but if they identify Great Britain as a continent, explain why it isn't.
8. Assess students' performance by having them apply their knowledge. For example, on a map of the world, have students label the seven continents for themselves and write, in their own words, a definition of *continent*.
9. To enhance retention and transfer, ask students to name famous people who came from the different continents. Or ask them, "On which continent does Nelson Mandela live?" "Where does Mel Gibson come from?" You may also review the concept "continent" and name the different continents at the beginning of the next lesson and occasionally thereafter.

## Gagné's Events of a Lesson

Gagné (Gagné & Driscoll, 1988) developed a model based on information-processing theory that views instruction in terms of nine sequential events:

1. Gain student attention.
2. Provide students with the goals or objectives of the lesson.
3. Retrieve prior knowledge.
4. Present stimulus material.
5. Guide learning.
6. Elicit student responses.
7. Provide feedback.
8. Assess performance.
9. Enhance retention and transfer.

## Planning for Transfer of Learning

In addition to helping students acquire more complex knowledge, teachers are also concerned with how students generalize learning from one situation to another. Students rarely encounter the same problems repeatedly; in fact, the very nature of learning involves an encounter with similar, but not identical, ideas or problems. A major educational goal is to equip students to **transfer** ideas previously learned to new materials or situations.

It is important to plan for transfer rather than assume it will take place. Students may need some guidance in understanding when their new knowledge is transferrable (and when it is not). In planning for transfer, give students opportunities to see how what they have learned relates to situations other than those in which they were taught. New knowledge should not be "welded" to a given situation, but be applicable to a variety of situations. Students must also grasp when

**12.7** ◎

*Identify ways to plan for transfer of learning and for individual differences among students.*

Transfer of learning is crucial. If students do not transfer new learning to appropriate situations, of what value is it?

---

**DIVERSITY MAKES A DIFFERENCE**

## Planning the Curriculum in a Multicultural World

The common practice in the United States has been to emphasize a Western historical and philosophical curriculum that focuses on the history and culture of Western Europe and the United States. In addition, the focus of the curriculum has been not only Western, but also predominately male.

Critics complain that the substantial contributions of ethnic and language minority groups and women are underrepresented or unrepresented in the curriculum, giving students a skewed view of the world. The United States, they note, is made up of people from a wide variety of cultural backgrounds that enhance society. They also claim that some students feel alienated from school because their own cultural background is not represented in the school culture (Banks & Banks, 1993; Bennett, 1995; Ogbu, 1992).

Educators, such as Hirsch (1987) and Ravitch and Finn (1987), however, note the valuable contributions of Western philosophy and thought to our present system of government and to the values and beliefs shared by the members of our society. They defend the traditional curriculum as upholding the tenets of a democratic culture and contend that all members of that society should share its values.

The argument does not present an all-or-none dilemma. Teachers can plan a curriculum that integrates the traditional curricula with opportunities for students to examine alternative methods of thinking and valuing.

While school boards, school districts, state legislatures, and other bodies often dictate a curriculum, teachers translate these directives into viable activities for the classroom. Curriculum guides reflect the basic attitudes society holds about relevant education at a particular time. Teachers, however, incorporate these goals into a workable plan and adapt the curriculum to fit their students' capabilities, backgrounds, and interests. Teachers allot time for various instructional areas to match their own beliefs about what is important. They accomplish long-range goals for each year in a variety of ways and through a variety of contexts and activities. Teachers select, test, and modify learning materials and texts to maximize student achievement. It is important to remember, however, that students are more likely to learn when they see the relevance of the subject matter and when they feel that their cultural group and gender are respected and included.

---

learning is *not* relevant. For example, students may learn that the letter *g* is silent when it appears before the letter *n* (e.g., *assign, gnat*). This knowledge can be transferred to other words that were not part of the lesson (e.g., *design, malign, gnome*), but not to words such as *indignation* or *designation*.

## Planning for Individual Differences

Vary your instruction to accommodate differences in students' background knowledge, learning styles, and instructional needs (Good & Brophy, 1991). You must decide when to use large- or small-group activities, pairs, or individualized instruction.

Assign students to small groups or pairs based on similarity of needs or complementary characteristics, a strategy called "planned heterogeneity." For example, rather than pairing two students who have similar needs, you could pair a student who understands a concept with one who doesn't; the first student benefits from "teaching," while the second student benefits from having someone who may be better equipped than the teacher to explain the concept in familiar terms.

Individual instruction can sometimes be used in classes where students are grouped heterogeneously. Some computer programs are designed for students to learn at their own pace and can be tailored to a student's specific instructional needs. A major drawback of individual instruction, however, is that it doesn't occur in a social context and, increasingly, educators are becoming aware of the value of the social environment in promoting learning.

# Planning and Implementation

Look at the following two sample lesson plans developed by Theresa Deady-Kabbez when she was a student teacher. Both are designed for third-grade students; one lesson is in math and the other is in science. What type of objectives has this teacher developed? How has the teacher used planned questions to promote students' understanding? How does the teacher use planned activities and guided discussion to meet the lesson's instructional objectives?

Planning and delivery of instruction are very much intertwined.

Planning is a time for reflection and revision; it can take place at any time, although some plans, such as those for setting routines and organizing the classroom, are best done at the beginning of the school year. Most importantly, planning is not a *fixed* phase, but rather is open to on-going modification and improvement. Planning can take place *before, during,* and *after* instruction. Most importantly, teachers need to step back from the activity of teaching and *reflect* on the process. Reflection is the precursor to useful planning.

## Sample Lesson Plans

### Sample One

*Title:*  Measuring with nonstandard units of measure.

*Goal:*  To introduce students to linear measure and help them recognize the need for a uniform set of measures.

*Aim:*  How many paper clips long are different objects?

*Objectives:*

1. Students will be able to measure the lengths of various objects using paper clips as units.
2. Students will be able to explore the nature of measurement using a variety of nonstandard methods.
3. Students will learn how estimation helps the process of measurement.

*Materials:*  Paper clips, teacher-designed activity cards, measurement worksheet.

*Procedure:*  Discuss measurement. *Questions:* What does it mean to measure something? What types of things do we measure? How do we measure objects? How can you use estimation to measure objects, distances, etc.?

Next, have students use their hands to measure the width of their desks. Compare the results of a few students. *Questions:* Your desks look the same length, don't they? Why do you think you have different measurements? How else could we check the size of these desks? (Use the same student's hand to measure several desks.) Discuss the importance of using the same unit of measurement when comparing objects. There must be a *common unit* so we can understand each other's results.

Then, have the same student measure the desk again without putting his/her hands end to end, leaving gaps. *Questions:* Why are the results different now? Why do we need to measure an object from end to end, without having gaps or overlapping? Explain how this changes the result. Give an example of measuring the blackboard.

*Development:*  Explain the next activity to students, using paper clips to measure various lengths of paper. Demonstrate in front of the class. Students record their results in their notebook; they should then trade cards and try to measure and record as many as they can. Hand out activity cards and paper clips.

After a period of exploring and measuring with paper clips, discuss results, problems, or differences in answers. Have students interpret their data by asking: Which card was the shortest? How do you know? Which card was the longest? How can you tell? Were there any cards that had the same measurement?

*Culmination:* Hand out worksheet. Now that students have worked with paper clips as a unit of measure, they can begin to estimate. They should first write down the number of paper clips they think might be enough for each object on the worksheet. Then they are to use their paper clips to find the exact measurement.

*Assessment:* Evaluate the students' use of the materials in measuring the various objects. Compare their estimates to the actual measure to see if they could judge a unit of measure based on the length of a paper clip.

*Follow-up:* Expand students' understanding of linear measure by introducing them to standard measures such as the inch, foot, and centimeter. Allow them to explore with these units the same way as the nonstandard unit.

## Sample Two

*Title:* Objects and their properties.

*Goal:* To have students learn that objects are described by their properties and that different objects may have some properties that are alike and other properties that are different.

*Aim:* What are the properties of the set of rocks presented to the class?

*Objectives:*
1. Students will observe a variety of objects and identify their properties.
2. Students will be able to classify objects based on their properties.
3. Students will be able to apply the concept of properties to new objects and different situations.

*Materials:* "Sylvester and the Magic Pebble"; assortment of rocks; assortment of other objects.

*Introduction:* Discuss the story "Sylvester and the Magic Pebble." *Questions:* What was Sylvester's hobby? What does it mean to collect things? Did Sylvester collect every rock he saw? What made certain rocks special (color, texture, size, shape)? Introduce the word *classifying* as a way of grouping something based on its size, shape, color, etc.

*Motivation:* Divide the class into groups of three or four. Give each group a container filled with a variety of rocks. Allow them time to explore the rocks. Tell them to observe their color, feel their texture and weight, and note their size and shape. Then have the students divide the rocks on their tray into groups. They can classify them by any means they choose.

*Development:* Have each group explain the observations they made. *Questions:* Why did you group the rocks the way you did? What do the rocks in each group have in common? List on the board the words they use to describe the rocks. Then introduce the word *property* as something that tells us about an object. We use *properties* of an object to *classify* objects into groups.

Then have the students look at one of their groups of rocks. *Questions:* Are all the rocks in that group the same in every property? Are they all big, black, rough, etc.? Explain how objects can be alike in one property but different in another.

*Conclusion:*    Hand out a variety of objects (e.g., ruler, pine cone, or cloth) so that each student has one object. Place in a bag a duplicate of six or seven of the objects you handed out.

Then have one student come up and pick an object out of that bag. While keeping it hidden from the rest of the class, have the student describe the properties of the object. The rest of the class listens to the properties and tries to figure out if their object is being described. The person who guesses the right object gets to come up and pick the next object and describe it to the class. While doing this activity, discuss any incorrect guesses.

*Evaluation:*    Were the students able to recognize the similarities in and the differences between the properties of the object being described and their own object?

*Follow-up:*    For homework, students should complete the worksheet on properties and objects. They are to find objects at home that either contain the property listed or list the property that describes the object listed. Discuss the different answers in class the next day.

## Worksheet Activity

| Object | Property |
|--------|----------|
| Sugar | _____ |
| _____ | Shiny |
| | Flaky |
| Door | _____ |
| Bed | _____ |
| _____ | Soft |
| Sponge | _____ |

## KEY POINTS

1. Teachers can use an ends-means model of planning or an integrated ends-means approach. Those who use the ends-means model focus initially on desired student performance outcomes, then develop instructional activities to achieve these goals, and specify student performance outcomes that are observable and measurable. Those who use the integrated ends-means model focus initially on instructional activities and allow student performance outcomes to evolve from the activities.

2. Teachers plan various activities to develop routines, create group cohesion among students, and vary the type of instruction to maintain student motivation.

3. Most teachers believe the most important time frame is unit planning, followed by weekly and daily planning. As teachers gain experience, their planning becomes routinized.

4. Planning consists of three stages: preactive (selecting activities and materials), interactive (carrying out and modifying instruction based on how students respond), and postactive (assessing the effectiveness of instruction once it has been completed).

5. Bloom's taxonomy of educational objectives classifies thinking into six types, hierarchically arranged by complexity. In practice, most teachers ask students questions that require thinking only at the two lowest levels of Bloom's taxonomy.

6. Ausubel's model of expository teaching is a deductive model that relies on the use of advance organizers to present new information in the form of general principles before examining specific examples.

7. Bruner's model of discovery learning is an inductive model in which students acquire general principles as a result of first examining numerous specific examples of the principles.

8. Gagné's nine-step model of instruction is based on an information-processing model of how students learn.

9. One controversy in planning is the extent to which the curriculum should reflect multicultural perspectives.

## SELF-STUDY EXERCISES

1. Select a unit you might want to teach to a group of students (e.g., magnetism, the Vietnam War, contributions of persons from various ethnic groups). Develop an instructional plan using the ends-means model for the entire unit and for a single lesson.

2. Using the unit you chose for the previous exercise, develop an instructional plan using the integrated ends-means model for the entire unit and for a single lesson.

3. Describe how you would develop a routine for returning students' corrected homework assignments.

4. Describe the cyclical nature of the preactive, interactive, and postactive stages of planning.

5. Describe how the instructional plans you developed for exercises 1 and 2 reflect your beliefs about the nature of schooling. Identify assumptions you are making that others might disagree with.

6. Using the unit you selected for exercises 1 and 2, construct one question at each level of Bloom's taxonomy of educational objectives.

7. Using the unit you selected for exercises 1 and 2, develop a lesson plan using one of the following models: Ausubel's, Bruner's, or Gagné's.

## FURTHER READINGS

Arends, R. I. (1988). *Learning to teach*. New York: Random House.

Goodlad, J. (1984). *A place called school*. New York: McGraw-Hill.

Kidder, T. (1989). *Among schoolchildren*. New York: Avon Books.

## REFERENCES

Arends, R. I. (1988). *Learning to teach*. New York: Random House.

Ausubel, D. P. (1960). The use of advance organizers in the learning and retention of meaningful material. *Journal of Educational Psychology, 51*, 267–272.

Ausubel, D. P. (1977). The facilitation of meaningful verbal learning in the classroom. *Educational Psychologist, 12*, 162–178.

Banks, J., & Banks, C. M. (1993). *Multicultural education: Issues and perspectives*. Boston: Allyn & Bacon.

Bennett, C. I. (1995). *Comprehensive multicultural education: Theory and practice*. Boston: Allyn & Bacon.

Berliner, D. (1986). In pursuit of the expert pedagogue. *Educational Leadership, 15*(7), 5–13.

Bloom, B. S., Engelhart, M. D., Frost, E. J., Hill, W. H., & Krathwohl, D. R. (1956). *Taxonomy of educational objectives: Handbook I: Cognitive domain*. New York: McKay.

Brickhouse, N. W. (1990). Teachers' beliefs about the nature of science and their relationship to classroom practice. *Journal of Teacher Education, 41*(3), 53–62.

Brown, D. S. (1988). Twelve middle-school teachers' planning. *The Elementary School Journal, 89*(1), 69–87.

Bruner, J. S. (1966). *Toward a theory of instruction*. New York: Norton.

Bullough, R. V. (1994). Digging at the roots: Discipline, management, and metaphor. *Action in Teacher Education, 16*(1), 1–10.

Carin, A. A., & Sund, R. B. (1985). *Teaching science through discovery*. Columbus, OH: Merrill.

Clark, C. (1988). Teacher preparation: Contribution of research on teachers' thinking. *Educational Researcher, 17*, 5–12.

Clark, C., & Lambert, M. (1986). The study of teacher thinking: Implications for teacher education. *Journal of Teacher Education, 37*(5), 27–31.

Clark, C., & Peterson, P. (1986). Teachers' thought processes. In M. Wittrock (Ed.), *Handbook on research on teaching* (3rd ed., pp. 255–296). New York: Macmillan.

Clark, C., & Yinger, R. (1988). Teacher planning. In I. Berliner & B. Rosenshine (Eds.), *Talks to teachers* (pp. 342–365). New York: Random House.

Cleary, M. J., & Groer, S. (1994). Inflight decisions of expert and novice health teachers. *Journal of School Health, 64*(3), 110–114.

Egeler, D. J. (1993). Factors that influence the instructional planning of teachers. *Educational Planning, 9*(3), 19–37.

Eisner, E. W. (1967). Educational objectives: Help or hindrance. *School Review, 75*, 250–266.

Fairbrother, R. (1975). The reliability of teachers' judgments of the abilities being tested by multiple-choice items. *Educational Researcher, 17*, 202–210.

Gagné, R., & Driscoll, M. (1988). *Essentials of learning for instruction* (2nd ed.). Englewood Cliffs, NJ: Prentice Hall.

Glidden, P. L. (1991). Teachers' reasons for instructional decisions. *Mathematics Teacher, 84*(8), 610–614.

Good, T. L., & Brophy, J. E. (1991). *Looking in classrooms* (5th ed.). New York: Harper Collins.

Goodlad, J. (1984). *A place called school*. New York: McGraw-Hill.

Gronlund, N. E. (1991). *How to write and use instructional objectives* (4th ed.). New York: Macmillan.

Gronlund, N. E. (1993). *How to make achievement tests and assessments* (5th ed.). Boston: Allyn & Bacon.

Hirsch, E. D., Jr. (1987). *Cultural literacy: What every American needs to know.* Boston: Houghton Mifflin.

Isenberg, J. P. (1990a). Reviews of research: Teachers' thinking and beliefs and classroom practice. *Childhood Education, 66*(5), 322–327.

Isenberg, J. P. (1990b). Teachers of the year: Their views, beliefs and concerns. *Childhood Education, 66*(5), 293–294.

Kennedy, M. F. (1994). Instructional design or personal heuristics in classroom instructional planning. *Educational Technology, 34*(3), 17–25.

Kidder, T. (1989). *Among schoolchildren.* New York: Avon Books.

Krathwohl, D., Bloom B. S., & Masia, B. (1964). *Taxonomy of educational objectives: The classification of education goals: Handbook 2. Affective domain.* New York: McKay.

Levin, B., & Ammon, P. (1992). The development of beginning teachers' pedagogical thinking: A longitudinal analysis of four cases. *Teacher Education Quarterly, 19*(4), 19–37.

Mager, R. (1975). *Preparing instructional objectives* (2nd ed.). Palo Alto, CA: Fearon.

Marland, P., & Osborne, B. (1990). Classroom theory, thinking and action. *Teaching and Teacher Education, 6*(1), 93–109.

McCutcheon, G. (1980). How do elementary teachers plan? The nature of planning and influences on it. *Elementary School Journal, 81*, 4–23.

McDonald, J. B. (1965). Myths about instruction. *Educational Leadership, 22*, 571–576.

McIntyre, J., & Pape, S. (1993). Using video protocols to enhance teacher reflective thinking. *Teacher Educator, 28*(3), 2–10.

McNamara, D. (1990). Research on teachers' thinking: Its contribution to educating student teachers to think critically. *Journal of Education for Teaching, 16*(2), 147–160.

Morine-Dershimer, G. (1978–1979). Planning and classroom reality: An in-depth look. *Educational Research Quarterly, 3*(4), 83–99.

Newell, A., & Simon, H. A. (1972). *Human problem solving.* Englewood Cliffs, NJ: Prentice Hall.

Ogbu, J. V. (1992). Understanding cultural diversity and learning. *Educational Researcher, 21*(8), 5–14.

Pearson, P. D., & Johnson, D. D. (1978). *Teaching reading comprehension.* New York: Holt, Rinehart & Winston.

Peterson, P., Marx, A., & Clark, C. (1978). Teacher planning, teacher behavior, and student achievement. *American Educational Research Journal, 15*, 417–432.

Peterson, P. L., & Comeaux, M. A. (1987). Teachers' schemata for classroom events: The mental scaffolding of teachers' thinking during classroom instruction. *Teaching and Teacher Education, 3*(4), 319–331.

Ravitch, D., & Finn, C. E., Jr. (1987). *What do our 17-year-olds know? A report on the first National Assessment of History and Literature.* New York: Harper & Row.

Roehler, L. R. (1988). Knowledge structures as incidence of the "personal": Bridging the gap from thought to practice. *Journal of Curriculum Studies 20*(2), 159–165.

Schon, D. (1987). *Educating the reflective practitioner.* San Francisco: Jossey-Bass.

Seddon, G. M. (1978). The properties of Bloom's taxonomy of educational objectives. *Review of Educational Research, 48*, 303–323.

Shavelson, R. J. (1983). Review of research on teachers' pedagogical judgments, plans and decisions. *The Elementary School Journal, 83*, 392–413.

Shavelson, R. J. (1987). Planning. In M. Dunkin (Ed.), *The international encyclopedia of teaching and teacher education* (pp. 483–486). New York: Pergamon.

Simon, H. (1980). Problem solving and education. In D. Tuma & F. Reif (Eds.), *Problem solving and education: Issues in teaching and research* (pp. 81–96). Hillsdale, NJ: Erlbaum.

Soodak, L. C., & Podell, D. M. (1994). Teachers' thinking about difficult-to-teach students. *Journal of Educational Research, 88*(1), 44–51.

Taylor, P. H. (1970). *How teachers plan their courses.* London: National Foundation of Educational Research.

Wolcott, L. L. (1994). Understanding how teachers plan: Strategies for successful instructional partnerships. *School Library Media Quarterly, 22*(3), 161–164.

Yinger, R. J. (1980). A study of teacher planning. *The Elementary School Journal, 80*(3), 107–127.

Yorke, D. B. (1988). Norm setting: Rules by and for the students. *Vocational Education Journal, 63*(5), 32–33.

Zahorik, J. (1975). Teachers' planning models. *Educational Leadership, 33*, 134–139.

Zahorik, J. A. (1970). The effects of planning on teaching. *Elementary School Journal, 71*(3), 143–151.

# 13

© Jeff Greenberg/Unicorn Stock Photos

# Student Assessment and Evaluation

# Chapter Outline

# Learning Objectives

13.1 Define *measurement, assessment,* and *evaluation.*

13.2 Describe how tests differ from other kinds of measuring instruments.

13.3 Describe how reliability and validity differ.

13.4 Describe standard scores and percentiles.

13.5 Identify the characteristics of norm-referenced and criterion-referenced tests.

13.6 Explain the purposes of evaluation.

13.7 Construct a classroom achievement test.

13.8 Name sources of bias in testing.

13.9 Describe the procedures used in performance-based and authentic assessment.

# Preview

This chapter explains various techniques of determining how well students have learned. It describes the principles of measurement underlying assessment and evaluation and the nature of tests and other measuring instruments. You will learn how to interpret scores used to report students' performance on standardized tests and how to construct high-quality tests of your own. ◉

# Measurement, Assessment, and Evaluation

Think back to your days as a student in elementary or high school and you will no doubt remember taking countless tests. Like it or not, testing plays a big role in our schools, and you can count on administering tests to your students. Before turning to a discussion of different kinds of tests, let us define some terms used in educational measurement.

Measurement and assessment are related, but not identical terms. **Measurement** is the process of gathering information and expressing it in numerical terms. We use measurement, for example, when we express the concept "distance" in numerical terms such as 6 inches, 20 centimeters, 4 feet, or 3 light-years, or when we express the concept "time" in numerical terms such as 15 seconds, 30 minutes, 2 decades, or 5 centuries.

**Assessment** is a broader term that includes the concept of measurement, but it also includes interpreting one or more measurements for the purpose of making decisions. We use assessment when we conclude that it would take twice as long for a car to travel 100 miles than to travel 50 miles if the driver maintains the same speed or that a car would have to go at twice the speed to cover 100 miles in the same time it takes to cover 50.

**13.1**
*Define* measurement, assessment, *and* evaluation.

# The Role of Tests in Educational Measurement and Assessment

Numerous physical concepts can be expressed numerically: temperature, weight, length, to name but a few. Measuring a physical concept requires only the use of an appropriate measuring instrument. If you want to measure temperature, you use a thermometer; weight, a scale; length, a ruler, etc.

Most concepts of interest to educators, however, are not physical in nature. Educators typically deal with nonphysical concepts such as academic achievement, academic aptitude, or student personality characteristics. Nevertheless, just as physical concepts are measured by appropriate measuring instruments, so are many nonphysical educational concepts. The most common form of educational measurement is a test. If you want to measure academic achievement, you use an academic achievement test; academic aptitude, an aptitude test; personality characteristics, a personality test, etc.

*Annual* **Edition**

unit **6**

Like it or not, testing plays a big role in our schools.

© Martin R. Jones/Unicorn Stock Photos

Psychologists use the Rorschach Test to measure personality characteristics by analyzing people's interpretations of ambiguous stimuli that look like inkblots.

© Will McIntyre/Photo Researchers

Other measurement tools in education include surveys, portfolios, interviews, rating scales, checklists, inventories, and observations.

Assessment in education typically takes the form of interpreting students' test scores in conjunction with other kinds of evidence, such as teachers' evaluations. For example, assessment of a student's performance on an intelligence test and several academic achievement tests may result in classifying the student as learning disabled. Or, assessment of a student's performance on some measure of intelligence may lead to classifying the student as gifted or as having mental retardation.

## Assessment and Evaluation

Assessment and **evaluation** are also related, but not identical, terms. Whereas assessment refers to the process of interpreting evidence, evaluation refers to the process of making a value judgment. A student's score on a reading test, for example, may lead to an assessment that the student is reading on the fifth-grade level. The evaluation of reading performance at the fifth-grade level would lead to the conclusion that the student is a superior reader if the student is a third-grader. The same performance by a ninth-grader, however, would lead to the conclusion that the student needs remediation in reading. In both cases, the conclusion is a value judgment based on one's notion of what constitutes good and poor reading ability.

# Properties of Tests and Measuring Instruments

13.2 ◎

*Describe how tests differ from other kinds of measuring instruments.*

There are numerous kinds of measuring instruments, such as questionnaires, inventories, rating scales, and tests. The term *test,* however, refers only to instruments containing items whose answers are right or wrong. An instrument designed to measure arithmetic achievement is an example of a test because each item has a correct answer. On the other hand, an instrument designed to measure attitudes toward mainstreaming is *not* a test because there are no right or wrong answers. Different answers to the same item are merely different, not right or wrong. Throughout the following discussion we have often used the term *test* rather than the phrase *test and measuring instrument* for the sake of brevity. The information we present about tests, however, applies to all measuring instruments.

Two properties determine how good a test is: reliability and validity.

# Reliability

**Reliability** pertains to the consistency of a measuring instrument. Before considering various kinds of reliability, it is important to note a fundamental principle. The more items a test has, the more reliable it will be. If you think of each item on a test as a sample of the behavior the test is measuring, it seems reasonable that the more samples of the behavior are obtained, the more consistent the measure of behavior will be.

**13.3** ◎

*Describe how reliability and validity differ.*

## Test-Retest Reliability

Suppose that hypothetically you could administer a test to a group of students and then completely erase their memories. If you administered the same test again to the same group of students under the same conditions and each student obtained the same score both times, the test would have perfect reliability.

The problem with this hypothetical description of reliability, of course, is that one cannot completely erase people's memories between the time the test is first administered and when it is administered again. We deal with this impossibility in two ways. The first way is to administer a test once and let time elapse before administering the test the second time. The question is how much time should elapse between the two test administrations. We want to allow a sufficiently long time to lapse so that we can be reasonably sure that the test takers will have forgotten most of the items on the test. On the other hand, the interval should not be so long that the test takers themselves have changed.

There is no hard and fast rule about how much time should elapse between the two test administrations. How much time a test developer decides on depends on the nature of the test and the nature of the test takers. It is not uncommon for the length of time that has elapsed between two administrations of the same test to range from one or two weeks to one or two months.

The procedure of checking a test's reliability by administering the same test twice is called the **test-retest method.** The same people must take the test twice. Administering the test once to one group of people and again to another group of people does not give any information about the test's reliability. The test-retest method of checking reliability is a fairly common way to determine the reliability of a test. The biggest drawback of the method is that there is no way to ensure that the test takers have really forgotten the items on the test. As we will see, however, no method of determining the reliability of a test is completely free of problems.

## Parallel Forms Reliability

A second way test developers overcome the impossibility of completely erasing test takers' memories between two administrations of the same test is to develop two forms of the same test. In other words, two tests are developed to measure the same thing, but the items on the two tests are different. The two tests developed to measure the same thing are usually called **parallel forms** or **equivalent forms.**

For example, a test developer interested in establishing the reliability of an arithmetic achievement test by means of parallel forms would develop two tests with similar, but different, items. If one function of the test is to measure how well students can add two one-digit numbers, on one form of the test an item might require the student to add 7 and 4; on the other form of the test the student might be required to add 5 and 8. Even though the two items are not identical, both items are basically measuring the same thing, which is the student's ability to add two one-digit numbers.

The advantage of using parallel forms rather than the test-retest method is that, with parallel forms, the problem of memory is completely eliminated because the two forms consist of different sets of items. The disadvantage of using parallel forms, however, is that precisely because the sets of items on the two forms are different, one cannot be completely sure that they are really measuring the same thing.

## Split-Half Reliability

One problem associated with both parallel forms and the test-retest method is the need to get the same group of people together twice to administer the tests. Often it is difficult to get a group of people together once for administering a test, and getting the same people together twice can be extremely difficult.

To determine the reliability of a test without having to arrange for testing the same group of people twice, test developers use the **split-half reliability** method. The split-half method is probably the most commonly used way of determining a test's reliability. It is used so frequently because it is so easy to do. The statistical calculations are exactly the same as those used with the test-retest method and with parallel forms, but the decided advantage is that the test needs to be administered only once. Furthermore, the split-half method also overcomes the problem of test takers' remembering questions from one test administration to another.

### *The Relationship Between Split-Half and Parallel Forms Reliability*

Conceptually, the split-half method is similar to the method of parallel forms. However, instead of administering two forms of the same test at different times, the test developer administers a single test at a single administration. To determine the test's reliability, however, the test developer conceptualizes the one test that has been administered as consisting of two halves, which may be regarded as two parallel forms of the same test.

The people taking the test are, of course, taking only one test, but the test developer treats the scores as though they have come from two parallel forms. For example, if a test consists of 100 items, the developer pretends that 50 items constitute one form of the test and the other 50 items constitute a parallel form of the same test. To determine the reliability of the test, one compares people's scores on the one set of 50 items with their scores on the other set. To the extent that the scores are the same on both sets of 50 items, the test is reliable.

By comparing two subtotal scores from the same test, one can determine the reliability of the test without having to administer the test more than once. Hypothetically, a test consisting of 100 items can be split a number of ways into two subtests, each of which is comprised of 50 items. For example, we could compare the scores on the first 50 items with the scores on the second 50 items. In other words, one subtotal could be calculated from the scores on items 1 through 50 and compared with the other subtotal calculated from the scores on items 51 through 100. We could combine the scores on items 1 through 25 with the scores on items 76 through 100 to get one subtotal and compare that subtotal with the subtotal calculated from the scores on items 26 through 75. In both cases we would be comparing the scores of one set of 50 items with the scores on a different set of 50 items.

### *Splitting Items into Halves*

In determining the reliability of a test using the split-half method, we always split the items into two halves consisting, respectively, of the odd-numbered and the even-numbered items. To obtain one subtotal score, we add up the scores on items 1, 3, 5, 7, and so forth until the scores on all odd-numbered items have been summed; then we add up the scores on all the even-numbered items to obtain the second subtotal score.

The reason we split the items into those with odd and even numbers is to counterbalance any effects that may be associated with the order in which items appear on a test. For example, it may be that the items on a test are arranged so that the further one proceeds in the test, the more difficult the items become. Obviously, if one took the score on the first half of the items, it is likely to be higher than the score on the second half of the items. If the items on a test are of uniform difficulty throughout the test, the beginning items might serve as a form of practice, and people's performance might get better and better as they continue. Again, splitting the items into the first and last halves would likely yield different subtotal scores. By splitting the items in an odd-even fashion, any effects associated with the placement of items on the test are likely to apply comparably to both groups of items.

# Validity

**Validity** refers to "the appropriateness, meaningfulness, and usefulness of the specific inferences made from test scores. . . ." The inferences regarding specific uses of a test are validated, not the test itself (American Psychological Association, American Educational Research Association, & National Council on Measurement in Education, 1985, p. 9). Validity is a necessary quality of a test whether we are speaking of commercially produced tests or teacher-made tests. A test is valid only for measuring a particular characteristic of a particular group of people under a particular set of circumstances. It is meaningless to speak of a test's validity in any absolute sense. A test designed to measure reading comprehension among North American second-graders is not a valid measure of intelligence among Australian second-graders.

A test may be valid for some purposes but not for others. Whether the National Teachers Examination (NTE) is a valid test of teachers' ability to teach may be debatable (e.g., Lovelace & Martin, 1984; Pugach & Raths, 1983), but there is no debate that the NTE is *not* a valid test of a physician's ability to perform surgery. The Graduate Record Examination (GRE) may be a valid measure of students' ability to pursue advanced academic degrees, but it surely would not be a valid measure of first-graders' levels of reading readiness.

Don't let a test's title mislead you. The fact that the title of a test may be "The XYZ Test of Arithmetic Achievement" is no guarantee that the test really measures arithmetic achievement. Suppose, for example, the "XYZ" test contains numerous word problems. Students' performance on the test may depend more on their ability to *read* than on their ability to do arithmetic.

Think of tests as falling into one of three relatively distinct categories: academic achievement, aptitude, and personality. Each test category has a different form of test validity, and each form of validity has its own distinctive set of validation procedures.

> Validity pertains to the extent to which a test measures a *particular* phenomenon (such as reading ability) among a *particular* population (such as third-graders in the United States).

> The type of validity that is appropriate for a particular test depends on what the test is designed to measure.

## Content Validity

**Content validity** is the form of test validity associated with academic achievement tests. You will use the principles of content validity to construct tests for students in your class.

To determine how well students have mastered any subject matter, you must first identify what material has been covered. In other words, what is the content of the subject matter? Think of the content of an academic subject area as a collection of particular kinds of knowledge and skills. An achievement test may then be thought of as a set of items dealing only with a sample of the entire collection of knowledge and skills (Crowl, 1996).

> Have you ever taken a test that you believed was unfair because the test material was not covered in the course? If this was the case, the test lacked content validity.

 **The Validity of Classroom Tests**

In determining the content of an instructional unit, ask yourself not only what topics you have covered but also what proportion of the total content each topic represents. Suppose a unit on electricity covered topics such as electrical conductors, resistance, current, electrodes, electromagnetism, electrolytes, insulating materials, and ways of generating electricity. What proportion of class time and textbook material was devoted to each topic?

Suppose that of the total material covered, 10 percent dealt with electrical conductors, 5 percent with resistance, 20 percent with current, and so forth. Continue the process until you have divided 100 percent of the total content proportionally among the various topics covered. When constructing your unit achievement test, make the proportion of the total number of test items dealing with each topic correspond to the proportion of the total content dealing with that topic. The resulting test will have content validity because the test items represent an accurate sample of the material covered.

Commercial test developers go through the same process of establishing content validity. For example, a publisher who wants to construct an academic achievement test for high school physics would probably examine the material included in the most commonly used high school physics textbooks to gauge what is being taught around the country. The publisher would probably also consult curriculum guides used in various school districts and perhaps talk with a sample of high school physics teachers. The publisher would then divide the total content of high school physics proportionally into various topics to determine the proportion of items on the achievement test that should deal with each topic.

## Criterion-Related Validity

Test developers use **criterion-related validity** to determine the validity of aptitude tests. The primary function of aptitude tests is to predict how well a person will perform in the future, prior to being given any formal instruction. In business, for example, you might take a sales aptitude test to determine how good a salesperson you are likely to be. In education, students might take a reading aptitude test in kindergarten to determine whether they are likely to have problems learning to read.

The validity of an aptitude test therefore is determined by how accurately the test predicts future performance, which is called the criterion measure. There are two forms of criterion-validity: **predictive** and **concurrent validity**. Predictive and concurrent validity differ only in terms of whether there is a lapse of time between the administration of the aptitude test and the measurement of the performance criterion.

Suppose a test developer wants to produce a test to measure students' aptitude for mastering calculus. After constructing the test, the developer would determine its validity by using either predictive or concurrent validity.

A test developer using predictive validity would administer the aptitude test to a group of students *before* they take calculus and then find out how well each student actually performed in the calculus course. The test would be valid to the extent that students' test performance accurately predicted their performance in the calculus course.

A test developer using concurrent validity would administer the aptitude test to a group of students *after* they have completed a course in calculus. Again, however, the test would be valid to the extent that students' test performance accurately predicted their performance in the calculus course.

Concurrent validity is used more frequently than predictive validity because it is easier to administer the aptitude test and obtain a measure of the criterion performance at the same time than to administer the aptitude test and then wait to measure criterion performance. Students who initially took the aptitude test may decide not to study calculus or may not complete the course. As a result, there may not be enough students who completed the course to yield an accurate measure of validity.

## Construct Validity

The terms we assign to various human characteristics or traits, such as authoritarianism, compulsivity, or paranoia, are often called hypothetical constructs. Such constructs are hypothetical in the sense that they are not observable in and of themselves, but instead are only terms used to describe regular patterns in an individual's behavior. When we say a teacher is authoritarian, for example, we are using the term to refer to a *set of behaviors* that differentiates authoritarian from nonauthoritarian teachers. We simply label the set of behaviors authoritarianism.

Personality tests are the most common example of tests used to measure hypothetical constructs, and the form of validity associated with such tests is called **construct validity**. Construct validity is the most comprehensive and abstract form of test validity because there is no clear-cut criterion to use as validating evidence. Establishing construct validity involves gathering evidence from numerous sources.

In education, the most commonly used aptitude tests are given to kindergartners and first-graders in the area of reading and math and to high school students in the area of particular careers.

Hypothetical constructs are derived from theories concerning (a) the nature of the construct, (b) characteristics of persons who exhibit the construct, and (c) factors that are likely to affect the construct. To validate a test that claims to measure a construct, it is usually necessary to study the three aspects of the theory underlying the construct (Wolf, 1982).

Suppose a test developer wants to establish the validity of a test that measures anxiety. The developer might administer the anxiety test as well as a test that measures neuroticism to a group of people. A finding that people's scores on the anxiety test are positively related to their scores on the neuroticism test would provide some evidence that the anxiety test is valid because, theoretically, anxiety and neuroticism are positively related. Similarly, the finding that a group of people classified as neurotic scored higher on the anxiety test than a group classified as nonneurotic would provide additional evidence that the anxiety test is valid because, theoretically, neurotics should display more anxiety than nonneurotics.

Just as one would expect anxiety and neuroticism to be positively related, one would expect to find no relationship between anxiety and various other kinds of constructs, such as mechanical aptitude, for example. Consequently, a finding that people's scores on the anxiety test are *not* positively related to their scores on a mechanical aptitude test provides further evidence that the anxiety test is valid.

Also, theoretically, people would be expected to display more anxiety in some situations than in others. For example, if the anxiety scores of a group of students who took the anxiety test immediately prior to taking a final exam are higher than the scores of students not taking the final exam, one would have additional evidence that the anxiety test is valid.

Construct validity is usually a concern in psychological tests. School psychologists often use tests of intelligence, cognitive ability, reading and math ability, and personality.

## The Relationship Between Reliability and Validity

Suppose we know that a test is reliable. Can we say anything about the test's validity? No. All we know is that the test is measuring something consistently. We do not know if the test is measuring what it claims to be measuring. A reliable test therefore may or may not be valid.

If we know a test is *not* reliable, can we say anything about its validity? Yes. If a test is not measuring anything consistently, it can't possibly be measuring what it claims to be measuring. A test that is not reliable cannot be valid. Reliability is a necessary but not sufficient prerequisite for validity.

## Reliability and Validity Coefficients

The reliability of a test is expressed as a **reliability coefficient**. The statistical symbol for the reliability coefficient is $r$ (which stands for relationship). An $r$ value of +1.00 designates perfect reliability.

For example, $r$ values that range from .70 to .80 indicate that people's test scores are reasonably consistent, but not totally so. As the value of $r$ approaches 0, the less consistent people's test scores are, indicating that the test lacks reliability.

Although content and construct validity are not expressed in numerical form, criterion-validity is expressed as a **validity coefficient**, which is also symbolized by $r$. Conceptually, the validity coefficient is identical to the reliability coefficient. The only difference is that instead of comparing people's scores on two tests, one compares their scores on a test and on the criterion measure. An algebra aptitude test that has a validity coefficient of .80, for example, means that the ranking of students according to their scores on the aptitude test is very similar to their ranking according to the grades they received in an algebra course.

## Standard Error of Measurement

There are no perfect tests or measuring instruments. Numerous sources of error may affect test scores, such as the physical and psychological condition of the test taker, the physical conditions of the test-taking situation, and the reliability of the

**Figure 13.1**

A normal, or bell-shaped, curve.

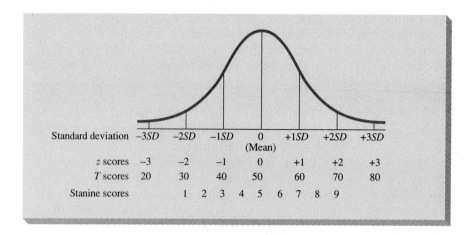

| Standard deviation | −3SD | −2SD | −1SD | 0 (Mean) | +1SD | +2SD | +3SD |
|---|---|---|---|---|---|---|---|
| z scores | −3 | −2 | −1 | 0 | +1 | +2 | +3 |
| T scores | 20 | 30 | 40 | 50 | 60 | 70 | 80 |
| Stanine scores | | 1 2 | 3 | 4 5 6 | 7 | 8 9 | |

When you use test scores to make decisions about a student, remember that no tests are fully reliable and all tests contain some degree of error. A person's score is therefore not "the last word" on that person's performance.

*Annual* **Edition**

unit 6

test. The term **true score** describes the hypothetical score a person would obtain if there were no sources of error. The score a person obtains on a test (the "obtained score") only approximates the person's true score.

How accurately an obtained score reflects a true score depends on a couple of factors, the most important of which in terms of our current discussion, is how reliable the test is. The more reliable a test, the more accurately the test score represents a person's true score.

The reliability coefficient $r$ describes how reliable a test is for a group of people. Often, however, we want to know the reliability of the test score of a single student. The statistical measure used to describe the accuracy of an obtained test score is called the **standard error of measurement**, symbolized as $SE_m$. The $SE_m$ allows test users to estimate a range, called a **confidence interval**, around an obtained score within which the test taker's true score likely falls. For example, if a student's obtained score is 55 and we know the test's $SE_m$ is 4, we create a confidence level by taking 55 and adding and subtracting 4. We conclude that the student's true score probably falls within the confidence interval of 51 and 59.

## Standardized Tests

Many tests produced by commercial test developers are **standardized**, which means that the procedures for administering the test, the materials used in the test, and the way in which the test is scored are held constant. A test manual accompanying the test gives precise instructions concerning how the examiner should administer and score the test. If the examiner follows these instructions, people who take the test at different times and in different places are all exposed to exactly the same conditions (Crowl, 1996).

The Scholastic Assessment Test (SAT) and the National Teachers Examination (NTE) are examples of standardized tests. One of the most important properties of standardized tests is the objectivity of the test scores. Standardized test scores require no subjective interpretation by the person scoring the test. A person's score on a standardized test would be the same no matter when or where the person took the test.

## The Normal Distribution

Before turning to a discussion of the normal distribution, note that the number of test items a student has answered correctly is called the **raw score**. If a student has a raw score of 45, it simply means that the student answered 45 items correctly.

The distribution of raw scores obtained by persons taking a standardized test often forms a **normal distribution**, which is sometimes called a normal, or a bell-shaped, curve. When scores are distributed normally, it simply means that few people score extremely well or extremely poorly on the test, and most score in the middle (see figure 13.1). Most phenomena that we wish to measure in education (i.e., IQ, reading achievement, mathematics ability) are normally distributed.

## Averages and Variability

There are three ways to express the average of a distribution of scores: the median, the mode, and the mean. The **median** is the score that would fall in the middle if you ranked all the scores from highest to lowest. Thus, half of all of the scores in the distribution fall above the median, and half fall below. The **mode** is the score that occurs most frequently. The **mean** is determined by adding all the students' scores and dividing the sum by the number of students.

The mean is what teachers usually have in mind when they speak of an average score. When a teacher says that the average score on a spelling test was 78, the teacher has simply added the spelling test scores of all students in the class and divided the total by the number of students.

The mean is the most frequently used average in educational measurement. It should also be noted that when scores are distributed normally, the mean, the median, and the mode are exactly the same. You can easily see that the score falling directly under the top of the curve in figure 13.1 is the mode. The highest point on the curve indicates the score most students have obtained.

It is also easy to see that the same score is the median, because half of the scores lie above and half lie below that score. It is also true, although not intuitively obvious from figure 13.1, that the score representing the median and the mode is also the mean.

### The Standard Deviation *(SD)*

Just as there are various ways of expressing the average score in a distribution, there are various ways of expressing how much variability a distribution of scores exhibits. Look at the two lists of scores below. Note that they both have a mean of 30.

> Group A: 28, 29, 30, 31, 32
> Group B: 10, 20, 30, 40, 50

Although they have the same mean, the two groups differ markedly. The scores in group A cluster close to the mean, but the scores in Group B do not. The scores in Group A exhibit less **variability** than those in Group B.

*Put differently, variability pertains to the extent to which a group is* homogeneous *or* heterogeneous.

The most common measure of variability is the **standard deviation**, symbolized as *SD*. The *SD* represents approximately how much, on the average, each score differs from the group's mean. The larger the *SD*, the more widely spread the scores are. Conversely, the smaller the *SD*, the more closely people's scores hover about the mean. In the previous example, Group A's *SD* is smaller than group B's.

## Properties of the Normal Curve

Students' scores can be graphed so that the horizontal axis represents the different scores and the vertical axis represents the number of scores at each point. This is called a **frequency distribution**. When the mean, median, and mode are equal, the frequency distribution is referred to as a **normal curve**.

There are hypothetically an infinite number of possible normal curves. Each curve is uniquely defined by its mean and *SD*. *All* normal curves, however, share certain known mathematical properties. One of the most important properties is that the percentage of people falling within different ranges of scores is always the same. When the distribution of scores is divided into parts based on the *SD* of the scores, there is a fixed percentage of scores falling into each of the areas under the curve.

Figure 13.2 shows that 68 percent of people's scores fall within a range defined by the mean plus and minus one *SD*. Thus, we can say that most people's scores fall within one *SD* of the mean. The vast majority, 95 percent, fall within a range defined by the mean plus and minus two *SD*s, and virtually 100 percent fall within a range defined by the mean plus and minus three *SD*s.

**Figure 13.2**

Areas under the normal curve as a function of the ranges defined by the mean and standard deviation units.

| Percent of area under the normal curve | Range |
|---|---|
| 68% | Mean $\pm 1$ $SD$ |
| 95% | Mean $\pm 2$ $SD$s |
| 100% | Mean $\pm 3$ $SD$s |

Suppose 1,000 fourth-graders are given a mathematics test. The mean of that group turns out to be 75, the standard deviation is 4, and the scores are normally distributed. We can conclude that 68 percent of the scores fall between 71 and 79 (75 plus or minus 4), 95 percent fall between 67 and 83 (75 plus or minus 8), and approximately 100 percent fall between 63 and 87 (75 plus or minus 12).

## Standard Scores

**13.4** ◎

*Describe standard scores and percentiles.*

Knowing that a student got 45 problems right on a math test tells us nothing about that student's performance relative to his or her peers. **Standard scores** allow us to interpret a score relative to the scores of others.

### z-Scores

Standard scores also allow you to compare one student's abilities across different tests.

One of the easiest standard scores to conceptualize is the **z-score**. The formula for computing z-scores is

$$z\text{-score} = (\text{raw score} - \text{mean})/SD$$

To convert a student's raw score into a z-score, subtract the mean from the student's score and divide the result by the value of the $SD$; z-scores always have a mean of 0 and an $SD$ of 1. Also, z-scores tell us how many standard deviations a person's score is from the mean. A z-score of 1.5, for example, means that the person's score is one and a half $SD$s above the mean; a z-score of –2.0 means that the person's score is two $SD$s below the mean.

Suppose a test yielded a normally distributed set of scores with a mean of 75 and an $SD$ of 5. A student who obtained a raw score of 80 on the test would have a z-score of +1.00 (i.e., $(80 - 75)/5 = +1.00$). A student who obtained a raw score of 70 would have a z-score of –1.00 (i.e., $(70 - 75)/5 = -1.00$).

If a student has a z-score of +1.00 on a test that has a mean of 46 and an $SD$ of 2, the student has a raw score of 48; if a student has a z-score of +1.00 on a test that has a mean of 70 and an $SD$ of 10, the student has a raw score of 80.

### The Function of Standard Scores

If a student receives a raw score of 76 on a math test and a raw score of 76 on a spelling test, it might appear that the student performs equally well in math and spelling. Such a conclusion is erroneous, however, since comparing raw scores on two different tests is analogous to comparing apples and oranges. Suppose we learn that the mean score on the math test was 80 and the mean score on the spelling test was 70. The student has scored below average on the math test but above average on the spelling test. Consequently, it would be more reasonable to conclude that the student performs better in spelling than in math.

Suppose a student has a raw score of 76 on both a math and a spelling test, and the average score on both tests is 70. The student has performed above average in both math and spelling. It would nevertheless still be wrong to conclude that the student performs equally well in math and spelling. Suppose, for example, the math test has an $SD$ of 6 and the spelling test has an $SD$ of 3. Given this information, we know the student has a z-score of +1.00 on the math test (i.e., $(76 - 70)/6 = +1.00$) and a z-score of +2.00 on the spelling test (i.e., $(76 - 70)/3 = +2.00$).

In other words, the student scored one *SD* above the mean in math and two *SD*s above the mean in spelling. Therefore, it is reasonable to conclude that the student performs better in spelling than in math. Converting test scores into standard scores permits us to compare students' performance on two different tests.

All standard scores convey the same information: how many standard deviations a raw score is from the mean. They simply use a different scale to accomplish this, much as length can be measured in inches, centimeters, miles, and so forth.

## Other Standard Scores

Many other standard scores are used in testing, some of which are specific to a particular test. SAT, GRE, and NTE scores are simply standard scores designed for those specific tests. Other standard scores are more generally applicable, and two of them are described below.

### *T*-Score

A *T*-score is like a *z*-score, but it avoids negative numbers and decimals. The formula for *T* is $T = 10z + 50$. So, it is easy to convert from *z*-score to *T*-score. A *z*-score of 0 is equivalent to a *T*-score of 50; a *z*-score of 1 is equivalent to a *T*-score of 60. The mean of *T*-scores is always 50 and the *SD* is always 10.

### Normal Curve Equivalent (NCE) Scores

**Normal curve equivalent (NCE) scores** are similar to *z*-scores in that both represent standardized scores and permit us to compare students' performance on different tests. The major difference is that *z*-scores have a mean of 0 and range from plus to minus 3, whereas NCE scores have a mean of 50 and range from 0 to 100. Having possible scores range from 0 to 100 has more intuitive appeal and, like the *T*-score, eliminates the use of negative values and decimals associated with *z*-scores.

Many school districts report test results to parents and teachers as NCE scores because of the appeal of the 0 to 100 scale. However, these scores can be easily misunderstood.

# Norm-Referenced and Criterion-Referenced Tests

Broadly speaking, academic achievement tests fall into two categories: norm-referenced and criterion-referenced.

**13.5**

*Identify the characteristics of norm-referenced and criterion-referenced tests.*

## Norm-Referenced Tests

**Norm-referenced tests (NRTs)** measure how well a student performs in comparison with others. In developing a norm-referenced test, test developers initially administer the test to a representative sample of students for whom the test has been designed. This sample is often called the **norming sample,** and the performance of this sample serves as the benchmark against which the performance of test takers in the future is compared. The test developer administers the test to the sample and determines the mean and standard deviation. Teachers later use this information to evaluate the scores of their students.

The members of the norming sample should be representative of the population of students in general because future students will be compared with them. Most test manuals give detailed information about the selection and demographic characteristics of the norming sample.

It is important to pay attention to the characteristics of the norming sample because, if the norming sample did not include the kinds of students you are testing, the test scores obtained may not be valid. For example, if a test was normed in the Northwest states, the norms may have little meaning when the test is administered to students in the Southeast. Or, if a test was normed on a sample of students who live in cities, it may not accurately measure characteristics of students living in rural settings. Most test developers select their sample with the intention of making it representative, and they often present a comparison of the sample with recent U.S. Census figures to demonstrate the representativeness of the sample.

**Figure 13.3**

A comparison of selected normal curve equivalent (NCE) scores, percentiles, and z-scores.

| NCE | Percentile | z-score |
|---|---|---|
| 99 | 99th | +2.33 |
| 90 | 97th | +1.90 |
| 80 | 92nd | +1.43 |
| 70 | 83rd | +0.95 |
| 60 | 68th | +0.48 |
| 50 | 50th | 0.00 |
| 40 | 32nd | −0.48 |
| 30 | 17th | −0.95 |
| 20 | 8th | −1.43 |
| 10 | 3rd | −1.90 |
| 1 | 1st | −2.33 |

## Percentiles

Norm-referenced test scores are reported in terms of how well each student has performed in comparison with students in the norming sample. Students' scores on a norm-referenced test are often reported as **percentiles**. A student scoring at the 90th percentile, for example, has performed better than 90 percent of students in the norming sample. Similarly, a student scoring at the 38th percentile has scored better than 38 percent of students in the norming sample. Figure 13.3 shows the relationship among percentiles, z-scores, and NCE scores.

It is important to distinguish between percentiles and percentages. When we say a student scored 80 percent on a test, we mean that the student answered 80 percent of the *test items* correctly. When we say a student scored at the 80th percentile, we mean the student scored higher than 80 percent of *the norming sample who took the test*.

Suppose a student has a raw score of 45 on a test. If the total number of items on the test is 50, a raw score of 45 indicates that the student has answered 90 percent of the items correctly; if the total number of items is 75, a raw score of 45 indicates that the student has answered 60 percent of the items correctly. The total number of items on a test plays no role in calculating percentiles. To convert a student's raw score into a percentile, it is only necessary to know what percentage of the norming group scored lower than that student.

There is no systematic relationship between percentiles and percentages. A student, for example, who scores at the 75th percentile may have answered far less than 75 percent of the test items correctly if the test is a difficult one or far more than 75 percent if the test is an easy one. Saying that a student scored at the 75th percentile tells us only that the student performed better than 75 percent of students in the norming group; it says nothing about the percentage of items the student answered correctly.

Percentiles are *ranks* rather than real "numbers" and, therefore, you should not perform mathematical operations on them, such as finding a mean.

## Grade Equivalent Scores

Students' raw scores on many norm-referenced tests are frequently converted to **grade equivalent scores**. A grade equivalent score is determined by the average raw score achieved by students at a particular grade level. For example, if the average raw score of students in the second month of the fourth grade is 71, any student who achieves a raw score of 71 receives a grade equivalent score of 4.2, which stands for second month of the fourth grade. A grade equivalent score of 5.3 is equal to the average raw score achieved by students in the third month of the fifth grade, and so forth. The higher the student's raw score, the higher the student's grade equivalent score.

Grade equivalent scores can be extremely misleading. Suppose a seventh-grade student receives a grade equivalent score of 9.2 on a math test. This score means that the student achieved a raw score equal to the average raw score achieved by students in the second month of the ninth grade. It does *not* mean that the student has mastered ninth-grade material. The average student in the second month of the ninth grade answered the same number of items correctly as the seventh-grade student, but the kinds of items answered correctly may be quite different.

The seventh-grader may have answered many easy items correctly but have incorrectly answered items requiring a knowledge of ninth-grade algebra. On the other hand, the ninth-grader may have incorrectly answered some of the easy items but correctly answered some of the algebra items. In both cases the total number of items answered correctly is identical, but it would be incorrect to conclude that the seventh-grader could perform satisfactorily in a ninth-grade algebra class. Most educators agree that instead of using grade equivalent scores, you should use percentiles or *z*-scores.

Despite the problems associated with grade equivalent scores, many test authors and school districts persist in using them.

## Criterion-Referenced Tests

**Criterion-referenced tests (CRTs)** measure which instructional objectives students have mastered. Consequently, CRTs are far more useful than NRTs for making decisions about instruction; NRTs are more useful for issues such as diagnosis of special needs or giftedness. The tests you develop in your own classroom will be CRTs.

# The Role of Evaluation in Classroom Instruction

Evaluation has many uses in classroom instruction. The four most common forms of evaluation teachers use to improve classroom instruction are placement evaluation, formative evaluation, diagnostic evaluation, and summative evaluation (Airasian & Madaus, 1972).

**13.6** ◎
*Explain the purposes of evaluation.*

## Placement Evaluation

The aim of **placement evaluation** is to find out how much students know about a subject before instruction, so you will have a better idea of where to begin and what kind of instructional techniques to use. Some typical questions that arise during placement evaluation are:

- Do students have the necessary prerequisite knowledge and skills on which to build further instruction?
- To what extent have students already mastered the objectives planned for the instructional unit?
- To what extent do students' interests and personalities point to the use of one instructional technique or another?

You can answer these questions by administering various kinds of tests, such as readiness tests, aptitude tests, pretests on course objectives, and self-report inventories. Also, make judgments about how and what to teach on the basis of observing students in the classroom.

Students who lack prerequisite skills, for example, may need individualized instruction or remedial instruction. On the other hand, students who have already mastered some of the instructional objectives may profit from independent study of topics that will enrich their understanding.

Psychological testing is often part of the diagnostic evaluation process.

## Formative Evaluation

The aim of **formative evaluation** is to give you ongoing feedback during instruction so that you and your students can identify what they have and have not mastered. The major goal of formative evaluation is to provide you guidelines for modifying instruction. On the basis of the information you gather, you may decide to spend more time on a particular topic or to give certain students more help with certain topics.

The results of formative evaluation tests are strictly to provide you and your students with feedback concerning their academic progress. Do *not* use the results of such tests as the basis for assigning grades. Teachers usually make up their own tests to carry out formative evaluations. Later in this chapter you will learn more about how to construct your own tests.

## Diagnostic Evaluation

Teachers usually use **diagnostic evaluation** only if the results of formative evaluation do not remedy students' problems. Diagnostic evaluation is more detailed and comprehensive than formative evaluation and frequently requires the services of specialized personnel, such as a school psychologist. The aim of diagnostic evaluation is to devise a plan for remediating serious learning problems. Special education placement often results from the use of diagnostic evaluation.

## Summative Evaluation

**Summative evaluation** occurs at the end of an instructional unit to determine how well students have mastered instructional objectives. Summative evaluation may take the form of teacher-constructed achievement tests and teachers' evaluations of student performance. The functions of summative evaluation are to assign students' grades and to evaluate the effectiveness of instruction.

# Commercially Available Tests

You undoubtedly know that publishers publish books to make money. You may not know that publishers publish tests for the same reason. Just as the quality of published books ranges from superior to poor, so does the quality of commercially available tests. Teachers sometimes mistakenly believe that any test that is published must be good. The fact that a test publisher has published a test, however, says nothing about the quality of the test.

There are two ways you can evaluate the quality of a commercially produced test. First, any good commercially available test is accompanied by a technical manual. The manual not only describes how to administer and score the test but also should contain information about the test's reliability and validity and a description of the norming sample.

The manual should list reliability coefficients either for the entire test or for various sections of the test and explain how each reliability coefficient was calculated. The manual should also describe the test's validity and the procedures used to determine validity. If the test has been validated by means of criterion-referenced validity, the validity coefficient should also be listed. If the manual does *not* contain information about reliability and validity, you probably shouldn't use the test.

Secondly, two reference books contain information about commercially available tests. *Tests in Print III* (Mitchell, 1983) lists the name of every test currently in print, along with the name and address of the publisher. It also contains a topic index listing all commercially available tests dealing with a particular topic.

Another reference is a series of books that have been revised periodically over the years, beginning in 1938. These books, called the *Mental Measurements Yearbooks* (Conoley & Kramer, 1989), contain information about various tests, such as the publisher's name and address, the cost of the test, validity and reliability information, a description of test booklets and items, and the kinds of people for whom the test is appropriate. Most importantly, each test is critically evaluated by experts in the field. These evaluations point out the strengths and weaknesses of a test and are more objective than information provided by the test publisher.

Consult these reference works before using a test because they may indicate problems with the test that may not be immediately apparent.

*Annual* **Edition**

unit 6

# Constructing Your Own Tests

It is best to construct your own test to measure the results of classroom instruction on a unit. You can focus precisely on the kinds of knowledge and skills you want students to have obtained as a result of the instructional unit. Constructing good tests takes time, but the payoff is enormous. Once you have constructed and administered a good test, you can further refine and use it for subsequent groups of students. Furthermore, good tests help students learn more and help teachers teach more effectively by pinpointing areas of instruction that need more attention.

**13.7** ◎

*Construct a classroom achievement test.*

## Planning: The First Step in Test Construction

Before beginning to construct a test, have clearly in mind what purposes the test is to serve. You will be constructing academic achievement tests. Academic achievement tests can help you learn (a) how well students have mastered what you have taught, and (b) how effective your instruction has been. Unless you have a clear set of instructional goals, it will be impossible to construct a good test.

Setting instructional goals and developing tests to measure how well students have achieved them are part of the same process. It is easiest to construct tests if you think about how you are going to determine how well students have learned at the same time you are devising instructional objectives. It is important, however, that your instructional goals dictate what kind of test you need to construct, not the other way around.

There are three important initial steps in planning a high-quality test:

1. Specify the content the test will cover.
2. State test objectives in behavioral terms.

Before their admission to any canine university,
dogs must first do well on the CATs.

3. Make sure that test items cover all six cognitive levels outlined in Bloom's (1956) taxonomy of educational objectives.

The best way to specify the content of the test is to apply the principles of content validity described earlier in this chapter.

Carry out steps 2 and 3 simultaneously by using action verbs to describe observable behaviors that reflect each level of cognition. You may combine all three steps to develop a test blueprint. Action verbs appear either in the description of the objective or the description of the content.

## Kinds of Teacher-Made Tests

Teacher-made tests consist of items falling into two broad categories: subjective and objective. Subjective items, such as essays and short-answer items, require students to construct their own responses. The scores you assign to students' responses rely to some extent on your subjective judgment. Multiple-choice, true-false, and matching items are objective because the scores you assign to students' responses require no subjective interpretation. Students do not have to construct responses to objective items but instead select responses from a list provided on the test.

Completion items fall at the border between subjective and objective items. Students must construct their own responses, but usually you do not have to rely on subjective interpretation to decide whether a response is correct.

### Essays and Short-Answer Items

One obvious difference between essays and short-answer items is the length of the expected response. Essays are particularly useful in evaluating students' higher-order thinking skills, but only if the essay question is phrased in a way that calls for higher-order thinking. The biggest problem in using essays is difficulty in scoring student responses reliably. Short-answer items are more narrowly focused than

The subjectivity inherent in scoring essays and short answers makes them less reliable than other test forms.

## Developing a System for Scoring Students' Essays

You can take several steps to improve the reliability of the scores you assign to students' essays (Goetz, Alexander, & Ash, 1992; Thorndike et al., 1991):

1. Grade essays holistically. Assign a grade in terms of your overall evaluation of how well the essay answers the question.
2. Before you begin to score essay responses, make sure you have a clear idea of what constitutes a correct response.
3. Conceal the name of the student whose essay you are grading so that the quality of the answer, not your impression of the student, will determine the score you assign.
4. If a test consists of more than one essay question, grade the responses of all students to the same essay question before moving on to the next question.

Do not grade the same student's responses to all essay questions before moving on to the next student's paper.

5. Before scoring any student's response to an essay question, read all of the students' answers. The procedure allows you to establish a set of anchor points that reflect the best and poorest answers in the group of essays to be scored.
6. Initially assign a tentative score to the essay. After assigning tentative scores to all responses to the essay question, reread each response and make any necessary adjustments to the scores initially assigned. If possible, have a colleague also score students' responses.
7. Put comments on students' papers that both justify the grade you have assigned and convince students that you have really read what they have written.

essay questions; consequently, they are not particularly well suited for evaluating higher-order thinking skills. On the other hand, because of their comparative brevity, the responses to short-answer items are more amenable to reliable scoring than essays are.

## Multiple-Choice Items

Multiple-choice items are one of the most frequently used (and misused) forms of test questions. These items consist of a stem, either in the form of a question or an incomplete statement, followed by a list of four or five possible responses, or **distractors,** only one of which is correct. It is possible to construct multiple-choice items to evaluate higher-order thinking skills, although the development of such items requires careful thought.

Teachers frequently misuse the multiple-choice test format by creating items that test only memorization and comprehension. Creating items that test lower-level thinking skills does not demand much time and effort, but such items typically result in trivial questions. The frequent use of such questions may cause some students to regard multiple-choice tests as measuring irrelevant material.

Another major misuse of multiple-choice items occurs when teachers do not consider the nature of the possible responses they construct. The nature of the distractors determines to a large extent the quality of the item. Each distractor should be plausible. Distractors that are "cute" but obviously wrong only contribute to the impression that multiple-choice items are silly. For example, it would be inappropriate to include among the distractors for an item dealing with the definition of the Piagetian concept of conservation the following: "a policy employed to curb the depletion of natural resources."

One of the most useful characteristics of multiple-choice items is the possibility of refining the questions for use on future tests by analyzing students' performance on previous tests. You can thus gradually accumulate a bank of refined multiple-choice items.

## Writing Good Multiple-Choice Items

You can take the following steps to improve the quality of your multiple-choice items (Thorndike et al., 1991):

1. Put as much of the item in the stem as possible and keep the wording of responses minimal.
2. Make sure that the stem contains a clear statement of a single problem. A common error in constructing multiple-choice items is to embed the statement of several different problems in the responses. Students should be able to identify the problem after reading the stem; they should not have to read each response option to determine what problems are being posed.

Below is an example of a *poorly* constructed item:

The field of educational psychology:
a. deals mainly with issues concerning human learning.
b. uses theoretical constructs stemming from developments in computer technology.
c. has little value to students who are not education majors.
d. developed as a result of Darwin's theory of evolution.

Below is an example of a *better* item:

The field of educational psychology deals mainly with:
a. human learning.
b. descriptive statistics.
c. theories of human intelligence.
d. mainstreaming students with disabilities.

3. Use only plausible distractors.

4. Make sure only one response is correct.
5. Avoid using "none of the above" and "all of the above" as responses. One way to circumvent the response of "all of the above" is to use combinations of responses as in the following example:

Which of the following are Japan's leading exports to the United States?
a. cars only
b. computer microchips only
c. cameras and cars only
d. computer microchips and cars only
e. computer microchips, cameras, and cars

6. Avoid the use of the word *not* in stems, such as "Which of the following is NOT an example of a standardized test score?"
7. Make sure that distractors contain approximately the same number of words as the correct response contains. Teachers tend to make correct responses longer than the distractors.
8. Avoid grammatical clues that make the correct response readily apparent, as in this example:

Public Law 94-142 mandates that every special student have an
a. Individualized Educational Plan (IEP).
b. resource room teacher.
c. rest period twice a day.
d. conference with a school psychologist at least once during each academic year.

9. Make sure that all items have the same number of possible responses.

## True-False Items

Most experts in measurement (e.g., Thorndike et al., 1991) discourage the use of true-false items, which are basically multiple-choice items with two responses. It is better to convert true-false items into conventional multiple-choice items with four or five responses (Goetz, Alexander, & Ash, 1992).

Students are likely to choose the correct response to a true-false item 50 percent of the time simply on the basis of chance (that is, by guessing). Furthermore, except for trivial statements, it is difficult to construct statements that are unequivocally true or false.

 If, however, you wish to use true-false items, you should follow these guidelines (Thorndike et al., 1991):

1. Make sure that each statement is unequivocally true or false.
2. Avoid the use of terms such as *always, never, all,* and *none.*
3. Avoid using the word *not.*
4. Restrict statements to a single idea.
5. Make the number of true statements equal to the number of false statements.
6. Keep the length of true and false statements comparable.

## Developing Good Matching Items

Matching items can be thought of as a variation on the multiple-choice test format. Many of the suggestions for improving multiple-choice items also apply to constructing matching items (Thorndike et al., 1991):

1. Make sure all of the terms or statements cover a relatively specific topic. If you wish to cover more than one topic, construct a separate set of matching items for each.
2. Do not construct a test consisting of more than 12 matching items (Goetz, Alexander, & Ash, 1992). Including too many items distracts students from focusing on the content of the items because of the necessity to keep track of which options have and have not been selected.

3. If the columns consist of statements of differing length, have students select options from the column with the shorter statements to match against the longer ones.
4. Label each column with a heading. If columns are not amenable to labeling, they probably contain statements focusing on too many different kinds of information.
5. Either have more options in the column from which selections are to be made than in the other column or permit the same option to be used more than once.
6. Specify in the directions the basis on which the options are to be matched and indicate whether options may be used more than once.

## Matching Items

Matching items consist of two columns of terms or statements. Students must select for each item in column A an option in column B that is related to that item. Use of matching items is an effective way to measure factual information but not higher-order thinking skills.

## Completion Items

Completion, or fill-in-the-blank, items contain statements in which a word or phase has been replaced with a blank. Students must fill in the blank with the correct word or phrase. The scoring of students' responses may be unreliable, particularly if the student supplies a word that is synonymous, but not identical to the correct response. It is difficult to use completion items to measure higher-order thinking skills.

# Item Analysis

Well-constructed multiple-choice items that measure students' higher-order thinking skills as well as knowledge and comprehension represent the best kind of testing format for teacher-constructed tests. Teachers can also improve multiple-choice items through repeated use. You can use the process of **item analysis** to improve the quality of any set of objective test items, but its use is especially effective with multiple-choice items.

You can carry out an item analysis in several ways, but the following discussion focuses only on procedures that you can *easily* use. Item analysis can help you refine tests you have already administered into sounder measures of student performance on future administrations.

## Item Difficulty

The first important bit of information revealed by item analysis is called **item difficulty**. You can determine the difficulty of every item on a test simply by determining what percentage of the students who attempted the item answered the item correctly. Suppose you administered a test to 28 students; if 14 students answered the item correctly, the item has a difficulty level of .50 (i.e., 14 divided by 28 = .50). If

21 students answered the item correctly, the item has a difficulty level of .75 (i.e., 21 divided by 28 = .75). Note that the higher the item difficulty level, the *easier* the item is. An item difficulty level of .90 indicates that 90 percent of the students answered the item correctly; an item difficulty of .10 indicates that only 10 percent of the students answered the item correctly.

One factor you want to consider when refining a test you have already administered is the overall difficulty of the test. How difficult was the test? To determine the overall difficulty of a previously administered test, you only need to figure out the difficulty level of each item and then calculate the average difficulty level for all items. In other words, if a test has 25 items, first determine the difficulty level for each item. By adding the 25 difficulty levels and dividing the sum by 25, you can determine the overall difficulty level of the entire test.

The next question is how difficult do you want the refined version of the test to be? The answer to this question depends on what kind of test you are designing. If the test is criterion-referenced, an acceptable difficulty level might be quite high. The purpose of a criterion-referenced test is to determine if students have mastered a specified body of subject matter. Theoretically, the best possible outcome of a criterion-referenced test would be for all students to achieve a perfect score; that is, the difficulty level of the test would be 1.00.

On the other hand, if you are constructing an achievement test to identify which students are best, which are average, and which are below average, it is necessary to include items that will not be answered correctly by all students. Some measurement experts suggest that the appropriate level of difficulty of a test should be approximately halfway between a perfect score and the score expected on the basis of chance (Thorndike et al., 1991). For example, if the items on a multiple-choice test have five possible responses, we would expect on the basis of chance that students would answer 20 percent of the items correctly simply by guessing (i.e., 1 divided by 5 = .20). The halfway point between 20 percent and 100 percent is 60 percent. Therefore, the appropriate test difficulty level would be approximately .60.

## Discrimination Index

In revising items for use on future tests, identify items that are good, those that need modification, and those that should be eliminated. You may think of a good item as one that measures what the test as a whole measures. In other words, an item is good to the extent that students who score well on the whole test answer the item correctly and students who do poorly on the whole test answer the item incorrectly. Correspondingly, an item is poor to the extent that students who score well on the whole test answer the item *incorrectly* or students who score poorly on the whole test answer the item correctly.

You can determine how good an item is by comparing the responses selected by students whose overall test scores are high with those selected by students whose overall test scores are low. First, rank students according to their overall test scores. Select the top and bottom 25 percent and compare their responses to each item. An item is good if most of the top 25 percent have answered it correctly and most of the bottom 25 percent have answered it incorrectly. Subtract the number of students in the bottom group who answered the item correctly from the number in the top group who answered the item correctly and divide the answer by the number of students in each group; this yields a measure called the **discrimination index**. The higher the discrimination index, the better the item is, which simply means that more of the better than the poorer students answered the item correctly.

## Improving Distractors

Item analysis also permits you to improve the set of response options to an item. Instead of examining each item by comparing how many high- and low-scoring students answered the item correctly, compare the actual response options selected by students in each group. The following example is based on the assumption that 40 students completed the item and the correct answer is response option *c*.

## Doing an Item Analysis

▣▣ Suppose you administer a 50-item multiple-choice test to a group of 40 students. An analysis of item number 1 reveals that all students responded to the item and 30 students answered it correctly. The difficulty level of the item is .75 (30 divided by 40 = .75).

After ranking students by their overall test scores, select the 10 tests with the highest and the 10 tests with the lowest scores (i.e., 25% × 40 = 10). Then ask how many in each group answered the item correctly. Suppose the results are as follows:

|  | Top 10 | Bottom 10 |
|---|---|---|
| Correct response | 9 | 1 |
| Incorrect response | 1 | 9 |

Calculate the discrimination index as follows:

$$(9 - 1)/10 = .80$$

This item is a good item because it effectively discriminates between students in the top and bottom groups.

Suppose, on the other hand, the results turned out to be:

|  | Top 10 | Bottom 10 |
|---|---|---|
| Correct response | 6 | 4 |
| Incorrect response | 4 | 6 |

The discrimination index would be .20 (i.e., (6 − 4)/10). This item is poor because it fails to discriminate between students in the top and bottom groups.

|  | Top 10 | Bottom 10 |
|---|---|---|
| Response a | 1 | 2 |
| Response b | 0 | 0 |
| Response c | 8 | 3 |
| Response d | 1 | 5 |

An inspection of these results indicates that response option *b* is a poor one because no student in either group selected it. Response option *d* is a good one because more students in the bottom than in the top group selected it. Response option *a* is only marginally effective because there is little difference between the number of students in each group who selected it.

# Bias in Testing

As a part of increasing national concern about providing equal opportunities to all, attention has focused on the role that tests play in determining the educational and occupational fate of many ordinary citizens. The well-known fact that students from lower socioeconomic and minority families score lower than white middle-class students on many standardized tests has raised the issue of whether such tests are biased (Gronlund & Linn, 1990). Critics argue that the content of IQ tests, for example, reflects experiences and values found only in the culture of middle-class whites and consequently discriminates unfairly against persons belonging to other cultural groups (Zoref & Williams, 1980).

13.8 ◎

*Name sources of bias in testing.*

## Minimizing Cultural Bias

Efforts to minimize cultural bias in testing have not always been effective. For example, researchers have failed to develop tests consisting of nonverbal items as a way of overcoming biases associated with language differences exhibited in various cultures (Anastasi, 1988). Test developers now typically consult experts from various cultural groups when constructing new tests so that potentially biased items may be detected and eliminated (Gronlund & Linn, 1990).

On the other hand, it should be noted that an item appearing to be culturally biased may not be, and conversely, an item appearing not to be culturally biased may be (Thorndike et al., 1991). Evidence suggests, however, that tests constructed in accordance with sound principles of measurement are not culturally biased against minority students who have been born in the United States (Reynolds, 1982a, 1982b).

No test is "culture-free," but test authors seek to make them "culture-fair."

Note that we discuss "minimizing" cultural bias, rather than "eliminating" it. Elimination of cultural bias is impossible: The moment you ask a question or present a task on a test, you are reflecting the values of a particular culture. The nature of the task and its content are reflections of the culture from which the test emerges. Therefore, the best we can hope for is to minimize the effect of cultural bias to the greatest degree possible.

## Test Bias and the Law

Largely as a result of the Civil Rights Act of 1964, which makes it illegal to use tests to discriminate against people on the basis of race, creed, color, gender, or national origin, the issue of test bias in educational settings has come before the courts and has sometimes resulted in inconsistent court rulings.

A California judge, for example, ruled that the Wechsler Intelligence Scale for Children (WISC) and the Stanford-Binet Intelligence Scale, which had been used as a basis for placing a group of African Americans in a class for students who have mental retardation, were racially biased. As a result, it is now illegal to use these tests for the class placement of minority students in California. In a similar court action in Illinois, however, a judge found the same tests not to be culturally biased. It is difficult to make sense of findings that the same test that is legally biased against African Americans in California is legally unbiased against African Americans in Illinois (Thorndike et al., 1991).

## Bias in Scoring Tests

The discussion of test bias so far has focused on the content of standardized tests as a potential source of bias. Test bias is probably even more likely to occur, however, when teachers must assign scores to nonstandardized tests that require students to write essays or give other kinds of open-ended responses. There is evidence, for example, that scores assigned to students' essays are biased as a result of the quality of

## DIVERSITY MAKES A DIFFERENCE

### Addressing Bias in Tests

The problem of cultural bias in testing has been a frustrating one for educators. The psychologist and sociologist Jane Mercer (1979) analyzed a number of possible solutions and described the difficulties associated with each:

#### Solution: Develop New Tests

1. Develop culture-free tests. (This can't be done.)
2. Develop culture-fair tests, that is, balance items so that they represent multiple cultures. (This is a desirable practice, but the tests will have low predictive value in monocultural schools.)
3. Develop culture-specific tests. (This solution also results in tests with low predictive value. Also, this practice would be expensive, and it would be difficult to define specific cultural groups because groups themselves are heterogeneous.)
4. Use Piagetian tests, that is assessment of performance on tasks such as

conservation, seriation, etc. (Even these tasks are not culture-free, and performance on them would have low predictive validity to school tasks.)

#### Solution: Modify Existing Tests

1. Translate the test. (In a translation, the item difficulty is changed, the precise meaning of the content is altered, and the test must be renormed.)
2. Change administration procedures, for example, by removing time limits. (Under these conditions the norms are no longer applicable.)
3. For achievement tests, use the difference between pre- and posttests to determine the effectiveness of instruction.
4. Use different norms for different groups on existing tests. (This practice would encourage the use of local norms but would be expensive initially. Also, it is difficult to define the cultural group, and some would argue against different "standards" for different groups.)

students' penmanship (Chase, 1968), spelling, punctuation, and grammatical usage (Marshall, 1967), even when examiners are specifically instructed to base their scores only on the content of the answer (Marshall, 1967).

Scoring bias may also occur when students are tested orally. For example, white teachers from the northern part of the United States gave significantly higher scores to tape-recorded oral answers spoken by white ninth-grade boys than answers spoken by African American ninth-grade boys, despite the fact that the answers spoken by the two groups were identical (Crowl & MacGinitie, 1974). Using the same tape-recorded answers, it was found that teachers from the southern part of the United States did exactly the opposite. They assigned higher scores to African American students' answers than they did to white students' answers. African American students' answers received higher scores from white as well as from African American teachers in the south (Crowl & Nurss, 1976).

# Performance-Based Assessment

As dismay with the poor quality of education has become a central national concern, legislators in many states have called for increasing the accountability of schools. Frequently, the call for accountability has led to statewide testing programs, which often use a multiple-choice testing format. Statewide testing programs frequently create a high-stakes situation because the public tends to use students' performance on such tests to judge the quality of the schools students attend.

Ranking schools according to students' test performance has pressured many educators to try to increase students' test performance, often by "teaching to the test" (O'Neil, 1992). As a result, statewide tests often influence what teachers teach and how they teach. Under such circumstances, test performance no longer represents a sample of students' performance; test performance represents the only performance that counts. This case of the "tail wagging the dog" raises a crucial question: Should the curriculum determine the test, or should the test determine the curriculum?

The criticism that multiple-choice tests too frequently measure only lower-order thinking skills has prompted the call for different ways of testing so that higher-order thinking skills can be measured. As a result, numerous test developers are now focusing on models of **performance-based assessment** or **authentic assessment.**

Performance-based assessment may take the form of writing an essay, conducting a group scientific experiment, or conversing in a foreign language with a foreign language teacher. Many educators incorrectly use the terms *performance-based assessment* and *authentic assessment* interchangeably. Both types of assessment require students to demonstrate the behavior that is to be measured. "For example, if the behavior to be measured is writing, the student writes. The student does not complete multiple-choice questions about sentences and paragraphs" (Meyer, 1992, p. 40). In authentic assessment, however, the behavior to be measured must occur in a real-life context.

A student's essay on the differences between North American and British forms of government is an example of performance-based assessment. A letter written by a student applying for a job is an example of authentic assessment.

## Portfolio Assessment

Performance-based assessment is often combined with the use of student **portfolios.** During the school year, students collect a portfolio of the various works they have produced. Periodically, the teacher and student review the contents of the portfolio together.

Teachers who use portfolio assessment in their classrooms attempt to balance their assessment of students' performance on standardized tests with perceptions of their students' developing abilities (Willis, 1992). In addition, they involve their students in the evaluation process; students select their best work for their portfolios. Assessment should reflect both the curriculum and the individual

**13.9** ◎
*Describe the procedures used in performance-based and authentic assessment.*

*Annual* **Edition**

unit 6

If you created a portfolio of your work in this course for the purpose of assessment, what might you include? What might be in your portfolio in a student teaching course?

*Annual* **Edition**

unit 6

An S.A.T. sample question is used to test students' sense of logic.

student. Students help determine the quality of the work to be done and the teacher provides models. The teacher assures that the student can carry out the assignment by providing the resources necessary to produce high-level work. All portfolios need not contain *only* good work. Students may also select earlier drafts and revised drafts of work and contrast their least polished work with their best efforts. Teachers may wish to analyze students' work over time by observing improvement in student performance rather than final products. According to Wolf, LeMahiew, and Eresh (1992), until now we have relied on tests that are accountable to others, and have neglected the importance of internal accountability that inspires teachers and students to look at what is worth knowing and achieving. These writers recommend that students and teachers periodically review work and select *typical* work to provide an honest basis for assessment. Over the long run, teachers and students can reflect on what is "worth documenting" (p. 11), and students can compare their typical and best work. At the end of a semester, students create a large portfolio, using it as a basis for conferences with their teacher or counselor. This final phase in portfolio assessment allows students to provide the best evidence of their progress. While portfolios may be used for reporting to parents, they are often used *in addition* to report cards to provide a broader evaluation of a student's achievement.

Wolf, LeMahiew, and Eresh (1992) describe some fundamental problems with portfolio assessment. For example, when test scores and portfolio assessments conflict, it often is not clear which assessment carries more weight. Similarly, they report that parents are concerned that portfolio work does not prepare their children for the real world, and that colleges will disregard portfolios when admitting students. In addition, the authors claim that measurement concerns have not been fully addressed, as Shavelson and Baxter (1992) have noted specifically in the area of science assessment. O'Neil (1992), while acknowledging the cost and time involved in portfolio assessment, suggests that performance tests, in general, have greater assessment power and often influence the appropriateness of instruction. For example, when some school districts have turned from multiple-choice tests to performance tests (as California did in writing assessment), teachers tended to assign more and different kinds of writing tasks and improve their students' writing efforts through analysis and practice (Herman, 1992; O'Neil, 1992).

As one form of performance assessment, the portfolio appears to be successful in writing instruction where drafts and early writing attempts can be evaluated over time and where reluctant writers are motivated to write (Frazier & Paulson, 1992). Similarly, there is evidence of increased learning in mathematics and reading in classrooms where portfolios have been used (Hetterscheidt et al., 1992; Knight, 1992). It appears, therefore, that the value of portfolios may lie as much in their instructional value as in their assessment value. When teachers spend less time "teaching to the test" and more time helping students prepare and evaluate their work, instruction is enhanced.

Assessment issues, however, still remain. Good assessment, according to Herman (1992), is "built on current theories of learning and cognition and grounded in views of what skills and capacities students will need for future success" (p. 75). While multiple-choice tests may test only *portions* of what students know and may, in some cases, interfere with students' ability to demonstrate what they know, these items can be tested for validity and reliability. Newer forms of assessment, such as portfolios, are in the design and prototyping stage (Herman, 1992), and we do not yet know about their reliability and validity.

> How could you enhance the reliability and validity of portfolio assessment?

## The Future of Performance-Based Assessment

Performance-based assessment is in its infancy, and it is difficult to predict what place it will ultimately hold in the evolution of educational assessment. According to Roy Hardy, who heads the Educational Testing Service office in Atlanta, "In many states, the question is no longer *if*, but *when* and *how* performance-based testing will be added to their programs" (Educational Testing Service, 1992, p. 4). John Frederiksen, a cognitive scientist at the Educational Testing Service, cautions, however, that "unless these new high-stakes [performance-based] tests can be made accountable, they may be an impediment to school reform rather than a tool for curricular change" (Educational Testing Service, 1992, p. 5).

Among the potential problems associated with performance-based assessment is the fact that in general they are costly, require an excessive amount of time to administer, and may not have psychometric properties that compare favorably to those of multiple-choice tests (O'Neil, 1992). Shavelson and Baxter (1992), for example, found that performance assessment in science requires an enormous undertaking to develop high quality assessments. They believe that short-circuiting this process will lead to poor quality assessments, which will lead to poor teaching.

The outcome of their work in science assessment, however, has yielded encouraging results. Raters, for example, were able to reliably rate students' hands-on performance, and such assessments were able to distinguish students who had different instructional experiences. In addition, they discovered that performance-based assessment did not duplicate information provided by multiple-choice tests. Performance assessment, therefore, can give a more complete picture of students' abilities and demonstrate their accomplishments over time.

## KEY POINTS

1. Measurement refers to the expression of a concept in numerical terms; assessment refers to the interpretation of one or more measurements; and evaluation refers to value judgments.

2. Measurement devices should have reliability, or consistency, which can be measured using the test-retest method, the equivalent forms method, or the split-half method.

3. Validity refers to the extent to which test scores permit one to draw appropriate, meaningful, and useful inferences. The different types of validity include content validity, criterion-related validity, and construct validity.

4. Standardized tests are those in which administration and scoring procedures are held constant.

5. Students' test scores often fall on the normal (or bell-shaped) curve. On

this curve, the mean, the median, and the mode are equal.

6. Standard scores, such as *z*-scores, *T*-scores, or NCE scores, allow a comparison of a student's test scores in different subjects.

7. Norm-referenced tests compare a student's performance to that of others; criterion-referenced tests determine a student's mastery of specific skills.

8. Percentiles indicate the percentage of people in the norming sample scoring below a specific score.

9. Student evaluation may be in the form of placement evaluation, formative evaluation, summative evaluation, or diagnostic evaluation.

10. When constructing their own tests, teachers should carefully plan the content and format of the test. The various types of items (essay, short-answer, true/false, multiple-choice, matching) have pros and cons, and teachers can take specific steps to maximize and measure their effectiveness.

11. All tests contain a degree of cultural bias, but it is important to minimize the impact of cultural bias in tests.

12. Performance-based assessment refers to assessment in which students' performance on an actual task (such as carrying out a scientific experiment) is assessed; authentic assessment refers to the use of tasks that occur in real-life settings.

13. Portfolio assessment refers to the use of collections of students' work to assess their performance. Portfolios may contain the best work, typical work, or work that has been revised and improved.

## SELF-STUDY EXERCISES

1. Explain the relationship and the distinctions among the terms *measurement, assessment,* and *evaluation.*

2. Define *reliability* and *validity.* How can a test developer demonstrate a test's reliability? How can a test be valid for one purpose and not another? What is the relationship between reliability and validity?

3. When is construct validity useful? Why is concurrent validity used more than predictive validity? When teachers make up their own tests, how can they apply the principles of content validity?

4. Describe the properties of normal distributions.

5. What does the standard deviation of a distribution of scores describe? Why is it important?

6. Explain the usefulness of standard scores.

7. Describe the differences between norm-referenced and criterion-referenced tests.

8. How can teachers determine the quality of a commercially made test? Name at least two sources of information about tests.

9. What are the differences between subjective and objective tests?

10. How can bias affect test results in different student populations? How can teachers avoid scoring bias?

11. What are the advantages in using performance-based and portfolio assessment? What are the drawbacks?

## FURTHER READINGS

Gronlund, N. E., & Linn, R. L. (1990). *Measurement and evaluation in teaching* (6th ed.). New York: Macmillan.

Thorndike, R. M., Cunningham, G. K., Thorndike, R. L., & Hagen, E. P. (1991). *Measurement and evaluation in psychology and education* (5th ed.). New York: Macmillan.

Witt, J. C., Elliott, S. N., Kramer, J. J., & Gresham, F. M. (1994). *Assessment of children: Fundamental methods and practices.* Madison, WI: Brown & Benchmark.

## REFERENCES

Airasian, P. W., & Madaus, G. J. (1972). Functional types of student evaluation. *Measurement and Evaluation in Guidance, 4,* 221–223.

American Psychological Association, American Educational Research Association, & National Council on Measurement in Education. (1985). *Standards for educational and psychological testing.* Washington, DC: American Psychological Association.

Anastasi, A. (1988). *Psychological testing* (6th ed.). New York: Macmillan.

Bloom, B. S. (Ed.). (1956). *Taxonomy of educational objectives: Handbook I. Cognitive domain.* New York: Longman, Green, and Company.

Chase, C. K. (1968). The impact of some obvious variables on essay test scores. *Journal of Educational Measurement, 5,* 315–318.

Conoley, J. C., & Kramer, J. J. (Eds.). (1989). *The tenth mental measurements yearbook.* Lincoln, NE: The Buros Institute of Mental Measurements, The University of Nebraska–Lincoln.

Crowl, T. K. (1996). *Fundamentals of educational research* (2nd ed.). Madison, WI: Brown & Benchmark.

Crowl, T. K., & MacGinitie, W. H. (1974). The influence of students' speech characteristics on teachers' evaluations of oral answers. *Journal of Educational Psychology, 66,* 304–308.

Crowl, T. K., & Nurss, J. R. (1976). Ethnic and regional influences on teachers' evaluations of oral answers. *Contemporary Educational Psychology, 1,* 236–240.

Educational Testing Service. (1992, Summer). Exploring the feasibility and educational potential of performance-based testing. *ETS Developments* (pp. 4–5). Princeton, NJ: Educational Testing Service.

Frazier, D. M., & Paulson, F. L. (1992). How portfolios motivate reluctant writers. *Educational Leadership, 49*(8), 62–65.

Goetz, E. T., Alexander, P. A., & Ash, M. J. (1992). *Educational psychology: A classroom perspective.* New York: Merrill/Macmillan.

Gronlund, N. E., & Linn, R. L. (1990). *Measurement and evaluation in teaching* (6th ed.). New York: Macmillan.

Herman, J. L. (1992). What research tells us about good assessment. *Educational Leadership, 49*(8), 74–78.

Hetterscheidt, J., Pott, L., Russell, K., & Tchang, J. (1992). Using the computer as a reading portfolio. *Educational Leadership, 49*(8), 73.

Knight, P. (1992). How I use portfolios in mathematics. *Educational Leadership, 49*(8), 71–72.

Lovelace, T., & Martin, C. E. (1984). *The revised National Teacher Examinations as a predictor of teachers' performance in public school classrooms.* Lafayette, LA: University of Southwestern Louisiana. (ERIC Document Reproduction Service No. ED 251 416)

Marshall, J. C. (1967). Composition errors and essay examination grades re-examined. *American Educational Research Journal, 4,* 375–386.

Mercer, J. R. (1979). *System of multicultural pluralistic assessment.* San Antonio: The Psychological Corporation.

Meyer, C. A. (1992). What's the difference between *authentic* and *performance* assessment? *Educational Leadership, 49*(8), 39–40.

Mitchell, J. V., Jr. (Ed.). (1983). *Tests in print III.* Lincoln, NB: The Buros Institute of Mental Measurements, The University of Nebraska–Lincoln.

O'Neil, J. (1992). Putting performance assessment to the test. *Educational Leadership, 49*(8), 14–19.

Pugach, M., & Raths, J. (1983). Testing teachers: Analysis and recommendations. *Journal of Teacher Education, 34*(1), 37–43.

Reynolds, C. R. (1982a). Methods for detecting construct and predictive bias. In R. A. Berk (Ed.), *Handbook of methods for detecting test bias* (pp. 192–227). Baltimore, MD: Johns Hopkins University Press.

Reynolds, C. R. (1982b). The problem of bias in educational assessment. In C. R. Reynolds & T. B. Gutkin (Eds.), *The handbook of school psychology* (pp. 178–208). New York: Wiley.

Shavelson, R. J., & Baxter, G. P. (1992). What we've learned about assessing hands-on science. *Educational Leadership, 49*(8), 20–25.

Thorndike, R. M., Cunningham, G. K., Thorndike, R. L., & Hagen, E. P. (1991). *Measurement and evaluation in psychology and education* (5th ed.). New York: Macmillan.

Willis, S. (1992). Quality by design through portfolios. *ASCD Update, 34*(5), 2.

Wolf, D. P., LeMahiew, P. G., & Eresh, J. (1992). Good measure: Assessment as a tool for educational reform. *Educational Leadership, 49*(8), 8–13.

Wolf, R. M. (1982). Validity of tests. In H. E. Mitzel (Ed.), *Encyclopedia of educational research* (5th ed., Vol. 4, pp. 1991–1998). New York: Free Press.

Zoref, L., & Williams, P. (1980). A look at content bias in IQ tests. *Journal of Educational Measurement, 17,* 313–322.

© Mike Penny/David Frazier

# Classroom Management

# Chapter Outline

# Learning Objectives

14.1 Explain why students demonstrate inappropriate behaviors in the classroom.

14.2 List techniques for maintaining a smoothly running classroom and avoiding and addressing disruptive behavior.

14.3 Describe the basic techniques of behavior modification, including positive reinforcement, negative reinforcement, extinction, and punishment.

14.4 Describe a variety of cognitive approaches to behavior management.

14.5 Explain how the classroom can be a model of a democratic society.

# Preview

Educational psychologists examine how students learn and how teachers plan and implement instruction. This chapter looks at how you can create a classroom environment that promotes learning and makes students feel welcome, comfortable, challenged, and safe.

This chapter also explores how you can create a productive learning environment by minimizing disruptive behavior, developing a healthy student-teacher relationship, keeping students on-task, maintaining a businesslike atmosphere, and communicating effectively with students. We explain how you can

establish classroom rules and consequences, and how to handle disruptive behavior if it occurs. We also describe behavior modification and the cognitive and humanistic approaches to behavior management. We conclude by considering the classroom as a model of a democratic society. ◉

# Establishing and Maintaining a Positive Classroom Environment

All teachers can create a positive classroom environment that promotes student learning, but establishing such an environment does not occur automatically. You have to learn the characteristics of well-managed classrooms (Emmer et al., 1994; Evertson et al., 1994) and how various classroom environments affect student behavior (Gottfredson, Gottfredson, & Hybl, 1993).

## The Causes of Disruptive Behavior

A large-scale survey reported that 81 percent of teachers believe that parents and society are largely responsible for students' misbehavior in the classroom, and 64 percent believe that schools can do little to improve student behavior (Jones & Jones, 1990). Some educators even believe that schools themselves contribute to students' disruptive behavior. Teachers expect students to behave in certain ways in the classroom: to stay seated for hours at a time, to speak only when called on, to conform academically to the norms of their grade, to find the topics of instruction interesting. If a student does not meet these expectations, teachers often blame the student. They regard the student as immature, emotionally disturbed, learning disabled, or simply unmanageable.

> We have to face the fact that the condition of [difficult students] is partially generated by the school. The problems these kids bring to school are exacerbated by the way they're treated by the discipline system and the ways teachers interact with them. There is also a substantial detrimental effect caused by the lack of interesting and engaging experiences to which they will be able to respond. (Turnbaugh, 1986, p. 8)

### Students' Needs

Many psychologists believe the failure of schools to meet students' basic needs results in much misbehavior in the classroom. Dreikurs, Grunwald, and Papper (1982) contend that students misbehave to get attention, power, and revenge, and

*Annual* **Edition**

unit *5*

**14.1** ◎

*Explain why students demonstrate inappropriate behaviors in the classroom.*

We assume that it is "normal" for students to sit still for extended periods of time and "abnormal" if they cannot.

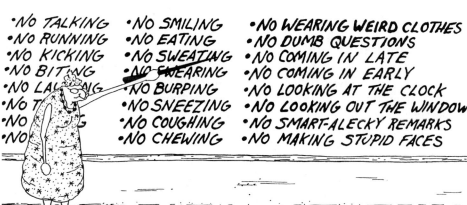

From John McPherson, *Life at McPherson High*. Copyright © 1991 by John McPherson. Reprinted by permission.

Mrs. Mutner went over a few of her rules on the first day of school.

**Figure 14.1**
Maslow's hierarchy of human needs.

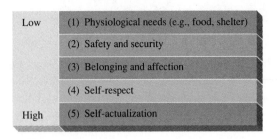

to cover up their sense of inadequacy. Students who fail to get the teacher's attention sometimes engage in disruptive behavior to validate their social status. If teachers fail to respond effectively to such attention-getting behaviors, students seek power. If the teacher frustrates their efforts to obtain power, students become discouraged and seek revenge.

According to Maslow (1968), human beings have five basic needs that are arranged in hierarchical order. Needs at the lower end of the hierarchy must be met before higher-level needs can be satisfied. Figure 14.1 shows Maslow's hierarchy of needs.

The need for food, physical comfort, and safety precedes other needs. If students are hungry or physically uncomfortable, for example, they will not be able to participate in basic classroom activities. Similarly, if they fear for their safety, they will not be able to learn. Do not assume that your students have fulfilled these basic needs. Some students come to school either hungry or worried about whether they will eat later. Students may worry about their physical safety not only in school, but also on the playground, on the streets, or in their homes. Even though these threats may lie beyond your control, it is important to recognize their effects on students' attitudes, behavior, and academic performance.

Students, as the rest of us, have a strong need for belonging and affection. You will better understand their feelings if you recall times you have felt uncomfortable in a social situation. Many of us feel uneasy and uncertain when we enroll in a new school or start a new job. Only after we have established relationships with other group members do we regain our composure. Establishing relationships with others, or "bonding" as it is sometimes called, provides us with support and respect.  You can facilitate the bonding process in your classroom by verbally expressing your affection for your students and encouraging them to demonstrate their attachment to one another. You can also use activities that promote group identity among students in your class.

Students with high self-esteem are likely to perform well academically. According to Coopersmith (1967), the development of self-esteem depends on the individual's sense of significance (being valued), competence (being able to perform valued skills), and power (being able to control one's own environment). To help  students build their self-esteem, demonstrate that you value them, recognize their achievements, and give them some control.

Only after students have fulfilled all other needs in the hierarchy are they able to try to meet their need for self-actualization, which according to Maslow, is the ability to reach one's potential and to express oneself creatively. The most important educational implication of Maslow's theory is that students have difficulty learning until their basic needs are met. Otherwise, they are likely to behave in maladaptive ways, which may include disruptive behavior in the classroom.

Students who behave disruptively in the classroom often drop out of school later on. Jones and Jones (1990) note common characteristics of students who are at-risk for dropping out. Each characteristic is associated with an accompanying need, as shown in figure 14.2.

| Characteristic | Need |
|---|---|
| 1. History of poor adult-child relationships | Positive, supportive relationships |
| 2. Tendency to lack a sense of personal efficacy or power | Experience of personal efficacy or power |
| 3. Focus on external factors as influencing one's own behavior | Learn to accept responsibility for one's own behavior; learn to control one's behavior |
| 4. Low self-esteem, particularly relating to academic achievement and peer relations | Develop and validate a positive self-image through school and social success |
| 5. Poor social cognition (awareness of the needs and emotions of others) | Learn to understand others and work cooperatively with others |
| 6. Poor problem-solving skills | Develop such skills |

**Figure 14.2**
Characteristics and needs of students at-risk for dropping out (Jones & Jones, 1990).

## The Issue of Control

Opinions vary about how much control teachers should have in the classroom. Beginning teachers sometimes try to exercise as much control in the classroom as possible to overcome their nervousness and anxiety. Student achievement, however, is greatest when teachers exercise a moderate level of control (Rim & Coller, 1979; Soar, 1983).

Teachers who maintain high levels of classroom control generally focus on instructional tasks that make only the minimal cognitive demands (e.g., memory) required on standardized tests. To have students engage in complex problem solving and creative activities, teachers must relinquish some of their control over the classroom (Johnson & Johnson, 1987; Soar & Soar, 1975). Corno (1987) found that students in a tightly controlled class scored higher on memory-oriented learning tasks but lower on measures of creativity than students in classrooms with less teacher control. The theories of Piaget, Vygotsky, and Bruner all suggest that students should have some control over their own learning.

## Maintaining a Smoothly Running Classroom

One way to reduce disruptive classroom behavior is to develop a healthy relationship with your students. Some teacher-student relationships are defined by narrow interpretations of the two roles: I am the teacher, you are the student; you must follow my rules. A healthier relationship develops, however, when both teachers and students acknowledge their respective roles and the responsibilities associated with these roles. In addition, they acknowledge that they are both human beings with common experiences and needs. Thus, both you and your students know that you are there to teach and they are there to learn; but you both also know that you both read books, have friends, go to movies, and have good days and bad days.

You can develop an effective teacher-student relationship by maintaining an honest dialogue with students, sharing some of your personal feelings with them, and encouraging them to share their feelings with you and with each other. Be aware, of course, of what is professionally appropriate. You may discuss your feelings about a new highway being built in town, for example, but not the strains in your marriage.

Expressing concern for and interest in students enhances the trust and attachment that students feel toward you. And understanding a student's interests allows you to better understand the student's needs and motivations.

### Communicating Your Interest and Concern

Teachers and students communicate with each other both verbally and nonverbally. Eye contact, gestures, and facial expressions reveal how interested you are in students and how you are interpreting their behavior. Although continuous direct eye

*Annual* **Edition**

unit *5*

**14.2** ◎
*List techniques for maintaining a smoothly running classroom and avoiding and addressing disruptive behavior.*

*A*⁺

Teachers need to find a comfortable and appropriate level of self-disclosure.

Videotape yourself teaching to gain insight about your nonverbal forms of communication.

Eye contact, gestures, and facial expressions reveal how interested teachers are in students.

© Tom McCarthy/Unicorn Stock Photos

contact tends to make people nervous, effective teachers monitor students by frequently looking around the room and making direct (although brief) eye contact with them (Jones, 1979). Make eye contact with *all* of your students, not just with the bright or disruptive ones. Eye contact communicates expectations; make sure to send *all* students the message that you have confidence they can learn.

Physical proximity is another nonverbal form of communication. We each have our own sense of "personal space," but for most people within the same culture, this distance is about the same. In the classroom, students seated nearest you tend to be the most motivated and those farthest from you the least motivated. Design your class and lessons so that you have ample opportunity to roam around the classroom to get physically close to all of your students.

Verbal communication and subtle differences in language usage also have a powerful influence on students. In the 1960s and 1970s, Haim Ginott wrote books on how parents and teachers could communicate more effectively with children. He noted the detrimental effect of labeling (Ginott, 1972). When teachers label students (e.g., "smart," "dumb," "lazy," or "sneaky"), they influence students' expectations of themselves as well as their self-esteem. Such labels may also affect teachers' behavior toward students, which further influences students' expectations and self-esteem.

Ginott notes that teachers should "describe" and not "characterize." That is, they should address the behavior and not the character of the student. Here are two examples of how one teacher "describes" and the other "characterizes."

> *During a poetry reading activity one student interrupts another who is reading her poem aloud, saying "That poem stinks! It could have been written by a kindergartner!"*
>
> *A teacher who* describes, *says, "Alice, it's Carrie's turn to read her poem. I am angry that you interrupted her. Your comment was rude. Carrie, please continue."*
>
> *A teacher who characterizes says, "Alice, you are rude and cruel. By insulting Carrie, you show us how obnoxious you are."*

Notice that in the first instance, the teacher honestly expresses anger and describes the student's comment as rude. The teacher perceives the particular *behavior* as rude; therefore, the student can earn the teacher's esteem by not acting rudely in the future. In the second instance, the teacher describes the student, not the comment, as rude. As a result, the student learns that the teacher believes that her character is flawed; the teacher sees her as a rude and cruel person and she will probably never be able to regain the teacher's esteem.

## Verbal and Nonverbal Communication

The verbal "rules" for interacting vary widely among different cultural groups. Some groups, such as Hispanic Americans and Asian Pacific Americans, expect a level of formality, whereas others, such as European Americans and African Americans, tend to be more informal and flexible (Grossman, 1995). Cultural groups also vary with regard to the level of emotionality that is typically expressed, whether communication is direct or indirect, and whether controversial topics are considered appropriate to discuss.

Nonverbal forms of communication also vary. In Asian cultures, for example, children learn to *avoid* eye contact with adults during conversation. In Anglo-American culture, the opposite is true. Asian American students tend to look down at the floor when a teacher speaks to them. In their culture, averting the

eyes is a sign of respect, not disrespect. To communicate effectively, you must take into account cultural differences in nonverbal communication and adjust your perceptions of social situations accordingly.

Cultures also vary with regard to how much "personal space," or space between you and another person, is comfortable. The need for space is related to context (e.g., your need is different on an elevator than in a classroom), but it is also related to culture.

Other nonverbal forms of communication, such as vocal tone and volume, hand gestures, and facial expressions also vary among individuals and among cultural groups. Don't make snap judgments about students based on their nonverbal behavior. Also, consider how students and their parents may misinterpret your actions because of your culture-bound nonverbal behavior.

## Maintaining Student Focus

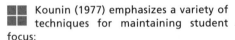

Kounin (1977) emphasizes a variety of techniques for maintaining student focus:

1. *Use strategies to maintain group focus on a specific topic.* Don't let a class discussion become a dialogue between you and one or two students; try to engage actively those who are slower or less motivated. Ask open-ended questions that are on the appropriate level and attempt to draw out individual students in a nonthreatening way.

2. *Provide students with ongoing feedback.* Feedback serves multiple functions: It allows students to know how they are doing, and it reduces boredom. Students tend to be more interested when they are receiving information about their own competence.

3. *Keep lessons challenging and vary your teaching approaches.* Students who are challenged and motivated are more likely to stay on-task and less likely to drift away from the activity and behave disruptively.

## Keeping Students On-Task

Keeping students actively engaged in learning is one of the best ways to avoid disruptive classroom behavior. Keeping students on-task, particularly when they are working in groups, pairs, or independently, is often difficult (Frick, 1990). Kounin (1977) investigated which teacher characteristics promote on-task behavior. He termed one such characteristic "withitness," which refers to a teacher's awareness of what is occurring in the classroom.

Kounin found that students decide whether a teacher has "withitness" by determining whether the teacher (a) consistently addresses disruptive behavior and identifies the student responsible for it, (b) can deal with the more disruptive behavior when two disruptions occur simultaneously, and (c) addresses disruptive behavior before it becomes a major problem. "Withitness" probably develops with experience and is a reflection of a teacher's own sense of comfort in the classroom.

## Creating a Businesslike Classroom Climate

■■ Cangelosi (1988) suggests that teachers
■■ create a "businesslike" atmosphere in
the classroom in which students understand
that they and the teacher have a shared goal:
to accomplish activities that promote learning. Naturally, other activities occur, such as
administrative functions (e.g., attendance),
personal functions (e.g., bathroom visits), and
social functions (e.g., a class birthday party),
but these activities are secondary to learning.

Cangelosi (1988) recommends five steps
for creating a businesslike atmosphere in the
classroom:

1. *Set the stage for cooperation at the
   beginning of a new school year.* Take
   advantage of students' initial
   uncertainty about you as a teacher to
   establish efficient on-task, cooperative
   behavior patterns. *Plan* for a favorable
   beginning of the school year; visualize
   what you want to happen. *Anticipate*
   the obstacles you may encounter.
   *Execute* learning activities in the first
   days that satisfy students so that they
   leave with a feeling of achievement and
   purpose.
2. *Be prepared and well organized.* Plan
   your lessons; when appropriate, consult
   with more experienced teachers. Have
   the materials you need at hand. If you
   model preparedness, students will
   themselves become better prepared and
   organized.
3. *Minimize transition time.* Develop
   efficient ways to carry out administrative
   duties, distribute materials, and give
   directions. One way is to establish cues
   for routines. For example, instead of
   saying, "Now form your social studies
   groups, and I want each group leader to
   get the group's textbooks from the shelf
   and distribute them," you might teach
   students a specific cue, such as "Get
   ready for social studies." You first have
   to teach what the cue refers to. Put
   detailed instructions on a wall chart for
   students to refer to. Students should
   know what they should be doing next.
   As Cangelosi (1986) notes, students
   waiting for a lesson to start tend to
   relieve their boredom by daydreaming,
   attention-getting, and being disruptive.

4. *Create a comfortable, nonthreatening
   atmosphere.* Students can't learn
   efficiently if they are scared. The Yerkes-
   Dodson law, or **arousal theory,** describes
   the relationship between arousal (or
   one's degree of excitement) and
   performance. As shown below, low
   levels of arousal are associated with low
   levels of performance. As arousal
   increases, so does performance.
   However, too much arousal is counter-
   productive and performance declines.
   Too much arousal may lead to anxiety.
   Alertness helps people learn, but anxiety
   hinders them.

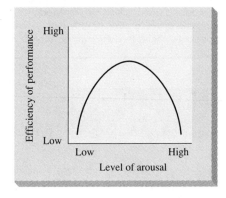

The Yerkes-Dodson law.

Students may fear criticism, ridicule,
and embarrassment by teachers or fellow students. Students who are failing
academically may fear loss of parental
love or teacher and peer respect. Cangelosi notes that parents and teachers
often communicate to students (sometimes inadvertently) that high achievement earns them self-respect and the
respect of others. Students who believe
that they are academically average or
below average may be unwilling to jeop-
ardize their self-esteem to engage in a
task they feel they are likely to fail.
5. *Establish clear expectations for conduct.*
   Make sure students know what you
   expect of them and why. Also ensure
   that they know the outcomes of
   deviations from these expectations.

How a teacher responds to disruptive behavior also influences its future occurrence. Kounin notes that threats, anger, or physically handling the student do
*not* decrease the likelihood that other students will demonstrate the same behavior
again. On the other hand, the likelihood is decreased when teachers explain *why* a
behavior is inappropriate.

## Handling Disruptive Behavior

A student sits in the back of the class-room and periodically throws paper wads at other students. A teacher who ignores the behavior risks the appearance of weakness and of giving over control of the class to the student. Ignoring the student's behavior also sends the message to all students that it is acceptable not to follow the class rules. It would be better for the teacher to explain to the student why the behavior is inappropriate and indicate the consequences of continuing it. If the behavior continues, it is important for the teacher to enforce the consequences.

Here are some guidelines for handling disruptive behavior:

1. *Deal in the present, not the past.* Deal with problems as soon as they develop. Address only the current problem; don't remind students of past misbehaviors.
2. *Talk to students, not about them.* Address students directly concerning inappropriate behavior. Complaining to other teachers or students about a disruptive student will further alienate the student. Speak directly with the student to ensure that he or she is aware of your feelings.
3. *Don't allow yourself to be provoked.* Some students may be disruptive to try to antagonize or annoy you. Stay calm and address the issue in a firm manner.

You are the adult. Always maintain your self-control while helping students reestablish theirs.

4. *Be aware of nonverbal messages, such as eye contact and body language.* This pertains to your own nonverbal messages as well as those of the student. In some situations, you may choose to ignore only slightly disruptive behaviors or use eye contact to convey that you are aware of the student's behavior. Also, attending to nonverbal messages helps you detect disruptive behavior before it happens.
5. *Diffuse student hostility by responding with concern.* If a student expresses hostility, a confrontational approach is likely only to make the situation worse. Instead, move close to the student and speak calmly and in soothing tones. In this way, you convey that you are aware of the student's anger and are concerned. Acknowledging students' feelings often reduces students' rage.
6. *Use "I" statements to indicate your needs.* "I" statements are an effective way to communicate to students; rather than saying "Interrupting me is unacceptable," you would say "When you interrupt me, *I* am unable to get across my thought to the class."

---

Kounin also found that maintaining student involvement in academic tasks was easier when teachers effectively moved the class from one activity to another. Clumsy, disorderly, and hurried transitions provide students opportunities to disrupt the class. In the confusion, students lose their focus. Carefully planned and executed transitions keep students focused and prevent opportunities for misbehaving.

Many people believe the lack of school discipline is one of the greatest problems in schools (Elam, Rose, & Gallup, 1993). Most teachers do not want to be disciplinarians, but successful teachers exert **assertive discipline;** that is, they apply classroom rules calmly and forcefully (Canter & Canter, 1992). Assertive teachers communicate classroom requirements to students, ensure that students comply with rules, but do not violate the students' interests. Teachers should set clear limits, follow through on limits, and reward students for behaving appropriately.

## School Violence

Violence in schools, which reflects the violence in the United States, is becoming a significant issue. Schools exist within communities; they border streets, playgrounds, homes, and shopping areas, and people are constantly coming and going. Schools are not islands untouched by the events and conditions surrounding them. The students and employees of the school also reflect the problems of the community, such as drug addiction, mental illness, or criminality.

*Annual* **Edition**

unit *7*

## Encouraging Mutual Respect and Courtesy

Many teachers complain that students lack respect for both teachers and each other. These guidelines can help you to develop mutual respect and courtesy in your students:

1. *Model a respectful, courteous manner.* By demonstrating respect for students, you send a message that respect is desirable and indicates maturity. Address students politely and respect their property. If you "confiscate" items (such as hand-held computer toys or comic books), protect the student's property until you return it. If you confiscate a note being passed between students, it is disrespectful to read it.
2. *Discuss the reasons individuals are respectful and courteous to one another.* The reasons may not be self-evident to all students.

3. *As a class, compose some classroom rules about courtesy and respect.* Then post the rules in a conspicuous place.
4. *Promote self-respect in students.* When students respect themselves, they are more likely to understand the importance of respecting others. Lack of self-respect underlies a great deal of the antagonism among students. Show students that you value them as members of the class.
5. *Reward instances of courtesy and respect.* Use compliments or a well-timed nod or smile to show students you recognize and appreciate polite behavior.
6. *Encourage students to take responsibility for the atmosphere of the classroom.* Encourage students to contribute to the tone of the room by presenting the classroom as a space shared by all. Present yourself as a participant, not as the controller.

Although school violence has increased in the past decade, violence itself may affect students less than the *fear* of violence. According to Maslow's hierarchy of needs, threats to our safety and security can prevent us from fulfilling other needs. Students who are fearful when they come to school will be unable to grow intellectually and socially. To try to make schools safer, some junior and senior high schools have hired security guards, and some have even installed metal detectors to screen for guns and knives. Despite these efforts, school safety continues to be a significant concern.

McCarthy (1992) believes the best way to prevent violence is to teach students about peace; others (Johnson et al., 1992; Scherer, 1992) think we should teach both students and teachers conflict mediation and negotiation techniques. Still others believe that schools need to teach values, a position that leads to the inevitable question in a multicultural society: Whose values should we teach?

*Annual* **Edition**

unit 5

## Rules and Consequences

To minimize disruptive behavior, many educators recommend that classrooms have stated "rules of conduct," or formal statements that give students broad guidelines indicating which behaviors are required and which are prohibited. Such rules should be general and apply to a wide variety of situations. Cangelosi (1988) recommends no more than ten rules, which should be posted where teachers, students, and visitors can easily consult them.

### Understanding Classroom Rules

Students must understand why a class *has* rules and why these particular rules have been formulated. Take time at the beginning of the school year to discuss both of these issues and allow students to ask questions and state their feelings about the rules. Useful classroom rules have four purposes:

1. To maximize on-task behaviors and minimize behaviors that are off-task or disruptive
2. To secure the safety and comfort of the learning environment

3. To prevent class activities from disturbing others
4. To maintain acceptable standards of behavior among students, school personnel, and visitors to the school (Cangelosi, 1988, p. 116).

Class rules that do not serve at least one of these four purposes should be dropped.

## Who Formulates Classroom Rules?

A democratic approach to teaching suggests that students participate in the formulation of rules. The appropriateness of this approach depends largely on the age and sophistication of the students. If necessary, you should amend rules as the school year progresses. Students may suggest new rules or you may need to devise new rules to cover unanticipated situations.

# Behavior Modification

**Behavior modification** (Alberto & Troutman, 1990) stems from B. F. Skinner's work on operant conditioning. According to the principles of operant conditioning, events that follow a behavior determine the likelihood that the behavior will be repeated. When a student's behavior is followed by a desirable consequence, the behavior is likely to occur again. When a student's behavior is followed by an undesirable consequence, the behavior is less likely to occur again.

You can control many aspects of students' behavior by applying behavior modification techniques. Although these techniques are often used in special education classes for students with severe behavioral problems or mental retardation, many regular education teachers also successfully apply them in a less formal manner to control students' behavior.

Operant conditioning involves presentation of a **stimulus** after a **response** has occurred. The response comes from the student, while the stimulus comes from the environment (e.g., the teacher or other students). The stimulus can either be desirable or undesirable, that is, a reward or a punishment. The stimulus can also be either presented or removed after the behavior has occurred. Thus, we have four different possibilities—positive reinforcement, extinction, punishment, and negative reinforcement—as shown in figure 14.3.

Positive reinforcement occurs when you reward students for demonstrating a behavior. Examples of positive reinforcement include:

- Giving students stickers or stars for good work
- Complimenting students on making quick and quiet transitions from one activity to another
- Allowing students who work cooperatively to earn points that they can "cash in" for time on computer games

Generally, positive reinforcement is a desirable approach because it avoids the unpleasant feelings that occur when you give punishment.

Teachers usually use tangible rewards, activity rewards, or social rewards. Tangible rewards may be in the form of stickers, stamps, or other small items. Choose tangible reinforcers in terms of students' interest and age. A high school student, for example, would probably not be interested in earning a sticker. Tangible rewards have two drawbacks: (a) you must continually replace them, which can become costly, and (b) items may lose their reinforcing power over time.

*Annual*  **Edition**

unit *5*

**14.3** ◎
*Describe the basic techniques of behavior modification, including positive reinforcement, negative reinforcement, extinction, and punishment.*

Choose reinforcers that are valuable to the student, but not easily accessible.

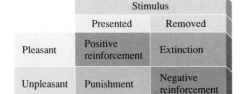

|  | Stimulus | |
|---|---|---|
|  | Presented | Removed |
| Pleasant | Positive reinforcement | Extinction |
| Unpleasant | Punishment | Negative reinforcement |

**Figure 14.3**
Operant conditioning methods.

## Using Positive Reinforcement Effectively

You can use positive reinforcement to increase desirable student behaviors if you keep in mind the following points:

1. *Because the students are not necessarily involved in selecting the reinforced behavior,* some teachers view behavior modification as manipulative. You can address this issue by working with students in establishing goals.
2. *The effectiveness of positive reinforcement depends on whether the student actually views the reinforcer as pleasant.* The power of a reinforcer is in the mind of the recipient; what one student finds positively reinforcing may not reinforce another.
3. *Positive reinforcement works best when the reinforcement is delivered immediately after the target behavior occurs.* If time passes between the behavior and the reward, the target behavior won't increase much.

Awards are a type of reinforcer that can be highly motivating, particularly to older students.

© Tom McCarthy/PhotoEdit

Activity rewards are based on the **Premack principle,** which states that a more interesting activity can be effectively used to positively reinforce a student for participating in a less interesting activity (Premack, 1959). For example, you might reward students who dislike math by allowing them to spend time playing a computer game after they have completed a math assignment.

Social reinforcers may take the form of compliments, a pat on the back, or an approving smile. For some students, however, teacher recognition means they won't "look cool" in the eyes of their peers. On the other hand, social reinforcers are easy to give, cost nothing, and do not need to be replenished.

One popular application of positive reinforcement in the classroom is the use of **token economies.** Using this approach, teachers reward desirable behavior with tokens a student can collect. When students earn enough tokens, they can "cash" them in for either tangible items or activities (Martin & Pear, 1992). Many educators feel that token economies help teach students to delay gratification, while at the same time maintaining the immediacy of positive reinforcement.

From John McPherson, *Life at McPherson High.*
Copyright © 1991 by John McPherson. Reprinted
by permission.

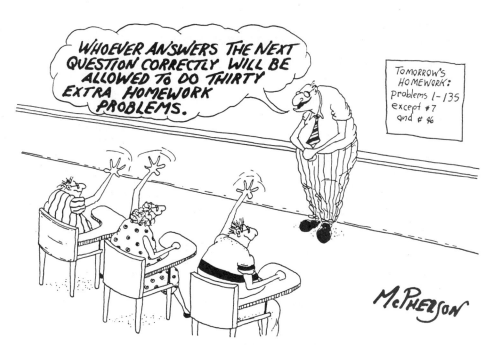

Mr. Glemply was a master of reverse psychology.

**Extinction,** which involves the removal of a desired reinforcer, is sometimes used to eliminate undesirable behaviors. For example, you may be inadvertently rewarding undesirable behaviors simply by paying attention to them. If you ignore the undesirable behavior, it will decrease in frequency and eventually stop completely.

You can increase the effects of extinction by combining it with positive reinforcement. If you ignore an undesirable behavior, reward the desirable opposite behavior. If you ignore students when they answer without being called on, reward them when they wait to be called on. This way, students realize that they can still earn rewards but that the rewards are contingent on their demonstrating socially appropriate behavior.

## Time-Out, Response Cost, and Punishment

A popular variation on extinction is the time-out method. Extinction can work only when you eliminate the positive reinforcer. You can accomplish this most easily when you are the supplier of the reinforcer. When the attention of other students positively reinforces the undesirable behavior of one student, the reinforcement is difficult to prevent. Removing the student demonstrating the undesirable behavior to an area away from the attention of the other students is called **time-out.** Thus, although you cannot stop other students from paying attention to a disruptive student, you can prevent the disruptive student from receiving attention.

In special education settings, a separate room is often used for time-out. For time-out to be effective, this room should be neither pleasant, which would make it a positive reinforcer, nor unpleasant, which would make it a punishment. The room should be neutral. It is difficult to create such an environment and to make sure that the student is supervised but not receiving attention. In regular education, the time-out area is often within the classroom, separated from the rest of the room by a divider or bookcase.

**Response-cost** differs from time-out in that it involves removal of an already-earned reward. For example, a teacher may award students points when they participate in class discussion. However, they lose points when they disrupt the class. Response-cost is a powerful method, but it tends to anger and frustrate students, thus creating an unpleasant classroom environment.

Time-out is used to remove a student from the environment in which an undesirable behavior is occurring.

© James L. Shaffer

## Minimizing the Negative Impact of Punishment

If you choose to use punishment to alter students' behavior, you should follow these rules:

1. *Use punishment as a last resort.* Try other methods before turning to punishment to decrease behavior.
2. *Make sure students understand the class rules and their rationale before you use punishment.* If students know the class rules and why they exist, punishment is less likely to be needed.
3. *Explain to students why you are punishing them.* If a student does not understand the relationship between the punishment and the behavior, the undesirable behavior will continue.

4. *Be certain that the punishment is appropriate.* Don't punish small infractions with major punishment or major infractions with minor punishment.
5. *Never use physical forms of punishment.* In most states, it is illegal to use physical forms of punishment.
6. *Do not use school-related activities as punishments.* Students should perceive school-related activities as pleasant.
7. *Combine punishment with positive reinforcement.* If you punish a student for disrupting the class, reward the student for *not* disrupting the class. Punishment is more effective when students also have opportunities to earn rewards.

---

When possible, avoid the use of punishment and find alternative methods of managing student behavior.

**Punishment** involves the presentation of an unpleasant stimulus. Although punishment is often effective, it has serious drawbacks. When punishment is used frequently, students eventually think of school as an oppressive place and the teacher as the oppressor. Frequently punished students are also likely to develop low self-esteem.

In addition, the vague difference between punishment and abuse is another serious problem. When does punishment become abuse? Most people agree that abuse occurs when punishment is physically harmful to the student, but there is less agreement about when punishment becomes psychologically harmful. Nevertheless, many parents and teachers argue that punishment is an important part of behavior management.

# Behavior Management from a Cognitive Perspective

**14.4** ◎

*Describe a variety of cognitive approaches to behavior management.*

Let us now look at managing student behavior from a cognitive perspective. This section explains how you can help students overcome behavior problems by having them examine their thoughts, attitudes, and beliefs.

## Rational-Emotive Therapy (RET)

*Annual* **Edition**

unit *5*

**Rational-emotive therapy (RET)** was developed by Albert Ellis (1962, 1973; Ellis & Dryden, 1987), who believed that people's thoughts control their emotions. For example, a student fails a math test and thinks "I'm lousy in math; I'll never succeed in math," which makes the student feel depressed.

The purpose of RET is to demonstrate to people the irrationality of their beliefs. In this case, the student's beliefs that "I'm lousy in math" and that "I'll never succeed" in math aren't necessarily true. Ellis defines irrational thoughts as those that are false or cannot be proven true. The belief that "I'm lousy in math" is not proven by having failed; there are many alternative explanations for failing a test (e.g., the test was poorly written or the student didn't study). The belief that "I'll never succeed" is also false because a student has no way to predict the future.

Ellis claims that a number of irrational beliefs are common in our culture, including the following:

1. You must be loved by and receive approval from virtually every other person.
2. You must always be thoroughly competent and achieving to be worthwhile.
3. Certain people are inherently bad and evil and should be blamed and punished.
4. When things do not go the way we want, life is awful and a terrible, horrible catastrophe.
5. Unhappiness comes from events outside of you, and you have no control over your unhappiness.
6. If some event is scary, you should dwell on it and be upset about it.
7. It is easier to avoid difficulties than to face them.
8. You should depend on people who are stronger than yourself.
9. A pattern that has occurred in your life will continue to occur.
10. You should be upset over other people's problems.
11. Things should turn out better than they do, and it is catastrophic if things don't turn out as you wish them to.

According to Ellis, people who have irrational beliefs often demonstrate one or more of these patterns: (a) they "awfulize," concluding that things are worse than they actually are; (b) they place unreasonable demands on life, expecting everything *must* turn out as they wish; (c) they cannot tolerate frustration, believing that, unless all their desires are met, "I can't stand it!" and (d) they damn themselves and others, believing that "I'm worthless" or "He deserves to suffer."

Teachers often hear students make statements that reflect irrational beliefs. You can point out to students the irrational nature of their beliefs. For example, "Just because you failed the math test doesn't mean you're bad at math. It doesn't mean you'll always fail math. It means you didn't do well on this particular test."

Research on RET has demonstrated its effectiveness in dealing with a variety of emotional problems, including anxiety about public speaking (Fremouw & Zitter, 1978), anxiety about participating in social interactions (DiLoreto, 1971), stuttering (Moleski & Tosi, 1976), and test anxiety (Holroyd, 1976).

## Cognitive Therapy

**Cognitive therapy,** developed by Aaron Beck (1976), differs from RET in one major way. In RET people try to erase irrational beliefs by reasoning and persuasion; in cognitive therapy, people test their beliefs against reality by obtaining external proof of (or evidence refuting) the beliefs. The crucial issue is not whether beliefs are irrational, but whether they are maladaptive. Beck argues that individuals may distort reality in a number of specific ways:

1. *Personalization:* blaming yourself for an occurrence out of your control (e.g., "My team lost because I struck out in the second inning").
2. *Polarized thinking:* interpreting everything in all-or-nothing terms (e.g., "Jessica didn't want to sit with me at lunch so she must hate me").
3. *Selective abstraction:* paying attention to a detail while ignoring the context (e.g., "I'm miserable because, even though I got an A on the test, I got question 7 wrong").
4. *Arbitrary inference:* jumping to conclusions without sufficient evidence (e.g., "I know the paper I wrote is lousy, so I'm not even going to hand it in").
5. *Overgeneralization:* drawing a sweeping conclusion from a single instance (e.g, "The teacher didn't call on me when I raised my hand today. She'll never call on me!")

## Cognitive Behavior Modification

Inner speech may also play an important role in many other aspects of learning.

**Cognitive behavior modification,** which was developed by Donald Meichenbaum (1977), is based on the idea that internal speech governs behavior. To change behavior, therefore, one must change one's internal speech.

Meichenbaum uses a five-step method to reduce the impulsivity of children who tend to act without thinking.

1. The teacher performs a task while saying aloud the instructions for performing it.
2. The student performs the task while the teacher continues to verbalize the instructions.
3. The student performs the task while saying the instructions aloud.
4. The student performs the task while whispering the instructions.
5. The student performs the task while saying the instructions in his or her mind (that is, thinking).

In the first step, the teacher models an approach to self-monitoring and self-instructing. Here is an example using a task that involves copying patterns of lines, so in the first step, the teacher uses these self-instructions:

> *Okay, what is it I have to do? You want me to copy the picture with the different lines. I have to go slowly and carefully. Okay, draw the line down, down, good; then to the right, that's it; now down some more and to the left. Good, I'm doing fine so far. Remember, go slowly. Now back up again. No, I was supposed to go down. That's okay. Just erase the line carefully. . . . Good. Even if I make an error I can go on slowly and carefully . . . Finished. I did it! (Meichenbaum & Goodman, 1971, p. 117)*

Notice that the monologue includes self-instruction, self-monitoring, self-correcting and self-reinforcing, which collectively are referred to as **metacognition,** or the awareness of one's own thinking. The goal of cognitive behavior modification is to enhance students' metacognitive abilities: The teacher models the self-evaluative and self-governing statements that the student internalizes after following the steps. Cognitive behavior modification has been shown to reduce impulsivity (Meichenbaum & Goodman, 1971), increase creativity (Meichenbaum, 1977), reduce test anxiety (Meichenbaum, 1972), and promote assertiveness (Kaplan, 1982).

## Self-Efficacy

Another cognitive approach to behavior management concerns **self-efficacy,** which refers to two beliefs: (a) that a particular behavior is effective in a specific situation and (b) that you are capable of that behavior (Bandura, 1977). Students who have sufficient self-efficacy concerning learning algebra believe that (a) algebra can be learned by studying and (b) they are capable of studying. Bandura asserts that self-efficacy is a strong predictor of behavior and behavior change.

Research concerning self-efficacy has focused largely on emotional problems, such as phobias and lack of assertiveness, and has primarily used modeling as a method of changing individuals' sense of their own efficacy (Masters et al., 1987).  Help students avoid maladaptive and disruptive ways by enhancing their self-efficacy.

## Attribution Theory

Another cognitive approach to managing student behavior is **attribution theory,** which is based on the idea that what we attribute events to influences our behavior. If, for example, you believe you failed a math test because you're simply not good at math, you may not bother to study for the next test. On the other hand, if you believe you failed because you didn't study hard enough, you may study harder next  time. Alter students' behavior by redirecting attributions toward those they can control (e.g., effort).

## Social Skills Instruction

U.S. schools focus primarily on academic skills; students are expected to learn social skills informally. Increasingly, however, teachers are beginning to teach social skills formally to ensure that students learn them just as they learn reading, writing, and arithmetic (Cartledge & Milburn, 1978; Jackson, Jackson, & Monroe, 1983; Waksman, Messmer, & Waksman, 1988).

Instruction usually focuses on common social skills, such as taking turns, sharing, and asking politely. Lessons may also focus on problem solving, such as how to solve interpersonal conflicts. Social skills instruction generally uses the same methods used in academic instruction but can also involve role playing. Teachers sometimes use situations presented in literature and film to stimulate discussion of social problem solving.

Social skills can be a part of the curriculum along with reading, mathematics, social studies, art, and science.

## Reality Therapy

**Reality therapy,** described by Glasser (1969) in his book *Schools Without Failure* is a seven-step approach to solving interpersonal problems.

1. *Be warm and caring.* Send the message that you are happy to have the student in class and that you care about him or her.
2. *When a problem occurs, have the student describe the disruptive behavior.* If the student is reluctant to discuss the problem, explain that you are not trying to place blame, but, rather, that you are going to solve the problem together.
3. *Help students judge whether their behavior was desirable.* Students must recognize that a particular behavior is undesirable before they can change it. Help them consider the long- and short-term advantages and disadvantages of their behavior.
4. *Once the student understands that the behavior should be changed, have him or her develop a plan for addressing the problem in a different way.* In this problem-solving phase, students learn to find their own solution rather than relying on the teacher.
5. *The student must make a commitment to implementing the new plan.* Without a firm commitment, the student may ignore or forget the new plan.
6. *Make a plan to follow up.* Discuss whether the student has actually stuck to the plan. When the student has successfully implemented the plan, give plenty of praise and review the plan's effectiveness.
7. *If the student hasn't followed the plan, encourage him or her to try again or make a new plan.* Maintain a positive, supportive attitude as you try to persuade the student to persevere.

Here is an example of a dialogue between a teacher and a student who are following Glasser's approach:

### Step 1

Teacher: Erik, I'd like to speak with you about what happened this morning. I'm concerned about how you're doing.

Student: Okay.

### Step 2

Teacher: What actually happened this morning?

Student: Do you mean the fight?

Teacher: Yes. I'm not interested in who was right or wrong; I just want to understand what happened.

Student: Albert called me a name and I told him to shut up. The next thing I knew we were fighting.

# TEACHERS ROUNDTABLE

# "We're Going to Make It Through the Year—Together"

**DMP:** Before we talk about disruptive students, let's turn the question around. What makes students behave?

**Angela:** If they're interested in what's happening, their eyes are focused. The discipline problems become very minor.

**Anthony:** Good material, good lessons, and a dynamic presentation.

**DMP:** Future teachers often ask themselves, "What am I going to do when kids start acting out?" I'm curious to know how you've dealt with disruptiveness among your students.

**Anthony:** You have to talk to children and listen to them. And hopefully, as you listen to them, maybe they'll listen a little bit to you. I don't believe in punishing children; I would never call an administrator or a parent. You give up all your power if you have to call a parent to help you discipline a child.

**Mary:** I disagree. The more cooperation you have from the parents, the more effective you can be. I would prefer to send home a happy note, but if I have a child who is acting out repeatedly, I try to make parents aware of it and get their support. In the classroom, I use time-out. If we are very busy and one student is interfering with the other students' learning through his acting out, I deal with it by giving him time-out for a few minutes. They get themselves collected before they come back to the group.

**Anthony:** At one point I had an old refrigerator box without a door and the kids decorated it. That was their time-out spot. They called it the "penalty box." Any time they had had too much in the classroom and just couldn't cope, they would go there and just sit. There were cushions and they might even have their feet up. It was fine—it removed them from a tension-filled situation.

**Angela:** I use a variety of strategies. I'm very expressive with my face and the kids kind of know. They can read my face and they know what I want them to do. I don't have to yell. By getting them aware of my facial expressions as well as different gestures, they become able to read me. Sometimes I compliment others: "Thank you for behaving so nicely." "Thank you for sitting." Or I'll say, "When you are ready, we can go on with the lesson." If a child is not working or is disrupting the lesson, I'll say, "When we finish the lesson, we can go on to computers." I try to use the curriculum to motivate them to complete one activity in anticipation of the next. Also, I sometimes try to remind a child what the appropriate behavior is. "Being ready means you're sitting up, that you're quiet, that you're waiting, that you're watching."

**Irwin:** When I started teaching many years ago, I was in what was considered one of the three most difficult junior high schools in New York City. And there was a little gray-haired old lady who was there for I don't know how many years. She seemed to have very few discipline problems. I asked myself how this could be; here I am, young and big and the kids should say, "Hey, watch out for this guy." But they really listened better to her. And she gave me advice that I've really followed. Her advice was, "What can you do to kids who come to school with such problems and have so many difficulties? Be positive. Don't challenge a kid. Give a kid an opportunity not to lose face. If a kid is ready to act

## Step 3

Teacher: Well, thanks for explaining it to me. It seems that you and Albert have trouble getting along. When he called you a name, did it help you to tell him to shut up?

Student: It caused us to get into the fight, so I guess it didn't exactly help me.

## Step 4

Teacher: I'll speak to Albert about this problem too, but I'm wondering what plan you and I could think of to deal with this if it ever happens again.

Student: I won't do it again.

Teacher: I'm glad, but let's think about what you could do if Albert or someone else did the same thing again.

Student: I could ignore him.

Teacher: That's true.

Student: Or I could walk away.

out, don't take down the kid in front of his peers and say, 'I'm going to call your mother up.' Remove the kid—let the kid be in an environment where he doesn't have to feel that if he listens or responds he is losing face." Face and respect are major, major issues for kids. So, you don't confront them; you are positive with them. You don't discipline them in front of one another. If a kid is disruptive, you allow a kid to feel that he is in charge of himself. And you give the kid options. You don't back him into a corner.

**Mary:** What options?

**Irwin:** If you have a kid who wants to attack another kid, you could step in front of him and grab him. But when you grab him, the whole scene starts. Instead, you move near the kid and show the kid where your hands are—open. You're not going to directly challenge him. You say, "Look, if you come to the Dean's office with me, I'm going to listen to everything you have to say. I won't interrupt. I want you to come with me—not as if I'm leading you; when we go inside it will be your opportunity to tell me everything. If you don't do this, what's going to happen? It's going to be a big fight. You will be automatically suspended from school. You don't need that kind of aggravation. Let's go inside and see if we can solve the problem." Does it always work? No. Does it work most of the time? It really does. When you go

inside, you have to listen. You have to let the kid ventilate. You look interested because you should be interested.

**SK:** Do students sometimes become disruptive because they don't feel that they're part of the classroom? Do you feel the classroom can function as a community?

**Angela:** Often, students are sent to me by other teachers. We do have a guidance counselor, but she's only there twice a week and she can't deal with everyone. But when these children come to my resource room, they have a chance to come to a very quiet space; we have a chance to really talk about what's going on. I try to give them different strategies and we talk a little about the children in the class who they feel are good role models. Sometimes I'll ask, "What does that student do that you are not doing?"

**Anthony:** What is helpful is to remember that the child is going to stay in your class for an entire year. You're going to have to develop strategies to live together for 10 months. The difficult child is not going to go away. You're going to have to make it until June.

**DMP:** But do you think that many teachers don't believe that and, instead, look to refer the difficult student to special education?

**Anthony:** Maybe everyone would like to get rid of a problem child, but where is he going to go? You are giving him to one of your colleagues. I've always believed in

the luck of the draw—when my 32 come in, they are *my* 32. I'm stuck with them and they're stuck with me. We're going to make it through the year—together.

**Mary:** However, sometimes you may have a child who is totally incapable of being in that environment, a child who is kicking out walls or hitting other children constantly. That's a child who cannot make it. I've only had two in the last few years. But, I think we often think that, because we've planned high-interest lessons and because we are working night and day, we're going to have no problems. We have a fairy-tale notion about human beings and about behavior. If you're a teacher, you're going to be dealing with behavior.

**Irwin:** At the high school level, it is a little bit different. Much of the frustration and acting out by students comes from their having tremendous difficulty coping with the material. It's very difficult for a 15-year-old boy looking stupid in front of his peers in the class. So I think that, as a teacher, you have to provide that kid with a possibility to be successful in the classroom. For him, success might be answering a question that is not factually based but based on his opinion instead. That way, the student is not embarrassed and he gains some status in the classroom.

## Step 5

Teacher: Do you think you could do that?

Student: Sure. I could walk away from Albert.

Teacher: It means a lot of self-control.

Student: I could do it.

Teacher: Let's agree that the next time this happens you'll ignore it and walk away.

Student: Okay.

(Some days later . . .)

## Step 6

Teacher: How has your new plan been working? Have you been in that same situation again?

Student: Yes, it did happen again and I just walked away.

Teacher: Good for you! How did that feel?

Student: It was okay because Albert didn't get the better of me.

Some teachers find Glasser's approach useful because they can implement it relatively quickly and learn the steps rather easily. If the process doesn't work, they can analyze each step to determine where the process broke down. Rather than placing teachers and students in antagonistic roles, this approach encourages them to work together to solve a problem with the teacher as the guide and the student as the problem solver. Placing the final responsibility for the problem solving on the student fosters self-management and independence.

# The Classroom as a Model of a Democratic Society

**14.5** ◎

*Explain how the classroom can be a model of a democratic society.*

Many people have expressed concern that schools in the United States are not preparing students to be responsible citizens who produce quality products in the workplace or who actively participate in their communities. These critics believe that what goes on in the classroom should mirror the needs of our democratic society.

## The Search for Quality

Glasser (1990) echoed the concerns of these critics in his book *The Quality School*. He notes the decline in the quality of U.S. education as compared to that of other industrial nations and argues that the primary goal of our schools should be *quality*. Glasser contends that quality can be achieved only through a democratic and participatory approach to education. He argues that coercive methods of managing students are doomed to failure.

Glasser has looked to the ideas of business leaders, such as Edward Deming, for successful models of managing people. Glasser believes that if we apply these business models to education that we, too, can turn out quality "products"—knowledgeable students. His book therefore details how teachers can "manage" students without coercion to produce citizens who are able and eager to participate in their workplace and community.

In applying these ideas to education, we need to consider how classrooms are like workplaces and how they are different.

Glasser makes a distinction between teachers who are "boss-managers" and "lead-managers." Boss-managers, he explains, want to be in charge. He notes that "boss-management" involves four basic behaviors:

1. The boss determines the task and the standards without input from the students. Students must adjust to the task and the standards as the boss has defined them.
2. The boss tells the students how the work should be done and does not ask for input regarding how it could be done better.
3. The boss inspects the work. However, because students have no role in evaluating the work, they tend to settle for just enough quality to pass inspection.
4. When students resist the boss's rules, the boss coerces them to conform; thus, the students and teachers are adversaries (Glasser, 1990).

Teachers who are lead-managers want to empower their "workers" and they have quality as their goal. Cooperative learning is an example of an approach in which teachers give students the power and responsibility of learning together and teaching each other. By choosing cooperative learning as an instructional approach, the teacher surrenders some power but in doing so empowers students. Four different elements typify "lead-managing":

1. The leader invites the students to discuss the quality of the work to be done and the time required to complete it; thus, students can contribute their input. The leader also attempts to fit the job to the students' skills and needs.
2. The leader demonstrates the job so the student understands exactly what is expected. The leader also asks students for their input about better approaches.

## Achieving a Quality School

To achieve a quality school, Glasser (1990) recommends the following:

1. *Allow students to participate in their own evaluation.* Encourage students to think about the quality of their work and to evaluate their own school.
2. *Try to eliminate or at least minimize coercion and criticism.* When students break rules or fail to work hard, don't threaten or punish, but rather help them resolve their problem. Develop a friendly, rather than an adversarial, relationship.
3. *Use cooperative learning as often as possible.* This strategy empowers students and encourages them to be responsible for their own learning.
4. *Encourage state governments to give bonuses to schools that succeed.* Money should be given to schools that have eliminated student dropouts, increased both student and teacher attendance, minimized discipline problems, and increased student achievement in hard and important courses. Specifically, he suggests that 75 percent of the money be shared among the faculty and that 25 percent be used to benefit the students.

---

**3.** The leader invites the students to inspect and evaluate the quality of their own work. The leader accepts that the students know a great deal about how to produce high-quality work and will therefore listen to what they say.

**4.** The leader does as much as possible to provide students with the best possible tools and "workplace" in a noncoercive, nonadversarial atmosphere (Glasser, 1990).

Glasser believes that boss-manager and lead-manager teachers use motivation differently. Boss-managers motivate students by offering rewards or punishments that encourage or discourage specific behaviors; lead-managers, however, know that they cannot motivate students to work hard if the work is not satisfying. Consequently, leaders need to find ways to make schoolwork satisfying to students. If U.S. education is to improve, both students and teachers will have to work hard, and students will work hard only if they achieve personal satisfaction in doing so.

When dealing with disruptive students, you should communicate, be consistent, and encourage students to recognize that the disruption is the student's problem, not the teacher's. Offer to help disruptive students but only after the students calm down. There are no "quick fixes," and long-term resolutions to student behavior problems can be found only when all parties are calm. Glasser further notes that students find it easier to follow the rules when they have helped to form them and understand their purpose.

While Glasser's approach may seem appealing, schools are different from businesses in many ways. Unlike businesses, public schools are funded by state governments. Schools work with children and adolescents who are developing as individuals, whereas businesses employ adults. Also, while both schools and businesses seek to create quality products, the nature of their products differs. The products of businesses are their various outputs, whereas the products of schools are knowledgeable, well-adjusted students who are ready to join the workforce and become responsible citizens. These differences certainly affect how well these principles apply to education.

Glasser's most important message is that students cannot be forced to learn or forced to behave. Rather, if students are to leave school as well-adjusted, well-prepared citizens and workers, they must understand the purpose of their learning and learn to be responsible for themselves.

Can we expect students to understand how democracies work when our schools and classrooms are run on very undemocratic principles?

## Learning About Democracy and Social Responsibility

One of the great ironies of U.S. education is that, while we hope to prepare students for their adult roles in our democratic society (Boyer, 1990), school itself is far from democratic. As Wood (1990) notes,

> We take for granted that our schools are communities, when, in fact, they are merely institutions that can become communities only when we work at it. But, with proper attention to all the individuals within the school, we can create an experience for students that demonstrates what it means to be a compassionate, involved citizen. For it is only within a community, not an institution, that we learn how to hold fast to such principles as working for the common good, empathy, equity, and self-respect. (p. 33)

In many schools, students seldom have the opportunity to participate actively in deciding major or minor issues. We run schools in a "top-down" manner with a chain of command from the principal to the assistant principal to the teacher. The student is not in the chain.

When students are permitted to make decisions as a group, they are often unequipped to do so because they have had no experience or preparation. Kohlberg (1981) suggested that the moral development of some individuals may be limited because they have never lived in a democracy.

Some countries, such as Denmark, make learning how to function as a democratic group a high-priority educational goal (Henriksen et al., 1986). The Danes believe that students can't function as responsible adults unless they have opportunities in school to learn how to participate in a democracy.

Parker (1990) believes it is difficult to help students develop a sense of social responsibility, and Fowler (1990) argues that to do so, schools should (a) use the classroom curriculum to instill democratic values and participation in government, (b) build hands-on community service programs into the curriculum, and (c) highlight in-school voter registration in the senior year of high school. Sobol (1990) believes that students learn social responsibility best by learning about the contributions of various ethnic groups in the United States.

Students learn about democracy and social responsibility by participating in democratic groups.

© Superstock

## Fostering an Understanding of Democracy

You can foster an understanding of democracy in several ways:

1. *Give students opportunities to make group decisions.* Such decisions should be about important issues; if the decisions concern insignificant matters, students will soon realize that their judgments are not truly valued.
2. *Discuss the mechanisms by which group decisions can be made.* Help students realize that debate and discussion in group decision making are valuable mechanisms for exploring an issue and persuading fellow students.
3. *Reflect on the relative roles and responsibilities of the individual and the group.* Have students discuss how we juggle our simultaneous rights and responsibilities as individuals and as members of a democratic group.
4. *Examine the situation of the "losers" in a general vote.* Pose questions like these: How does it feel to have your position voted down? What are the needs of the "minority"? Are there situations in which the "minority" may need to be protected from the "majority"?
5. *Explore the social responsibilities of the majority for the protection of the minority.* Ask students to consider how a majority can ensure that they do not impinge on the rights of the minority.

## KEY POINTS

1. Students often misbehave in class because schools do not meet their basic needs. Maslow (1968) theorizes that there is a hierarchy of needs, and each must be satisfied before the next can be met. The five basic needs are physiological needs, safety and security, belonging and affection, self-respect, and self-actualization.

2. Student achievement is greatest when teachers exercise a moderate level of control. High levels of teacher control are generally associated with teaching that emphasizes low-level tasks (e.g., memory), which are often required in standardized tests; less teacher control is associated with higher-level tasks (e.g., creative or critical thinking).

3. One way to prevent disruptive behavior in the classroom is to develop a healthy teacher-student relationship based on an honest exchange of ideas and an acknowledgment that both teachers and students have roles other than those in the classroom.

4. Effective classroom management depends on teachers' ability to communicate effectively with students, a skill that includes nonverbal communication (eye contact, gestures, facial expression, and respect for an individual's body space). Cultural groups differ in their interpretation of nonverbal communication.

5. You can prevent disruptive behavior by keeping students on-task, making smooth transitions, expressing your displeasure with students' disruptive behavior rather than with students, dealing with the present and not the past, talking *to* students and not *about* them, not allowing yourself to be provoked, expressing concern, and using "I" messages to indicate your needs.

6. Students should know the classroom rules, why the rules exist, and when possible, help develop them.

7. Behavior modification changes students' behavior through four types of interventions: positive reinforcement, negative reinforcement, extinction, and punishment.

8. Positive reinforcement is the presentation of rewards for desirable behavior; teachers should be careful to reward desirable, not undesirable student behaviors.

9. Time-out is an effective behavior modification method in which disruptive students are removed from the classroom to prevent them from being reinforced by other students.

10. Punishment is a frequently used method of behavior modification that makes students dislike school and learning and develop low self-esteem.

11. Rational-emotive therapy is a cognitive approach to behavior change, in which teachers help students recognize and change irrational beliefs that underlie behavior. Cognitive therapy is a technique in which students test their beliefs against reality. In cognitive behavior modification, students learn self-instruction, self-reinforcing, and self-monitoring techniques to govern their own behavior. Altering students' beliefs in their self-efficacy and attributional beliefs can also modify student behavior.

12. Behavior management approaches also include teaching students social skills directly, and Glasser's reality therapy in which teachers encourage students to find new ways of dealing with interpersonal problems.

13. Glasser argues that teachers should act as leaders, not bosses, to increase student motivation and improve the quality of teaching.

14. Educators are responsible for helping students understand democracy and teaching them the skills to participate in democratic decision making.

## SELF-STUDY EXERCISES

1. Identify three ways teachers can be more effective communicators.

2. Why is it important for students to participate in rule making in the classroom?

3. What are the drawbacks of punishment as a method of behavior management?

4. How are the various cognitive approaches to behavior management similar? How are they different?

5. How can teachers help students learn to participate in democratic decision making?

## FURTHER READINGS

Alberto, P., & Troutman, A. C. (1990). *Applied behavior analysis for teachers: Influencing student performance* (3rd ed.). Columbus, OH: Merrill.

Emmer, E. T., Evertson, C. M., Clements, B. S., & Worsham, M. E. (1994). *Classroom management for secondary teachers* (3rd ed.). Boston: Allyn & Bacon.

Evertson, C. M., Emmer, E. T., Clements, B. S., & Worsham, M. E. (1994). *Classroom management for elementary teachers* (3rd ed.). Boston: Allyn & Bacon.

Glasser, W. (1990). *The quality school: Managing students without coercion.* New York: Harper & Row.

Grossman, H. (1995). *Classroom behavior management in a diverse society* (2nd ed.). Mountain View, CA: Mayfield.

## REFERENCES

Alberto, P., & Troutman, A. C. (1990). *Applied behavior analysis for teachers: Influencing student performance* (3rd ed.). Columbus, OH: Merrill.

Bandura, A. (1977). Self-efficacy: Toward a unifying theory of behavioral change. *Psychological Review, 84,* 191–215.

Beck, A. T. (1976). *Cognitive therapy and the emotional disorders.* New York: Guilford.

Boyer, E. L. (1990). Civic education for responsible citizens. *Educational Leadership, 48*(3), 4–7.

Cangelosi, J. S. (1986). *Cooperation in the classroom: Students and teachers together.* Washington, DC: National Education Association.

Cangelosi, J. S. (1988). *Classroom management strategies: Gaining and maintaining students' cooperation.* New York: Longman.

Canter, L., & Canter, M. (1992). *Lee Canter's assertive discipline: Positive behavior management for today's classroom.* Santa Monica, CA: Lee Canter & Associates.

Cartledge, G., & Milburn, J. (1978). The case for teaching social skills in the classroom: A review. *Review of Educational Research, 48,* 133–156.

Coopersmith, S. (1967). *The antecedents of self-esteem.* San Francisco: Freeman.

Corno, L. (1987). Teaching and self-regulated learning. In D. Berliner & B. Rosenshine (Eds.), *Talks to teachers* (pp. 249–266). New York: Random House.

DiLoreto, A. O. (1971). *Comparative psychotherapy.* Chicago: Aldine-Atherton.

Dreikurs, R., Grunwald, B., & Papper, F. (1982). *Maintaining sanity in the classroom: Classroom management techniques* (2nd ed.). New York: Harper & Row.

Elam, S. E., Rose, L. C., & Gallup, A. M. (1993). The 25th annual Gallup Poll of the public's attitudes toward the public schools. *Phi Delta Kappan, 75,* 137–157.

Ellis, A. (1962). *Reason and emotion in psychotherapy.* New York: Lyle Stuart.

Ellis, A. (1973). *Humanistic psychotherapy: The rational-emotive approach.* New York: McGraw-Hill.

Ellis, A., & Dryden, W. (1987). *The practice of rational-emotive therapy.* New York: Springer.

Emmer, E. T., Evertson, C. M., Clements, B. S., & Worsham, M. E. (1994). *Classroom management for secondary teachers* (3rd ed.). Boston: Allyn & Bacon.

Evertson, C. M., Emmer, E. T., Clements, B. S., & Worsham, M. E. (1994). *Classroom management for elementary teachers* (3rd ed.). Boston: Allyn & Bacon.

Fowler, D. (1990). Democracy's next generation. *Educational Leadership, 48*(3), 10–15.

Fremouw, W. J., & Zitter, R. E. (1978). A comparison of skills training and cognitive restructuring-relaxation for the treatment of speech anxiety. *Behavior Therapy, 9,* 248–259.

Frick, T. W. (1990). Analysis of patterns in time: A method of recording and quantifying temporal relations in education. *American Educational Research Journal, 27,* 180–204.

Ginott, H. G. (1972). *Teacher and child.* New York: Avon Books.

Glasser, W. (1969). *Schools without failure.* New York: Harper & Row.

Glasser, W. (1990). *The quality school: Managing students without coercion.* New York: Harper & Row.

Gottfredson, D. C., Gottfredson, G. D., & Hybl, L. G. (1993). Managing adolescent behavior: A multiyear, multischool study. *American Educational Research Journal, 30,* 179–217.

Grossman, H. (1995). *Classroom management in a diverse society* (2nd ed.). Mountain View, CA: Mayfield.

Henriksen, S., Hesselholdt, S., Jensen, K., & Larsen, O. B. (1986). *The democratization of education.* Copenhagen: The Royal Danish School of Educational Studies.

Holroyd, K. A. (1976). Cognition and desensitization in the group treatment of test anxiety. *Journal of Consulting and Clinical Psychology, 44,* 991–1001.

Jackson, N., Jackson, D., & Monroe, C. (1983). *Getting along with others: Teaching social effectiveness in children.* Champaign, IL: Research Press.

Johnson, D., & Johnson, R. (1987). *Learning together and alone: Cooperative, competitive, and individualistic learning* (2nd ed.). Englewood Cliffs, NJ: Prentice Hall.

Johnson, D. W., Johnson, R. T., Dudley, B., & Burnett, B. (1992). Teaching students to be peer mediators. *Educational Leadership, 50*(1), 10–13.

Jones, F. (1979). The gentle art of classroom discipline. *National Elementary Principal, 58,* 26–32.

Jones, V. F., & Jones, L. S. (1990). *Comprehensive classroom management: Motivating and managing students* (3rd ed.). Boston: Allyn & Bacon.

Kaplan, D. A. (1982). Behavioral, cognitive, and behavioral-cognitive approaches to group assertion training therapy. *Cognitive Therapy and Research, 6,* 301–314.

Kohlberg, L. (1981). *The philosophy of moral development.* New York: Harper & Row.

Kounin, J. (1977). *Discipline and group management in classrooms.* New York: Holt, Rinehart & Winston.

Martin, G., & Pear, J. (1992). *Behavior modification: What is it and how to do it* (4th ed.). Englewood Cliffs, NJ: Prentice Hall.

Maslow, A. (1968). *Toward a psychology of being.* New York: D. Van Nostrand.

Masters, J. C., Burish, T. G., Hollon, S. D., & Rimm, D. C. (1987). *Behavior therapy: Techniques and empirical findings* (3rd ed.). Fort Worth, TX: Harcourt Brace Jovanovich.

McCarthy, C. (1992). Why we must teach peace. *Educational Leadership, 50*(1), 6–9.

Meichenbaum, D. H. (1972). Cognitive modification of test-anxious college students. *Journal of Consulting and Clinical Psychology, 39,* 370–380.

Meichenbaum, D. H. (1977). *Cognitive-behavior modification.* New York: Plenum.

Meichenbaum, D. H., & Goodman, J. (1971). Training impulsive children to talk to themselves: A means of developing self-control. *Journal of Abnormal Psychology, 77,* 115–126.

Moleski, R., & Tosi, D. J. (1976). Comparative psychotherapy: Rational-emotive therapy versus systematic desensitization in the treatment of stuttering. *Journal of Consulting and Clinical Psychology, 44,* 309–311.

Parker, W. C. (1990). Assessing citizenship. *Educational Leadership, 48*(3), 17–22.

Premack, D. (1959). Toward empirical behavior laws: I. Positive reinforcement. *Psychological Review, 66,* 219–223.

Rim, E., & Coller, R. (1979). In search of nonlinear process-product functions in existing schooling-effects data: A reanalysis of the first grade reading and mathematics data from the Stallings and Kaskowitz follow-through study. *JSAS Catalog of Selected Documents in Psychology, 9,* 92.

Scherer, M. (1992). Solving conflicts—Not just for children. *Educational Leadership, 50*(1), 14–18.

Soar, R. (1983). *Impact of context variables on teacher and learner behavior.* Paper presented at the annual meeting of the American Association of Colleges of Teacher Education, Detroit.

Soar, R., & Soar, R. (1975). Classroom behavior, pupil characteristics and pupil growth for the school year and the summer. *JSAS Catalog of Selected Documents in Psychology, 5,* 873.

Sobol, T. (1990). Understanding diversity. *Educational Leadership, 48*(3), 27–30.

Turnbaugh, A. (1986). A view from the center. *National Center on Effective Secondary Schools Newsletter, 1,* 8–10.

Waksman, S., Messmer, C., & Waksman, D. (1988). *The Waksman social skills curriculum: An assertive behavior program for adolescents.* Portland, OR: Applied Systems Instruction Evaluation Publishing.

Wood, G. H. (1990). Teaching for democracy. *Educational Leadership, 48*(3), 32–36.

# 15

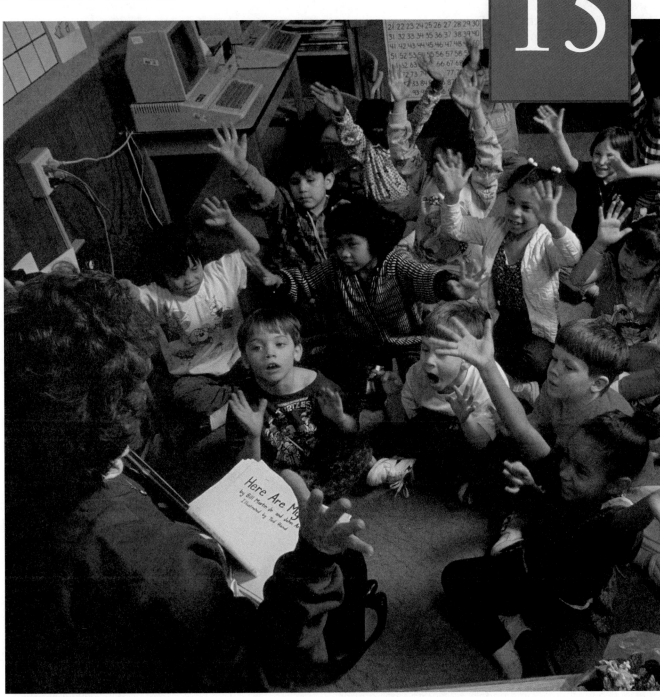

© Jeffry W. Myers/Corbis Media

# How to Teach Effectively

# Chapter Outline

# Learning Objectives

15.1  Identify the various ways of grouping students and list the pros and cons of each.

15.2  Describe techniques that teachers can use to make cooperative learning groups more effective.

15.3  Describe ways of maximizing instructional time.

15.4  Describe teacher behaviors that promote student achievement.

15.5  Compare teacher-centered and student-centered philosophies of instruction.

15.6  Describe the direct instruction, learning strategies, and cognitive apprenticeship models of teaching.

15.7  Describe teaching strategies suggested by our knowledge of students' cognitive development.

15.8  Describe methods of fostering student independence and involvement.

15.9  Explain how teachers can adapt their instruction to meet the needs and characteristics of all students.

# Preview

This chapter discusses *how* to teach. More specifically, we examine what the field of educational psychology has contributed to our understanding of effective teaching. Some people believe that good teaching comes from instinct; however, research in educational psychology shows that certain skills, knowledge, and attitudes make individuals effective teachers.

One aspect of effective teaching is knowing how to group students, both within a school and within a class. Another aspect is knowing which instructional methods to use when working with a whole class or with small groups.

The classroom is a complex environment with multiple events occurring simultaneously and on different levels. This chapter describes teacher behaviors that promote student achievement and maximize instructional time. We describe the teacher-centered and student-

centered philosophies of teaching and three models of teaching: direct teaching, strategy teaching, and cognitive apprenticeship. We explain how cognitive theory provides the basis for effective classroom instruction by identifying ways to promote student autonomy and involvement and to adapt instruction to different learners. We also examine cultural bias in schools and instructional materials. ◉

# Thinking About Teaching

*Annual* **Edition**

unit *4*

This chapter focuses on *how* to teach. We know that there is no *one* best way to teach. Good teaching cannot be reduced to a recipe. Good teaching depends on two factors: (a) the objectives of the lesson and (b) the characteristics of the students. Different lessons have objectives that demand different teaching strategies. Teaching a group of ninth-graders algebra, for example, demands a different set of teaching techniques than teaching the same group of students how to write creatively. Similarly, teaching different age levels often requires different teaching strategies. For example, teaching algebra to ninth-graders requires different teaching techniques than teaching basic number concepts to first-graders.

The ultimate test for determining a teacher's skill is how well students master the lesson's objectives. Figure 15.1 lists some teacher behaviors that researchers have found improve student academic performance. Some factors that affect students' academic performance are beyond the teacher's control. These factors include the quality of students' prior learning, and their study strategies and work habits. Students from better educated and wealthier families tend to perform better in school than students from lower socioeconomic families (Good & Brophy, 1986; Ornstein, 1991). However, when students' socioeconomic background is controlled, differences between high and low academic achievers are associated with the quality of the students' teachers. Students who perform well academically have better teachers than students who perform poorly (Heyneman & Losely, 1983).

Rosenshine and Stevens (1986) studied teaching strategies and found that effective teachers:

1. Begin each new lesson with a review
2. State the goal of the lesson
3. Present new material in small steps
4. Give clear instructions and explanations
5. Give students much time to practice
6. Ask numerous questions
7. Guide initial practice
8. Provide feedback and corrections
9. Provide explicit instructions for seatwork
10. Hold weekly and monthly reviews

These points can serve as guidelines for good teaching. In the end, the quality of your teaching will be a function of your planning, your knowledge of your students, your knowledge of the content, your creativity, and your ability to think fast on your feet.

---

- Stresses the development of student skills (Brophy & Good, 1986)
- Spends considerable class time on academic tasks (Brophy & Good, 1986)
- Exhibits confidence in teaching ability (Johnston, 1990)
- Sets high standards for student performance (Johnston, 1990)
- Believes students have the ability to learn (Johnston, 1990)
- Is warm, enthusiastic and businesslike when dealing with students (Rosenshine, 1983)
- Provides variety in materials and academic activities (Rosenshine, 1983)
- Uses probing questions in following up initial questions (Smith, 1985)
- Is enthusiastic (Stallings, Cory, Fairweather, & Needles, 1978)
- Provides students with corrective feedback by clarifying incorrect or partially incorrect responses (Stallings, Cory, Fairweather, & Needles, 1978)
- Monitors student activities and minimizes transitional periods from one activity to another (Brophy, 1983; Crawford, 1983)
- Gives students sufficient time to answer oral questions (Tobin, 1980; Tobin & Capie, 1982)

**Figure 15.1**
Teacher behaviors positively related to student academic performance.

*Annual* **Edition**

unit *3*

The debate over ability grouping has continued for decades and does not appear likely to be resolved soon. Homogeneous and heterogeneous groupings come in and out of fashion, depending on social climate, regardless of research findings.

# Many Individuals, One Class

One of the toughest jobs you will face as a teacher is taking a room of individual students and molding it into a "class." Each student has a unique personality, and unique needs, beliefs, and attitudes. Each enters the class with different background knowledge and different school experiences. You face the difficult tasks of making the group a coherent whole and making instruction meaningful to all students.

You rarely have any choice in how students are selected for class membership. Generally, school administrators or school boards determine the composition of classrooms. In the United States, students are generally grouped by grade, although some schools combine grades in a class. For example, a school may combine a class of first- and second-graders, either because there are insufficient numbers of students in each grade to make up a class, or because it is hoped that the combination of the two grades will be instructionally beneficial.

You do, however, have choices regarding how to organize each group of students. You can use whole-group activities, such as lectures or discussions, small-group activities, or individualized instruction. To a large extent, the grouping you choose depends on your lesson objectives. A good rule of thumb is not to cling to one method; vary your technique to match the nature of your group and the instructional objectives you seek to achieve.

## Ability Grouping

Some schools group students homogeneously according to academic performance (often on a reading achievement test), which is usually referred to as **ability grouping.** Other schools group students heterogeneously, without regard to achievement or ability. The issue of grouping students homogeneously or heterogeneously is fraught with controversy. Ultimately, however, no matter how students are grouped, you will find much variability in your classroom and need to accommodate these differences.

Studies typically find that homogeneous grouping has no positive effect on students' academic performance (Manning & Lucking, 1990; Slavin, 1987, 1990). One study, however, found that homogeneous grouping positively affected the academic performance of high-ability students in honors classes (Kulik & Kulik, 1982), and another study found that both higher- and lower-ability junior high school students achieved better in higher-ability classes (Veldman & Sanford, 1984).

Even homogeneously grouped classes have a wide variety of ability levels among students.

© Jeffry W. Myers/Corbis Media

Homogeneous grouping, however, does seem to affect how teachers run their classes. Classes for less able students tend to be less stimulating (Dar & Resh, 1986; Eder, 1981) than classes for higher-ability students, who are provided an enriched intellectual environment. Durkin (1990) claims that ability grouping is ineffective because it encourages the use of a standardized curriculum and inhibits teachers from individualizing instruction.

Most advocates of homogeneous grouping argue that it is academically better for all students; others argue that, even if it is not best for all, teachers must keep the brightest students stimulated and prepare them for higher education and to contribute to society. Opponents argue that heterogeneous grouping is more academically sound, is a more equitable approach, and will teach students how to live among others whose abilities are different from their own. Some also claim that ability grouping is inherently racist because different groups have not had equal opportunities prior to entering school. Consequently, some groups of students are unfairly penalized when they are placed in lower-ability groups.

## Organizing Instruction *Within* the Class

Another form of grouping occurs *within* the class (Evans, 1994). Even homogeneously grouped classes have students whose abilities vary, although individual differences are even greater in heterogeneously grouped classes. Teachers often place students with similar abilities and academic needs in small groups to ensure that instruction is on the appropriate level for all.

In most schools teachers have the freedom to choose how they organize their classes: in large groups, small groups, or individualized instruction. To a large extent, this decision is based on the teacher's intentions, the subject matter, and students' characteristics (e.g., age, level of achievement). Teachers must also consider what kind of learning atmosphere they wish to create and whether a cooperative arrangement or competitive arrangement would be more beneficial for student learning.

### Whole-Class Instruction

The most traditional form of teaching is whole-class instruction, in which the teacher presents a lesson to all the students simultaneously, with all students getting the same assignments afterwards. Usually, whole-class instruction takes the form of a **lecture** in which the teacher presents information orally, perhaps in conjunction with diagrams, pictures, or demonstrations.

Whole class instruction is one of the most traditional forms of teaching.

© Jeffry W. Myers/Corbis Media

The lecture has remained a popular teaching method because teachers can prepare their material beforehand, present it in an almost scripted fashion, and follow up with assignments or tests that are directly related to the information presented. Lectures are effective in getting a good deal of information across relatively quickly. Teachers may also lecture because that is how they were taught.

Lectures, however, have crucial disadvantages. First, they are based on the premise that all students have the same learning needs and possess the same background knowledge. This is very seldom true; students have many individual differences and learning styles. Second, some students find it difficult to maintain their attention to a lengthy lecture. Although they may appear to be attending, in reality, they may be thinking about things that have nothing to do with the lecture topic. Third, the lecture format places students in a passive role. Cognitive and constructivist theory indicates that learning occurs best when students actively construct their own knowledge.

One way to mix lecture with active student learning is a **lecture-recitation** format, in which teachers not only lecture, but also ask students follow-up questions. For students, the process of searching for answers promotes mental activity; they must process the information acquired in the lecture to answer the questions. The lecture-recitation format forces teachers to design questions that are mentally challenging and stimulating.

Another whole-class method of instruction is **discussion,** in which teachers encourage students to think critically, state their ideas, and evaluate those of their classmates. Having a good discussion is difficult. Students who have had little experience in class discussions may initially find it difficult to take an active role. Others may be reluctant to present their ideas, fearing ridicule. A good discussion also depends on students being prepared, having read assigned passages. And, a good discussion depends on how adept the teacher is at preparing some opening questions and creating an atmosphere that encourages students to express their views.

Teachers often have difficulty changing from their role as a transmitter of information to a facilitator or group leader in a discussion (Dillon, 1987). Discussion, when executed well, can improve both academic learning and students' social skills. In addition to engaging in higher-level thinking skills, students learn to wait their turn, attend to others, criticize constructively, tolerate criticism of their own ideas, and accept that others have views differing from their own.

Even new teachers, fresh from their preservice training, tend to fall back on old patterns they learned from their teachers when they were students, regardless of the methods advocated in their education courses.

Some students are uncomfortable with the recitation format because they feel put "on the spot" to answer the teacher's questions and are afraid of offering a "wrong" answer.

As opposed to lectures, class discussion promotes student participation and a lively exchange of ideas.
© Mary Kate Denny/PhotoEdit

## Cooperative Learning

**Cooperative learning** is an instructional strategy in which students engage in activities that promote collaboration and teamwork, and individual achievement is sometimes overlooked in favor of group accomplishment (Johnson & Johnson, 1987, 1991). Peer collaboration often requires teachers to establish new criteria for student evaluation and feedback and to monitor, rather than to direct, the interaction among students. Cooperative learning succeeds when teachers ask students to brainstorm ideas or evaluate each other's work. Cooperative learning is also effective when students collaborate to write a class newspaper, produce a class play, research information, or plan classroom events.

*Annual* **Edition**

unit *4*

In cooperative learning, students engage in activities that promote collaboration and teamwork.

© Jeffry W. Myers/Corbis Media

 **Making Cooperative Learning Work**

◼◼ Simply grouping students is not likely to
◼◼ be enough for cooperative learning to work. True cooperative groups need to be structured by the teacher to be effective. Here are some suggestions for making cooperative learning work:

1. *Determine clear objectives* (Johnson & Johnson, 1987). For example, you might assign each group to research the geographical characteristics of a particular country.
2. *Group students heterogeneously.* Groups should include students at different achievement levels, from different cultural backgrounds, and both genders (Johnson & Johnson, 1987, 1991).
3. *Make sure group success depends on the contribution of each group member* (Johnson & Johnson, 1991). One way to make group members interdependent is to use the **jigsaw technique,** which consists of structuring the group so each student performs a function without which the group cannot succeed. In the example of the geography assignment, one student in each group could be responsible for constructing a map of the

country, while another gathers information about climate, another collects data about the economy, and another researches the political system.
4. *Give groups opportunities to evaluate their performance.* In addition to evaluating whatever product emerges from the group effort, students should evaluate their performance as a group. Did each member contribute? Did group members discuss issues and resolve differences in opinion to reach consensus?
5. *Provide rewards for the group's successful achievement of its goals.* Providing some kind of acknowledgment of the group's success not only motivates students, but it helps solidify the feeling of group membership and shared responsibility.
6. *Vary group membership.* Varying group membership for different projects allows students to learn from a wider variety of peers and to get to know one another socially. It also prevents elitism and cliquishness among groups. Students can learn a great deal from one another, both academically and socially.

**15.2**

*Describe techniques that teachers can use to make cooperative learning groups more effective.*

According to Johnson and Johnson (1987), for cooperative learning to be successful, students must believe that their goals are attainable only if others also reach those goals; in competitive learning students believe that their goals are reached only if others do not reach those goals.

## Competitive Learning

**Competitive learning** pits student groups against one another so that one group will ultimately "win." When participating in competitive groups for extrinsic rewards, students learn how to strive for success within a group and learn that the effort of each member is critical. Competing for rewards, however, may result in some students always losing. Use only activities that can promote worthwhile competition without endangering the self-worth of individual students (Johnson & Johnson, 1987).

A drawback of competitive learning groups is that they may detract from the sense of solidarity that students may feel for their class; in addition, there tends to be one team of winners and many losers.

## Individualized Learning

Some activities, such as learning specific skills (e.g., mathematics facts or handwriting) and personal activities (e.g., individual writing efforts) are best taught through **individualized instruction,** where each student works independently. For example, one student may be working on learning to write capital letters, while another may concentrate on lowercase letters. Individualized instruction is most productive for activities that require self-direction, self-pacing, and self-interest and when students need extra practice to achieve a skill. Sometimes only a few students need practice, and you can set aside time for them to work alone. Use individualized instruction in situations where students need personal space and time, such as when they are reading silently, writing creatively, or working on personal projects.

## Peer Tutoring

**Peer tutoring,** an approach in which one student tutors another, can be applied in either of two ways. In the first, the students are classmates, but in the second, **cross-age tutoring,** the students are in different grades. Some students are more willing to accept tutoring from an older student than from a same-age classmate.

Peer tutoring provides highly individualized instruction. The tutor can work on precisely the skills the tutee is lacking. In addition, peer tutoring frees the teacher to work with other students in large or small groups. The teacher, nevertheless, needs to prepare the tutors and monitor the pair's progress. Training and monitoring tutors is crucial to the success of peer tutoring (Jenkins & Jenkins,

"I think it's called team teaching."

1987). Peer tutoring strengthens the *tutor's* grasp of the material (Rekrut, 1992). You will find out when you teach that nothing strengthens learning better than teaching.

Peer tutoring has some disadvantages, however. Tutees may feel uncomfortable being tutored by other students. There is also a risk that the tutor is providing the tutee with *misinformation* and that the tutor is abusing the role by making the tutee feel inadequate. To avoid these problems, match tutors to tutees with some attention to their personalities and the tutee's knowledge. Monitor the activities of the peers closely.

## Class Size

Class size may influence your decisions about group arrangements or classroom procedures, although to date little research has explored this possibility. Research on class size has focused primarily on student achievement and student attitudes (Finn & Achilles, 1990; Harder, 1990; Holliday, 1992; Johnston, 1990; Preece, 1987; Slavin, 1990). Glass and Smith (1978) examined the findings of numerous studies of class size carried out in the 1970s and concluded that small class size has a positive influence on student achievement.

On the other hand, several studies have found that other factors, such as peer and cross-age tutoring (Berliner & Casanova, 1988) or the presence of a teacher's aide (Johnston, 1990) are more beneficial for achievement and more cost effective than reducing class size. In some cases, however, reduced class size improves the atmosphere and morale of the school (Slavin, 1990) and yields significant benefits for minority students (Achilles, 1993).

Apart from class size, *teachers' beliefs* about the effects of class size influence the kinds of instructional strategies they use. In a large study conducted to measure the effect of reduced class size (Filby, 1980), teachers reported that classroom management seemed more effective in smaller classes. Teachers also believed that they included more enrichment activities in their teaching, prepared lessons in greater depth, and experienced a sense of freedom from constraints imposed by larger classes.

Comparisons of class sizes across six different nations (McAdams, 1993) indicate that the average class size in U.S. schools (between 20 and 30 students) is similar to those of other industrialized countries, such as Canada, England, and Germany (see figure 15.2). With an average of about 40 students, class size is greater in Japan, where educational achievement is currently higher than it is in the United States. On the other hand, the Japanese school year contains approximately 44 percent more days than ours, including 40 half-day classes on Saturdays.

| | Canada | Denmark | England | Germany | Japan | U.S. |
|---|---|---|---|---|---|---|
| Daily hours of attendance in elementary school | 5 to 6 hours | 3 to 4 hours | 5 to 6 hours | 4 to 5 hours | 4 hours in first grade, 6 after third grade | 5 to 6 hours |
| Length of school year | 190 to 200 days; no Saturdays | 200 days; no Saturdays | 190 days; no Saturdays | 195 to 226 days; some half-day Saturdays | 240 days, including 40 half-day Saturdays | 180 days; no Saturdays |
| Average class size | 20 to 30 students per class | 15 to 20 students per class | 20 to 30 students per class | 20 to 30 students per class | 40 students per class | 20 to 30 students per class |
| Grouping for instruction | Mixed-ability groups until tenth grade | Mixed-ability groups until ninth grade | Mixed-ability groups until seventh grade | Mixed-ability groups until seventh grade | Mixed-ability groups until tenth grade | Tracking begins in mid-elementary school |

**Figure 15.2**

Comparisons of education in the United States and selected other countries.

From R. P. McAdams, *Lessons From Abroad: How Other Countries Educate Their Children.* Copyright © 1993 Technomic Publishing Co., Lancaster, Pennsylvania. Reprinted by permission.

# The Teaching "Act"

The "act" of teaching is simultaneously a public performance, a juggling act, and a thought-out, reasoned set of activities. While in the act of teaching, teachers make moment-by-moment decisions and record information in their heads for later use. Consider the following scenario:

*A sixth-grade math teacher has planned a lesson on the volume of three-dimensional figures. She designed the lesson to start with a demonstration using figures she has created, followed by students, in groups of three and four, creating their own cardboard figures and using rulers to determine each figure's volume. She carefully grouped together higher and lower achievers. At the end of the lesson, each group was to show the class their figures and demonstrate how they computed their figure's volume.*

*During her initial demonstration, loudspeaker announcements interrupt twice, and the assistant principal walks in unannounced to observe her teach. Although she is initially uncomfortable, she collects herself and continues. Just after forming her groups, the music teacher enters and announces that six of the students must come with him for a special chorus practice prior to tomorrow's concert. The carefully selected groups are now in complete disarray.*

*The teacher reformulates the groups on the spot, making quick decisions about who will work together. Two students who are now grouped together do not want to be in the same group and begin to argue. The teacher rearranges the groups before the argument breaks into a fight. She begins to distribute the cardboard and rulers but discovers that she has only half of the cardboard and rulers she will need because another teacher has borrowed them without asking. She decides to use some file folders in place of the cardboard and to turn other file folders into rulers by marking inches on the side of the folder.*

This scenario probably occurs more often than you think. The ability to plan a good lesson is crucial in good teaching, but so is thinking on your feet. While the lesson may not have turned out as well as planned, the teacher was flexible and imaginative and thereby saved the day.

## The Complexity of the Classroom

While novices may be overwhelmed by the complexity of the classroom, experts have become adept at handling the demands of a complex classroom environment.

The scenario illustrates the complexity of the classroom. Many events occur simultaneously. The various individuals in the room (the teacher, the students) have different agendas, different interests, different background knowledge, and are having different experiences. Complexities of a typical classroom include multidimensionality, simultaneity, immediacy, unpredictability, publicness, and history (Doyle, 1986).

### Multidimensionality

Multidimensionality refers to the many events that occur in the classroom, such as keeping records, scheduling content to be taught, ordering supplies, planning instruction, carrying out instruction, motivating students, monitoring their behavior, and assessing and analyzing student learning. At any given moment, the teacher may be performing one or more of these tasks. The activities are not only interrelated, but often dependent on one another. For example, when teachers order supplies or plan for instruction, they base their decisions on many factors, including student achievement, curricular requirements, and allocation of classroom time. Similarly, students must play multidimensional roles as learners, as members of a group, and as individuals interacting with rules, ideas, materials, and assignments.

## Simultaneity

Multiple classroom events often occur simultaneously. Teachers, for example, may be directing their attention to particular students who need help, but they simultaneously monitor the behavior of students working alone or in groups. This overlapping of behaviors becomes the repertoire of every experienced teacher (Kounin, 1970). How successfully teachers handle these simultaneous roles depends on how aware and skillful they are.

## Immediacy

The rapid exchange of teacher-student interactions often requires teachers to react on the spot. Maintaining the flow of instruction and juggling the many requirements for order, discipline, and movement from one activity to the next allow teachers little time to reflect. These actions are sometimes further complicated by unpredictable events.

## Unpredictability

All experienced teachers know that interruptions, diversions, and confusion can occur in the classroom at any time. Teachers must respond to these occurrences while maintaining the threads of the activity in which they are engaged. Or they must temporarily leave the ongoing activity. Many experienced teachers learn how to prepare their students for unanticipated events; new teachers often find dealing with unpredictable classroom events and disruptive student behavior the most frustrating part of their work.

## Publicness

Few jobs are as public as teaching. Teachers carry out most of their tasks in front of someone else. Students can observe how the teacher handles other students; they often judge the effectiveness of their teacher by these observations. In addition, supervisors, parents, colleagues, or students from other classes may enter the classroom at any time. Mistakes in judgment become public knowledge fast.

## History

Classes meet several times a week over a long period of time. Frequently, the way a new school year begins affects the way the class will run for the rest of the year. Early planning, establishing rules, and maintaining the flow of instruction are basic requirements for effective teaching. When teachers make students aware of their expectations early in the school year, they have laid the groundwork for successful learning.

The more experienced a teacher becomes, the easier it is to manage all of the pressures in the classroom. In other words, some of the behaviors teachers must perform to maintain the functioning of a classroom become **automatic**. Teachers are able to do more than one thing at a time by having many automatic responses and actions. The teacher can then focus on the most important events.

# Allocating Instructional Time

One of the most important decisions teachers make about teaching is how to use class time. The amount of time students spend in school is not equivalent to the amount of time spent teaching or learning. Much time in schools is spent in administrative functions (e.g., as taking attendance), transitions, noninstructional activities (e.g., lunch), and, simply, "down time" when nothing is being done.

In recent years, education in the United States has been criticized as being "soft" on our students as compared to other countries, in particular, Japan. Students in the United States attend school five days per week for about six and a half hours; students in Japan attend school six days a week and often for longer hours and more weeks in the year (Sato, 1990). On the other hand, the use of time in

**15.3** ◎
*Describe ways of maximizing instructional time.*

Japan's schools is different; that is, in Japan, students have longer lunch hours, more time is devoted to the arts or science in afterschool activities, and teachers have more time to work with students individually and more time to prepare for their work (McAdams, 1993; Stevenson & Stigler, 1992). In some other Western countries such as Germany and Denmark, school days are shorter than in the United States with a greater number of breaks; however, these countries have more school days in the year than in the United States and teachers generally have less responsibility for administrative and nonteaching tasks and behavior management.

When discussing instructional time, it is important to differentiate between mandated time allotment (the amount of time the state or school district requires for different subject areas) and the amount of time spent on actual teaching and learning. Teachers have little control over the first, although they can often make decisions about how to organize that time, over days or weeks.

Research indicates that only two-thirds of actual time spent in school is spent in instruction (Fisher et al., 1980). The time students spend listening or carrying out an assignment or engaged in verbal interactions with the teacher and other class-mates is called time-on-task, or **engaged time.** Not surprisingly, high-achieving students are more focused on tasks than low-achieving students (Evertson, 1986; Nystrand & Gamoran, 1989). Since low-achieving students may not be actually learning or may be confused or frustrated with the schoolwork, their attention often wanders. Boredom can also explain why some students daydream or lose their concentration. When students experience success and are interested in the material presented, they are more likely to expend effort on learning.

## Maximizing Instructional Time

After all the administrative functions, bathroom breaks, and transitions are accounted for, the time available for teaching and learning is limited. When you do not use instructional time well, you squander actual time spent learning. The following suggestions will help you maximize the use of instructional time:

1. *Keep students motivated.* Students need a reason to participate; some may genuinely enjoy learning, but others may need an explanation of the value of the learning or some form of extrinsic reinforcement to apply themselves.
2. *Keep instruction on students' levels.* Instruction that students find either too difficult or too simple will result in lack of interest and engagement. Because students have various abilities and background knowledge, finding the proper instructional level is particularly challenging. Some teachers solve the problem by grouping students or individualizing instruction.
3. *Keep students active.* When you design lessons with student activities built in, students have fewer opportunities to become disengaged with the lesson.

However, it is important that the activities are meaningful and promote the learning objectives of the lesson.
4. *Be organized and prepared; anticipate problems.* The better prepared you are and the more you anticipate interruptions in a lesson, the more likely you will use instructional time efficiently. Experience helps in this area.
5. *Delegate responsibilities when appropriate.* In most classes, you can call on responsible students to help with administrative functions, freeing you to do more teaching. Giving responsibilities to students often heightens their self-esteem and their sense of belonging to the class.
6. *Turn on your "radar" and watch for students whose attention is drifting.* In larger classes, it is difficult to keep all students engaged; however, by circulating through the room and surveying the room with your eyes, you can often detect students whose attention has drifted away from the lesson. Re-engage them without embarrassing or humiliating them and compliment them later for staying engaged.

## The Effects of Teacher Behavior

*How* you teach may have as powerful an effect as *what* you teach. The actions you take as a teacher directly affect what your students learn. For example, effective teachers stress skill development, spend considerable time on academic tasks, exhibit confidence, work well with supervisors, stress academics in the classroom, emphasize good classroom management, are optimistic about their students' ability to learn, and set high standards for achievement (Miller & Ellsworth, 1985; Rosenshine, 1983; Stallings, 1991).

In addition, effective teachers are warm, enthusiastic, and businesslike, provide variety in materials and academic activities (Rosenshine, 1983), teach with clarity (Smith, 1985), and use probing questions to follow initial questioning. Teachers' nonverbal signs of approval, their use of student ideas, and the amount of teacher talk have little bearing on student achievement.

Student achievement also improves when teachers structure content well (Stallings et al., 1978; Wright & Nuthall, 1971), provide opportunities for review and discussion, and give students corrective feedback (Stallings et al., 1978). Clarifying incorrect or partially incorrect responses has a positive effect on learning (Coker, Medley, & Soar, 1980; Crawford, 1983; Dunkin, 1978; Evertson, 1986). When teachers monitor activities, minimize transitional periods, and maximize task engagement, student outcomes tend to be successful (Brophy, 1983; Crawford, 1983). When teachers increase "wait-time" (the amount of time they give students to respond), student learning increases (Tobin, 1980; Tobin & Capie, 1982), particularly when combined with high-level questioning (Tobin & Capie, 1982).

Although it seems obvious that low-achieving students need more opportunities to learn (Murphy, 1986; Woolfolk & Brooks, 1985), teachers frequently give less content and less instructional time to low-achieving students (Murphy, 1986). This pattern contributes to low-achieving students' developing low self-esteem and negative attitudes toward school. Teachers' nonverbal behavior, such as facial expressions and eye contact, also sends students messages about teachers' expectations of the students' performance.

## Practicing Good Teaching Behavior

Effective teachers (a) use clear and varied methods of presentation, (b) provide corrective feedback, (c) emphasize academic instruction, (d) maintain students' task engagement in academic activities for most of classroom time, (e) manage and organize classrooms as efficient learning environments, (f) implement classroom rules and procedures, and (g) keep the pace of instruction moving smoothly.

## Managing Behavior

Maintaining order is a major concern for new teachers. Managing student behavior, however, does not imply rigidity or authoritarianism. In fact, the most successful teachers involve their students in learning as a way to maintain order and promote successful achievement. By focusing on task engagement, rather than disciplinary methods, these teachers establish an orderly classroom in which students learn (Berliner, 1986; Claridge & Berliner, 1991; Denham & Leiberman, 1980; Evertson et al., 1983; Kounin, 1970; McLaughlin, 1994). When students disrupt the classroom, attempts to manage their behavior through work-related activities are often more practical than disciplinary measures. Successful teachers focus on classroom organization techniques that are best for the group. Of course, when a student disrupts learning or presents a threat to others, teachers must focus on that individual student.

In typical day-to-day classroom management teachers must consider the physical arrangement of the classroom, the time allotted to various subject matter instruction, the rules for transitions from one activity to another, the rules for group and individual behavior, and the types of activities that occur. In other words, classroom management consists of *where* activities take place, *when* and *for how long* the activities occur, *how* the activities are carried out, *who* participates, and *what* is

**15.4** ◎
*Describe teacher behaviors that promote student achievement.*

Many teachers have difficulty formulating high-level questions; many also have difficulty pausing long enough for students to formulate answers. They are sometimes concerned that, by waiting, the lesson loses momentum.

expected of all the participants in the classroom. Teachers make many decisions that affect how successful they will be in promoting learning. One of the most important decisions teachers make is their choice of a model of teaching.

# Teacher-Centered or Student-Centered Instruction

15.5 ◎

*Compare teacher-centered and student-centered philosophies of instruction.*

Neither "teacher-centered" nor "student-centered" teaching is the *right* philosophy of teaching. Both are valid ways of understanding learning and classroom instruction.

One of the most important teaching decisions you will make is who controls the learning process: the students or you. This decision depends largely on your beliefs about how students learn. You may be unaware of the theories you hold, so it is important for you to begin examining your own viewpoints about learning. Reflect on your own learning and identify the ways in which you learn best. Also, observe students learning a particularly difficult task and ask yourself how they are acquiring the skill or knowledge.

You will no doubt discover that some kinds of learning seem to be best directed by the learner, whereas other kinds of learning require the regulation of the teacher or other adult. Consider, for example, the way you may have learned the various theories of cognitive psychologists mentioned in this book. You may have had to encounter the ideas or theories in several contexts, to discuss these ideas with some of your classmates, to ask your instructor many questions, and to incorporate these ideas into others you may have learned in previous psychology and education courses. Your instructor probably facilitated your acquisition of difficult ideas, but much of what you learned developed from your own complex thinking.

Contrast this with how you may have learned to operate a computer; although higher-order thinking may be required for certain levels of computer application, your initial encounter with the machine was probably through direct teacher instruction. Few people have the courage to sit down and try to "conquer" the computer by themselves; most ask a more knowledgeable computer user to show them how to use the machine. In this instance, the learning is more "teacher-directed" in that the more experienced computer user is directing the learning activity.

# Models of Teaching

15.6 ◎

*Describe the direct instruction, learning strategies, and cognitive apprenticeship models of teaching.*

Your philosophy of teaching you hold has direct bearing on the model of teaching you select. If you tend to be more teacher-centered in your philosophy, you are likely to select direct instruction as your model of teaching. If you are more student-centered, you are more likely to choose a cognitive apprenticeship model. When you teach, you may find yourself applying both models in your work.

## Direct Instruction

Educators who tend to be teacher-centered advocate a model of teaching called **direct instruction,** which is sometimes referred to as explicit teaching. Supporters of this approach suggest that well-structured and carefully sequenced learning activities lead to student success (Anderson, Evertson, & Brophy, 1982; Emmer et al., 1982; Fitzpatrick, 1982; Good & Grouws, 1979; Porter & Brophy, 1988; Stallings, 1991).

### The Phases of Direct Instruction

*A+*

Direct instruction consists of four phases: introduction and review, presentation, guided practice, and independent practice. First, the teacher introduces a lesson to students, explaining its purpose and format and reviewing pertinent material presented previously. Second, the teacher presents new concepts, perhaps providing examples, demonstrating an activity, and asking students questions. Third, students practice using the new knowledge with the teacher's guidance and, finally, students work independently.

Suppose you are teaching students how to format a formal letter. In the introduction and review phase, you may ask students if they have written letters before, to whom, and for what purpose. You might discuss various situations in which they would write letters in the future (mostly eliciting ideas from the students themselves). And you may review ideas that you have previously covered (e.g., leaving margins and double spacing). In the presentation phase, you might model on the board a letter to the neighboring class inviting them to a party, identifying the various elements of the letter, such as the date, the greeting, and the closing. In the guided practice phase, students would work on a letter of their own, while you circulate through the room looking over their letters and providing feedback. Finally, in the independent practice phase, you may have students work on a letter on their own as a homework assignment.

## The Effects of Direct Instruction

Most research investigating direct instruction has compared teachers who have received training in specific instructional strategies with teachers who have not received training. Fitzpatrick (1982), for example, found that algebra and foreign language teachers who received explicit training in a sequential instructional design maintained the attention of students, provided immediate feedback, had fewer interruptions, and set clearer goals than teachers who received no training. In other words, trained teachers received higher ratings than untrained teachers.

## When Direct Instruction Works Best

Direct instruction is most successful with young children, children who learn slowly, students with learning disabilities, and in situations where one is teaching well-structured skills or knowledge that can be broken into steps (Berliner, 1982; Gettinger, 1982, 1993). These might include arithmetic facts, spelling, decoding skills, grammar, factual information in science and history, and skills related to cooking, electronics, or other manual arts. Advocates of direct instruction believe that difficult material should be taught in small steps with much practice so that students can process small amounts of information without overtaxing working memory (Tobias, 1981).

Skill development and factual information that is readily "automatized" can be taught better through direct instruction. Direct instruction in comprehension can also be effective, particularly when teachers show students how to generate ideas while reading (Carnine et al., 1983) or how to select appropriate study skills for various study tasks (Archambeault, 1992). Information-processing theory also supports direct instruction by suggesting that learning is enhanced by review, rehearsal, and summarizing (Gagné, 1985).

Ill-structured content, such as writing compositions, literature analysis, or content that requires problem solving and decision making, is less amenable to direct instruction (Mayer & Cook, 1980; Rosenshine & Stevens, 1986). It is best *not* to use direct instruction when learning objectives involve evaluation, appreciation, critiquing, or analyzing and synthesizing information.

## Teaching Learning Strategies

Instructional approaches have recently focused on teaching the learner *how* to learn. This approach draws on several sources for its rationale: (a) current research on metacognition (or students' awareness of their own thinking), (b) the recognition that learning strategies can be explicitly taught, and (c) the perspective that learners should actively engage in learning.

**Learning strategies** are techniques that can be applied in a variety of situations to promote recall or comprehension. Generating a set of prereading questions based on the title of a book is a learning strategy that promotes comprehension. When taught this strategy, students can apply it in various reading situations, including reading in the content areas, such as science and social

When teaching learning strategies, try to ensure that students not only learn the strategies, but that they *generalize* them to appropriate situations.

studies. Four learning strategies students can use and apply either to basic or more complex tasks are rehearsal, elaboration, organization, and monitoring (Weinstein & Mayer, 1986).

### Rehearsal

Weinstein and Mayer (1986) found that age is a critical factor in the *spontaneous* use of learning strategies; for example, a child in nursery school does not use rehearsal strategies, but a fourth-grade child may consistently use rehearsal strategies to memorize new information (Flavell, Friedrichs, & Hoyt, 1970). Students who use rehearsal techniques perform better on memory tasks than students who do not (Flavell & Wellman, 1977). Mayer and Cook (1980) examined the effects of using rehearsal strategies to learn complex tasks. They found that rehearsers remembered more details, but the control group remembered more concepts, a finding that suggests rehearsal strategies may be more useful for basic than for complex tasks. Rehearsal helps students master complex tasks only if they are mature enough to master the task. For example, students below the sixth grade who copied or underlined important facts in a reading passage were unable to identify the important information (Brown & Smiley, 1977).

### Elaboration

Elaboration strategies used in basic tasks sometimes entail forming mental images or constructing a sentence that connects two or more items. Elaboration for complex tasks includes paraphrasing, summarizing, creating analogies, and question answering. The most difficult elaboration strategy for complex tasks appears to be notetaking, although older students who receive sufficient training can benefit (Carrier & Titus, 1981; Peper & Mayer, 1986). Since most students below the sixth grade have difficulty distinguishing between more and less important sentences or facts, notetaking is most useful in upper-grade and secondary school classrooms.

### Organizational Strategies

Organizational strategies involve categorizing and clustering similar objects or ideas. Young children, ages 5 to 7, do not use organizational strategies spontaneously when asked to memorize pictures, but 10-year-olds do. Nine-year-olds who fail to use the strategy spontaneously can be taught to use it (Flavell, Friedrichs, & Hoyt, 1970). Although students' competence in using organizational strategies follows a developmental progression, training in this strategy can be effective (Bjorklund, Ornstein, & Haig, 1977; Rossi & Wittrock, 1971). Students can successfully use organizational strategies for more complex tasks, particularly when they are constructing relationships among ideas in working memory (Farnham-Diggory, 1992; Mayer, 1982, 1984). Outlining, organizing items in meaningful tasks, networking ideas in a text, and identifying different types of prose structures are some of the strategies that students can be taught.

### Monitoring

Students who monitor their own performance perform better than those who simply perform a task and never check themselves. Self-monitoring is part of a student's metacognitive awareness; it is the first step in diagnosing and remediating one's own learning (Brown & Palincsar, 1982; Collins, Brown, & Newman, 1989).

The learning strategies model calls for teachers to make explicit the way they themselves learn. For example, Graves (1983) teaches students how to write by writing along with them; Chall (1983) believes that reading comprehension can be enhanced by teaching students, through modeling, how to monitor their comprehension, reread for memory, and summarize for getting the gist of the material.

## Explicit Teaching of Learning Strategies

The learning strategies just described can be taught explicitly. Collins and Smith (1980) studied learning strategies by developing a taxonomy of comprehension failures (such as meeting a novel word or failure to understand a sentence or its relationship to other sentences) and the ways in which readers can remediate these failures: by (a) ignoring and reading on, (b) suspending judgment, (c) forming a tentative hypothesis, (d) rereading, and (e) going to an expert source, such as a dictionary, person, or glossary. Furthermore, Collins and Smith suggest that instruction should take place in two phases. First the teacher models comprehension strategies and then the teacher coaches students as they try out the strategies.

## Reciprocal Teaching

Brown and Palincsar (1982) extended the ideas of Collins and Smith and developed a model of instruction called **reciprocal teaching,** in which a teacher or a fellow student models effective learning strategies. Four basic strategies foster comprehension: (a) summarizing, (b) clarification of difficulties, (c) asking a question that might appear on a test, and (d) making predictions. After reading a passage, a small group meets to discuss it. The teacher (or a student) uses the four strategies out loud, saying, for example, "What do I think will happen next? I think the sun will melt the snowman." The students then engage in the same strategies. Later, the students take turns playing the role of "teacher."

Brown and Palincsar (1982) found that students who used this approach not only improved their comprehension, but maintained their improvement some months later. Reciprocal teaching is effective for students from first grade through college.

To determine whether the strategies identified in the Collins and Smith (1980) and Brown and Palincsar (1982) studies are actually strategies that skilled comprehenders use, Bereiter and Bird (1985) asked ten adults to think aloud while reading passages. Verifying that expert readers do use metacognitive strategies uncovered in the earlier studies, Bereiter and Bird taught seventh-graders these strategies. Results showed that students who received training improved almost three grade levels, whereas those who did not receive the training improved about a half a grade.

Other demonstrated effective learning strategies include note taking, summarizing, predicting, thinking aloud, generating hypotheses, memorizing, and question asking (King, 1991; Palincsar, 1991; Paris, 1991).

# A Cognitive Apprenticeship Approach to Teaching and Learning

Recent developments in the field of cognitive psychology have led to the development of models of instruction that address newer theories of learning (Brown, Collins, & Duguid, 1989; Collins, Brown, & Newman, 1989; Farnham-Diggory, 1990; Resnick, 1989). One potentially powerful model is based on Collins, Brown, and Newman's (1989) cognitive apprenticeships, which stem from the ideas of the Russian psychologist Lev S. Vygotsky. Although apprenticeships are generally thought of in terms of crafts, such a model can be applied to cognitive activities as well. Apprenticeships involve experts and novices working together on important projects that are meaningful to both groups. The experts demonstrate their methods and encourage the apprentices to reenact their task-related behavior. Experts then coach and provide **scaffolding,** or supporting structure. They gradually increase the complexity of the task and turn over more responsibility to the learner (the apprentice). Along the way, the experts ask the apprentices to describe what they are doing and to identify the general principles they are applying. In such a model, the work is cooperative; both the experts and the apprentices care about the outcomes, and the experts want apprentices to become competent.

Because it makes learning a collective experience, the reciprocal teaching method encourages students to become a community of learners.

In cognitive apprenticeship, experts (teachers) gradually turn over more responsibility to apprentices (students).

© Jeffry W. Myers/Corbis Media

An excellent example of apprenticeship in cognitive activity is the curriculum by Rendell (undated, as cited in Farnham-Diggory, 1990), which has features similar to the apprenticeship model of Collins, Brown, & Newman (1989). Based on what he calls a topic study, Rendell has created curricula around hundreds of themes or topics that last two or more semesters and that integrate all of the subject matter commonly used in the elementary school (reading, math, science, social studies, etc.). Each topic study is (a) based on the idea that the world is complex and that students need to find out how it works; (b) developed around a storyline that captures students' interest and imagination; (c) problem oriented; and (d) designed to encourage critical thinking and have students actively participate as decision makers in the learning process.

Collins, Brown, and Newman (1989) identify four categories within the apprenticeship model: *content, method, sequence,* and *sociology.*

## Content

**Domain specific knowledge** refers to specific facts in a particular area (e.g., a whale is a mammal; the Navajo tribe inhabited what we now call Arizona and New Mexico). Domain knowledge does not tell students *how* they may use the knowledge. When learners cannot apply domain specific knowledge, it can become inert, or unavailable, which Flavell and colleagues (1981) call a production deficiency. Collins, Brown, & Newman (1989) believe that domain specific knowledge is what is essentially taught in today's schools.

To activate knowledge, students must learn three types of procedural knowledge: problem-solving strategies, control strategies, and learning strategies. Problem-solving strategies include asking questions and repetition or reactivation of what the problem solver believes has been learned.

Control strategies help learners construct efficient "working programs" or organized thinking strategies, which experts generally use but which novices generally lack. Control strategies include monitoring, predicting, diagnosing one's own thinking patterns, and deciding how to fix unsuccessful thinking approaches. These self-checking strategies control how the individual studies problems.

Learning strategies refer to techniques people use to learn domain specific knowledge, the kind of strategies you use when you have to learn new vocabulary or when you are studying for an examination.

## Method

In the apprenticeship model of teaching, the learner serves as an "apprentice" to the teacher until the student has achieved mastery. The teacher uses various instructional strategies, including **modeling,** which means showing students how to do something while verbally describing what you are doing.

Coaching follows modeling. Students perform the task and the teacher (the expert) gives feedback and guidance. Coaching brings the student closer to expert performance; *approximation* of expert performance is the goal, since it takes a long time to become an expert. The purpose of coaching is to keep students on the right track.

Scaffolding refers to support the teacher gives until the student can work independently, and **fading** refers to the gradual removal of the support. As the student achieves greater competence, the teacher withdraws support in increments that allow the learner to gain control.

**Articulation** is based on the principle that verbalization enhances learning (Bower & Hilgard, 1981). It involves asking students to verbalize how they are solving a problem. Articulation forces students to *attend* to the control process they are using; it provides linguistic support for what the student is doing (Farnham-Diggory, 1992).

**Reflection** requires students to compare their activities with those used by the expert or other students. Collins, Brown, & Newman (1989) call this abstracted replay, or identifying the principles underlying task-related behavior. The object of this phase of learning is to help students understand task requirements and to increase their repertoire of working programs, or mental organizations of knowledge. By making such comparisons, students discover flaws in their own approach or in the approaches of others. Reflection promotes analysis, evaluation, and problem solving.

The final phase is exploration, when students try out newer or more challenging applications of their knowledge. Students try to figure out how and when their skills are relevant and to find new ways to apply their knowledge.

## Sequence

Sequencing instruction is the teacher's most difficult task. Collins, Brown, and Newman (1989) recommend three overarching principles of sequencing: (a) present "global" tasks prior to "local" tasks, (b) gradually increase the complexity of tasks, and (c) gradually increase the diversity of the tasks.

## Sociology

This apprenticeship model also takes into account that learning is situated, that is, learning takes place within a physical and sociocultural space that defines the nature of meaning itself (Collins, Brown, & Newman, 1989). Miller and Gildea (1987) distinguish between meaning that is learned from dictionaries and meaning that is learned in everyday life. Traditional teaching focuses on dictionary meanings; everyday experiences with ideas reflect the "cumulative wisdom of the culture" (Brown, Collins, & Duguid, 1989). Students learn cultural meaning from practitioners. In this model, experts work closely with students to impart knowledge. Farnham-Diggory (1992) believes this type of cooperative learning environment fosters intrinsic motivation.

# Teaching Strategies and Cognitive Development

Let us now examine how the complex nature of cognitive development influences the way teachers teach. The teacher's understanding of how students learn and how cognition develops is fundamental to the selection of appropriate teaching strategies.

15.7 ◎

*Describe teaching strategies suggested by our knowledge of students' cognitive development.*

In the 1960s, Jerome Bruner began the "cognitive revolution" in education, and since then, U.S. educators have looked carefully at the work of Piaget, Vygotsky, and the information-processing theorists to understand better how to promote learning. Increasingly, educators in the United States are concerned with changing students' cognitions; students need to learn thought processes, rules, and strategies, not only memorize information. For example, when students perform a particular science experiment, they not only learn the findings of the experiment; they also learn about scientific inquiry, hypothesis testing, and the nature of scientific experimentation.

## Increasing Connectivity

Farnham-Diggory (1992) has identified qualitative shifts that contemporary researchers have experienced in their search for underlying cognitive mechanisms that produce wide-ranging changes in cognitive ability. One of these mechanisms is increasing connectivity, which allows students to interconnect symbols, make inferences, and apply previously learned knowledge. It is the ability to "put two and two together" (Farnham-Diggory, 1992, p. 180). Farnham-Diggory suggests that one source of increasing connectivity is the growth of the brain. As the brain grows, neural connections become more numerous and more complex.

Young children do not automatically make connections; as they mature, however, they spontaneously make connections that form the foundation for more complex thinking. They also begin to elaborate on information and make inferences. Schmidt and Paris (1983) found that among children age 5 to 9, older children make more inferences than younger children and integrate information in more ways to make inferences. Paris, Cross, and Lipson (1984) used these ideas to develop a program to teach reading that emphasizes discussion and teaches children strategies to connect their ideas.

## Detecting Patterns

Gibson (1969) studied perceptual learning and found that, with age, children are better able to perceive differences in incoming information. Young children, for example, may respond to all dogs in the same way; as they mature, they begin to distinguish between pets and other dogs (Farnham-Diggory, 1992). The development of this ability coincides with the development of a longer attention span and the emergence of an ability to *decide* what to pay attention to. As children are better able to focus, they also begin to recognize patterns instead of perceiving each individual stimulus separately. Recognizing patterns is an important cognitive ability because it promotes thinking that is more sophisticated, efficient, and economical. Reading instruction that focuses on letter and word patterns is based on Gibson's work (Gibson & Levin, 1975).

## Rules and Strategies

Children also become increasingly able to retrieve and use complex rules (procedures) and strategies. Children's knowledge of rules is a critical aspect of cognitive development (Seigler, 1986). As children mature, they increase their knowledge of rules and they start to encounter more complex rules in school (Klahr & Robinson, 1981; Seigler, 1986). Think, for example, of how rules in mathematics range from simple (how to add without regrouping) to more complex (how to add fractions with unlike denominators).

## Working Memory Programs

According to Karmiloff-Smith (1979), children go through three phases in mastering a new task. In Phase 1, children's task behavior is data-driven; that is, they respond to external stimuli sequentially, with no overall plan. These responses may be quite skilled, but the child has not yet looked at the relationships among the stimuli.

With age, children are better able to perceive and recognize patterns.

© Wolfgang Kaehler/Corbis Media

In Phase 2, children become aware of some pattern in their responses. For example, they may note that a sequence of responses is really one response, which they have been repeating. At this point, they can make the response into a rule. Karmiloff-Smith (1979) points out that while this is a very important cognitive step, it can lead to errors, since general rules do not always apply. (Think, for example, of pronunciation rules in English: Contrast the pronunciation of *taught, caught,* and *fraught* with the pronunciation of *laughter*).

Can you think of other pronunciation rules in English that do not always apply?

In Phase 3, children begin to realize that they need to develop more elaborate and flexible plans to account for situations where the general rule does not apply. Karmiloff-Smith (1979) refers to this three-phase process as **metaprocedural control**. In Phase 1, the child responds to each discrete stimulus on a trial-and-error basis. In Phase 2, the child observes a pattern in his or her responses and uses metaprocedural knowledge, rather than just procedural, to make decisions. In Phase 3, the child understands when general rules apply and when exceptions are necessary.

## Interlocking Working Memory Programs

Working memory becomes larger and more complex because of the individual's ability to interlock various working memory programs through chaining (hooking one program on to another), or embedding (creating subprograms as computer programmers do). Students tend to remember important information better than less important information regardless of age. Age, however, is a factor in the students' ability to select the most important, rank it, and discard irrelevant material. Most students through fifth grade are not able to summarize effectively; this skill develops in later childhood and adolescence (Brown, Day, & Jones, 1983; Brown & Smiley, 1977).

## Cognitive Shifts and Instruction

Cognitive shifts occur as a result of brain development and children's experiences. As children get older, they become better able to deal with more connections, more complex patterns, more rules and strategies, and to operate within more complex working programs. Cognitive development occurs best in classrooms with stimulating learning environments that permit students to test and explore various ideas.

# Fostering Student Independence and Involvement

One of the most difficult challenges facing teachers is producing independent learners while maintaining student interest and involvement. The cognitive model of apprenticeship can help solve this dilemma. Students in a classroom may appear "involved" as they respond to fast-paced, recitation-type questions requiring them to "stay on their toes" and get ready for rapid-fire interactions with their teacher. However, the *quality* of that involvement is debatable if the questions are like these: "In the passage we just read who was the main character? Where did the story take place?" The students are involved in the sense that they are participating; however, this type of interaction doesn't create interest that is long-ranging and important to the student. In fact, teacher-controlled recitations can lead to simplistic thought processes and "right-answer" questions, rather than thought-provoking problems that require meaningful analysis.

15.8
*Describe methods of fostering student independence and involvement.*

Think of your classroom as a workplace in which the students have several jobs that need to be accomplished in different ways. They need to learn skills, examine ideas, and produce written work, and they need time to consolidate, discuss, and integrate what they have learned. They also must learn how to cooperate, to work alone, to address differences among their classmates, and to appreciate the work of others. Your job is to make this possible through the materials you offer, the behavior you model, the information you impart, and the experiences you devise.

Allowing students to pace their own learning encourages them to become autonomous learners.

© Tom McCarthy/Unicorn Stock Photos

Most teachers believe they accomplish these goals in their classrooms; unfortunately, the need to control student behavior sometimes overshadows the goals. The more choices students are given and the more students are permitted to move about the classroom, the greater the demand for the teacher to monitor and manage behavior (Doyle, 1986). When students control what is to be learned, how learning should take place, and the pacing of activities, they are more task-involved. The dilemma for every teacher, then, is to organize the classroom to accomplish two seemingly opposing goals, namely, *developing student autonomy* and *managing student behavior*.

## Student Autonomy

Individualized and small-group instruction in which students are allowed to pace their own learning and to select learning materials promote student autonomy. Learning how to work alone, how to monitor one's own behavior, how to assess one's own learning, and how to work cooperatively are aspects of autonomy. To develop autonomy, students must believe that they control their own learning. They must also feel that making mistakes is part of learning and is useful toward achieving eventual mastery. In other words, students need to make hypotheses, test them, and confirm their hunches. They need to approximate accuracy without achieving precision immediately. Students need to believe in their own effectiveness and in their ability to become autonomous learners.

The physical arrangement of a classroom that encourages student autonomy differs from traditional whole-class instruction in which all students work on the same task. To allow for student mobility, the classroom must be arranged for movement; to allow for independent study, the classroom must have space where individuals can work quietly. Individuals and small groups can rearrange chairs and desks for different tasks; and spaces should be set aside for specific individual and small-group tasks, such as centers for reading alone, writing, working on research, and conducting scientific experiments.

*A*⁺ Establish specific procedures for conduct within these spaces; allot different amounts of time for different activities. Carefully implement how students are allowed to move and change activities.

## Student Involvement

Some studies have shown that students remain more task-oriented when the teacher controls the events of the classroom (Doyle, 1986). When students' work is externally paced (through recitations or tests), their involvement is high (Kounin & Gump, 1974). Student involvement is particularly high in situations where teacher-paced instruction is accompanied by appropriate materials and clearly defined student learning goals. Students are off-task more often when lessons are centered around class discussion, group projects, or role playing. On the other hand, Kounin and Gump found that when students work on individual tasks that are insulated from intrusion, on-task behavior is high.

Differences in student involvement also vary according to student characteristics. For example, high achievers tend to maintain involvement longer than low achievers (Shimron, 1976); this is not unusual since success generally generates continued involvement (and vice versa). Unfortunately, some of the differences in student involvement may have more to do with teachers' responses to high- and low-ability groups than to an inherent difference between the two groups.

# Adapting Teaching for Different Learners

The most difficult and important job for a teacher is to adapt teaching strategies that take into account student differences, such as aptitude, variations in cultural perceptions and language, or individual preferences for learning. Given students' varying levels of aptitude and achievement, their cultural diversity, and their varying socioeconomic backgrounds, this challenge can be particularly daunting.

15.9
*Explain how teachers can adapt their instruction to meet the needs and characteristics of all students.*

## Aptitude and Achievement

Because students differ markedly in their aptitude or ability to learn various tasks, teachers need to address the importance of aptitude in relationship to educational goals. These goals can be either collective or individual. Collective goals are those that educational institutions and the prevailing culture regard as important for everyone. Individual goals are those that individuals evolve for themselves.

Teachers must determine how differences in aptitude influence what is taught. They have two choices regardless of whether the educational goal is common or individual: (a) help students develop the aptitude or (b) help them circumvent or compensate for their lack of aptitude.

Corno and Snow (1986) have described education as a long-term effort to develop aptitude. Educational systems are dedicated to developing aptitudes for problem solving, literacy, numeracy, and learning-to-learn strategies; these are the goals of a modern, technological, and literate society. On the other hand, individual differences in aptitude can create barriers to the successful attainment of these desired goals.

In some cases, teachers supplement instruction by using tutors or computers to work directly with students who need more help or time in acquiring a skill. At other times, teachers can teach to a student's strength, capitalizing on that strength to bypass lack of aptitude or weakness. The decision to teach to strength or teach to weakness is not mutually exclusive; both can be used, depending on the educational goal, the nature of the student's deficiency, the flexibility of the aptitude, and the availability of alternative learning materials. For example, for students who cannot read well enough to understand complex texts, the teacher may provide instruction in social studies or science by using other materials, such as films, TV, or computer simulations; on the other hand, the teacher may decide that social studies learning is better delayed until students achieve higher levels of reading proficiency. Since our technology provides many alternatives to texts, teachers can easily provide instruction despite students' inadequacy in reading ability.

Computers show great promise for helping students who need more practice to acquire a skill. You must be careful, however, to select a software program that addresses the specific skill the student lacks.

Strategy training supports a more direct approach to the teaching of the skill or aptitude. Although research shows that many low-achieving students do not use cognitive strategies in higher-order thinking tasks that their higher-achieving counterparts use spontaneously, attempts to teach the strategies have been successful (Knight & Padron, 1988; Waxman, Knight, & Owens, 1990).

Individual goals can also determine how and what to teach; our curricula in secondary and higher education provide students with many electives so they can select areas of instruction in which they have sufficient aptitude.

While grouping by ability would seem to be a logical solution to teaching for differences, it is not necessarily successful. In fact, grouping by ability appears to widen the gap in performance between high-ability and lower-ability students and stigmatizes lower-achieving students with loss of self-esteem and motivation (Good & Stipek, 1983; Rosenholtz & Wilson, 1980). Teachers also set lower-level goals and objectives for low-ability groups (Shavelson & Stern, 1981; Woolfolk & Brooks, 1985).

Corno and Snow (1986) suggest that teachers adapt their teaching to differences by manipulating the organizational structures of the classroom, such as varying the materials, creating learning centers, varying the reward structure, and keeping grouping flexible and short term. Additionally, they recommend that teachers vary instruction by reinforcing correct responses, encouraging students to retry if they are incorrect, and altering or varying the level of questioning. Teachers can orchestrate group and individual learning without separating students on the basis of ability and without sacrificing the needs or self-esteem of individual students.

## Cultural Diversity

Perhaps even more challenging to the teacher are the differences that arise from cultural variations among the students in a classroom. These differences are often subtle and may lead to misunderstandings between teachers and students. Schools have only partially solved the communication problems that arise when teachers and students have different expectations about schooling and learning.

In the past, schools have promoted discrimination in a number of ways, including grouping methods, testing policies, design of curriculum, and selection of curriculum materials. Recently, increased efforts have been made to reduce these instances of bias and intolerance.

## Socioeconomic Background

Students from lower socioeconomic families often lack materials (e.g., computers, books, etc.) and experiences (e.g., visiting the zoo, going to the library, etc.) that enhance school learning. You can help such students overcome this disadvantage by providing them enriching activities, such as taking them on field trips, teaching them how to use computers and other technological devices, and exposing them to a wide variety of books, magazines, and newspapers.

You can also vary your teaching strategies to provide experiences that some students may lack. For example, use various grouping arrangements and ask open-ended questions to encourage active student participation. Similarly, capitalize on different experiences some students bring with them to the classroom. Acknowledging students' backgrounds promotes a sense of pride in students and broadens all students' knowledge of the world in which they live.

*Annual* **Edition**

unit *3*

Why do you think schools have been places where one culture tends to dominate another?

# DIVERSITY MAKES A DIFFERENCE

## Bias in Instructional Materials

Throughout this book, as we have discussed multicultural issues in education, the issue of *bias* has periodically arisen. Teachers can be biased in their behavior toward groups of students and policies can be biased to help or hinder groups of students. In this section, we discuss how instructional materials can be biased to reflect a set of cultural beliefs that all students in a classroom may not share.

Fortunately, there is far less bias in instructional materials now than even five years ago; textbook authors and publishers are very sensitive to how different ethnic groups and how men and women are portrayed. Teachers must attend to bias when deciding what materials to use.

Hernandez (1989) has noted three primary types of bias:

1. *Stereotyping.* Stereotyping occurs when all members of a group are described as having the same characteristics. When this happens, differences between groups are exaggerated and the differences within groups are hidden. Think, for example, of how the elderly are often portrayed in literature: wise, kindly, and helpful. Other stereotypes are not as benign, with Puerto Ricans characterized as being poor or Native Americans portrayed as warlike. People with disabilities are often portrayed as helpless. Stereotypes also occur when group members are shown in a narrow range of situations, occupations, or performing the same activities.
2. *Omissions and distortions.* Omissions refer to information that is left out; distortions are erroneous "facts." The contributions of women, ethnic minorities, and religious minorities are often omitted or presented in a distorted way. For example, the experience of African Americans as slaves may be included in a history book, but their contribution to the movement to settle the North American West is almost universally overlooked. Omissions are a particularly insidious type of bias, because an author cannot be accused of lying. For example, a history textbook may say that slaves were freed after the Civil War, but may omit descriptions of how African Americans were treated in the century that followed.
3. *Biased use of language.* The use of language can bias the reader in subtle, not easily detectable ways. The most obvious example is the use of masculine pronouns *he* and *him* when the author is really discussing both males and females. Many other terms reflect bias. For example, have you ever wondered why we call the body of water separating England and France the "English Channel"? The French don't! The term reflects an "Anglo-centric" orientation. Many of our terms in history and literature reflect an Anglo-North American orientation that not all groups share.

The Association of American Publishers (1984) has established guidelines concerning the content, illustrations, and language of instructional materials. Bias-free instructional materials do the following:

### Content
- Represent diverse groups of people in a variety of activities, occupations, and careers, including positions of leadership.
- Represent fairly and accurately the historic and contemporary achievements of people in society within a wide range of areas.
- Integrate materials by and about minorities, women, and members of other cultural groups that provide a range of perspectives and reflect intragroup diversity.
- Include materials that honestly convey the positive and negative political, social, and economic realities that have been part of the American experience for members of various cultural groups and segments of society.
- Represent all groups in a variety of settings—urban, suburban, and rural—and socioeconomic levels.

### Illustrations
- Provide a fair, reasonable, and balanced representation with respect to race, religion, ethnicity, age, socioeconomic level, sex, and national origin.
- Include positive role models for male and female students of different ethnic backgrounds.
- Avoid stereotyping groups and individuals.
- Show men and women from different cultural groups in positions of prominence and leadership.

### Language
- Encompass members of both sexes by (1) avoiding use of terms that exclude women, and (2) designate occupations by work performed.
- Reflect cultural diversity through inclusion of varied ethnic names as well as more common Anglo-Saxon ones.
- Avoid words that are loaded or convey biased connotations and assumptions.

# DIVERSITY MAKES A DIFFERENCE

## How Schools Promote Discrimination

Discrimination of individuals based on gender, race, culture, sexual preference, disability status, or religion occurs because of people's attitudes and beliefs. Often the educational policies and practices we adopt also promote discrimination. Sometimes this occurs intentionally, and other times it is purely accidental. Nieto (1992) notes that educational practices that help some students may sometimes hurt others. Schools must then choose which students' needs have a higher priority. Such decisions are often a function of who has the most power within a school.

Nieto (1992) notes some practices that detract from the success of many students and maintain social inequality:

1. *Tracking.* Tracking refers to homogeneously grouping students based on ability or achievement; this is often accomplished by grouping students with similar test scores. Thus, within a grade, you might find that one class is the "high" class, one is the "middle" class, and a third is the "low" class. As Goodlad (1984) notes, once students are tracked, they tend to remain in that track for the remainder of their school years.

    Many studies of the ethnic distribution in homogeneously grouped classes in urban school districts have shown that African American, Latino, and Native American students are disproportionately overrepresented in the lower classes as compared to whites (Braddock & Dawkins, 1993). In Boston, for example, African American and Hispanic students were overrepresented in the lower-track classes, whereas whites were overrepresented in the higher-track classes (Massachusetts Advocacy Center, 1990). This disproportionate representation of different groups is alarming enough; an additional concern is that teachers often use very different instructional strategies in high- versus low-track classes. Thus, students of different ethnic

groups may be exposed to inferior types of teaching practices.

2. *Testing.* Tests themselves can be culturally biased, and the person who administers a test can be biased. Since testing is almost invariably used in tracking students (and in placing students in special education), it is not surprising that this practice promotes discrimination.

3. *The curriculum.* The curriculum can foster discrimination when it represents cultural information and values of the "mainstream" culture and fails to acknowledge the diversity of cultures. Despite ongoing discussion of multiculturalism in the curriculum, textbooks and curriculum guides still tend to reflect a male-dominated European North American perspective that may send the message to students that this perspective is the "right" one and that other perspectives are inappropriate or incorrect. In an examination of textbooks used in various subject areas in grades 1 through 8, Sleeter and Grant (1993) found that:

    • The achievements of whites are noted to a far greater extent than those of any other groups.
    • Women and non-whites are portrayed in more limited roles than white males.
    • The issues that most concern women and ethnic minorities are poorly covered.
    • The relations between groups are depicted as harmonious, and minority groups are portrayed as being contented.

4. *Pedagogy.* Nieto (1992) uses the term *pedagogy* to describe both the instructional practices used by teachers and their beliefs and assumptions about learners. She notes that teachers are often hindered by their own ignorance about how students vary and how such variability may influence learning. When teachers treat all students equally by giving them the

same type of instruction, they may be overlooking critical ways in which differences among students call for different approaches to teaching.

5. *Physical Structure of a School.* The physical structure of a school can profoundly affect students' attitudes about learning. Unfortunately, many urban schools bear a striking resemblance to prisons and factories (McNeil, 1986), whereas suburban schools more often are spacious and in better physical condition (National Coalition of Advocates for Students, 1985). Given that most students from ethnic minorities attend urban schools, they may perceive school negatively, not see school as a part of the community, and view themselves as being imprisoned from 8:30 to 3:00, where the teachers are the jailors and the principal is the warden.

6. *Disciplinary Policies.* Schools' disciplinary policies have been found to discriminate against some students, particularly when teachers misunderstand or are intolerant of cultural differences. When teachers perceive student behavior as rebellious or disruptive (rather than as an expression of individuality or group identity), they may discipline the student; indeed, minority group students are suspended more often for disruptive behavior than are white students, and schools with high suspension rates also have high drop-out rates (Felice, 1981).

7. *Parent Involvement.* Parent involvement is widely known to contribute to the success of schools. However, parents are generally less involved when they are poor or do not speak English as a native language or when they themselves had negative experiences in school. Because minority group parents are more likely than whites to fall into these groups, this factor also contributes to differences in the quality of education between whites and other groups.

# TEACHERS ROUNDTABLE

## "Every Year You Get Better"

**DMP:** Could you share some thoughts at this point with college students who are planning to be teachers? What are your recommendations to them?

**Donna:** I'd like to emphasize the small successes. You give your students an opportunity, and you encourage them to succeed. Also, it's important to remember that fair doesn't necessarily mean equal. I may give more help to one student and less to another. Some may not be able to do what every other child is doing; or they may not have the ability to sit and do work for the period of time you're asking them to. You have to provide them with the opportunities for success so they will want to go on and tackle the next lesson. You also have to be knowledgeable and sensitive to the social aspects. You have to know their personalities.

**Mary:** To new teachers, I would say count your successes. New teachers are often very hard on themselves. It's difficult to be the teacher. Sometimes it's frustrating. So, to help yourself, you have to focus on the successes.

**Anthony:** And remember that you can't be a perfect teacher the first year of teaching; you make improvements every year. And every year you get a little bit better. You do it a step at a time. There is no substitute for experience.

**Angela:** And continue to learn. Take a course; read journals. Not only do you get wonderful information, but you're learning about other teachers and what they have tried, faced with the same types of problem you may have. And as you grow as a person, you automatically grow as a teacher because you have more to share.

**Irwin:** The first thing I would tell teachers is that it is a very difficult job. It requires a great deal of work and a great deal of planning. You have to be prepared. You also have to learn from the students who are in front of you. You have to learn about them, their egos, their needs. You have to deal with all different kinds of kids in the classroom. So not only do you have to plan the material in order to be prepared (because otherwise you'll stumble), but you also have to learn continuously from the kids who are in front of you.

**Donna:** My first few weeks, my head was spinning. "She's doing this, but he's doing that." I kept thinking about how the kids *should* be and how I *should* be. Now, I'm really finding my own way. It's very difficult, but suddenly the days and weeks go by, and you realize you've found your own style.

**Irwin:** The single most important factor in the classroom is that the teacher must make connections with a class. You can always teach better—you can ask better questions and you can know the curriculum better. But when you connect with that class, when your personality is present, then the kids believe that you and they are in this together. Then you're a successful teacher.

## KEY POINTS

1. The choice of the best teaching method is influenced by factors such as grade, student ability and background knowledge, and instructional goals.

2. Effective teachers stress skill development, spend considerable time on academic tasks, exhibit confidence, work well with supervisors, emphasize good classroom management, are optimistic about their students' ability to learn, and set high standards for achievement. In addition, they are warm, enthusiastic, and businesslike, provide variety in materials and academic activities, teach with clarity, and use probing questions to follow initial questioning.

3. The combination of teacher wait-time and higher-level questioning further contributes to student achievement, as do minimizing transitional periods and maximizing task engagement.

4. Teachers must orchestrate a complicated system of interactions among ideas, events, and persons within the classroom.

5. The way the classroom is organized for instruction (i.e., cooperative, competitive, or individualized learning) has much to do with the teacher's intentions, the subject matter, and the characteristics of students (e.g., age and level of achievement).

6. Class size and method of student grouping (ability versus heterogeneous) are usually determined by a school district, but they seem to influence how teachers teach.

7. The amount of time in the school day actually allocated for instruction and the effectiveness of teachers' classroom management methods also affect student achievement.

8. Direct instruction involves well-structured and carefully sequenced learning activities. In this approach, the six teaching functions that are the most effective include review, presentation, guided practice, correction and feedback, independent practice, and weekly and monthly reviews.

9. Educators are increasingly teaching students *how* to learn, that is, teaching them strategies they can use to learn independently. These strategies include rehearsal, elaboration, organization, and self-monitoring.

10. One potentially powerful instructional model based on cognitive theory is Collins and Brown's cognitive apprenticeship, in which experts and novices work together on important projects that are meaningful to both.

11. Fundamental to the selection of appropriate teaching strategies is the understanding of how students learn and how cognition develops. Increasingly, U.S. educators are concerned with changing students' thought processes.

12. In selecting an instructional approach, teachers must strike a balance between developing student autonomy and controlling student behavior.

13. Teachers must decide how to address the various levels of student aptitude that exist within the same class; one approach is to develop individual goals for students that match their particular needs.

14. In a variety of ways, including tracking and testing, schools can foster discrimination. Instructional materials can contain bias pertaining to age, gender, cultural background, and ethnicity.

## SELF-STUDY EXERCISES

1. List 10 activities that contribute to effective teaching.

2. What are the pros and cons of heterogeneous and homogeneous grouping in schools? Why is the issue so controversial?

3. What are the merits of whole-group lectures, discussions, cooperative grouping, peer tutoring, and individualized learning? What are the disadvantages of each?

4. In what situations is it preferable to use direct instruction?

5. Describe the learning strategies teachers can teach students. Why are they useful?

6. Describe the cognitive apprenticeship model and relate it to the ideas of Vygotsky.

7. Why is it difficult to strike a balance between student autonomy and management of student behavior?

8. What should teachers look for when they review instructional materials for possible gender, age, ethnic, and cultural bias?

## FURTHER READINGS

Johnson, D. W., & Johnson, R. T. (1987). *Learning together and alone.* Englewood Cliffs, NJ: Prentice Hall.

Nieto, S. (1992). *Affirming diversity: The sociopolitical context of multicultural education.* New York: Longman.

Waxman, H. C., & Walberg, H. J. (1991). *Effective teaching: Current research.* Berkeley, CA: McCutchan.

## REFERENCES

Achilles, C. M. (1993). Creating successful schools for all children: A proven step. *Journal of School Leadership, 3,* 606–621.

Anderson, L. M., Evertson, C. M., & Brophy, J. E. (1982). *Principles of small-group instruction in elementary reading.* East Lansing, MI: Institute for Research on Teaching, Michigan State University.

Archambeault, B. (1992). Personalizing study skills in secondary students. *Journal of Reading, 35,* 468–472.

Association of American Publishers. (1984). *Statement on bias-free materials.* New York: Association of American Publishers.

Bereiter, C., & Bird, M. (1985). Use of thinking aloud in identification and teaching of reading comprehension strategies. *Cognition and Instruction, 2,* 131–156.

Berliner, D. (1982). '82 issue: Should teachers be expected to learn and use direct instruction? *ASCD Update, 24,* 5.

Berliner, D. (1986). In pursuit of the expert pedagogue. *Educational Leadership, 15*(7), 5–13.

Berliner, D., & Casanova, U. (1988). Peer tutoring: A new look at a popular practice. *Instructor, 87*(5), 14–15.

Bjorklund, D. F., Ornstein, P. A., & Haig, J. R. (1977). Developmental differences in organization and recall: Training in the use of organizational techniques. *Developmental Psychology, 13,* 175–183.

Bower, G. H., & Hilgard, E. R. (1981). *Theories of learning* (5th ed.). Englewood Cliffs, NJ: Prentice Hall.

Braddock, J. H., II, & Dawkins, M. P. (1993). Ability grouping, aspirations, and attainments: Evidence from the National Educational Longitudinal Study of 1988. *Journal of Negro Education, 62,* 324–336.

Brophy, J. (1983). Improving instruction: Effective classroom management. *School Administrator, 40*(7), 33–36.

Brown, A. L., Day, J. D., & Jones, R. S. (1983). The development of plans for summarizing texts. *Child Development, 54,* 968–979.

Brown, A. L., & Palincsar, A. S. (1982). Inducing strategic learning texts by means of informed, self-control training. *Topics in Learning and Learning Disabilities, 2,* 1–17.

Brown, A. L., & Smiley, S. S. (1977). Rating the importance of structural units of prose passages: A problem of metacognitive development. *Child Development, 48,* 1–8.

Brown, J., Collins, A., & Duguid, P. (1989). Situated cognition and the culture of learning. *Educational Researcher, 18,* 32–42.

Carnine, D., Kuder, J., Salvino, M., & Moore, J. (1983). *The use of generative and question-asking strategies for the improvement of reading comprehension.* Paper presented at the annual meeting of the American Educational Research Association, Montreal.

Carrier, C., & Titus, A. (1981). Effects of notetaking pretraining and text mode expectations on learning from lectures. *American Educational Research Journal, 18,* 385–397.

Chall, J. S. (1983). *Stages of reading development.* New York: McGraw-Hill.

Claridge, P. B., & Berliner, D. C. (1991). Perceptions of student behavior as a function of expertise. *Journal of Classroom Interaction, 26*(1), 1–8.

Coker, H., Medley, D., & Soar, R. (1980). How valid are expert opinions about effective teaching? *Phi Delta Kappan, 62,* 131–134.

Collins, A., Brown, J. S., & Newman, S. E. (1989). Cognitive apprenticeship: Teaching the craft of reading, writing and mathematics. In L. B. Resnick (Ed.), *Knowing, learning and instruction: Essays in honor of Robert Glaser* (pp. 453–454). Hillsdale, NJ: Erlbaum.

Collins, A., & Smith, E. (1980). Teaching the process of reading comprehension. (Tech. Rep. No. 182). Cambridge, MA: Bolt, Beranek, & Newman.

Corno, L., & Snow, R. E. (1986). Adapting teaching to individual differences among learners. In M. C. Wittrock (Ed.), *Handbook of research in teaching* (3rd ed., pp. 605–629). New York: Macmillan.

Crawford, J. (1983). A study of instructional processes in Title I classes: 1981–82. *Journal of Research and Evaluation of the Oklahoma City Public Schools, 13*(1).

Dar, Y., & Resh, N. (1986). Classroom intellectual and academic achievement. *American Educational Research Journal, 23,* 357–374.

Denham, C., & Leiberman, A. (Eds.). (1980). *Time to learn.* Washington, DC: National Institute of Education.

Dillon, J. (1987). *Questioning and discussion: A multidisciplinary study.* Norwood, NJ: Ablex.

Doyle, W. (1986). Classroom management and organization. In M. Wittrock (Ed.), *Handbook of research on teaching* (3rd ed., pp. 392–431). New York: Macmillan.

Dunkin, M. (1978). Student characteristics, classroom processes, and student achievement. *Journal of Educational Psychology, 70,* 998–1009.

Durkin, D. (1990). Matching classroom instruction with reading abilities: An unmet need. *Remedial and Special Education, 11*(3), 23–28.

Eder, D. (1981). Ability grouping as a self-fulfilling prophecy: A micro-analysis of teacher-student interaction. *Sociology of Education, 54*(3), 151–162.

Emmer, E. T., Evertson, C., Sanford, J., & Clements, B. S. (1982). *Improving classroom management: An experimental study in junior high classrooms.* Austin, TX: Research and Development Center for Teacher Education, University of Texas.

Evans, M. D. (1994). Dividing classes for more effective instruction. *Schools in the Middle, 4*(1), 35–36.

Evertson, C. M. (1986). Do teachers make a difference? Issues for the eighties. *Education and Urban Society, 18*(2), 195–210.

Evertson, C. M., Emmer, E. T., Sanford, J. P., & Clements, B. S. (1983). Improving classroom management: An experiment in elementary classrooms. *Elementary School Journal, 84*(2), 173–188.

Farnham-Diggory, S. (1990). *Schooling.* Cambridge, MA: Harvard University Press.

Farnham-Diggory, S. (1992). *Cognitive processes in education* (2nd ed.). New York: Harper.

Felice, L. G. (1981). Black student dropout behavior: Disengagement from school, rejection and racial discrimination. *Journal of Negro Education, 50,* 415–424.

Filby, N. (1980). *What happens in smaller classes?: A summary report of a field study. Class size and instruction project.* (ERIC Document Reproduction Service No. ED 219 365).

Finn, J. D., & Achilles, C. M. (1990). Answers and questions about class size: A statewide experiment. *American Educational Research Journal, 27,* 557–577.

Fisher, C., Berliner, D., Filby, N., Marliave, R., Cohen, K., & Dishaw, M. (1980). Teaching behaviors, academic learning time and student achievement: An overview. In C. Denham & A. Lieberman (Eds.), *Time to learn* (pp. 7–32). Washington, DC: National Institute for Education.

Fitzpatrick, K. A. (1982). *The effect of a secondary classroom management training program on teacher and student behavior.* Paper presented at the annual meeting of the American Educational Research Association, New York.

Flavell, J. H., Friedrichs, A. H., & Hoyt, J. D. (1970). Developmental changes in memorization processes. *Cognitive Psychology, 1,* 324–340.

Flavell, J. H., Speer, J. R., Green, F. L., & August, D. L. (1981). The development of comprehension monitoring and knowledge about communication. *Monographs of the Society for Research in Child Development,* Serial No. 192.

Flavell, J. H., & Wellman, H. M. (1977). Metamemory. In R. V. Kail, Jr. & J. W. Hagen (Eds.), *Perspectives on the development of memory and cognition* (pp. 3–33). Hillsdale, NJ: Erlbaum.

Gagné, E. D. (1985). *The cognitive psychology of school learning.* Boston: Little Brown.

Gettinger, M. (1982). Improving classroom behaviors and achievement of learning disabled children using direct instruction. *School Psychology Review, 11*(3), 329–336.

Gettinger, M. (1993). Effects of invented spelling and direct instruction on spelling performance of second grade boys. *Journal of Applied Behavior Analysis, 26,* 281–291.

Gibson, E. J. (1969). *Principles of perceptual learning and development.* New York: Appleton-Century-Crofts.

Gibson, E. J., & Levin, H. (1975). *The psychology of reading.* Cambridge, MA: MIT Press.

Glass, G., & Smith, M. (1978). *Meta-analysis of research on the relationship of class size and achievement.* Boulder, CO: University of Boulder, Laboratory of Educational Research.

Good, T. L., & Brophy, J. E. (1986). School effects. In M. Wittrock (Ed.), *Handbook of research on teaching* (3rd ed., pp. 570–602). New York: Macmillan.

Good, T. L., & Grouws, D. A. (1979). The Missouri mathematics effectiveness project. *Journal of Educational Psychology, 71,* 355–362.

Good, T. L., & Stipek, D. J. (1983). Individual differences in the classroom: A psychological perspective. In G. D. Fenstermacher & J. I. Goodlad (Eds.), *Individual differences and the common curriculum* (82nd Yearbook of the National Society for the Study of Education, Part 1, pp. 9–44). Chicago: University of Chicago Press.

Goodlad, J. (1984). *A place called school.* New York: McGraw-Hill.

Graves, D. H. (1983). *Writing: Teachers and children at work.* Portsmouth, NH: Heinemann.

Harder, H. (1990). A critical look at reduced class size. *Contemporary Education, 62*(1), 28–30.

Hernandez, H. (1989). *Multicultural education: A teacher's guide to content and process.* Columbus, OH: Merrill.

Heyneman, S., & Losely, S. (1983). The effect of primary school quality on academic achievement across twenty-nine high- and low-income countries. *American Journal of Sociology, 88,* 1162–1194.

Holliday, W. G. (1992). Should we reduce class size? *Science Teacher, 59,* 14–17.

Jenkins, J. R., & Jenkins, L. M. (1987). Making peer tutoring work. *Educational Leadership, 44*(6), 64–68.

Johnson, D. W., & Johnson, R. T. (1987). *Learning together and alone: Cooperative, competitive, and individualistic learning* (2nd ed.). Englewood Cliffs, NJ: Prentice Hall.

Johnson, D. W., & Johnson, R. T. (1991). Classroom instruction and cooperative learning. In H. C. Waxman & H. J. Walberg (Eds.), *Effective teaching: Current research* (pp. 277–294). Berkeley, CA: McCutchan.

Johnston, J. M. (1990). *Effects of class size on classroom processes and teacher behaviors in kindergarten through third grade.* (ERIC Document Reproduction Service No. ED 321 848).

Karmiloff-Smith, A. (1979). *A functional approach to child language.* Cambridge: Cambridge University Press.

King, A. (1991). Effects of training in strategic questioning on children's problem-solving performance. *Journal of Educational Psychology, 83,* 307–317.

Klahr, D., & Robinson, M. (1981). Formal assessment of problem solving and planning processes in preschool children. *Cognitive Psychology, 13,* 113–148.

Knight, S. L., & Padron, Y. N. (1988). Teaching cognitive reading strategies to at-risk students. In H. C. Waxman, S. L. Knight, & Y. N. Padron (Eds.), *Teaching strategies that promote higher-level thinking skills for at-risk learners* (pp. 8–17). LaMarque, TX: Consortium for the Advancement of Professional Excellence.

Kounin, J. S. (1970). *Discipline and group management in classrooms.* New York: Holt, Rinehart & Winston.

Kounin, J. S., & Gump, P. V. (1974). Signal systems of lesson settings and the task-related behavior of preschool children. *Journal of Educational Psychology, 12,* 71–78.

Kulik, C. C., & Kulik, J. A. (1982). Research synthesis on ability grouping. *Educational Leadership, 38,* 619–621.

Manning, M. L., & Lucking, R. (1990). Ability grouping: Realities and alternatives. *Childhood Education, 66,* 254–258.

Massachusetts Advocacy Center. (1990). *Locked in/locked out: Tracking and placement practices in Boston Public Schools.* Boston: Massachusetts Advocacy Center.

Mayer, R. E. (1982). Instructional variables in text processing. In A. Flammer & W. Kintsch (Eds.), *Discourse processing.* Amsterdam: North-Holland.

Mayer, R. E. (1984). Aids to prose comprehension. *Educational Psychologist, 19,* 30–42.

Mayer, R. E., & Cook, L. K. (1980). Effects of shadowing on prose comprehension and problem solving. *Memory & Cognition, 8,* 101–109.

McAdams, R. P. (1993). *Lessons from abroad: How other countries educate their children.* Lancaster, PA: Technomic Publishing Co.

McLaughlin, H. J. (1994). From negation to negotiation: Moving away from the management metaphor. *Action in Teacher Education, 16*(1), 75–84.

McNeil, L. M. (1986). *Contradiction of control: School structure and school knowledge.* New York: Methuen/Routledge & Kegan Paul.

Miller, G. A., & Gildea, P. M. (1987). How children learn words. *Scientific American, 257*(3), 94–99.

Miller, J. W., & Ellsworth, R. (1985). The evaluation of a two-year program to improve teacher effectiveness in reading instruction. *Elementary School Journal, 85,* 485–496.

Murphy, J. (1986). Inequitable allocations of alterable learning variables. *Journal of Teacher Education, 37*(6), 21–26.

National Coalition of Advocates for Students. (1985). *Barriers to excellence: Our children at risk.* Boston: National Coalition of Advocates for Students.

Nieto, S. (1992). *Affirming diversity: The sociopolitical context of multicultural education.* New York: Longman.

Nystrand, M., & Gamoran, A. (1989). *Instructional discourse and student engagement.* Paper presented at the annual meeting of the American Educational Research Association, San Francisco.

Ornstein, A. C. (1991). Teacher effectiveness research: Theoretical considerations. In H. C. Waxman & H. J. Walberg (Eds.), *Effective teaching: Current research* (pp. 63–80). Berkeley, CA: McCutchan.

Palincsar, A. S. (1991). Examining the context of strategy instruction. *Remedial and Special Education, 12*(3), 43–53.

Paris, S. G. (1991). Assessment and remediation of metacognitive aspects of children's reading comprehension. *Topics in Language Disorders, 12*(1), 32–50.

Paris, S. G., Cross, D. R., & Lipson, M. Y. (1984). Informed strategies for learning: A program to improve children's reading awareness and comprehension. *Journal of Educational Psychology, 76,* 1239–1252.

Peper, R. J., & Mayer, R. E. (1986). Generative effects of note taking during science lectures. *Journal of Educational Psychology, 78,* 34–38.

Porter, A. C., & Brophy, J. (1988). Synthesis of research on good teaching: Insights from the work of the Institute for Research on Teaching. *Educational Leadership, 45*(8), 74–85.

Preece, P. (1987). Class size and learning: A theoretical model. *Journal of Educational Research, 80*(6), 77–79.

Rekrut, M. D. (1992). *Teaching to learn: Cross-age tutoring to enhance strategy acquisition.* Paper presented at the annual meeting of the American Educational Research Association, San Francisco.

Rendell, F. (undated). *Topic study: How and why?* Glasgow: Jordanhill College of Education.

Resnick, L. B. (1989). *Knowing, learning and instruction: Essays in honor of Robert Glaser.* Hillsdale, NJ: Erlbaum.

Rosenholtz, S. J., & Wilson, B. (1980). The effect of classroom structure on shared perceptions of ability. *American Educational Research Journal, 17,* 75–82.

Rosenshine, B. (1983). Teaching functions in instructional programs. *Elementary School Journal, 83,* 335–351.

Rosenshine, B., & Stevens, R. (1986). Teaching functions. In M. Wittrock (Ed.), *Handbook of research on teaching* (3rd ed., pp. 376–391). New York: Macmillan.

Rossi, S., & Wittrock, M. C. (1971). Developmental shifts in verbal recall between mental ages two and five. *Child Development, 42,* 333–338.

Sato, N. (1990). Context matters: Teaching in Japan and in the United States. *Phi Delta Kappan, 73*(5), 359–366.

Schmidt, C. R., & Paris, S. G. (1983). Children's use of successive clues to generate and monitor inferences. *Child Development, 54,* 742–759.

Seigler, R. S. (1986). *Children's thinking* (2nd ed.). Englewood Cliffs, NJ: Prentice Hall.

Shavelson, R. J., & Stern, P. (1981). Research on teachers' pedagogical thoughts, judgments, decisions, and behavior. *Review of Educational Research, 51,* 455–498.

Shimron, J. (1976). Learning activities in individually prescribed instruction. *Instructional Science, 5,* 391–401.

Slavin, R. E. (1987). Ability grouping and student achievement in elementary schools: A best evidence synthesis. *Review of Educational Research, 57,* 293–336.

Slavin, R. E. (1990). Achievement effects of ability grouping in secondary schools: A best-evidence synthesis. *Review of Educational Research, 60,* 471–499.

Sleeter, C. E., & Grant, C. A. (1993). *Making choices for multicultural education.* Columbus, OH: Merrill.

Smith, L. (1985). Teacher clarifying behaviors: Effects on student achievement and perceptions. *Journal of Experimental Education, 53*(3), 162–169.

Stallings, J. (1991). Learning how to teach in the inner city. *Educational Leadership, 49*(3), 25–27.

Stallings, J., Cory, R., Fairweather, J., & Needles, M. (1978). *A study of basic reading skills taught in secondary schools.* Menlo Park, CA: SRI International.

Stevenson, H. W., & Stigler, J. W. (1992). *The learning gap: Why our schools are failing and what we can learn from Japanese and Chinese education.* New York: Summit Books.

Tobias, S. (1981). When do instructional methods make a difference? *Educational Researcher, 11,* 4–10.

Tobin, K. (1980). The effect of an extended teacher wait-time on science achievement. *Journal of Research in Science Teaching, 17,* 469–475.

Tobin, K., & Capie, W. (1982). Relationships between classroom process variables and middle-school science achievement. *Journal of Educational Psychology, 74,* 441–454.

Veldman, D. K., & Sanford, J. P. (1984). The influence of ability level on student achievement and classroom behavior. *American Educational Research Journal, 21,* 629–644.

Waxman, H. C., Knight, S. L., & Owens, E. W. (1990). The relations between the classroom learning environment and students' problem-solving strategies in mathematics. In H. C. Waxman & C. D. Ellett (Eds.), *The study of learning environments* (Vol. 4, pp. 94–103). Houston, TX: University of Houston.

Weinstein, C. E., & Mayer, R. E. (1986). The teaching of learning strategies. In M. C. Wittrock (Ed.), *Handbook of research on teaching* (pp. 315–327). New York: Macmillan.

Woolfolk, A. E., & Brooks, D. M. (1985). The influence of teachers' nonverbal behaviors on students' perceptions and performance. *Elementary School Journal, 85,* 513–528.

Wright, C., & Nuthall, G. (1971). Relationships between teacher behaviors and pupil achievement in three experimental elementary science lessons. *American Educational Research Journal, 7,* 477–491.

# GLOSSARY

## A

**ability grouping:** Grouping students homogeneously by placing together students with similar academic ability; this is usually done within a grade.

**abstract concept:** A concept that has no physical existence, such as "liberty."

**abstracted replay:** Identifying the principles that underlie a behavior; the purpose of abstracted replay is to help students gain insight about their own thinking.

**accommodation:** In Piaget's theory, the tendency of people to change their schemata when faced with evidence that contradicts their current understanding.

**achievement motivation:** A construct that personality theorists believe controls the desire to achieve; it is the product of the need to achieve success and the need to avoid failure.

**adaptive skills:** Skills used by individuals to function in their environment.

**adolescent egocentrism:** A "rebirth" of egocentrism that occurs in the stage of formal operations in which adolescents believe, for example, that they are invulnerable or that people are listening to their thoughts.

**advance organizers:** General information presented about a new topic before instruction to help students relate new information to what they already know.

**amalgamation:** A synthesis of the majority and minority cultures arising from interaction between them.

**American Sign Language (ASL):** The language used by many people with hearing impairment in the United States to communicate using hand gestures.

**anxiety:** A feeling of tension or foreboding.

**arousal theory:** The idea that, to achieve optimally, people must have a level of arousal and that the task must be neither too easy nor too difficult.

**articulation:** Having students verbalize their problem-solving activities (e.g., "Well, first I thought about whether this was an addition question or a multiplication question . . .").

**artificial intelligence:** The field that examines how computers can be designed and programmed to process information in ways similar to human information processing.

**assertive discipline:** A program advocated by Lee Canter based on the idea that successful teachers apply rules calmly but forcefully, communicate requirements clearly to students, and respond effectively to students' violations of classroom rules.

**assessment:** Interpreting one or more measurements to make a decision.

**assimilation:** In Piaget's theory, the tendency to change or distort evidence from the outside world to fit into one's existing schema; the process by which the values and beliefs of a majority group gradually displace the values of a minority group.

**attention:** The ability to focus our awareness on a particular stimulus.

**attention deficit/hyperactivity disorder (ADHD):** A learning disability characterized by inattention, impulsivity, and hyperactivity at levels greater than usually seen in individuals at comparable levels of development.

**attribute:** A feature or characteristic of a concept.

**attribution theory:** The idea that students' beliefs about the causes of their successes and failure will influence their motivation in subsequent situations.

**authentic assessment:** Assessment that relies on the demonstration of a specific skill in a real-life context.

**authoritarian parenting:** A style of parenting in which the parent values conformity, is detached, and does not explain rules but expects compliance from the child.

**authoritative parenting:** A style of parenting in which the parent is firm but caring, and explains the reasons for rules.

**automatic behaviors:** Behaviors that occur without effort or attention; some teaching behaviors, such as providing students with social rewards such as smiles or compliments, can become automatic, allowing teachers to attend to other activities.

**automatic processing:** Mental activity that requires little attention and may occur without conscious awareness; it is usually used when a task is very well learned.

## B

**babbling:** The production of random sounds by babies, which is a precursor for the production of words.

**behaviorism:** The psychological school of thought that emphasizes the study of observable, measurable behavior.

**behavior modification:** The application of behavioral principles for the purpose of changing an individual's behavior.

## C

**center:** To focus on one dimension of a stimulus, which results in the failure to attend to other relevant dimensions.

**central processing unit (CPU):** The part of a computer that carries out logical functions.

**chaining:** In behavior modification, the systematic instruction and rewarding of small sub-steps that are part of a more complex, multi-step behavior; in cognitive psychology, the establishing of connections between working memory programs (e.g., ranking tasks by importance and allocating study time proportionately).

**child abuse:** The harmful treatment and violation of the human rights of children by adults.

**chronological age:** An individual's age expressed in time units.

**classical conditioning:** The process by which a new stimulus elicits a response formerly elicited by another stimulus.

**classification:** Grouping objects that have the same physical or functional characteristic (e.g., sorting animals by the type of environment they live in).

**class inclusion:** The ability to classify objects as being in more than one category simultaneously (e.g., an object can be both red and small).

**clinical interview:** *See* semi-structured interview.

**coaching:** Providing feedback and guidance to students as they perform an assigned task; for example, telling a student what she is doing correctly and incorrectly and suggesting alternative ways as she attempts to compute the volume of a cube.

**cognitive behavior modification:** A technique in which people use self-instruction and self-monitoring techniques to change their behavior.

**cognitive-developmental model:** An approach to learning that focuses on the development of thinking as a series of stages individuals go through.

**cognitive processes:** Mental activities such as attending, perceiving, thinking, remembering, problem solving, decision making, and creativity.

**cognitive styles:** Patterns that determine how people process information (e.g., reflectively or impulsively).

**cognitive therapy:** A technique that teaches individuals to test their beliefs against reality.

**cognitivism:** The psychological school of thought that emphasizes the study of human beings' mental processes.

**collective monologues:** Conversations of groups of children in the preoperations stage in which one child's speech has nothing to do with the other children's speech.

**communicative competence:** The ability to understand and use language appropriately in a variety of situations.

**competitive learning:** An instructional strategy in which students are placed in groups that compete with one another such that one group "wins" by accomplishing a goal better or faster than the other groups.

**comprehension:** The process of constructing meaning from new information.

**computer-assisted instruction (CAI):** The use of computers to present information, followed by small tests or quizzes that determine the learner's progress in an instructional unit.

**concept:** Classifications of a set of related ideas or events.

**conceptual competence:** The ability to apply what one knows, reorganize one's knowledge, and embellish one's understanding.

**conceptual knowledge:** The classifications of a set of related information into an organized idea.

**concrete concept:** A concept that is tangible, such as "chair."

**concrete operations stage:** In Piaget's theory, the developmental stage (from approximately ages 6–12) in which children can apply adult-like logic to actual (but not hypothetical) situations.

**concurrent validity:** The extent to which performance on a test (usually an aptitude test) correlates positively with performance on the criterion measure when both measures are made at the same time.

**conditioned response:** In classical conditioning, a response (or behavior) that occurs in the presence of a conditioned stimulus as the result of repeated pairing with an unconditioned stimulus. In Pavlov's experiment, his dog salivated (conditioned response) when hearing the footsteps of the researchers (conditioned stimulus).

**conditioned stimulus:** In classical conditioning, a stimulus that has been repeatedly paired with an unconditioned stimulus so that it leads to a conditioned response. In Pavlov's experiment, the conditioned stimulus (the sound of the researcher's footsteps), having been paired with an unconditioned stimulus (meat powder), led to a conditioned response (salivation).

**conditioning:** A form of learning in which a person's behavior becomes associated with a particular stimulus in the environment.

**confidence interval:** A range around a person's obtained test score into which the individual's true score is likely to fall.

**conservation:** The ability of concrete operational children to understand that changing something's shape does not change its quantity. For example, pouring liquid from a tall, thin beaker into a short, wide one does not change the amount of liquid even though it may look different.

**constructivism:** The psychological school of thought that assumes people construct or create knowledge.

**construct validity:** The extent to which a test measures the psychological trait or construct it is intended to measure.

**content validity:** The extent to which the content of a test (usually an achievement test) reflects the content of an instructional unit.

**control processes:** Components of information processing, such as attention and rehearsal, that are under the control of the individual.

**control strategies:** Organized mental activities, such as monitoring, predicting, and analyzing one's own thinking, that promote more efficient thinking and learning.

**convergent thinking:** Thinking that leads to the single solution of a problem.

**cooperative learning:** An instructional strategy in which students work in small groups to meet a specific goal; in cooperative groups, teamwork and collaboration are considered more important than individual achievement.

**co-regulation:** The process in which adults give children control in gradually increasing degrees.

**creativity:** The ability to construct new and inventive ideas and solutions to problems.

**criterion-referenced tests:** Tests designed to compare a student's academic performance to an established performance standard.

**criterion-related validity:** The extent to which a test (usually an aptitude test) predicts performance on another measure of performance (i.e., a criterion).

**critical period:** A biologically determined period in some organisms in which learning can take place most easily.

**critical thinking:** Higher-level mental activity characterized by analyzing and evaluating arguments and opinions.

**cross-age tutoring:** A variation on peer-tutoring in which the tutor is older than the tutee.

**crystallized intelligence:** Knowledge of the ideas deemed important in a given culture.

**cultural pluralism:** The process in which different cultural groups maintain their own values and beliefs while participating in the majority culture.

**culture:** A system of shared beliefs, values, and customs that people in a social group collectively construct.

## D

**database software:** Computer programs people use to store records for later use.

**decenter:** The ability to attend to more than one dimension of a stimulus.

**declarative knowledge:** Knowledge of factual information.

**depth of processing:** A model that explains how we process new information, varying from shallow to deep.

**desktop publishing:** Computer programs that enable people to produce written material that looks as though it has been printed professionally.

**development:** Changes in behavior that result from learning, experience, or maturation.

**diagnostic evaluation:** The use of assessment information to make diagnostic or classification decisions (e.g., regarding learning disabilities or mental retardation).

**dialects:** Normal variations of speech that evolve within subgroups in most language communities.

**direct instruction:** A highly structured (often scripted) instructional approach emphasizing the teaching of specific skills that a student has not mastered.

**discovery learning:** An instructional approach promoted by Bruner in which students learn concepts and ideas through firsthand experience.

**discrimination index:** A comparison of the percentage of high test-scorers getting an individual item correct with the percentage of low test-scorers getting the item correct.

**discussion:** A form of whole-class instruction in which teachers encourage students to state their ideas, think critically, and evaluate the ideas of others.

**disk drive:** The part of a microcomputer that reads information stored on a floppy or hard disk.

**distractors:** The incorrect alternatives in a multiple-choice test item.

**distributed practice:** Practice occurring over time with breaks between study periods.

**divergent thinking:** Thinking that leads to many possible solutions of a problem.

**domain-specific knowledge:** Knowledge about a specific topic or subject matter area.

**dramatic play:** Play typical of the preoperations stage, in which objects take on imaginary qualities (e.g., when a child pretends that a block is a fire truck).

**drill-and-practice programs:** Computer tutorial programs for practicing basic skills.

# E

**efficacy expectation:** The belief that one's behavior will lead to a particular reward based on prior experience.

**effortful processing:** Conscious mental activity that requires attention and is usually used when first learning a task.

**egocentrism:** The inability to take the perspective of others, characteristic of the preoperations stage.

**elaborated code:** A form of speech that uses relatively complex language with explicit explanations of meaning.

**elaborative rehearsal:** Rehearsal that helps information move from short-term to long-term memory.

**elementary processes:** In Vygotsky's theory, mental activities that are automatic, immediate, and usually necessary for survival (e.g., attending to the loud pop of a balloon).

**embedding:** Creating a subprogram for working memory in a manner similar to sub-programs of computer programs; for example, as a student checks her answers to multiple-choice questions, she may write down key words on items she answered incorrectly for later studying.

**emergent literacy:** The knowledge that children develop about reading and writing through informal experiences with books and other printed matter.

**emotional disturbance:** A disability characterized by behavior that significantly differs from the norm and disrupts the classroom.

**empirical research:** A firsthand investigation in which researchers observe a phenomenon.

**empiricism:** The philosophy that knowledge is based on experience; this philosophy underlies behaviorism.

**enactive stage:** In Bruner's theory, the stage in which children acquire knowledge through active engagement.

**ends-means planning:** A planning model in which teachers formulate objectives and choose instructional methods appropriate for reaching their goals.

**engaged time:** The amount of time in a classroom in which students are actually engaged in learning; this may include the time in which students are listening, verbally interacting with the teacher or other students, or carrying out an activity.

**episodic LTM:** Long-term memory for the events of our lives.

**equilibration:** The pursuit of equilibrium between one's understanding of the world (schema) and conflicting evidence from the environment.

**equivalent forms reliability:** The consistency of a measuring instrument as determined by comparing the scores of the same group of people who have taken two versions of the same test.

**ethnocentrism:** The tendency to assume that the views of one's own culture are correct.

**evaluation:** Using assessment information to make a value judgment.

**events of a lesson:** A nine-step instructional model including gaining attention, retrieving prior knowledge, guiding learning, providing feedback, and assessing performance.

**example:** Cases that illustrate a particular concept (e.g., "oxygen" is an example of the concept "element").

**experiential aspects of intelligence:** The use of prior experience to solve new and unfamiliar problems.

**exploration:** Engaging in behavior that leads to new territory; trying to apply one's knowledge in new ways and in new situations.

**expository teaching:** An instructional approach that relies heavily on teachers' explanations and explicit instruction.

**external locus of control:** The belief that other people or events control the outcomes of one's actions.

**extinction:** The gradual disappearance of a learned response when behavior is not reinforced (e.g., when a teacher ceases to pay attention to students calling out).

**extrinsic motivation:** Motivation that comes from outside the learner, such as reinforcement from rewards, prizes, or compliments.

**eyewitness testimony:** An area of research in cognitive psychology focusing on the reliability of individuals reporting events they have witnessed.

# F

**fading:** The gradual removal of support provided to a student that occurs as the student gains competence; for example, a teacher may coach a student on a moment-by-moment basis as he is learning to use cursive writing and, gradually, give the student fewer and fewer words of guidance as the student becomes more proficient at the task.

**fetal alcohol syndrome (FAS):** A group of birth defects sometimes found in infants whose mothers consumed alcohol during pregnancy.

**field dependence:** An individual's ability to use external factors as guides in processing information.

**field independence:** An individual's ability to use internal, independent factors as guides in processing information.

**fluid intelligence:** Thinking and reasoning abilities that are independent of any given culture.

**formal operations stage:** In Piaget's theory, the developmental stage (from about age 12–adult) in which individuals can apply logic not only to actual situations, but to abstract and hypothetical situations.

**formative evaluation:** The process of obtaining ongoing feedback during instruction so that teachers can modify their behavior in terms of what students have and have not mastered.

**frequency distribution:** A graph showing how many individuals received each score on a test.

## G

**general knowledge:** Knowledge that one uses in a broad range of situations.

**generative knowledge:** Knowledge that can be used to help interpret new situations and solve problems.

**generative model of learning:** The view that learning occurs when learners derive meaning from information and identify the relationships between ideas.

**genetic epistemology:** The branch of philosophy that examines how human beings obtain knowledge.

**genotype:** An individual's genetic makeup.

**Gestalt psychology:** The school of psychology based on the idea that humans tend to perceive objects as wholes, rather than as discrete stimuli.

**given:** The information available in solving a problem.

**goal:** The desired outcome of solving a problem.

**grade equivalent score:** The average raw score achieved by students at a particular grade level.

**guided discovery:** In Bruner's theory, an instructional approach in which teachers arrange data or examples so students can induce ideas and relationships contained in the situations.

## H

**hearing impairment:** A disability characterized by diminished or absent hearing ability.

**hemispherality:** The idea that one side of the brain is dominant in an individual.

**heuristics:** General rules ("rules of thumb") that are often helpful in problem solving.

**hierarchy:** A graphic "tree" showing subordinate (lower) and superordinate (higher) ideas.

**higher mental functions:** In Vygotsky's theory, mental activities in which we exercise our own will (e.g., paying attention to the architecture of a building).

**holophrases:** One-word utterances used by young children as substitutes for whole phrases or sentences.

**human immunodeficiency virus (HIV):** The virus that causes acquired immunodeficiency syndrome (AIDS).

**humanist approach:** An approach to learning that focuses on the affective or emotional components of learning.

## I

**iconic stage:** In Bruner's theory, the stage in which children learn through visual stimuli, such as pictures or charts.

**identity crisis:** The difficulty encountered by some adolescents who struggle to choose a set of beliefs, behaviors, and goals.

**imaginary audience:** The phenomenon in which adolescents believe others are watching what they do or listening to their thoughts.

**impulsivity:** The tendency to act immediately and without consideration.

**inclusion:** The integration of students with disabilities in age-appropriate regular classrooms.

**individual differences:** Variations among learners, such as in intelligence or moral development.

**Individualized Education Plan (IEP):** A statement of long-term and short-term instructional goals, instructional methods, and materials written for each student placed in special education.

**individualized instruction:** An instructional strategy in which each student works independently on goals that are specific to him or her.

**inductive reasoning:** The use of specific examples to identify general principles.

**inert knowledge:** Knowledge a learner has acquired, but is not accessible to or retrievable by the learner.

**information-processing model:** An approach that describes the human mind as if it were a computer with storage, transformation, and retrieval of information.

**inner speech:** According to Vygotsky's theory, the use of words in our thinking to guide our actions.

**integrated ends-means planning:** A model of planning in which activities are selected before instructional objectives.

**intelligence quotient (IQ):** A score determined by a person's performance on an intelligence test. Originally, IQ was the ratio of a student's mental age and chronological age. Currently, IQ is based on the distance between an individual's score and the average for his or her age group.

**intelligent tutoring systems:** Sophisticated computer programs that help people discover systematic errors in their thinking.

**interactive laser discs:** Laser discs that permit users' responses to determine the computer program.

**interactive stage:** Teacher planning that occurs during instruction.

**interference:** The inability to access information from long-term memory because of the presence of other learning.

**internal locus of control:** The belief that individuals control the outcomes of their actions.

**Internet:** An enormous network of linked computers allowing the exchange of data through modems.

**intrinsic motivation:** The tendency of individuals to act because of an internal desire to achieve or understand.

**introspection:** A method used in early psychological experiments in which subjects analyzed their own thought processes.

**item analysis:** The examination of the effectiveness of individual test items in measuring the qualities the test maker seeks to measure.

**item difficulty:** The percentage of test takers giving a correct response to a particular test item.

## J

**jigsaw technique:** A method of structuring cooperative groups such that each student is assigned a function within the group; all the functions of the individual students are necessary for the group to succeed in its task.

## K

**knowledge-acquisition components:** According to Sternberg, aspects of intelligence that help people organize incoming information.

## L

**laser discs:** A variation on the CD-ROM that contains digitally coded information.

**lateral thinking:** Thinking that reformulates a problem or "goes around" the problem.

**law of effect:** Thorndike's belief that an organism will repeat an action if that action is followed by a pleasant or satisfying stimulus.

**learned helplessness:** The belief that one's efforts are unrelated to outcomes, leading to a decreased willingness to try.

**learning:** Changes in an individual due to experience.

**learning disabilities:** A set of disabilities characterized by significant academic difficulty in one or more areas among persons with normal levels of intelligence.

**learning strategies:** Instructional techniques that can be applied to a variety of situations that are designed to help students recall or comprehend information. For example, students may learn to engage in a self-questioning technique ("What is the main idea of the passage I am reading?") to help them comprehend the text.

**least restrictive environment:** An educational setting that is as normal as possible but still meets the special needs of students with disabilities.

**lecture:** Instructional approach in which the teacher presents information verbally to a class of students, sometimes with visual aids (such as a blackboard or overheads) and demonstrations.

**lecture-recitation format:** A form of whole-class instruction in which teachers present information orally and then ask follow-up questions.

**levels of processing:** Depth of our processing of new information from a shallow level (in which it is poorly integrated with existing knowledge) to deeper levels (in which it is well integrated with existing knowledge).

**limited English proficiency:** Minimal competence in English as a second language.

**linear array:** A line on which events are sequenced according to the time at which they took place.

**linguistic competence:** One's knowledge of the structure of a language.

**literacy:** The ability to read and write.

**local area network (LAN):** A set of linked microcomputers that simultaneously run the same program.

**locus of control:** One's belief regarding whether internal or external forces control events.

**long-term memory (LTM):** The storehouse of information that has been previously processed and stored by our information-processing system.

**low achiever:** A nondisabled student whose academic performance is poor.

## M

**magical thinking:** Thinking typical in the preoperations stage in which children believe that fantastic and impossible situations are possible (e.g., children believing that they have superpowers or that witches fly).

**mainstreaming:** The practice of educating students with disabilities in regular classroom settings to the greatest extent possible.

**maintenance rehearsal:** Rehearsal that keeps information "alive" in short-term memory.

**massed practice:** Practice occurring in one, long sitting.

**mastery goals:** Goals that pertain to competence in skills and achieving a sense of self-satisfaction.

**matrix:** A graphic presentation of information along multiple dimensions (e.g., a matrix in geography might show demographic characteristics along the top of the page and the names of various countries on the left-hand side).

**maturation:** The normal sequence of growth that humans experience as they get older.

**mean:** The arithmetic average of a set of scores.

**measurement:** Gathering information and expressing it in numerical terms.

**median** The score that falls in the middle when scores are ranked from highest to lowest.

**mediation:** The process of working between two entities (e.g., language mediates between a task and the performer of a task).

**mental age:** The age at which a given score on an intelligence test is typical.

**mental retardation:** A disability characterized by significantly below average intelligence and deficits in adaptive skills.

**metacognition:** The awareness and monitoring of one's own thinking activities.

**metacomponents:** According to Sternberg, aspects of intelligence that involve recognizing the existence of a problem, defining its nature, generating a set of steps to solve the problem, putting the steps in the best sequence, allocating the mental resources to solve the problem, and monitoring the solution to the problem.

**metaprocedural control:** A three phase process, according to Karmoliff-Smith (1979), in which a learner moves from trial-and-error, responding to detection of patterns and, finally, to recognition of general rules and exceptions.

**method of solution:** A component of a problem that indicates the problem-solving approach.

**minimal brain dysfunction (MBD):** A disorder characterized by poor attention, hyperactivity, and academic failure; this term is currently seldom used.

**mnemonic devices:** Techniques that help students remember information by forming associations, such as the use of acronyms (e.g., *HOMES* for the five Great Lakes).

**mode:** The most frequent score in a set of scores.

**modeling:** Demonstrating to students how to perform an act while verbally describing what is being done.

**modem:** A device that permits computers to send and receive information by means of telephone lines.

**modified cultural pluralism:** An educational approach to multiculturalism in which the values of the majority culture are emphasized, while the values of minority cultures are also presented.

**morpheme:** The smallest unit of meaning in a language.

**motivation:** An internal state that activates and gives direction to thoughts, feelings, and actions.

**multicultural education:** An approach to education in which individual variations are respected and the cultures of different groups are part of the curriculum.

**multidisciplinary team:** A group of professionals representing a variety of perspectives (e.g., education, social work, and psychology).

## N

**negative reinforcement:** The strengthening of a behavior by removal of an unpleasant (or aversive) stimulus following the behavior (e.g., when other students in a class stop making fun of a student with a stutter, increasing the frequency of the student's efforts to produce words).

**neglect:** The failure of parents or caretakers to provide adequate food, shelter, or other care for children.

**network:** A graphic image depicting the links among various ideas.

**neuropsychology:** The branch of psychology that examines how brain activity relates to cognitive processing, emotion, and behavior.

**nondiscriminatory evaluation:** Assessment of children in which their ethnic background, language background, race, and gender do not bias assessment results.

**nonexample:** An item that is not part of the set encompassed by a concept (e.g., "lizard" is a nonexample of the concept "mammal").

**normal curve:** *See* normal distribution.

**normal curve equivalent (NCE) scores:** A standard score that distributes scores on a range from 0 to 100 with a mean of 50.

**normal distribution:** The distribution of scores falling on a symmetric, bell-shaped curve. In such a distribution the mean, median, and mode are equal.

**normalization:** The concept that individuals with disabilities should live as normally as possible.

**norming sample:** The group of individuals whose scores on a test provide the basis of comparison for future test takers.

**norm-referenced tests:** Tests that measure a student's performance against the scores of a norming sample.

## O

**object permanence:** The understanding that objects continue to exist when they are not in view.

**obtained score:** The score a person obtains on a test.

**open classroom:** Classroom settings in which various learning stations are placed around the room, allowing students to pursue and develop their own interests.

**open education:** Educational settings where students largely take charge of their own learning and in which teachers emphasize the development of creativity and emotional growth.

**operant conditioning:** The process in which a response is followed by a stimulus that either leads to an increase or a decrease in the frequency of the response.

**overgeneralization:** The application of language rules to situations beyond those for which rules apply (e.g., making the word *think* past tense by adding *ed* to form *thinked*).

## P

**parallel forms reliability:** *See* equivalent forms reliability.

**parallel play:** In the preoperations stage, playing near but not with another child.

**peer-tutoring:** An instructional strategy in which one student is assigned to tutor or coach another student; in peer-tutoring, the tutor and the tutee are usually classmates.

**percentile:** The percentage of students in the norming sample performing at or below a given score.

**perception:** The process of making sense of, attaching meaning to, or interpreting incoming stimuli.

**performance:** Demonstration of a behavior, which is the true test of whether learning has occurred.

**performance-based assessment:** Assessment that relies on the demonstration or execution of a specific skill.

**performance components:** According to Sternberg, aspects of intelligence involving operations that are required to carry out a task, such as drawing inferences and perceiving relationships between concepts.

**performance goals:** Goals that pertain to obtaining positive judgments from the teacher about one's competence.

**permissive parenting:** A style of parenting in which the parent gives the child total freedom and has few expectations or demands.

**personal and social epistemologies:** Ideas held by individuals or by social groups about their own thinking and acquisition of knowledge.

**personal fable:** The belief by adolescents that they are invulnerable to harm.

**personality:** The collection of attributes, including attitudes, traits, behavior patterns, and values that characterize an individual.

**phoneme:** The smallest unit of sound in a language.

**physical disabilities:** Disabilities characterized by difficulty with physical or motor control.

**P.L. 94-142:** The Education for All Handicapped Children Act of 1975, a landmark federal law that guarantees a free and appropriate education for all school-age children, regardless of their handicapping condition.

**P.L. 99-457:** The Education of Handicapped Children Act Amendment of 1986 that extends P.L. 94-142 to the age of 3 and assists states in developing programs for infants and toddlers with disabilities.

**P.L. 101-476:** The Individuals with Disabilities Act of 1990 (IDEA), a law that reauthorizes and extends P.L. 94-142.

**placement evaluation:** The use of assessment information to determine how much a student knows about a subject before instruction has begun.

**portfolio assessment:** Assessment involving the use of portfolios, or collections of student work and other material developed over a semester or year.

**portfolios:** Collections of students' work, such as student-selected best work, typical work and revised drafts of ongoing work with the teacher's and students' comments.

**positive reinforcement:** Strengthening a behavior by presenting a pleasant stimulus after the occurrence of the behavior.

**postactive stage:** Teacher planning that occurs after instruction.

**pragmatics:** The relationship of language to the situation in which it is used; the social aspects of language.

**preactive stage:** Teacher planning that occurs before instruction.

**predictive validity:** A type of criterion-related validity pertaining to the extent to which a test predicts performance after a passage of time.

**Premack principle:** The idea that an activity students enjoy can be used to reinforce with an activity they are less interested in to increase the frequency of the latter activity.

**preoperations stage:** In Piaget's theory, the developmental stage (from ages 2–7) in which children develop language skills, use symbolic thought, are egocentric, and lack adult-like logic.

**principle:** A general statement that describes the relationship between or among concepts.

**proactive interference:** Difficulty in learning new information because of the presence of existing knowledge.

**problem-solving strategies:** Generalizable activities that students can use to help resolve a problem, such as identifying the elements of the problem or defining the nature of the problem.

**procedural knowledge:** Knowledge of rules and steps that need to be followed to accomplish a task.

**production deficiency:** A student's inability to gain access to and apply previously learned knowledge.

**programmed instruction:** An instructional approach in which individuals are given small amounts of information followed by questions; their progress through instructional units is based on their performance on the questions.

**prototype:** An instance of a concept that first comes to mind and possesses the attributes of the most typical examples of a concept (e.g., the prototype of the concept "bird" may be, for some, a canary).

**psychometrics:** The process of measuring psychological traits.

**punishment:** The weakening of a behavior by presenting an unpleasant, or aversive, stimulus following the occurrence of the behavior.

**Q**

**qualitative research methods:** Methods used to examine questions that can best be answered by verbally describing how participants in a study perceive and interpret various aspects of their environment.

**quantitative research methods:** Methods used to examine questions that can best be answered by collecting and statistically analyzing numerical data.

**R**

**random access memory (RAM):** The location of the program and data currently being used in a microcomputer.

**rational-emotive therapy (RET):** A technique in which individuals' irrational beliefs are made clear to them with the goal of changing their behavior.

**rationalism:** The philosophy that knowledge is based on reasoning; this philosophy underlies cognitivism.

**raw scores:** The number of test items answered correctly.

**reading readiness:** The assumption that children must reach a specific level of physical, emotional, and cognitive maturity to benefit from reading instruction.

**read-only memory:** The location of information held for long-term use in a microcomputer.

**reality therapy:** A therapeutic approach in which students are encouraged to describe their own behavior, judge its

desirability, develop a plan for changing, and put the plan into effect.

**reciprocal questioning:** An instructional method in which students in pairs or small groups ask each other questions about the material they have been taught.

**reciprocal teaching:** An instructional approach in which a teacher or a student models an effective learning strategy, such as making predictions, for the benefit of other students. It can be used to encourage students to develop higher-order thinking skills.

**reflection:** Considering and analyzing a past event, perhaps by comparing the event with other events or comparing one's perception of it with the perceptions of other individuals.

**reflectivity:** The tendency to take time and consider before acting.

**register:** The way of speaking associated with a particular social or professional role.

**rehearsal:** Mental repetition of information for remembering information.

**reinforcer:** A stimulus that occurs after a response that can be either pleasant or unpleasant to the learner. Presenting pleasant reinforcers or removing unpleasant reinforcers leads to an increase in the frequency of the behavior.

**reliability:** The extent to which a measuring instrument is consistent.

**reliability coefficient:** The reliability of a test expressed in numerical form.

**resource room:** A separate room in which special education teachers work with small groups of mainstreamed students for part of the day.

**response:** The behavior exhibited by an individual as a result of stimuli.

**response-cost:** A behavior modification method in which students lose rewards previously earned when they demonstrate undesirable behavior.

**restricted code:** A form of speech that uses simple, idiomatic, and repetitive language to generate common understandings.

**retroactive interference:** The loss of learned information from memory because of interference from new knowledge.

**reversibility:** The concept understood by concrete operational children that an object whose appearance has been changed (e.g., a flat pancake of clay that was once a ball of clay) can be reversed to its original form, with no addition or removal of material.

**rote learning:** Remembering through repetition.

**S**

**savant syndrome:** A condition in which an individual has an exceptional talent in a narrow, specific area but who otherwise has mental retardation.

**scaffolding:** The instructional support adults give students as they attempt to solve problems that go beyond their current knowledge.

**schema (plural, schemata):** One's understanding of how the world works (e.g., one's understanding of where babies come from).

**schema theory:** The approach to learning that examines how individuals create relationships between concepts.

**scorer bias:** The tendency of test scorers to be influenced by irrelevant characteristics of a student (such as gender, physical appearance, or ethnicity).

**script theory:** The theory that, in our long-term memory, we possess sequences of steps, or scripts, that we use in specific situations, such that each situation is not viewed as unique.

**selective combination:** Putting relevant pieces of information together in an effective combination to solve problems.

**selective comparison:** Relating new information to preexisting knowledge to solve problems.

**selective encoding:** Choosing the important aspects of a problem and ignoring the irrelevant aspects.

**self-concept:** Our perceptions of who we are and what we are like.

**self-efficacy:** Our perceptions that a particular behavior is effective in a specific situation and that we are capable of demonstrating that behavior.

**self-schema:** A cognitive structure that we construct based on information we receive about ourselves.

**semantic LTM:** Long-term memory for words and verbal concepts.

**semantics:** The system of meanings of words within their contexts.

**semi-structured interview:** Method used by Jean Piaget to ask subjects the same opening questions followed by various questions depending on the subjects' responses.

**sensation:** The process of receiving stimuli from the environment through our various senses.

**sensorimotor stage:** In Piaget's theory, the developmental stage (from birth–about age 2) in which infants and toddlers acquire skills and develop schemata as a result of their sensory and motor experiences.

**sensory register:** A structural feature in the memory in which information is stored for an extremely brief period (i.e., less than one second).

**seriation:** The ability to arrange objects in a logical order (e.g., from smallest to largest).

**shaping:** The process of reinforcing successive approximations of a desired behavior (e.g., rewarding pronunciations of words in a foreign language until the learner produces closer and closer approximations of the correct pronunciation).

**short-term memory (STM):** The storehouse of information used in our current thinking, also called "working memory"; it retains 7 plus or minus 2 "chunks" of information for about 20 seconds.

**simulation programs:** Computer programs that simulate real-life situations.

**situated cognition:** Thinking that takes place in a specific physical and social context.

**social cognition:** The way we remember, analyze, and make sense of information about our social world.

**socialization:** The process in which we acquire the values and beliefs of our culture and learn what is expected of us and how we should behave in our culture.

**social learning theory:** The theory that we learn through the experience of others through observing, modeling, and imitation.

**social mobility:** The ability of people to move from one social class to another.

**social stratification:** Hierarchical ranking of individual members of a group in terms of wealth, status, or power.

**software:** Any computer program stored on disks.

**special education:** The branch of education designed for students whose needs cannot be met in regular educational settings.

**spiral curriculum:** A curriculum in which learners return periodically to topics already covered but each time in a more sophisticated manner, relating a topic to information learned in the interim.

**split-half reliability:** The consistency of a measuring instrument as determined by comparing people's subtotal scores on the odd- and even-numbered items.

**spreadsheet programs:** Computer programs people use to enter and analyze numerical data.

**standard deviation:** A statistical measure of the spread of scores around the mean; approximately the average distance of scores from their mean.

**standard error of measurement:** A statistical measure that estimates the expected variation in an individual's obtained score.

**standardized test:** A test in which the procedures for administering the test, the materials used in the test, and the way in which the test is scored are held constant.

**standard scores:** Scores indicating the performance of individuals in terms of distance from the mean.

**state:** A temporary condition of an individual.

**stimulus:** An event occurring in the environment.

**stimulus discrimination:** The tendency for responses to occur in the presence of some stimuli, but not in the presence of others (e.g., saying *a* is appropriate when you see *A* or *a*, but not *H*).

**stimulus generalization:** The tendency for similar stimuli to elicit the same response. For example, silent *e* at the end of a word makes a vowel long whether the vowel is *a* (*made*), *e* (*cede*), *i* (*bite*), *o* (*dote*), or *u* (*mute*).

**story grammars:** The knowledge of the structure and rules that govern stories.

**strategy training:** An instructional approach that emphasizes teaching students learning strategies that apply in a variety of situations.

**structural features:** Components of information processing, such as short-term and long-term memory, that are static and not amenable to change.

**student-centered teaching:** An approach in which the teacher facilitates learning by providing structure and guidance.

**student-talk register:** The conventions students are expected to follow when communicating in the classroom.

**summative evaluation:** Tests, quizzes, homework and other measures that help assess students' performance at the end of an instructional unit to determine their degree of mastery.

**support services:** Services provided to students with special needs, including speech therapy, physical therapy, and occupational therapy.

**symbolic stage:** In Bruner's theory, the stage in which children learn through the use of symbols, such as words and mathematical and scientific notations.

**syntax:** The way in which words are organized in a language to produce meaningful sentences.

## T

**teacher efficacy:** Teachers' beliefs in their ability to effect change in their students and their belief that teaching can overcome other influences on students.

**telegraphic speech:** Early speech by children whose sentences omit nonessential words but convey the essential meaning of an utterance (e.g., "Baby go home").

**test-retest reliability:** The consistency of a measuring instrument as determined by comparing the scores of the same group of people who have taken the same test twice.

**thinking skills program:** Curricula designed to teach students how to think.

**time-out:** A behavior modification method in which students are removed from the normal setting to prevent them from being rewarded; they are usually placed in a neutral time-out room or area.

**token economy:** A method of behavior modification in which students earn tokens by demonstrating desirable behavior; the tokens can later be "cashed in" for desired reinforcers.

**total communication:** A communication system used by many individuals who have hearing impairment employing American Sign Language, manual signing, finger spelling, speech, and speech reading.

**trait:** A relatively stable characteristic of an individual.

**transfer:** The appropriate application of previously learned information to new situations.

**transitivity:** The logical operation involving the understanding that if A equals B, and B equals C, then A must equal C; children acquire this understanding in the concrete operations stage.

**true scores:** The hypothetical scores a person would obtain if there were no sources of error.

**T-score:** A standard score using a mean of 50 and a standard deviation of 10.

**tutorial programs:** Computer programs that help people learn new information on their own.

## U

**unconditioned response:** An involuntary reaction that occurs following an unconditioned stimulus. For example, the smell of a steak (an unconditioned stimulus) leads to salivation (an unconditioned response).

**unconditioned stimulus:** A stimulus that leads to an involuntary response (unconditioned response). For example, a loud noise (unconditioned stimulus) leads to a startle reaction (unconditioned response).

## V

**validity:** The appropriateness, meaningfulness, and usefulness of inferences made from test scores.

**validity coefficient:** The expression of the criterion-related validity of a test in numerical form.

**values:** Any one of a set of mutually exclusive characteristics that a variable may have.

**values clarification:** An approach in which teachers engage students in discussions of moral issues to explore different ideas and select beliefs with which the students feel most comfortable.

**variability:** The extent to which scores in a set differ from each other.

**variable:** An entity that may take on one of two or more mutually exclusive values.

**verbal elaboration:** A method of enhancing memory in which the learner uses words to elaborate new information.

**vertical thinking:** Thinking that involves refining existing ideas.

**vicarious reinforcement:** In social learning theory, when an individual learns through the reinforcement of another person, i.e., a model.

**visual imagery:** A method of enhancing memory in which the learner paints an internal mental picture of something to be remembered.

**visual impairment:** A disability characterized by diminished or absent vision.

## W

**word processing programs:** Programs that enable people to write, revise and save written work on a computer.

**working self-concepts:** Beliefs about oneself that are open to change as individuals encounter new experiences and receive new feedback.

## Z

**zone of proximal development:** The distance between the level at which one can solve problems independently and the level at which one can solve problems with guidance from a parent or teacher.

**z-scores:** A standard score designed to have a mean of zero and a standard deviation of 1.

# NAME INDEX

# SUBJECT INDEX